Handbook for International Management Research

2nd Edition

Handbook for International Management Research

2nd Edition

Edited by Betty Jane Punnett and Oded Shenkar

THE UNIVERSITY OF MICHIGAN PRESS
ANN ARBOR

Copyright © by the University of Michigan 2004
All rights reserved
Published in the United States of America by
The University of Michigan Press
Manufactured in the United States of America
♾ Printed on acid-free paper

2007   2006   2005   2004   4   3   2   1

A CIP catalog record for this book is available from the British Library.

Library of Congress Cataloging-in-Publication Data

Handbook for international management research / edited by Betty Jane
    Punnett and Oded Shenkar. — 2nd ed.
        p.   cm.
    Includes bibliographical references and index.
    ISBN 0-472-09837-3 (cloth : alk. paper) — ISBN 0-472-06837-7
(pbk. : alk. paper)
        1. Management—Research—International cooperation.   2.
    International business enterprises—Management—Research.   I.
    Punnett, Betty Jane.   II. Shenkar, Oded.
    HD30.4   .H345   2003
    658'.0072—dc21   2003011959

To Don, Amanda, and Justin
and Miriam, Keshet, Joshua, and Rakefet

CONTENTS

Part I

INTRODUCTION

INTRODUCTION

Betty Jane Punnett and Oded Shenkar

At the dawn of the twenty-first century, the internationalization of the business world is taken for granted. Both trade and foreign investment continue to increase at a rapid pace, and with them management is becoming increasingly international. In the past we used to ask how managerial systems compared with each other, a field of inquiry called "comparative management." Today we are mostly interested in how diverse managerial systems intersect and in how to operate in a business environment spanning national boundaries, a field titled "international management." We often forget, however, that comparative management offers a critical base on which international management rests. Unfortunately, the relationship between comparative and international management has greatly weakened over the years, to the detriment of both. The *Handbook for International Management Research* is a partial response to the emerging gap between these two inseparable realms. While the handbook is aimed at increasing rigor in international management research, it is equally concerned with its comparative management roots as well as the theoretical and practical relevance of international management research in a global economy.

This new edition of the *Handbook for International Management Research* is intended to do the following:

- provide readers with a thorough understanding of past, current, and future research in international management
- retain the vital comparative perspective on which international management rests while showing its applicability in the current global environment

- highlight select international management issues and the research strategies and methodologies their study necessitates
- consider where research in the field is and should be heading
- guide those undertaking research in the field, offering methodological paths anchored in theory and relevant in practice

We prepared this introduction for the handbook in January 2002, some four months after the terrorist attacks of September 11, 2001. The events underscored the importance of understanding global issues and the interconnectedness of people from different parts of the world—in terms of economics, politics, culture, technology, trade, investment, and security. Consider some aspects of the organization that carried out the terrorist attacks, which

- drew members from many countries of the world
- was headquartered in Afghanistan, but whose leaders were Egyptian, Pakistani, and Saudi Arabian
- consisted of a loose network of cells located in countries and regions throughout the world, including the United States
- was financed by global activities, both legal and illegal, in many countries
- forged strategic alliances with other terrorist groups around the world—in Europe, North America, Asia, Latin America, and Africa
- moved people and money around the world, using modern technology
- was known to have committed terrorist acts in Afghanistan, Africa, Europe, the former Soviet Union, and the United States

This organization was clearly global in strategy, structure, and operations. If it had not been engaged in activities that most people of the world consider repugnant, this organization would have been acknowledged as a successful international organization. To be successful in business today, it is especially important to understand the nature of globalization and its impact on managers. Many academics have turned their attention to international management phenomena over the past ten years, and research in the field has increased dramatically (as illustrated in the chapters in this handbook). Internationalization brings new challenges to the research process. International research, by its very nature, is expensive in terms of time and money and is considerably more complex than domestic research. International research involves travel to and time in foreign countries, as well as interaction with scholars, respondents, and government officials from different backgrounds and with different attitudes toward such research. Doing international research right the first time is vital—there are few opportunities to do a research project a second time. The planning of international projects is critical, and researchers undertaking such projects need to understand the opportunities and pitfalls of various methodologies in an international context, as well as to possess a thorough grounding in the literature in their particular field, not only that published in their own language.

A number of authors have addressed the essentials of good international research and specific issues such as sampling, equivalence, and biases from an international perspective. Reviews of streams of international management literature, such as culture, leadership, and joint ventures, are also available. However, there is no definitive source that can serve as a reference point to which researchers can turn when they plan to undertake an international management research project. The *Handbook for International Management Research* is intended to provide such a source. The handbook is aimed at a global audience of university and college researchers, doctoral- and master-level students, as well as business professionals involved in research, whether in business firms or consulting companies. The book is particularly directed at those with an interest in international and comparative management; however, those undertaking international research in a variety of fields (for example, anthropology, sociology, or gender studies) will find the book useful as well. A globalization of research is one outcome of the broader process of globalization, making the understanding of the international aspects a must for all researchers.

CONTENTS

The field of international and comparative management, the primary focus of the handbook, is a broad one. A major challenge, therefore, for us as the book's editors was to decide what to include in the handbook (and thus what to exclude). We would have liked to include "everything," but space did not allow this luxury. We asked ourselves, "What would *we* find most helpful in doing international management research?" Our answers are reflected in the contents of the handbook. From our perspective, there were two broad areas that needed to be included in the handbook:

- the development of effective, rigorous, and theory-based research design for international management research
- the state of the art in international management research as illustrated through select but key topics in such research

We were fortunate that colleagues who are experts in their respective fields agreed to prepare the chapters that constitute this handbook. It is the work of these colleagues that makes the handbook valuable. Our role as editors was to initiate, guide, coordinate, and cajole. Their role was to provide the valuable knowledge and intriguing insights of which this book is made. We hope that, as in any cooperative venture, the individual inputs have created synergies that go beyond the sum of the individual parts. Thus, the handbook should provide both a comprehensive survey of current international management research and a zoomed focus onto specific realms that might be of particular interest to the reader contemplating or doing research in that area.

CHAPTER CONTENT

The chapters on *effective research design* focus on international and comparative/cross-national issues. We chose to focus on three aspects of research that we believe are fundamental, given the state of the art in the field. The first aspect, survey research, was chosen because it is widely used yet remains a challenge to international management researchers and the subject of much debate in the literature. The second aspect, qualitative research, was chosen because, while often touted as vital, it is underutilized at a time when many researchers opt for large-scale quantitative studies for which data is more readily available and whose analysis is more codified. The third aspect, experimental research, is also underutilized in international management research despite its demonstrated promise in other areas. Following are summaries of the three design-oriented chapters.

"The Essence of Performing Meaningful Comparative International Survey Research," by Harpaz, provides a thorough exploration of the "do's" and "don'ts" in doing survey research internationally. Since most international management research contains a survey component, this chapter is relevant even for those whose research uses alternative methods. The chapter carefully explains how to make sure that the survey results are reliable and valid and how to interpret them meaningfully.

"The Need for International Qualitative Research," by Wright, documents why qualitative research is necessary to move international management research forward. Wright stresses the need for multiple methods and convincingly argues for the role of qualitative methods as one of these. The chapter also identifies the challenges associated with qualitative approaches in a cross-cultural context and provides suggestions for dealing with these challenges.

"Experimental Methods for Research on Culture and Management," by Leung and Su, looks at the strengths and weaknesses of experimentation, relative to other methodologies, available to the international researcher. Experimentation provides important insights—in particular, it allows the researcher to demonstrate causality—and this chapter does an excellent job of outlining and discussing the reasons for international experimentation. The chapter also identifies the drawbacks of experimental methods.

Chapters on the *state of the art in the field* focus on selected topics identified for their importance, currency, and research priority. We selected the topic of *culture* for its ongoing centrality in international management research and for the superficiality with which this subject is handled in other disciplines. The focus on culture is seen in the inclusion of three chapters that deal with the topic in a separate part.

"Conceptualizing Culture: Elucidating the Streams of Research in International Cross-Cultural Management," by Boyacigiller, Kleinberg, Phillips, and Sackmann, is a comprehensive elucidation of the many facets of culture, particularly as they relate to management. This chapter helps us understand the term "culture," the many faces of culture, and the impact of culture on people doing business around the world. It provides valuable insights for those whose research focuses directly on cultural issues, as well as for all who recognize the important role of culture in all aspects of business and management.

"Cultural Distance Revisited: Toward a More Rigorous Conceptualization and Measurement of Cultural Differences," by Shenkar, explores the widely used construct of cultural distance, which has been applied to issues such as foreign investment expansion, entry mode choice, selection and training of international assignees, and the performance of foreign-invested affiliates. This chapter constitutes a critical review of the cultural distance construct, outlining the hidden assumptions that underlie the construct and challenging its theoretical and methodological properties. A comprehensive framework for the treatment of the construct is developed, and concrete steps aimed at enhancing rigor are outlined.

"The Role of Subjective Culture in Organizations: Progress and Pitfalls Twenty Years Later," by Bhagat, Kedia, Perez, and Moustafa, reviews research in the field of cross-cultural and intercultural studies of organizational processes from the perspective presented in Bhagat and McQuaid's "Role of Subjective Culture in Organizations: A Review and Directions for Future Research" (*Journal of Applied Psychology Monograph* 67, no. 5 [1982]: 653–85). The essence of this chapter is to reexamine and revitalize theoretical rigor and methodological robustness to help the field of cross-cultural management achieve the goals to which scholars around the world aspire. The tables and figures specifically developed for this chapter provide evidence of the progress and pitfalls in the field twenty years after the original article was published. The authors suggest avenues for future research and hope that an accelerated rate of research will advance transcultural understanding of human beings in dissimilar cultures.

Part 4 includes a number of key topics. We selected international *human resource management* as a functional business area that very much relies on and benefits from international management research. We selected *leadership* as a key, visible behavioral construct with major implications for both the theory and practice of management. We chose *negotiations* because they underlie all business transactions. Finally, we selected the topics of *alliances* and *mergers/acquisitions* because of their prominence in management research and practice and the growing importance of international transactions in this realm. Following are brief highlights of each of the topical chapters.

"International Alliances," by Parkhe, provides a picture of the growth in international alliances and the accompanying growth in research in this area. The chapter includes a summary of alliance studies published between 1995 and 2000, as well as an integrative framework of core concepts, focusing on "soft" aspects of collaboration; knowledge and organizational learning; network embeddedness; and the intersection of theories, methods, and levels in the field. This chapter is an invaluable resource for those doing research in the international alliance field, and it allows those whose work is peripheral to alliances to realize how they can also contribute to the understanding of alliances.

"Cross-Border Mergers and Acquisitions: What Have We Learned?" by A. Arikan, provides a description and analysis of one of the fastest growing, yet little known, research areas in international management. While the volume of cross-border mergers has now surpassed that of domestic mergers, much of the literature in the area remains focused on domestic issues. Yet there is considerable evidence emerging suggesting that cross-border mergers may be fundamentally different from domestic mergers in terms of both strategy and implementation. This chapter reviews this evidence and provides guidelines for researchers on how to approach this increasingly important topic.

"International and Cross-Cultural Leadership Research," by Dorfman, illustrates the burgeoning interest in leadership in a cross-cultural context. Although leadership research and an interest in leadership in different cultures go back a long way, this chapter identifies and discusses the substantial progress that has been made in the past decade. The chapter provides a detailed description of both published leadership studies and those currently under way. It examines diverse methodological issues in leadership research and suggests areas for future research. Related issues, such as motivation and communications, are also discussed.

"International Human Resource Management," by Schuler, Budhwar, and Florkowski, is a wide-ranging discussion of the many aspects of international human resource management (IHRM). The chapter begins with an integrative framework, including exogenous and endogenous factors; strategic components; IHRM issues, functions, policies, and practices; and multinational enterprise (MNE) effectiveness. This framework serves to guide the discussion of what we know, and need to know, about IHRM. This chapter provides valuable guidance for all those interested in doing research in this field.

"International Business Negotiations Research: Revisiting 'Bricks, Mortar, and Prospects,'" by Weiss, begins by illustrating the ubiquitous nature of negotiations for international managers. This serves to underscore the need to understand how negotiations take place in different locations and the characteristics of effective negotiations. The chapter incorporates a variety of models of negotiations and an analysis of articles on international business negotiations that appeared in the *Journal of International Business Studies* between 1976 and 2001, concluding with an extensive consideration of future directions for research on international business negotiations.

The final chapter in the handbook, "International Management Research at the Dawn of the Twenty-first Century," by Punnett and Shenkar, seeks to highlight the realities of the business world today. It focuses on the increased interaction and interdependence in the global marketplace—how international managers must familiarize themselves with the expectations and desires of colleagues, superiors, and subordinates from multiple and varied locations while concomitantly supporting the coordination and control of dispersed activities that are crucial for success in a globally competitive marketplace. The authors contend that now, more than ever, managers need to understand the intersection of the forces of globalization and localization, as well as their ramifications for the managerial role, contradictory as these may be. This chapter examines those ramifications and considers the role of international management research in this environment.

In addition to the challenges discussed in the two broad areas identified for coverage in this handbook, many researchers face a substantial challenge in terms of finding relevant information for developing and carrying out an international management research project. For this reason we include an appendix—"Retrieving Information for International Management Research: Electronic and Print Sources," by I. Arikan and Meredith—that provides the details of library and Internet sources that are of particular relevance to international management researchers. The appendix discusses the pluses and minuses of Internet research and gives practical advice on topics such as information retrieval, evaluation of resources, and documentation. An important resource for researchers is the listing and description of libraries, databases, and indices, as well as print resources appropriate for international management research.

The chapters in the handbook deal with different topics, but, not surprisingly, there are overlaps in the material they cover. Culture, for example, is a consideration in leadership, joint ventures, mergers, negotiations, and human resource management; leadership is a consideration in joint ventures, mergers, negotiations, and human resource management. Similarly, emic and etic trade-offs are necessary in surveys, qualitative research, and experimental research, and these trade-offs need to be considered in all of the various research topic areas. We have not attempted to eliminate these overlaps because we believe the discussion, within the context of each chapter, is appropriate. We think that many readers will focus on particular chapters of interest and will read the entire book at a later point; therefore, we decided it was appropriate to retain material relative to each chapter, even where it might be essentially repeated in another.

Two important topics—electronic media and ethics—are addressed as part of the discussion in several chapters and in the appendix. Nevertheless, we felt these two topics deserved special attention here. The following sections briefly outline some of our thoughts on these two issues.

ELECTRONIC COMMUNICATION AND THE INTERNET

A major change for researchers in today's environment is access to electronic media. While academics have used email for more than two decades, it is only in the last decade that the use of email has become common and that the Internet has developed as a widespread means to access information. The spread of electronic communication and use of the Internet have affected the way research is carried out. Increasingly, researchers in international management are involved in virtual, cross-cultural teams that, for the most part, communicate electronically. This has greatly increased the ability of researchers to carry out multicountry studies without incurring the costs associated with international travel. Working with virtual, cross-cultural teams provides new challenges for researchers (some of which are discussed in Harpaz's chapter on survey research and in Dorfman's chapter on leadership). We encourage international management researchers to seek ways to broaden research horizons through electronic communication and the Internet, but we also caution that such research is not easy and needs to be planned and executed with care.

The Internet and electronic communication, now that they have become relatively commonplace, also provide new avenues for accessing information (some of which are discussed in the appendix). Gone are the days when a researcher spent many weeks in the library, laboriously looking up material and tracking references. No longer are researchers limited to material available locally, which has helped researchers immeasurably. Researchers may look for investment in Canada and end up taking a tour of native communities. Learning to access information efficiently and effectively on the Internet is critical to researchers. Evaluating the information that is received through the Internet is also critical. Libraries provide a safeguard not available with the Internet—a librarian evaluates material before deciding to purchase it for the library.

The possibility for accessing potential subjects has also changed because of electronic communication and the Internet. It is not yet well understood how widespread or effective electronic surveys or interviews are. These media do provide the opportunity to reach a large number of potential respondents in countries around the world at relatively low cost. The concerns raised in the chapters regarding surveys and interviews apply to electronic ones as well. In addition, researchers should be conscious that, in many parts of the developing world, access to electronic communication is still minimal. In many parts of the world, those who do regularly use electronic media represent a very select sample. It is also likely that response rates to electronic surveys differ significantly for different groups. Researchers using these media need to identify these differences and to interpret responses meaningfully. In essence, the use of electronic media for research has its biases and drawbacks as well as its advantages.

ETHICS IN INTERNATIONAL
MANAGEMENT RESEARCH

A special issue that international management researchers face is that of dealing internationally with ethics. Many North American and European organizations and universities, as well as ethical oversight committees, have clearly defined research codes of ethics. The same is not true in the rest of the world. A researcher working in such locations does not have experts who can advise on the ethics of a particular research situation. Equally important for researchers is the fact that what is considered ethical in their country (say, North America) may actually be unethical in a foreign location. Consider the situation in the People's Republic of China, for example.

Despite substantial reforms, for the Chinese, contact with foreigners can be considered a liability, and information considered ordinary in the West may be classified or considered as potentially harmful to national interests. Chinese respondents who are fully debriefed regarding the purpose of a research project may thus be put at risk if they are later deemed to have knowingly worked with a foreigner on a research project questioned by the authorities. For similar reasons, Chinese colleagues who would normally be listed as co-authors may prefer not to be so publicly associated with a particular research project. At one point in the early 1990s, *any* social survey research by foreigners in the People's Republic of China was prohibited. Under these circumstances, it seemed unethical to us, in our research in China, to ask respondents to a survey for any demographic information that could potentially identify them as research participants.

As researchers, we have to deal with at least two sets of values. We have to consider the requirements of our home country and ensure that our research activities meet these requirements. We also have to consider the requirements of the host country and ensure that our activities satisfy them. In North America and Europe, the operationalization of ethical requirements is largely standardized—for example, signed consent forms. But these may be meaningless elsewhere, for example, where subjects cannot read and write. The challenge is to achieve the underlying ethical requirement—in this case, that subjects participate voluntarily—in a way that is appropriate in the particular research setting.

Ethical concerns are valid no matter where research is carried out, but they may be even more important in the international context because the environment is unfamiliar. Paying attention to ethical issues is vital in international settings, even where the foreign community may not have defined ethical guidelines for research. We believe that discussions with such groups as potential participants, local academics, and researchers can help the foreign researcher understand the local implications of a project. Such discussions can clarify what is ethical, considering local conditions, and will help ensure that researchers meet all ethical standards.

CONCLUSION

In today's global business environment, it is especially important that international management research be rigorous and provide reliable and valid results that can offer practical guidance for managers. We hope that this book will go some way in assisting researchers to undertake such research effectively. We particularly appreciate the efforts of all of the contributors to this handbook. We recognize the substantial work that has gone into preparing these chapters and thank our colleagues, who have so generously given of their time and expertise. We also appreciate the enthusiasm of the editorial staff at the University of Michigan Press and, in particular, Ellen McCarthy for this project. We enjoyed working with them to ensure that the handbook achieved its objectives.

Part 2

DESIGNING EFFECTIVE RESEARCH

THE ESSENCE OF PERFORMING MEANINGFUL COMPARATIVE INTERNATIONAL SURVEY RESEARCH

Itzhak Harpaz

Meaningful scientific survey research requires adherence to basic principles of research methods. Design considerations, administrative issues, sampling, and data collection are just some of the concerns that a researcher must address in order to conduct a meaningful research project. Neglect of such issues will undoubtedly affect the outcomes of the survey. In the case of international comparative survey research, these considerations are combined with a host of additional complex issues particular to that area. The issues that are fundamental to the pursuit of meaningful survey research are the focus of this chapter.

Survey research is probably one of the most commonly used instruments in international research. It was defined by Frey (1970, 175–76) as a "method for systematically obtaining specific information from a relatively large number of individuals ordinarily through questioning." The problems inherent in international survey research are not necessarily confined to this type of research. They may also occur in a research program survey of a single country even though the researcher may be less aware of them.

A review of the literature reveals that the terms "culture" and "nation" are often used synonymously. For instance, Bhagat and McQuaid (1982)

~

The author is grateful to Liora Rothschild-Shaked for her assistance with the literature search.

claim that national differences found in the characteristics of organizations are frequently explained as cultural differences. Kelly, Whatley, and Worthley (1987) contend that usually national rather than cultural comparisons are made; however, the interpretations of the comparative results for the most part turn on culture. Earley and Singh (1995) propose that an important criterion for the execution of valuable cross-cultural or international management research is comprehension of the context in which individuals and organizations operate and function. Hence, comparative studies should neither wholly rely on nor disregard any country's characteristics (Earley and Singh 1995). Consequently, in the present chapter, rather than trying to resolve this issue, the term "international" is applied interchangeably with "culture" and "nation."

International survey research studies human phenomena by selecting and investigating samples chosen from populations (cross-nationally or cross-culturally) to discover the relative occurrence, distribution, and interrelations of selected variables or issues. Survey researchers study samples, since it is hardly possible to collect data on a whole culture or an entire country. Inferences are drawn from these samples for the characteristics of the target population. International survey research ordinarily focuses on people and some important phenomena in their behavior, such as perceptions, beliefs, opinions, attitudes, norms, and values, with the emphasis on international comparisons.

This chapter is mainly concerned with the conduct of international survey research. It considers different aspects of the survey process, particularly highlighting equivalence and comparability, translation, sampling, measurement instruments, and data collection. It is within these areas that the most critical problems of conducting an international survey may arise. Specific data analysis techniques are not discussed or evaluated, as similar methods are applicable in national and international comparative studies.

FORMS OF INTERNATIONAL
SURVEY RESEARCH

Adler (1983) presents a classic typology of six different approaches for conducting international management research. They range from what she terms "parochial research" to ethnocentric, polycentric, comparative, geocentric, and synergistic research. Each of these approaches focuses on different issues: the way culture is addressed, approaches to similarity and difference, assumptions about universality, type of study, primary questions each study asks, and the main methodological issues that must be settled. Table 2.1 describes the various types of international management research and the kinds of issues that they address.

Three distinct forms of international survey research have been identified in the literature (Drenth and Wilpert 1980; MOW International Research Team 1987): "safari" or replication research; adaptation research; and decentralized collective research.

"SAFARI" OR REPLICATION RESEARCH

This research fashion is devised, evolved, executed, and managed by a researcher in one center or country. The same research is repeated in other countries by the project originator or local collaborators. According to Drenth and Wilpert (1980), an advantage of this form of research is the central control of the project; however, a possible problem may arise from the lack of enculturation of methods and intracultural data explanations.

An example of this research mode can be found in Ali's (1989) study on managerial beliefs about work in Arab states. A similar study, conducted by Jaeger (1989), focused on organizational development. Jaeger examined organizational development in five different countries, and in each he was assisted by colleagues in data collection.

ADAPTATION RESEARCH

Usually one researcher or research team organizes this kind of research, but then scholars from other countries adopt the study and carry it out in their own native state with an idiosyncratic elaboration of the central design. Ownership of data in this type of research is frequently decentralized. This may result in greater responsibility and identification of the national team, as well as in a different distribution of influence on the conclusions of the research. Tannenbaum's (1968) study on control in organizations is an example of this semidecentralized research. Another such example is England's (1974, 1975) cross-cultural study of managers' values. England originally studied managers' values in the United States; his colleagues subsequently utilized the same instrument in Australia, India, Japan, and Korea.

DECENTRALIZED COLLECTIVE RESEARCH

In this form of collaboration, researchers from different nations/cultures join in the formulation, design, development, implementation, and data

TABLE 2.1. Types of Cross-Cultural Management Research

Title	Culture	Approach to Similarity/Difference	Approach to Universality	Type of Study	Primary Question	Main Methodological Issues
Parochial research	Single culture studies	Assumed similarity	Assumed universality	Domestic management studies	What is the behavior of people like in work organizations? Study is only applicable to management in one culture, and yet it is assumed to be applicable to management in many cultures.	*Traditional methodologies:* All of the traditional methodological issues concerning design, sampling, instrumentation, analysis, and interpretation without reference to culture.
Ethnocentric research	Second culture studies	Search for similarity	Questioned universality	Replication in foreign cultures of domestic management studies	Can we use home country theories abroad? Can this theory that is applicable to organizations in country A be extended to organizations in country B?	*Standardization and translation:* How can management research be standardized across cultures? How can instruments be literally translated? Replication should be identical to original study with the exception of language.
Polycentric research	Studies in many cultures	Search for difference	Denied universality	Individual studies of organizations in specific foreign cultures	How do managers manage and employees behave in country X? What is the pattern of organizational relationship in country X?	*Description:* How can country X's organizations be studied without using either home country theories or models and without using obtrusive measures? Focus is on inductive methods and unobtrusive measures.
Comparative research	Studies contrasting many cultures	Search for both similarity and difference	Emergent universality	Studies comparing organizations in many foreign cultures	How are the management and employee styles similar and different across cultures? Which theories hold across cultures and which do not?	*Equivalence:* Is the methodology equivalent at each stage in the research process? Are the meanings of key concepts defined equivalently? Has the research been designed such that the samples, instrumentation, analysis, and interpretation are equivalent with reference to the cultures included?

Geocentric research	International management studies	Search for similarity	Extended universality	Studies of multinational organizations	How do multinational organizations function?	*Geographical dispersion:* All of the traditional methodological questions are relevant with the added complexity of geographical distance. Translation is often less of a problem since most MNOs have a common language across all countries in which they operate. The primary question is to develop an approach for studying the complexity of a large organization. Culture is frequently ignored.
Synergistic research	Intercultural management studies	Use of similarities and differences as a resource	Created universality	Studies of intercultural interaction within work settings	How can the intercultural interaction within a domestic or international organization be managed? How can organizations create structures and processes that will be effective in working with members of all cultures?	*Interaction models and integrating process:* What are effective ways to study cross-cultural interaction within organizational settings? How can universal and culturally specific patterns of management be distinguished? What is the appropriate balance between culturally specific and universal processes within one organization? How can the proactive use of cultural differences to create universally accepted organizational patterns be studied?

Source: Adler 1983. *The Journal of International Business Studies*, the Nature Publishing Group at Palgrave Macmillan. Reprinted with permission.

analysis of the project. Willingness to compromise and flexibility of individuals, as well as the degree of consensus and the level of collaboration reached by participants of the international research team, will determine the success of the project. Some pioneering projects that adopted this formulation are the Industrial Democracy Systems in Europe (IDE International Research Group 1979), the Meaning of Work study (MOW International Research Team 1987), and the Work Socialization of Youth (WOSY International Research Group 1989, 1992; Whitely, Peiro, and Sarchielli 1992). Two more recent examples of this approach are the World Values Survey (WVS) and the International Social Survey Program (ISSP). The WVS, a worldwide investigation of sociocultural and political change, was initiated in 1981 as the European Values Surveys. It was repeated several times during the 1990s. Its fourth wave was in 1999–2000, when it was carried out on representative national surveys focusing on basic values and beliefs of publics in more than sixty-five countries (World Values Survey 2000). Coordination and distribution of data are based at the Institute for Social Research of the University of Michigan, under the direction of Ronald Inglehart (World Values Survey 2000). The ISSP is a continuing, annual program of cross-national collaboration consisting of more than thirty countries located on five continents (International Social Survey Program 2000).

The social dynamics of any research group is an important determinant of its ability to achieve its research agenda, especially if its membership is multinational (Fourcade and Wilpert 1981). Since the early 1960s researchers have attempted to create workable models that can both illustrate and facilitate interdisciplinary and international studies. Still, very little research has been conducted on aspects related to the structure or composition of research teams (Drenth and Wilpert 1980). Difficulties may arise from the need for the team to remain together, often for lengthy spells. Moreover, aspects such as ownership of the instruments and data, authorship, and proper acknowledgment of sponsorship are some of the hurdles that must be overcome in this type of research. A procedure to control these problems was suggested by Drenth and Wilpert (1980), namely drawing up a written "social contract" that regulates all administrative, ethical, and other possible issues that may cause disagreement or misunderstanding.

A social contract, according to Drenth and Wilpert (1980), is an essential tool for any international research project. It serves to resolve issues such as responsibility for the study, ownership of instruments and data, proper acknowledgment of sponsors and co-workers, integration of national and cross-national analysis and publications, and royalties. These authors suggest that a contract such as this should be drawn up at a very early stage of any research, with every member of the research team committed to it. The purpose is to foresee possible points of conflict and to resolve them before they arise or at least to prepare for their occurrence.

The objective of the social contract is thus to ensure a continuing harmonious and productive relationship among members of a large multinational research team over the years. Such an approach was utilized in the twelve-nation comparison of Industrial Democracy Systems in Europe (IDE 1979), the eight-country study focusing on the Meaning of Work (MOW International Research Team 1987), and the eight-country project comparing Work Socialization of Youth (WOSY International Research Group 1989, 1992; Whitely, Peiro, and Sarchielli 1992).

Bulmer (1998) adds to these sets of considerations two additional aspects to be adopted by international research teams. The first is *informed consent* by those participating in any study, especially in societies or organizations where gatekeepers can limit right of entry to parts of a society or where individuals or organizations may be forced into participating. The second is *science versus ideology* and the need to take into consideration the likelihood of one's research being misinterpreted or abused to serve political ends.

To determine the effect of team culture on the performance of multicultural research teams, Earley and Mosakowski (2000) created a model of transnational team dynamics. This model examines the role of factors such as nationality, race, gender, and religion in such a study. It was developed through a qualitative field research, whose hypotheses were then confirmed by two laboratory studies. The conclusions of these studies and the ensuing model can be summed up as follows: nationality is the factor having the most effect on a person's identity (especially relevant in multicultural research teams). In transnational research teams, a hybrid team culture (consisting of rules, norms, expectations, and roles shared and enacted by team members) is created over time. This culture serves to facilitate team interaction and performance.

Homogeneous and highly heterogeneous teams outperform moderately heterogeneous ones. This is because in homogeneous teams conflicts are less prevalent on account of a shared worldview, and in heterogeneous teams a hybrid culture emerges, making a group solution possible for any conflicts that may arise. In a moderately heterogeneous team the preexistence of subgroups dictates a fallback to these groups and the creation of factions whenever trouble surfaces (Earley and Mosakowski 2000).

Decentralized collective survey research has some clear advantages over the other approaches (MOW International Research Team 1987): the scientific value is intensified by each country being able to assess international differences from its own perspective; international teams often consist of members representing multidisciplinary fields and accordingly are capable of contributing to fertility of methods and explanations of outcomes; international teams usually include individuals of diverse backgrounds and values, which makes for a more objective evaluation of results; and, finally, decentralization permits equal contribution to international survey design. This last issue is often a target for criticism in the scientific literature, where a single instrument is designed in the United States or Europe and then sent to or adopted by "hired hands" in other countries (Hofstede 1980a; Roberts and Boyacigiller 1984; Warwick and Lininger 1975).

Another aspect to be considered in this type of research setting is that problems may arise in comparisons between modern and developing countries, which may cause difficulties in the interpretation of findings. Even in comparisons among countries in a similar developmental state or level of modernity, problems may arise from the level of measurement, for example, individual versus institutional, which calls for a good middle-level theory to deal with discrepancies (Scheuch 1993).

Finally, an additional important issue in any social research undertaking is reflexivity. It stems from the idea that no social researcher can be detached from the phenomenon he or she is observing. Easterby-Smith and Malina (1999) suggest that in a multinational research project techniques of mirroring (realizing that features observed may be attributed to the observer) and contrasting (focusing on the other in order to gain an understanding of how one is different) be used to facilitate not only better research but also the building of mutual trust and respect between the parties involved.

EQUIVALENCE AND COMPARABILITY

Each culture views life in a unique fashion. This is usually based on the norms, values, attitudes, and experiences particular to that specific culture. Thus, the comparability of any phenomenon could pose a major methodological problem in international research (Bulmer 1998). Surveys should be conducted in a manner that makes them purposeful to a given culture, as well as secures their comparability and suitability for international comparison. Questionnaires or interviews should contain *culture-specific* items to allow the collection of valid data that genuinely represent that culture. According to Berry (1969), however, any meaningful international comparison of findings requires the collected data to be *functionally equivalent;* that is, concepts or structures should have the same role in a particular system (Teune 1990).

> Functional equivalence of behavior exists when the behavior in question has developed in response to a problem shared by two or more social/cultural groups, even though the behavior in one society does not appear to be related to its counterpart in another society. These functional equivalences must pre-exist as naturally occurring phenomena; they are discovered and cannot be created or manipulated by the cross-cultural researchers. Without this equivalence, it is suggested, no valid cross-cultural behavioral comparisons may be made. (Berry 1969, 122)

Graen et al. (1997) rightly argue that identifying functionally equivalent constructs across cultures is harder than it might seem. As a case in point, if one wishes to compare the concept of work centrality in the United States, Japan, and Israel, ascertaining its functional equivalence requires assessment of construct functions in all three countries. Performing such an assessment necessitates a thorough conceptualization and operationalization of work centrality in these nations. To realize functional equivalence as a construct, work centrality must mean and encompass equivalent functions in the United States, Japan, and Israel, as substantiated by analogous nomological networks of relationships both between and within constructs.

A related issue is *conceptual equivalence,* namely whether the concepts used in the comparative survey research have the same meaning in the countries/cultures under study. Moreover, a difference may exist with regard to the prominence of the concept for a culture/nation or a subgroup within a culture. Brett et al. (1997) contend that a construct may be considered conceptually equivalent in two or more cultures when it can be meaningfully discussed in each culture and has a comparable meaning across all cultures involved. Consequently, a construct displaying conceptual equivalence in several countries can be said to have a universal concept for those countries. Mitchell (1983) points out that a conceptual equivalence problem may occur with such concepts as time, future, distance, or height in regard to visual scaling devices, as well as with various concepts evaluative in nature, such as table manners. Warwick and Lininger (1975) indicate that an important concept in many international studies on work and employment is that of "looking for work," which may be irrelevant to many peasant societies in developing countries. Adler, Campbell, and Laurent's (1989) study of managerial behavior in the People's Republic of China provides another example of conceptual equivalence. An application of Laurent's management questionnaire failed to produce a valid and reliable description of Chinese managerial behavior. Adler, Campbell, and Laurent realized that several items in that questionnaire incorporate the Western notion of "truth," which, according to the authors, is irrelevant in Confucian thinking.

Attempting to achieve conceptual equivalence may require several questions in one nation versus only one question in another. Mitchell (1983) claims that such a situation creates potential problems for comparative research since major terms in the questions are often different and diverse procedures are utilized to obtain the same type of information.

Several solutions are suggested for overcoming some of the problems introduced by conceptual equivalence in international survey research. Mitchell (1983) asserts that substantial familiarity with the local culture and language may facilitate conceptual equivalence. This usually can be attained if the international research team includes members who actually represent all the relevant cultures.

Warwick and Lininger (1975, 44–45) offer some additional considerations for achieving equivalence.

1. The choice of countries in a cross-national study should be meaningful. For instance, if a study attempts to generalize about "developing nations" it is vital that the countries involved represent this population.
2. All countries or units under study must use comparable sampling procedures (see more on sampling later in the chapter).
3. Questions used in the research should be equivalent in meaning

from country to country (or culture) rather than have an identical formal translation.

4. The equivalence criterion should be applied to the attributes of the interviewers, the supervision and training provided to the interviewers, and the concrete field methods used.
5. Attention should be given to issues of considerable refusal rates or minimum completion rates. Data analysis would be complicated if there were significant differences in the response rates between countries.
6. Comparability in administration and data analysis should be planned and developed if these are to be carried out locally in each of the participating countries.

Przewroski and Teune (1973) also propose a solution to the equivalence issue. They contend that international surveys should contain components that are culture-specific aspects of concepts or behaviors—namely, emic—as well as culture-common aspects—namely, etic. Through the incorporation of both, a valid measurement instrument can be devised for obtaining reliable information of a similar phenomenon in different countries.

Jowell (1998) also stresses the importance of the equivalence of meaning in questions and the divestment of special coding schemes to ensure correct interpretation of those answers. To mitigate these and some of the other problems that may arise in such a situation, Jowell (1998, 174–76) advances rules of thumb to be followed in international comparative surveys.

1. Scientists should not attempt to interpret data from a country they know little about and should avoid the comparison of too many countries at once.
2. Attention should be given to the choices and compilation of aggregate-level contextual variables, not only individual-level dependent and independent ones.
3. Take into account limitations of explanatory powers.
4. Ground rules should be developed for such research concerning issues such as sample coverage, sampling methods, and fieldwork periods.
5. Analysts should try to suspend belief in any findings revealing

intercountry differences until other interfering variables can be ruled out.

6. The collective development of experimentation, scale construction, and piloting should be carried out in all participating nations.
7. Secondary analysis, detailed methodological reports, and success rates should be provided, highlighting variations among countries.
8. Methodological experiments should be included in such research.

A third type of equivalence, *metric equivalence,* has also received attention in the literature (Berry 1980). Metric equivalence prevails when the psychometric values in different populations representing several data sets (cultures or nations) demonstrate virtually similar composition or adherence. Basically, there are two requirements for establishing metric equivalence (Berry 1980). The first requirement demands that statistical association among dependent and independent variables stay relatively stable, regardless of whether the obtained variance is used within a state/culture or internationally. According to this approach, covariation among variables should be constant irrespective of the cause of variation. The second requirement is that, before any comparisons are made, statistical relationships among dependent variables should be formed congruently in the involved nations/cultures. This may be evinced via similarity in correlation matrices or by common factor structures (Berry 1980). Measurement instruments should be designed in a similar manner within cultures/ nations before any international comparisons are drawn. Ordinarily, it is possible to institute metric equivalence only after completion of data collection and analysis.

Comparability may be established once the three types of equivalence— *functional, conceptual,* and *metric*—are substantiated. However, theoretical conceptualization is required as well, to make meaningful interpretations of international findings.

TRANSLATION

Some of the major complications in international survey research are highlighted by attempts at translation. This issue has received considerable attention in the literature (Brislin 1976; Bulmer 1998; Jowell 1998; Pareek and Rao 1980; Philips, de Hernandez, and de Ardon 1994; Kuechler 1998; Ronen 1986; Small et al. 1999a; Triandis 1976; Warwick and Lininger 1975). Iyengar (1983) claims that linguistic diversity is a problem peculiar to international surveys but may also be an issue in single-country studies. For instance, Iyengar notes that in 44 percent of all nation-states, three-quarters or less of the population speak the dominant language.

Instrumentation and administration of surveys should use language that is equivalent across nations rather than literally identical. The notion of functional equivalence rather than literal conversion in translation has been emphasized since the 1960s (Adler 1982; Kuechler 1998; Scheuch 1968). Almond and Verba (1963) suggest the utilization of a common vocabulary, constructed mainly of concrete, frequently used expressions. Brislin (1983) proposes the employment of simple sentences, nouns, and specific terms and the avoidance of metaphors and colloquialisms, subjunctive mood, possessive forms, and vague words. In addition, he suggests that, to increase chances of understanding the intended meaning, it is advisable to include a redundancy and to add any necessary context for difficult phrases. According to Adler (1982), the redundancy can be used for hypothesis testing, as well as for distinguishing the effects of the experimental variables from those of the cultural variables. It is desirable to represent every concept investigated in an international survey research project by at least two questions phrased in different words. If the different questions show similar responses, a stronger case could be established for the reliability and validity of the instrument, as well as for the claim that the acquired outcomes are not due to translation errors. For a study on attitudes toward management, an example question might be, "Do management personnel work effectively in this organization? *How* well do managers do their jobs?" Such redundant questions may allow the translator to be more confident of the meaning when converting thoughts from one language to another. If a word or idea is missed in one phrase it may be secured from another. Redundancy also enhances the chance that the prospective respondent will better understand the intended purpose of the question.

Four basic translation techniques could be used in survey research (Brislin 1983): back translation, bilingual method, committee procedure, and pretest technique.

BACK TRANSLATION

In back translation, the subject matter in one language is translated into another language, and then a second person independently translates the material back into the original language. Retranslation into the original language by someone other than the original translator ensures that the meaning has been retained. Nevertheless, failure to translate exactly back into the original language does not necessarily mean that the translation was wrong, since the connotations of words may be different in other languages. The process of back translation ensures literal accuracy and facilitates the recognition of mistakes; yet it may lead the investigator to assume that equivalence has been achieved when it has not (Bulmer and Warwick 1983). Some concepts may not have equivalents in another language, and even when they do, the exact meaning may be utterly different. For example, Adler (1982) claims that in French there is no word for "achievement," while in Japanese there seems to be no word for "decision making." There are also some indications that the concept of "commitment," which receives much attention in the management literature, may not be applied to non-Western cultures (Near 1989; Randall 1993).

Back translation helps provide literal accuracy and also has the advantage of ensuring that no one culture or language will dominate a comparative research project. According to Sekaran (1983), good back translation secures vocabulary equivalence, idiomatic equivalence, grammatical equivalence, and experimental equivalence, which are all important for measurement instrumentation.

BILINGUAL METHOD

In this method, an instrument is administered to bilingual individuals in the two languages that they know. Differences in responses, or inconsistencies in responses, between the two languages may be identified and corrected. One problem that may evolve from this method is that the instrument created is based on the reactions of bilinguals, who constitute a unique group.

COMMITTEE PROCEDURE

In this procedure, a committee formed by bilinguals translates the research instrument from one language to another. Any difficulties or mistakes made by one person can be discussed and corrected. Brislin (1983) warns that a disadvantage of this procedure lies in the process that may develop in the committee, in which one member may not want to criticize another.

PRETEST TECHNIQUE

Like any type of instrument developed for research, the translated instrument should be pretested in a pilot study prior to being administered to the target population. This is particularly important with translated material to ensure comprehension.

All of these translation methods can be used or even combined for the specific purposes of a research project, as long as the advantages and disadvantages of each are considered and acknowledged. Small et al. (1999a) contend that all of these methods should be employed in comparative international research. Nonetheless, they found that a translation scheme that went further than a simple translation and back translation produced more reliable and apt translations. Finally, they recommend documenting the translation process in the published reports resulting from the research, as well as in the taping of interviews for future reference, in addition to testing interviewer effects at the point of data analysis (Small et al. 1999b).

SAMPLING

Sampling design in international survey research involves complicated strategies and decision making regarding sample size, nations involved, and organizations and individuals to be sampled. Many international studies lack a sampling plan, and the researchers tend to interview individuals who are readily available and seem to be intelligent, talkative, and cooperative (Brislin, Lonner, and Thorndike 1973). In many developing countries, it is often difficult to obtain lists of homes, streets, or even communities. In addition, Brislin, Lonner, and Thorndike (1973) claim that the outcomes of a cross-cultural survey on two random samples drawn from different cultures may be attributed to any of several aspects of these cultures.

In many countries dominated by several major subcultures (e.g., Belgium, India, and Switzerland) differences are so vast that any sample selected from a specific geographic region cannot be used to make generalizations about the whole country. Therefore, a major problem in international survey research is the ability to select representative and random samples of a nation (Brislin, Lonner, and Thorndike 1973).

Drenth and Groenendijk (1984) contend that the selection of countries for participation in international surveys should be based on theoretical, as well as methodological, grounds. They argue that these are usually ignored and that the selection of countries ordinarily is determined by pragmatic decisions and considerations. Based on his experience with the multination ISSP, Kuechler (1998) recommends that countries selected for participation in international surveys should be similar with regard to their residents' familiarity and experience with attitude surveys. Besides, respondents should share similar social norms related to behavior, which are the study's core subject matter.

Drenth and Groenendijk (1984) suggest two criteria for choosing countries: maximum similarity among countries and maximum differences among countries. Maximum similarity among countries is preferred when the effect of a certain independent variable on some organizational phenomenon is being investigated. An example of this proposition would be an examination of the effect of union domination and power on the extent of industrial democracy. Countries should be selected with large differences in the specified variables but with as many similarities as possible in the rest of the variables. According to Drenth and Groenendijk (1984), it is very hard to achieve the last condition, since countries differ on a multitude of other dimensions that may lead to the formulation of plausible alternative interpretations.

Maximum differences among countries are preferred when a theoretical or a causal relationship is entailed. If the goal of the study is to show, for example, that the level of inflation or unemployment affects grievance procedures, it is preferable to select a group of countries with great differences among them. Drenth and Groenendijk (1984) believe that different cases in the sample are highly consequential for making generalizations. Namely, if similar findings may result from countries exhibiting large differences (e.g., poor versus rich), such may be related to a common theory or casual relationships. Both approaches for selection of countries are appropriate; the choice of one approach rather than the other will depend on the goals of the study.

One alternative to a representative national sample is the utilization of matched samples (Sekaran 1983). The latter are functionally equivalent but are not identical across various nations. Such matching minimizes possible contamination by extraneous variables that may influence the interpretation of results. Hofstede (1980a, 1990) used this approach in his study of employees in IBM subsidiaries in forty different countries. All individuals in the samples worked for the same employer (IBM) and were matched for jobs, gender, and age. Matching samples was also utilized in Bynner and Heinz's (1991) study of labor market entry in England and Germany. In that study the use of this method allowed comparisons over and above occupational categories, including differences at the national level, within and between labor markets, between career trajectories, and between occupational types within each trajectory. Other studies that have used matched samples include Ali's (1989) comparison of managerial beliefs about work in Iraq and Saudi Arabia and Dorfman and Howell's (1988) research on dimensions of national culture and effective leadership patterns.

A different method to improve sampling in international survey research, as suggested by Campbell (1968), is the *plausible rival hypothesis* approach. In using this approach the researcher should probe what other plausible interpretations (other than the hypothesized theoretical conceptualization) are made possible by the research setting and the measurement processes. Plausible alternatives may include various methodological errors, such as inaccuracies in sampling, instrumentation, understanding of interviewees, or representatives of activities executed on a test basis versus normal activities performed. Each alternative explanation of the data should be considered individually. The fewer of these, and the more *implausible* each is, the more validity can be ascribed to the comparison.

Consideration should also be given to the selection of the organizations that will participate in the international survey. The ideal in this regard should be to choose organizations in each country that are as similar as possible to organizations in other countries based on criteria such as technology, size, and so forth (Drenth and Groenendijk 1984). This was the basis for selection of organizations in the Industrial Democracy Systems in Europe project conducted in twelve countries (IDE 1981). However, in practice, organizations are not always chosen for surveying as just described, and practical considerations may influence selection (e.g., availability of organizations). In addition, Drenth and Groenendijk (1984) contend that problems may arise out of the possible wide variation in the concept of "organization" from country to country.

Another approach for improvement of sampling design in international surveys is *sampling frames* for selection of individuals (Naroll, Michik, and Naroll 1980). According to this scheme, a list is created that helps raise the representativeness of the sample with regard to a particular population. Examples of sampling frames may be found in records of people obtained from a village's or a city's municipality or from a list of school graduates. After the decision about the sampling frame is made, careful consideration should be given to the selection of respondents or households to be included in the study. Cautiously choosing a stratified random sample ensures that the various strata of the population under study will be represented in the sample.

Brislin, Lonner, and Thorndike (1973) provide an example, somewhat related to the sampling frame, of how the problem of sampling can be addressed. They point to a study of blue-collar workers in the United States and Japan (by Whitehill and Tazekawa) and show that the sampling problem was partially solved since the workers were selected from "specified equivalent industries" (25). In another study, Brislin, Lonner, and Thorndike (1973) quote Berrien, who sampled workers from enterprises "having equivalent objectives in two or more countries" (23). Thus, because the organizations share similar objectives, the resulting differences should be attributed to cultural/national values.

Berry (1997) distinguishes two types of study, those aimed at *testing* a phenomenon and those *generalizing* it. He suggests that the sampling strategy should be chosen according to the goal of the study. If the goal of an international comparative research project is to *test* an explicit hypothesized relationship between a national/cultural and a sociopsychological phenomenon, a small number of distinctively well-selected national/cultural contexts possibly will be adequate, for instance, the relationship between the degree of individualism in a society and the degree of instrumental orientation among people in that society. Conversely, if the purpose of the study is to make a *generalization* about such an association, a larger representative sample would be essential.

Finally, Brislin and Baumgardner (1971) argue that random samples should be described carefully, so that subsequent researchers may take advantage of data from others' pretest work or select different samples that may demonstrate differences that are theoretically based. According to these authors, sample descriptions should include all important characteristics of individuals, organizations, or societies that could affect interpretations of research outcomes. Some such peculiarities are age, sex, educational level, income, occupation, special training or education, and habitation.

MEASUREMENT INSTRUMENT AND
DATA COLLECTION

Unique and special issues arise in measuring and collecting data in international research surveys (Brislin 1983; Bulmer 1998; Kohn 1989; Sekaran 1983; Warwick and Lininger 1975). Some grave mistakes occur from faulty assumptions about the feasibility of carrying out certain types of studies in distinct regions. Moreover, some occasions for producing good research outcomes are lost due to the application of erroneous methods. A prevalent misapplied strategy may be observed when a self-administered questionnaire is used in regions that are not prepared for it culturally, psychologically, or politically. The loss is not only in terms of bungled research but also in terms of a missed opportunity for a study of a more appropriate kind, such as a structured or unstructured interview approach.

The most common methods of data collection in survey research include a *structured interview, telephone interview, mail questionnaire,* and *self-administered questionnaire,* that is, various forms of questionnaire utilization. In a review of all comparative international research appearing in twenty-four leading English-language journals between 1981 and 1987, Peng, Peterson, and Shyi (1991) found that questionnaires were used in about 70 percent of all international studies and interviews were used in about 5 percent. Questionnaires were used to collect data mainly from lower level employees while interviews were applied for collecting data from higher echelon managers. Pareek and Rao (1980) also assert that questionnaires are the most widely used instrument for data collection. They claim that most of the studies comparing questionnaires and interviews found no differences in the responses elicited through the two methods. Thus, both can be used, depending on the goals, constraints, samples, and so forth, in the study. There are various advantages and disadvantages to the utilization of each of these methods.

In international surveys, awareness of the constraints common to national or cultural differences is essential from the outset. A major hurdle may be the extent to which respondents will understand the selected methodology and, conversely, be viable in the field. It is senseless to carry out a pretentious survey if a substantial number of respondents in remote areas misunderstand the purpose of the research or fear authorities' (e.g., government, union) repression if they cooperate with the study. Another important consideration should be research in areas that may place the interviewer at substantial risk, a real likelihood in areas of civil conflict, illegal operations, or infectious diseases.

Attention should also be given to the specific instruments to be used in the comparative survey. In the past two decades, *telephone interviewing* has become a popular means in the United States for conducting all kinds of surveys. However, it can be used only in countries enjoying a well-developed telephone system, as well as a high rate of people who own a telephone and are willing to respond to an intrusion on their privacy. Hence, while telephone interviewing has become a favorite mode for survey research in the United States, it is less acceptable in Europe. In most other countries, it is not an option worth considering since many people do not have a telephone and those who do are unwilling to answer it for purposes of a survey, much less to give out the necessary information.

Conducting a *mail survey* may yield better results; however, it is appropriate only when the majority of the population is literate. There are other criteria to be met in order to make this a viable method: the postal service in the particular country must be reliable, every person should have an address that can be reached, and when potential respondents are habituated to this mode of data collection, they must be willing to cooperate by completing and returning the questionnaire. The response rate to mail surveys is admittedly problematic, even in the most advanced industrial nations (Oppenheim 1966).

In the literature considerable attention is paid to *interviewing* practices in international surveys (Brislin, Lonner, and Thorndike 1973; Pareek and Rao 1980; Brislin 1983; Ronen 1986). All studies caution against the pitfalls and provide useful suggestions and guidelines on the process of interviewing in comparative surveys.

Pareek and Rao (1980, 128) introduce the concept of *authenticity,* which is the ability of the interviewer to obtain trustworthy, sincere, and pertinent information from the respondent. According to them, four categories of factors affect authenticity:

1. *interviewer-related factors:* interviewer's affiliation, interviewer's image, respondent-interviewer distance, respondent's relevance, and interviewer's bias;
2. *the interview and its setting:* the setting, thematic relevance, thematic sensitivity, cultural relevance, social desirability, capacity to reach depth, length, and structure;

3. *respondent-related factors:* private-public opinion gap, omniscience syndrome, previous experience, saturation, and response set;
4. *cultural factors:* courtesy norm, reticence, and game-playing norm.

Brislin, Lonner, and Thorndike (1973) provide several important points associated with the selection and training of interviewers, as well as the means of dealing with interviewer-respondent communication problems, in comparative research surveys. Some major selection standards include being an inhabitant of the surveyed region, preferably a member of the same racial group, mastery of local dialect, and extensive familiarity with local culture. Small et al. (1999b) emphasize the importance of incorporating language assessments into the interview process; they view it as potentially problematic because of issues of different culture and language affecting the research process and analysis. In international settings, they recommend that interviewers be proficient in English and the local language, as well as possess a good understanding of the two cultures taking part in the research. Regarding the training of interviewers over and above that regularly provided, lectures on the objectives of the survey and its nature may improve interviewers' performance.

The following list includes several biases that could lead to communication problems between the interviewer and respondents. All of these biases may be overcome with proper attention, training, and awareness.

- *Being able to answer any question:* giving an answer to any question regardless of knowledge.
- *The courtesy bias:* providing the interviewer with a certain answer that the respondent thinks the interviewer wants; this is especially prevalent in China, Indonesia, and Japan (Drenth and Groenendijk 1984).
- *The sucker bias:* the tendencies in some cultures to give ridiculous answers and make fun of the interviewer.
- *The reticent-loquacious bias:* members of some cultures (e.g., Chinese residing in Malaysia) are very quiet and reserved during interviews, while members of other cultures (e.g., Indians residing in Malaysia) are so outgoing and happy to talk that their responses may be underweighted or overweighed, respectively.
- *The individual-group opinion bias:* the inability in some cultures to

obtain responses from individuals alone as others constantly surround them. In such situations, it is possible for the same individuals to give different answers to questions when interviewed alone and when in the presence of others (Brislin, Lonner, and Thorndike 1973).

The extraordinary recent growth in electronic-based means for both communication and business, linked with the unique technological capabilities of the medium, has opened particular opportunities for collecting and disseminating electronic-based (Internet or email) survey research data. Concurrently, *e-surveys* raise several ethical and technical issues, which must be addressed if this method is to be used reliably and validly for comparative international survey research.

Two basic forms of electronic surveys may be distinguished. One intends the survey for a general population that is invited to participate, which involves a heavy self-selection process. The other, more promising method is when the survey is directed toward a specific target population selected by a probability mechanism. Such populations, certainly those with access to some form of an electronic communications, may be currently relatively sparse, but they are increasing in number. Examples of typical target populations are certain professional associations or some groups of firms and organizations that make regular use of electronic communications methods. A distinctive example of the latter may be the survey I am currently conducting on the role conflict between work and home among telecommuters employed in the high technology industry. Obviously, all of the participants in that study routinely use electronic means of communications as part of their regular working pattern, which makes them an ideal target population for an electronic-based survey. Moreover, this method is especially appropriate in the context of mixed-style surveys, where respondents have different types of interviewing modes (personal, telephone, Internet) available.

Some obvious advantages of the Internet or email over traditional survey media (telephone, mail, and face-to-face interviews) include the relatively low cost of the fieldwork, potentially quick response and turnaround times, lower refusal rates, lower respondent error, broader stimuli potential, flexibility in the form of adaptive questioning, the possibility of very large sample sizes, the saving of paper, and a greater flexibility (postal mail, fax, or email) in response (Forrest 1999; Kehoe and Pitkow 1996; Stanton 1998).

On the other hand, a problem may exist with the fact that electronic-based surveying is not yet a mainstream research method and that relatively little is yet known about it. There is difficulty in the administration of long surveys, safeguarding the anonymity and confidentiality of respondents, sampling and representatives issues, and administration of incentives for respondents, just to name a few (Brennan, Rae, and Parackal 1999; DSS 2000). There is little published information about these factors or about the problems that may be encountered in the conduct of a survey via electronic means.

In contrast to the rapid growth of electronic-based surveys—mainly in marketing (e.g., Basi 1999; Brennan, Rae, and Parackal 1999) and web surveys methodology (e.g., Cho and LaRose 1999; Zhang 2000)—comparative international surveys are very rare, especially in management. An example of a general (nonmanagement) international comparative study is provided by Coomber (1997), who conducted a study on the adulteration/dilution practices of drug dealers across national borders. Coomber, whose research was carried out through the Internet and the World Wide Web, obtained eighty responses from fourteen countries and four continents. Not surprisingly, U.S. dominance of the Internet was illustrated by the fact that 40 percent of all responses were attained from that country. The rest were from countries such as the United Kingdom, Canada, Australia, Finland, South Africa, and New Zealand, all technologically advanced countries and relatively firm Internet users.

Another general example of an international comparative survey is provided by Bainbridge (1999), who reported a wide-scale complex initiative by Witte. In 1998 the latter led a team that carried out a web-based survey centering on migration and regional culture. More than sixty-five thousand people from thirty-three nations (at least one hundred individuals from each country) responded to a half-hour on-line survey. The questionnaire, although simple from the respondents' position, was technically remarkably composite on account of the exceptionally large number of optional items contingent on answers to previous items.

Utilization of electronic surveys for comparative international management studies is in its infancy. Presently, the status of the Internet may perhaps be compared with the introduction of the telephone for survey research several decades ago, exhibiting some similar patterns concerning its application, namely novelty, unfamiliarity, suspicion, limited exposure and availability, relatively high cost, and technical difficulties, to name just a few. Furthermore, it will be a while before we are able to see its employment in countries with less developed technological infrastructure. Likewise, that the Internet is relatively inexpensive to use and difficult to regulate means that it can be open to misuse by less experienced or less scrupulous researchers.

Nevertheless, it seems that electronic surveys will become extremely important in the near future. With ever-larger segments of the population worldwide gaining excess to the Internet, the possibilities of sampling the general population will dramatically increase, particularly for business and organizational surveys. Technological improvements also will help the future of electronic surveys. Cheaper and more powerful computers, in addition to enhanced possibilities of multimedia, have great potential for significantly improving the scope and the quality of such surveys. Before long, the global information network evolving out of the Internet and the World Wide Web will no doubt become a mainstream instrument of international comparative surveys.

Regardless of the specific instrument chosen for data collection, some problems with question wording (in any type of questionnaire or interview) and content are particularly salient in international surveys. One problem is the adequacy of the respondent's frame of reference for answering the question. Bulmer and Warwick (1983) assert that the likelihood of trying to measure opinions that do not exist among individuals with low socioeconomic backgrounds, or with minimal exposure to an urban lifestyle, is very high. They suggest that it is preferable to ascertain the extent to which respondents have thought about the subject matter rather than to collect data whose meaning is doubtful.

Another complication may result from sensitive topics included in the questionnaire. Some questions may be embarrassing or even offensive to certain respondents (e.g., income, marital status, religion, etc.). Questions probing into attitudes toward the government or political orientations may also create resentment or even fear in certain countries.

Additional difficulties may arise when answers are sought to questions that are hypothetical, highly complex, or remote from respondents' normal experiences. Asking hypothetical questions of individuals who are not familiar with thinking in conditional terms may result in unreliability (Bulmer and Warwick 1983). A related issue has to do with response categories on a questionnaire, such as "often," "sometimes," and so forth. These can vary considerably in meaning from country (or culture) to country. In some countries (e.g., India, Philippines), an occasional consultation with a superior may be considered "often," while in other countries (e.g., Israel, Denmark), it will be deemed "seldom." To overcome this potential problem, Drenth and Groenendijk (1984) suggest the formulation of response categories that are as concrete as possible.

The problems of questionnaire and interview designs for international surveys are immense, and the solutions are often complicated. Kuechler (1987) suggests one way to improve instrumentation for international surveys:

> Conceptualization and questionnaire development should be a team effort. For each nation the research team should include at least one scholar with intimate knowledge of this nation (this includes, but is not restricted to, native tongue equivalent language proficiency). Ideally, each nation should be represented by at least one researcher native to this country and still residing there. (237)

Pilot testing the research instruments can control many of the problems in questionnaires and interview developments. An example of this approach is provided by the eight-country Meaning of Work Project (MOW International Research Team 1987). Extensive pilot studies were carried out in all countries but one. The size of the pilot samples ranged from 79 to 104 cases in each country, with a combined total of 669 cases. In the pilot studies, the selected questionnaires and scales were evaluated for their applicability to the populations in question, their reliability, and other required or desired characteristics. Moreover, changes and adaptations were made on the basis of the information gathered during the pilot phase.

Another suggestion regarding instrumentation and data collection, provided by England and Harpaz (1983) and Peterson (1986), concerns the importance of using multiple methods of measurement for conceptual ideas or domains. Specifically, one method is not inherently superior to another, but the particular method or combination of methods chosen must be appropriate to the problem or issue in question. Finally, Sekaran (1983) believes that the adoption of uniform data collection procedures in all participating countries will ensure *response equivalence,* thereby minimizing variance due to measurement errors.

According to Nasif et al. (1991), achieving response equivalence is possible when international researchers attain equivalence in (a) the respondents' familiarity with the test, (b) anxiety levels and other psychological responses, (c) experimenter effect, (d) demand characteristics, (e) characteristics of the researchers, and (f) characteristics of the presentations. Response equivalence can usually be achieved if the international research team utilizes similar procedures and methods for data collection and analysis.

CONCLUSION

This chapter has attempted to highlight and integrate some major aspects important for conducting significant comparative international survey research. No attempt was made to cover all potential issues to be considered when international survey research is conducted. A full volume devoted to this topic alone would be needed to fulfill that objective. The execution of high-quality international survey research is by no means an easy or simple task, as was demonstrated in this chapter. The methodological pitfalls discussed here with regard to equivalence and comparability, translation, sampling, measurement instrument, and data collection are complex and may severely hinder international comparisons.

In addition to the issues raised in this chapter, note that conducting international surveys may be an extremely costly enterprise (Brislin, Lonner, and Thorndike 1973; Heller 1985; Kohn 1989), which may limit large-scale surveys. From my own experience in international research, funds should also be allotted for the meetings, plenary sessions, and workshops that are a necessary condition for the success of such projects. Additional costs may accrue from the fact that it takes longer to launch and to carry out such a comparative project.

Another important consideration has to do with outcomes of international survey research. Country differences should be interpreted very cautiously, including drawing firm conclusions in relation to culture. The complex issues involved in inferring national differences from comparative research results were addressed by England and Negandhi (1979):

> As comparative researchers, we would argue that one should not get
> overly excited about observed national differences, unless they are
> rather large in magnitude, in an absolute sense and in a relative sense,
> when compared to observed differences within a given country. It is
> only when national differences are large in both an absolute and a rel-

ative sense that it seems worthwhile to pursue the very difficult issues surrounding the reasons (cultural and other) why such differences exist, and what the consequences of such differences could be. (188)

Additional reflection on improving international surveys was provided by Peng, Peterson, and Shyi (1991). They suggest that, in addition to quantitative data collection methods, qualitative descriptions should be included, containing examples of the context and consequent meanings of questionnaire items. This procedure may allow the handling of cultural subtleties that could not be treated adequately by quantitative methods, thus improving researchers' ability to explain more accurately the phenomena under study.

Communications problems and even possible friction among participants may be created by the fact that researchers from diverse cultural backgrounds with different working styles and methodological vigor have to work jointly (Heller 1988; Sarapata 1985). Standardizing survey techniques demands tenacity and proficiency, as well as some originality. Even with the most cooperative and skillful group of international researchers, it is not practical to anticipate the same level of uniformity or consonance reached by a single-country team. Nevertheless, one of the best ways to overcome most of the hurdles discussed here and to achieve good results in international research surveys is to establish collaborative relationships among team members. This is very hard to accomplish, as authentically described by Kohn (1989):

> If a good collaboration is like a good marriage, rewarding yet difficult, then a good cross-national collaboration is akin to a cross-cultural marriage that manages to succeed despite the spouses living much of the time in different countries, sometimes with considerable uncertainty about passports, visas, and the reliability and timeliness of mail delivery, and despite working in different institutional settings with conflicting demands and rewards. (96)

Hence, the first and principal step toward the execution of a sound and well-grounded international survey research can be taken only through a meaningful cooperative effort by researchers from the participating countries. This kind of effort could be aided, in part, by what Szalai (1993) terms "social science centers," namely, places equipped to serve as bases for coordination and management of such international projects, which will back such undertakings and promote their acceptance in the field.

Finally, the purpose of this chapter was to review some of the major considerations in conducting a meaningful comparative international research survey. Such a discussion should not cast a shadow over the important issue of selecting a meaningful topic for an international research project. Without the latter, by and large, the pursuit of international research is probably not merited. The future of international management research will depend on its contribution to the advancement of theory in the area (Arvey, Bhagat, and Salas 1991). Utilization of research methods will only serve as a means of revealing essential aspects about employees and managerial behavior in organizations from an international perspective. International survey projects are very complex and intricate endeavors; addressing the issues raised in this chapter may somewhat alleviate the problems associated with them and may contribute to an improvement in the conduct of such research and better realizations of its goals.

REFERENCES

Adler, N. J. 1982. Understanding the ways of understanding: Cross-cultural management methodology reviewed. In R. N. Farmer, ed., *Comparative management: Essays in contemporary thought.* Greenwich, CT: JAI Press.

———. 1983. A typology of management studies involving culture. *Journal of International Business Studies* 14:29–47.

Adler, N. J., N. Campbell, and A. Laurent. 1989. In search of appropriate methodology: From outside the People's Republic of China looking in. *Journal of International Business Studies* 20:61–74.

Ali, A. 1989. A comparative study of managerial beliefs about work in the Arab states. In S. B. Prasad, ed., *Advances in international comparative management,* vol. 4. London: JAI Press.

Almond, C., and S. Verba. 1963. *The civic culture: Political attitudes and democracy in five nations.* Princeton: Princeton University Press.

Arvey, R. D., R. S. Bhagat, and E. Salas. 1991. Cross-cultural and cross-national research in personnel and human resources management: Where do we go from here? In G. R. Ferris and K. M. Rowland, eds., *Research in personnel and human resources management,* 9:367–407. Greenwich, CT: JAI Press.

Bainbridge, W. S. 1999. Cyberspace: Sociology's natural domain. *Contemporary Sociology* 28:664–67.

Basi, R. K. 1999. WWW response rates to socio-demographic items. *Journal of the Market Research Society* 41 (4): 397–401.

Bhagat, R. S., and S. J. McQuaid. 1982. Role of subjective culture in organizations: A review and direction for future research. *Journal of Applied Psychology Monograph* 67 (5): 635–85.

Berry, J. W. 1969. On cross-cultural comparability. *International Journal of Psychology* 4:119–28.

———. 1980. Introduction to methodology. In H. C. Triandis and J. W. Berry, eds., *Handbook of cross-cultural psychology,* vol. 2. Boston: Allyn and Bacon.

———. 1997. An ecological approach to the study of cross-cultural industrial/organizational psychology. In C. Earley and M. Erez, eds., *New perspectives on international/industrial organizational psychology,* 130–47. San Francisco: New Lexington.

Brennan, M., N. Rae, and M. Parackal. 1999. Survey-based experimental research via the Web: Some observations. *Marketing Bulletin* 10:83–92.

Brett, J. M., C. H. Tinsley, M. Janssens, Z. I. Barsness, and A. Louise Lytle. 1997. New approaches to the study of cultural in industrial/organizational psychology. In P. C. Earley and M. Erez, eds., *New perspectives on international/industrial organizational psychology,* 75–129. San Francisco: New Lexington.

Brislin, R. W. 1976. *Translation, applications, and research.* New York: Wiley/Halsted.

———. 1983. Cross-cultural research in psychology. *Annual Review of Psychology* 34:363–400.

Brislin, R., and S. Baumgardner. 1971. Nonrandom sampling of individuals in cross-cultural research. *Journal of Cross-Cultural Psychology* 2:397–400.

Brislin, R., W. Lonner, and R. Thorndike. 1973. *Cross-cultural research methods.* New York: Wiley.

Bulmer, M. 1998. The problem of exporting social survey research. *American Behavioral Scientist* 42:153–67.

Bulmer, M., and D. P. Warwick. 1983. Data collection. In M. Bulmer and D. P. Warwick, eds., *Social research in developing countries.* New York: Wiley.

Bynner, J., and W. Heinz. 1991. Matching samples and analyzing their differences in a cross-national study of labor market entry in England and West Germany. *International Journal of Comparative Sociology* 32:137–53.

Campbell, D. 1968. A cooperative multinational opinion sample exchange. *Journal of Social Issues* 24:245–58.

Cho, H., and R. LaRose. 1999. Privacy issues in Internet surveys. *Social Science Computer Review* 17:421–34.

Coomber, R. 1997. Using the Internet for survey research. *Sociological Research Online* 2. <http://www.socresonline.org.uk/socresonline/2/2/2.html>

Dorfman, Peter W., and P. Jon Howell. 1988. Dimensions of national culture and effective leadership patterns. In R. N. Farmer and E. G. McGoun, eds., *Advances in international comparative management,* 127–50. London: JAI Press.

Drenth, P. J. D., and B. Groenendijk. 1984. Work and organizational psychology in cross-cultural perspective. In P. J. D. Drenth, H. Thierry, P. J. Willems, and C. J. de Wolff, eds., *Handbook of work and organizational psychology.* New York: Wiley.

Drenth, P. J. D., and B. Wilpert. 1980. The role of "social contracts" in cross-cultural research. *International Review of Applied Psychology* 29 (3): 293–306.

DSS. 2000. Creative research and information solutions. <http://www.dssresearch.com>

Earley, P. C., and H. Singh. 1995. International and intercultural management research: What's next? *Academy of Management Journal* 38:327–40.

Earley, P. C., and E. Mosakowski. 2000. Creating hybrid team cultures: An empirical test of transnational team functioning. *Academy of Management Journal* 43:26–49.

Easterby-Smith, M., and D. Malina. 1999. Cross-cultural collaborative research: Toward reflexivity. *Academy of Management Journal* 42:76–86.

England, G. W. 1974. *The manager and the man.* Kent, OH: Kent State University Press.

———. 1975. *The manager and his values.* Cambridge, MA: Balinger.

England, G. W., and I. Harpaz. 1983. Some methodological and analytic considerations in cross-national comparative research. *Journal of International Business Studies* 14:49–60.

England, G. W., and A. R. Negandhi. 1979. National contexts and technology as determinants of employees' perceptions. In G. W. England, A. R. Negandhi, and B. Wilpert, eds., *Organizational functioning in a cross-cultural perspective.* Kent, OH: Kent State University Press.

Forrest, E. 1999. *Internet marketing research.* Sydney: McGraw-Hill.

Fourcade, J. M., and B. Wilpert. 1981. Group dynamics and management problems of an international interdisciplinary research team. In F. A. Heller and B. Wilpert, eds., *Competence and power in managerial decision-making.* Chichester: Wiley.

Frey, F. 1970. Cross-cultural survey research in political science. In R. Holt and J. Turner, eds., *The methodology of comparative research,* 173–264. New York: Free Press.

Graen, G. B., C. Hui, M. Wakabayashi, and Z-M Wang. 1997. Cross-cultural research alliances in organizational research: Cross-cultural partnership-making in action. In P. C. Earley and M. Erez, eds., *New perspectives on international/industrial organizational psychology,* 160–89. San Francisco: New Lexington.

Heller, F. A. 1985. Some theoretical and practical problems in multinational and cross-cultural research on organizations. In P. Joynt and M. Warner, eds., *Managing in different cultures.* Oslo, Norway: Universitetsforlaget.

———. 1988. Cost benefits of multinational research on organizations. In B. J. Punnett, ed., *International Studies of Management and Organization* 18:5–18.

Hofstede, G. 1980a. Motivation, leadership, and organizations: Do American theories apply abroad? *Organizational Dynamics* 9:42–63.

———. 1980b. *Cultures consequences: International differences in work-related values.* Beverly Hills: Sage.

———. 1990. A reply to and comment on Jogider P. Singh: Managerial culture and work-related values in India. *Organization Studies* 11:103–6.

IDE International Research Group. 1979. Participation: Formal rules, influence, and involvement. *Industrial Relations* 18:273–94.

———. 1981. *Industrial democracy in Europe.* Oxford: Oxford University Press.

International Social Survey Program. 2000. <http://www.issp.org/info.htm>

Iyengar, S. 1983. Assessing linguistic equivalence in multilingual surveys. In M. Bulmer and D. P. Warwick, eds., *Social research in developing countries.* New York: Wiley.

Jaeger, M. Alfred. 1989. Organizational development methods in practice. In S. B. Prasad, ed., *Advances in international comparative management,* 4:113–30. London: JAI.

Jowell, R. 1998. How comparative is comparative research? *American Behavioral Scientist* 42:168–77.

Kehoe, C. M., and J. E. Pitkow. 1996. Surveying the territory: GVU's five WWW user surveys. *World Wide Web Journal* 1 (3).

Kelly, L., A. Whatley, and R. Worthley. 1987. Assessing the effects of culture on managerial attitudes: A three-culture test. *Journal of International Business Studies* 2:17–30.

Kohn, M. L. 1989. Cross-national research as an analytic strategy. In M. L. Kohn, ed., *Cross-national research in sociology.* Newbury Park, CA: Sage.

Kuechler, M. 1987. The utility of surveys for cross-national research. *Social Science Research* 16:229–44.

———. 1998. The survey method. *American Behavioral Scientist* 42:178–200.

Mitchell, R. E. 1983. Survey materials collected in the developing countries: Sampling, measurement, and interviewing obstacles to international and international comparisons. In M. Bulmer and D. P. Warwick, eds., *Social research in developing countries.* New York: Wiley.

MOW International Research Team. 1987. *The meaning of working.* London: Academic Press.

Naroll, R., G. L. Michik, and F. Naroll. 1980. Holocultural research methods. In H. C. Triandis and J. W. Berry, eds., *Handbook of cross-cultural psychology,* vol. 2, *Methodology.* Boston: Allyn and Bacon.

Nasif, E. G., H. Al-Daea, B. Ebrahimi, and M. S. Thibodeaux. 1991. Methodological problems in cross-cultural research: An updated review. *Management International Review* 31:79–91.

Near, J. P. 1989. Organizational commitment among Japanese and U.S. workers. *Organization Studies* 10:281–300.

Oppenheim, A. N. 1966. *Questionnaire design and attitude measurement.* New York: Basic Books.

Pareek, U., and T. V. Rao. 1980. Cross cultural survey and interviewing. In H. C. Triandis and J. W. Berry, eds., *Handbook of cross-cultural psychology,* vol. 2, *Methodology.* Boston: Allyn and Bacon.

Peng, T. K., M. F. Peterson, and Y. P. Shyi. 1991. Quantitative methods in cross-national management research: Trends and equivalence issues. *Journal of Organizational Behavior* 12:87–107.

Peterson, R. 1986. Future directions in comparative management research: Where we have been and where we should be going. Paper presented at the annual meeting of the Academy of Management, Chicago.

Philips, L. R., I. L. de Hernandez, and E. T. de Ardon. 1994. Strategies for achieving cultural equivalence. *Research in Nursing and Health* 17:149–54.

Przewroski, A., and H. Teune. 1973. Equivalence in cross-cultural research. In D. P. Warwick and S. Osherson, eds., *Comparative research methods,* 119–37. Englewood Cliffs, NJ: Prentice-Hall.

Randall, D. M. 1993. Cross-cultural research on organizational commitment: A review and application of Hofstede's value survey module. *Journal of Business Research* 26:91–110.

Roberts, K. H., and N. A. Boyacigiller. 1984. Cross-national organizational research: The group of the blind men. In B. M. Staw and E. E. Cummings, eds., *Research in organizational behavior,* 6:423–75. Greenwich, CT: JAI Press.

Ronen, S. 1986. *Comparative and multinational management.* New York: Wiley.

Sarapata, A. 1985. Researchers' habits and orientations as factors which condition international cooperation in research. *Science of Science* 5:157–82.

Scheuch, E. K. 1968. The cross-national use of sample surveys: Problem of comparability. In S. Rokkan, ed., *Comparative research across cultures and nations,* 176–209. Paris: Mouton.

———. 1993. Theoretical implications of comparative survey research: Why the wheel of cross-cultural methodology keeps on being reinvented. *Historical-Social Research* 18:172–95.

Sekaran, U. 1983. Methodological and theoretical issues and advancement in cross-cultural research. *Journal of International Business Studies* 14:61–73.

Small, R., J. Yelland, J. Lumley, P. L. Rice, V. Cotronei, and R. Warren. 1999a. Cross-cultural research: Trying to do it better. 1. Issues in study design. *Australian and New Zealand Journal of Public Health* 23:385–89.

———. 1999b. Cross-cultural research: Trying to do it better. 2. Enhancing data quality. *Australian and New Zealand Journal of Public Health* 23:390–95.

Stanton, J. M. 1998. An empirical assessment of data collection using the Internet. *Personnel Psychology* 51 (3): 709–25.

Szalai, A. 1993. The organization and execution of cross-national survey research projects. *Historical Social Research* 18:139–71.

Tannenbaum, A. S. 1968. *Control in organizations.* New York: McGraw-Hill.

Teune, H. 1990. Comparing countries: Lessons learned. In E. Oyen, ed., *Comparative methodology.* London: Sage.

Triandis, H. 1976. Approaches toward minimizing translation. In R. Brislin, ed., *Translation: Applications and research,* 247–60. New York: Wiley/Hasted.

Warwick, D. P., and C. A. Lininger. 1975. *The sample survey: Theory and practice.* New York: McGraw-Hill.

Whitely, W., J. Peiro, and G. Sarchielli. 1992. Work socialization of youth theoretical framework research methodology and potential implications. *International Review of Social Psychology* 5:9–36.

World Values Survey. 2000. <http://wvs.isr.umich.edu/index.html>

WOSY International Research Group. 1989. Socializacion laboral del joven: un estudio transnacional. *Papeles del Psicologo* 39/40:32–35.

———. 1992. Work Socialization of Youth. *International Review of Social Psychology* 5 (1).

Zhang, Y. 2000. Using the Internet for survey research: A case study. *Journal of the American Society for Information Science* 51:57–68.

THE NEED FOR INTERNATIONAL QUALITATIVE RESEARCH

Lorna L. Wright

Unlike the position that exists in the physical sciences, in economics and other disciplines that deal with essentially complex phenomena, the aspects of the events to be accounted for about which we can get quantitative data are necessarily limited and may not include the important ones. (Hayek 1974)

Hayek had his own discipline of economics primarily in mind when he wrote these words in his Nobel Memorial Lecture (1974), but the sentiments are also applicable to management research and, even more so, to international management research. We are only beginning to know the right questions to ask, and if we are straight-jacketed into looking only at that which can be measured, we will miss out on much that is important.

In the social sciences, certain disciplines have been more open to qualitative methods than others. Sociology and anthropology have traditionally relied to a greater extent on the qualitative methods, while psychology and economics have adhered much more rigidly to the more quantitative methods. Management has tended to follow its closer cousins, psychology and economics. However, this perennial debate among academics about the relevant merits of quantitative versus qualitative research, and rigor versus relevance, with the assumption that quantitative is the more rigorous, is an example of a false dichotomy that is dangerous to make. One method is not a priori better than the other. Both have merits and both have weaknesses.

A better question to ask would be, How do we use quantitative and qualitative methods together to strengthen both? Research methodologists (e.g., Triandis 1976; Brewer and Hunter 1989; McGrath, Martin, and Kulka 1982) have long advocated triangulation—using more than one method in conducting a research study to garner more reliable results. Adding qualitative research techniques to the researcher's arsenal of quantitative techniques helps guard against the danger of research driving us in the direction of "knowing more and more about less and less." The larger questions and complex issues that are the important areas of inquiry in international management are not always amenable to neat statistical analysis. Worse, trying to force the fit leads to biased results—biases even more dangerous for not being recognized. For example, much of the empirical research into international negotiations has revolved around bargaining over price, because this helps simplify a complex phenomenon, making it more amenable to statistical analysis. In the process, however, we may lose sight of the fact that, for most international negotiations, price is only one aspect to be negotiated and often not the most important. Other "softer" aspects such as relationships, social or political goals, technical goals, and the presence of third parties may actually be more salient in the real world and lead to different results than those obtained in laboratory experiments (Wright 1991).

At the same time, we need to avoid the other extreme of saying that whatever can be measured should be disregarded. Quantitative research can add to our sum total of knowledge, particularly when it is married to more qualitative methods. Ulijn (2000), for example, argues that for the study of cross-cultural negotiations, combining real life studies with simulations can lead to the highest reliability and internal and external validity.

Before delving deeper into the reasons for the importance of qualitative research, it is useful to set out a working definition of the term. Different authors use different terms for what I call "qualitative research." Clark (1991) uses the term "descriptive study"; Schatzman and Strauss (1973) "field research"; Jorgensen (1989) "participant observation"; Yin (1994) "case study"; Judd, Smith, and Kidder (1991) "naturalistic research." I will be using "qualitative research" to mean any research where large samples and statistical techniques are not the central issues, where an attempt is made to get close to the collection of data in its natural setting. Methods include not only the generally considered participant observation and case studies (in their meanings that are narrower than those used by the authors previously cited) but also such techniques as content analysis, formal and informal interviewing, videotaping, unobtrusive measures, archival data surveys, frame analysis, issue-area analysis, ethnomethodology, and discourse analysis.

An interest in qualitative methods in the social sciences is growing (e.g., Fielding 1999; Sutton 1997), fueled by a disenchantment with the results of many of the quantitative studies. Van Maanen, Dabbs, and Faulkner (1982) sum up some of the sources of discontent as "the relatively trivial amounts of explained variance, the abstract and remote character of key variables, the lack of comparability across studies, the failure to achieve much predictive validity, the high level of technical and notational sophistication rendering many research publications incomprehensible to all but a highly trained few, and the causal complexity of multivariate analysis, which, even when understood, makes change oriented actions difficult to contemplate" (13).

In the field of management, in particular, this interest is indicated by an increasing number of articles appearing in publications such as *Academy of Management Review* and *Journal of International Business Studies* calling for a leavening of the purely quantitative research with more qualitative methods for the better advancement of organizational theory in general and international management theory in particular (e.g., Boyacigiller and Adler 1991; Brewer 1992; Daniels 1991; Jacques 1992; Parkhe 1993; Priem, Lyon, and Dess 1999). Parkhe (1993, 227), in discussing the literature related to international joint ventures (IJV), points out that "current empirical IJV research, which boasts a large number of methodologically impeccable studies, fails to address concepts that are theoretically deemed central to the IJV relationship." Priem, Lyon, and Dess (1999), in writing about top management teams, advocate integrating qualitative research with quantitative as a base for developing research questions that are more informed, salient, and interesting.

The reverse of this picture is that researchers, when they submit more qualitative work for publication, are still receiving comments from reviewers such as "this is old frontier work," "needs testable hypotheses," and "where are the numbers?" As Graham and Gronhaug (quoted in Boyacigiller and Adler 1991, 270) conclude, "the dissident . . . scientist . . . is rather likely to suffer the slow burnout of never emerging from the journals' revision purgatories." The procedure of peer review ensures that published research is most likely to be in the logical empiricist mode. Change occurs slowly. In a study of international management articles published between 1984 and 1990, Mendenhall, Beaty, and Oddou (1993) found that only 14 percent used qualitative methods and only 4 percent used joint methodologies. Even in 1997, an article in *Organization Science* titled "The Virtues of Qualitative Research" advocated that there are times when it is best to conceal or downplay the role qualitative data played in developing an idea (Sutton 1997).

This chapter will examine theoretical and practical reasons for encouraging more qualitative research in international management research and will then touch on some of the difficulties researchers encounter in attempting such work.

THEORETICAL REASONS FOR QUALITATIVE RESEARCH IN INTERNATIONAL MANAGEMENT

As many authors (e.g., Ricks 1993; Miller 1993; Nasif et al. 1991; Black and Mendenhall 1990; Sekaran 1983; Adler 1983) have pointed out, international management is still a field characterized by a lack of theoretical understanding. This is one of the strongest theoretical reasons for advocating the importance of qualitative research in the field, since qualitative research is the most robust way of generating theory.

Glaser and Strauss (1967) in their seminal work on grounded theory delineate clearly the domains of theory generation and theory verification. They give a succinct explanation for the difference between verification of theory, to which rigorous quantitative methods are more germane, and the important prior step of generating theory, to which qualitative methods are more appropriate. As indicated previously, many researchers in the international management field are still looking for the right questions to ask, realizing a need to be cautious about the cultural biases brought to every research project.

Theory generated from data (i.e., inductive) has greater staying power than theory generated from deductive hypotheses, because, even though it may be modified by input from later data, it is very unlikely to be proved totally wrong. The researcher is not as likely to be led astray by ungrounded assumptions pertaining to the generalizability of concepts such as "power," "motivation," "organization," and so forth. The question of whether these are viewed in the same way by all people everywhere needs to be asked. The likelihood is that they are not, but if a researcher has an idea of those concepts firmly fixed in his or her mind before undertaking the research, there will be a greater tendency to force-fit the data into the existing paradigm. As Glaser and Strauss (1967) put it, "The verifier may find that the speculative theory has nothing to do with his evidence unless he *forces* a connection" (29).

Glaser and Strauss state that comparative analysis can be used to generate substantive (that is, developed for a substantive or empirical area; for example, focusing on selected organizational problems such as conflict resolution, joint venture partner selection) and formal (that is, developed for a formal or conceptual area; for example, permitting higher order normative implications) theory. They designate both of these types as "middle-range" theories, falling between "minor working hypotheses" and "all-inclusive" grand theories. This is exactly the area where the most useful work in international management research lies. Weick (1989, 521) describes middle range theories as "solutions to problems that contain a limited number of assumptions and considerable accuracy and detail in the problem specification." Both of these types of theories must be grounded in data (that is, the data comes first, with the theory deriving out of inductive reasoning from the real world). "Indeed it is presumptuous to assume that one begins to know the relevant categories and hypotheses until the 'first days in the field,' at least, are over" (Glaser and Strauss 1967, 34). A substantive theory must first be generated from the data, and this in turn helps to generate new grounded formal theories and reformulates previously established ones.

This is graphically illustrated by the changes Hofstede made in his original cultural dimensions after further research was conducted using questions generated by Chinese researchers (Hofstede and Bond 1988; Yeh 1989). The instrument on which the original research was based was developed by Western researchers. Hofstede and Bond then asked the question, "Can we assume that the respondents' answers accurately reflect the essence of their own cultures?" (15). As the results of the new research show, the answer is "no." Of the new dimension discovered—Confucian Dynamism—it is telling how its impact is described: "we were stunned to discover that our new dimension, Confucian dynamism, is strongly associated with economic growth" (Hofstede and Bond 1988, 16).

Although the research by Hofstede and Bond is not of itself qualitative, it serves to illustrate how qualitative research might have helped to strengthen Hofstede's original questionnaire survey research. If interviews and/or participant observation had been utilized in the original research, it might have been discovered sooner that the research was not capturing much of what was important in Asian cultures. As Hofstede and Bond admit, "It took the Chinese Value Survey to identify this dimension. This is a powerful illustration of how fundamental a phenomenon culture really is. It not only affects our daily practices . . . ; it also affects the theories we are able to develop to explain our practices" (19).

Hofstede and Bond are at least more optimistic about the ability of researchers to shed these cultural shackles than Holbrook (1981): "I discovered that Westerners understand very little about Chinese science and are equipped, if 'highly educated,' *not* to be able to understand it" (11). Holbrook speaks for other writers who have decried the fact that many researchers are ruled by their methodology—that they end up "searching for problems that are amenable to favored research procedures" (Schatzman and Strauss 1973). This becomes not only a case of the "tail wagging the dog" but fertile ground for being unequipped to see anything beyond the bounds of those procedures. Boyacigiller and Adler (1991) mention the lack of fit between much of the research in North American social science, with its dependence on rigorous quantitative methods and internal validity, and the nature of international studies, which is dependent on context, necessitating high levels of external validity. They point out that "[t]he general acceptance of laboratory studies in American social science exemplifies this acceptance of context-free methodology" (269). They go on to say that "research methods are driving knowledge production rather than the problems and needs of managers, policy makers, and students" (270). This view is echoed by Parkhe (1993) in the subfield of international joint ventures.

Studies have also indicated the extent to which current research techniques themselves are culture bound. Many authors (e.g., Brislin 1976; Triandis 1976; Hofstede and Bond 1988; Adler, Campbell, and Laurent 1989) have made the observation that an instrument developed in one culture may have limited applicability in another where people may not attach the same value to the concepts. As Adler, Campbell, and Laurent (1989) point out: "Choosing a methodology determines what we can study as well as the range of possible results and conclusions" (61). In their own questionnaire research in China, they discovered a pattern of bimodality, a nonnormal distribution that made the standard statistical analyses, which assume normality, of questionable value. They were also left with the unanswered question of why this pattern appeared. Was it because of a diversity of opinions or a lack of correspondence between Western and Asian conceptions of management? Each explanation would lead to very different interpretations of the results.

Again, application of qualitative research could have indicated the likelihood of this happening and could possibly have prevented it, thus leading to better insight. Adler, Campbell, and Laurent end their article with the following insight: "This, of course, brings into question much of the research that is currently being conducted in Japan and China by western and western-trained researchers using predominately western models and instrumentation. The question is: Are we asking the right questions to understand them? . . . Will we need to develop more indigenous models, questions, and methods—perhaps more fundamentally based on anthropological methods?" (71). Usunier (1997) goes further to say that qualitative approaches favor the emergence of unique features, while quantitative approaches favor the emergence of similarities because they are based on standardized models and instruments.

Even psychologists, who tend to favor experiments, testing, and statistical techniques in a domestic setting, are acknowledging the value of qualitative methods in cross-cultural research. Brislin (1976) advocates perusing the anthropological literature, which tends to be based on ethnographic research, as a basis for discovering the core items to inform cross-cultural psychological research procedures. He also states: "I hope that participant observation in cross-cultural psychology is developed as a method so that it can take a prominent place along with experiments, correlational analyses, psychometrics, and so forth" (221). Frijda and Jahoda (1966) make similar observations: "the development of observational methods and factual interviews . . . put comparative study on a somewhat more solid footing" (123). Conger (1998) in relation to leadership research promotes qualitative studies as "the richest of studies," responsible for paradigm shifts, insight into the role of context, and longitudinal perspectives that other methods cannot capture.

The processes of data collection and analysis and theory generation are much more closely linked in qualitative research than in quantitative (Jorgensen 1989; Glaser and Strauss 1967). "When he begins to hypothesize with the explicit purpose of generating theory, the researcher is no longer a passive receiver of impressions but is drawn naturally into actively generating and verifying his hypotheses through comparison of groups. Characteristically, in this kind of joint data collection and analysis, multiple hypotheses are pursued simultaneously" (Glaser and Strauss 1967, 39).

Qualitative research emphasizes comprehensive, interdependent, holistic structures that are dynamic and predictive. Because of this, it can reconcile contradictory findings of individual studies because the role of any given variable is seen as the outcome of different combinations of variables, and what is important is the interaction (Kleiner and Okeke 1991). This perspective allows the researcher to better understand complex cross-cultural phenomena. A distinguishing feature of much qualitative research is that it usually utilizes multiple sources of data rather than one alone (Van Maanen, Dabbs, and Faulkner 1982). This in itself makes it a valuable addition to quantitative methods, which dominate many of North America's top journals.

It may be helpful at this point to look at a comparison of traditional, quantitative methods and what researchers are advocating as more appropriate qualitative methods for illuminating the international management situation. Table 3.1 sets out the underlying assumptions of each method. For all the reasons that have previously been outlined, it is apparent that the quantitative methods by themselves are not sufficient to carry us further in the study of international management. We need the capability to study the nonlinear, interactive, interdependent phenomena that make up the field. It is only through qualitative methods that we will obtain that capability. Because of the dangers of hypothesizing in advance of our data in such unknown waters, we also need the inductive approach that is more common to the qualitative methods. This will help ameliorate the cultural biases that are a constant danger as well.

TABLE 3.1.   Comparison of Methods in Cross-Cultural Research

Quantitative Methods	Qualitative Methods
Independence	Interdependence
Linear	Linear and nonlinear
Cumulative, additive	Multiplicative, interactive
Deriving realities from measures of other realities	Independent measures of the various realities
Deductive	Inductive

Source: Adapted from Kleiner and Okeke 1991, 519

PRACTICAL REASONS FOR QUALITATIVE RESEARCH IN INTERNATIONAL MANAGEMENT

In addition to the theoretical reasons for qualitative research, there are several practical reasons. International management involves "messy" problems and complex issues. Qualitative research gives the researcher more flexibility. It allows one to take advantage of the richness of data and thus to obtain more meaningful results. It affords the opportunity to examine the processes "why" and "how," not just "what," and to explore the complex, interdependent issues that constitute international management. The "what" are the factors that need to be considered; the "how" refers to how they are related; and the "why" are the underlying psychological, economic, or social dynamics that justify the selection of those factors and their relationships. As Parkhe (1993) shows in his study of the IJV literature, many studies focus on factors (e.g., partner selection characteristics, motives, performance), but few show any linking mechanisms between them. He diagrams a "soft" core of concepts consisting of reciprocity, trust, opportunism, and forbearance, but complains that the "hard" data sources of large sample multivariate statistical studies favored by IJV researchers are unlikely to capture such "soft" concepts. The "why" does not appear at all.

Participant observation allows a researcher to better understand the "how" because of the ability to place an individual in an organizational context to gain a realistic perspective on the dynamics of individual and group behavior. Also, the observation of one particular event can lead the researcher to a generalization that might not otherwise have arisen. An example of this is Stoever's (1981) differentiation between negotiation and renegotiation, based on his case study research. It can also lead to significant discoveries that were not anticipated (Whyte 1984; Munroe and Munroe 1986). Walton and McKersie's (1965) seminal work on labor negotiations, which they extended into the international area, grew out of field research. Vernon's (1971) influential theory of MNE-government relations arose from case studies. Hall's (1959) description of a silent language was also based on field research and has grown in influence beyond its home discipline of anthropology to be accepted in the cross-cultural management field as well.

Case studies are holistic, so that one can see the relation of the parts to the whole and not just collections of parts (Chetty 1997; Ragin 1987; Munroe and Munroe 1986; Marshall and Rossman 1999). This makes for better interpretation, as can be seen from Parkhe's previous description of the work being done in IJVs. The danger in using a single case study lies in not being able to generalize to larger populations. However, that drawback can be minimized by using more than one case and matching cases as far as possible along some variables—for example, choosing companies according to a set of common criteria such as the same industry or similar size and entering a foreign market within the same time period.

In addition to this problem of not being able to generalize, qualitative methods are prone to several other problems that must be addressed if the methods are to be as valuable as they potentially can be.

PROBLEMS TO OVERCOME

The problems encountered in conducting international field research have been set out in Wright, Lane, and Beamish (1988), where they were broken down into two categories—methodological and practical. Barrett and Cason (1997) cover the practical problems well in their guide to overseas research. Here, it is the methodological type of problem that concerns us most. The areas of greatest concern, particularly in trying to develop theory, are the complex, interdependent nature of the topics themselves, language barriers, cultural bias, and the atheoretical nature of most of the research that has been done to date.

NATURE OF THE RESEARCH TOPIC

Most of the questions of interest in international management are complex, unstructured problems with multiple important interactive relationships that cannot be studied in a quick or easy fashion (e.g., the relationship between multinational enterprises and host governments, cross-cultural negotiations, and the formation of international joint ventures). The quantitative methods favored by many management researchers do not work well here. They generally are not adequate to capture the problem and may provide misleading information since critical interactions and interactive effects may be excluded in the analysis, as has been indicated in the descriptions given earlier. Even if this distortion does not occur, one is still left with the question of whether the issue or variable under consideration is worth the study.

However, this "messy" nature also makes the topic difficult to study by qualitative means. Although the statistical rigor that is characteristic of quantitative methods is difficult to obtain here, qualitative research has its own criteria for rigor. For example, as Judd, Smith, and Kidder (1991) explain, in participant observation research, a technique called "negative case analysis" takes the place of statistical analysis. This means that the researchers constantly revise their hypotheses as their research progresses. They must constantly look for data that would disconfirm the hypothesis. When a single negative case is found, the hypothesis is revised to account for that case. Hypotheses are checked not only against subsequent data but against all previously collected data. They maintain that in some respects this is an even more stringent analysis than statistical analysis, because it tolerates no deviation from the rule.

A frequent criticism of qualitative research is that it allows researchers to go on a "fishing trip," choosing data that fits with their view or interpreting the data in the way they want. If this happens, then they have a bad piece of qualitative research, just as they would have bad quantitative research if they fudged the results. Good qualitative research rigorously searches for that negative case. Qualitative researchers are constantly checking for any bias that might enter into their interpretation of the data.

Another common criticism leveled at qualitative research is that the multitude of relations means a clear picture of anything never emerges. This is inherent in the complex nature of the problems examined, so this criticism has some validity. It is a problem that researchers must deal with in the design phase of their study, choosing case studies so they can be matched on certain criteria, for example, so that there is a possibility of gleaning an understanding of some of these complex relationships. Although all parts of the research process are important, it might be fair to say that the design phase of a qualitative study is the critical aspect, while the data analysis stage is the critical point for quantitative studies. (This is *not* to say that the analysis is not important for qualitative studies, nor that design is not important for quantitative studies—merely that the relative weight is different.)

LANGUAGE

At this point in the history of international management research, it should be a given that cross-cultural studies should not be carried out in a unilingual English language fashion. However, one can still occasionally find such studies being done, although it is more common in survey research than in qualitative research.

Not only is there a problem with concepts having different meanings in different cultures (as discussed in further detail in the section dealing with cultural bias), but there is the problem of people not being comfortable using English. If they are not comfortable, respondents either restrict themselves to short answers, depriving the researcher of much valuable information, or withdraw from the research because they do not want to be embarrassed. This withdrawal introduces another source of error, because those who are fluent in English may have different attitudes and behaviors than those who are not. There is also the probability of misunderstanding. A third source of error is that one also thinks differently in a different language, and a researcher may get subtly different answers to questions, depending on the language in which they are asked (Wright, Lane, and Beamish 1988). A graphic example of this is provided by B. J. Punnett (personal communication 1994): "I had students (a small number) fill out the PRF [Personality Research Form] questionnaire, both in English and in Mandarin (Chinese students studying here [in Canada]) and we looked at the differences. Interestingly, they had nothing to do with the translation (my original focus)—instead, in English they responded as they feel in Canada; in Mandarin they responded as they used to feel in China. For example, to the statement 'I spend a lot of time with my friends' they might say 'False' when responding to the English and 'True' when responding to the Mandarin."

These language problems can be ameliorated by working with a team of international researchers, a process advocated by many (e.g., Daniels 1991; Boyacigiller and Adler 1991; Eisenhardt 1989), or by hiring a good interpreter and/or translator. In both cases it is important to work closely with the people to ensure that they have a clear understanding of the concepts and language, because "translation" in and of itself will not necessarily solve all the problems related to language. There is never a one-to-one correspondence of concepts between languages. A literal translation can often be the worst thing possible. You need people who understand the purpose of the research and the meaning of the concepts, who can then ensure that the translation, although not word for word, will convey the meaning precisely. For example, when conducting research into Thai negotiation styles (Wright 1992), the initial translation of the pivotal term "negotiation" was the commonly used "kaan tok long kan." However, that term carries the sense of an "agreement," which is not the sense conveyed by the English term. By working with interpreters who also had a knowledge of business, we were able to settle on the term "kaan jiraca tooroo," which carries more of the sense of give-and-take bargaining that the English word "negotiation" does.

CULTURAL BIAS

All researchers bring to their studies assumptions, values, biases, and beliefs. Most researchers do not realize this or see how it affects their work. The North American predilection for the deductive approach to theory building, hypothesis testing, and statistical analysis is in itself rooted in North American culture, which assumes that the nature of organizations is an objective one, amenable to impartial exploration and discovery. Gioia and Pitre (1990) use this argument to illustrate how the functionalist paradigm has come to dominate over interpretivist, radical humanist, or radical structuralist paradigms in North American organizational theory and research.

Even when a researcher's assumptions and biases are realized, it can be very difficult to guard against them. It is very important to remember to check all assumptions periodically. There are some aspects of international management where the biases may be less important, but in anything to do with personnel of an organization, the possibilities of these biases must be foremost in the researcher's mind. This brings to mind the old cultural divergence-convergence debate, which dissolves when you divide the studies supporting each side into those dealing with micro, individual-based issues (divergence) and those dealing with macro, structure-based issues (convergence) (Adler 2001).

Every culture has its own set of beliefs, values, and assumptions, and there are well-documented differences in thinking and logic patterns, not to mention different perspectives on concepts we take for granted. For example, "power" in a Javanese context is quite different from "power" in the Western context (Wright 1991). To a North American, power is something to be achieved. To a Javanese, power is an ascribed characteristic. You either have it or you do not, and no amount of striving will obtain it if you do not have it. The study of power in organizations would thus need to start from different premises in these two cultures. Boyacigiller and Adler (1991) show that organizational commitment means different things in a collectivist culture than it does in an individualistic culture. If we try to apply the North American understanding in these cases, we will have an inaccurate perception of the reality in that culture. Hofstede (1980) found that "achievement," a central concept for most of the English-speaking world, could not be translated into some languages. And these are only three of a myriad of examples.

Researchers must be constantly on the alert for alternate interpretations of what they are observing or hearing. This is where the multiple sources of data that the qualitative researcher uses are very important (Wright 1991; Hall and Rist 1999). In research carried out by the author into cross-cultural negotiations that utilized case studies, observation, and interviews, each method revealed potential bias on the researcher's part and served as a check on the others. For example, in observing the ongoing negotiation, the researcher interpreted the proceedings as the foreign (Western) negotiator bending over backwards to be accommodating. Only after interviewing the other side after the negotiations had ended was it apparent that, far from feeling that the Westerner had been accommodating, the Indonesians felt he had been particularly inflexible. The difference in interpretation, it transpired, occurred because the researcher had focused on the part of the negotiation that the literature indicated was most important (price), while to the Indonesian side the principles on which the bargaining was based were more important. The Westerner had been flexible on price but stuck rigidly to his criteria (Wright 1991).

Another way to minimize cultural bias in case studies is to ensure that you talk to all the people involved. Many case studies in the literature are marred because they only present one side of the story—the one that was easiest to get in English. In joint ventures, negotiations, strategic alliances, and so forth, the different sides may have very different views of the situation. Two studies that did look at both sides in research into joint ventures are Beamish 1984 and Schaan 1983.

BUILDING ON ESTABLISHED THEORY

A common complaint of many of the qualitative studies in international management is that they do not build on established theory. There must be some connection to what has gone before if the field is to advance and not be just a series of stand-alone studies. How does this fit with what has been argued throughout the chapter—that one must derive the theory from the data? No researcher comes to a problem with a tabula rasa, but the important thing is to keep an open mind—to start the process with assumptions as opposed to full-blown hypotheses and to allow room to revise as the data indicates. The strength of qualitative research is that it allows that revision. Even if researchers go ahead and do the study first, there is merit in then going back and seeing how it can build on what has previously been done. Schatzman and Strauss (1973) characterize the field researcher as one who finds it more important to link his or her findings to other discoveries rather than "nailing it down"—that is, measuring or testing the findings. Only after the linking, the placing in context, either logically, theoretically, or empirically, does he or she measure or test it.

CONCLUSION

This chapter has attempted to present the case for the importance of qualitative research in international management. We can see this importance in both theoretical and practical terms. Theoretically, qualitative research allows us to generate better, more durable theories because it is induced from actual data. It allows us to address the broader, more complex issues that are the important areas of consideration in international management. Practically, it gives us flexibility and a way to address the "how" and "why" as well as the "what" questions. It helps us avoid the cultural biases and instrumentation blinkering to which more quantitative methods are prone.

However, qualitative research is not a panacea. It must be used judiciously, and it is helpful if it is used in conjunction with quantitative methods in multimethod fashion. If international management research is viewed on a continuum, as shown in figure 3.1, the vast majority of the research conducted would benefit from a triangulation of both types of methods. At either end of the continuum we can see that qualitative methods have the greatest strengths in the area of theory generation, while quantitative methods are most useful for testing the generalizability of particular factors.

The downfall of qualitative methods is in four areas: the "messy" nature of the research topic, language, cultural bias, and not building on established theory. These are areas of caution for the researcher, but they can all be overcome, and so they should not be viewed as inescapable flaws. (It should also be kept in mind that language and cultural biases are of equal concern with more quantitative methods.)

If researchers who have been trained to use quantitative methods can learn to add qualitative methods to their repertoire, resulting research will be much more meaningful and will have a greater probability of being valid—of actually measuring what it purports to measure. Researchers then will have less tendency to be slaves to their methodology. They will

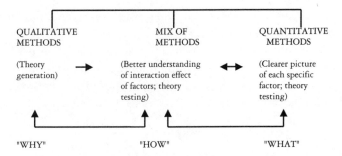

FIGURE 3.1. Appropriate use of qualitative and quantitative methods in international management research

be less concerned with whether their techniques are "scientific" and more with whether specific operations might lead to the most meaningful information (Schatzman and Strauss 1973). Then the field of international management research will be progressing, and we will avoid the trap that Weick (1989, 516) describes of "theorists often writ[ing] trivial theories because their process of theory construction is hemmed in by methodological strictures that favor validation rather than usefulness."

The criteria for the evaluation of research put forward by the British Sociological Association Medical Sociology Group in 1996 (Silverman 2000; table 3.2) can usefully be adapted by international management scholars as well. The questions present a useful checklist, not only to decide

TABLE 3.2.   Criteria for the Evaluation of Research

1. Are the methods of research appropriate to the nature of the question being asked?
2. Is the connection to an existing body of knowledge or theory clear?
3. Are there clear accounts of the criteria used for the selection of cases for study and of the data collection and analysis?
4. Does the sensitivity of the methods match the needs of the research question?
5. Was the data collection and record keeping systematic?
6. Is reference made to accepted procedures for analysis?
7. How systematic is the analysis?
8. Is there adequate discussion of how themes, concepts, and categories were derived from the data?
9. Is there adequate discussion of the evidence for and against the researcher's arguments?
10. Is there a clear distinction made between the data and their interpretation?

Source: Silverman 2000, 12

whether quantitative or qualitative methods will be more suitable, but to ensure that the design of the study—whether qualitative or quantitative—is the best it can be.

REFERENCES

Adler, N. J. 1983. Cross-cultural management research: The ostrich and the trend. *Academy of Management Review* 8 (2): 226–32.

———. 2001. *International dimensions of organizational behavior.* 4th ed. Mason, OH: Southwestern.

Adler, N. J., N. Campbell, and A. Laurent. 1989. In search of appropriate methodology: From outside the People's Republic of China looking in. *Journal of International Business Studies* 20 (1): 61–74.

Barrett, C. B., and J. W. Cason. 1997. *Overseas research: A practical guide.* Baltimore: John Hopkins University Press.

Beamish, P. 1984. Joint venture performance in developing countries. Ph.D. diss., University of Western Ontario.

Black, J. S., and M. Mendenhall. 1990. Cross-cultural training effectiveness: A review and a theoretical framework for future research. *Academy of Management Review* 15 (1): 113–36.

Boyacigiller, N., and N. J. Adler. 1991. The parochial dinosaur: Organizational science in a global context. *Academy of Management Review* 16 (2): 262–90.

Brewer, J., and A. Hunter. 1989. *Multimethod research: A synthesis of styles.* Newbury Park, CA: Sage.

Brewer, T. L. 1992. An issue-area approach to the analysis of MNE-government relations. *Journal of International Business Studies* 23 (2): 295–309.

Brislin, R. W. 1976. Comparative research methodology: Cross-cultural studies. *International Journal of Psychology* 11 (3): 215–29.

Chetty, S. 1997. The case study method for research in small- and medium-sized firms. *International Small Business Journal* 15 (1): 73–85.

Clark, R. A. 1991. *Studying interpersonal communication: The research experience.* Newbury Park, CA: Sage.

Conger, J. A. 1998. Qualitative research as the cornerstone methodology for understanding leadership. *Leadership Quarterly* 9 (1): 107–21.

Daniels, J. D. 1991. Relevance in international business research: A need for more linkages. *Journal of International Business Studies* 22 (2): 177–86.

Eisenhardt, K. M. 1989. Building theories from case study research. *Academy of Management Review* 14 (4): 532–50.

Fielding, N. G. 1999. The norm and the text: Denzin and Lincoln's handbooks of qualitative method. *British Journal of Sociology* 50 (3): 525–34.

Frijda, N., and G. Jahoda. 1966. On the scope and methods of cross-cultural research. *International Journal of Psychology* 1(2): 109–27

Gioia, D. A., and E. Pitre. 1990. Multiparadigm perspectives on theory building. *Academy of Management Review* 15 (4): 584–602.

Glaser, B. G., and A. L. Strauss. 1967. *The discovery of grounded theory: Strategies for qualitative research.* Chicago: Aldine.

Hall, A. L., and R. C. Rist. 1999. Integrating multiple qualitative research methods (or avoiding the precariousness of a one-legged stool). *Psychology and Marketing* 16 (4): 291–304.

Hall, E. T. 1959. *The silent language.* New York: Doubleday.

Hayek, F. A. 1974. The pretence of knowledge. <http://www.nobel.se/economics/laureates/1974/hayek-lecture.html>. Accessed 17 January 2003.

Hofstede, G. 1980. *Culture's consequences: International differences in work-related values.* Beverly Hills, CA: Sage.

Hofstede, G., and M. H. Bond. 1988. The Confucius connection: From cultural roots to economic growth. *Organizational Dynamics* (spring):4–21.

Holbrook, B. 1981. *The stone monkey: An alternative, Chinese-scientific, reality.* New York: William Morrow.

Jacques, R. 1992. Critique and theory building: Producing knowledge "from the kitchen." *Academy of Management Review* 17 (3): 582–606.

Jorgensen, D. L. 1989. *Participant observation: A methodology for human studies.* Newbury Park, CA: Sage.

Judd, C. M., E. R. Smith, and L. H. Kidder. 1991. *Research methods in social relations.* 6th ed. New York: Holt, Rinehart, and Winston.

Kleiner, R. J., and B. I. Okeke. 1991. Advances in field theory: New approaches and methods in cross-cultural research. *Journal of Cross-Cultural Psychology* 22 (4): 509–24.

Marshall, C., and G. B. Rossman. 1999. *Designing qualitative research.* 3d ed. Thousand Oaks, CA: Sage.

McGrath, J. E., J. Martin, and R. A. Kulka. 1982. *Judgment calls in research.* Beverly Hills, CA: Sage.

Mendenhall, M., D. Beaty, and G. R. Oddou. 1993. Where have all the theorists gone? An archival review of the international management literature. *International Journal of Management* 3:24–31.

Miller, E. L. 1993. International management: A field in transition—What will it take to reach maturity? In D. Wong-Rieger and F. Rieger, eds., *International management research: Looking to the future.* New York: Walter de Gruyter.

Munroe, R. L., and R. H. Munroe. 1986. Field work in cross-cultural psychology. In W. J. Loner and J. W. Berry, eds., *Field methods in cross-cultural research.* Newbury Park, CA: Sage.

Nasif, E. G., H. Al-Daeaj, B. Ebrahimi, and M. S. Thibodeaux. 1991. Methodological problems in cross-cultural research: An updated review. *Management International Review* 31 (1): 79–91.

Parkhe, A. 1993. "Messy" research, methodological predispositions, and theory development in international joint ventures. *Academy of Management Review* 18 (2): 227–68.

Priem, R. L., D. W. Lyon, and G. G. Dess. 1999. Inherent limitations of demographic proxies in top management team heterogeneity research. *Journal of Management* 25 (6): 935–53.

Ragin, C. C. 1987. *The comparative method: Moving beyond qualitative and quantitative strategies.* Berkeley: University of California Press.

Ricks, D. 1993. International management research: Past, present, and future. In D. Wong-Rieger and F. Rieger, eds., *International management research: Looking to the future.* New York: Walter de Gruyter.

Schaan, J. 1983. Parent control in joint ventures: The case of Mexico. Ph.D. diss., University of Western Ontario.

Schatzman, L., and A. L. Strauss. 1973. *Field research: Strategies for a natural sociology.* Englewood Cliffs, NJ: Prentice-Hall.

Sekaran, U. 1983. Methodological and theoretical issues and advancements in cross-cultural research. *Journal of International Business Studies* 14 (2): 61–73.

Silverman, D. 2000. *Doing qualitative research.* Thousand Oaks, CA: Sage.

Stoever, W. 1981. *Renegotiations in international business transactions.* Lexington, MA: Lexington Books.

Sutton, R. I. 1997. The virtues of qualitative research. *Organizational Science* 8 (1): 97–106.

Triandis, H. C. 1976. Methodological problems of comparative research. *International Journal of Psychology* 11 (3): 155–59.

Ulijn, J. 2000. Innovation and international business communication: Can European research help to increase the validity and reliability for our business and teaching practice? *The Journal of Business Communication* 37 (2): 173–87.

Usunier, J-C. 1997. Atomistic versus organic approaches. *International Studies of Management and Organization* 26 (4): 90–112.

Van Maanen, J., J. M. Dabbs Jr., and R. R. Faulkner. 1982. *Varieties of qualitative research.* Beverly Hills, CA: Sage.

Vernon, R. 1971. *Sovereignty at bay.* New York: Basic Books.

Walton, R. E., and R. B. McKersie. 1965. *A behavioral theory of labor negotiations.* New York: McGraw Hill.

Weick, K. E. 1989. Theory construction as disciplined imagination. *Academy of Management Review* 14 (4): 516–31.

Whyte, W. F. 1984. *Learning from the field: A guide from experience.* Beverly Hills, CA: Sage.

Wright, L. L. 1991. Cross-cultural project negotiations in the consulting engineering industry: A study of Canadian-Indonesian negotiations. Ph.D. diss., University of Western Ontario.

———. 1992. A comparison of Thai, Indonesian, and Canadian perceptions of negotiation. Working paper, Queen's University School of Business.

Wright, L. L., H. W. Lane, and P. W. Beamish. 1988. International management research: Lessons from the field. *International Studies of Management and Organization* 18 (3): 55–71.

Yeh, R. 1989. On Hofstede's treatment of Chinese and Japanese values. *Asia Pacific Journal of Management* 6 (1): 149–60.

Yin, R. K. 1994. *Case study research: Design and methods.* 2d ed. Thousand Oaks, CA: Sage.

EXPERIMENTAL METHODS
FOR RESEARCH ON CULTURE
AND MANAGEMENT

Kwok Leung and Steven K. Su

Researchers of international management choose from several prominent and widely recognized disciplinary methodologies. With a particular methodology come potential strengths and limitations. In this chapter, we focus on experimentation, a methodology that has been richly utilized in psychology to study cultural and intercultural phenomena. Despite this tradition, experimentation is surprisingly underemphasized in the more practitioner-oriented field of international management. Instead, greater emphasis has been given to methodologies such as case study, ethnography, and survey research. We will argue that experimental studies of culture offer some distinct advantages that can contribute importantly to understanding culture and management. Throughout this chapter, we will provide examples that illustrate strategies to manage potential pitfalls and to capitalize on its strengths. Specifically, we begin by reviewing the relative merits of experimentation in comparison to the other research methodologies. We then consider a central concern in cross-cultural experimentation, the challenge of maintaining cross-cultural equivalence, and discuss methods for strengthening causal inferences. Finally, the chapter ends with a discussion of important directions for future development.

~

This chapter is an update of a similar chapter written by Earley and Mosakowski (1996) for the previous edition of this handbook. We gratefully borrow from their organizing framework and provide updates on recent progress and new insights in the field.

EXPERIMENTATION IN INTERNATIONAL MANAGEMENT RESEARCH

EXPERIMENTATION IN METHODOLOGICAL CONTEXT

In studying a phenomenon, researchers are wise to consider the relative strengths, weaknesses, and requirements of available methodologies. Many excellent methodologies exist, but none is perfect for every use. Differences in the environmental context, the facets of the phenomenon that are of greatest theoretical interest, and the resources available may impact which methodology is optimal. Furthermore, a multimethod approach is essential to overcome the inherent weaknesses of each methodology. This perspective suggests that, if a particular methodology has rarely been utilized in the study of a phenomenon, collective oversights are likely in current scholarship. To discuss these considerations, we compare experimentation to case study, ethnography, and correlational/survey study, three important methodologies in international management research.

Perhaps the methodology that speaks most directly to the immediate interests of practitioners and management students is the case study. A case study is simply any manuscript that devotes itself to describing a person, organization, or business in detail. One widely circulated form is the business school case, which describes the history of a company up to a specific point in time involving a critical decision. Cases often encompass primary data collection through interviews but may be based solely upon secondary sources. Because of the relatively unrestrictive methodology and the tendency to report on companies of great public interest, the case study is virtually ubiquitous. Thousands of business cases are available through outlets such as the European Case Clearinghouse and Harvard Business Publishing.

Ethnography is a methodology that yields richly descriptive accounts with the potential to provide a deep and nuanced understanding of culture. The researcher typically studies firsthand a native community for long periods of time, immersing himself or herself as a participant-observer. In becoming part of the situation, the researcher attempts to deeply enter its reality, pushing beyond surface statements and representations. Ethnographies focus on creating a "thick" description that decodes the culture being studied. Classic examples include Hallowell 1955, Malinowski 1944, Crozier 1964, and Trist and Bamford 1951.

In correlational research, quantitative measures are taken of various aspects of a subject matter, and the degree of relationship between these various "variables" are determined through statistical analyses. The measurement instrument is often a survey, for instance, with questions about the extent to which one values different aspects of work. As surveys are relatively easy to administer, researchers can collect responses to many questions from large numbers of respondents from different cultures. With the application of powerful statistical procedures, large amounts of data can be distilled into basic underlying psychological dimensions. A simplified theoretical framework can then be created so that different cultures can be ranked and arrayed relative to each other. One of the most widely referenced studies in international management is Hofstede's (1980) large-scale survey measuring work attitudes of IBM employees in more than forty countries. This single dataset allowed him to derive the now classic typology of cultural dimensions, a single theoretical framework that differentiates various nations along broad cultural dimensions such as individualism-collectivism and power distance.

Compared to these methodologies, experimentation differs most distinctively in its rigorous exploration of cause-effect relationships. In an experiment, a researcher intentionally varies conditions of the environment believed to influence the occurrence of another event (Fromkin and Streufert 1976). For instance, Leung and Bond (1984) hypothesized that allocation condition (public vs. private) shows a similar impact on the way American and Chinese participants allocate a monetary reward with a co-worker. Upon completion of a joint task with another person, each participant in an experiment was given an envelope of money. The participant was instructed to take his or her share of the money, either in public or in private, leaving the remainder for the other person to collect at a later time. No guidelines were given regarding how the reward should be allocated. In this experiment, Leung and Bond manipulated the independent variable, public or private allocation of the reward, to see if there would be any measurable differences on the dependent variable, the amount of money left for the other person. The results found that, indeed, this manipulation led to different patterns of allocation. For both cultural groups, participants were more likely to allocate more money to their co-worker if the allocation was made in public than in private.

In an experiment, results are assessed by comparison of outcomes across the manipulated conditions. A critical requirement is control, or features designed to ensure that any systematic differences observed in the dependent variables are actually due to the manipulation of the independent variable. The experimental setting is strictly regulated so that treatment of the participants is as uniform as possible and varies only by the intended manipulation. In the Leung and Bond experiment, all participants engaged in exactly the same activities and received the same materials. The only difference was that participants in one condition allocated the reward in public, while participants in another condition allocated the money in private. Within each of these conditions, there were no differences in the treatment received by the participants.

Experimenters also attempt to control for preexisting differences in participants. For instance, if participants in one condition were wealthier than those in another condition, this preexisting difference could account for any observed differences in allocation behavior. To guard against such possibilities, participants are randomly assigned to experimental conditions. With large enough numbers of participants in each condition, random assignment reduces to a very low, and hence acceptable, likelihood that systematic preexisting differences exist across conditions.

Another important aspect of experimentation is quantitative analysis of results. Any differences in behavior that were observed across conditions are statistically analyzed for significance. Whereas individuals have cognitive limits and can be biased to see patterns that do not actually exist in the data, the experimental methodology imposes an impartial and objective authority, statistical theories, as the judge. Statistical analysis, of course, requires data of a numeric format. In some cases, this is simple, as behaviors such as allocation of money can be easily quantified or counted. Other experiments require respondents to evaluate their agreement with various statements on a numeric scale. Yet other experiments employ coders to report numeric values for qualitative data. For instance, a person is employed to count the number of times certain references are made in a written statement.

Experimentation has been applied to cross-cultural settings to study many issues, such as group productivity (Erez and Somech 1996), group and individual training (Earley 1994), social loafing (Earley 1989), negotiation behavior (Kelley et al. 1970), preferences for conflict resolution mechanisms (Leung and Lind 1986; Leung 1987), and justice perceptions (Brockner et al. 2000; Leung, Su, and Morris 2001).

Table 4.1 lays out many differences between experimentation and the other methodologies. Across the various categories, the methodologies can be differentiated along two broad types of differences. The first broad difference is the emphasis on naturally occurring behaviors and responses versus the emphasis on behaviors and reactions in contrived conditions. In ethnography, case study, and even survey research, participants are studied while they are in their natural work context, engaged in their normal activities, and embedded in their webs of continuing relationships and obligations. In contrast, in experimentation participants are taken out of their normal environment, placed in a controlled context, and asked to perform activities that are of short time duration and very much standardized and predesignated by the researcher. In experimentation, the primary focus is not on learning about the participants themselves but on examining the impact of the experimental manipulations. Indeed, the random assignment of participants to conditions is a direct attempt to make the participants in the manipulated conditions more uniform.

The second broad difference is the degree to which the methodologies are dependent on the distinctive attributes of the researcher. In ethnography, the researcher is an actual participant in the community being studied. He or she develops different types of relationships and engages in different types of activities with each informant. The researcher is also the sole data gatherer, recording his or her personal observations or impressions in field notes. In short, the findings are very much dependent on the researcher: the behaviors of the natives depend on the behavior and social inclinations of the researcher, and the interpretive lens that is applied depends on his or her training and academic orientations as well as sensibilities and life experiences. No methodology is ever independent of the researcher, but in experimentation there is greater likelihood that one researcher can replicate the work of another. Experimentation makes specific effort to utilize standardized procedures. The closely controlled manipulation procedures are designed to be simple and straightforward, as they have to be administered in an identical fashion to many participants. These procedures, as well as manipulation and measurement materials, are made available to readers. Data analysis conforms to statistical theories and to commonly held disciplinary standards on significance levels.

The methodologies also differ regarding the types of resources that will be demanded in data collection. Experiments require considerable effort in producing the measurement and manipulation materials, in recruiting respondents, and in executing the manipulations. This demand is drastically escalated if the manipulation procedure must be repeated separately

TABLE 4.1. Comparison of Methodologies

	Case Study	Ethnography	Correlation/ Survey Study	Experiment
Examination of causal relationship	Observes naturally occurring distribution of independent and dependent variables			Deliberately manipulates independent variables in controlled context
Respondents and context	Respondents chosen for important knowledge about organization	Respondents are native informants at the site	Respondents are selected to be representative of a population or segment	Participants are randomly assigned to condition manipulated by researcher
Interaction with respondents	Researcher interviews key players	Researcher participates in community over long period of time, developing relationships with informants	Each respondent receives identical survey	Participants within each condition receive identical treatment
Data format	Interviews and/or secondary data sources	Personal observations of researcher are recorded in field notes	Numeric: ensured either by requiring participants to respond on a numeric scale or by a coder who imposes one on the data	
Data processing/analysis	Researcher qualitatively identifies patterns in data		Mathematical analysis is utilized to identify statistically significant relationships	

for each individual respondent. Surveys require considerable time to construct the questions but can be relatively simple to administer. One central challenge is ensuring that the sample of respondents is representative of the target population, as differential response rates from different segments can skew the results. Ethnographies require the researcher to spend extended periods of time on-site and large amounts of time and care in taking field notes and collecting artifacts. Finally, the type of effort for data collection varies for case study, as there are no strict requirements that there even be primary data collection.

RELATIVE STRENGTHS AND WEAKNESSES
OF EXPERIMENTATION

The principal advantage of experimentation over the other methodologies is its superior ability to demonstrate causality. As the other methodologies observe naturally occurring distributions of independent and dependent variables, they infer causality based upon covariation or co-occurrence. Such inferences of causality are weaker, as covariation can occur even when the observed variables do not in fact causally affect each other. For instance, the observed correlation may be spurious: whenever several unrelated variables are observed, some will co-vary merely due to chance. Alternatively, covariation of two causally unrelated observed variables may occur because each is causally affected by a third unobserved variable. Moreover, even if a causal relationship does exist between two observed variables, the direction of causality may flow in a direction opposite to the hypothesis.

The manipulation of the hypothesized independent variable in a controlled context is a method that is not vulnerable to these rival explanations. This is certainly an important advantage in international management, where practitioners look to researchers to provide guidance on the likely outcome of various actions. Yet another advantage is that experimenters are not constrained to report on practices that currently exist. The ability to design and specify manipulations gives experimenters the ability to evaluate untried techniques and innovations.

Finally, standardization and ease of replication are also important strengths of experimentation. The ability to easily replicate one's own experiment makes it easier for researchers to evaluate new variants of their procedures, and to further refine their theory. The relative ease with which others can replicate one's experiments provides a mechanism for the research community to correct errors of a particular experiment or experimenter. Standardization also enables others to build on and add to a promising program of research.

Experimentation is not without its drawbacks, with most complaints centering on its weaker ability to capture "real world" phenomena and "mundane realism." Experimental contexts often bear little resemblance to the workplace, and participants are removed from any real stakes and longer-term considerations that are critical antecedents of workplace behavior. With low "external validity," doubt may be raised as to whether the cause-effect relationship found in the experiment extends to govern actual work behavior

It is also argued that controlled experiments focus so narrowly on a particular planned manipulation or a limited set of predefined set of measures that it is virtually impossible for them to address the full complexity of the cultural experience. Qualitatively oriented critics suggest that in order to provide a rich description of cultural reality, researchers must have the freedom to inductively discover and investigate the innumerable facets of another culture. Ethnographers also suggest that long periods of time spent on-site is necessary in order to build the relationships and understanding necessary to delve beyond surface attributes of culture.

Experiments may also lack breadth since they tend not to examine a causal relationship along a large number of levels of the independent variable. Typical experiments manipulate only two or three levels of the independent variable because relatively large numbers of participants are necessary for each condition. This barrier becomes even more prohibitive when the causal relationship involves many explanatory variables, an important reason why most experiments do not involve more than three independent variables. In contrast, correlational studies typically examine naturally occurring variation in many explanatory variables in a continuous fashion.

Finally, the experimental technique necessarily assumes hypothesized cause-effect relationships that can be invoked under appropriate conditions. However, certain theories focus on causal relationships involving macrolevel explanatory variables, such as the impact of organizational climate on business values. Such broad and multifaceted conditions would be difficult, if not impossible, for an experimenter to replicate in the laboratory.

DIFFERENT TYPES OF EXPERIMENTS

Experiments can be categorized in a tripartite fashion: laboratory, field, and quasi (Cook and Campbell 1976; Fromkin and Struefert 1976; Brown and Sechrest 1980). In a laboratory experiment, the participant is put in an artificially constructed and controlled environment. In a field experiment, the investigator attempts to manipulate and control the pertinent variables in a natural setting. Participants may be in their normal context engaged in work activities in the presence of co-workers. Early field studies manipulated physical working conditions, such as rest periods, refreshments, and lighting, and collected measures of performance (Roethlisberger and Dickson 1939). More recently, Earley (1986) conducted a field experiment in goal setting. Tire-tread laborers in comparable factories in the United States and the United Kingdom were exposed to a goal manipulation by either their supervisor or a shop steward. The manipulation attempted to influence the participants' ongoing work activities in their normal work setting.

A quasi-experiment is a field experiment in which a truly random assignment of participants to experimental treatments is absent or less than perfect. This may occur in a variety of situations, such as when researchers withhold a treatment from a preassigned control group or when differential attrition occurs across conditions. The main weakness of this design is that the experimenter cannot ensure that there are no systematic preexisting differences in the participants across conditions. Yet quasi-experiments can be powerfully instructive. For example, a company that planned to institute pay cuts gave one type of explanation to employees in one division and a different explanation to those of another division. Researchers found that this difference in treatment led to different levels of theft in the divisions (Greenberg 1990). As experimenters do not have the ability to plan a controlled experiment in which real pay cuts are made, the quasi-experimental technique allowed researchers to study the consequences of a dramatic real-world action.

WHAT IS INTERNATIONAL MANAGEMENT RESEARCH?

A basic but perplexing issue revolves around the question of what exactly qualifies a research program as international or intercultural. Is a study international if it is conducted in a non-Anglo-American or non-Western setting? Such an approach might argue that, to the extent a discipline has its historical origins in one dominant national perspective, any work that improves the understanding of other cultural settings is international. Others might argue, however, that truly international research requires a direct comparison of cultures, so that we can compare and contrast them along important dimensions.

This debate is a reflection of two different philosophies regarding "origin of constructs," a term that refers to the source of the ideas or constructs utilized in a program of research. A common distinction in intercultural research is the emic versus etic distinction (Pike 1954). In the emic approach, behavior can only be meaningfully understood in the context of the cultural meaning system in which it is embedded. As any criteria or definitions used in such analyses are internal to the culture, only a single culture can be studied at a time. In the etic approach, however, multiple cultural systems can be assessed and compared with one another for similarities or differences. The analyst can create or impose a conceptual structure, wherein the criteria used are considered absolute or culturally universal (see Headland, Pike, and Harris 1990 for a review).

In ethnography, the emic approach has been predominant, with the objective of yielding a deep, rich description of one culture. As early ethnographers had focused on studying a single jungle tribe at a time, more recent work has focused on single organizations such as the Body Shop (Martin, Knopoff, and Beckman 1998) and Disney in Japan (Raz 1999). In psychology, however, cross-cultural research has typically taken the etic approach of trying to identify universal dimensions to distinguish various cultures. This is perhaps best demonstrated by Hofstede's IBM survey research, upon which dimensions of power distance and collectivism were derived. More recently, it has become apparent that a purely etic approach can overlook important concepts unique to a given culture. For instance, while Hofstede identified the etic notion of power distance, he initially failed to uncover the more nuanced dimension salient in East Asian culture, namely Confucian Dynamism (Hofstede and Bond 1988).

As a result of such revelations, a more balanced approach has emerged, as more specific cultural constructs are being introduced. Instead of imposing one culturally universal dimension of individualism-collectivism, more culturally specific types are being proposed (e.g., Triandis and Gelfand 1998). Researchers also increasingly frame their claims in terms of specific contexts that cue different norms or criteria in observers from different cultures (e.g., Leung 1997). Observing this trend, Morris et al. (1999) argue that the emic and etic perspectives can stimulate and enrich each other. A synergistic approach incorporating both approaches in an iterative manner is most conducive to theory development.

This negotiation between the emic and etic approaches both helps to demonstrate the versatility of the experimental approach and foreshadows an important challenge. Experiments may be conducted solely in one country to develop a nuanced understanding of local meaning systems or in multiple countries to allow contrasts and comparisons. The cross-cultural comparisons enabled by the etic approach are especially important in international management, as they gauge the extent to which practices that are commonplace in one culture might be received differently elsewhere. The following sections will discuss, however, the many difficulties and challenges inherent to experiments conducted simultaneously in multiple cultures.

CROSS-CULTURAL EQUIVALENCE

As we mentioned, experimenters attempt to control the context so that the only between-condition differences are the intentionally manipulated levels of the hypothesized explanatory variables. A fundamental requirement is that all nonmanipulated factors in the various experimental conditions should be equivalent. In a cross-cultural experiment, researchers must also ensure that the manipulations are equivalent across cultures, in the sense that the experimental manipulations have the same meaning in the various cultures. In the current section we employ cross-cultural equivalence as the organizing theme and delineate the difficulties that often pose a threat to internal validity of cross-cultural experiments.

EQUIVALENCE OF PARTICIPANTS

Participants of an experiment may be recruited in different ways: as paid or unpaid volunteers, as participants of training courses in which the experiment is a learning exercise, as students fulfilling a course requirement, as employees who are sponsored by their companies to participate, or as employees working in their natural setting as part of a field experiment. One basic guideline in experimentation is that participants in different cultures should be comparable with respect to the circumstances of participation. If participants in one culture are paid volunteers while those in another are fulfilling a course requirement, this difference in recruitment method may constitute a significant rival hypothesis for any differences observed in the two samples. If payment is involved, the experimenter should seek to ensure that the amounts are equivalent across cultures, in light of the underlying economic differences that may exist. In short, it is a wise practice to match as closely as possible the circumstances under which participants take part in an experiment across cultures.

A similar guideline is that the experimenter should attempt to match the demographic profile of the participants in the different cultures, since factors such as gender, education, or wealth may affect responses. Unfortunately, a simple matching on education or wealth may be insufficient. Societies differ widely on their average demographic profiles, and a similar profile may have very different meanings in different societal contexts. For instance, cross-cultural comparisons of samples of MBA students with similar age and gender compositions may seem fine at the first glance. However, the comparisons may be problematic if the social status of being an MBA student varies widely across cultures. Take the comparison of China and the United States as an example. At present, MBA programs in China are mostly for the elites due to the scarcity of such programs, whereas MBA programs abound in the United States and many programs are not highly selective. Thus, a simple comparison of MBA students from China and the United States may confound career success with cultural differences.

Participants should also be similarly familiar with the experimental context, as well as the stimulus and measurement instruments used. If, for example, participants in one culture are less familiar with the stimulus materials, any between-culture differences that are observed may be due to stimulus familiarity rather than other substantive causes. A classic demonstration is provided by Serpell (1979), who found that Scottish children performed better than Zambian children in sorting photos of animals and motor vehicles. When miniature models were used, these two cultural groups showed similar levels of performance, suggesting that Scottish children's higher familiarity with photos may have accounted for the earlier results. In the arena of international management research, a potentially parallel example may be familiarity with computers. Cross-cultural experiments may involve the use of computers as a communication tool. If one cultural group is less familiar with the use of computers than other cultural groups, the cross-cultural comparisons may be biased.

CONCEPTUAL EQUIVALENCE

In cross-cultural research, a concept must have a similar meaning across cultures before it can be compared (van de Vijver and Leung 1997, ch. 2). In the context of an experiment, the independent and dependent variables should be conceptually equivalent across cultures. For instance, one may be interested in the effect of prior achievement on subsequent performance. However, it is now known that achievement is primarily conceptualized in personal terms in individualist societies, such as the United States, whereas it has a noticeable collective element in collectivistic societies, such as Taiwan (Yu 1996). Thus, the concept of achievement is not equivalent across the United States and Taiwan, and a comparison of the antecedents and consequences of achievement without distinguishing its individual and collective elements may be misleading. In an experimental context, an individual-oriented manipulation of achievement may have a weaker effect in Taiwan than in the United States. If only individual-oriented achievement is manipulated, and the effect is found to be weaker in Taiwan than in the United States, it is not accurate to conclude that achievement has a weak effect in Taiwan. The effect of group-oriented achievement should also be evaluated for a fuller picture of the dynamics involved.

Even when concepts can be said to be equivalent, there may be calibration differences across cultures. For instance, a manipulation that provides an incentive of ten U.S. dollars to participants in the United States and in Mexico may not be equivalent, as the United States has a higher GDP per capita than Mexico. Thus, an experiment that employs an identical instead of an equivalent operational definition of incentives (i.e., an equivalent amount of monetary incentive) in these two countries will run into the problem of nonequivalence. To overcome this problem, some researchers have equated incentives across cultures in terms of purchasing power (Roth, Prasnikar, and Okuno-Fujiwara 1991). In sum, the operation of the variables must be equivalent in their meaning and intensity across cultures for the results to be interpretable.

EQUIVALENCE OF THE EXPERIMENTAL PROCEDURE

It is well known that subtle differences in experimental procedures may potentially have major consequences on the experimental results. For instance, a slight variation in experimental instructions led to very different results of an assigned work goal on performance (Latham, Erez, and Locke 1988). The problem of nonequivalent experimental procedures is more threatening in cross-cultural experiments, because they are typically conducted by different experimenters in different countries. Different experimenters may unwittingly execute the experiment in subtly different manners.

Another well-known type of confounding influence has been called the "experimenter expectancy effect," which refers to the influence of the expectations of experimenters on the participant's behavior (Rosenthal 1968). If experimenters in different countries have different expectations about the findings, the experimenter expectancy effect may bias the results differentially across cultures. In fact, the appearance, demographic background, and unintended behaviors of experimenters may also affect the behavior and responses of the participants (e.g., Cotter, Cohen, and Coulter 1982). Cross-cultural differences in these background factors will introduce systematic biases in the data. One effective method to reduce this problem is to gather the experimenters from different countries to rehearse the experimental procedure together so that cross-cultural variations in experimental procedures and other background factors are minimized (Roth, Prasnikar, and Okuno-Fujiwara 1991). The double-blind technique, which requires both the participants and the experimenters to be blind to the hypotheses, provides an effective way to reduce the expectancy effect of the experimenter.

Even if extreme care is taken to equate the demographic backgrounds and the behavior of the experimenters across cultures, experimenters may trigger cultural values and practices that are salient in some cultures and thus bias the results. For instance, experimenters as a class of people may generate a higher level of demand characteristics in high rather than in low power distance societies. There is no perfect way to eliminate the influence of these cultural values, and the best strategy is to explore their effects as part of the experimental design, so that their effects can be systematically documented and explicated.

EQUIVALENCE OF THE EXPERIMENTAL CONTEXT

Ideally, the physical context of an experiment should be identical across conditions. This goal presents a major challenge to cross-cultural experiments, especially to field experiments, in which experimental control is relatively low. For instance, physical settings affect people's behavior, and unintended cultural variations in physical settings may render observed cultural differences uninterpretable. As an illustration, consider the case in which participants in one culture are put in a small room and as a result communicate more frequently because of closer proximity. In another culture, participants are put in a much bigger room, and the larger distance between participants may discourage interpersonal communication.

SPECIAL CONCERNS IN CROSS-CULTURAL EXPERIMENTS

Several concerns are particularly important for cross-cultural experiments because of the need to compare and contrast results from multiple cultures.

NATURE OF MANIPULATION:
REAL-LIFE VERSUS HYPOTHETIC

In most monocultural experiments, the experimental manipulation involves real-life, real-time stimuli, such as instructions from an experimenter or an experimental task. In cross-cultural experiments, the vignette approach is more prevalent. In a vignette experiment, participants are asked to respond to a hypothetical situation, often presented in a written form, either as an imagined actor or as an observer. For instance, Kim, Park, and Suzuki (1990) compared how Americans, Koreans, and Japanese distributed a hypothetical reward. Leung, Su, and Morris (2001) compared how MBA students in Hong Kong and the United States reacted to hypothetical criticism from a supervisor. There are many reasons for the popularity of this approach. Because the materials can be administered in much the same fashion as a survey, there is no need for intricate manipulations of the environment and data can be collected from large numbers of respondents at the same time. Vignettes can also be easily adapted and standardized across cultures through translation and back translation. And, finally, many situations that are difficult to enact can be easily captured by a vignette.

Despite these advantages, the vignette approach does have weaknesses. First, establishing the equivalence of a vignette across several cultures may prove to be very challenging. Assume, for example, that one is interested in how incentives affect work performance across several cultures and has decided to employ a restaurant vignette in an experiment. Of course, there are cultural differences in how restaurants operate. In some countries, waiters rely heavily on tips as their income, work on preassigned tables individually, and often work part-time. In some other countries, waiters do not expect tipping, work as a team, and are mostly full-time. Developing a restaurant vignette that is simple, clear, and equivalent across many cultures may prove to be elusive. This difficulty can be extended to social situations, as cultures differ dramatically with respect to the scripts that are associated with particular occasions.

Another concern is that hypothetical and real-life stimuli may elicit different responses, and findings based on vignettes may differ from those based on real-life experimental studies. It is an empirical question whether vignette-based results diverge from those derived from real-life analogues, and our view is that a categorical rejection of this approach is untenable. In fact, some of the most influential work in psychology is based on vignettes: the best known of which are perhaps the vignette experiments conducted by Tversky and Kahneman (1974) for demonstrating their well-known decision heuristics. There is also evidence showing that some responses to vignettes correspond to real behaviors. For instance, Leung and Bond (1984) showed that the tendency for Chinese to divide a reward equally is found in distributive behaviors as well as in hypothetical distributions in response to a vignette. One major factor that determines the usefulness of the vignette approach may lie in the nature of the responses. If the responses are often enacted in real-life and are based on salient norms or attitudes, they are likely to be valid despite their hypothetical nature. Nevertheless, it is always important to triangulate vignette-based results with other methods to ascertain their validity.

INTRACULTURAL VERSUS CROSS-CULTURAL INTERACTION

Cross-cultural experiments can be classified into two types: those that are designed to study *intra*cultural interactions and those that study *cross*-cultural interactions. In studies of an intra-cultural phenomenon, a similar experiment is conducted within each of the different cultural groups, and the results are compared across cultures. In studies of a cross-cultural phenomenon, however, a single experiment that involves the interaction of two or more cultural groups is conducted. The issue of interest is often how the cultural backgrounds of the participants affect the interaction. Some cross-cultural studies on bargaining include both approaches in a single study and provide a good illustration of how these two designs shed light on the relationship between culture and bargaining outcomes. In intracultural bargaining studies, the same bargaining experiment is conducted in different cultural groups, and their results are compared. In experiments of cross-cultural bargaining, two cultural groups are typically asked to bargain with each other, and the results are interpreted in the light of the cultural backgrounds of the bargainers (e.g., Adair, Okumura, and Brett 2001; Brett and Okumura 1998).

Cross-cultural experiments must contend with a set of confounding variables that usually do not affect intracultural experiments. Culture constitutes one set of variables in such experiments, but intergroup variables that are more transient than cultural variables may play a bigger role in shaping the processes and outcomes of such intercultural interactions. The relative social status of two cultural groups, the stereotype that each group holds about the other, and the perceived meaning of the interaction, just to name a few factors, may override the effects of culture and shape the interaction in significant ways. Even the perceived cultural identity of the experimenter and his or her relationship with the other cultural groups may alter the behaviors of the interactants (e.g., Reese et al. 1986). These intergroup processes are legitimate and important topics of scientific enquiry (e.g., Hogg and Terry 2000), but if the research focus is on the effects of culture, these processes are a source of validity threats to conclusions based on cultural considerations. There is no perfect way to fully control for these intergroup variables; they just have to be taken into account when intercultural experiments are designed. When in doubt, it is always desirable to develop rival hypotheses based on these intergroup variables and to test their validity against the cultural hypotheses.

DEPENDENT VARIABLES

The instruments used to measure dependent variables in cross-cultural experiments fall into two broad categories: paper-and-pencil and behavioral. Pencil-and-pencil measures, including attitudinal measures, judgments, and behavioral intentions, are common in part because vignette studies are popular, and these studies typically employ paper-and-pencil measures. Moreover, paper-and-pencil measures can include many items, rendering them amenable to multivariate statistical analyses, such as factor analysis and regression for evaluating cross-cultural equivalence (van de Vijver and Leung 1997). In contrast, behavioral measures are usually single-item, and it is hard to demonstrate their cross-cultural equivalence statistically. Other than face validity, the major way to demonstrate the validity of behavioral measures is triangulation, which seeks converging results of conceptually similar behaviors. For instance, Chatman and Barsade (1995) used three unrelated measures to index cooperative behavior. Triangulation of behavioral measures may sometimes be difficult to carry out, and a more practical approach is to employ hybrid designs, in which paper-and-pencil results are checked against behavioral results. For instance, Earley (1994) used results based on self-rated effort to check against results based on task performance.

DECEPTION

Because of ethical concerns, deception has grown out of favor in experimental research. For the most part, only mild forms are employed now, such as the provision of misleading information and the withholding of vital information. When deception is used, it is always the burden of the experimenter to show that it would not lead to artificial results. In cross-cultural studies, a major worry of this experimental technique is that they may have differential effects across cultures. For instance, one group may be more suspicious than another group, and it is hard to tell how different levels of skepticism about the experimental instructions may affect the cross-cultural results obtained. In fact, it is interesting to note that some cultural groups may come to see deception as an integral part of most experiments, and this belief may shape their behavior even if deception is not employed. This stereotypical belief, if showing variations across cultures, may lead to observed cultural differences that are unrelated to the cultural hypotheses being evaluated.

CAUSALITY IN CROSS-CULTURAL EXPERIMENTAL RESEARCH

As mentioned before, the primary advantage of the experimental method is its superior ability to ascertain causality. However, the fact that cultures can be neither manipulated nor randomized severely constrains our ability to draw firm causal inferences in the cross-cultural context. In this section, we explore ways to improve the confidence that we can place on causal conclusions derived from cross-cultural experiments.

CULTURE AS BACKGROUND OR CAUSE

Cross-cultural experiments can be placed into two broad types according to their objectives with respect to causality. In the first type, referred to as generalizability studies by van de Vijver and Leung (1997), the main purpose is to evaluate the generalizability of a causal relationship across cultures. Culture is simply a background variable, and its role in the casual process is to be ruled out. For instance, Leung, Su, and Morris (2001, study 1) hypothesized that the positive effects of the perceived fairness of a criticism on reactions to the criticism should be culture-general. This pattern was indeed obtained across a number of experimental conditions for both Chinese and American participants. In general, the validity of the causal conclusions of these experiments is easier to establish because true experiments are being conducted in each cultural group. As long as these experiments are equivalent across the cultures involved, causality can be demonstrated with a high degree of confidence.

Most cross-cultural experiments are of the second type, in which some aspects of culture are hypothesized to play a significant role in the causal processes, either as an antecedent or as a moderator. For instance, individualism-collectivism has been shown in experimental studies to affect social loafing (Earley 1989), reward allocation (Leung and Bond 1984), and bargaining behavior (Gelfand and Christakopoulou 1999). Brockner et al. (2000) have shown that self-construal moderates the joint effects of perceived justice and outcome. Causal claims that arise from this type must contend with potentially serious problems of internal reliability for the simple reason that we cannot manipulate culture nor randomize participants to different cultural groups.

THE COVARIATE APPROACH

Van de Vijver and Leung (1997) have proposed a number of techniques to strengthen the causal claims derived from cross-cultural studies, which are refined and expanded in the following discussion. The *covariate approach* is a frequently employed technique that involves a direct test of the cultural elements concerned in the form of a covariate analysis. In this approach, culture is conceptualized and operationalized as an individual differences variable, and its causal role is supported by its covariation with the observed between-group difference in the dependent variables. For instance, Brockner et al. (2001) have shown that the effect of voice is stronger in cultural groups with a lower power distance. When power distance was controlled for in a covariate analysis, the cultural differences in the effect of voice disappeared. Analyses of covariance or regression are common statistical techniques used in this approach.

There are at least two other variants of the covariate approach, the first of which may be termed the *single-group covariate approach*. This approach categorizes individuals by their standing on the individual differences variable that corresponds to a cultural dimension and uses this individual-level variable for the assignment of participants into different experimental conditions. To control for confounding variables due to cross-cultural variation, a single culture is often used. A good example comes from an experimental study by Chatman and Barsade (1995), who classified their American participants as individualists or collectivists based on their level of measured individualism-collectivism. These two groups of participants were then randomly assigned to either an individualistic or a collectivistic culture, both of which were experimentally induced. In support of their person-culture fit model, the results indicate that collectivists behaved more cooperatively in a collectivist rather than individualist culture, whereas the cooperative behavior of individualists was not affected by the dominant culture.

The second variant of the covariate approach may be described as the *fixed-group covariate approach.* Here, existing groups from a single culture that vary on the cultural dimension of interest are used to evaluate a hypothesized causal relationship. For instance, kibutz and non-kibutz groups in Israel have been contrasted in experimental studies because these two groups vary in levels of individualism-collectivism (e.g., Erez and Earley 1987). The fact that they share a similar cultural background helps sidestep many confounding problems in multicultural experiments. A recent study by Kurman (2001) has contrasted four groups in Israel: religious kibutz members, nonreligious kibutz members, religious urban Israelis, and nonreligious urban Israelis. The kibutz membership provides the variation in individualism-collectivism, whereas religiosity provides variation in modesty. With this four-group design, she was able to show that the tendency for self-enhancement is not related to individualism-collectivism but to a modesty norm.

THE CULTURAL MANIPULATION APPROACH

Recently, a new approach has been used to demonstrate the causal role of culture by experimentally manipulating the strength of a cultural element and demonstrating that this manipulation influences the dependent variable in a predictable way. Cohen et al. (1996) labeled this approach "experimental ethnography," but we prefer the label "cultural manipulation." Cohen et al. (1996) are interested in the effect of a culture of honor on aggressiveness in the Southern region of the United States. To demonstrate its causal effects, they conducted an experiment in which participants from the South and the North were insulted in the experimental condition. While Southerners and Northerners behaved similarly in the control condition in which there was no insult, Southerners were more likely to report that their masculine reputation was threatened and to display more aggressive behavior after they were insulted in the experimental condition. The insult triggered the culture of honor among the Southerners, which led to their aggressive reactions. Another example comes from the experimental work of Hong et al. (2000), who argue that, compared to people from collectivist cultures, people from individualist cultures are more likely to attribute the cause of other people's behaviors to internal reasons, such as their personality traits (as opposed to external reasons, such as the situation). Hong et al. (2000) argue that a priming technique can be used to manipulate the individualist or collectivist mind-set. A group of Hong Kong Chinese were randomly exposed to one of two sets of experimental stimuli. One set included well-known American icons such as Superman, and the other set contained well-known Chinese icons such as Monkey King, from a well-known classical novel that provides the template for the main character of the popular Japanese cartoon series *Dragon Ball.* In support of their cultural explanation, exposure to the American primes resulted in a stronger tendency to make internal attributions than did exposure to the Chinese primes.

In our opinion, the cultural manipulation approach provides a powerful means to ascertain causal claims in cross-cultural experiments. However, an effective way to manipulate the cultural element that is assumed to play a causal role must first be identified, which may not be easy. This approach is currently uncommon in cross-cultural experiments in management research but holds great promise as a tool in future research.

FUTURE DIRECTIONS

DEVELOPMENTS IN EXPERIMENTAL RESEARCH ON CULTURE AND MANAGEMENT

In the last decade, considerable progress has been made in cross-cultural experimentation, and exciting breakthroughs are even more likely in this coming decade, as researchers are now equipped with better knowledge about culture and cross-cultural experimentation. At present, the bulk of cross-cultural management research is based on surveys, but as theories on culture and management become more precise, the need for experimental work will increase dramatically.

We see at least four important developments in experimental research on culture and management. First, triangulation is important in helping to overcome the weaknesses of any particular methodology, and we expect that the field will demand researchers to demonstrate the validity of their results by multiple methods. Survey results will need to be checked against experimental results, and paper-and-pencil responses will need to be verified with behavioral responses. Convergence will be required before results can be taken as valid. In the coming years, multimethod approaches will become the rule rather than the exception, and experimentation is a pivotal part of this process because of its strength in internal validity.

Second, there is a strong need to expand the geographical boundaries of cross-cultural experimental work. At present, most such work targets North America and East Asia, primarily because of their economic prominence. However, there are often sound theoretical reasons for venturing into relatively uncharted regions. For instance, there has been interest in the conception of time and negotiation (Tinsley 1998), and the understanding of cross-cultural issues will be advanced as it is studied in the South American context. Experimental research on culture and management needs to span the globe in a more systematically and theoretically driven fashion.

Third, the trend to *unpackage* culture, to trace observed cultural differences to specific cultural elements, will continue (van de Vijver and Leung 1997, ch. 1). It is simply inadequate to speculate on why two cultures are different; we need to know what exactly is causing the difference. The unpackaging of culture will lead to new individual differences variables, such as self-construal—the way one views oneself (Markus and Kitayama 1991)—and *guanxi*—the way an individual is related to others (Farh et al. 1998). Structural aspects of culture will also emerge as explanatory variables of cultural differences. For instance, in the heyday of Japanese management, the pros and cons of lifetime employment and a generalist career track were often discussed because these two arrangements were less common in the West (Ouchi and Price 1993). We expect that some structural elements of cultures that are amenable to experimental exploration, such as the cultural diversity of a group (Thomas 1999), will receive more attention and enrich theories on culture and management.

Fourth, in monocultural experiments, confounding variables are typically eliminated by a good experimental design. In cross-cultural experiments, however, confounding variables sometimes point to legitimate and important substantive questions. For instance, Japanese bargainers are found to display more silence than Brazilians and Americans in bargaining (Graham 1985). In a bargaining experiment, if the bargaining time is equalized for these three cultural groups, the Japanese results may be confounded by a shorter duration for verbal exchanges for Japanese bargainers. An experimenter may develop an ingenious way to control for the confounding influence of this variable, but cultural differences in silence during bargaining are an interesting phenomenon in their own right. A more informative approach may be to include the bargaining time allowed as an independent variable and explore its effect on the bargaining process and outcomes. We expect that systematic exploration rather than the control of culture-related confounding variables will be more common in the future.

THE CENTRAL ROLE OF THEORY
IN EXPERIMENTATION

Van de Vijver and Leung (2001) suggest that theory should take a central role in cross-cultural studies. Research methods, no matter how sophisticated and meticulous, cannot compensate for imprecise and incoherent theories. The best safeguard against experimental artifacts and confounding variables is perhaps sound theory and precise predictions. Significant developments in theorizing on culture and management are on the horizon and will encourage the integration of culture in management theories. In particular, the synergistic integration between etic and emic perspectives for the development of universal theories proposed by Morris et al. (1999) is noteworthy. In addition, the convergence approach advocated by van de Vijver and Leung (2001), which calls for the juxtaposition and integration of theories of different cultural origins, can facilitate the diversity and richness of management theories. Well-known examples of this approach include the Global Leadership and Organizational Behavior Effectiveness (GLOBE) project on leadership (House et al. 1999) and the event management project orchestrated by Smith and Peterson (e.g., Smith, Peterson, and Wang 1996). Both projects are multicentered because the research questions and working hypotheses involved were derived from multiple cultural perspectives at an early stage. Hopefully, these exciting metatheoretical developments will render cross-cultural theories of the next generation more comprehensive, coherent, and precise. We see theory development and advances in experimental methods as interdependent and necessary for real progress in the field.

FRUITFUL AREAS FOR CROSS-CULTURAL EXPERIMENTAL RESEARCH

In this final section, we speculate on the substantive areas that are likely to benefit from cross-cultural experimentation. Part of our judgment is guided by where most previous cross-cultural experimentation is concentrated, and part of it is based on the pros and cons of this methodology. Given that most laboratory experimentations involve artificial settings and short durations, work and managerial processes that are not distorted in significant ways by these characteristics are natural candidates for experimentation. Therefore, it is not accidental that, as reviewed before, the bulk of cross-cultural experimentation is concerned with group dynamics and interpersonal interactions, such as negotiation and performance on well-defined tasks. However, many other behavioral phenomena, such as decision-making and motivational processes, are amenable to experimentation, but they are rarely the target of cross-cultural experimental work. We expect to see an increasing number of cross-cultural experiments in these new areas.

It is true that cross-cultural experimentation is typically employed to explore behavioral issues, but our review suggests that culture as a set of macrolevel antecedents is amenable to experimentation as well. There are now a number of ingenious ways to simulate the effects of cultural elements on individuals. A good example is the design employed by Chatman and Barsade (1995) to simulate collectivistic and individualistic work climates. Researchers who are interested in the effects of structural or firm-level variables on individual or group behaviors across cultures should find experimentation an important addition to their tool set.

Finally, for work and managerial processes that take a long duration to evaluate, such as chronic effects of stress or effects of leadership styles on productivity, field experiments are more appropriate. Unfortunately, field experiments are difficult to set up, and cross-cultural field experiments are even harder. However, because of their unique capability in the evaluation of causal relationships in vitro, they should definitely be encouraged.

REFERENCES

Adair, W. L., T. Okumura, and J. M. Brett. 2001. Negotiation behavior when cultures collide: The United States and Japan. *Journal of Applied Psychology* 86:371–85.

Brett, J., and T. Okumura. 1998. Inter and intracultural negotiation: U.S. and Japanese negotiators. *Academy of Management Journal* 41:495–510.

Brockner, J., G. Ackerman, J. Greenberg, M. J. Gelfand, A. M. Francesco, Z. X. Chen, K. Leung, G. Bierbrauer, C. Gomez, B. L. Kirkman, and D. Shapiro. 2001. Culture and procedural justice: The influence of power distance on reactions to voice. *Journal of Experimental Social Psychology* 37:300–315.

Brockner, J., Y. R. Chen, E. A. Mannix, K. Leung, and D. P. Skarlicki. 2000. Cross-cultural variation in the interactive relationship between procedural fairness and outcome favorability: The case of self-construal. *Administrative Science Quarterly* 45:138–59.

Brown, E. D., and L. Sechrest. 1980. Experiments in cross-cultural research. In J. W. Berry, M. H. Segall, and C. Kagitcibasi, eds., *Handbook of cross-cultural psychology,* vol. 2. Boston: Allyn and Bacon.

Chatman, J. A., and S. G. Barsade. 1995. Personality, organizational culture, and cooperation: Evidence from a business simulation. *Administrative Science Quarterly* 40:423–43.

Cohen, D., R. E. Nisbett, B. F. Bowdle, and N. Schwarz. 1996. Insult, aggression, and the southern culture of honor: An "experimental ethnography." *Journal of Personality and Social Psychology* 70:945–60.

Cook, T. D., and D. T. Campbell. 1976. The design and conduct of quasi-experiments and true experiments in field settings. In M. D. Dunnette, ed., *Handbook of industrial and organizational psychology.* Chicago: Rand McNally.

Cotter, P. R., J. Cohen, and P. Coulter. 1982. Race-of-interviewer effects in telephone interviews. *Public Opinion Quarterly* 46:278–84.

Crozier, M. 1964. *The bureaucratic phenomenon.* Chicago: University of Chicago Press.

Earley, P. C. 1986. Supervisors and shop stewards as sources of contextual information in goal-setting: A comparison of the U.S. with England. *Journal of Applied Psychology* 71:111–18.

———. 1989. Social loafing and collectivism: A comparison of the United States and the People's Republic of China. *Administrative Science Quarterly* 34:565–81.

———. 1994. Self or group? Cultural effects of training on self-efficacy and performance. *Administrative Science Quarterly* 39:89–117.

Earley, P. C., and E. Mosakowski. 1996. Experimental international management research. In B. J. Punnett and O. Shenkar, eds., *Handbook for international management research.* Cambridge, MA: Blackwell.

Erez, M., and P. C. Earley. 1987. Comparative analysis of goal-setting strategies across cultures. *Journal of Applied Psychology* 72:658–65.

Erez, M., and A. Somech. 1996. Is group productivity loss the rule or the exception? Effects of culture and group-based motivation. *Academy of Management Journal* 39:1513–37.

Farh, J. L., A. S. Tsui, K. Xin, and B. S. Cheng. 1998. The influence of relational demography and Guanxi: The Chinese case. *Organization Science* 9:471–88.

Fromkin, H. L., and S. Streufert. 1976. Laboratory experimentation. In M. D. Dunnette, ed., *Handbook of industrial and organizational psychology.* Chicago: Rand McNally.

Gelfand, M. J., and S. Christakopoulou. 1999. Culture and negotiator cognition: Judgment accuracy and negotiation processes in individualistic and collectivistic cultures. *Organizational Behavior and Human Decision Processes* 79:248–69.

Graham, J. 1985. The influence of culture on business negotiations. *Journal of International Business Studies* 16:81–96.

Greenberg, J. 1990. Employee theft as a reaction to underpayment inequity: The hidden costs of pay cuts. *Journal of Applied Psychology* 75:561–68.

Hallowell, A. I. 1955. *Culture and experience*. Philadelphia: University of Pennsylvania Press.

Headland, T. N., K. L. Pike, and M. Harris. 1990. *Emics and etics: The insider/outsider debate*. Newbury Park, CA: Sage.

Hofstede, G. 1980. *Culture's consequences: International differences in work-related values*. Beverly Hills, CA: Sage.

———. 1991. *Cultures and organizations: Software of the mind*. London: McGraw-Hill.

Hofstede, G., and M. H. Bond. 1988. The Confucius connection: From cultural roots to economic growth. *Organizational Dynamics* (spring):4–21.

Hogg, M., and D. J. Terry. 2000. Social identity and self-categorization processes in organizational contexts. *Academy of Management Review* 25:121–40.

Hong, Y. Y., M. W. Morris, C. Y. Chiu, and V. Benet-Martinez. 2000. Multicultural minds: A dynamic constructivist approach to culture and cognition. *American Psychologist* 55:709–20.

House, R. J., P. J. Hanges, S. A. Ruiz-Quintanilla, P. W. Dorfman, M. Javidan, M. Dickson, and V. Gupta. 1999. Cultural influences on leadership and organizations: Project GLOBE. *Advances in global leadership* 1:171–233.

Kelley, H. H., G. H. Sure, M. Deutsch, C. Faucheux, J. T. Lanzetta, S. Moscovici, J. M. Nuttin, and J. M. Rabbie. 1970. A comparative study of negotiation behavior. *Journal of Personality and Social Psychology* 16:411–38.

Kim, K. I., H. J. Park, and N. Suzuki. 1990. Reward allocations in the United States, Japan, and Korea: A comparison of individualistic and collectivistic cultures. *Academy of Management Journal* 33:188–98.

Kurman, J. 2001. Is self-enhancement related to modesty or to individualism-collectivism? A test with four Israeli groups. *Asian Journal of Social Psychology* 4:225–37.

Latham, G. P., M. Erez, and E. A. Locke. 1988. Resolving scientific disputes by the joint design of crucial experiments by the antagonists: Application to the Erez-Latham dispute regarding participation in goal setting. *Journal of Applied Psychology* 73:753–72.

Leung, K. 1987. Some determinants of reactions to procedural models for conflict resolution: A cross-national study. *Journal of Personality and Social Psychology* 53:898–908.

———. 1997. Negotiation and reward allocations across cultures. In P. C. Earley and M. Erez, eds., *New perspectives on international industrial and organizational psychology*. San Francisco: Jossey Bass.

Leung, K., and M. H. Bond. 1984. The impact of cultural collectivism on reward allocation. *Journal of Personality and Social Psychology* 47:793–804.

Leung, K., and E. A. Lind. 1986. Procedure and culture: Effects of culture, gender, and investigator status on procedural preferences. *Journal of Personality and Social Psychology* 50:1134–40.

Leung, K., S. K. Su, and M. W. Morris. 2001. When is criticism not constructive? The roles of fairness perceptions and dispositional attributions in employee acceptance of critical supervisory feedback. *Human Relations* 54:1155–87.

Malinowski, B. 1944. *A scientific theory of culture*. Chapel Hill: University of North Carolina Press.

Markus, H., and S. Kitayama. 1991. Culture and the self: Implications for cognition, emotion, and motivation. *Psychological Review* 98:224–53.

Martin, J., K. Knopoff, and C. Beckman. 1998. An alternative to bureaucratic impersonality and emotional labor: Bounded emotionality at The Body Shop. *Administrative Science Quarterly* 43:429–69.

Morris, M. W., K. Leung, D. Ames, and B. Lickel. 1999. Incorporating perspectives from inside and outside: Synergy between emic and etic research on culture and justice. *Academy of Management Review* 24:781–96.

Ouchi, W. G., and R. L. Price. 1993. Hierarchies, clans, and theory Z: A new perspective on organization development. *Organizational Dynamics* 21 (spring): 62–70.

Pike, R. 1954. *Language in relation to a united theory of the structure of human behavior.* Glendale, AZ: Summer Institute of Linguistics.

Raz, A. E. 1999. *Riding the black ship.* Cambridge, MA: Harvard University Press.

Reese, S. D., W. A. Danielson, P. J. Shoemaker, T. Chang, and H. L. Hsu. 1986. Ethnicity-of-interviewer effects among Mexican Americans and Anglos. *Public Opinion Quarterly* 50:563–72.

Roethlisberger, F. J., and W. J. Dickson. 1939. *Management and the worker.* Cambridge, MA: Harvard University Press.

Rosenthal, R. 1968. Experimenter expectancy and the reassuring nature of the null hypothesis decision procedure. *Psychological Bulletin* 70:30–47.

Roth, A., V. Prasnikar, and M. Okuno-Fujiwara. 1991. Bargaining and market behavior in Jerusalem, Ljubljana, Pittsburgh, and Tokyo: An experimental study. *American Economic Review* 81:1068–95.

Schwartz, S. H. 1992. Universals in the content and structure of values: Theoretical advances and empirical tests in twenty countries. In M. P. Zanna, ed., *Advances in experimental and social psychology.* San Diego: Academic Press.

Schwartz, S. H., and W. Bilsky. 1987. Toward a universal psychological structure of human values. *Journal of Personality and Social Psychology* 53:550–62.

Serpell, R. 1979. How specific are perceptual skills? *British Journal of Psychology* 70:365–80.

Smith, P. B., M. F. Peterson, and Z. M. Wang. 1996. The manager as mediator of alternative meanings: A pilot study from China, the USA, and U.K. *Journal of International Business Studies* 27:115–37.

Thomas, D. C. 1999. Cultural diversity and work group effectiveness: An experimental study. *Journal of Cross Cultural Psychology* 30:242–63.

Tinsley, C. 1998. Models of conflict resolution in Japanese, German, and American cultures. *Journal of Applied Psychology* 83:316–23.

Triandis, H. C., and M. J. Gelfand. 1998. Converging measurement of horizontal and vertical individualism and collectivism. *Journal of Personality and Social Psychology* 74:118–28.

Trist, E. L., and K. W. Bamford. 1951. Social and psychological consequences of the Longwall method of coal-getting. *Human Relations* 4:3–28.

Tversky, A., and D. Kahneman. 1974. Judgment under uncertainty: Heuristics and biases. *Science* 185:1124–31.

van de Vijver, F., and K. Leung. 1997. *Methods and data analysis for cross-cultural research.* California: Sage.

———. 2001. Personality in cultural context: Methodological issues. *Journal of Personality:* 69:979–1031.

Yu, A. B. 1996. Ultimate life concerns, self, and Chinese achievement motivation. In M. H. Bond, ed., *Handbook of Chinese psychology.* Hong Kong: Oxford University Press.

Part 3

THE ROLE OF CULTURE IN INTERNATIONAL MANAGEMENT RESEARCH

CONCEPTUALIZING CULTURE

ELUCIDATING THE STREAMS OF RESEARCH IN
INTERNATIONAL CROSS-CULTURAL MANAGEMENT

*Nakiye A. Boyacigiller, Jill Kleinberg, Margaret E. Phillips,
and Sonja A. Sackmann*

It is, I believe, both presumptuous and self-defeating to help spread the attitude that, in spite of our conviction that culture is important, we are only in the very early stages of dealing with it. In so far as we are confused, we would, I suggest, be advised to consider carefully the body of already produced materials on the history of, debates about and, above all, circumstances which are currently encouraging interest in culture. (Robertson 1992, 32)

"Culture" is a powerful social construct. From the early days of academic anthropology, various and often competing conceptualizations of culture have offered social scientists both a framework and a vocabulary for distinguishing one group of people from another in terms of their differing systems of meaning, patterns of behavior, and levels of technology.[2] Debate about such matters as the construct's defining characteristics and about its relevance for understanding and explaining a vast array of human social phenomena touches all fields of study that are concerned with human

~
The authors of this chapter are listed in alphabetical order.[1] *We wish to thank Noriko Yagi of the University of Kansas and Pritica Shah of the Graziadio School at Pepperdine University for their helpful assistance with research for this chapter.*

behavior. That area of research we identify as the study of management or organization is no exception.

In 1970, Roberts called on researchers engaged in cross-national, cross-cultural organizational analysis to reassess the value—indeed, the logic—of continuing research until some fundamental issues were more explicitly and systematically addressed. Chief among those fundamental issues was the construct "culture." To quote Roberts, "without some theoretical notions explaining culture and predicting its effect on other variables, we cannot make sense of cross-cultural comparisons" (1970, 33). Much progress has occurred in the thirty-plus years since Roberts's seminal review (see Boyacigiller and Adler 1994; Boyacigiller et al. 1996; Child 1981; Earley and Erez 1997; Earley and Singh 1995; Gannon and Newman 2002; Maznevski, Gibson, and Kirkman 2000; Redding 1994; Roberts and Boyacigiller 1984; Sullivan 1994). Yet, in the words of John Berry, for many researchers and practitioners, culture continues to be "the c-word, mysterious, frightening and to be avoided" (1997, 144).

In this chapter we take stock of the way culture has been conceptualized in the international cross-cultural management (ICCM) literature,[3] recognizing and examining different schools of thought. We build upon our chapter in the first edition of this handbook (Boyacigiller et al. 1996), as well as upon Sackmann, Phillips, Kleinberg, and Boyacigiller 1997, and integrate the significant developments that have been occurring in the field. We work from the premise that a concept of culture begins with a definition of culture. But, in addition, this chapter encompasses notions of how culture comes into being, what culture does, why it is important, how we can discover culture, and how we can convey a representation of culture as a social construct in verbal form (Kleinberg 1998). Like organization and management scholars in general, many ICCM researchers have come to share a set of assumptions about culture (see Adler 2002; Deresky 2000; Harris and Moran 1991).[4] Whether they are stated explicitly or merely implied through the text, these assumptions include the following:

the core of culture is composed of explicit and tacit assumptions or understandings commonly held by a group of people; a particular configuration of assumptions/understandings is distinctive to the group; these assumptions/understandings serve as guides to acceptable and unacceptable perceptions, thoughts, feelings and behaviors; they are learned and passed on to new members of the group through social interaction; culture is dynamic—it changes over time. (adapted from Kleinberg 1989; Louis 1983; Phillips 1994; Sackmann 1992b; and Schein 1985)

Nonetheless, these common assumptions about culture do not indicate a commonly accepted concept of culture. In fact, it can be argued that such broad agreement on particular points oftentimes obscures critical differences among researchers in their overall conceptual framework and concomitant research agenda. The illusion of commonality has had the effect of impeding the advancement of culture theory. In the 1996 edition of this handbook, we noted that a strong motivation for this chapter comes from the changing nature of the world in which we live and work. This point has become even more critical in the period since that first writing. Therefore, this chapter is both a "taking stock" and a "forging ahead." Globalization is causing us to question traditional, conventional ways of viewing culture. As our organizational contexts become more complex, and simultaneously more diverse, we are challenged to seek the most appropriate way to conceptualize this social construct. Embedded in this issue are assumptions about the nature and mandate of scientific inquiry. How does the nature and mandate of ICCM research reflect the social, political, and economic context of the time? Does the rapid globalization of business make different demands on the type of ICCM research that should be done? What is it that we seek to learn from cross-cultural research?

In our review of the ICCM literature, we find evidence of three streams of research, each with a relatively distinct interpretation of the culture construct. These three streams grew out of different social, economic, political, and intellectual contexts. The different concepts of culture, therefore, have implications for the theoretical underpinnings of each perspective, the focus and goals of the research, the methodologies employed, and, consequently, the insights created by each perspective. We label these streams of research (1) ICCM studies with a focus on *cross-national comparison;* (2) ICCM studies with an *intercultural interaction* focus, and (3) ICCM studies from a *multiple cultures* perspective.[5]

For each stream of research, we address the following issues: the context that framed and encouraged the stream of research; theoretical drivers, underlying assumptions, and frameworks, including the resultant research foci and goals; research methods typically employed; and contributions to knowledge.

Following our review of the three streams, we address implications for future research and practice. Our overarching goal is to assess what we have learned from ICCM research to date and to explore what can be learned from the comparison of the streams of research examined here. This is not an exhaustive review of the literature, which is burgeoning, but rather an illustrative review of the last thirty-plus years of research, with the goal of highlighting different approaches.[6]

CROSS-NATIONAL COMPARISON

THE CONTEXT OF CROSS-NATIONAL COMPARATIVE RESEARCH

Just as organizations are imprinted during their early years and enduringly influenced, so is social inquiry (Stinchcombe 1965). Even today, the field of ICCM bears the imprint of its early years. Interest in cross-cultural management research first arose in the United States during the late 1950s and mid-1960s, led by the pioneering work of Harbison and Myers (1959), Farmer and Richman (1965), and Haire, Ghiselli, and Porter (1966). The intellectual foundations of that era continue to be reflected in the dominant stream of ICCM research—cross-national comparison—and in its strong conceptualization of culture as a nation-based independent variable.

World War II had left most of the industrialized economies of the world decimated. Thus, following the war, the United States accounted for 75 percent of the world's GNP (Thurow 1988). The 1960s were characterized by continued American economic dominance (Servan-Schreiber 1968; Thurow 1988), most dramatically symbolized by the international reach of U.S. corporations. As the United States moved into ever-expanding markets around the globe (Vernon 1971), the growing importance of multinational corporations and the reality of operating in different economic and political environments created a need to understand different national contexts and the implications of these contexts for the management of organizations.

Furthermore, the Western political context of the time, complemented and encouraged by the economic expansion of the United States, promoted a great concern with development. The comparative study of management became important, as management was viewed as "the single most critical social activity in connection with economic progress" (Farmer and Richman 1965, 1).[7] Thus, the economic and political context encouraged attention to cross-*national* differences, and, from a practical standpoint, cross-cultural management research was undertaken to better understand how to conduct business in and with other *nations*. Consequently, the early movers in ICCM adopted the nation-state as the logical unit of analysis.

While later many would question the appropriateness of using "nation-state" as a surrogate for "culture" (Boyacigiller and Adler 1994), this clearly was not of concern in the early days of the field. Harbison and Myers (1959), who first studied cross-national management, did not even have culture in their index. Rather, they focused on national demographic and economic variables. This is understandable given the belief of many researchers at the time that *no universal definition of culture* existed (Farmer and Richman 1965, citing Kroeber and Kluckhohn 1952). Also, given the very real logistical difficulties of data collection for international research, researchers were attracted by the relative ease of conducting research that assumes that cultural and national borders are synonymous.

At the same time, academic management research was primarily a Western and, to a large degree, a U.S. enterprise (Boyacigiller and Adler 1991; Lawrence 1987). In addition to the interest in U.S. management practices bred by the economic success of the United States, institutional forces, such as the leadership of key journal editorial boards and academic professional organizations and the minimal international content of doctoral programs, encouraged a parochial approach to management inquiry. Few researchers explicitly addressed the influence of American cultural values on the largely U.S.-based organization science (Adler and Jelinek 1986; Boyacigiller and Adler 1991; Burrell and Morgan 1979; Hofstede 1980b, 1984; Laurent 1983; Newman 1972). These contextual, institutional, and cultural factors led to an implicit universalism in much of organization science: the unspoken assumption that most research in the field was applicable across cultural boundaries.

In recent years, scholars who conduct cross-national comparative research have been exposed to a discourse in organizational studies that encourages a more complex notion both of the relationship between culture and nation and of the construct of culture than that reflected in the work of the field's pioneers. It is a discourse stimulated by globalization of the economy with the accompanying increase in cross-national business and organizational activity. Globalization and the comparatively rapid growth of certain transitional economies have led to a burgeoning interest in understanding management practices within their own context and cultural frame of reference (e.g., Lovett, Simmons and Kali 1999). Yet, despite a growing appreciation that nation and culture cannot be equated, that nations are not unified cultural entities, and that national culture might not always be the most salient cultural focus, the cross-national comparative stream of research continues to dominate the field of ICCM.

Why this continued dominance? One reason for the persistence of cross-national comparison is that the nation-state continues to be an important economic actor. From a theoretical and practical standpoint, it is important to understand how management differs across national boundaries. Moreover, in countries undergoing massive economic and organizational transformation in particular, there is a great demand for professional management practices and management training. Given the economic success of the United States during the twentieth century and its early focus on management education and training, U.S.-influenced management practices and training methods continue to be exported by the United States and imported by other countries. Cultural receptivity at the national level, therefore, remains an issue of academic and practical interest. We would add that another reason for the continued pervasiveness of cross-national comparative research lies in the inherently conservative nature of academic enterprise. As will be discussed, the particular construct of national culture that characterizes the bulk of the research lends itself to the positivist research paradigm that dominates the field.

THEORETICAL DRIVERS, ASSUMPTIONS, AND FRAMEWORKS OF CROSS-NATIONAL COMPARATIVE RESEARCH

Two differing sets of concerns emerged from the pioneering work in the field of ICCM, each with different implications for the conceptualization of culture in subsequent cross-national comparative research: (1) an interest in the relationship between management and economic development and in comparative systems of management; and (2) an interest in the link between cultural values and managerial attitudes and behaviors.

The work of Harbison and Myers (1959) and Farmer and Richman (1965) stimulated a sizeable body of research centering on the relationship between management and economic development and on comparing systems of management (Nath 1986). In these early studies, culture per se was not a research issue. This work was strongly multidisciplinary in orientation, especially that of Farmer and Richman (1965), who included educational/cultural, sociological/cultural, political/legal, and economic variables in their model. The research was premised on the convergence hypothesis of socioeconomic development. It predicted the "convergence of cultures, as well as applicable management principles and practices, throughout the industrial world" even if "this type of universal convergence is likely to take decades, generations, and even centuries in some extreme cases" (Farmer and Richman 1965, 394).

While no longer articulated with the same optimism or force, the convergence thesis continues to maintain an important philosophical place in cross-national comparative research (Kerr 1983). Furthermore, scholars who focus on management in developing countries (Austin 1990; Jaeger and Kanungo 1990; Kiggundu 1989) continue to take a multidisciplinary approach, but, while acknowledging the importance of culture, they do not consider it a prime interest. Today we see an increasing recognition of a distinction between a cultural approach to organizations in an international context and a broader institutional approach (e.g., Kostova 1996). An institutional approach is particularly favored by scholars who study the consequences of the breakup of the Soviet Union and the recent movement toward free-market economies in Russia, China, and other nations. Furthermore, evidence of significant variation among capitalist systems renders the classic question of convergence (Kerr 1983) more problematic (Hampden-Turner and Trompenaars 1996; Clegg and Redding 1990; Whitley 1999).

Haire, Ghiselli, and Porter's groundbreaking work, *Managerial Thinking: An International Study* (1966), with its explicit focus on managerial attitudes, was the precursor to later studies that seek to understand the link between cultural values and managerial attitudes and behaviors. This research sought to determine whether managers around the world held similar attitudes. It was the first large-scale empirical study in international cross-cultural management, and it reflected certain assumptions about the culture construct that were prevalent at the time. Cultural boundaries were assumed to coincide with national boundaries,[8] and national, and hence cultural, identity was assumed to be a given, single, and immutable characteristic of an individual. However, the dependent variable of interest was managerial attitudes, not culture. In fact, culture was not defined a priori in Haire, Ghiselli, and Porter's research, nor was it explicitly measured. Culture was considered an independent variable and, if significant differences could be found across nations, holding other factors constant, these differences were attributed to cultural differences.

The lack of explicit attention to culture continued unabated in most cross-national research throughout the 1970s. In 1970, Ajiferuke and Boddewyn found that, of twenty-two studies they reviewed that had culture as an independent variable, only two even attempted to define it. A significant exception to this trend was Triandis's (1972) framework for conceptualizing culture, composed of the following constructs: distal cultural antecedents, proximal cultural antecedents, basic psychological processes, subjective culture, and consequences of subjective culture. Subjective culture encompassed "a cultural group's characteristic way of perceiving the man-made part of its environment" (4).[9] Triandis himself noted, however, that the utility of his framework was limited by the absence of middle-range theory specifying how the particular variables subsumed under each of the constructs related to one another (24).

Hofstede's seminal book, *Culture's Consequences: International Differences in Work-Related Values* (1980a), filled an important vacuum in the field, as cross-national comparative researchers gained a readily accessible set of universal dimensions from which measures of culture could be derived. Hofstede grounded his research in an extensive literature review—including the values orientations work of Kluckhohn (1951), Kluckhohn and Strodtbeck (1961), and Kroeber and Parsons (1958)—and on one of the largest databases ever analyzed (attitude surveys of 116,000 IBM employees). Defining culture as "the collective programming of the mind which distinguishes members of one human group from another" (1980a, 25), Hofstede initially found four "universal categories of culture" around which programming occurs. The now well-known dimensions are individualism-collectivism, power-distance, uncertainty avoidance, and femininity-masculinity. The dimension of Confucian dynamism was added later, developed in a subsequent study with Michael Bond and his Chinese colleagues (Chinese Culture Connection 1987).[10] These universal dimensions of culture "describe basic problems of humanity with which every society has to cope; and the variation of country scores along these dimensions shows that different societies do cope with these problems in different ways" (Hofstede 1980a, 313).

Hofstede's research and arguments are compelling. The parsimony of his framework, its strong face validity for researchers and managers alike, and the ease with which it can be used in empirical studies have led to a virtual explosion of interest in cross-cultural research. *Culture's Consequences* has become a classic and is one of the most cited sources in the Social Science Citation Index (Hofstede 2001). Not only has Hofstede tremendously influenced scholarly work, but his numerous books and articles (e.g., 1983, 1984, 1991) have had a profound influence on practitioners as well. Trompenaars (1993, iii) gives credit to Hofstede "for opening management's eyes to the importance of the [cross-cultural management] subject" (cited in Kirkman, Lowe, and Gibson 2000).

The conceptual framework presented in *Culture's Consequences* has not escaped criticism, as will be described later (Dorfman and Howell 1988; Roberts and Boyacigiller 1984; Singh 1990a, 1990b; Smith, Dugan, and Trompenaars 1996, Trompenaars 1993). Indeed, Hofstede cautioned scholars against the wholesale adoption of his measures (Hofstede 1990, 1991). A vast literature on a wide array of topics using his dimensions nevertheless has evolved.[11] The individualism-collectivism dimension continues to be the main focus of most research.[12] (For sample studies, see Earley 1989, 1993; Earley, Gibson, and Chen 1999; Gomez, Kirkman, and Shapiro 2000; Leung and Iwawaki 1988; Morris, Davis, and Allen 1994.) Other research has utilized power distance (Bochner and Hesketh 1994; Earley 1986; Kanungo and Wright 1983), uncertainty avoidance (Schneider and de Meyer 1991), masculinity (Hofstede et al. 1998; Kim, Park, and Suzuki 1990; Newman and Nollen 1996), and power distance and uncertainty avoidance (Birnbaum and Wong 1985). In addition, a quantitative measure that allows computation of cultural distance has been derived from all four dimensions (e.g., Barkema and Vermeulen 1997; Benito and Gripsrud 1992; Gomez-Mejia and Palich 1997; Kogut and Singh 1988; Li and Guisinger 1991; Roth and O'Donnell 1996; Shenkar and Zeira 1992). All these studies mentioned reflect the basic concept of culture that informed the work of Haire, Ghiselli, and Porter (1966). They expand the notion of an immutable, individual-carried national culture by elaborating "culture" in terms of a standardized, universally applicable set of dimensions.

Dimensions-based conceptualizations of culture existed before Hofstede's in disciplines outside the field of cross-national comparative ICCM (e.g., Hall 1959; Kluckhohn 1951; Kluckhohn and Strodtbeck 1961; Parsons and Shils 1951). However, little empirical work based on these frameworks, beyond that of the original authors, appears to have been conducted.[13] Recently, we have seen expanding interest in what might be called "value models of culture" among ICCM researchers who engage in cross-national comparison that offer alternatives to Hofstede's model (Erez and Earley 1993). Maznevski, DiStefano, and Nason (1995) have developed an instrument that operationalizes the Kluckhohn and Strodtbeck (1961) values orientations.[14] Trompenaars (1993) and Smith, Dugan, and Trompenaars (1996) offer another framework, also based on the work of Kluckhohn and Strodtbeck (1961), that is gaining acceptance in Europe.[15] Schwartz and his colleagues (Sagiv and Schwartz 1995; Schwartz 1992; 1994; Schwartz and Bilsky 1990) have developed a framework that includes the seven cultural value dimensions of egalitarianism, harmony, embeddedness, hierarchy, mastery, affective autonomy, and intellectual autonomy. Nevertheless, Hofstede's framework (1980a), "where the questions and the dimensions are used as taken-for-granted assumptions" (Søndergaard 1994, 453), continues its paradigmatic hold on the field, and "much of the research attention continues to be an extrapolation of Hofstede's values system" (Earley and Singh 2000, 2). Publication of the second edition of *Culture's Consequences* (Hofstede 2001), with data from ten additional countries and a substantially expanded list of references citing the original work, is likely to continue this framework's dominance.

An emerging and promising alternative to Hofstede's framework is the conceptualization of culture developed by Robert House and his colleagues as part of the GLOBE (Global Leadership and Organizational Behavior Effectiveness) project (see Dickson, Aditya, and Chhokar 2000; House et al. 1999). GLOBE "is both a research program and a social entity . . . comprised of a network of 170 social scientists and management scholars from 62 cultures throughout the world" (House et al. 1999, 171). Much more than a study of leadership, the GLOBE project seeks to understand culture's influence on leadership and an array of other variables that relate to organizational effectiveness. The central theoretical proposition of the GLOBE program is as follows:

> attributes and entities that distinguish a given culture from other
> cultures are predictive of the practices of organizations and leader
> attributes and behaviors that are most frequently enacted, acceptable,
> and effective in the culture. (House et al. 1999, 187)

Building on previous research and utilizing both etic and emic approaches, the GLOBE researchers developed nine unidimensional culture scales, all of which exhibited satisfactory psychometric properties (Dickson, Aditya, and Chhokar 2000, 448):

1. Avoidance of uncertainty
2. Power distance
3. Collectivism 1 (Societal emphasis of collectivism)
4. Collectivism 2 (Family collectivism)
5. Assertiveness
6. Gender egalitarianism
7. Future orientation
8. Performance orientation
9. Humane orientation

In an extension of Hofstede's work, the GLOBE study has multiple measures of culture based on shared values of organizational or society members, on current organizational and societal practices, and on unobtrusive measures. It assesses organizational culture using an organizationally focused frame of reference and assesses societal culture using a societally focused frame of reference (Dickson, Aditya, and Chhokar 2000, 453). The sheer number of countries included in the project and its etic and emic focus, with qualitative reports written on many of the countries studied, suggest that the GLOBE project is going to have a lasting effect on the field. Whether its model will supplant Hofstede's framework remains to be seen.

The GLOBE project defines culture as "shared motives, values, beliefs, identities, and interpretations or meanings of significant events that result from common experiences of members of collectives and are transmitted across age generations" (House et al. 1999, 184). Given this definition of culture, combined with its fuller appreciation of context and its multimethod research approach, the GLOBE project brings us closer to the conceptualizations of culture and methods of cultural inquiry espoused in the other streams of ICCM research: intercultural interaction and multiple culture perspectives.

In addition, globalization and the relatively rapid growth of transitional economies have, in general, created a burgeoning interest in understanding the management practices of various countries in their own context and within their own frame of reference. East Asia especially receives attention. Management scholars, for example, have studied *guanxi,* the expectations and patterns of social interaction surrounding personal "connections" in China (Fahr, Tsui, Xin, and Cheng 1996; Lovett, Simmons, and Kali 1999; Xin and Pearce 1996). Others have studied the role of "face" in Chinese organizational behavior (Earley 1997; Redding and Ng 1982). In a broader frame, Redding (1990) writes about Chinese capitalism and Whitley (1990, 1992) analyzes East Asian business systems and enterprise structures. These management studies may or may not be written from a comparative perspective, but their goal is to facilitate cross-national comparison.

METHODS EMPLOYED IN CROSS-NATIONAL COMPARATIVE RESEARCH

Parallel to the development of cross-national comparative research, the scientific norms of the physical sciences were becoming the norms for the social sciences (Redding 1994; Sullivan 1994). Cross-national comparative research, therefore, has followed a natural science model from a positivist perspective. The natural science model "presents scientific knowledge and truth as though they were transcendent, independent of any society or historical period" (Sampson 1978, 1332). Large-scale quantitative studies became the normative form of research. This focus on large-scale, multivariate, empirical research discourages attention to understanding the particular culture in situ—that is, as a *context.* Instead, culture as a *variable,* easily defined as nation-state, is but one of many independent variables considered.

The methodology of cross-national comparative ICCM research has been the subject of many critiques (Adler 1984; Bhagat and McQuaid 1982; Earley and Singh 1995, 2000; Earley and Erez 1997; Maznevski, Gibson, and Kirkman 2000; Roberts 1970; Roberts and Boyacigiller 1984; Ronen 1986; Sekaran 1983). Concerns regarding functional equivalence, instrumentation, sampling issues, measurement, and analysis have been widely expressed. Among the methodological issues unique to cross-national comparative research is what Triandis (1972) called "pseudo-etic" research, in which "instruments based on American theories, using items reflecting American conditions, are simply translated and used in other cultures" (Bhagat and McQuaid 1982, 662). Another crucial concern has been isolating the impact of culture from other explanatory variables.

Given the dominance of Hofstede's framework, a discussion of methodological issues facing the field of ICCM is necessarily tied up to a discussion of research based on Hofstede's work. Kirkman, Lowe, and Gibson's (2000) analysis of twenty years of empirical research utilizing Hofstede's framework focuses on the 138 articles published in the top peer-reviewed journals in management and applied psychology fields and leads to numerous insights. Kirkman and his colleagues conclude that in

Reviewing the body of research that was inspired by Hofstede's [1980a] framework, at least three general statements can be made. First, cultural values have pervasive direct and moderating effects at each of the four levels of analysis for a variety of different criterion variables. Second, the specific level of analysis being investigated does impact the type of findings that are obtained in these studies. *Finally, causal relationships are seldom demonstrated in this domain of research, and thus causal claims should be interpreted with extreme caution.* (2000, 34; emphasis added)

Kirkman, Lowe, and Gibson (2000) offer three recommendations to scholars intending to build on Hofstede's framework. First, scholars need to include measures of cultural values rather than assigning country measures to individuals within a study; second, it is necessary to move beyond single cultural value studies; and, third, there is a need to explore new territory in terms of criterion variables.

ICCM studies have overemphasized a quantitative approach to the study of culture and, arguably, do not represent the full array of approaches available to study the subject nor, in fact, the heated disputes (Martin 2002) around the topic. This is in no small measure due to the continued dominance of quantitative methods in North American academia (Bond and Smith 1996). Understandable though it may be, the need for more diverse methods continues, with the Globe project offering one important step in such a direction.

CONTRIBUTIONS TO KNOWLEDGE FROM THE
CROSS-NATIONAL COMPARATIVE PERSPECTIVE

Research in the cross-national comparative stream has provided us with great momentum and allowed us to make significant strides toward understanding cultural differences. As noted previously, it has motivated the development of various typologies or dimensions of culture for understanding these differences. In addition, the cultural clusters approach (Ronen and Shenkar 1985), an outcropping of the focus on national culture, has given researchers and practitioners alike a sense that culture is tractable—that we can make certain generalizations across national units. Thus, the empirical evidence of commonalities between countries within the Anglo, Germanic, Nordic, Latin European, and Latin American clusters that have strong support (Ronen 1986) has influenced our sense that one can "learn culture" and that certain lessons can be applicable within certain geographical areas.

We have made progress in testing organizational theories cross-nationally. We now know more about how a number of organizational processes and practices differ in different national contexts. The literature includes studies on *leadership* (e.g., Dorfman 1996 and his chapter in this volume; Dorfman and Howell 1997; Helgstrand and Stuhlmacher 1999; Pillai and Meindl 1998; Smith and Peterson 2002; House et al. 1999; Zander 1997); *motivation* (e.g., Erez 1997; Markus and Kitayama 1991; Redding and Wong 1986; Steers and Sanchez-Runde 2002); *socialization* (e.g., Granrose 1997); *teamwork/team performance and group effectiveness* (e.g., Eby and Dobbins 1997; Elron 1997; Gibson 1999); *role ambiguity* (e.g., Peterson et al.1995); *job satisfaction* (e.g., Lincoln and Kalleberg 1990; Redding, Norman, and Schlander 1993); *decision making* (e.g., Ali 1993; Mitchell et al. 2000); *negotiation and/or conflict resolution* (e.g., Graham, Mintu, and Rogers 1994; Leung 1987; Tinsley and Pillutla 1998; Weiss 1983); *organizational citizenship* (e.g., Moorman and Blakely 1995); and *entrepreneurship* (e.g., Morris, Davis, and Allen 1994).

A framework that emphasizes a finite set of cultural dimensions has facilitated the relatively straightforward inclusion of cultural variables into cross-national research in other management-related fields. A dimensions-based framework informs research in the areas of *strategy* (e.g., Barkema and Vermeulen 1997; Li and Guisinger 1991; Kogut and Singh 1988; Zaheer and Zaheer 1997); *marketing* (Eramilli 1991; Kale 1995; Lynn and Gelb 1996); *accounting* (Gray, Radebaugh, and Roberts 1990); *human resource management* (e.g., Ramamoorthy and Carroll 1998); and *economics* with regard to economic growth (e.g., Franke, Hofstede, and Bond 1991). The related notion of cultural distance has influenced research on investment and entry strategies (Barkema, Bell, and Pennings 1996; Peterson, Rodrigues, and Smith 2000), as well as on human resource management practices (Black and Mendenhall 1992; Rosenzweig and Nohria 1994). In these studies, the difficulty of adjusting to a foreign culture is seen as a function of the host culture's distance from one's own culture.[16]

Although we continue to know comparatively little about countries outside of the G-7, progress is being made in this regard.[17] Today most journal editors have made a concerted effort to internationalize their editorial boards, which hopefully will expand the geographic scope of ICCM research (Boyacigiller 2000). The new *International Journal of Cross-Cultural Management* actively encourages papers on cultural perspectives "from non-western societies which represent indigenous management theory" with the goal of including contributions that may be overlooked in other international journals (*IJCCM* 2001). The recent explosion of research on China (e.g., Child 1994; Earley 1997; Luo and Peng 1999; Xin and Pearce 1996) is also a good illustration of another important change beginning to occur in the ICCM field: an internationally informed approach to theory construction.[18] Convergence may be occurring in ways quite different from that initially formulated by the pioneers of the field.

Finally, some of the most conceptually revealing insights from the cross-national comparative approach have been self-reflective in nature. Among them are an increased understanding of U.S. cultural characteristics (the country of origin of a large percentage of the research), an appreciation of the parochialism of American organization theory (so widely in use internationally), and increased attentiveness to the difficulty of transferring American management techniques to other nations (Adler 2002; Hofstede 1980b; Jaeger 1986; Shenkar and Von Glinow 1994). We have, in addition, gained insight into the difficulty of doing collaborative international multicultural research (Teagarden et al. 1995).

We still are grappling with the fundamental questions posed by Lammers and Hickson in *Organizations Alike and Unlike* (1979): Is organizational science, as it currently conceived, applicable across all countries? and to what extent must organizational theorizing be modified by national differences? (see also Boyacigiller and Adler 1991; Earley and Singh 1995; Earley and Erez 1997; Maznevski, Gibson, and Kirkman 2000; Hofstede 1980b, 2001). Moreover, as noted by Earley and Singh (1995), there has also been a noticeable convergence of "an interest in improving understanding of fundamental theories of management with research on international management" (429).

Conceptually and methodologically, however, cross-national comparative research is subject to some critical limitations and weaknesses in its development. Though rising to a higher level of consciousness among researchers in the field, these limitations need to be overcome within the research itself for the perspective to have continuing relevance in the multicultural world we are facing today. In particular, two critical factors continue to afflict the majority of research (some exceptions are noted later) from the cross-national comparative perspective: (1) the use of nation-state as the surrogate for culture and (2) the assumption that national culture is a given, single, and immutable characteristic of an individual.

These two factors intertwine to allow a simplified approach to research. Moreover, the research is concerned with cultures in parallel but seldom addresses intercultural behavior (Adler 1984; Godkin, Braye, and Caunch 1989; Peng, Peterson, and Shyi 1991). As Bond and Smith warn, although

> most studies use national affiliation, . . . the existing and increasing cultural diversity of many nations makes this strategy unsatisfactory. . . . the growing cultural heterogeneity both of nations and of smaller social systems within them will require that researchers progress from documenting contrasts between different [national] cultures toward examining the ways in which individuals and groups from different [national] cultures relate to one another. (1996, 227)

We see movement away from the assumption that culture and nation-state are synonymous in the work of Lenartowicz and Roth (2001). Using a multimethod approach, these researchers surface four distinct regional subcultures within a single country, suggesting that national culture and regional subcultures may simultaneously exist and influence business performance. Similarly, Au (1999) found that intracultural variation on certain constructs was greater than intercultural variation when comparing multiple countries. While still working within the paradigm of cross-national comparison, this work begins to link with defining elements of the intercultural interaction and multiple cultures perspectives.

The dominant cross-national comparative approach has also tended to obscure important cultural differences at other levels of analysis.[19] Table 5.1 depicts the distribution of the 138 articles that form the basis of a review conducted by Kirkman, Lowe, and Gibson (2000) across four levels of analysis (individual, group, organization, country) and three cultural foci (culture as a direct effect, moderator, or criterion variable).[20] It is inter-

TABLE 5.1. Classification Scheme Used for Literature Review and Number of Articles Included

	Individual Level	Group Level	Organization Level	Country Level	Total
Culture as a direct effect	49	5	4	42	100
Culture as a moderator	13	4	4	2	23
Culture as a criterion variable	3	0	0	1	4
Total	65	9	8	45	127

Source: Kirkman, Lowe, and Gibson 2000

esting to note the limited number of studies at the group and organization level of analysis and, in particular at these levels, the complete void of studies that look at culture as a criterion variable.

Furthermore, the large-scale inclusion of national dimensions in cross-national comparative research generally means foregoing any fine-grained understanding of how culture impacts individual behavior. While we have learned that national differences may be important, we still do not have a good understanding of how cultural differences influence the behavior in and of organizations.[21] This speaks to the need for midrange theory, the building of which continues to be a weakness of the field (see Earley and Gibson 1998; Earley and Singh 1995; Redding 1994), jeopardizing a clear understanding of "when culture matters" (Maznevski, Gibson, and Kirkman 2000). Earley and Gibson forcefully argue that the field needs "serious conceptual work . . . relating cultural constructs to organizational phenomena" and suggest further that

> arguments such as "Collectivists are more group oriented than individualists. Therefore, we hypothesize that collectivists will enjoy teamwork more than individualists" are *unacceptable*. Instead, researchers need to draw from existing theory (or create their own coherent framework) and posit why cultural effects may guide action in a particular fashion. (1998, 301; emphasis added)

Erez and Earley's self-representation model (1993) exemplifies one type of theoretical development from the cross-national comparative perspective that may fill this gap and help lead us to a clearer understanding of how culture influences work behavior. For these scholars, the self seems to be the link between culture and employees' work behavior. On the one hand, it is shaped by cultural values and norms; on the other, it directs employees' behavior toward self-enhancement. Therefore, it captures the cultural characteristics which are most relevant for work behavior. (1993, 21)

Erez and Earley argue that much of the organization behavior literature may be reinterpreted in line with their model.

Two different recommendations have emerged from the critiques of the methodology of cross-national comparative research. One is for ICCM research to continue on its current path but to become more rigorous and more inventive in its research designs (Earley and Singh 1995, 2000; Lytle et al. 1995). For example, Earley and Mosakowski's (2000) lab and field experiments are an underutilized methodology that provides researchers an opportunity to test "the precise way culture may influence organizational phenomena" (Earley and Mosakowski 1996). Earley and Singh (1995, 2000) identify four general forms of research styles currently employed and advocate using a hybrid form of styles in multiple national contexts to produce cross-national generalizations or "universals."

[W]e suggest that the field integrate its working definitions of nation and culture and create an understanding based on various facets of nations and cultures, including economic, legal, cultural, and political systems. The key to conducting quality international or intercultural management research is to understand the contexts in which firms and individuals function and operate. However, underlying the legal context of a society is its culture. Thus a researcher should neither entirely rely on nor ignore any aspect of a country. Effective hybrid research emphasizes understanding all major systems in a given nation rather than a focus on some to the detriment of others. (Earley and Singh 1995, 338)

Others have questioned the appropriateness of the methodological assumptions that have underpinned the cross-national comparison perspective. For example, Redding (1994) concludes that the vast majority of cross-national comparative research has been positivist, descriptive, and concerned with fact. He advocates a reorientation of the field to include more interpretative work and to move from idiographic microtheory to more midrange theories. Momentum in this direction can already be detected in the two other streams of ICCM research.

INTERCULTURAL INTERACTION

THE CONTEXT OF INTERCULTURAL INTERACTION RESEARCH

"Interaction, not merely comparison, is the essence of most managerial action." These words were addressed to cross-national comparative researchers by Adler, Doktor, and Redding in 1986. They express a felt need to refocus the attention of those working in the dominant stream of ICCM research toward certain issues of escalating significance in the increasingly globalized business environment. Of immediate concern was the interaction of persons from different nations in organizational contexts—specifically, what impact does the meeting of national cultures have on an organization and its members?

Two interrelated trends prompted unprecedented interest among management scholars and practitioners in the interaction of national cultures and its consequences. One was the changing balance of global economic power. As the locus of energy shifted from the United States toward Japan and the newly developing Asian countries, attention focused on the issue of competitiveness. In the United States, as in many other countries (Fukuda 1988), this meant a preoccupation with Japan. The assumption that a unique Japanese culture contributes to the success of Japanese industrial organizations underlay this preoccupation (Drucker 1971; Ouchi 1981; Pascale and Athos 1981; Vogel 1979). Westerners not only studied how the Japanese organize for success, they contemplated what could be borrowed from Japan and applied at home to strengthen domestic industry (Drucker 1971; Ouchi 1981; Pascale and Athos 1981;Takezawa 1966).

This highlights a second global trend—the dramatic increase in direct foreign investment in the form of joint ventures, foreign-owned subsidiaries, or multinational corporations. Whether in the realm of business negotiation or organizational operation, we began to be interested in the impact of national culture on successful outcomes. Again, from the Western perspective, Japan loomed large. A host of articles and books examined how to negotiate with the Japanese (e.g., Black and Mendenhall 1993; Graham and Sano 1984). The proliferating Japanese "transplant" firms received similar scrutiny. Initial optimism about the smooth transfer of

Japanese cultural norms, ideologies, and organizational practices from expatriate Japanese managers to host-country employees (Johnson and Ouchi 1974) nevertheless gave way to the recognition that intercultural processes are exceedingly complex (Kleinberg 1989). While the image of Japan as a paragon of management has been challenged by an uninterrupted economic slump since 1991, research on Japanese firms outside Japan continues to contribute toward a dynamic cultural perspective on organization (Brannen and Kleinberg 2000).

THEORETICAL DRIVERS, ASSUMPTIONS, AND FRAMEWORKS OF INTERCULTURAL INTERACTION RESEARCH

The historical context described previously predisposed early intercultural interaction research in ICCM toward a cross-national, cross-cultural focus. Several concurrent and, to some degree, intersecting developments in organizational research have contributed to the emerging framework for conceptualizing interaction between persons in multinational organizational settings. These developments include (1) a growing body of work on "organizational culture"; (2) a tenacious, if minority, interest in interpretive frameworks; and (3) the application of anthropological theory and methodology to organizational analysis. In addition, a model of intercultural interaction drawn from communication studies influences the research.

ORGANIZATIONAL CULTURE RESEARCH

The organization culture literature exhibits considerable variation in focus and methods (Ashkanasy, Wilderom, and Peterson 2000; Cooper, Cartwright, and Earley 2001; Hatch 1993; Martin 1992, 2002; Martin and Frost 1996; Schultz and Hatch 1996). As frequently noted, conceptualizations of culture range from viewing it as an independent variable that managers can manipulate for desired ends (Davis 1984)—that is, something an organization "has"—to viewing it as something an organization "is" (Smircich 1983). Our discussion of the multiple cultures perspective will say more about different approaches to the study of organizational culture. Here it is important to recognize that, among organizational researchers, those concerned with the phenomenon of organizational culture have gone furthest toward offering clear definitions of culture, a way of representing culture as a social construct, and a basis for examining the implications of culture for organization. Intercultural interaction research has emerged along with a developing view in organizational culture research that organizations encompass a multiplicity of cultures (Martin 1992; Sackmann 1991; Sackmann and Phillips 1992). Although intercultural interaction research to date places emphasis on the construct of national culture, its concern with the way in which cultures in an organization form, intersect, or otherwise influence one another is relevant to broader organization culture theory building.

THE INTERPRETIVE PARADIGM

Organizational scholars interested in interpretive research basically ask how organizational participants make sense of their social world (Jones 1988; Pondy et al. 1983; Putnam and Pacanowsky 1983; Schultz and Hatch 1996). Interpretive studies fall within a naturalistic research paradigm (e.g., Lincoln and Guba 1985). According to the paradigm, reality is socially constructed, and different sets of actors within an organization may define their reality differently. Furthermore, reality cannot be fragmented into independent variables and processes that enable direct cause-and-effect relationships to be posited. Instead, all entities are "in a state of mutual and simultaneous shaping" (Lincoln and Guba 1985). These assumptions contrast sharply with those that underlie cross-national comparative research (e.g., Earley and Singh's hybrid research form [1995, 2000]), Thus, in place of generalization and prediction, naturalistic inquiry emphasizes the transferability of research findings—specifically, under similar conditions, similar outcomes can be anticipated.

Not all researchers of an interpretive bent use the term "culture" to refer to their reconstruction of their subjects' system of meaning. For anthropologist Clifford Geertz (1973, 5), however, whose ethnographic writing has greatly influenced interpretive research, the "webs of significance" that are revealed by these researchers are indeed cultural. Furthermore, interpretive researchers generally describe their approach as "ethnographic" (a term implying attention to cultural phenomena), as they adopt the methods of anthropological ethnography—that is, intensive, open-ended interviews and participant observation.

APPLICATION OF ANTHROPOLOGICAL THEORY AND METHODS TO ORGANIZATIONAL ANALYSIS

To anthropologists, ethnography "is the science—and art—of cultural description" (Frake 1983, 60). The goal of cultural description is to sort out, represent, and contextually explain the meanings that humans create for themselves through social interaction (Geertz 1973). Despite broad agreement on what ethnography is, several currents of thought coexist with regard to what culture is and how to represent it in written form. Organizational scholars doing interpretive research are part of this dialogue (Fine 1984; Schultz and Hatch 1996; Smircich 1983; Smircich and Calas 1987; Van Maanen 1988).

Many organizational researchers have adopted a concept of culture drawn from cognitive anthropology (Frake 1983; Goodenough 1981; Spradley 1980). Gregory (1983) introduced this approach to organizational studies in an early article on mapping "native-view paradigms." The researcher's task is to discover the shared "cultural knowledge" that is the essence of culture. Cultural knowledge, which may be explicit or tacit, reflects the way members of a culture make sense of their social setting; it helps to guide the way they interpret experience and to generate "cultural" behavior. Tacit cultural knowledge generally is thought to be most resistant to change.

The assumptions or understandings or sense making that comprise cultural knowledge are inferred from the "doings and sayings" (Frake 1983) of organizational participants, normally through some kind of content analysis (e.g., Spradley 1980). The assumptions that are surfaced sometimes are represented as broad, encompassing categories of cultural knowledge (termed "cultural themes" by Spradley 1980), which organize into constituent subcategories of cultural knowledge (Gregory 1983; Sackmann 1992b). Sometimes member assumptions or understandings are represented merely in terms of cultural themes, without the emphasis on taxonomy (Martin 1992). Cognitive anthropologists typically do not presume a priori cultural dimensions of culture such as those proposed by Kluckhohn and Strodtbeck (1961) or Hofstede (1980a). Some organizational culture researchers, however, have surfaced cultural knowledge through content analysis but have organized the revealed cultural knowledge around such universal dimensions (Dyer 1985; Phillips 1994).

Among anthropologists, cognitive anthropology has been criticized for imposing on the construct of culture a coherence and an inflexibility that culture does not really exhibit. It has, in addition, been criticized for leaving critical contextual analysis out of the cultural description (Geertz 1973). These criticisms may be true of cognitive anthropology in its most formalized form. However, Frake's metaphor of culture as cognitive "sketch maps" (1977, quoted in Spradley 1980, 7) indicates that cognitive anthropologists need not have such a coherent vision. Moreover, many scholars who borrow methods of discovering and representing culture from cognitive anthropology share with critics an emphasis on explaining a culture within its historical, political, and economic context.

As an alternative mode of cultural representation, Geertz (1973) offers what he labels "thick description." Through finely detailed, multilayered descriptions of people, events, and actions, in both present and historical time, the ethnographer arrives at an interpretation of the "interworked systems of construable signs"(Geertz 1973, 14)—that is, an interpretation of the meanings that are culture. Rohlen's (1974) ethnographic study of a Japanese bank and Silin's (1976) ethnographic study of leadership in Taiwanese large-scale enterprise are two examples of thick description that vividly illustrate the interplay between national culture and behavior in and of an organization. Geertz's (1979) more esoteric study of the bazaar economy in a Moroccan town, however, offers the quintessential illustration of Geertzian thick description.

Geertz's thick description, in turn, has been criticized for being too local in its conceptualization of history and, consequently, for presenting too self-contained and unified a representation of culture (Roseberry 1989). An alternative view sees the cultural other as a product of a history that itself is connected to a larger set of economic, political, social, and cultural processes (Appadurai 1991; Clifford 1986; Marcus 1986; Roseberry 1989; and Wolf 1982). Appadurai (1991) speaks of these connections in terms of a transnational, deterritorialized "ethnoscape." Within a broad political economy framework, culture "shifts from being some sort of inert, local substance to being a rather more volatile form of difference" (Appadurai 1991, 205). Indeed, culture may be viewed as actively negotiated (Giddens 1979, 1984) on an ongoing basis. Quoting Clifford,

> If "culture" is not an object to be described, neither is it a unified corpus of symbols and meanings that can be definitively interpreted. Culture is contested, temporal, and emergent. Representation and explanation—both by insiders and outsiders—is implicated in this emergence. (1986, 19)

In the organizational culture literature, the cultural fragmentation perspective that Meyerson and Martin (1987) describe best reflects the view of culture in today's complex organizations as being ambiguous, incongruent, and actively negotiated.

INTERCULTURAL COMMUNICATION IN THE WORKPLACE

A basic model of intercultural communication (Samovar and Porter 1991; Samovar, Porter, and Jain 1981) informs a theory of culture that is widely accepted in the field of international and cross-cultural management (Adler 2002; Erez and Earley 1993; Kleinberg 1989, 1998). Nonetheless, this framework often is not explicitly integrated into research design (e.g., Lincoln, Hanada, and Olson 1981; Lincoln, Kerbo, and Wittenhagen 1995; Lincoln, Olson, and Hanada 1978; Linowes 1994). That theory states that members of a nation are seen as bearers of a common culture that influences the behavior in and of organizations. Thus, people from different national backgrounds acquire different expectations about the formal structures of firms and the informal patterns by which work is accomplished. These expectations then color the way people respond to unfamiliar or unexpected behaviors when they work with, negotiate with, or generally do business with counterparts from another society. The implication is that, all too often, cross-national, cross-cultural encounters result in misperception, misinterpretation, and a negative evaluation of the cultural other's intentions and abilities.[22]

A cultural synergy model of interaction, which builds on the intercultural communication model, currently attracts organizational scholars dealing with either international or domestic cultural diversity (Adler 2002; Moran and Harris 1981). This model assumes that successful intercultural communication and, therefore, successful task accomplishment hinge on conscious management of both differences and similarities. In effect, organizational members learn to "create new forms of management and organization that transcend the individual cultures of their members" (Adler 2002, 116). The accepted notion of cultural synergy essentially concerns the conscious construction of new (cultural) understandings at the work group or organization-wide level; it does not consider the unconscious construction of cultural synergy that may occur (Kleinberg 1994a).

EMERGING FRAMEWORK FOR
INTERCULTURAL INTERACTION

So far, intercultural interaction research predominantly concerns Japanese-owned and -managed firms located outside of Japan, what we refer to here as "binational" organizations. Studies include Bonazzi and Botti 1995;

Brannen 1994, 1995; Brannen and Salk 2000; Kleinberg 1989, 1994a, 1994b, 1998; Lincoln, Kerbo, and Wittenhagen 1995; Linowes 1993; Rao and Hashimoto 1996; Sharpe 1997; and Sumihara 1992.[23] Other country foci, however, exist, as in the study of British-Italian joint venture by Salk and Shenkar (2001).[24] Due to the many and sometimes contradictory theoretical influences, discussed previously, the emerging framework for considering intercultural interaction in organizations is loosely constructed. Nevertheless, some common threads connect the existing research.

A number of assumptions about culture and its consequences underlie the intercultural interaction framework. Researchers generally conceptualize culture as a group-level phenomenon—a social construct that encompasses shared understandings. National culture is considered not only salient but of critical importance. Researchers assume that national cultural identity remains separate and distinct throughout the process of interaction (while recognizing that an individual's thinking and behavior may be temporarily or enduringly altered as a result of their intercultural experiences). In addition, researchers assume that national culture is reflected in a work-related cultural subset that members of each nation bring to the multinational setting. Along with national culture, the original organizational culture of a binational firm's employees may be relevant (Brannen 1994; Brannen and Salk 2000; Kleinberg 1998; Salk 1993; Salk and Shenkar 2001). The organizational culture comprises a set of understandings different from national culture or a nation-specific work culture but still theoretically (Enz 1986) connected to the wider national culture.[25] Finally, researchers believe that cultural differences may affect communication processes in much the same way as described by the intercultural communication model—with misperception, misinterpretation, and misunderstanding evident.

Several researchers, namely those with roots in social or cultural anthropology, view the binational organization, in addition, as a context for the construction of new understandings, as participants interactively make sense of an extraordinary, unfamiliar organizational terrain (Brannen 1994; Brannen and Salk 2000; Kleinberg 1994a, 1994b, 1998; Sumihara 1992). Therefore, the focal question—"What is it that representatives of different national cultures create through their interaction?"—anticipates the development of a new organizational culture (or cultures). In addition to the content and form of emergent organizational culture, of key concern is the *process* of culture formation.

Studies of emergent culture in binational organizations arrive at different, but not inconsistent, frameworks for explaining and representing culture formation. These differences are explained in part by different organizational circumstances and in part by the particular emphasis of the researcher. For example, Kleinberg's (1994a, 1994b) study of a U.S.-based Japanese subsidiary focuses on emergent organizational cultures at three levels: an organization-wide culture; Japanese (expatriate) and American subgroup cultures; and individual work group cultures.

The framework emphasizes that emergent cultural understandings are strongly influenced by national cultural differences in expectations about work. The construct of "nation-specific work sketch maps," derived from a pilot study of Japanese firms in southern California (Kleinberg 1989) and based on ethnographic interviews of Japanese and American employees, captures some specific differences. The framework also emphasizes the interconnections among the various cultures that emerge within the binational firm. Shared understandings of each cultural grouping are shown to largely reflect enhanced awareness of cultural difference resulting from cross-national interaction. Nevertheless, analysis of one particular work group (Kleinberg 1994a) shows that, despite the understanding at the organization-wide level that "we are a company divided," spontaneously created intercultural harmony and synergy are possible. In this research, Kleinberg represents culture as cognitive structures or "sketch maps for navigation" (Frake 1977), combined with thick description.

Other research places even more emphasis on the nature of the face-to-face interaction through which cultural understandings are created. A "negotiated culture" framework is evolving from this work (Brannen 1994, 1995; Brannen and Kleinberg 2000; Brannen and Salk 2000; Kleinberg 1998; Sumihara 1992). For example, Brannen's (1994) study of a U.S.-based Japanese takeover firm describes the process by which a "bicultural" organizational culture evolves as particular issues trigger cultural negotiations among individuals. An individual may be "marginally normal," "culturally norm(al)," or "hyper-normal" with regard to any specific cultural foci—nation, organization of origin, binational organization, or even organizational issue. Brannen's representation of Japanese and American national culture draws mainly from the anthropological and sociological literature (e.g., Dore 1973; Lebra 1976; Nakane 1970; Rohlen 1974). In a study of negotiated culture in a German-Japanese joint venture, however, Brannen and Salk (2000) devise an innovative technique for assessing the degree to which individual joint venture participants matched a cultural profile constructed from existing literature. In the negotiated culture research, cultural understandings typically are represented through thick description.

METHODS EMPLOYED IN INTERCULTURAL INTERACTION RESEARCH

The methodology for doing intercultural interaction research that is grounded in social or cultural anthropology has been described in some detail already. In summary, researchers employ the traditional inductive methods of their discipline. Long-term participant observation is undertaken in conjunction with an extensive series of ethnographic interviews conducted with a wide range of informants. The ability to interpret culture in a social setting is developed through the researcher's prolonged engagement with the research site (Lincoln and Guba 1985; Van Maanen 1988). In most of the cases cited, the ethnographers spent from eighteen months to more than four years gathering data. Furthermore, cultural interpretation is best accomplished if the researcher has a high degree of linguistic and cultural fluency in the national cultures being studied. Researchers arrive at a cultural interpretation primarily through qualitative data analysis, often including content analysis, described earlier. Cultural description may involve a representation of cognitive structures, enriched by thick description, or thick description alone.

Other intercultural interaction research that we have mentioned but not highlighted largely rests on data collected through personal interviews and/or survey-based interviews and on either qualitative or quantitative analysis of the data. Many of the cultural insights parallel those gained from long-term ethnographic research. In this work, however, descriptions of both the processes and the outcomes of cross-national, cross-cultural interaction tend to be less detailed.

CONTRIBUTIONS TO KNOWLEDGE FROM THE INTERCULTURAL INTERACTION PERSPECTIVE

As a result of a variety of historical, theoretical, and methodological influences, intercultural interaction research focuses initially on the cross-national nature of the interaction but recognizes that the organization provides a cultural context for this exchange and that the organization itself will be shaped by the exchange. Thus, the intercultural interaction perspective offers to ICCM research the insight that cultural identity must be assumed to be broader than the given, single, and immutable national culture of the cross-national comparative perspective. Intercultural interaction researchers view national culture and emerging and evolving forms of organizational culture as all being relevant to the identity of the individual acting within the setting of the multinational organization.

Detailed cultural description gives insight into how individuals interactively construct shared understandings. We are forced, for example, to reexamine conventional models of intercultural communication that fail to take into account the phenomenon of "cultural cross-knowledge"—that is, what is known or understood about the cultural other (see Sumihara 1992). Cultural cross-knowledge may well be faulty, but it nonetheless affects sense making among organizational participants (Weisinger and Salipante 2000). We are reminded of the "international comparison fallacy," the mistaken assumption that individuals think or behave the same in interactions with domestic colleagues as they do with foreign counterparts (Adler and Graham 1989). Cultural description also helps illuminate the interplay of cultural factors and noncultural contextual variables. Research, for instance, indicates the importance of contextual factors in binational firms, such as the relative power held by Japanese and host-country employees and the nature of relations between the U.S. operation and the Japanese headquarters. External environmental variables relating to industry, labor markets, and national and international politics are shown to be similarly important (Brannen 1994; Brannen and Salk 2000; Kleinberg 1994a, 1994b).

Finally, the research on intercultural interaction has made considerable progress in making culture a visible construct. It has drawn attention to issues of representation, or "writing culture" (Clifford and Marcus 1986), whether culture is viewed as relatively stable or, as in the negotiated culture framework, as contested and temporal.

Naturalistic, ethnographic research usually does not address certain issues that the dominant positivistic paradigm provides insight into and that also are important to practitioners and theorists. For instance, it is not amenable to generalization and prediction about structural features of the firm or individual attitudes, as they relate to the presence of persons from different nations.[26] We have an indication, however, of the potential of the joint application of ethnographic and more conventional quantitative approaches for synergistic research outcomes (Brannen 1996; Brannen and Salk 2000).

While the research described here begins to address intriguing challenges and has made valuable contributions to theory development, much more conceptual and theoretical work is needed with regard to intercultural interaction. We need to learn more about the factors that affect intercultural interaction in organizational contexts, both what they are and how they exert influence. We especially need a deeper understanding of the process by which shared understandings are negotiated and by which negotiated understandings help to shape formal and informal organizational practices. More studies, and studies of greater rigor, need to be conducted in a variety of research settings so that the research findings across sites can be compared. Different sorts of binational or multinational organizations may exhibit very different responses to national cultural differences than the organizations studied to date. As the following discussion of the multiple cultures perspective will argue, national culture may not be as salient a factor in all situations.

MULTIPLE CULTURES

THE CONTEXT OF RESEARCH FROM
A MULTIPLE CULTURES PERSPECTIVE

The past decades have introduced many changes in all spheres of life, turning commonly accepted rules and assumptions upside down. A key assumption in traditional ICCM research, the central importance of nations and of national cultures, has been called into question by developments in world economies, politics, technology, and the social sphere.

In the political sphere, established national boundaries have been challenged and in some cases destroyed as ethnic or regional identities have grown stronger. Vivid examples are seen in Central and Eastern Europe (the former USSR, the former Yugoslavia, the former Czechoslovakia), in Asia (the Koreas), and in Western Europe. The separatist movements and the striving toward stronger regional independence prevalent in Western European countries such as Ireland, Italy, Spain, Belgium, and even Germany are further evidence of the relative meaning and impact of nation-state as the boundary for businesses and their daily operations.[27]

Economic as well as political questions are increasingly discussed in regard to regions or continents, such as the European Union, NAFTA, the Pacific Rim or ASEAN, Mercasor, the Tiger countries, or the NICs. If a firm wants to succeed in these new economies, it has to reach beyond national boundaries. This has been accomplished predominantly by initiating operations in foreign locations; by creating international, multinational, or global firms; by acquiring or merging with firms already established in a desirable market; and/or by forming strategic alliances and networks (e.g., Conlon and Giovagnoli 1998; Davis 2001; Hamel, Doz, and Prahalad 1989; Siegwart and Neugebauer 1998). As a result, interdependencies have grown dramatically around the globe (Dunning 1988; de la Torre 1990).

The number of joint ventures, strategic alliances, mergers, and acquisitions has rapidly increased during the past two decades, providing all companies, regardless of size, the opportunity to stay competitive and to participate in resource-intensive, long-term projects. The resultant workforces are diverse in interests, backgrounds, training, and nationalities—even within the same firm and the same geographic location. The "expatriate" assignment frequently is replaced by "transpatriate" activity. For example, at Asea Brown Boveri, the Swiss-Swedish merger, it is not uncommon for 125 employees of a department (or "profit center") to share among themselves twenty-five passports. More commonly, as in this description of work at Eastman Kodak Company,

> people of many nationalities . . . lead multicultural teams, work on
> multi-country projects, and travel monthly outside their home coun-
> tries. In any year, they may work in Paris, Shanghai, Istanbul,
> Moscow, or Buenos Aires with colleagues from a different set of
> countries. (quoted in Delano 2000, 77)

In such multicultural contexts, binational, bicultural interactions—the initial focus of intercultural interaction research—seldom are of central importance.

Radical developments in communication technology have enabled a global economy to evolve, in which companies and individuals have access to markets far beyond those in which they are geographically located. The pervasiveness and power of the Internet have made the entire globe the potential marketplace and workplace, fostering the rise of distant work and virtual teams (DiStefano and Maznevski 2000). These "non-co-located" teams of international, multinational, or global corporations tend to be multinational and multicultural in composition.

In addition (and independent of firm-sponsored transfers), the ever-growing global movement of people has also contributed to an increasingly multicultural workforce worldwide. From North America and Europe to

Singapore and Hong Kong, managers and management researchers alike take note of the increased representation of a variety of national cultures within the workforce. This is coupled with growing attention to differences in ethnicity, gender, age, and sexual preference among workers. The mosaic of cultural diversity presents a major workplace challenge, and there is growing recognition that "the skills and core competencies traditionally required of executives on international assignments will also be required of managers in a domestic context" (Tung 1997, 163).

THEORETICAL DRIVERS, ASSUMPTIONS, AND FRAMEWORKS OF RESEARCH FROM A MULTIPLE CULTURES PERSPECTIVE

It has long been recognized that multiple cultures exist within larger societies and organizations, and research into their source and nature has been conducted.[28] However, their study was predominantly bound to *preselected subcultures*—groups with minority representation identified a priori as they seemed relevant in the existing context. The multiple cultures perspective in organization studies derived its initial momentum from a countercurrent in the developing field of organization culture. As interest in this new area of organization theory was rising in the late 1970s and early 1980s, leading researchers in the organization culture field conceptualized an organization as the carrier of a single, unique, and monolithic culture (e.g., Deal and Kennedy 1982; Ouchi 1981; Pascale and Athos 1981; Peters and Waterman 1982; Pettigrew 1979; Schein 1983). In borrowing the term "culture" from the field of anthropology, this dominant group of organization culture theorists also incorporated what they assumed was an anthropological presupposition of "one culture to a society" (Phillips 1990, 21).

In contrast, a second conception of cultural groupings in organizational settings was emerging, fed by the findings of a small set of organization researchers largely engaged in inductive research (e.g., Gregory 1983; Louis 1983; Martin and Siehl 1983; Martin, Sitkin, and Boehm 1985; Sackmann 1985; Van Maanen and Barley 1983). These researchers observed that an organization is not a simple, primitive society, as was the traditional field site of anthropological research; rather, it is a heterogeneous, pluralistic system whose members live within a larger complex society. Therefore, they recognized that organization members may develop shared sets of assumptions within the organization setting but that they can also bring with them the various sets of assumptions that they acquire outside of the organization. Thus, the organization is viewed as the potential carrier of a multiplicity of separate, overlapping, superimposed, or nested cultures, with the organization's participants maintaining simultaneous membership in any number of these cultural groups.

For example, the membership body of any particular group may be nested within the organization, forming *suborganizational cultures* according to function or functional domains (Handy 1978; Sackmann 1991, 1992b); tenure and hierarchy (Martin, Sitkin, and Boehm 1985; Sarnin 1989); ethnicity (Gregory 1983); nationality (Kleinberg 1994b); gender (Blackhurst 1986; Burrus 1997; Eberle 1997; Symons 1986); role (Rusted 1986); plant site (Bushe 1988); work group (Kleinberg 1994a); and countermovement (Dent 1986). At the *organizational* level, cultural boundaries have been drawn around a single business (e.g., Pacanowsky 1987; Pederson 1987; Rosen 1986; Rusted 1986; Schein 1985; Schumacher 1997; Ybema 1997); a global enterprise (Garsten 1990); a conglomerate (Pettigrew 1985; Sackmann 1991; Tunstall 1985); and a family firm (Dyer 1986). Professions or guilds, as a form of *transorganizational* culture, have been found to exist in research by Barley (1984), Dubinskas (1988), Geist and Hardesty (1987), and Gregory (1983), as have project-focused groups such as the "directed interorganizational systems" studied by Lawless (1980). At the *supraorganizational* level, cultural boundaries have been drawn around nation (Hofstede et al. 1990; Kleinberg 1989; Meek and Song 1990) or nationally influenced practices (Globokar 1997; Jang and Chung 1997); geographical region within a country (Weiss and Delbecq 1987); economic region (Hickson 1993); industry (Grinyer and Spender 1979; Kreiner and Schultz 1990; Laurila 1997; Lilja, Räsänen, and Tainio 1992; Pederson 1987; Phillips 1990, 1994; Räsänen and Whipp 1992); and ideologies, such as religion (Aktouf 1988) and differences between Eastern and Western civilizations (Westwood and Kirkbride 1989).

Organizational culture researchers holding a multiple culture perspective believe that any and all of these types of cultural groupings may exist and coexist within an organizational setting. That is, organizations, and the people who compose them, do not simply carry one specific culture (e.g., national culture); instead, they are embedded in a pluralistic cultural context (Louis 1983; Kopper 1992; Phillips, Goodman, and Sackmann 1992). Nonetheless, the *actual existence* of any particular cultural grouping within, coincidental with, crosscutting, or overlaid upon the organization *is an empirical question,* not *an a priori assumption.* The researcher's task, therefore, is to identify the culture(s) impacting the organization at any given time, around any specific issue, in any particular circumstance, and to any certain degree, as shown, for example, in studies by Eberle (1997), Sackmann (1992b), Sharpe (1997), and Ybema (1997). This precludes, then, the strong and purposeful focus on national culture as *the* single cultural grouping of certain relevance to the organization, as is assumed in earlier cross-national intercultural interaction ICCM research, and as a culture of permanent identity for the individual, as is assumed in cross-national comparative ICCM research.

At the individual level, people may identify with and hold membership in several cultural groups simultaneously. This notion has been long accepted in social categorization and social identity theory (Tajfel 1974, 1981; Tajfel et al. 1971). Tajfel considers social identity as being that part of an individual's self-concept that is derived from personal knowledge about one's membership in a social group, including the value and emotional significance attached to that particular membership. Applied to today's business organizations, members are most likely to belong to several groups from which they derive social identity (Ashforth and Mael 1989; Pratt 1998).

> Our understanding of identification and disidentification is also simplistic in that we have tended to focus on how a single, social identity is either adopted or lost within an organization context. Members will, however, simultaneously be identifying and disidentifying with a whole host of social identities. (Pratt 1998, 201)

Acknowledging a complex organizational environment, the multiple culture perspective argues, therefore, that organizational members' identity may be composed of or constituted by multiple cultural identities (Goodman, Phillips, and Sackmann 1999; Phillips et al. 1992; Sackmann 1997). This more complex view, not only of organizations but also of individuals operating within organizations and making sense of events within that context, has been supported by findings from recent identity research (e.g., Pratt and Rafaeli 1997; Pratt 1998). It is also supported by more recent theoretical and empirical diversity research that goes beyond the visible differences of gender, race, and age to acknowledge cognitive differences such as educational background and profession (Bissels, Sackmann, and Bissels, 2001; Milliken and Martins 1996; Nemetz and Christensen 1996;

Sackmann, Bissels, and Bissels, 2002). In addition, some recent cross-national intercultural interaction research (e.g., Brannen and Kleinberg 2000; Brannen and Salk 2000; Salk and Brannen 2000; Salk and Shenkar 2001) has examined some of the empirical questions that arise regarding multiple cultural identities.[29] Salk and Shenkar, in their study of a British-Italian joint venture, ask, for example, "what cultural identity is most salient (national vs. joint venture vs. home company)?" Their findings suggest that

> social identity enactments (using particular boundaries to define primary social identities) by team members mediate the relationship of contextual variables, both environmental and structural, with group and organizational outcomes (such as role investment and job satisfaction). (2001, 161)

Underpinning the multiple cultures conception of cultural groupings in organization settings is a conceptualization of the key construct—culture—that accounts for potential cultural diversity and is sensitive to emerging cultural groupings at various levels. This conceptualization, shared by cross-national intercultural interaction researchers and elucidated earlier in this chapter, has several implications for theory, research, and the carriers of culture—organizations and individuals alike.

Of theoretical importance is the definitional implication that culture is a collective social phenomenon that is created, rather than only inherited, by group members. Once in existence, these assumptions subtly influence perceiving, thinking, acting, and feeling in ways that are consistent with the cultural reality of that group. As guidelines for "map making and navigation" (Frake 1977), these basic assumptions guide selection, interpretation, and communication of information in ways that are meaningful to the group. They channel the choices of actions in ways considered appropriate by the group.

This conceptualization implies that the essence or core of culture is cognitive rather than factual or symbolic in nature (Sackmann 1983). Values, norms, symbolic events (e.g., rites, rituals, ceremonies), and artifacts are at a more accessible level of culture (Schein 1985) and can be considered part of the cultural network (Sackmann 1983). However, their specific meanings need to be inferred in a given cultural context since the same symbols or artifacts may be attributed with different meanings in different cultural contexts (e.g., Bjerke 1999; Bochner 1982; Sackmann 1992b). This deciphering process is only possible by understanding the underlying basic assumptions.

Furthermore, this conceptualization implies that a culture may exist or emerge whenever a set of basic assumptions is commonly held by a group of people. This has led multiple cultures researchers to focus on identifying commonalities in assumptions as the precursor to drawing boundaries around the cultural group. Tentative boundaries are sometimes drawn around anticipated or hypothesized groups, then cultural commonalities are surfaced to support maintaining or reconfiguring those boundaries of shared understandings (e.g., Burrus 1997; Dahler-Larsen 1997; Eberle 1997; Gregory 1983; Grinyer and Spender 1979; Laurila 1997; Martin, Sitkin, and Boehm 1985; Phillips 1990, 1994; Sackmann 1985; Schumacher 1997; Sharpe 1997; Van Maanen and Barley 1984; de Vries 1997; Ybema 1997). Consequently, unanticipated groupings can be identified, as can emergent cultures, a common product of cross-national intercultural interaction research. It is also possible to identify some of the cultural dynamics inherent in organizational settings at different levels of analysis. For example, researchers have looked at sense making and active identity work at the individual level (Bissels et al. 2001); interpersonal as well as intergroup dynamics at the group level (Sackmann 1991); subculture interplay at the organizational level (Sackmann 1992b); as well as the evolving dynamics of intercultural engagement in strategic alliances, mergers, and acquisitions (Sackmann 2001a). But unlike the intercultural interaction research, which focuses on the *nature and the product of the interaction* between two cultural groups within an organization, the focus of the multiple cultures perspective has been *primarily* on identity work and the interplay of different cultural identities.

An individual's cultural nature is also addressed by this conceptualization. Since individuals are seen as simultaneous carriers of several cultural identities, depending on the issue at hand, a different cultural identity may become salient at a given moment (e.g., Pratt 1998). When, how, and to what extent a particular cultural identity becomes salient are, again, empirical questions, not a priori assumptions. The business reality of multiple cultural identities and their potential impact has been illustrated for an individual practicing manager (Phillips et al. 1992) and for an international project team (Phillips, Sackmann, and Goodman 1992). And researchers recently have started to focus explicitly on the emergence, existence, and interplay of individuals' multiple cultural identities within organizational contexts. Their results seriously question both monolithic identities and the unquestioned equation of culture with nation (Dahler-Larsen 1997; Hernes 1997; Pratt and Rafaeli 1997; Sackmann 1999, 2001a; Salk and Brannen 2000).

Because the multiple cultures perspective illustrates that organizations do not simply operate within one specific cultural context, critical questions arise that differ substantially from those posed by the other streams of research:

- When and under which conditions do certain cultural groups become salient and more relevant than others?
- How do the various cultures interact under different circumstances?
- How do individuals deal with their multiple identities?
- What are the implications for managerial practice?

METHODS EMPLOYED IN RESEARCH FROM A MULTIPLE CULTURES PERSPECTIVE

A wide variety of methods for data collection, analysis, and representation are employed by multiple cultures researchers, reflecting the newness of the field and the absence of strong roots in any single academic discipline. Because this stream of research flows from organization theory—a hybrid field composed of sociologists, psychologists, anthropologists, economists, and industrial engineers—no single methodology predominates. In contrast with the dominance of state-of-the-art anthropological ethnographic methods used in cross-national intercultural interaction research, the multiple cultures perspective reflects pluralistic methods based on a naturalistic inquiry paradigm (Brett et al. 1997; Sackmann 1991).

However, in seeking to identify the boundaries of commonly held assumption sets, toward the end of surfacing the extant cultural groupings within organization settings, the definitional notion that the particular configuration of assumptions is distinctive to the group implies an emic approach (Sackmann 1991). To decipher the specific meaning of a given cultural group in context requires in-depth probing to gain an insider's view rather than imposing an outsider's perspective. Consequently, multiple cultures researchers generally tend to advocate, though not necessarily purely employ, empirical investigations involving inductive methodologies and field data collection. Similar to the manner in which cross-national intercultural interaction researchers have tailored methodologies to their organizational settings and research interests, multiple cultures researchers have employed specifically tailored combinations of ethnographic and quasi-ethnographic methods such as participant observation (Burrus 1997; Gregory 1983; Sapienza 1985; Schumacher 1997; Sharpe 1997), action research (Globokar 1997), storytelling (Martin et al. 1983), in-depth interviews (Dahler-Larsen 1997; Phillips 1990, 1994; Sackmann 1991; Schein 1985; Vinton 1983), group discussions (Schein 1985), assumptional analysis (Kilmann 1983), cognitive mapping methods such as causal mapping (Axelrod 1976; Narayanan and Fahey 1990), the repertory grid technique (Langan-Fox and Tan 1997; Reger 1990), argument mapping (Fletcher and Huff 1990), narrative semiotics (Fiol 1990), the twenty statements test (Walker, Symon, and Davies 1996), the critical incidents technique (Gundry and Rousseau 1994), historical analysis (Rowlinson and Procter 1999), multidimensional scaling (Brodbeck et al. 2000), and neural network analysis (Veiga et al. 2000).

These different data collection and data analysis techniques involve different degrees of "engagement" with the research subjects and produce different depths of understanding with regard to the research setting (Sackmann 1991, 2001b). The more extensive and intensive the ethnographic nature of the engagement, the more detailed the view of the cultural assumptions (Martin 1992). Choices of technique appear to be related to the researcher's long-term interest in theory building versus practical application. In the latter case, it is related to managers' needs to better understand an existing situation and their search for help with a given problem situation (e.g., Globokar 1997). Interests and choices in this regard are certainly influenced by the time-frame issues previously discussed, as well as by practical logistics and operational pressures.

In order to condense, systematize, and report the collected data, some researchers have applied the categories of a priori developed frameworks and delineated the cultural assumptions in terms of the framework's dimensions or typology (e.g., Handy 1978; Sackmann and Phillips 1992; Pümpin 1984). Others have used the categories of empirically derived frameworks (e.g., Hofstede [see Kirkman, Lowe, and Gibson 2000]; Nagel 1995; Hofstede et al. 1990; Phillips 1994; Sackmann 1991; Schein 1985). A third approach, primarily employed in cross-national intercultural interaction research, is to let the relevant dimensions of a given culture emerge from the research and to use these in the organization and presentation of the findings (e.g., Eberle 1997; Globokar 1997; Kleinberg 1989; Schumacher 1997; Sharpe 1997; Van Maanen 1979; Ybema 1997). Whether framework dimensions are applied or induced, resultant research from this perspective tends to surface a broad range of cultural characteristics of the extant group and reveals these with rich in situ examples. This reinforces the assumption that it is a *set* of cultural characteristics, not single elements (solely, e.g., individualism or collectivism), that distinguishes the cultural group and thus is in strong contrast with assumptions and common practice in cross-national comparative research methodology.

CONTRIBUTIONS TO KNOWLEDGE FROM THE MULTIPLE CULTURES PERSPECTIVE

Researchers working in the multiple cultures perspective acknowledge the inherent complexity and contradictions that the new social, political, and economic realities have created for organizations and for individuals in organizations in the construal of one's identity. Such recognition can be considered the major contribution of this perspective. In addition, studies from this perspective have identified and delineated the cultural assumptions of a variety of different groups existing and coexisting within organizations and more recently have started to focus on practical implications, as well as the impact of culture on performance.

The research has established convincingly that the cultural group of importance in an organizational setting is not a given, nor is it necessarily equivalent with national culture. The mere distinction between nations is no longer sufficient for understanding today's cross-cultural issues (Bond and Smith 1996; Salk and Brannen 2000; Salk and Shenkar 2001). As a result of their investigation of a multinational team in a German-Japanese joint venture, for example, Salk and Brannen acknowledge that national "culture is important but that its role is far more complex than past research and theory suggest" (2000, 199). Therefore, we now are aware that researchers have to make a conscious choice about the focal cultural context of their study—to determine not only if the focal culture exists within the organizational setting but also if it is salient to the circumstance. We are aware as well that researchers need to pay attention to the other cultural contexts most likely to interact with the one of central concern.

Multiple cultures research has advanced our understanding of cultural interaction in an important way, by highlighting the notion of cultural identity within a framework of social identity theory. Following the logic of Laurent's (1983) and Kleinberg's (1989) observations with regard to the conditions that make national culture salient, we can hypothesize that the salience of any particular cultural identity would increase when that identity is confronted or perceived to be threatened. This hypothesis finds support in cross-cultural social psychology research on group formation and conflict (Dahler-Larsen 1997; Hogg and Turner 1985; Pratt 1998; Turner 1984).[30] We have learned from studies conducted in the Western Hemisphere that the differences that separate interacting people tend to become salient (e.g., Bochner 1982; Bochner and Ohsako 1977).[31] It is further suggested that the larger the differences between interacting groups, regardless of whether these differences are real or imagined, the more likely are individuals to distinguish between "we" and "them," or in-group and out-group membership.

The most obvious differentiating characteristics seem to be highly visible ones, such as race, skin color, language, and religion (Klineberg 1971), as shown in the first wave of diversity research, or common national stereotypes, as shown in recent research on a German-French joint venture (Sackmann 1995). We have some indication that these more obvious differentiating criteria may also be used for convenience to explain differences within a socially acceptable framework (e.g., national stereotypes) or because of the lack of other cognitive categories available to the individuals.[32]

Although known to ICCM researchers, these findings have only recently been applied in ICCM research. Further research is needed to determine their applicability in ICCM settings or their transferability to the individual level, as well as to Asian contexts. Future studies need to determine the usefulness of these findings in resolving individual cultural identity issues, such as which cultural identity will become most important, how various cultural identities are "managed" by an individual, and the larger group salience issues. The studies by Earley and Laubach (2002), Pratt and Rafaeli (1997), Pratt (1998), Salk and Brannen (2000), and Salk and Shenkar (2001) can be seen as first steps in this direction.

The multiple cultures perspective also provides a way of exploring issues of synergy that are raised in the cross-national comparison and intercultural interaction perspectives (Adler 1991; Moran and Harris 1981) and encouraged in the latter stream of research. Rather than finding ways to *bridge differences* of national cultures, the question may become how to *build on similarities* engendered in other commonly held cultures for creative solutions and how to use and manage differences. Thus, the multiple cultures perspective helps us to address the primary difficulty that most strategic alliances, mergers, and acquisitions face today: how to realize the synergies that were initially promised and expected (Jansen 2001; Jansen and Körner 2000).

Concern with the issue of synergy has motivated recent research efforts on the impact and outcomes of culture, including recommendations for managerial practice. Research on multinational teams by DiStefano and Maznevski (2000) suggests, for example, that synergy may not just happen in multicultural teams in terms of members' national culture. Instead, it requires active work through a team development process that is based on tolerance and appreciation of differences.[33] In addition, research results from a longitudinal study of top management team heterogeneity, and from the reinterpretation of prior studies on this topic, suggest that, if adjusted for power, cognitive diversity in regard to functional background (profession/industry) has a positive impact on organizational performance (Pitcher and Smith 2001). These recent research efforts demonstrate a move toward a more differentiated treatment of the culture concept and a concern with practical implications and performance.

Finally, on a practical level, the multiple cultures perspective suggests that, to effectively live in the new global business reality, people need to develop an appreciation for multiple cultures that exist simultaneously. This requires that practitioners develop special skills to help them deal with this multicultural context and handle the differences in synergistic ways rather than considering cultural differences as a problem with which one must cope. ICCM research, which has always exhibited a heightened awareness of and sense of responsibility for practical application, is particularly geared toward clarifying and developing those necessary skills for reading the multiple cultural context and managing it in sensitive ways (Sackmann 1992a).

IMPLICATIONS FOR FUTURE RESEARCH

We have examined the nature and content of international cross-cultural management research within a framework of three research streams—cross-national comparison, intercultural interaction, and multiple cultures research. Despite superficial acknowledgment of a shared definition of culture, inherent in each stream is a relatively distinct conceptualization of culture as a social construct. As we have shown, these different interpretations of the culture construct emerge from different political, social, economic, and intellectual milieus and are underpinned by different sets of assumptions and theories. The result is inquiry into different questions, using different models for analysis and methods of investigation and providing different insights into the field of ICCM.

Our exploration of the culture construct, of how it has been and currently is being conceptualized, was motivated not just by our recognition that significant diversity existed (e.g., Sackmann 1991, ch. 2). It was becoming equally apparent that, across these differences, little conversation was occurring. Many researchers seemed to be oblivious of alternative conceptualizations of culture and of the implications of using one conceptualization as opposed to another. While many voiced criticism of the dominant research stream of cross-national comparison with regard to its concept of culture, few provided much insight into the source of their concerns or into constructive directions for future research. In the years since the first edition of this handbook was published, however, Robertson's words quoted at the beginning of our chapter are even more meaningful. It is, indeed, "both presumptuous and self-defeating to help spread the attitude that, in spite of our conviction that culture is important, we are only in the very early stages of dealing with it" (1992, 32). Scholars debating the conceptualization of culture in ICCM research finally have begun to establish a constructive dialogue that promises to have far-reaching implications.

In the paragraphs that follow, we summarize the areas of divergence and intersection in the culture debate among researchers representing the three perspectives we have described. Our discussion will focus on the set of assumptions implicitly or explicitly encompassed in any conceptualization of culture—assumptions about what culture is, how it comes into being, what it does, why it is important, how we can discover it, and how we can convey a representation of it in verbal form.

CONCEPTUALIZATIONS OF CULTURE

Far more than cross-national comparison research, intercultural interaction and multiple cultures research are concerned with expanding our knowledge of culture as a social construct; with grasping *what culture is*. Researchers who focus on cross-national comparison, however, are paying more attention than previously to making culture a clearly articulated social construct that far transcends the common "culture as nation" equation in its analytical utility. The "values research" (Earley and Singh 2000, 3), organized around universal dimensions of culture, that increasingly drives cross-national comparison provides a bridge to that multiple cultures research that organizes its concept of culture around a values dimensions construct. The research that offers an interpretation of nation-specific cultural constructs such as face- or nation-specific concepts of (presumably) universal processes such as leadership provides a bridge to intercultural interaction research, as well as multiple cultures research. Both directions in cross-national comparison share with the other two streams of research the assumption that culture, in essence, is a cognitive phenomenon that influences thought and behavior. Nonetheless, whichever the stream of research, a vast distance separates that which is based on unelaborated dimensions of culture, such as power distance, from research that attempts to capture the country-specific meaning of power distance, as implied in shared understandings about the relationship between superiors and subordinates (see Tayeb 2001).

The construct of national culture—the critical and almost exclusive focus of cross-national comparison—continues to lack the dynamism of the culture construct that informs the other research perspectives. Culture is assumed to be a coherent and enduring set of values that members of the nation-state carry and invariably act upon. In contrast, much of the research from the other two streams assumes not just that culture is carried but that the shared understandings that constitute culture actively are created (i.e., negotiated) through social interaction. This research may further recognize variation among individuals in how strongly any particular shared understanding is held as well as the contextual influences on individual interpretations of culture (see Osland and Bird 2000). The degrees of a culture's coherence and endurance frequently are research questions.

Research in the cross-national comparison stream implicitly assumes that culture is learned as one is socialized into a national culture. *How culture comes into being* has not been an issue of interest. In contrast, much of the intercultural interaction and multiple cultures research adopts a social constructionist approach. The view of culture as emergent, arising from the interaction among people as they make sense of the setting in which they live and work, leads researchers from these perspectives to be cognizant of the various kinds of contextual factors that help to shape emergent culture. A good deal of the research, in fact, seeks to understand how various cultures influence one another within an organization. The most significant difference between cross-national intercultural interaction research and multiple cultures research lies in the relative emphasis each places on national culture. Intercultural interaction research has taken as its starting point the assumption that, at least in the binational settings that have been studied, national culture is a powerful force in shaping sense making and action within an organization. The multiple cultures perspective that we have described makes no such a priori assumption.

Cross-national comparison research primarily is concerned with the issue of *what culture does*. But, as previously indicated, the impact of national culture on emergent organizational cultures is never what is being "explained." Rather, the research assumes a linkage between culture and the behavior or attitudes of individuals in organizations, the behavior of groups in organizations, or the behavior of organizations as entities. Culture is important because it constitutes one key variable in research typically designed around belief in the explanatory power of statistical correlation. With the rare exception, as in Erez and Earley's (1993) model of cultural self-representation, correlation between culture and behavior is viewed as direct, and little insight into the process by which culture influences behavior is offered.

With regard to *what culture does,* the intercultural interaction and multiple cultures perspectives also assume a linkage between culture and behavior of people in organizations. And, as in cross-national comparison research, that linkage may be construed as having implications for organizational effectiveness (e.g., Brannen 1994; Globokar 1997; Kleinberg 1994a; Schumacher 1997; Sumihara 1992). But most of the intercultural interaction research and much of the multiple cultures research stress culture as a reflection of sense making. Researchers assume that one of the most important things culture does is to enable people mentally to order their social world—to construct, in Frake's (1977) vocabulary, sketch maps that guide thinking and generate actions. Guiding this research is an interest in how the linkage between culture, thought, and behavior plays out within the framework of sense making rather than statistical correlation between culture and behavior. We gain an understanding of the importance of contextual factors, such as the relative power of the organizational actors, of how cultural identity is constructed and enacted, and of the effect of the intercultural communicative process on cultural negotiation.

How to discover culture is a question that engages many intercultural interaction and multiple culture researchers but relatively fewer cross-national comparison researchers. This is not surprising since the question follows naturally from an interest in *what culture is.* The formulation of relevant dimensions of culture in cross-national comparison research constitutes a kind of discovery, but, as noted, the resulting analysis generally does not lead to an emic interpretation of any group's shared sense making. Earlier discussion of the multiple cultures perspective shows that a wide variety of techniques for discovering shared sense making is utilized, including participant observation, in-depth interviews, causal mapping, and the critical incidents technique. In this stream of research, however, the typical combinations of ethnographic and quasi-ethnographic methods cannot reveal culture in the detail and depth that the long-term ethnographic inquiry conducted by some intercultural interaction researchers enables.

Choices concerning *how to represent culture* flow from a researcher's stance on the other questions that have been posed with regard to a conceptualization of culture. Analyses in which culture and nation are synonymous essentially avoid the issue of representation. In much of the values-based research, the representation of culture exhibits a descriptive economy, which is constrained by the particular dimensions that have been determined to be relevant and by the short sequence of words that have been selected to capture the essence of each dimension (e.g., individualism or collectivism, masculinity or femininity). Cross-national comparison researchers rarely engage in cultural representation that attempts to put into words the shared understandings, or sense making, or the cultural assumptions that describe this sense making contextually (with or without the frame of a dimensions schema). This kind of representation is found in intercultural interaction research (e.g., Brannen 1994; Kleinberg 1989) and, although less frequently, in multiple cultures research as well (e.g., Sackmann 1991; Sharpe 1997).

ENRICHING OUR THEORIES OF CULTURE
AND ORGANIZATION

Our review of ICCM research shows that cross-stream learning is occurring and indicates that the field as a whole will benefit tremendously from the heightening of such activity. A number of ICCM scholars have called for greater attention to midrange theory building as a way to integrate cross-cultural research into a body of literature that describes the effects of culture (Earley and Singh 1995, 2000; Lytle et al. 1995). A necessary step in this direction is to explicitly acknowledge that ICCM research by definition involves a theory of culture (Bjerke 1999; Kleinberg 1998; Lytle et al. 1995) and to incorporate this understanding into our research design. Cross-stream learning with regard to the concept of culture should not change the viewpoint expressed by Adler:

> in the future, the field [of international cross-cultural management will] continue its eclectic approach. In studying complex worldwide phenomena, it is important that researchers neither limit themselves to narrow conceptual maps nor rigid methodological approaches. (1983, 45)

Calls for midrange theory building so far have come from scholars working within a positivist research paradigm. An emphasis on explanation, as it is conceived by positivists, and an emphasis on understanding, as it is conceived by scholars working within an interpretive paradigm, each imply a theory of culture that differs from the other in important ways.

> It is clear that no matter what definition is given to "culture," it is an abstraction and a model (if you are an explanaticist) or a concretization and an interpretation (if a hermeneuticist). . . . So any definition of culture is also a theory of culture. (Dredge 1985, 411)

We are reminded by Bjerke that "the usefulness of such a definition/ description should be judged when applied" (1999, 17). If we cannot, and perhaps should not, expect convergence with regard to an overarching theory of culture, we can and should encourage researchers to be aware of how their particular conceptualization of culture is like or unlike others. While we anticipate that eclecticism will continue to characterize ICCM research, we predict that increasingly this will be an informed eclecticism.

The changing nature of the business and organizational environment makes different demands on the type of ICCM research that is undertaken. As we, among many other commentators, have noted, globalization drives rapid realignments and interdependencies among and within nations as well as among and within organizations. The people whose social interaction makes up these constructs of nation and organization draw on past cultural experience in order to create new cultural understandings that enable them to make sense of and live in a world in which frequent and often wrenching change is commonplace. Researchers are challenged to provide the insights that facilitate both meaningful cross-cultural comparison (cross-national or other) and an understanding of cross-cultural interaction (cross-national or other). When we consider the field of ICCM broadly, these should not be viewed as unrelated endeavors.

Finally, although we do not advocate that more recent perspectives supplant former ones, today's business and organizational environment demands that researchers at least *recognize* that multiple cultures exist. We can say with even greater confidence now than we did five years ago that new directions in cross-national comparison and cross-national intercultural interaction demonstrate such recognition. It is these bodies of research that draw most heavily on theories and concepts from other disciplines (particularly anthropology, sociology, and psychology) for ways to comprehend the various organizational issues and social phenomena that require our understanding. Continuing this multidisciplinary approach, while incorporating a multiple cultures perspective, enriches organizational theory in general, as it broadens and deepens our understanding of culture and its relevance to management research and practice.

NOTES

1. This is an invited update of the chapter "Conceptualizing Culture," prepared by the same authors for the first edition of the *Handbook* (Punnett and Shenkar 1996). An abridged version of that chapter appeared as Sackmann, Phillips, Kleinberg, and Boyacigiller in Sackmann 1997.

2. See Sackmann 1991 (10–12) for a detailed exposition of the main anthropological approaches; Rohner 1984 for the main approaches toward culture in the psychological literature; Thompson, Ellis, and Wildavsky 1990 for the main approaches in political science; and Smircich 1983 for the approaches in organization theory.

3. This rather pedantic description is necessary because cross-cultural research need not be international and international management is not always cross-cultural (further elaborated in Jackson and Aycan 2001).

4. For Harris and Moran, culture is "the way of living developed and transmitted by a group of human beings, consciously or unconsciously, to subsequent generations. More precisely, ideas, habits, attitudes, customs and traditions become accepted and somewhat standardized in a particular group as an attempt to meet continuing needs. Culture is overt and covert coping ways, or mechanisms that make a people unique in their adaptation to their environment and its changing conditions" (1991, 135). For Deresky, culture "of a society comprises the shared values, understandings, assumptions and goals that are learned from earlier generations, imposed by present members of a society, and passed on to succeeding generations" (2000, 105).

5. We developed this three-school scheme as a heuristic device in the first handbook (Boyacigiller et al.1996), and although recent research has made overlaps across streams more substantive we still find the demarcations helpful.

6. It is important to note that, while we are a multinational, multidisciplinary, and multilingual research team, we all received our doctorates in the United States. Thus, while we endeavor to include scholarship from outside of North America, the overwhelming majority of research cited is U.S.-based.

7. Unfortunately, this interest in development was lost in the 1970s and 1980s. However, it has seen a resurgence (e.g., Austin 1990; Jaeger and Kanungo 1990; Kiggundu 1989), which has been particularly bolstered by the interest in transitional economies (e.g., Child 1994).

8. The bicultural nature of Belgium was an exception that was recognized with questionnaire instruments in French and Flemish and with the resultant grouping of the two regions into two different clusters.

9. In Triandis's (1972) model, *distal antecedents* refer to physical-environmental resources and historical events; *proximal antecedents* refer to such things as occupation, language, and religion; basic *psychological processes* refer to cognitive learning and conditioning; *subjective culture* refers to a complex interplay of roles, norms, tasks, affect, cognitive structures, and behavioral intentions; and *consequences* refers to patterns of actions.

10. Definitions of the dimensions are not provided, given the widespread use of this perspective in ICCM (interested readers are urged to refer to Hofstede's own work [1980a, 2001]).

11. A cursory review would not do them justice. We recommend Kirkman, Lowe, and Gibson 2000 for readers seeking a thorough review.

12. Earley and Gibson (1998) provide a comprehensive review of this literature.

13. In fact, John Daniels, in his presidential address to the Academy of International Business (1991), cited Hall's research as an example of literature that has endured within the field without much empirical testing.

14. Kluckhohn and Strodtbeck's values orientations model (1961) includes the dimensions of human nature orientation, relationship to nature orientation, time orientation, activity orientation, relational orientation, and space orientation (see Lane, DiStefano, and Maznevski 1997 for a detailed discussion).

15. The Trompenaars framework is based on solutions to three universal problems: relationships with people, attitudes toward time, and attitudes toward the environment. The first dimension, relationships with people, is composed of five different orientations: universalism versus particularism, individualism versus collectivism, neutral versus emotional, specific versus diffuse, and achievement versus ascription. Trompenaars's work has gained greater acceptance in Europe, perhaps because it is more contextually based, includes more European countries, and doesn't assume that the dimensions are orthogonal.

16. Kirkman, Lowe, and Gibson (2000) recommend not using aggregate cultural distance measures (e.g., Kogut and Singh 1988) but rather, if a cultural distance score is necessary, computing a more specific distance measure based on each cultural value separately (e.g., Barkema and Vermeulen 1997; Shenkar and Zeira 1992).

17. Thomas, Shenkar, and Clarke (1994), in their review of articles published in the

Journal of International Business Studies (*JIBS*) during its twenty-four-year history, show the relatively narrow mental map of *JIBS* researchers. They conclude that, with "the exception of Italy, the top research locations have been confined to the G-7 nations, mirroring the prominence of those countries that have traditionally accounted for the majority of world trade" (677). Given that *JIBS*'s mandate is to publish *international* articles, one could argue that their researchers had arguably *broader* mental maps than most of their colleagues publishing in the mainline management journals.

18. For example, Lovett, Simmons, and Kali (1999) argue that, given today's business context, business relationships based on trust have increasing importance in Eastern and Western societies. Citing the relationship between Chinese management researchers' findings about *guanxi* and Western studies of *relationship marketing,* they argue that countries may be converging on a type of business relationship where trust is essential.

19. See, e.g., Schneider 1988 on the relationship between organizational and national cultures.

20. The review is of empirical research using Hofstede's cultural dimensions.

21. Triandis (1972) offers an exception.

22. A subset of intercultural communication research concerns cross-national, cross-cultural negotiations. This is a burgeoning field that, for space considerations, we have chosen not to incorporate into this paper. Some of the recent research relevant to this topic includes Brett and Okumura 1998; Gabrielidis et al. 1997; George, Jones, and Gonzalez 1998; Kleinberg 1998; Leung 1987; Tinsley and Pillutla 1998; and Triandis et al. 2001.

23. Previous discussion of contextual factors influencing and encouraging intercultural interaction research helps explain why more research effort revolves around the U.S.-based Japanese firm than other possible foci of cross-national interaction.

24. The main objective of Salk and Shenkar (2001) is to investigate social identity in an international joint venture. They consider cultural identity to be one type of social identity, stating that "Cultural identities have been viewed as interpretive lenses for sense making and signification" (163). Because of the focus on social identity rather than on cultural knowledge per se, this research is discussed in more depth in the section on a multiple cultures perspective in ICCM research.

25. See Holden 2001 for a discussion of how the conservative organizational culture of Matsushita Electric hinders localization efforts, despite a discourse of globalization.

26. See studies by Lincoln, Hanada, and Olson (1981); Lincoln, Olson, and Hanada (1978); and Pascale (1978) for a positivist approach to American-Japanese interaction.

27. Ronen and Shenkar's (1985) findings of the significance of regional boundaries to cultural issues have been further supported by recent GLOBE project results (e.g., Brodbeck et al. 2000) in which European cultural clusters were more or less replicated.

28. See, e.g., Bochner 1982 and Sackmann 1992b for references to and critiques of this research.

29. However, Salk and Shenkar carefully avoid the concept of multiple cultural identities by basing their arguments in other, mostly social-psychological, literature.

30. Dahler-Larsen (1997) reports from his study of the strike at Scandinavian Airlines System (SAS) that the salience of flight attendant cultural identities (profession, organization, nationality) may change depending on the issue at hand and the identities being

threatened. Pratt's initial findings from his ongoing research suggest that "as physicians are coming to identify with their organization and profession, other social identities (e.g., spouse, athlete) are becoming less salient or lost" (1998, 201).

31. Research on group formation and interaction shows factors influencing the identification with a group to be the distinctiveness of the group values and practices in relation to those of comparable groups (Oakes and Turner 1986), including negatively valued distinctions (van Knippenberg 1984); the prestige of the group (Chatman, Bell, and Staw 1986); the salience of the out-group(s) (Allen, Wilder, and Atkinson 1983; Turner 1981; Kanter 1977); the degree of intergroup competition (Brown and Ross 1982; van Knippenberg 1984); and factors associated with group formation such as interpersonal interaction, similarity, liking, proximity, shared goals or threats, and common history (Hogg and Turner 1985; Turner 1984).

32. Sackmann observed that national stereotypes (socially acceptable, since much more obvious) were predominantly used to explain difficulties that emerged in daily work, despite the fact that regional and organizational culture differences tended to be stronger than these national differences in this German-French joint venture.

33. In fact, the results of a qualitative field study, combined with two confirmatory laboratory studies from the cross-national comparative perspective, further specify that (nationally) homogeneous and (nationally) highly heterogeneous teams outperform moderately heterogeneous teams in the long run (Earley and Mosakowski 2000).

REFERENCES

Adler, N. J. 1983. Typology of management studies involving culture. *Journal of International Business Studies* (fall):29–47.

———. 1984. Understanding the ways of understanding: Cross-cultural management methodology reviewed. In R. N. Farmer, ed., *Advances in international comparative management,* 31–67. Greenwich, CT: JAI Press.

———. 2002. *International dimensions of organizational behavior.* 4th ed. Boston: Kent Publishing.

Adler, N. J., R. Doktor, and S. G. Redding. 1986. From the Atlantic to the Pacific century: Cross-cultural management reviewed. *Journal of Management* 12 (2): 295–318.

Adler, N. J., and J. L. Graham. 1989. Cross-cultural interaction: The international comparison fallacy? *Journal of International Business Studies* (fall):515–37.

Adler, N. J., and M. S. Jelinek. 1986. Is "organization culture" culture bound? *Human Resource Management* 25 (1): 73–90.

Ajiferuke, M., and J. Boddewyn. 1970. Culture and other explanatory variables in comparative management studies. *Academy of Management Journal* 35:153–64.

Aktouf, O. 1988. Corporate culture, the Catholic ethic, and the spirit of capitalism. Paper presented at the Standing Conference on Organizational Symbolism, Istanbul, Turkey.

Ali, A. J. 1993. Decision-making style, individualism, and attitudes toward risk of Arab executives. *International Studies of Management and Organization* 23:53–73.

Allen, V. L., D. A. Wilder, and M. L. Atkinson. 1983. Multiple group membership and social identity. In T. R. Sarabin and K. E. Scheibe, eds., *Studies in social identity,* 92–115. New York: Praeger.

Appadurai, A. 1991. Global ethnoscapes: Notes and queries for a transnational anthropology. In R. G. Fox, ed., *Recapturing anthropology: Working in the present,* 191–210. Santa Fe, NM: School of American Research Press.

Ashforth, B. E., and F. Mael. 1989. Social identity in the organization. *Academy of Management Review* 14:20–39.

Ashkanasy, N. M., C. P. M. Wilderom, M. F. Peterson, eds. 2000. *Handbook of organizational culture and climate.* Thousand Oaks: Sage.

Au, K.Y. 1999. Intra-cultural variation: Evidence and implications for international business. *Journal of International Business Studies* 30:799–812.

Austin, J. E. 1990. *Managing in developing countries: Strategic analysis and operating techniques.* New York: Free Press.

Axelrod, R. 1976. *Structure of decision.* Princeton, NJ: Princeton University Press.

Barkema, H. G., J. H. J. Bell, and J. M. Pennings. 1996. Foreign entry, cultural barriers, and learning. *Strategic Management Journal* 17:151–66.

Barkema, H. G., and F. Vermeulen. 1997. What differences in the cultural backgrounds of partners are detrimental for international joint ventures? *Journal of International Business Studies* 28:845–64.

Barkema, H. G., and F. Vermeulen. 1998. International expansion through start-up or acquisition: A learning perspective. *Academy of Management Journal* 41:7–26.

Barley, S. R. 1984. The professional, the semi-professional, and the machine: The social ramifications of computer-based imaging in radiology. Ph.D. diss., Sloan School of Management, Massachusetts Institute of Technology.

Benito, G. R. G., and G. Gripsrud. 1992. The expansion of foreign direct investments: Discrete rational location choices or a cultural learning process? *Journal of International Business Studies* 23 (3): 461–76.

Berry, J. W. 1997. An ecocultural approach to the study of cross-cultural industrial/organizational psychology. In P. C. Earley and M. Erez, eds., *New perspectives on international industrial/organizational psychology,* 130–47. San Francisco: New Lexington Press.

Bhagat, R. S., and S. J. McQuaid. 1982. Role of subjective culture in organizations: A review and direction for future research. *Journal of Applied Psychology Monograph* 67 (5): 653–85.

Birnbaum, P. H., and G. Y. Y. Wong. 1985. Organizational structure of multinational banks in Hong Kong from a culture-free perspective. *Administrative Science Quarterly* 30 (2): 262–77.

Bissels, S., S. A. Sackmann, and T. Bissels. 2001. Kulturelle Vielfalt in Organisationen [Cultural diversity in organizations]. *Soziale Welt* 52 (4):403–26.

Bjerke, B. 1999. *Business leadership and culture: National management styles in the global economy.* Cheltenham, UK: Edward Elgar.

Black, J., and M. Mendenhall. 1992. The u-curve adjustment hypothesis revised: A review and theoretical framework, *Journal of International Business Studies* 22 (2): 225–48.

———. 1993. Resolving conflicts with the Japanese: Mission impossible? *Sloan Management Review* (spring):49–59.

Blackhurst, M. 1986. The role of culture in affirmative action strategy. Paper presented at the International Conference on Organizational Symbolism and Corporate Culture, Montreal.

Bochner, S. 1982. The social psychology of cross-cultural relations. In S. Bochner, ed., *Cultures in contact*, 5–44. Oxford, NY: Pergamon Press.

Bochner, S., and B. Hesketh. 1994. Power distance, individualism/collectivism, and job-related attitudes in a culturally diverse work group. *Journal of Cross-Cultural Psychology* 25:233–57.

Bochner, S., and T. Ohsako. 1977. Ethnic role salience in racially homogenous and heterogenous societies. *Journal of Cross-Cultural Psychology* 8:477–92.

Bonazzi, G., and H. Botti. 1995. Asymmetric expectations: Cross-national coalitions in a Japanese transplant in Italy. *International Executive* 37 (4): 395–414.

Bond, M. H., and P. B. Smith. 1996. Cross-cultural social and organizational psychology. *Annual Review of Psychology* 47:205–35.

Boyacigiller, N. A. 2000. Orgut biliminde Turk yontecilerin alacagi dersler: Bazi uyarilar ve oneriler [The relevance of organization science for Turkish executives: A cautionary tale]. In Zeynep Aycan, ed., *Turkiye'de yonetim, liderlik ve insan kaynaklari ugumalari* [Management, leadership, and human resource applications in Turkey], 3–23. Ankara: Turk Psikologlar Dernegi Yayinlari, no. 21.

Boyacigiller, N. A., and N. J. Adler. 1991. The parochial dinosaur: Organizational science in a global context. *Academy of Management Review* 16 (2): 262–90.

———. 1994. Insiders and outsiders: Bridging the worlds of organizational behavior and international management. In B. Toyne and D. Nigh, eds., *International business inquiry: An emerging vision*. Columbia: University of South Carolina Press.

Boyacigiller, N. A., M. J. Kleinberg, M. E. Phillips, and S. A. Sackmann. 1996. Conceptualizing culture. In B. J. Punnett and O. Shenkar, eds., *Handbook for international management research*, 157–208. New York: Blackwell.

Brannen, M. Y. 1994. Your next boss is Japanese: Negotiating cultural change at a western Massachusetts paper plant. Ph.D. diss., University of Massachusetts, Amherst.

———. 1996. Ethnographic international management research. In B. J. Punnett and O. Shenkar, eds., *Handbook for international management research*, 115–43. New York: Blackwell.

Brannen, M. Y., and J. Kleinberg. 2000. Images of Japanese management and the development of organizational culture theory. In N. M. Ashkanasy, C. P. M. Wilderom, and M. F. Peterson, eds., *Handbook of organizational culture and climate*, 387–400. Thousand Oaks, CA: Sage.

Brannen, M. Y., and J. Salk. 2000. Partnering across borders: Negotiating organizational culture in a German-Japanese joint venture. *Human Relations* 52:451–87.

Brett, J. M., and T. Okumura. 1998. Inter- and intracultural negotiation: U.S. and Japanese negotiators. *Academy of Management Journal* 41 (5): 495–510.

Brett, J. M., C. H. Tinsley, M. Janssens, Z. I. Barsness, and A. L. Lytle. 1997. New approaches to the study of culture in industrial/organizational psychology. In P. C. Earley and M. Erez, eds., *New perspectives on international/industrial organizational psychology*. San Francisco: New Lexington Press.

Brodbeck, F. C., et al. 2000. Cultural variation of leadership prototypes across twenty-two European countries. *Journal of Occupational and Organizational Psychology* 73:1–29.

Brown, R. J., and G. F. Ross. 1982. The battle for acceptance: An investigation into the dynamics of intergroup behavior. In H. Tajfel, ed., *Social identity and intergroup relations,* 155–78. Cambridge: Cambridge University Press.

Burrell, G., and G. Morgan. 1979. *Sociological paradigms and organizational analysis.* London: Heinemann.

Burrus, K. 1997. National culture and gender diversity within one of the universal Swiss banks: An experiential description of a professional woman officer and president of the Women Managers' Association. In S. A. Sackmann, ed., *Cultural complexity in organizations: Inherent contrasts and contradictions,* 209–27. Thousand Oaks, CA: Sage.

Bushe, G. R. 1988. Cultural contradictions of statistical process control in American manufacturing organizations. *Journal of Management* 14 (1): 19–31.

Chatman, J. A., N. E. Bell, and B. M. Staw. 1986. The managed thought: The role of self-justification and impression management in organizational settings. In H. P. Sims Jr. and D. A. Gioia, eds., *The thinking organization: Dynamics of organizational social cognition,* 191–214. San Francisco: Jossey-Bass.

Child, J. 1981. Culture, contingency, and capitalism in the cross-national study of organizations. In L. L. Cummings and B. M. Staw, eds., *Research in organizational behavior,* 3:303–56. Greenwich, CT: JAI Press.

———. 1994. *Managing in China during the age of reform.* Cambridge: Cambridge University Press.

Chinese Culture Connection. 1987. Chinese values and the search for culture-free dimensions of culture. *Journal of Cross-Cultural Psychology* 18 (2): 143–64.

Clegg, S. R., and S. G. Redding, eds. 1990. *Capitalism in contrasting cultures.* New York: Walter de Gruyter.

Clifford, J. 1986. Introduction: Partial truths. In J. Clifford and G. E. Marcus, eds., *Writing culture: The poetics and politics of ethnography,* 1–26. Berkeley: University of California Press.

Clifford, J., and G. E. Marcus, eds. 1986. *Writing culture: The poetics and politics of ethnography.* Berkeley: University of California Press.

Conlon, J. K., and M. Giovagnoli. 1998. *The power of two: How companies of all sizes can build alliance networks that generate business opportunities.* San Francisco: Jossey-Bass.

Cooper, C. L., S. Cartwright, and P. C. Earley. 2001. *Handbook of organizational culture and climate.* Chichester, NY: John Wiley and Sons.

Dahler-Larsen, P. 1997. Organizational identity as a "crowded category": A case of multiple and quickly shifting "we" typifications. In S. A. Sackmann, ed., *Cultural complexity in organizations: Inherent contrasts and contradictions,* 367–89. Thousand Oaks, CA: Sage.

Daniels, J. D. 1991. Relevance in international business research: A need for more linkages. *Journal of International Business Studies* 22 (2): 177–86.

Davis, S. I. 2001. *Bank mergers: Lessons for the future.* New York: Palgrave.

Davis, S. M. 1984. *Managing corporate culture.* Cambridge, MA: Ballinger.

de la Torre, J. 1990. Managing in a changing global economy. Paper presented at the Advanced Executive Program, John E. Anderson Graduate School of Management, University of California, Los Angeles.

Deal, T. E., and A. A. Kennedy. 1982. *Corporate cultures.* Reading, MA: Addison-Wesley.

Delano, J. 2000. Executive commentary to J. S. Osland and A. Bird, beyond sophisticated stereotyping: Cultural sensemaking in context. *Academy of Management Executive* 14 (1): 77–78.

Dent, J. F. 1986. A case study of emergence of a new organizational reality. Paper presented at the International Conference on Organizational Symbolism and Corporate Culture, Montreal.

Deresky, H. 2000. *International management: Managing across borders and cultures.* 3d ed. Upper Saddle River, NJ: Prentice Hall.

de Vries, S. 1997. Ethnic diversity in organizations: A Dutch experience. In S. A. Sackmann, ed., *Cultural complexity in organizations: Inherent contrasts and contradictions,* 297–314. Thousand Oaks, CA: Sage.

Dickson, M. W., R. N. Aditya, and J. S. Chhokar. 2000. Definition and interpretation in cross-cultural organizational culture research: Some pointers from the GLOBE Research Program. In N. M. Ashkanasy, C. P. M. Wilderom, and M. F. Peterson, eds., *Handbook of organizational culture and climate,* 447–64. Thousand Oaks, CA: Sage.

DiStefano, J. J., and M. L. Maznevski. 2000. Creating value with diverse teams in global management. *Organizational Dynamics* 29 (1): 45–63.

Dore, R. 1973. *British factory—Japanese factory: The origins of national diversity in industrial relations.* Berkeley: University of California Press.

Dorfman, P. W. 1996. International and cross-cultural leadership. In P. J. Punnett and O. Shenkar, eds., *Handbook for international management research,* 267–350. Cambridge, MA: Blackwell.

Dorfman, P. W., and J. P. Howell. 1988. Dimensions of national culture and effective leadership patterns: Hofstede revisited. *Advances in International Comparative Management* 3:127–50.

———. 1997. Managerial leadership in the United States and Mexico: Distant neighbors or close cousins? In C. S. Granrose and S. Oskamp, eds., *Cross-cultural work groups,* 234–64. Thousand Oaks, CA: Sage.

Dredge, C. P. 1985. Corporate culture: The challenge to expatriate managers and multinational corporations. In H. V. Wortzel and L. H. Wortzel, eds., *Strategic management of multinational corporations: The essentials,* 410–24. New York: John Wiley and Sons.

Drucker, P. F. 1971. *Men, ideas, and politics: Essays.* New York: Harper and Row.

Dubinskas, F. A. 1988. Janus organizations: Scientists and managers in genetic engineering firms. In F. A. Dubinskas, ed., *Making time: Ethnographies of high-technology organizations,* 170–232. Philadelphia: Temple University Press.

Dunning, J. H. 1988. The future of the multinational enterprise. In J. C. Baker, J. K. Ryans Jr., and D. G. Howard, eds., *International business classics,* 55–71. Lexington, MA: D.C. Heath.

Dyer, W. G., Jr. 1985. The cycle of cultural evolution in organizations. In R. H. Kilmann, M. J. Saxton, and R. Serpa, eds., *Gaining control of the corporate culture,* 200–29. San Francisco: Jossey-Bass.

———. 1986. *Cultural change in family firms.* San Francisco: Jossey-Bass.

Earley, P. C. 1986. Trust, perceived importance of praise and criticism, and work performance: An examination of feedback in the United States and England. *Journal of Management* 12:457–73.

————. 1989. Social loafing and collectivism: A comparison of the United States and the People's Republic of China. *Administrative Science Quarterly* 34 (4): 565–81.

————. 1993. East meets West meets Mideast: Further explorations of collectivistic and individualistic work groups. *Academy of Management Journal* 36 (2): 317–48.

————. 1997. *Face, harmony, and social structure: An analysis of organizational behavior across cultures.* New York: Oxford University Press.

Earley, P. C., and M. Erez. 1997. *New perspectives on international industrial/organizational psychology.* San Francisco: New Lexington Press.

Earley, P. C., and Gibson, C. B. 1998. Taking stock in our progress on individualism-collectivism: One hundred years of solidarity and community. *Journal of Management* 24 (3): 265–305.

Earley, P. C., C. B. Gibson, and C. C. Chen. 1999. How did I do? vs. How did we do? Cultural contrasts of performance feedback use and self-efficacy. *Journal of Cross-Cultural Psychology* 30:594–619.

Earley, P. C., and M. Laubach. 2002. Structural identity theory and the dynamics of cross-cultural work groups. In M. J. Gannon and K. L. Newman, eds., *Handbook of cross-cultural management,* 256–82. Oxford: Blackwell.

Earley, P. C., and E. Mosakowski. 1996. Experimental international management research. In B. J. Punnett and O. Shenkar, eds., *Handbook for international management research,* 83–114. New York: Blackwell.

————. 2000. Creating hybrid team cultures: An empirical test of transnational team functioning. *Academy of Management Journal* 43 (1): 26–49.

Earley, P. C., and H. Singh. 1995. International and intercultural management research: What's next? *Academy of Management Journal* 38 (2): 327–40.

————, eds. 2000. *Innovations in international and cross-cultural management.* Thousand Oaks, CA: Sage.

Eberle, T. S. 1997. Cultural contrasts in a democratic nonprofit organization: The case of a Swiss reading society. In S. A. Sackmann, ed., *Cultural complexity in organizations: Inherent contrasts and contradictions,* 133–59. Thousand Oaks, CA: Sage.

Eby. L. T., and G. H. Dobbins. 1997. Collectivism orientation in teams: An individual and group-level analysis. *Journal of Organizational Behavior* 18:275–95.

Elron, E. 1997. Top management teams within multinational corporations: Effects of cultural heterogeneity. *Leadership Quarterly* 8:393–412.

Enz, C. A. 1986. New directions for cross-cultural studies: Linking organizational and societal cultures. In R. N. Farmer, ed., *Advances in international comparative management,* 2:173–89. Greenwich, CT: JAI Press.

Eramilli, M. K. 1991. The experience factor in foreign market entry behavior of service firms. *Journal of International Business Studies* 22 (3): 479–501.

Erez, M. 1997. A culture-based model of work motivation. In P. C. Earley and M. Erez, eds., *New perspectives on international industrial/organizational psychology,* 193–242. San Francisco: New Lexington Press.

Erez, M., and P. C. Earley. 1993. *Culture, self-identity, and work.* New York: Oxford.

Farh, J. L., A. S. Tsui, K. R. Xin, and B. S. Cheng. 1998. The influence of relational demography and guanxi: The Chinese case. *Organization Science* 9 (2): 1–18.

Farmer, R. N., and B. N. Richman. 1965. *Comparative management and economic progress.* Homewood, IL: Richard D. Irwin.

Fine, G. A. 1984. Negotiated orders and organizational cultures. *Annual Review of Sociology* 10:239–62.

Fiol, M. C. 1990. Narrative semiotics: Theory, procedures, and illustration. In A. S. Huff, ed., *Mapping strategic thought.* New York: John Wiley.

Fletcher, K. E., and A. S. Huff. 1990. Argument mapping. In A. S. Huff, ed., *Mapping strategic thought.* New York: John Wiley.

Frake, C. O. 1977. Plying frames can be dangerous: Some reflections on methodology in cognitive anthropology. *Quarterly Newsletter of the Institute for Comparative Human Development* 3:1–7.

———. 1983. Ethnography. In R. E. Emerson, ed., *Contemporary field research,* 60–67. Prospect Heights, IL: Waveland Press.

Franke, R. H., G. Hofstede, and M. H. Bond. 1991. Cultural roots of economic performance: A research note. *Strategic Management Journal* 12:165–73.

Fukuda, K. J. 1988. *Japanese-style management transferred: The experience of East Asia.* London: Routledge.

Gabrielidis, C., W. G. Stephan, O. Ybarra, V. M. Dos Santos Pearson, and L. Villareal. 1997. Preferred styles of conflict resolution: Mexico and the United States. *Journal of Cross-Cultural Psychology* 28 (6): 661–77.

Gannon, M. J., and K. L. Newman. 2002. *Handbook of cross-cultural management.* Oxford: Blackwell.

Garsten, C. 1990. The fluidity of space and time: The amorphous culture of global high-technology companies. Paper presented at the International Conference on Organizational Symbolism and Corporate Culture, Saarbrucken, West Germany.

Geertz, C. 1973. *The interpretation of cultures.* New York: Basic Books.

———. 1979. Suq: The bazaar economy in Sefrou. In C. Geertz, H. Geertz, and L. Rosen, eds., *Meaning and order in Moroccan society,* 123–264. Cambridge: Cambridge University Press.

Geist, P., and M. Hardesty. 1987. The symbolics of quality care: The intangible product of the hospital organization. Paper presented at the International Conference on Organizational Symbolism and Corporate Culture, Milan.

George, J. M., G. Jones, and J. A. Gonzalez. 1998. The role of affect in cross-cultural negotiations. *Journal of International Business Studies* 29 (4): 749–72.

Gibson, C. B. 1999. Do they do what they believe they can? Group efficacy and group effectiveness across tasks and cultures. *Academy of Management Journal* 42 (2): 138–52.

Giddens, A. 1979. *Central problems in social theory: Action, structure, and contradiction in social analysis.* Berkeley: University of California Press.

———. 1984. *The Constitution of Society.* Berkeley: University of California Press.

Globokar, T. 1997. Eastern Europe meets West: An empirical study on French management in a Solavenian plant. In S. A. Sackmann, ed., *Cultural complexity in organizations: Inherent contrasts and contradictions,* 72–86. Thousand Oaks, CA: Sage.

Godkin, I., C. E. Braye, and C. L. Caunch. 1989. U.S.-based cross-cultural management research in the eighties. *Journal of Business and Economic Perspectives* 15 (2): 37–45.

Gomez, C., B. L. Kirkman, and D. L. Shapiro. 2000. The impact of collectivism and in-group/out-group membership on the evaluation generosity of team members. *Academy of Management Journal* 43 (6): 1097–106.

Gomez-Mejia, L. R., and L. E. Palich. 1997. Cultural diversity and the performance of multinational firms. *Journal of International Business Studies* 28:309–35.

Goodenough, W. H. 1981. *Culture, language, and society.* Menlo Park, CA: Benjamin/Cummings.

Goodman, R. A., M. E. Phillips, and S. A. Sackmann. 1999. The complex culture of international project teams. In R. A. Goodman, ed., *Modern organizations and emerging conundrums: Exploring the post-industrial sub-culture of the third millennium*, 23–33. San Francisco: New Lexington Press.

Graham, J. L., A. T. Mintu, and W. Rogers. 1994. Explorations of negotiation behaviors in ten foreign cultures using a model developed in the United States. *Management Science* 40:72–95.

Graham, J. L., and Y. Sano. 1984. *Smart bargaining: Doing business with the Japanese.* Cambridge, MA: Ballinger.

Granrose, C. S. 1997. Cross-cultural socialization of Asian employees in U.S. organizations. In C. S. Granrose and S. Oskamp, eds., *Cross-cultural work groups*, 61–89. Thousand Oaks, CA: Sage.

Gray, S. J., L. H. Radebaugh, and C. B. Roberts. 1990. International perceptions of cost constraints on voluntary information disclosures: A comparative study of U.K. and U.S. multinationals. *Journal of International Business* 21 (4): 597–622.

Gregory, K. 1983. Native-view paradigms: Multiple cultures and culture conflicts in organizations. *Administrative Science Quarterly* 28:359–76.

Grinyer, P. H., and J. C. Spender. 1979. Recipes, crises, and adaptation in mature businesses. *International Studies of Management and Organization* 9 (3): 113–33.

Gundry, L., and D. Rousseau. 1994. Critical incidents in communicating culture to newcomers: The meaning is the message. *Human Relations* 46:1391–409.

Haire, M., E. E. Ghiselli, and L. Porter. 1966. *Managerial thinking: An international study.* New York: Wiley.

Hall, E. T. 1959. *The silent language.* New York: Doubleday.

Hamel, G., Y. L. Doz, and C. K. Prahalad. 1989. Collaborate with your competitors— and win. *Harvard Business Review* (January–February):133–39.

Hampden-Turner, C. M., and F. Trompenaars. 1993. *The seven cultures of capitalism: Value systems for creating wealth in the United States, Japan, Germany, France, Britain, Sweden, and the Netherlands.* Garden City, NY: Doubleday.

Handy, C. B. 1978. Zur entwicklung der organisations-kultur durch management development methoden [Developing organizational culture through management development]. *Zeitschrift fuer Organisation* 7:404–10.

Harbison, F., and C. A. Myers. 1959. *Management in the industrial world: An international analysis.* New York: McGraw.

Harris, P. R., and R. T. Moran. 1991. *Managing cultural differences.* 3d ed. Houston: Gulf.

Hatch, M. J. 1993. The dynamics of organizational culture. *Academy of Management Review* 18 (4): 657–93.

Helgstrand, K. K., and A. F. Stuhlmacher. 1999. National culture: An influence on leader evaluations? *International Journal of Organizational Analysis* 7:153–68.

Hernes, H. 1997. Social identity as a critical concept in dealing with complex cultural settings. In S. A. Sackmann, ed., *Cultural complexity in organizations: Inherent contrasts and contradictions,* 343–66. Thousand Oaks, CA: Sage.

Hickson, D. J., ed. 1993. *Management in Western Europe.* Berlin: Walter de Gruyter.

Hofstede, G. 1980a. *Culture's consequences: International differences in work-related values.* Beverly Hills: Sage.

———. 1980b. Motivation, leadership, and organization: Do American theories apply abroad? *Organizational Dynamics* (summer): 42–63.

———. 1983. The cultural relativity of organizational practices and theories. *Journal of International Business Studies* 14:75–89.

———. 1984. *Culture's consequences: International differences in work-related values.* Abbrev. ed. Beverly Hills: Sage.

———. 1990. Pitfalls in replication culture surveys. *Organization Studies* 11 (1): 103–6.

———. 1991. *Cultures and organizations: Software of the mind.* London: McGraw-Hill.

———. 2001. *Culture's consequences: Comparing values, behaviors, institutions, and organizations across nations.* 2d ed. Thousand Oaks, CA: Sage.

Hofstede, G., and Associates. 1998. *Masculinity and femininity: The taboo dimension of national cultures.* Thousand Oaks, CA: Sage.

Hofstede, G., and M. Bond. 1988. The Confucius connection: From cultural roots to economic growth. *Organizational Dynamics* 16 (4): 4–21.

Hofstede, G., B. Neuijen, D. D. Ohayv, and G. Sanders. 1990. Measuring organizational cultures: A qualitative and quantitative study across twenty cases. *Administrative Science Quarterly* 35 (2): 286–316.

Hogg, M. A., and J. C. Turner. 1985. Interpersonal attraction, social identification, and psychological group formation. *European Journal of Social Psychology* 15:51–66.

Holden, N. 2001. Why globalizing with a conservative corporate culture inhibits localization of management: The telling case of Matsushita Electric. *International Journal of Cross-Cultural Management* 1 (1): 53–72.

House, R. J., P. Hanges, S. A. Ruiz-Quintanilla, P. W. Dorfman, M. Javidan, M. Dickson, V. Gupta, and 170 co-authors. 1999. Cultural influences on leadership and organizations: Project *GLOBE.* In W. F. Mobley, M. J. Gessner, and V. Arnold, eds., *Advances in global leadership,* 1:171–233. Stamford, CT: JAI Press.

IJCCM (International Journal of Cross-Cultural Management). 2001. Aim and scope, 1 (1): inside back cover.

Jackson, T., and Z. Aycan. 2001. *International Journal of Cross-Cultural Management:* Towards the future. *International Journal of Cross-Cultural Management* 1 (1): 5–9.

Jaeger, A. M. 1986. Organizational development and national culture: Where's the fit? *Academy of Management Review* 11 (1): 178–90.

Jaeger, A. M., and R. N. Kanungo, eds. 1990. *Management in developing countries.* London: Routledge.

Jang, S., and M-H. Chung. 1997. Discursive contradiction of tradition and modernity in Korean management practices: A case study of Samsung's new management. In S.A. Sackmann, ed., *Cultural complexity in organizations: Inherent contrasts and contradictions,* 51–71. Thousand Oaks, CA: Sage.

Jansen, S. A. 2001. *Mergers and Acquisitions.* Wiesbaden: Gabler Verlag.

Jansen, S. A., and K. Körner. 2000. Szenen einiger Unternehmensehen: Vier Hochzeiten und drei Todesfälle [Scenes of some corporate marriages: Four weddings and three funerals]. *Frankfurter Allgemeine Zeitung* 260, no. 8 (November): 49.

Johnson, R. T., and W. G. Ouchi. 1974. Made in America (under Japanese management). *Harvard Business Review* 5:61–69.

Jones, M. O. 1988. In search of meaning: Using qualitative methods in research and application. In M. O. Jones, J. D. Moore, and R. C. Snyder, eds., *Inside organizations: Understanding the human dimension,* 31–47. Newbury Park, CA: Sage.

Kale, S. H. 1995. Grouping Euroconsumers: A culture-based clustering approach. *Journal of International Marketing* 2023:35–48.

Kanter, R. M. 1977. Some effects of proportions on group life: Skewed sex ratios and responses to Token women. *American Journal of Sociology* 82:965–90.

Kanungo, R. N., and R. M. Wright. 1983. A cross-cultural comparative study of managerial job attitudes. *Journal of International Business Studies* (fall):115–29.

Kerr, C. 1983. *The future of industrial societies.* Cambridge, MA: Harvard University Press.

Kiggundu, M. N. 1989. *Managing organizations in developing countries: An operational and strategic approach.* West Hartford, CT: Kumarian Press.

Kilmann, R. H. 1983. A dialectical approach to formulating and testing social science theories: Assumptional analysis. *Human Relations* 36 (1): 1–22.

Kim, K. I., H. Park, and N. Suzuki. 1990. Reward allocations in the United States, Japan, and Korea: A comparison of individualistic and collectivistic cultures. *Academy of Management Journal* 33 (1): 188–98.

Kirkman, B. L., K. B. Lowe, and C. B. Gibson. 2000. Twenty years of culture's consequences: A review of the empirical research on Hofstede's cultural value dimensions. Working paper. University of North Carolina at Greensboro.

Kleinberg, J. 1989. Cultural clash between managers: America's Japanese firms. In S. B. Prasad, ed., *Advances in international comparative management,* 4:221–44. Greenwich, CT: JAI Press.

———. 1994a. The crazy group: Emergent culture in a Japanese-American binational work group. In S. Beechler and A. Bird, eds., *Research in international business and international relations,* 6:1–45. Greenwich, CT: JAI Press. Special issue on Japanese management.

———. 1994b. Practical implications of organizational culture where Americans and Japanese work together. *National Association for the Practice of Anthropology Bulletin* 14:48–65. Washington, DC: American Anthropological Association.

———. 1998. An ethnographic perspective on cross-cultural negotiation and cultural production. In J. Wagner, ed., *Advances in qualitative organization research,* 1:201–49. Greenwich, CT: JAI Press.

Klineberg, O. 1971. Black and white in international perspective. *American Psychologist* 26:119–128.

Kluckhohn, C. 1951. Values and value-orientation in the theory of action: An exploration in definition and classification. In T. Parsons and E. A. Shils, eds., *Toward a general theory of action*, 388–433. Cambridge, MA: Harvard University Press.

Kluckhohn, F. R., and F. L. Strodtbeck. 1961. *Variations in value orientations*. Evanston, IL: Row, Peterson.

Kogut, B., and H. Singh. 1988. The effect of national culture on the choice of entry mode. *Journal of International Business Studies* 19 (3): 411–32.

Kopper, E. 1992. Multicultural workgroups and project teams. In N. Bergemann and A. L. J. Sourisseaux, eds., *Interkulturelles Management* [Intercultural management], 229–51. Heidelberg: Physica-Verlag.

Kostova, T. 1996. Success of the transnational transfer of organizational practices within multinational corporations. Ph.D. diss., University of Minnesota, Minneapolis.

Kreiner, K., and M. Schultz. 1990. Cultures in collaboration—The genetic code of conduct in biotechnology. Paper presented at the International Conference on Organizational Symbolism and Corporate Culture, Saarbrucken, West Germany.

Kroeber, A. L., and C. Kluckhohn. 1952. Culture: A critical review of concepts and definitions. *Papers of the Peabody Museum of American Archaeology and Ethnology* 47 (1). Cambridge, MA: Harvard University.

Kroeber, A. L., and T. Parsons. 1958. The concepts of culture and of social system. *American Sociological Review* 23:582–83.

Lammers, C. J., and D. J. Hickson. 1979. Towards a comparative sociology of organizations. In C. J. Lammers and D. J. Hickson, eds., *Organizations alike and unlike: International and interinstitutional studies in the sociology of organizations,* 3–20. London: Routledge and Kegan Paul.

Lane, H. W., J. J. DiStefano, and M. L. Maznevski. 1997. *International management behavior.* 3d ed. Cambridge, MA: Blackwell.

Langan-Fox, J., and P. Tan. 1997. Images of culture in transition: Personal constructs of organizational stability and change. *Journal of Occupational and Organizational Psychology* 70:273–94.

Laurent, A. 1983. The cultural diversity of Western conceptions of management. *International Studies of Management and Organization* 13 (1–2): 75–96.

Laurila, J. 1997. Discontinuous technological change as a trigger for temporary reconciliation of managerial subcultures: A case study of a Finnish paper industry company. In S. A. Sackmann, ed., *Cultural complexity in organizations: Inherent contrasts and contradictions,* 252–72. Thousand Oaks, CA: Sage.

Lawless, M. W. 1980. Toward a theory of policy making for directed interorganizational systems. Ph.D. diss., Graduate School of Management, University of California, Los Angeles.

Lawrence, P. R. 1987. The historical development of organizational behavior. In J. W. Lorsch, ed., *Handbook of organizational behavior.* Englewood Cliffs, NJ: Prentice-Hall.

Lebra, T. S. 1976. *Japanese patterns of behavior.* Honolulu: University of Hawaii Press.

Lenartowicz, T., and K. Roth. 2001. Does subculture within a country matter? A cross-cultural study of motivational domains and business performance in Brazil. *Journal of International Business Studies* 32 (2): 305–26.

Leung, K. 1987. Some determinants of reactions to procedural models for conflict resolution: A cross-national study. *Journal of Personality and Social Psychology* 53:898–908.

Leung, K., and S. Iwawaki. 1988. Cultural collectivism and distributive behavior. *Journal of Cross-Cultural Psychology* 19:35–49.

Li, J., and S. Guisinger. 1991. Comparative business failures of foreign-controlled firms in the United States. *Journal of InternationalBusiness Studies* 22 (2): 209–24.

Lilja, K., K. Räsänen, and R. Tainio. 1992. A dominant business recipe: The forest sector in Finland. In R. Whitley, ed., *European business systems: Firms and markets in their national contexts,* 137–54. London: Sage.

Lincoln, J. R., M. Hanada, and J. Olson. 1981. Cultural orientations and individual reactions to organizations: A study of employees of Japanese-owned firms. *Administrative Science Quarterly* 26:93–115.

Lincoln, J. R., and A. L. Kalleberg. 1990. *Culture, control, and commitment: A study of work organization and work attitudes in the United States and Japan.* Cambridge: Cambridge University Press.

Lincoln, J. R., H. R. Kerbo, and E. Wittenhagen. 1995. Japanese companies in Germany: A case study in cross-cultural management. *Industrial Relations* 34 (3): 417–40.

Lincoln, J. R., J. Olson, and M. Hanada. 1978. Cultural effects on organizational structure: The case of Japanese firms in the United States. *American Sociological Review* 43:829–47.

Lincoln, Y. S., and E. G. Guba. 1985. *Naturalistic inquiry.* Beverly Hills: Sage.

Linowes, R. G. 1994. The design of Japanese and American bicultural work teams. In M. G. Serapio, S. Beechler, and A. Bird, eds., *Research in International Business and International Relations* 6:47–71.

Louis, M. R. 1983. Organizations as culture-bearing milieux. In L. R. Pondy, P. J. Frost, G. Morgan, and T. C. Dandridge, eds., *Organizational symbolism,* 39–54. Greenwich, CT: JAI Press.

Lovett, S., L. C. Simmons, and R. Kali. 1999. *Guanxi* versus the market: Ethics and efficiency. *Journal of International Business Studies* 30 (2): 231–47.

Luo, Y., and M. W. Peng. 1999. Learning to compete in a transition economy: Experience, environment, and performance. *Journal of International Business Studies* 30 (2): 278–307.

Lynn, M., and B. D. Gelb. 1996. Identifying innovative national markets for technical consumer goods. *International Marketing Review* 13 (6): 43–57.

Lytle, A. L., J. M. Brett, Z. I. Barness, C. H. Tinsley, and M. Janssens. 1995. A paradigm for confirmatory cross-cultural research in organizational behavior. In L. L. Cummings and B. M. Staw, eds., *Research in organizational behavior,* 17:167–214. Greenwich, CT: JAI Press.

Marcus, G. E. 1986. Contemporary problems of ethnography in the modern world system. In J. Clifford and G. E. Marcus, eds., *Writing culture: The poetics and politics of ethnography,* 165–93.. Berkeley: University of California Press.

Markus, H. R., and S. Kitayama. 1991. Culture and self: Implications for cognition, emotion, and motivation. *Psychological Review* 98:224–253.

Martin, J. 1992. *Cultures in organizations: Three perspectives.* New York: Oxford University Press.

———. 2002. *Organizational culture: Mapping the terrain.* Thousand Oaks, CA: Sage.

Martin, J., M. Feldman, M. J. Hatch, and S. Sitkin. 1983. The uniqueness paradox in organization studies. *Administrative Science Quarterly* 28:438–53.

Martin, J., and P. Frost. 1996. The organizational culture war games: A struggle for intellectual dominance. In S. Clegg, C. Hardy, and W. Nord, eds., *Handbook of organization studies,* 559–621. London: Sage.

Martin, J., and C. Siehl. 1983. Organizational culture and counter-culture: An uneasy symbiosis. *Organizational Dynamics* 12 (2): 52–64.

Martin, J., S. B. Sitkin, and M. Boehm. 1985. Founders and the elusiveness of a cultural legacy. In P. J. Frost, L. F. Moore, M. R. Louis, C. C. Lundberg, and J. Martin, eds., *Organizational culture,* 99–124. Beverly Hills, CA: Sage.

Maznevski, M. L., J. J. DiStefano, and S. Nason. 1995. *Cultural perspectives questionnaire.* Ontario, Canada: University of Western Ontario, London; and Charlottesville: University of Virginia.

Maznevski, M. L., C. R. Gibson, B. L. Kirkman. 2000. When does culture matter? Working Paper. McIntire School of Commerce, University of Virginia.

Meek, C. B., and Y. H. Song. 1990. The impact of national culture on management and organization: Lessons from the Land of the Morning Calm. Paper presented at the annual meeting of the Academy of Management, San Francisco.

Meyerson, D. E., and J. Martin. 1987. Cultural change: An integration of three different views. *Journal of Management Studies* 24:623–47.

Milliken, F. J., and L. I. Martins. 1996. Searching for common threads: Understanding the multiple effects of diversity in organizational groups. *Academy of Management Review* 21 (4): 402–33.

Mitchell, R. K., B. Smith, K. W. Seawright, and E. A. Morse. 2000. Cross-cultural cognitions and the venture creation decision. *Academy of Management Journal* 43:974–93.

Moorman, R. H., and G. L. Blakely. 1995. Individualism-collectivism as an individual difference predictor of organizational citizenship behavior. *Journal of Organizational Behavior* 16 (2): 127–2.

Moran, R. T., and P. R. Harris. 1981. *Managing cultural synergy.* Houston: Gulf.

Morris, M. H., D. L. Davis, and J. W. Allen. 1994. Fostering corporate entrepreneurship: Cross-cultural comparisons of the importance of individualism versus collectivism. *Journal of International Business* 25 (1): 65–89.

Nagel, C. 1995. *Zur Kultur der Organisation: Eine Organisationspsychologische Untersuchung in der Automobilindustrie* [The culture of organizations: An organizational psychological study in the automotive industry]. Frankfurt am Main: Lang.

Nakane, C. 1970. *Japanese society.* Berkeley: University of California Press.

Narayanan, V. K., and L. Fahey. 1990. Evolution of revealed causal maps during decline: A case study of Admiral. In A. S. Huff, ed., *Mapping strategic thought,* 109–33. New York: John Wiley.

Nath, R. 1986. The role of culture in cross-cultural and organizational research. In R. N. Farmer, ed., *Advances in international comparative management,* 2:249–67. Greenwich, CT: JAI Press.

Nemetz, P. L., and S. L. Christensen. 1996. The challenge of cultural diversity: Harnessing a diversity of views to understand multiculturalism. *Academy of Management Review* 21 (4): 434–62.

Newman, K. L., and S. D. Nollen. 1996. Culture and congruence: The fit between management practices and national culture. *Journal of International Business Studies* 29:729–48.

Newman, W. H. 1972. Cultural assumptions underlying U.S. management concepts. In J. L. Massie and S. Laytie, eds., *Management in an international context,* 327–52. New York: Harper and Row.

Oakes, P. J., and J. C. Turner. 1986. Distinctiveness and the salience of social category memberships: Is there an automatic perceptual bias towards novelty? *European Journal of Social Psychology* 16:325–44.

Osland, J. S., and A. Bird. 2000. Beyond sophisticated stereotyping: Cultural sensemaking in context. *Academy of Management Executive* 14 (1): 77–78.

Ouchi, W. G. 1981. *Theory Z.* Reading, MA: Addison-Wesley.

Pacanowsky, M. 1987. Communication in the empowering organization. In J. A. Anderson, ed., *ICA yearbook* 11. Beverly Hills, CA: Sage.

Parsons, T., and E. A. Shils, eds. 1951. *Towards a general theory of action.* Cambridge, MA: Harvard University Press.

Pascale, R. T. 1978. Employment practices and employee attitudes: A study of Japanese and American managed firms in the United States. *Human Relations* 38 (7): 597–615.

Pascale, R. T., and A. G. Athos. 1981. *The art of Japanese management.* New York: Warner Books.

Pederson, J. S. 1987. Organizational cultures within computer firms. Paper presented at the International Conference on Organizational Symbolism and Corporate Culture, Milan.

Peng, T. K., M. F. Peterson, and Y. P. Shyi. 1991. Quantitative methods in cross-national management research: Trends and equivalence issues. *Journal of Organizational Behavior* 12 (2): 87–108.

Peters, T. J., and R. J. Waterman, Jr. 1982. *In search of excellence: Lessons from America's best-run companies.* New York: Harper and Row.

Peterson, M. F., C. L. Rodrigues, and P. B. Smith. 2000. Extending agency theory with event management and foreign direct investment theories. In P. C. Earley and H. Singh, eds., *Innovations in international and cross-cultural management,* 131–82. Thousand Oaks, CA: Sage.

Peterson, M. F., P. B. Smith, D. Akande, S. Ayestaran, S. Bochner, V. Callan, N. G. Cho, J. Correia Jesuino, M. D'Amorim, P. H. Francois, K. Hofmann, P. L. Koopman, K. Leung, T. K. Lim, S. Mortazavi, J. Munene, M. Radfort, A. Ropo, G. Savage, B. Setiadi, T. N. Sinha, R. Sorenson, and C. Viedge. 1995. Role conflict, ambiguity, and overload by national culture: A twenty-one nation study. *Academy of Management Journal* 38:429–52.

Pettigrew, A. M. 1979. On studying organizational cultures. *Administrative Science Quarterly* 23 (4): 570–81.

———. 1985. *The awakening giant.* Oxford: Basil Blackwell.

Phillips, M. E. 1990. Industry as a cultural grouping. Ph.D. diss., Graduate School of Management, University of California, Los Angeles.

————. 1994. Industry mindsets: Exploring the cultures of two macro-organizational settings. *Organization Science* 5 (3): 384–402.

Phillips, M. E., N. A. Boyacigiller, S. A. Sackmann, and M. K. Bolton. 1992. Multiple cultural mindsets as a normal state: A cultural perspective on European organizational life. Paper presented at the International Conference of the Western Academy of Business, Leuven, Belgium.

Phillips, M. E., R. A. Goodman, and S. A. Sackmann. 1992. Exploring the complex cultural milieu of project teams. *pmNETwork—Professional Magazine of the Project Management Institute* 8:20–26.

Phillips, M. E., S. A. Sackmann, and R. A. Goodman. 1992. The cultural environment of project teams: An expanded view of their complex nature. Paper presented at the EIASM Workshop on Managing in Different Cultures, Cergy-Pontoise, France.

Pillai, R., and J. R. Meindl. 1998. Context and charisma: A meso level examination of the relationship of organic structure, collectivism, and crisis to charismatic leadership. *Journal of Management* 24:643–71.

Pitcher, P., and A. D. Smith. 2001. Top management team heterogeneity: Personality, power, and proxies. *Organization Science* 12 (1): 1–18.

Pondy, L. R., P. J. Frost, G. Morgan, and T. C. Dandridge, eds. 1983. *Organizational symbolism.* Greenwich, CT: JAI Press.

Pratt, M. 1998. To be or not to be? Central questions in organizational identification. In D. A. Whetten and P. C. Godfrey, eds., *Identity in organizations,* 171–207. Thousand Oaks, CA: Sage.

Pratt, M., and A. Rafaeli. 1997. Organizational dress as symbol of multilayered social identities. *Academy of Management Journal* 40 (4): 862–98.

Pümpin, C. 1984. Unternehmenskultur, unternehmensstrategie und unternehmenserfolg [Corporate culture, corporate strategy and corporate performance]. Paper presented at the ATAG Conference on the Importance of Corporate Culture for the Future Success of Your Firm, Zurich.

Punnett, B. J., and O. Shenkar, eds. 1996. *Handbook for international management research.* Oxford: Blackwell.

Putnam, L. L., and M. E. Pacanowsky. 1983. *Communication and organizations: An interpretive approach.* Beverly Hills, CA: Sage.

Ramamoorthy, N., and S. J. Carroll. 1998. Individualism/collectivism orientations and reactions toward alternative human resource management practices. *Human Relations* 51:571–88.

Rao, A., and K. Hashimoto. 1996. Intercultural influence: A study of Japanese expatriate managers in Canada. *Journal of International Business Studies* (third quarter):443–65.

Räsänen, K., and R. Whipp. 1992. National business recipes: A sector perspective. In R. Whitley, ed., *European business systems: Firms and markets in their national contexts,* 46–60. London: Sage.

Redding, S. G. 1990. *The Spirit of Chinese Capitalism.* New York: Walter de Gruyter.

————. 1994. The comparative management theory zoo: Getting the elephants and ostriches and even dinosaurs from the jungle into the iron cages. In B. Toyne and D. Nigh, eds., *International business inquiry: An emerging vision,* 416–39. Columbia: University of South Carolina Press.

Redding, S. G., A. Norman, and A. Schlander. 1993. The nature of individual attachment to the organization: A review of East Asian variations. In M. D. Dunnette, ed., *Handbook of industrial and organizational psychology,* 4:647–88. Palo Alto: Consulting Psychologists Press.

Redding, S. G., and M. Ng. 1982. The role of "face" in the organizational perceptions of Chinese managers. *Organization Studies* 3 (3): 201–19.

Redding, S. G., and G. Y. Y. Wong. 1986. The psychology of Chinese organizational behavior. In M. H. Bond, ed., *The psychology of the Chinese People,* 267–95. Hong Kong: Oxford University Press.

Reger, R. K. 1990. The repertory grid technique for eliciting the content and structure of cognitive constructive systems. In A. S. Huff, ed., *Mapping strategic thought,* 71–88. New York: John Wiley.

Roberts, K. H. 1970. On looking at an elephant: An evaluation of cross-cultural research related to organizations. *Psychological Bulletin* 74 (5): 327–50.

Roberts, K. H., and N. A. Boyacigiller. 1984. Cross-national organizational research: The grasp of the blind men. In B. M. Staw and L. L. Cummings, eds., *Research in organizational behavior,* 6:423–75. Greenwich, CT: JAI Press.

Robertson, R. 1992. *Globalization: Social theory and global culture.* London: Sage.

Rohlen, T. P. 1974. *For harmony and strength: Japanese white-collar organization in anthropological perspective.* Berkeley: University of California Press.

Rohner, R, 1984. Toward a conception of culture for cross-cultural psychology. *Journal of Cross-Cultural Psychology* 15 (2): 111–38.

Ronen, S. 1986. *Comparative management and multinational management.* New York: John Wiley.

Ronen, S., and O. Shenkar. 1985. Clustering countries on attitudinal dimensions: A review and synthesis. *Academy of Management Review* 10 (3): 435–54.

Roseberry, W. 1989. *Anthropologies and Histories: Essays in Culture, History, and Political Economy.* New Brunswick, NJ: Rutgers University Press.

Rosen, M. 1986. Christmas time and control: An exploration in the social structure of formal organizations. Paper presented at the International Conference on Organizational Symbolism and Corporate Culture, Montreal, Quebec.

Rosenzweig, P. R., and N. Nohria. 1994. Influences on human resource management practices in multinational corporations. *Journal of International Business Studies* 25 (2): 229–52.

Roth, K., and S. O'Donnell. 1996. Foreign subsidiary compensation strategy: An agency theory perspective. *Academy of Management Journal* 39:678–703.

Rowlinson, M., and S. Procter. 1999. Organizational culture and business history. *Organization Studies* 20:369–96.

Rusted, B. 1986. Corporate entertainment as social action: The case of a service organization. Paper presented at the International Conference on Organizational Symbolism and Corporate Culture, Montreal, Quebec.

Sackmann, S. A. 1983. Organisationskultur—Die unsichtbare Einflussgrosse [Organizational culture—The invisible influence]. *Gruppendynamik* 14:393–406.

———. 1985. Cultural knowledge in organizations: The link between strategy and organizational processes. Ph.D. diss., Graduate School of Management, University of California, Los Angeles.

———. 1991. *Cultural knowledge in organizations: Exploring the collective mind.* Newbury Park, CA: Sage.

———. 1992a. Culture and management development in a global economy. In R. M. Schwartz, ed., *Managing organizational transitions in a global economy,* 57:31–56. Monograph and Research Series, Institute of Industrial Relations, University of California, Los Angeles.

———. 1992b. Cultures and subcultures: An analysis of organizational knowledge. *Administrative Science Quarterly* 37 (1): 140–61.

———. 1995. Analyse und Diagnose der Organisationskultur bei DBA, Projektbereicht [Project Report]. Institute for Human Resources and Organization Studies, University Bw Munich.

———. 1999. When cultures meet. . . . Managing the post merger integration. Paper presented at Dürr AG, Paris.

———. 2001a. Issues of culture in globalizing firms. Paper presented at the European Congress on Work and Organizational Psychology, Prague.

———. 2001b. Cultural complexity in organizations: The value and limitations of qualitative methodology and approaches. In C. L. Cooper, S. Cartwright, and P. C. Earley, eds., *Organizational culture and climate,* 143–63. New York: Wiley.

———, ed. 1997. *Cultural complexity in organizations: Inherent contrasts and contradictions.* Thousand Oaks: Sage.

Sackmann, S. A., S. Bissels, and T. Bissels. 2002. Kulturelle Vielfalt in Organisationen: Ansätze zum Umgang mit einem vernachlässigten Thema der Organisationswissenschaften [Cultural diversity in organization: Ways to deal with a neglected topic in the organizational sciences]. *Die Betriebswirtschaft* 62 (1): 43–58.

Sackmann, S. A., and M. E. Phillips. 1992. Mapping the cultural terrain in organizational settings: Current boundaries and future directions for empirical research. CIBER Working Paper 92-05. Center for International Business, Anderson Graduate School of Management, University of California, Los Angeles.

Sackmann, S. A., M. E. Phillips, M. J. Kleinberg, and N. A. Boyacigiller. 1997. Single and multiple cultures in international cross-cultural management research: An overview. In S. A. Sackmann, ed., *Cultural Complexity in Organizations: Inherent Contrasts and Contradictions,* 14–48. Thousand Oaks, CA: Sage.

Sagiv, L., and S. H. Schwartz. 1995. Value priorities and readiness for outgroup social contact. *Journal of Personality and Social Psychology* 69:437–48.

Salk, J. E. 1993. Partners and other strangers: Cultural boundaries and the negotiated order developed in bi-cultural and joint venture teams. Paper presented at the annual meeting of the Academy of Management, Atlanta.

Salk, J., and M. Y. Brannen. 2000. National culture, networks, and individual influence in a multinational management team. *Academy of Management Journal* 43 (2): 191–202.

Salk, J., and O. Shenkar. 2001. Social identities in an international joint venture: An exploratory case study. *Organization Science* 12 (2): 161–78.

Samovar, L. A., and R. E. Porter, eds. 1991. *Intercultural communication: A reader.* Belmont, CA: Wadsworth.

Samovar, L. A., R. E. Porter, and N. C. Jain. 1981. *Understanding intercultural communication.* Belmont, CA: Wadsworth.

Sampson, E. E. 1978. Scientific paradigms and social values: Wanted—a scientific revolution. *Journal of Personality and Social Psychology* 36 (11): 1332–43.

Sapienza, A. M. 1985. Believing is seeing: How organizational culture influences the decisions top managers make. In R. H. Kilmann, M. J. Saxton, and R. Serpa, eds., *Gaining control of the corporate culture,* 66–83. San Francisco: Jossey-Bass.

Sarnin, P. 1989. Stability of leaders' cognitions in the firm and the need for strategic change: The role of socio-cognitive conflict in a service company. Paper presented at the International Conference on Organizational Symbolism and Corporate Culture, Fontainebleau, France.

Schein, E. 1983. The role of the founder in creating organizational culture. *Organizational Dynamics* 12 (1): 13–28.

———. 1985. *Organizational culture and leadership.* San Francisco: Jossey-Bass.

Schneider, S. C. 1988. National vs. corporate culture: Implications for human resource management. *Human Resource Management* 27 (2): 231–46.

Schneider, S. C., and A. de Meyer. 1991. Interpreting and responding to strategic issues: The impact of national culture. *Strategic Management Journal* 12:307–20.

Schultz, M., and M. J. Hatch. 1996. Living with multiple paradigms: The case of paradigm interplay in organizational culture studies. *Academy of Management Review* 21 (2): 529–57.

Schumacher, T. 1997. West coast Camelot: The rise and fall of an organizational culture. In S. A. Sackmann, ed., *Cultural complexity in organizations: Inherent contrasts and contradictions,* 107–32. Thousand Oaks, CA: Sage.

Schwartz, S. H. 1992. Universals in the content and structure of values: Theoretical advances and empirical tests in twenty countries. In M. P. Zanna, ed., *Advances in experimental social psychology,* 1–65. San Diego, CA: Academic Press.

———. 1994. Beyond individualism/collectivism: New dimensions of values. In U. Kim, H. C. Triandis, C. Kagit ibasi, S. C. Choi, and G. Yoon, eds., *Individualism and collectivism: Theory, applications, and methods,* 85–119. Thousand Oaks, CA: Sage.

Schwartz, S. H., and W. Bilsky. 1990. Toward a theory of the universal content and structure of values. *Journal of Personality and Social Psychology* 58 (5): 878–91.

Sekaran, U. 1983. Methodological and theoretical issues and advancements in cross-cultural research. *Journal of International Business Studies* (fall):61–72.

Servan-Schreiber, J. J. 1968. *The American challenge.* Trans. R. Steel. New York: Atheneum.

Sharpe, D. 1997. Managerial control strategies and subcultural processes: On the shop floor in a Japanese manufacturing organization in the United Kingdom. In S. A. Sackmann, ed., *Cultural complexity in organizations: Inherent contrasts and contradictions,* 228–51. Thousand Oaks, CA: Sage.

Shenkar, O., and M. A. Von Glinow. 1994. Paradoxes of organizational theory and research: Using the case of China to illustrate national contingency. *Management Science* 40 (1): 56–71.

Shenkar, O., and Y. Zeira. 1992. Role conflict and role ambiguity of chief executive officers in international joint ventures. *Journal of International Business* 23 (1): 55–75.

Siegwart, H., and G. Neugebauer, eds. 1998. *Mega-fusionen mega-mergers.* Bern: Verlag Paul Haupt.

Silin, R. H. 1976. *Leadership and Values: The Organization of Large Scale Taiwanese Enterprises.* Cambridge: MA: East Asian Research Center, Harvard University.

Singh, J. P. 1990a. Managerial culture and work-related values in India. *Organization Studies* 11 (1): 75–102.

———. 1990b. A comment on Hofstede's reply. *Organization Studies* 11 (1): 106.

Smircich, L. 1983. Concepts of culture and organizational analysis. *Administrative Science Quarterly* 28, no. 3 (September): 339–58.

Smircich, L., and M. B. Calas. 1987. Organizational culture: A critical assessment. In F. M. Jablin, L. L. Putnam, K. H. Roberts, and L. W. Porter, eds., *Handbook of organizational communication,* 228–63. Newbury Park, CA: Sage.

Smith, P. B., S. Dugan, and F. Trompenaars. 1996. National culture and managerial values: A dimensional analysis across forty-three nations. *Journal of Cross-Cultural Psychology* 27:231–64.

Smith, P. B., and M. F. Peterson. 2002. Cross-cultural leadership. In M. J. Gannon and K. L. Newman, eds., *Handbook of cross-cultural management,* 217–35. Oxford: Blackwell.

Søndergaard, M. 1994. Research note: Hofstede's consequences: A study of reviews, citations, and replications. *Organization Studies* 15 (3): 447–56. Special issue on cross-national organization culture.

Spradley, J. P. 1980. *Participant observation.* New York: Holt, Rinehart, and Winston.

Steers, R. M., and C. J. Sanchez-Runde. 2002. Culture, motivation, and work behavior. In M. J. Gannon and K. L. Newman, eds., *Handbook of cross-cultural management,* 190–216. Oxford: Blackwell.

Stinchcombe, A. L. 1965. Social structure and organizations. In J. G. March, ed., *Handbook of organizations,* 142–93. Chicago: Rand McNally.

Sullivan, J. 1994. Theory development in international business research: The decline of culture. In B. Toyne and D. Nigh, eds., *International business inquiry: An emerging vision.* Columbia: University of South Carolina Press.

Sumihara, N. 1992. A case study of structuration in a bicultural work organization: A study of a Japanese-owned and -managed corporation in the U.S.A. Ph.D. diss., Department of Anthropology, New York University.

Symons, G. L. 1986. Corporate culture, managerial women, and organizational change. Paper presented at the International Conference on Organizational Symbolism and Corporate Culture, Montreal.

Tajfel, H. 1974. Social identity and intergroup behaviour. *Social Science Information* 13:65–93.

———. 1981. *Human groups and social categories: Studies in social psychology.* New York: Cambridge University Press.

Tajfel, H., C. Flament, M. G. Billig, and R. F. Bundy. 1971. Social categorization and intergroup behaviour. *European Journal of Social Psychology* 1:149–77.

Takezawa, S. I. 1966. Socio-cultural aspects of management in Japan: Historical development and new challenges. *International Labour Review* 94:148–74.

Tayeb, M. 2001. Conducting research across cultures: Overcoming drawbacks and obstacles. *International Journal of Cross Cultural Management* 1 (1): 91–108.

Teagarden, M. B., et al. 1995. Toward a theory of comparative management research: An idiographic case study of the best international human resources management project. *Academy of Management Journal* 38 (5): 1261–87.

Thomas, A. S., O. Shenkar, and L. Clarke. 1994. The globalization of our mental maps: Evaluating the geographic scope of JIBS coverage. *Journal of International Business Studies* 25 (4): 675–86.

Thompson, M., R. Ellis, and A. Wildavsky. 1990. *Cultural theory.* Boulder, CO: Westview Press.

Thurow, L. 1988. Keynote address, Western Academy of Management, Big Sky, MT.

Tinsley, C. H., and M. M. Pillutla. 1998. Negotiating in the United States and Hong Kong. *Journal of International Business Studies* 29:712–28.

Triandis, H. C. 1972. *The analysis of subjective culture.* New York: Wiley.

———. 1992. Cross-cultural industrial and organizational psychology. In M. D. Dunnette, ed., *Handbook of industrial and organizational psychology,* vol. 4. Palo Alto, CA: Consulting Psychologists Press.

Triandis, H. C., P. Carnevale, M. Gelfand, C. Robert, S. A. Wasti, T. Probst, E. Kashima, T. Dragonas, D. Chan, X. P. Chen, U. Kim, C. de Dreu, E. van de Vliert, S. Iwao, K. Ohbuchi, and P. Schmitz. 2001. Culture and deception in business negotiations: A multilevel analysis. *International Journal of Cross-Cultural Management* 1 (1): 73–90.

Trompenaars, F. 1993. *Riding the waves of culture: Understanding diversity in global business.* Chicago, IL: Irwin.

Tung, R. L. 1997. International and intranational diversity. In C. S. Granrose and S. Oscamp, eds., *Cross-cultural work groups,* 163–85. Thousand Oaks, CA: Sage.

Tunstall, W. B. 1985. Breakup of the Bell system: A case study in cultural transformation. In R. H. Kilmann, M. J. Saxton, and R. Serpa, eds., *Gaining control of the corporate culture,* 44–65. San Francisco: Jossey-Bass.

Turner, J. C. 1981. The experimental social psychology of intergroup behavior. In J. C. Turner and H. Giles, eds., *Intergroup behavior,* 66–101. Chicago: University of Chicago Press.

———. 1984. Social identification and psychological group formation. In H. Tajfel, ed., *The social dimension: European developments in social psychology,* 2:518–38. Cambridge: University Press.

van Knippenberg, A. F. M. 1984. Intergroup differences in group perceptions. In H. Tajfel, ed., *The social dimension: European developments in social psychology,* 2:560–78. Cambridge: Cambridge University Press.

Van Maanen, J. 1979. The fact of fiction in organizational ethnography. *Administrative Science Quarterly* 24:539–50.

———. 1988. *Tales of the field: On writing ethnography.* Chicago: University of Chicago Press.

Van Maanen, J., and S. Barley. 1983. Cultural organization: Fragments of a theory. Paper presented at the annual meeting of the Academy of Management, Dallas, TX.

———. 1984. Occupational communities: Culture and control in organizations. In B. M. Staw and L. L. Cummings, eds., *Research in organizational behavior,* 6:287–365. Greenwich, CT: JAI Press.

Veiga, J. F., M. Lubakin, R. Calori, P. Very, and Y. A. Tung. 2000. Using neural network analysis to uncover the trace effects of national culture. *Journal of International Business Studies* 31 (2): 223–38.

Vernon, R. 1971. *Sovereignty at bay: The multinational spread of U.S. enterprises.* New York: Basic Books.

Vinton, K. 1983. Humor in the work-place: It's more than telling jokes. Paper presented at the annual meeting of the Western Academy of Management, Santa Barbara.

Vogel, E. 1979. *Japan as number one: Lessons for America.* Cambridge, MA: Harvard University Press.

Walker, H., G. Symon, and B. Davies. 1996. Assessing organizational culture: A comparison of methods. *International Journal of Selection and Assessment* 4:96–105.

Weisinger, J. Y., and P. F. Salipante. 2000. Cultural knowing as practicing: Extending our conceptions of culture. *Journal of Management Inquiry* 9 (4): 376–90.

Weiss, S. E. 1983. Analysis of complex negotiations in international business: The RBC perspective. *Organization Science* 4 (2): 269–300.

Weiss, J., and A. Delbecq. 1987. High-technology cultures and management: Silicon Valley and Route 128. *Group and Organization Studies* 12, no. 1 (March): 39–54.

Westwood, R. I., and P. S. Kirkbride. 1989. Jonathan Livingston Seagull is alive and well and living in Hong Kong: Cultural disjuncture in the symbolization of corporate leadership. Paper presented at the International Conference on Organizational Symbolism and Corporate Culture, Fontainebleau, France.

Whitley, R. D. 1990. East Asian enterprise structures and the comparative analysis of forms of business organization. *Organization Studies* 11 (1): 47–74.

———. 1992. *Business systems in East Asia.* London: Sage.

———. 1999. *Divergent capitalisms: The social structuring and change of business systems.* Oxford: Oxford University Press.

Wolf, E. R. 1982. *Europe and the people without history.* Berkeley: University of California Press.

Xin, K. R., and J. L. Pearce. 1996. *Guanxi:* Connections as substitutes for formal institutional support. *Academy of Management Journal* 39 (6): 1641–48.

Ybema, S. B. 1997. Telling tales: Contrasts and commonalities within the organization of an amusement park—confronting and combining different perspectives. In S. A. Sackmann, ed., *Cultural complexity in organizations: Inherent contrasts and contradictions,* 160–86. Thousand Oaks: Sage.

Zaheer, S., and A. Zaheer. 1997. Country effects on information seeking in global electronic networks. *Journal of International Business Studies* 28:77–100.

Zander, L. 1997. The license to lead: An eighteen-country study of the relationship between employees' preferences regarding interpersonal leadership and national culture. Ph.D. diss., Institute for International Business, Stockholm School of Economics.

CULTURAL DISTANCE
REVISITED

TOWARD A MORE RIGOROUS CONCEPTUALIZATION AND
MEASUREMENT OF CULTURAL DIFFERENCES

Oded Shenkar

Few constructs have gained broader acceptance in the international business literature than cultural distance (CD). Presumably measuring the extent to which different cultures are similar or different, the construct has been applied to most business administration disciplines, that is, management, marketing, finance, and accounting. In management, CD has been used as a key variable in strategy, management, organization behavior, and human resource management. The construct has been applied to a multitude of research questions, from innovation and organizational transformation to foreign expansion and technology transfer (Gomez-Mejia and Palich 1997) and from affiliate performance to expatriate adjustment (Black and Mendenhall 1991). It is in the area of foreign direct investment (FDI), however, that the construct has had its greatest impact.

To understand the appeal of the CD construct, it is useful to recall the nature of the phenomenon it is set to capture. Complex, intangible, and subtle, culture has been notoriously difficult to conceptualize and scale (Boyacigiller et al. 1996). Establishing a measure gauging the "distance" between cultures has understandably presented an even greater challenge. By presenting a seemingly simple and standardized measure of cultural

Originally published in Journal of International Business Studies *22 (3): 519–35.* © *2001,* The Academy of International Business.

differences, the CD construct has offered a tangible and convenient tool with which to bypass the complexities and intricacies of culture, yielding a quantitative measure to be employed in combination with other "hard" data (see Kogut and Singh 1988).

The appeal of the CD construct is, unfortunately, illusory. It masks serious problems in conceptualization and measurement, from unsupported hidden assumptions to questionable methodological properties, undermining the validity of the construct and challenging its theoretical role and application. Those problems, their implications, and their remedies are the focus of this chapter.

CULTURAL DISTANCE IN THE FOREIGN INVESTMENT LITERATURE

For almost three decades, CD and its proxies have been applied to multiple areas of business, from strategy to organization behavior to accounting and auditing, in both domestic and international contexts. The construct found its most loyal following in international business, where it has been used in such realms as FDI, headquarter-subsidiary relations, and expatriate selection and adjustment. By and large, FDI represents the most popular arena for the application of the CD construct, most often in the form of an index compiled by Kogut and Singh (1988) from Hofstede's (1980) cultural dimensions.

In the FDI literature, CD has had three primary thrusts. The first thrust has been to explain the foreign market investment location and especially the sequence of such investment by multinational enterprises (MNEs). The second thrust has been to predict the choice of mode of entry into foreign markets. A third application has been to account for the variable success, failure, and performance of MNE affiliates in international markets. A brief review of each of the three thrusts follows.

CULTURAL DISTANCE AND THE LAUNCH/SEQUENCE OF FOREIGN INVESTMENT

The first use of CD in the FDI literature has been to account for the very decision of firms to invest in a foreign country. A theory of familiarity emerged, arguing that firms were less likely to invest in culturally distant markets. Yoshino (1976) and Ozawa (1979) viewed Japan's CD from Western nations as a constraint on Japanese FDI in the West. In a similar vein, Davidson (1980) attributed the large U.S. investment in Canada and the United Kingdom—well beyond what their market size, growth, tariffs, and proximity would have predicted—to cultural similarity. Dunning (1988), in contrast, argued that larger CD between home and host markets encouraged FDI as a way of overcoming transactional and market failures.

A related and eventually more influential use of the CD construct within the expansion stream has been to predict the sequence of multiple foreign entries. This work is closely associated with that of Johanson and Vahlne (1977), who observed that Swedish firms progressively expanded from their home base into countries with greater "psychic distance." This thesis has later become known as the Uppsala process model, or the "Scandinavian school" (Johanson and Wiedersheim-Paul 1975; Luostarinen 1980; Engwall 1984; Welch and Luostarinen 1988; Forgsren 1989; Axelsson and Johanson 1992). Support for the Scandinavian thesis has been limited (Turnbull 1987; Engwall and Wallenstal 1988). Both Benito and Gripsrud (1992) and Sullivan and Bauerschmidt (1990) failed to find CD to be a predictor of FDI sequence per Johanson and Vahlne's thesis.

CULTURAL DISTANCE AND ENTRY MODE

The Scandinavian school also predicted an incremental increase in investment commitment from exports into FDI. It was not clear whether the two trends—incremental distance and incremental commitment—were to occur in tandem, however, a first of many omissions in the area. Eventually, the thesis predicting a relationship between CD and FDI mode became synonymous with transaction cost theory (Williamson 1985). The higher the CD, the more control the MNE was likely to maintain over its foreign operations (Root 1987; Davidson and McFeteridge 1985; Kim and Hwang 1992). Control was phrased as a choice between licensing and FDI but more often as a choice between the wholly owned subsidiary (WOS) and the partially controlled international joint venture (IJV) (Agarwal 1994; Cho and Padmanabhan 1995; Erramilli 1991; Erramilli and Rao 1993; Kogut and Singh 1988; Larimo 1993; Padmanabhan and Cho 1994).

The loosening of control in culturally distant locations was alternatively seen as a way of reducing uncertainty and information costs (Alpander 1976; Richman and Copen 1972). As Goodnow and Hansz (1972, 46) put it, the "degree of control declines as the environment becomes less favorable." In predicting entry mode, transaction cost theorists associate higher distance with a higher cost of transaction, due to information costs and the difficulty of transferring competencies and skills (Buckley and Casson

1976; Vachani 1991). In transaction costs, internalization is imperative when market agents are likely to take advantage of a firm's limited knowledge and when future transaction contingencies could not be specified because of uncertainty or complexity (Williamson 1975; Beamish and Banks 1987). In the absence of internalization, it will not be possible to verify claims by agents and reduce operational uncertainty or to reverse the investment altogether (Williamson 1981).

The underlying though implicit assumption in incorporating CD into the transaction costs argument is that international operations are highly uncertain. Presumably, it will be more difficult to verify claims by culturally distant agents, since the agents will make claims rooted in an unfamiliar environment while buffered from enforcement by an MNE. Roth and O'Donnell (1996) argue that agency costs increase as a function of CD because complete and accurate information on agents' (subsidiaries') performance becomes more difficult and more costly to obtain, resulting in higher dependence of headquarters upon the subsidiary.

Gatignon and Anderson (1988) acknowledge that CD does not fit very well within the transaction costs argument. Logically, the theory can accommodate opposite predictions of the CD-control mode relation. A firm may prefer low control to compensate for its lack of knowledge in high CD situations, relying on a local partner to contribute local knowledge. Or it may opt for high control, such as a WOS, as a way of reducing dependence upon agents whose actions are poorly understood. Anderson and Gatignon (1986) suggest that high control is perhaps more efficient when the entrant's methods confer a transaction-specific advantage that cannot be easily imitated by other firms. "On occasion, operation methods that do not fit local culture will constitute the necessary advantage that enables foreigners to compete with locals on their home ground" (Anderson and Gatignon 1986, 18). Indeed, from a resource-based perspective (Barney 1991), the very ability to bridge CD confers a unique advantage.

Empirical results regarding the impact of CD on entry mode are mixed (Benito and Gripsrud 1992; Padmanabhan and Cho 1994). Erramilli and Rao (1993) found that low CD resulted in low control, though the relationship was mediated by levels of experience and asset specificity. Pan (1996) found that the larger the CD, the more likely it was for a foreign partner to have an equal or a majority stake in their Chinese IJV. Boyacigiller (1990) found that CD was positively related to control (defined as the proportion of U.S. nationals in the foreign affiliate). On the other hand,

Kogut and Singh (1988) and Kim and Hwang (1992) report low control modes at high CD levels. Kogut and Singh (1988) found that greater CD increased the likelihood of greenfield IJVs over both greenfield WOSs and the acquisition of a controlling stake in an existing operation. While the contradictory results can be partially attributed to the firms studied (the service firms by Erramilli and Rao and Boyacigiller could have lower control costs than the manufacturing enterprises researched by Kim and Hwang and Kogut and Singh), this is unlikely to explain the full spectrum of inconsistent results.

CULTURAL DISTANCE AND
AFFILIATE PERFORMANCE

In this third application, CD has largely been taken to represent a hindrance to the performance of the MNE and its affiliates. According to Chang (1995), CD limits the ability of an MNE to generate rent when entering new domains. Empirical results have been mixed. Li and Guisinger (1991) found that U.S. affiliates whose foreign partners came from culturally dissimilar countries were more likely to fail. Barkema et al. (1997) found that firms that have gradually ventured into more culturally distant locations were less likely to have their affiliates terminated prematurely; controlling for experience, IJV longevity decreased with the CD to the host country. Johnson, Cullen, and Sakano (1991) reported that "cultural congruence" between IJV partners had no effect on the Japanese partner's perceptions of success, and Park and Ungson (1997) found that a larger CD was actually associated with a lower rate of joint venture dissolution.

HIDDEN ASSUMPTIONS IN THE CULTURAL
DISTANCE CONSTRUCT

The inconsistent results obtained for the three FDI thrusts may be the result of the conceptual and/or methodological properties of the CD construct. In this section, these properties are culled from an extensive review of the literature applying the CD construct to the domain of FDI and enriched with insights from the broader literature on culture, FDI, and related areas. The properties are presented in the form of hidden assumptions that largely go unnoticed but are not supported by either logic or empirical evidence.

The hidden assumptions appear in two clusters, one emanating from the conceptual properties of the construct and the other from its methodological properties. Conceptual properties produce illusions that are at the core of the CD construct and undermine its validity within the context of FDI theories. Methodological properties present instrumentation and measurement biases that distort the accurate measurement of cultural differences; they are most closely associated with the Kogut and Singh (1988) index but address broader measurement issues as well. While the two sets of properties are intertwined, they represent distinct sets of problems that require different sets of remedies and are hence presented in separate clusters.

CONCEPTUAL PROPERTIES

THE ILLUSION OF SYMMETRY

"Distance," by definition, is symmetric: the distance from point A to point B is identical to the distance from point B to point A. CD symmetry is, however, difficult to defend in the context of FDI. It suggests an identical role for the home and host cultures—for instance, that a Dutch firm investing in China is faced with the same CD as a Chinese firm investing in the Netherlands. There is no support for such assumption. Numerous studies have shown the importance of investor culture in predicting investment, entry mode, and performance (e.g., Pan 1996; Kogut and Singh 1988; Tallman 1988). Other studies have shown a role for the host culture. However, there are no studies showing symmetry between the two, nor is there a reason to assume one. On the contrary, home and host country effects are different in nature, the former being embedded in the firm and the latter in a national environment.

THE ILLUSION OF STABILITY

Measured at a single point in time, CD is implicitly assumed to be constant. Cultures change over time, however. The culture measured at market entry time may have changed by the time performance is measured. Furthermore, a convergence thesis (Webber 1969) would predict CD narrowing over time as more investors flock into the market and local employees become knowledgeable of MNE management methods (Richman and Copen 1972). As firms learn more about a market, their CD to that market decreases. Stopford and Wells (1972) found that when a firm had more experience in a country, it was more likely to choose a WOS than an IJV (see also Dubin 1975). Hennart (1991) found that experience in the United States has led Japanese firms to look more favorably at a WOS than at an IJV. International experience may also lead firms to prefer acquisition to greenfield investment (Caves and Mehra 1986), a preference that is not captured by the control thesis yet significantly influences the availability of WOS versus IJV investment.

THE ILLUSION OF LINEARITY

Also embedded in the distance metaphor is the assumption of linear impact on investment, entry mode, and performance. The higher the distance between cultures, the higher the likelihood that investment will occur at a later stage in the investment sequence and that a less controlling entry mode will be chosen and the worse the performance of foreign affiliates will be. These are all questionable assumptions. On the contrary, the Scandinavian school acknowledges that the time lag between expansion waves will vary due to differences in learning curves. Erramilli (1991) showed that CD and experience interacted to influence ownership in a nonlinear fashion. Davidson (1980) suggested that firms taking their first investment steps were more likely to prefer culturally similar countries than those firms in an advanced stage of internationalization (see also Bilkey 1978). Pan (1996) found that foreign partners who already held a majority equity stake in a joint venture were not interested in further increasing this stake when CD was large.

Parkhe (1991) points out that CD, like other "diversity variables," plays a different role at the strategic choice and operational phases. At the strategic phase, cultural differences may be a basis for synergy while at the operational phase they may erode the applicability of the parent's competencies (see also Brown, Rugman, and Verbeke 1989; Chowdhury 1992; Gomes-Casseres 1989; Harrigan 1985, 1988; Hergert and Morris 1988; Lorange and Roos 1991). The expatriate literature suggests that adaptation to a foreign culture may be U-shaped (Black and Mendenhall 1991) and reports that adjustment to a relatively similar culture is often as difficult as adjustment to a distant one because differences are not anticipated (e.g., Brewster 1995; O'Grady and Lane 1996).

THE ILLUSION OF CAUSALITY

Implicit assumption in much of the literature is that CD has a causal effect on FDI pattern, sequence, and performance. The connotation is that culture is the only determinant of distance with relevance to FDI. Earlier work has been tuned to the problem and has attempted to compensate by incorporating nonculture variables in a broader distance measure. Johanson and Vahlne's (1977) definition of "psychic distance" refers to the "sum of factors" affecting information to the market. Goodnow and Hansz (1972) treat "geo-cultural distance" as one of a number of variables (also including level of development, political stability) making a country a "hot" or "cold" investment opportunity. Richman and Copen's (1972) measure of "socio-cultural distance" includes such variables as the foreign education of local executives.

As Boyacigiller (1990, 363) offers, "key characteristics of nations such as dominant religion, business language, form of government, economic development and levels of emigration to the US indicate a country's cultural distance from the US." Factors such as language (Buckley and Casson 1976, 1979); political instability (Thunnell 1977); and level of development, market size, and sophistication (Davidson and McFetridge 1985) all play a role in establishing "distance." Barkema et al. (1997), in their study of the FDI of Dutch firms, found the effect of CD to be significant for IJVs in developing countries but not for IJVs in developed countries. A similar point is made by Beamish (1993) vis-à-vis investment in China's transitional economy. Brown, Rugman, and Verbeke (1989) argue that the combination of economic and cultural factors creates firm-specific assets, which can cause failure.

THE ILLUSION OF DISCORDANCE

The implicit assumption that differences in cultures produce lack of fit and hence an obstacle to transaction is questionable. First, not every cultural gap is critical to performance. As Tallman and Shenkar (1994, 108) note, "different aspects of firm culture may be more or less central, more or less difficult to transmit, and more or less critical to operations." Second, cultural differences may be complementary and hence have a positive synergetic effect on investment and performance. For instance, as global cooperation demands both concern for performance (masculine) and concern for relationships (feminine), the two may be mutually supportive (Hofstede 1989; Haspeslagh and Jemison 1991). Similar evidence can be found in the FDI (Barkema and Vermeulen 1998), merger and acquisition (e.g., Haspeslagh and Jemison 1991; Morosini 1998), and IJVs literature (Shenkar and Zeira 1992).

METHODOLOGICAL PROPERTIES

THE ASSUMPTION OF CORPORATE HOMOGENEITY

The CD index used to measure the construct relies on national culture measures and implicitly assumes lack of corporate culture variance, an assumption that lacks support (e.g., Hofstede et al. 1990). Laurent (1986) proposes that corporate culture can modify the behavior and beliefs associated with national culture, a proposition confirmed by Weber, Shenkar, and Raveh (1996) for international mergers. Corporate culture alters the dynamics of national CD though not necessarily in the way of reducing its impact. As Schneider (1988, 243) notes, "national culture may play a stronger role in the face of a strong corporate culture. The pressures to conform may create the need to reassert autonomy and identity, creating a national mosaic rather than a melting pot."

THE ASSUMPTION OF SPATIAL HOMOGENEITY

Measuring distance from one national culture to another, the CD index assumes uniformity within the national unit. Quite to the contrary, evidence suggests that intracultural variation explains as much as, if not more than, intercultural variation (Au 2000). Neither the spatial location of the firm in the home or host country nor the actual physical distance between the locations has an impact upon the CD measure calculated. This masks actual investment conditions, for instance, a "border effect" formed across contiguous regions divided by a national border (Mariotti and Piscitello 1995). A somewhat similar argument can be made regarding the variable location of industries from the cultural milieu, as, for instance, in the case of "cultural industries."

THE ASSUMPTION OF EQUIVALENCE

The Kogut and Singh (1988) index is a rather simplistic aggregate of Hofstede's (1980) dimensions and is hence liable to the same criticism leveled against Hofstede, for example, nonexhaustiveness, reliance on single company data, and so forth (e.g., Schwartz and Bilsky 1990; Schwartz 1994; Drenth 1983; Goodstein and Hunt 1981). The index amplifies the problems associated with the Hofstede framework in two important ways.

First, the index has not been updated to incorporate latter work by Hofstede and others, for instance, the fifth dimension of Confucian dynamism or Long Term Orientation (LTO) (Hofstede and Bond 1988). Derived from a Chinese instrument, this dimension captures a facet that is critical to corporate strategy. Because of LTO's relationship to Confucianism, failure to include it in CD measures involving East Asian countries, for instance, those used in studies of Japanese FDI (e.g., Yoshino 1976; Ozawa 1979; Li and Guisinger 1991), are especially open to challenge.

The second and most important way in which the Kogut and Singh's measure amplifies the measurement problems associated with Hofstede is by making an invalid assumption of equivalence. Hofstede (1989) offers that some cultural gaps are less disruptive than others and that differences in uncertainty avoidance are potentially the most problematic for international cooperation due to their correlates in terms of differential tolerances toward risk, formalization, and so forth. Kogut and Singh (1988) themselves examined the role of uncertainty avoidance separately from their index. Both Barkema et al. (1997) and Barkema and Vermeulen (1998) supported Hofstede's (1989) contention and found that uncertainty avoidance was more important than other cultural dimensions in predicting FDI success. Other studies have shown individualism to have a special effect on FDI (e.g., Hamel, Doz, and Prahalad 1989; Shane 1992; Dickson and Weaver 1997). The aggregate measure may hence provide false readings regarding meaningful cultural differences.

INTEGRATION AND CONSTRUCT DEVELOPMENT

The significant conceptual and methodological inadequacies relating to the CD construct carry important implications for theory and research. For example, the illusion of symmetry pinpoints divergent transaction costs and the prospect of conflict between partners as each seeks to minimize its cost of the transaction regardless of the cost incurred by the other party, necessitating convergence of transaction and bargaining models. By showing that certain cultural combinations possess synergetic rather than disruptive potential, the illusion of discordance may explain the inconsistent results obtained for the transaction cost argument regarding control and performance. The illusion of causality may explain the inconsistent results obtained for CD and FDI sequence. For instance, Benito and Gripsrud (1992) proposed that their lack of support for the gradual expansion thesis might have been the result of similarity in labor costs among countries within the same cultural cluster. The assumption of spatial homogeneity may explain obtaining inconsistent results for the same pair of countries.

In the following sections, an integrative framework for the treatment of

CD construct is developed. In a departure from the existing metaphor that is focused on what sets cultures apart, we also consider mechanisms closing CD. Then, we incorporate a crucial yet missing element in the current conceptualization of CD, namely, the interface among transacting parties and its accorded friction. Taken together, the two serve to form a basis from which a comprehensive framework for the treatment of the CD construct is launched.

CLOSING CULTURAL DISTANCE

A product of the use of a metaphor can be the framing of one's frame of reference (Morgan 1986). In the case of CD, the "distance" metaphor is translated into a focus on what sets cultures apart but not on what might bring them together. A balanced analysis of the relations between social or organizational entities should, however, consider both opening and closing mechanisms. A number of key mechanisms with the potential of closing cultural distance follow.

GLOBALIZATION AND CONVERGENCE

Increased communication and interaction bridge CD by encouraging the convergence of cultural systems (Webber 1969). This implies a trend toward lower CD over time albeit at different paces across the globe. The World Competitiveness Yearbook (2000) publishes an index of openness to foreign influences, showing substantial differences between relatively open countries such as the Netherlands and closed countries such as France and Korea.

GEOGRAPHICAL PROXIMITY

Often confused with CD (as in the case of Canada as a first foreign investment for Eastern and Midwestern U.S. firms), geographic proximity reduces entry barriers (Buckley and Casson 1979; see also Mariotti and Piscitello 1995), subject to transportation and information processing requirements. Geographical proximity lowers the costs of managerial coordination and control and reduces the cost of monitoring agents' behavior. It can also facilitate the personal contact that is necessary for effective transfer of knowledge and other resources (Vachani 1991).

FOREIGN EXPERIENCE

The literature acknowledges the importance of foreign experience as a CD-closing mechanism. It is not always clear, however, whether it is international experience per se or experience in the host culture and to what extent the experience of individual managers can substitute for corporate experience, a point that would be especially important to smaller firms (see also the following discussion on acculturation).

ACCULTURATION

Acculturation has been defined as "changes induced in systems as a result of the diffusion of cultural elements in both directions" (Berry 1980, 217). Acculturation can generally be assumed to reduce the CD to the host country. It is interesting that in describing one exception to the pattern of gradual involvement that they observed (the establishment of a sale subsidiary in a new market), Johanson and Vahlne (1977) explain that the decision maker in that case was partly educated in the other country. Nor is acculturation dependent upon actual experience. Black, Mendenhall, and Oddou (1991, 310) suggest that "individuals make anticipatory adjustments before they actually encounter the new situation." A corporation may do the same thing, in effect closing the CD to a country even prior to the establishment of operations there. Another intriguing question is whether the reentry syndrome described by Adler (1981) would apply at the corporate level.

CULTURAL ATTRACTIVENESS

Certain cultures are considered attractive to other cultures. A foreign culture's perceived attributes may be a major reason for the preferences expressed by potential partners and host countries (Gould 1966). From a cognitive perspective (Sackmann 1983; Boyacigiller et al. 1996), even when attractiveness is absent, adjustment to a relatively similar culture is often as difficult as adjustment to a distant one. This is explained by the expatriate literature in that executives do not expect differences in relatively similar cultures (e.g., Brewster 1995; O'Grady and Lane 1996).

STAFFING

Staffing is not only a means of control but also a venue through which groups and individuals bring their cultural properties into a system. Shenkar (1992) discusses the role of employee groups as mechanisms affecting the national and corporate CD in an IJV. For instance, foreign parent expatriates bring with them both the national and corporate culture of the parent while third-country nationals recruited by the foreign parent will likely bring the parent firm's culture into the venture, but less of its national culture. The merger and acquisition (M&A) literature makes the point that such senior managers have a major influence on the motivation of the other employees and play the most significant role in shaping and transmitting corporate culture signals to the broader membership (see Weber, Shenkar, and Raveh 1996). Bicultural individuals play an especially important role in closing the CD between the foreign and host countries. By virtue of their familiarity with both cultures, such individuals bring the two countries together by serving as emissaries and interpreters of culturally embedded signals and behaviors. The presence of such individuals in a company, especially in senior positions, may hence serve as a mechanism closing CD.

CULTURAL INTERACTION AS FRICTION

While the existence of mechanisms opening and closing CD can be accommodated within the "distance" metaphor, a closer look into the reality of FDI points at interaction as the key issue. After all, how different one culture is from another has little meaning until those cultures are brought into contact with one another. Hence, we suggest replacing the "distance" metaphor with that of "friction," the term used by Williamson (1975) in his original treaty on transaction costs theory. By "friction," we mean the scale and essence of the interface between interacting cultures and the "drag" produced by that interface for the operation of those systems.

As an example, let us consider the difference in the cultural interface between an IJV and an international M&A. An IJV is, by definition, an entity separate from its parent firms. While the parents maintain direct contact as well, the bulk of the interaction is mediated by the IJV, whose activities remain compartmentalized from those of the parents. The cultural differences between the parent firms produce friction only to the extent of their involvement with the new entity. Individuals and units in the parent firms who are not involved with the IJV operations do not produce friction. In contrast, a merger brings together the entire set of operations on both sides, producing, at least on the onset, much greater friction. In many M&As, integration is a key goal (see Weber, Shenkar, and Raveh 1996 for a summary). The intensity makes the interaction more dramatic, and the ensuing conflict makes differences salient (Sales and Mirvis 1984). Weber, Shenkar, and Raveh (1996) found that the top managers in acquired firms have made anticipatory adjustment toward the acquiring organization. In contrast, officers of the acquiring firm may find little reason to do the same.

Obviously, friction varies within the M&A population as well. Where the acquiring firm determines goals, strategic choices, and other operations for the acquired company, more friction can be initially expected, but such friction may decline faster than where each firm retains its autonomy. "Modes of acculturation," such as integration, assimilation, separation, and deculturation (Nahavandi and Malekzadeh 1988), will hence influence friction levels. For similar reasons, friction is also likely to differ between acquisition and greenfield investment. In an acquisition, the potential friction is greater, because the acquired firm has already a corporate culture in place. Indeed, lower CD was found to increase the rate of acquisitions over greenfield investments (Dubin 1975), while high CD has been suggested as a reason why Japanese investors in the United States prefer greenfield investments and partial over complete acquisitions (Hennart 1991). Li and Guisinger (1991), among others, report that foreign acquisitions of U.S. firms tend to fail more than greenfield investment, possibly the result of cultural friction.

The friction among cultural systems is also the product of strategic objectives, that is, how closely firms want the other system to be positioned vis-à-vis their own. The tighter the control to be maintained, the greater the friction potential. Hence, control (and, in extension, entry mode) is not only the product of cultural distance, it is also a potential trigger of cultural friction. Furthermore, culture itself is a means of control (Schneider 1988). A strong corporate culture could, in theory, lower the transaction cost as the subsidiary becomes similar to the parent, though results by Laurent (1986) suggest that corporate culture actually accentuates national culture differences.

RECOMMENDATIONS

While the theory development effort delineated earlier will eventually result in new CD measures, a number of key steps can be taken now. First, the Kogut and Singh (1988) index must be supplemented by LTO (Confucian Dynamism), especially where East Asian countries are involved. The use of the aggregate index must be theoretically justified and, where appropriate, substituted by CD measures calculated separately for one or more of the five dimensions as necessitated by theoretical and domain considerations. Both aggregate and one-dimensional measures should also be drawn from alternative classifications, for example, Schwartz's (1994) measures, with multiple measures employed wherever possible.

Second, measures of general cultural similarity, such as Ronen and Shenkar's (1985) measures (for applications see Barkema et al. 1997; Park and Ungson 1997; Vachani 1991), which do not assume linearity, additivity, and normal distribution, should be used in conjunction with other measures. Findings showing a relationship between CD and governance for select country clusters (e.g., Gatignon and Anderson 1988) suggest supplementing those approaches with measures of cultural diversity, such as Gomez-Mejia and Palich's (1997) indices of intercluster and intracluster diversity.

Third, national-level data should be supplemented by cognitive CD measures (e.g., Sullivan and Bauerschmidt 1990). An example can be found in Boyacigiller 1990, where executives were asked to rank adjustment difficulties in countries where they have served in the past. Retrospective data should be considered in deriving such cognitive measures. Evidence suggests such data do not become less accurate over time periods as long as ten years (Finkelstein 1992; Huber and Power 1985) and are especially helpful when anchored in dramatic events such as mergers that tend to make culture and cultural differences more salient. A recent example can be found in Veiga, Lubatkin, Calori, and Very 2000 (see also Veiga, Lubatkin, Calori, Very, and Tung 2000). Qualitative, emic data should be added wherever feasible.

Fourth, control for closing distance mechanisms such as cultural attraction, acculturation and foreign experience, geographical distance (Balabanis 2000), language, level of development, home market, and company size (Erramilli 1996), which have already been found to correlate with CD or to mediate or moderate its impact on FDI. Be sure to control for CD at the corporate level, using the wide repertoire of corporate culture instruments while remaining aware of both instrument design (Geringer 1998) and interaction effects (Weber, Shenkar, and Raveh 1996) across the two levels.

Fifth, consider CD not only as an independent variable predicting FDI governance, sequence, and performance (or other variables as the case may be) but also as a dependent variable. CD is as much the product as the consequence of entry mode, and FDI sequence and even performance may have an impact on the perceived distance. Consider culture also as a quasi-moderator variable (Sharma et al. 1981), altering the form but not the strength of the relationship between environmental and strategic variables.

Finally, consider cultural differences as having the potential for both synergy and disruption (Morosini 1998; Parkhe 1991). This point cannot be overstated, as it lies at the intersection of strategic logic and operational challenges that underline FDI, expatriate adjustment or auditing, and other international business issues. Replacing "distance" with "friction" as the underlying metaphor for cultural differences is a natural step from there. Not merely semantic, this change implies focusing on the interface between transacting entities rather than on the void between them.

REFERENCES

Adler, N. J. 1981. Re-entry: Managing cross-cultural transitions. *Group and Organization Studies* 6:341–56.

Agarwal, S. 1994. Socio-cultural distance and the choice of joint ventures: A contingency perspective. *Journal of International Marketing* 2 (2): 63–80.

Alpander, G. G. 1976. Use of quantitative methods in international operations by U.S. vs. overseas executives. *Management International Review* 16 (1): 71–77.

Anderson, E., and H. Gatignon. 1986. Modes of foreign entry: A transaction cost analysis and propositions. *Journal of International Business Studies* 17 (2): 1–26.

Au, K. Y. 2000. Inter-cultural variation as another construct of international management: A study based on secondary data of forty-two countries. *Journal of International Management* 6:217–38.

Axelsson, B., and J. Johanson. 1992. Foreign market entry: The textbook versus the network view. In B. Axelsson and G. Easton, eds., *Industrial networks: A new view of reality,* 218–34. London, UK: Routledge.

Balabanis, G. I. 2000. Factors affecting export intermediaries' service offerings: The British example. *Journal of International Business Studies* 31 (1): 83–99.

Barkema, H., O. Shenkar, F. Vermeulen, and J. H. Bell. 1997. Working abroad, working with others: How firms learn to operate international joint ventures. *Academy of Management Journal* 40 (2): 426–42.

Barkema, H., and F. Vermeulen. 1998. International expansion through start-up or acquisition: A learning perspective. *Academy of Management Journal* 41 (1): 7–26.

Barney, J. B. 1991. Firm resources and sustained competitive advantage. *Journal of Management* 17 (1): 99–120.

Beamish, P. 1993. The characteristics of joint ventures in the People's Republic of China. *Journal of International Marketing* 1 (2): 29–48.

Beamish, P. W., and J. C. Banks. 1987. Equity joint ventures and the theory of the multinational enterprise. *Journal of International Business Studies* (summer):1–16.

Benito, R. G., and G. Gripsrud. 1992. The expansion of foreign direct investments: Discrete rational location choices or a cultural learning process? *Journal of International Business Studies* 3:461–76.

Berry, J. W. 1980. Social and cultural change. In H. C. Triandis and R. W. Brislin, eds., *Handbook of cross-cultural psychology,* 5:211–79. Boston: Allyn and Bacon.

Bilkey, W. J. 1978. An attempted integration of the literature on the export behavior of firms. *Journal of International Business Studies* 9:33–46.

Black, J. S., and M. Mendenhall. 1991. The U-curve adjustment hypothesis revisited: A review and theoretical framework. *Journal of International Business Studies* 22 (2): 225–47.

Black, J. S., M. Mendenhall, and G. Oddou. 1991. Toward a comprehensive model of international adjustment: An integration of multiple theoretical perspectives. *Academy of Management Review* 16:291–317.

Boyacigiller, N. 1990. The role of expatriates in the management of interdependence. *Journal of International Business Studies* 21 (3): 357–81.

Boyacigiller, N., M. J. Kleinberg, M. Phillips, and S. Sackmann. 1996. Conceptualizing culture. In B. J. Punnett and O. Shenkar, eds., *Handbook for international management research.* Cambridge, MA: Blackwell.

Brewster, C. 1995. Effective expatriate training. In J. Selmer, ed., *Expatriate management: New ideas for international business.* Westport, CT: Quorum.

Brown, L. T., A. M. Rugman, and A. Verbeke. 1989. Japanese joint ventures with Western multinational: Synthesizing the economic and cultural explanations of failure. *Asia Pacific Journal of Management* 6:225–42.

Buckley, P. J., and M. Casson. 1976. *The future of the multinational enterprise.* London: Macmillan.

———. 1979. A theory of international operation. In J. Leontiades and M. Ghertman, eds., *European research in international business.* Amsterdam and London: North-Holland.

Caves, R. E., and S. K. Mehra. 1986. Entry of foreign multinationals into U.S. manufacturing industries. In Michael E. Porter, ed., *Competition in global industries.* Boston: Harvard Business School.

Chang, S. J. 1995. International expansion strategy of Japanese firms: Capability building through sequential entry. *Academy of Management Journal* 38:383–407.

Cho, K. R., and P. Padmanabhan. 1995. Acquisition versus new venture: The choice of foreign establishment mode by Japanese firms. *Journal of International Management* 1 (3): 255–85.

Chowdhury, J. 1992, Performance of international joint ventures and wholly owned foreign subsidiaries: A comparative perspective. *Management International Review* 32 (2): 115–33.

Davidson, W. H. 1980. The location of foreign direct investment activity: Country characteristics and experience effects. *Journal of International Business Studies* 11 (2): 9–22.

Davidson, W. H., and D. J. McFeteridge. 1985. Key characteristics in the choice of international technology transfer mode. *Journal of International Business Studies* 16 (summer): 5–22.

Dickson, P. H., and K. M. Weaver. 1997. Environmental determinants and individual-level moderators of alliance use. *Academy of Management Journal* 40 (2): 404–25.

Drenth, P. J. D. 1983. Cross-cultural organizational psychology: Challenges and limitations. In S. H. Irvine and J. W. Berry, eds., *Human assessment and cultural factors.* New York: Plenum Press.

Dubin, M. 1975. Foreign acquisitions and the spread of the multinational firm. DBA thesis, Harvard University.

Dunning, J. H. 1988. The eclectic paradigm of international production: A restatement and some possible extensions. *Journal of International Business Studies* 19:1–31.

Engwall, L., ed. 1984. *Uppsala contributions to business research.* Uppsala, Sweden: Acta Universitatis Upsaliensis.

Engwall, L., and M. Wallenstal. 1988. Tit for tat in small steps: The internationalization of Swedish banks. *Scandinavian Journal of Management* 4 (3/4): 147–55.

Erramilli, M. K. 1991. The experience factor in foreign market entry behavior of service firms. *Journal of International Business Studies* 22 (3): 479–501.

———. 1996. Nationality and subsidiary patterns in multinational corporations. *Journal of International Business Studies* 27:225–48.

Erramilli, M. K., and C. P. Rao. 1993. Service firms, international entry mode choice: A modified transaction-cost analysis approach. *Journal of Marketing* 57 (July): 19–38.

Finkelstein, S. 1992. Power in top management teams: Dimensions, measurement, and validation. *Academy of Management Journal* 35:505–38.

Forgsren, M. 1989. Managing the internationalization process: The Swedish case. London, UK: Routledge.

Gatignon, H., and E. Anderson. 1988. The multinational corporation's degree of control over foreign subsidiaries: An empirical test of a transaction cost explanation. *Journal of Law, Economics, and Organization* 4 (2): 305–36.

Geringer, J. M. 1998. Assessing replication and extension. A commentary on Glaister and Buckley: Measures of performance in U.K. international alliances. *Organization Studies* 19 (1): 119–38.

Gomes-Casseres, B. 1989. Ownership structures of foreign subsidiaries: Theory and evidence. *Journal of Economic Behaviour and Organization* 11:1–25.

Gomez-Mejia, L. R., and L. Palich. 1997. Cultural diversity and the performance of multinational firms. *Journal of International Business Studies* 28:309–35.

Goodnow, J. D., and J. E. Hanz. 1972. Environmental determinants of overseas market entry strategies. *Journal of International Business Studies* 3:33–50.

Goodstein, L. D., and J. W. Hunt. 1981. Commentary: Do American theories apply abroad? *Organizational Dynamics* 10 (1): 49–62.

Gould, P. 1966. On mental maps. Discussion paper no. 9, Department of Geography, University of Michigan.

Hamel, G., Y. L. Doz, and C. K. Prahalad. 1989. Collaborate with your competitors—and win. *Harvard Business Review* 67 (1): 133–39.

Harrigan, K. R. 1985. *Strategies for joint ventures.* Lexington, MA: Lexington Books.

———. 1988. Strategic alliances and partner asymmetries. In F. J. Contractor and P. Lorange, eds., *Cooperative strategies in international business,* 205–26. Lexington, MA: Lexington Books.

Haspeslagh, P. C., and D. B. Jemison. 1991. *Managing acquisitions: Creating value through corporate renewal.* New York: Free Press.

Hennart, J-F. 1991. The transaction costs theory of joint ventures: An empirical study of Japanese subsidiaries in the United States. *Management Science* 37 (4): 483–97.

Hergert, M., and D. Morris. 1988. Trends in international collaborative agreements. In F. J. Contractor and P. Lorange, eds., *Cooperative strategies in international business,* 99–110. Lexington, MA: Lexington Books.

Hofstede, G. 1980. *Culture's consequences.* New York: Sage.

―――. 1989. Organizing for cultural diversity. *European Management Journal* 7 (4): 390–97.

Hofstede, G., and M. H. Bond. 1988. The Confucius connection: From cultural roots to economic growth. *Organizational Dynamics* 16 (4): 4–21.

Hofstede, G., B. Neuijen, D. D. Ohavy, and G. Sanders. 1990. Measuring organizational cultures: A qualitative and quantitative studies across twenty cases. *Administrative Science Quarterly* 35:386–16.

Huber, G. P., and D. J. Power. 1985. Retrospective reports of strategic level managers: Guidelines for increasing their accuracy. *Strategic Management Journal* 6:171–80.

Johanson, J., and J. E. Vahlne. 1977. The internationalization process of the firm: A model of knowledge development and increasing foreign market commitments. *Journal of International Business Studies* 8 (spring/summer): 23–32.

Johanson, J., and F. Wiedersheim-Paul. 1975. The internationalization of the firm: Four Swedish cases. *Journal of Management Studies* 12 (3): 305–22.

Johnson, J. L., J. B. Cullen, and T. Sakano. 1991. Cultural congruency in international joint ventures: Does it matter? Proceedings of the Eastern Academy of Management fourth biennial international conference, Nice, France, June.

Kim, W. C., and P. Hwang. 1992. Global strategy and multinational entry mode choice. *Journal of International Business Studies* 23 (1): 29–53.

Kogut, B., and H. Singh. 1988. The effect of national culture on the choice of entry mode. *Journal of International Business Studies* 19 (3): 411–32.

Larimo, J. 1993. *Foreign direct investment behaviour and performance: An analysis of Finnish direct manaufacturing investments in OECD countries.* Acta Wasaensia, no. 32. Faasa, Finland: University of Vaasa.

Laurent, A. 1986. The cross-cultural puzzle of international human resource management. *Human Resource Management* 25 (1): 91–102.

Li, J. T., and S. Guisinger. 1991. Comparative business failures of foreign-controlled firms in the United States. *Journal of International Business Studies* 22 (2): 209–24.

Lorange, P., and J. Roos. 1991. Why some strategic alliances succeed and others fail. *The Journal of Business Strategy* (January/February):25–30.

Luostarinen, R. 1980. *Internationalization of the firm.* Helsinki: Helsinki School of Economics.

Mariotti, S., and L. Piscitello. 1995. Information costs and location of FDIs within the host country: Empirical evidence from Italy. *Journal of International Business Studies* 26 (4): 815–41.

Morgan, G. 1986. *Images of organization.* Beverly Hills: Sage.

Morosini, P. 1998. *Managing cultural differences.* Oxford, U.K.: Pergamon.

Nahavandi, A., and A. Malekzadeh. 1988. Acculturation in mergers and acquisitions. *Academy of Management Review* 13:79–90.

O'Grady, S., and H. W. Lane. 1996. The psychic distance paradox. *Journal of International Business Studies* 27 (2): 309–33.

Ozawa, Terutomo. 1979. International investment and industrial structure: New theoretical implications from the Japanese experience. *Oxford Economic Papers* 31 (1): 72–92.

Padmanabhan, P., and K. R. Cho. 1994. Ownership strategy for a foreign affiliate: An empirical investigation of Japanese firms. *Management International Review* 36 (1): 45–65.

Pan, Y. 1996. Influences on foreign equity ownership level in joint ventures in China. *Journal of International Business Studies* 77 (1): 1–26.

Park, S. H., and G. R. Ungson. 1997. The effect of national culture, organizational complementarity, and economic motivation on joint venture dissolution. *Academy of Management Journal* 40 (2): 279–307.

Parkhe, A. 1991. Interfirm diversity, organizational learning, and longevity in global strategic alliances. *Journal of International Business Studies* 22 (4): 579–600.

Richman, B. M., and M. Copen. 1972. *International management and economic development.* New York: McGraw-Hill.

Ronen, S., and O. Shenkar. 1985. Clustering countries on attitudinal dimensions: A review and synthesis. *Academy of Management Review* 10 (3): 435–54.

Root, F. 1987. *Entry strategies for international markets.* Lexington, MA: Lexington Books.

Roth, K., and S. O'Donnell. 1996. Foreign subsidiary compensation strategy: An agency theory perspective. *Academy of Management Journal* 39 (3): 678–703.

Sackmann, S. A. 1983. Organizationskultur: Die unsichtbare einflussgrosse (Organizational culture: The invisible influence). *Gruppendynamick* 14:393–406.

Sales, M. S., and P. H. Mirvis. 1984. When cultures collide: Issues in acquisitions. In J. R. Kimberly and R. E. Quinn, eds., *Managing organizational transitions.* Homewood, IL: Irwin.

Schneider, S. C. 1988. National vs. corporate culture: Implications for human resource management. *Human Resource Management* 27:231–46.

Schwartz, S. H. 1994. Beyond individualism/collectivism: New cultural dimensions of values. *Individualism and collectivism: Theory, method, and applications,* ed. Uichol Kim et al., 85–119. Thousand Oaks, CA: Sage.

Schwartz, S. H., and W. Bilsky. 1990. Toward a theory of the universal content and structure of values: Extensions and cross-cultural replications. *Journal of Personality and Social Psychology* 58 (5): 878–91.

Shane, S. A. 1992. The effect of national cultural differences in perceptions of transaction costs on national differences in the preferences for licensing. Academy of Management best papers proceedings.

Sharma, S., R. M. Durand, and O. Gur-Arie. 1981. Identification and analysis of moderator variables. *Journal of Marketing Research* 18 (August): 291–300.

Shenkar, O. 1992. The corporate/national culture matrix in international joint venture. Paper presented at the AIB annual meeting, Brussels, Belgium.

Shenkar, O., and Y. Zeira. 1992. Role conflict and role ambiguity of chief executive officers in international joint ventures. *Journal of International Business Studies* 23:55–75.

Stopford, J. M., and L. T. Wells Jr. 1972. *Managing the multinational enterprise: Organisation of the firm and ownership of the subsidiaries.* New York: Basic Books.

Sullivan, D., and A. Bauerschmidt. 1990. Incremental internationalization: A test of Johanson and Vahlne's thesis. *Management International Review* 30:19–30.

Tallman, S. B. 1988. Home country political risk and foreign direct investment. *Journal of International Business Studies* 19 (2): 219–34.

Tallman, S., and O. Shenkar. 1994. A managerial decision model of international cooperative venture formation. *Journal of International Business Studies* 25:91–113.

Thunnell, L. H. 1977. *Political risk in international business.* New York: Praeger.

Turnbull, P. W. 1987. A challenge to the stages theory of the internationalization process. In S. Reid and P. Rosson, eds., *Managing export entry and expansion,* 21–40. New York: Praeger.

Vachani, S. 1991. Distinguishing between related and unrelated international geographic diversification: A comprehensive measure of global diversification. *Journal of International Business Studies* 22 (2): 307–22.

Veiga, J., M. Lubatkin, R. Calori, and P. Very. 2000. Measuring organizational culture clashes: A two-nation post-hoc analysis of cultural compatibility index. *Human Relations* 53 (4): 539–57.

Veiga, J., M. Lubatkin, R. Calori, P. Very, and Y. A. Tung. 2000. Using neutral network analysis to uncover the trace effects of national culture. *Journal of International Business Studies* 31 (2): 223–38.

Webber, R. 1969. Convergence or divergence? *Columbia Journal of World Business* 4, 3.

Weber, Y., O. Shenkar, and A. Raveh. 1996. National and corporate cultural fit in mergers/acquisition: An exploratory study. *Management Science* 42 (8): 1215–27.

Welch, L. S., and R. Luostarinen. 1988. Internationalization: Evolution of a concept. *Journal of General Management* 14 (2): 34–55.

Williamson, O. E. 1975. *Markets and hierarchies, analysis and antitrust implications: A study in the economics of internal organization.* New York: Free Press.

———. 1981. The economics of organization: The transaction cost approach. *American Journal of Sociology* 87 (3): 548–77.

———. 1985. *The economic institutions of capitalism.* New York: Free Press.

World competitiveness yearbook. 2000. Lausanne, Switzerland: International Institute for Management Development.

Yoshino, Michael Y. 1976. *Japan's multinational enterprises.* Cambridge, MA: Harvard University Press.

THE ROLE OF SUBJECTIVE CULTURE IN ORGANIZATIONS

PROGRESS AND PITFALLS TWENTY YEARS LATER

Rabi S. Bhagat, Ben L. Kedia, Liliana M. Perez,
and Karen South Moustafa

With the advent of globalization and tremendous increases in foreign direct investment since World War II, there has been a significant increase in understanding the functioning of organizations in distinctive cultural milieus around the world. The cross-cultural study of organizations is concerned with systematic investigations of the behavior and experience of participants in different cultures. Though theories of international management that were developed immediately after World War II did not pay much attention to the dynamics of cultural variations, there has been a significant shift toward incorporating the role of cultural intricacies in our attempts to understand effectiveness of various activities dealing with globalizing the world even further. Research involving cultural variations has accelerated, especially after the publication of two main publications. The first publication was Geert Hofstede's (1980) *Culture's Consequences,* which provided a firmer grasp of national differences in forty countries with respect to four cultural dimensions. The second publication was William Ouchi's (1981) *Theory Z,* which provided substantial evidence in favor of linking organizational culture to organizational performance, especially in the context of Japanese work organizations. The rate of publication in this cross-cultural area since Hofstede's and Ouchi's works has increased, and we seem to have come closer toward a better understanding of how cultural processes in different parts of the world affect various organizational outcomes, including organizational effectiveness.

CROSS-CULTURAL STUDIES IN
A HISTORICAL PERSPECTIVE

In her extensive review of literature, Roberts (1970) noted that there was considerable disappointment with the progress in the cross-cultural study of organizations. No systematic paradigms had emerged, and the findings were rarely integrated with the mainstream literature on organizational functioning. Child (1981) went a step further in characterizing the tendency of the researchers to use culture as an excuse for *intellectual laziness*. National differences found in the characteristics of organizations or of their members were often interpreted as cultural differences, and no conceptual grounding was advanced as to why cultural differences would be synonymous with national differences. Bhagat and McQuaid (1982), in their research monograph exploring the role of subjective culture (a more precise term coined by Triandis and his colleagues, referring to a group's characteristic way of perceiving and interpreting its social environment) in organizations, commented on the following topics.

ON THEORETICAL RIGOR

Cross-cultural research conducted prior to 1982 compared mean group differences without attempting to understand or explain why cultures should differ on the variables that were being investigated. The construct of *culture* was rarely operationalized consistently across numerous studies involving cultural variations. No systematic attempts were made to explain the differences in the phenomenon in terms of more precise nomothetic considerations. There was hardly any attempt made to relate cross-cultural findings with mainstream research and theory of organizational functioning. Cultures were often selected as "targets of opportunity" and oftentimes in accordance with the travel plans of the principal investigator. Furthermore, the flow of knowledge seemed to proceed from a unicultural view of organizational functioning to a multicultural view without appropriate explanations or conceptual grounding.

ON METHODOLOGICAL ROBUSTNESS

On this front, "static-group designs" (Campbell and Stanley 1966) were often employed, and the cultural variations were not systematically understood in terms of different levels of the treatment variable on subjects who were randomly assigned. Complicating this issue was the ample display of "ignorance of the mind of the other" (Malpass 1977, 1072). Bhagat and

McQuaid (1982) noted that, in order to correctly ascertain the behavior of people and work organizations in unfamiliar cultural settings, the researcher must educate himself or herself about the various contextual influences as well as the sociocultural and culture-specific (i.e., emic) antecedents of behavior. The old adage that differences between people are best interpreted against a background of similarity was hardly incorporated, even in its elementary form. That some of the problems could indeed arise from the principal investigator's lack of emic issues—that is, understanding of local customs and mores—resulted in the superimposition of Western theoretical perspectives on local phenomena. It seemed as though we started knowing more and more about less and less.

ORGANIZATION OF THE PRESENT CHAPTER

In this chapter, we review some of the major empirical research conducted in the area of cultural variations in management and organizational processes. While our review is not meant to be exhaustive, we believe it should be able to ascertain the current state of theory and research on the role of subjective culture in organizations in terms of progress and pitfalls twenty years later. We also discuss some of the major studies that have become hallmarks of the field since the publication of Bhagat and McQuaid's (1982) research monograph on evaluating the role of subjective culture in organizations. Other broad reviews were published by Drenth (1985) and Ronen and Kumar (1986), which echoed similar concerns expressed by Bhagat and McQuaid in 1982 and by Roberts in 1970. Triandis, in his classic chapter in the *Handbook of Industrial and Organizational Psychology* (1994a), explored various theoretical and methodological issues involving the construct of culture. He traced the development of the field by noting various research gaps, drawing the following conclusions:

1. It was no longer acceptable to develop theories that have limited generalizabilities and that can be applied only under very restricted cultural conditions.
2. Variables reflecting cultural variations ought to become parameters in our theories in describing various organizational processes, and such theories ought to be the norm as opposed to the exception.
3. Since culture change is an ongoing process and best understood from a developmental perspective, it is crucial that researchers in

the international management area develop the capability to monitor all of the manifestations of cultural change and incorporate such manifestations in developing theories of organizational functioning.

In writing the present chapter for the second edition of the *Handbook for International Management Research,* we have been guided by the concerns reflected in the earlier reviews (Bhagat and McQuaid 1982; Roberts and Boyacigiller 1984; Triandis 1994a). First, we conduct a review of noteworthy studies in the field; then we provide our assessment of the developments that have taken place and discuss other issues that make acquisition of knowledge in the domain of cross-cultural studies of organizational functioning tricky at best.

CURRENT STATUS OF THEORY AND RESEARCH

In table 7.1, we provide a summary of the studies in terms of countries and cultures considered, whether the primary focus was etic or emic, the kind of samples employed in the investigation, the theoretical foundations, and methodology.

Ali 1993 is an emic study of decision-making styles, individualism, and attributes toward risk in Arab executives; it used a modified version of the scale developed in Ali 1987. Cultural variations were assumed, following Hofstede's framework. The study is noteworthy in that it explores decision-making styles in a Middle Eastern sample—an investigation rarely attempted by Western scholars.

Earley (1993) conducted a rigorous study of the way individualism-collectivism and group membership interact to influence individual performance. This etic study of Israeli, Chinese, and American managers used an experimental model that simulated managerial activities and a follow-up field study that replicated the results. Earley used Hofstede's dimension of individualism-collectivism and Triandis and his colleagues' work on individualism-collectivism to arrive at his conclusions. In 1994, Earley conducted another mixed design–based study involving both emic and etic constructs. A laboratory experiment followed by a field experiment were conducted in Hong Kong, China, and the United States. We applaud this effort for its sustained focus on providing rigorously validated findings. More studies of this type are bound to provide insight into the functioning of the role of cultural variations on organizational processes and outcomes.

Peterson et al. (1995) examined the effect of culture on role stresses,

Author(s)	Countries/Cultures	Primary Focus	Sample Size and Type	Theoretical Foundations	Research Methodology
Ali (1993)	Majority Saudi subjects; in addition, 1 Bahrani, 1 Omani, and 2 Qatari subjects	Emic	117 managers who attended the Arab Gulf Management Development Conference in Saudi Arabia	Nomological validity Decision-making styles used by many other researchers: Likert (1967), Heller (1971), Vroom and Yetton (1973), Bass and Valenzi (1974), and Muna (1980) Individualism based on Hofstede's dimension of individualism-collectivism Decision-making style, individualism, and attributes toward risk of Arab executives	Questionnaire. Used a modified version of the scale developed by Ali (1987). Survey of Management and Organization in the Arab World (SMOAW). Reliable and valid instrument. ANOVA, MANOVA
Earley (1993)	Chinese, Israeli, and American subjects	Etic	45 Israeli, 60 Chinese, and 60 American managers	Hofstede's dimension of individualism-collectivism Triandis and colleagues' work on individualism-collectivism How individualism-collectivism and group membership interact to influence individual performance	Validation of measurement model with factor analysis. 1. Experiment that simulated managerial activities. Different language versions To test hypotheses: hierarchical moderated regression analysis 2. Follow-up field survey (which replicated the results)
Earley (1994)	Hong Kong, People's Republic of China, and U.S.	Etic and emic	Study 1: 67 Hong Kong Chinese, 96 Chinese from China, and 87 American managers Study 2: 46 Chinese from the People's Republic of China and 62 American service representatives from similar communication companies	Relationship of training and individualism-collectivism to self-efficacy (a person's estimate of his or her ability to perform a task) and performance How individualism-collectivism and group membership interact to influence individual performance Etic (training will increase self-efficacy, no matter the culture) Emic (certain types of training have a stronger effect on self-efficacy and	1. Laboratory experiment, which simulated managerial activities To test hypotheses: hierarchical regression analysis 2. Sixth-month field experiment (which replicated the results) To test the hypotheses: hierarchical regression analysis

(continued)

TABLE 7.1.—Continued

Author(s)	Countries/Cultures	Primary Focus	Sample Size and Type	Theoretical Foundations	Research Methodology
				performance depending on the culture as determined by individualism-collectivism)	
Peterson et al. (1995)	21 countries	Emic in purpose but has an etic ingredient	Around 100 middle managers of each country: Australia, Brazil, Finland, France, Germany, Hong Kong-Macao, India, Indonesia, Iran, Japan, Korea, Mexico, Netherlands, Nigeria, Portugal, Singapore, South Africa, Spain, Uganda, U.K., and U.S.	Hofstede's 4 culture dimensions The effect of culture on role stresses (role conflict, role ambiguity, and role overload) Has authors from different cultural backgrounds Etic ingredients (i.e., they found 13 role stress items that retain their meaning across all countries)	Adapted role stress scales devised by Rizzo, House, and Lirtzman (1970) and revised by House, Schuler, and Levanoni (1983) Multigroup confirmatory factor analysis to validate instrument of role stress Back translation and parallel translation To test hypotheses: hierarchical regression analysis
Gibson (1995)	Norway, Sweden, Australia, U.S.	Etic and emic	45 Norwegians, 55 Swedes, 64 Australians, and 45 Americans; 55% male; majority were midlevel managers	Eagly's (1987) gender differences Hofstede's 4 dimensions of culture Flamholtz's (1986) leadership framework Effects of gender and culture (country) on leadership Etic—gender differences across four countries Emic—Australian leadership	Flamholtz's (1986) leadership effectiveness questionnaire 2 x 4 MANOVA SAS general linear models procedure
Weber, Shenkar, and Raveh (1996)	U.S., Netherlands, Canada, Germany, and France	Etic	2 samples: 8 international M&A, and 8 domestic M&A. Either international firms acquiring an American company or an American company acquiring another American company. In the IM&A, 3 mergers with firms from	Relative role of national and corporate cultural fit in predicting effective integration between merger partners Etic (national and organizational culture are separate constructs)	Questionnaire sent to top managers in firms (average of 7 managers in TMT) Innovative, nonparametric coplot method is introduced to test hypothesis. National differences using Hofstede's dimensions Corporate culture differences using

Study	Country	Emic/Etic	Sample	Theory / Focus	Method
			with firms from Canada, 2 mergers with firms from Germany, and 1 merger with 1 French firm.		Survey Hierarchical regression analysis
Sanchez and Brock (1996)	Chilean, Cuban, Puerto Rican, and Spaniard individuals	Emic	139 Hispanic employees of multiple organizations located in Dade County, FL, U.S. 60% were Cuban, 41% were born outside the U.S., 59% were from Hispanic origin but born in U.S.	Social identity theory Acculturation research Effect of perceived discrimination on employee outcomes Emic—discrimination of Hispanics in U.S. (only Florida)	Questionnaire Acculturative stress using items suggested by Hofstede (1980), Bond (1987), Denison (1990), and Chatterjee et al. (1992) Hofstede's 4 dimensions of culture Accounted for confounding variables Tested for interrater reliability ANOVA Regression analysis
Very, Lubatkin, and Calori (1996)	Great Britain, France, and U.S.	Etic	62 top managers of French-acquired firms and 95 top managers of British-acquired firms. 16 French firms acquired by French firms, 16 French firms acquired by British firms, 10 French firms acquired by U.S. firms, 24 British firms acquired by French firms, 20 British firms acquired by British firms, 20 British firms acquired by U.S. firms. A total of 106 mergers.	Hofstede's 4 dimensions of culture Effect of culture on acculturative stress and relationship between acculturative stress and merger performance The group of researchers was cross-national (France and U.S.)	
Farh, Earley, and Lin (1997)	Taiwan	The study identifies emic and etic dimensions of the Western OCB and the Chinese OCB.	2 samples in study 1: 109 Chinese students and employees pursuing an MBA at the National Chengchi University in Taiwan; 75 managers from 10 different organizations. 1 sample in study 2: 227 employees from 8 companies in the electronics business	The moderating effect of culture on the relationship between citizenship behavior and organizational justice Culture was identified through 2 dimensions: traditionality and modernity They try to find evidence of the etic value that citizenship behavior has on cultures in which expectations for employees are different.	2 studies: Study 1: development of the Chinese OCB scale. It is contrasted to the Western OCB scale developed by Organ (1988) and operationalized by Podsakoff et al. (1990). Used factor analyses. Study 2: Test of hypotheses (moderating effect of culture) Questionnaire developed in study 1 Used LISREL 8 and regression

(continued)

TABLE 7.1.—*Continued*

Author(s)	Countries/ Cultures	Primary Focus	Sample Size and Type	Theoretical Foundations	Research Methodology
Martínez and Dorfman (1998)	Mexico	Emic	6 Mexican *empresarios* (entrepreneurs)	The study aimed at a greater understanding of leadership in Mexico. Identifies 6 core roles of the Mexican entrepreneur through an inductive approach.	Ethnographic methods Interviews Inductive
Brett and Okumura (1998)	Japan and U.S.	Etic	30 intercultural negotiations, 47 U.S.-U.S. intracultural, and 18 Japanese-Japanese intracultural simulated negotiations	Effects of inter- and intracultural negotiations on joint gains, on the understanding of the priorities of the other party, and on the utility of a compatible issue Hofstede's individualism-collectivism dimension, Schwartz's hierarchical-egalitarian dimension	Simulated negotiations Schwartz's survey of values to measure cultural dimensions Simples correlations Chi-squares, MANOVA, ANOVA
Roberson (2000)	Chile, Australia, U.S.	Etic and emic	64 Chilean, 72 Australian, and 53 American workers at all levels in the organization	Hofstede and Bond's cultural values Hofstede's 4 culture dimensions Tests whether Confucian Dynamism exists in non-Confucian nations at the individual level and whether future and past/present orientations are different across countries Etic (Confucian Dynamism exists in non-Confucian nations) Emic (future and past/present orientations are different across countries)	Survey Correlational analysis, multiple regression analyses, *t*-tests Used control variables (age, education, and gender)
Lenartowicz and Roth (2001)	Brazil	Etic and emic	Study 1: 189 workers in kiosks (small retail businesses) from 4 Brazilian subcultures: 31 Mineiros from the Minas Gerais state, 49 Cariocas from Greater Rio de Janeiro,	Effects of within-country subcultures on business outcomes Schwartz and Bilsky's (1987, 1990) theory of the universal structure of values Etic (individual values vary across	Selection of country based on prior research (not guided by convenience, as is usually the case) Used Rokeach Values Survey (RVS) Did 2 studies Study 1: MANOVA Regression analysis

	Countries	Emic/Etic	Sample	Research Question/Hypothesis	Methods
			Paulo state and 47 Gauchos from the Rio Grande do Sul state. Study 2: 5,947 kiosks: 2,053 kiosks from Greater Rio de Janeiro, 2,038 from Sao Paulo, and 1,856 from the Rio Grande do Sul.	Emic (business performance will vary by subculture)	
Stottinger and Holzmuller (2001)	U.S. and Austria	It has an etic focus, but the results prove to be emic.	104 American companies (private sector manufacturing firms with 50 to 100 employees) (Austrian companies had been used in a previous study.)	Whether a model developed in one national context (Austria) applies in another national context (U.S.) Model of Export performance by Holzmuller and Kasper (1990, 1991) Austria is a small open economy. U.S. has a large home market.	Drop-in-questionnaire (i.e., the interviewer asks the respondent to fill in a questionnaire in his/her presence) Cross-cultural collaboration of authors (one is from Austria, the other from Germany) Path modeling Factor analysis to test measurement model Selection of country to compare based on size of the market and other factors that show that Austria and U.S. are different indeed (and not guided by convenience)
Marshall and Boush (2001)	U.S. and Peru	Emic	500 American (U.S. Exporters' Directory) and 500 Peruvian (Asociacion de Exportadores Membership Guide) export managers	Hofstede's individualism-collectivism dimension Effects of culture on trust and cooperation in exports	Simulation: A sequence of 3 simulated interactions of Peruvian and American export managers with business partners Multinomial logit analysis

assuming Hofstede's four cultural dimensions in twenty-one countries. The study was essentially emic in its design but had an etic component. The authors adapted role stress scales devised by Rizzo, House, and Lirtzman (1970) and revised by House, Schuler, and Levanoni (1983). Studies of this kind are rare in the field, and the findings that power distance and collectivism were negatively related to role ambiguity and positively related to role overload across these twenty-one nations are indeed helpful for researchers concerned with human stress and cognition in organizational settings. The major problem with this study is the tendency to equate culture with nation.

Gibson (1995) used a questionnaire-based method to examine the effects of gender and country culture on leadership. The subjects in this design with both etic and emic components were Norwegian, Swedish, Australian, and American midlevel managers. The study assumed Eagly's (1987) gender differences theory, Hofstede's four dimensions of culture, and Flamholtz's (1986) leadership framework. The findings are helpful for researchers wishing to explore the role of cultural variations on leadership effectiveness.

Weber, Shenkar, and Raveh (1996) examined the relative role of national and corporate cultural fit in predicting effective integration between merger partners. In this etic study, questionnaires were sent to top managers in firms in the United States, Netherlands, Canada, Germany, and France. The authors assumed national differences using Hofstede's dimensions and measured corporate culture differences using Chatterjee et al.'s (1992) instrument. The research identified national and organizational culture as separate constructs. For researchers interested in incorporating the roles of national and organizational cultures in predicting merger- and joint venture–related activities, this study is indeed a step in the right direction.

Sanchez and Brock (1996) utilized social identity theory and themes from acculturation research to examine the effects of perceived discrimination on employee outcomes. This emic study, which analyzed the experience of discrimination in Hispanic samples in Florida, has significant implications for researchers concerned with the effects of cultural diversity on individually and organizationally valued outcomes.

Very, Lubatkin, and Calori (1996) examined the effects of culture on acculturative stress and the relationship between acculturative stress and merger performance. These researchers studied top managers of French-acquired firms and British-acquired firms in Great Britain, France, and the United States. Acculturative stress was measured using items suggested by Hofstede (1980), Bond (1987), Denison (1990), and Chatterjee et al. (1992). Hofstede's four dimensions of culture were assumed. They account for confounding variables, providing alternative explanations for their findings. As suggested by Bhagat and McQuaid (1982) and Roberts (1970), they used collaborative methods to obtain results. The authors found that acculturative stress is affected by culture and that the specific impact of performance may be specific to country and culture.

Farh, Earley, and Lin (1997) identified emic and etic dimensions of the Western organizational citizenship behavior (OCB) scale and the Chinese OCB scale. The moderating effect of culture on the relationship between citizenship behavior and organizational justice was examined, and culture was operationalized along the dimension of traditionality versus modernity. The goal of the study was to examine the external validity of OCB, a well-known U.S.-based organizational construct, in China—a non-Western culture. Once again, studies of this kind are indeed very helpful, and our overall impression is that the various steps leading to the findings were carefully executed.

Martínez and Dorfman (1998) investigated leadership effectiveness in Mexico using an emic technique, which was essentially based on an inductive approach of ethnographic methodology, coupled with field-based interviews. While this study has limited generalizability, studies of this kind have the potential to assist us in developing a greater understanding of the phenomenon in each country in a qualitative vein. As Bhagat and McQuaid (1982) hoped, studies of this kind, which are Type III studies (ethnographically motivated studies), do indeed reflect the kind of studies one should undertake in the initial stages of investigation.

Brett and Okumura (1998) undertook an etic study of the effects of within-culture and between-culture variations on negotiations for joint gains, on the understanding of the priorities of the other part, and on the utility of a compatible issue. The authors used simulated negotiations and Schwartz's survey of values to measure cultural dimensions among within-culture and between-culture variations on negotiations in the United States and Japan. Hofstede's individualism-collectivism dimension was the underlying dimension of cultural variation. As a cross-cultural study involving simulation, this study is indeed a laudable achievement.

Robertson (2000) examined both etic and emic theories to test whether

Confucian Dynamism exists in non-Confucian nations at the individual level and whether future and past/present orientations are different across countries. He used a survey instrument to examine Chilean, Australian, and U.S. workers at all levels of the organization. Hofstede and Bond's cultural values were examined, and Hofstede's four cultural dimensions were assumed. He used control variables to account for some of the variance, such as age, education, and gender. Robertson's study adds credence to the concept that cultural traits are interdependent at an individual level of analysis. His identification of the link between uncertainty avoidance and future values in the Confucian Dynamism scale will help bridge the gap between the definitions and identify similarities between these two concepts.

Lenartowicz and Roth (2001) undertook a study with both etic and emic design of the effects of within-country subcultures on business outcomes in Brazil, using the Rokeach Values Survey. They were testing the effects of within-country cultures on business outcomes. The selection of the country was based on prior research. The importance of this study is the use of actual cultural differences within a national border rather than the assumption of national border homogeneity. In our careful scrutiny of this study and others covered in this review, we are particularly pleased that a study of this kind did indeed take place in the new millennium. While most studies have equated nations with culture, a tendency that is difficult to overcome despite repeated pleas to the contrary (e.g., Bhagat and McQuaid 1982; Malpass 1977), this study is one of the very few that has overcome this significant hurdle in cross-cultural management research.

Stottinger and Holzmuller (2001) took an etic focus, but the results prove to be emic in character. These authors examined whether a model developed in one national context (Austria) applies in another national context (U.S.) using the model of export performance by Holzmuller and Kasper (1990, 1991). They selected the United States because, theoretically, the United States was a national context almost diametrically opposed to that of Austria. In terms of transferability of management practices from the European context to the North American context, this investigation stands out as a good attempt.

Marshall and Boush (2001) developed an emic study to examine the effects of culture on trust and cooperation in export firms using a simulation of interactions using Peruvian and American managers and their export partners. Hofstede's individualism-collectivism dimension was assumed. The aim of the study was to determine whether Peruvians or Americans would be more trusting after three interactions. Peruvians reflected less trust in the initial stage, which reflected differences between Peruvians and Americans in their behavior toward in-group versus out-group members. They found, however, that the influence of cultural differences gradually decreases and personal characteristics and relationship-specific history become more important to developing trusting relationships. In terms of effects of culture change on repeated exposure to important stimuli from the environment, this study went beyond what would have ordinarily been expected from studies of this kind.

AN ASSESSMENT

ON THEORETICAL RIGOR

We get the clear impression that the studies reviewed in this chapter are definitely better focused and often derived from a theoretical base that is supported in the U.S. or European management literature. A significant portion of the studies reviewed was conducted by researchers who have traveled and taught management courses outside their own countries. The proliferation of various international academic conferences focusing on advanced issues in conducting cross-cultural and cross-national research, as well as international learning facilities in various institutions of higher learning in the United States, Europe, and various parts of Asia, have also aided the process of theory construction. Although the number of studies has increased greatly since the publication of Bhagat and McQuaid's (1982) research monograph on the role of subjective culture in organizations, an assessment of the significance of this research clearly reaches the following conclusions.

The scope of the topics needs to expand significantly. The work environment has changed greatly in the electronic age. Issues concerning virtual organizations, virtual teams, shift work, telecommuting, flexi-space, and Internet-related work activities have increased exponentially, not only in the United States but also in other parts in the world. India, from the South Asian context, would ordinarily be viewed by Western scholars as a developing country. However, recent developments in the software industry clearly put India ahead of many other European countries in terms of emphasis on electronic work in the software industry. Any attempts to understand the organizational processes of these organizations in India should be relatively free from previous conceptualizations regarding how Indian organizations functioned in the 1970s and 1980s.

With respect to depth, following Hui and Luk's (1997) analysis, we also feel that there is a bias toward research on issues that are more theoretical than pragmatic. For example, although there has been significant progress in the area of managerial values and intercultural negotiation, research is needed in the areas of organizational stress and cognition, the dynamics of entrepreneurship, adoption of new technology, and absorptive capacities of firms. Research on practical issues is characterized by anecdotal and impressionistic evidence, and while this evidence constitutes a good starting point we believe it is time to move beyond these methodologies. Although we are favorably biased toward developing etic-based theoretical frameworks, we must admit that there is a need for broadening the scope of investigations to include more practical concerns, such as the ones just described. The viability of the research, including pragmatic issues of funding, is contingent on the practical utility of the findings for managers functioning in the rapidly globalizing marketplace.

The constructs of individualism versus collectivism and, to a lesser extent, power distance have been the dominant dimensions of cultural variation, but again, echoing Hui and Luk's (1997) observation, we also reassert the relevance of examining the world in terms of other dimensions. While individualism-collectivism is unquestionably the most important dimension of cultural variation (Triandis 1989, 1994a, 1995, 1998; Hofstede 1980, 1991, 2001), excessive emphasis on this dimension may have the inadvertent consequences of dichotomizing the world in a manner that might have an adverse impact on developing fine-grained theories of organizational functioning around the globe. While two of the authors of the present chapter are also responsible for emphasizing the role of individualism-collectivism on the cross-border transfer of organizational knowledge (Bhagat et al. 2002), we did note the significance of other dimensions as possible predictors of other types of organizational knowledge. The work of Lytle et al. (1995), which lists other dimensions of culture and provides background information on each of these dimensions, should be referred to before embarking on developing a theory purely based on the dimension of individualism-collectivism. For example, decision-making processes in organizations, including the launching of new products and services in the marketplace, have more to do with uncertainty-avoidance processes than with individualism-collectivism. Our point is simple: Efficient construction of comprehensive theoretical frameworks that specify a priori the various kinds of relationships that are likely to be found once the analysis is completed is the starting point for building a storehouse of knowledge on examining the role of subjective culture in organizations.

Based on a careful review of the studies, we are of the opinion that researchers have overcome some of the persistent problems of poor theory in the studies reviewed in Bhagat and McQuaid 1982 and in other broad reviews conducted since then. Next, we examine the methodological robustness of the studies.

ON METHODOLOGICAL ROBUSTNESS

On this dimension, we have indeed witnessed solid progress. However, the journey is not over. Studies by Earley (1993, 1994) and his colleagues (Farh, Earley, and Lin 1997), Bhagat et al. (1994, 2001), Lenartowicz, and Roth (2001), the GLOBE project at the Wharton School, Hofstede and his colleagues (1990) (on comparative studies of organizational culture in the Nordic countries), Shenkar and von Glinow (1994), and others have demonstrated ample methodological robustness of a nature not found in studies prior to the 1990s. While not all of the methodological pitfalls have been avoided, we are indeed on a path to developing a body of knowledge on various aspects of cross-cultural variations of organizational phenomena that is relatively free from certain types of biases. Problems of response consistency have been avoided in studies by Bhagat and his colleagues (1994, 2001). Problems of multimethod convergency have been addressed by House and his colleagues in the GLOBE project (1999). Issues concerning emic methodologies have been addressed by Dorfman (1996) and by Martínez and Dorfman (1998) on studies of Mexican entrepreneurship.

One of the noted examples of theory-based and methodologically sophisticated cross-cultural research was conducted by Bhawuk (2001) on the evolution of culture assimilators, and once again it stands out in our judgment as reflecting the development of a positive trend. This trend, which we would like to see continue in the future, essentially consists of researchers who are fundamentally knowledgeable of the basic theoretical underpinnings of a given organizational phenomenon and are willing to adopt rigorous and robust methodological designs. We believe that, in order to contribute to a finely integrated body of knowledge involving cross-cultural variations of organizational phenomenon in the international context, an investigator must possess certain characteristics.

First, the investigator must possess a willingness to spend the necessary time investigating the emic aspects of the phenomenon in the cultures of interest. The cultures should be appropriately selected in order to reflect their standing on various points on one or more dimensions of culture. These cultural dimensions, in turn, should be responsible for creating and sustaining the necessary variance in the phenomenon.

Second, there must be a willingness to collaborate with a team of researchers from the cultures under investigation and to be open to their suggestions regarding methodological improvements and theoretical frameworks. From our experience and from the experience of other established scholars, we often find that researchers from developing countries are reluctant or shy about sharing their valuable insights for the fear of losing face with Western scholars.

Triandis noted numerous times in his commentary on various developments of cross-cultural phenomena that research of this kind is indeed difficult to execute. However, when conducted with care and executed with as much precision as one can bring to bear, cross-cultural research has the potential to enrich the intellectual development of the field of international management in ways one cannot easily conceive.

WHERE DO WE GO FROM HERE?

Arvey, Bhagat, and Salas (1991) noted in their review of cross-cultural research on personnel and human resources management that the research tended to be highly atheoretical and opportunistic. We do not find the same trend present in the studies reviewed in this chapter. While traces of opportunism do exist, we have come a fairly long way on our path to create a body of sound knowledge in understanding the role of subjective culture in organizations. There are reasons for optimism, and the numbers of researchers that are well trained to conduct research on cross-cultural and cross-national variations of organizational phenomena have dramatically increased in various parts of the world. Gone are the days when knowledge in the area of cross-cultural research on organizations was highly dependent on the travel schedules of principal investigators from the United States and Western Europe and when researchers from countries of interest in the developing parts of the world had limited chances to collaborate. Today, it is possible for even a young researcher from Japan or India or Poland to conduct sustained research on a topic of interest by using the technology of the Internet and computer-mediated communication networks. While we do not advocate this method of conducting research all of the time, research using electronic networks has the potential to build relationships among international collaborators and to remove misconceptions and misjudgments concerning the scope, methodology, and possible impact of the findings.

As Bhagat and McQuaid (1982, 681) noted, "for those who feel the challenge is too great, the longest journey begins with a single step." Our review in this chapter has clearly demonstrated that we have gone far beyond the first single step.

REFERENCES

Ali, A. 1987. Scaling an Islamic work ethic. *Journal of Social Psychology* 128 (5): 575–83.
———. 1993. Decision-making style, individualism, and attributes toward risk of Arab executives. *International Studies of Management and Organization* 23 (3): 53–73.
Arvey, R. D., R. S. Bhagat, and E. Salas. 1991. Cross-cultural and cross-national issues in personnel and human resources management: Where do we go from here? In K. M. Rowland and G. Ferris, eds., *Research in personnel and human resources management*, 9:367–407. Greenwich, CT: JAI Press.
Bhagat, R. S., D. L. Ford Jr., M. P. O'Driscoll, L. Frey, E. Babakus, and M. Mahanyele. 2001. Do South African managers cope differently from American managers? A cross-cultural investigation. *International Journal of Intercultural Relations* 25:301–13.
Bhagat, R. S., B. L. Kedia, P. Harveston, and H. C. Triandis. 2002. Cultural variations in the cross-border transfer of organizational knowledge: An integrative framework. *Academy of Management Review* 27 (2): 1–18.
Bhagat, R. S., and S. J. McQuaid. 1982. Role of subjective culture in organizations: A review and directions for future research. *Journal of Applied Psychology Monograph* 67 (5): 653–85.
Bhagat, R. S., M. P. O'Driscoll, E. Babakus, and L. T. Frey. 1994. Organizational stress and coping in seven national contexts: A cross-cultural investigation. In G. P Keita and J. J. Hurrell Jr., eds., *Job stress in a changing workforce*. Washington, DC: American Psychological Association.
Bhawuk, D. P. S. 2001. Evolution of culture assimilators: Toward theory-based assimilators. *International Journal of Intercultural Relations* 25:141–63.
Bond, M. 1987. Chinese values and the search for culture-free dimensions of culture. *Journal of Cross-Cultural Psychology* 18 (2): 143–64.
Brett, J. M., and T. Okumura. 1998. Inter and intracultural negotiation: U.S. and Japanese negotiators. *Academy of Management Journal* 41(5): 495–510.
Campbell, D. T., and J. Stanley. 1966. *Experimental and quasi-experimental design for research*. Chicago: Rand-McNally.
Chatterjee, S., M. Lubatkin, O. Schweiger, and Y. Weber. 1992. Cultural differences and shareholder value in related mergers: Linking equity and human capital. *Strategic Management Journal* 13:319–34.

Child, J. 1981. Culture, contingency, and capitalism in the cross-national study of organizations. In L. L. Cummings and B. M. Staw, eds., *Research in organizational behavior,* vol. 3. Greenwich, CT: JAI Press.

Denison, D. 1990. *Corporate culture and organizational effectiveness.* New York: Free Press.

Dorfman, P. 1996. International and cross-cultural leadership. In B. J. Punnett and O. Shenkar, eds., *Handbook for international management research.* Cambridge, MA: Blackwell.

Drenth, P. J. D. 1985. Cross-cultural organizational psychology: Challenges and limitations. In P. Joynt and M. Warner, eds., *Managing in different cultures.* Amsterdam: Universitetsforlaget.

Eagly, A. H. 1987. *Sex differences in social behavior: A social-role interpretation.* Hillsdale, NJ: Erlbaum.

Earley, P. C. 1993. East meets West meets Mideast: Further explorations of collectivist and individualist work groups. *Academy of Management Journal* 36 (2): 319–48.

———. 1994. Self or group? Cultural effects of training on self-efficacy and performance. *Administrative Science Quarterly* 39 (March): 89–117.

Farh, J-L., P. C. Earley, and S-C. Lin. 1997. Impetus for action: A cultural analysis of justice and organizational citizenship behavior. *Administrative Science Quarterly* 42 (September): 421–44.

Flamholtz, E. G. 1986. *How to make the transition from entrepreneurship to a professionally managed firm.* San Francisco: Jossey-Bass.

Gibson, C. B. 1995. An investigation of gender differences in leadership across four countries. *Journal of International Business Studies* 26 (2): 255-79.

Hofstede, G. 1980. *Culture's consequences: International differences in work-related values.* Beverly Hills, CA: Sage.

———. 1991. *Cultures and organizations: Software of the mind.* London: McGraw-Hill.

———. 1994. Management scientists are human. *Management Science* 40:4–13.

———. 2001. *Culture's consequences: Comparing values, behaviors, institutions, and organizations across nations.* 2d ed. Thousand Oaks, CA: Sage.

Hofstede, G., B. Neuijen, D. D. Ohayv, and G. Sanders. 1990. Measuring organizational cultures: A qualitative and quantitative study across twenty cases. *Administrative Science Quarterly* 35:286–316.

Holzmuller, H. H., and H. Kasper. 1990. The decision maker and export activity: A cross-national comparison of the foreign orientation of Austrian managers. *Management International Review* 30 (3): 217–30.

———. 1991. On a theory of export performance: Personal and organizational determinants of export trade activities observed in small and medium-sized firms. *Management International Review* 31:45–70. Special issue.

House, R. J., P. J. Hanges, S. A. Ruiz-Quintanilla, P. W. Dorfman, M. Javidan, M. Dickson, V. Gupta, and GLOBE Country Co-investigators. 1999. Cultural influences on leadership and organizations: Project GLOBE. In W. H. Mobley, M. J. Gessner, and V. Arnold, eds., *Advances in global leadership,* vol. 1, 171–234. Stamford, CT: JAI Press.

House, R. J., R. S. Schuler, and E. Levanoni. 1983. Role conflict and ambiguity scales: Reality or artifacts? *Journal of Applied Psychology* 68 (2): 334–37.

Hui, C. H., and C. L. Luk. 1997. Industrial/organizational psychology. In J. W. Berry,

M. H. Segall, and C. Kagitcibasi, eds., *Handbook of cross-cultural psychology,* 3:371–412, 2d ed. Needham Heights, MA: Allyn and Bacon.

Lenartowicz, T., and K. Roth. 2001. Does subculture within a country matter? A cross-cultural study of motivational domains and business performance in Brazil. *Journal of International Business Studies* 32 (2): 305–25.

Likert, R. 1967. *The human organization.* New York: McGraw-Hill.

Lytle, A. L., J. M. Brett, Z. I. Barsness, C. H. Tinsley, and M. Janssens. 1995. A paradigm for confirmatory cross-cultural research in organizational behavior. In L. L. Cummings and B. M. Staw, eds., *Research in organizational behavior* 17:167–214. Greenwich, CT: JAI Press.

Malpass, R. S. 1977. Theory and method in cross-cultural psychology. *American Psychologist* 32:1069–79.

Marshall, R. S. T., and D. M. Boush. 2001. Dynamic decision-making: A cross-cultural comparison of U.S. and Peruvian export managers. *Journal of International Business Studies* 32 (4): 873–93.

Martínez, S. M., and P. W. Dorfman. 1998. The Mexican entrepreneur: An ethnographic study of the Mexican *empresario.* *International Studies of Management and Organization* 28 (2): 97–123.

Ouchi, W. G. 1981. *Theory Z: How American business can meet the Japanese challenge.* New York: Perseus.

Peterson, M. F., P. B. Smith, A. Akande, S. Ayestaran, S. Bochner, V. Callan, N. G. Cho, J. Correira-Jesuino, M. D'Amorim, P-H. Francois, K. Hofman, P. L. Koopman, K. Leung, T. K. Lim, S. Mortazavi, J. Munene, M. Radford, A. Ropo, G. Savage, B. Setiadi, T. N. Sinha, R. Sorenson, and C. Viedge. 1995. Role conflict, ambiguity, and overload: A twenty-one-nation study. *Academy of Management Journal* 38 (2): 429–52.

Rizzo, J., R. S. House, and S. I. Lirtzman. 1970. Role conflict and ambiguity in complex organizations. *Administrative Science Quarterly* 15:150–63.

Roberts, K. H. 1970. On looking at an elephant: An evaluation of cross-cultural research related to organizations. *Psychological Bulletin* 74:327–50.

Roberts, K. H., and N. A. Boyacigiller. 1984. Cross-national organizational research: The grasp of the blind men. *Research in Organizational Behavior* 6:423–75.

Robertson, C. J. 2000. The global dispersion of Chinese values: A three-country study of Confucian dynamism. *Management International Review* 40 (3): 253–68.

Ronen, S., and R. Kumar. 1986. Comparative management: A developmental perspective. In B. M. Bass, P. Weissenberg, and F. Heller, eds., *Handbook of cross-cultural organizational psychology.* Beverly Hills, CA: Sage.

Sanchez, J. I., and P. Brock. 1996. Outcomes of perceived discrimination among Hispanic employees: Is diversity management a luxury or a necessity? *Academy of Management Journal* 39 (3): 704–19.

Schwartz, S. H., and W. Bilsky. 1987. Toward a universal psychological structure of human values. *Journal of Personality and Social Psychology* 53:550–62.

———. 1990. Toward a theory of the universal content and structure of values. *Journal of Personality and Social Psychology* 58 (5): 878–91.

Shenkar, O., and M. A. von Glinow. 1994. Paradoxes of organizational theory and research: Using the case of China to illustrate national contingency. *Management Science* 40 (1): 56–71.

Stottinger, B., and H. H. Holzmuller. 2001. Cross-national stability of an export performance model: A comparative study of Austria and the U.S. *Management International Review* 41 (1): 7–28.

Triandis, H. C. 1989. The self and social behavior in differing cultural contexts. *Psychological Review* 96:269–89.

———. 1990. Cross-cultural studies of individualism and collectivism. In J. J. Berman, ed., *Nebraska symposium on motivation,* 37: 41–133. Lincoln: University of Nebraska Press.

———. 1994a. Cross-cultural industrial and organizational psychology. In H. C. Triandis, M. D. Dunnette, and L. M. Hough, eds., *Handbook of industrial and organizational psychology,* 4:103–72, 2d ed. Palo Alto, CA: Consulting Psychologists Press.

———. 1994b. *Culture and social behavior.* New York: McGraw-Hill.

———. 1995. *Individualism and collectivism.* Boulder, CO: Westview Press.

———. 1998. Vertical and horizontal individualism and collectivism: theory and research implications for international comparative management. In J. L. Cheng and R. B. Peterson, eds., *Advances in International Comparative Management* 12:7–35.

Very, P., M. Lubatkin, and R. Calori. 1996. A cross-national assessment of acculturative stress in recent European mergers. *International Studies of Management and Organization* 26 (1): 59–86.

Vroom, V. H., and P. W. Yetton. 1973. *Leadership and decision-making.* Pittsburgh: University of Pittsburgh Press.

Weber, Y., O. Shenkar, and A. Raveh. 1996. National and corporate cultural fit in mergers/acquisitions: An exploratory study. *Management Science* 42 (8): 1215–27.

Part 4

TOPICAL ISSUES
IN INTERNATIONAL
MANAGEMENT RESEARCH

INTERNATIONAL ALLIANCES

Arvind Parkhe

Back in 1966, General Motors (GM) Corporation boldly declared in its annual report that "Unified ownership for coordinated policy control of all of our operations throughout the world is essential for our effective performance as a worldwide corporation." That was then. Today, virtually all companies, including former corporate loners such as GM, are forsaking their emphasis on unified ownership in favor of alliances, which represent shared control and, frequently, combined ownership. With the growing globalization of business, such alliances are often international in scope. The trend toward international alliances, already conspicuous during the 1980s (Hergert and Morris 1988), continued to accelerate through the 1990s (Knecht 1994; Andersen Consulting 1999). The Andersen Consulting study suggests that (a) 82 percent of executives believe alliances will be a prime vehicle for future growth; (b) alliances will continue to increase in importance, accounting for as much as 25 percent of median company value within five years; and (c) for the advanced economies as a whole, alliances will represent somewhere between $25 trillion and $40 trillion in value within five years.

These are impressive, even astonishing, growth statistics. In the wake of this rapid growth, research on the topic of alliances has also grown exponentially in recent years. The purpose of this chapter is to briefly assess past achievements, present status, and future opportunities for alliance research. Toward this end, the chapter outline reflects the following structure. First, the place and role of alliances are examined against the broader backdrop of global business. Next, the core theoretical dimensions of existing alliance research are identified and the typical methodologies employed in empirical research are critically evaluated. Based on this assessment, significant conceptual and methodological gaps in the alliance literature are noted. The gaps, in turn, suggest promising prospects for future research. The chapter concludes with general observations of potential interest for scholars pursuing—or contemplating—research in international alliances.

I should note at the outset that the present chapter builds on and extends my earlier chapter in the first edition of this handbook (Parkhe 1996). The extension is temporal as well as thematic. Temporally, I have updated my review and synthesis of the alliance literature to include the latest available research. Thematically, whereas the previous chapter focused only on international joint ventures, this chapter casts a wider conceptual net to include international alliances of various other types as well, which I describe next.

ALLIANCES IN THE CONTEXT OF GLOBAL BUSINESS

The global business environment is in unprecedented turmoil. This turmoil is fueled by factors at various analytical levels, including converging consumer tastes and escalating fixed costs (Ohmae 1989), shortening product life cycles and accelerating pace of technological change (Harrigan 1988), and declining trade and investment barriers (Luo 1999). Companies competing in this environment often find that, at the same time as savage global competition is raising the bar for quality, innovation, productivity, and customer value, the scope of what a firm can do alone is shrinking.

It is in this challenging context that alliances are emerging as an increasingly used organizational structure, not necessarily as a first choice but often as the last resort. Following Gulati (1998), for purposes of this chapter alliances are broadly defined as "voluntary arrangements between firms involving exchange, sharing, or codevelopment of products, technologies, or services" (1998, 293). It is considered to be an international alliance if at least one partner is headquartered outside the alliance's country of operation or if the alliance has a significant level of operation in more than one country (Geringer and Hebert 1989).

As Wille (1988) noted, the selection of a joint command structure represented by alliances is hardly a novel phenomenon. Early nation-states often cooperated as a means of countering external threats to their sovereignty that exceeded their individual resources and capabilities. Similarly, modern multinational companies are increasingly serving foreign markets via international alliances rather than the organizational alternatives. In the vast literature on foreign market entry modes (e.g., Root 1987; Luo 1999), entry modes for international expansion are typically classified into three categories: export entry modes (indirect, direct agent/distributor, direct branch/subsidiary); contractual entry modes (licensing, franchising, technical agreements, service contracts, management contracts, construction/turnkey contracts, contract manufacture, and coproduction agreements); and investment entry modes (joint ventures, acquisitions, and greenfield sole ventures). The broad definition of international alliances cited previously encompasses most of these entry modes, with the exception of acquisitions, greenfield sole ventures, and direct exports through a company's wholly owned foreign branches or subsidiaries. I do not view mergers or acquisitions as interfirm alliances, and therefore I excluded these important organizational forms from consideration in this chapter. A substantial variety of international alliances remains on the table, however. As the next section shows, despite the mix of strategic motives, the range of tight and loose couplings, and diverse organizational forms and legal structures, important substratal commonalities may be uncovered from the major streams of research emphasized in the alliance literature.

THEORETICAL UNDERPINNINGS OF EXTANT ALLIANCE RESEARCH

A computer search of databases revealed that to date hundreds of books and more than eleven thousand articles have been published on alliances, the majority of them within the past decade. This massive body of work has undoubtedly added rich insights into our understanding of various aspects of alliances. Yet as Oliver observed, "The study of interorganizational relationships (IORs) has begun to suffer the consequences of its own growth in importance. . . . We no longer know what we know about the formation of IORs" (1990, 241). Oliver described the literature on IORs as vast but highly fragmented.

In a preliminary attempt to overcome this fragmentation, and to organize the impressive theoretical and empirical advances made by prior studies into a coherent theoretical structure, Parkhe (1993a) extracted four interconnected theoretical dimensions that have received primary emphasis in the current alliance literature. As shown in figure 8.1, these dimensions are motives for alliance formation, partner selection/characteristics, control/conflict, and alliance stability/performance. As discussed later in this chapter, each of these four dimensions can be effectively linked with

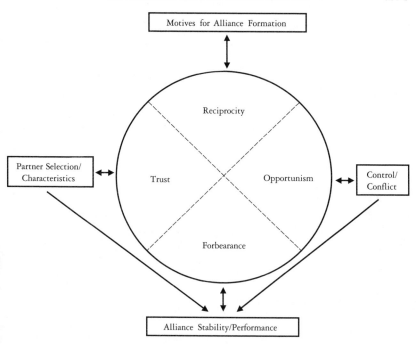

FIGURE 8.1. An integrative framework for core alliance concepts

core behavioral variables that are, according to leading scholars (e.g., Buckley and Casson 1988), at the heart of voluntary interfirm cooperation.

MOTIVES FOR ALLIANCE FORMATION

A large number of studies have sought to shed light on a basic question about the alliance phenomenon: Why alliances? In their chapter titled "Why Should Firms Cooperate?" Contractor and Lorange (1988) maintained that seven more or less overlapping objectives constitute the rationales for entering into cooperative ventures: (1) risk reduction, (2) economies of scale and/or rationalization, (3) technology exchanges, (4) coopting or blocking competition, (5) overcoming government-mandated trade or investment barriers, (6) facilitating initial international expansion, and (7) vertical quasi-integration advantages of linking the complementary contributions of the partners in a value chain. It is clear that the reasons for forming alliances are manifold and reach into all areas of business strategy. These motivations can usefully be distilled into three categories: resource-driven alliances, market-driven alliances, and risk-driven alliances (Wille 1988).

The three categories are often interrelated, and modern alliances are distinguishable from their traditional counterparts by their straddling of multiple motivations, which suggests a more expansive scope of alliance operations in worldwide corporate activities. For example, the focus now is on the creation of new products and technologies rather than on the distribution of existing ones, and partnerships are often forged during industry transitions when competitive positions are shifting and the very basis of building and sustaining competitive advantage is being defined (Bartlett and Ghoshal 2000). Little wonder, then, that alliances appear to be moving closer to parent firms' core technologies, products, and markets (Harrigan 1986) rather than occupying a fringe position in the corporate mission.

Strategic behavior improving the competitive positioning of a firm vis-à-vis its rivals is one of the motivations to collaborate (Kogut 1988). In addition, Kogut analyzed alliances as a means by which firms learn or seek to retain their capabilities (the organizational learning motive) and as organizational choices that minimize the sum of production and transaction costs (the transaction cost motive). The latter, drawing upon the work of Williamson (1975, 1985), has received especially widespread attention in alliance research.

For instance, using the transaction cost paradigm, Stuckey (1983) studied the conditions under which alliances provide a superior means for firms pursuing international vertical integration, while Beamish and Banks (1987) examined the choice of alliances in the context of international horizontal diversification. Hennart (1988) took the thought further to propose a transaction cost theory of equity joint ventures and applied this theory to study Japanese subsidiaries in the United States (Hennart 1991). The theory distinguishes between "scale" and "link" alliances. Scale alliances arise when parents seek to internalize a failing market, but indivisibilities due to scale or scope economies make full ownership of the relevant assets inefficient. Link alliances are motivated by the simultaneous failure of the markets for the services of two or more assets whenever these assets are firm-specific public goods, and acquisition of the firm owning them would entail significant management costs. Thus, Hennart (1988) concluded, alliances represent a first-best strategy in a limited number of specific circumstances.

Research in recent years reflects two (sometimes related) motives for alliance formation: organizational learning and network membership. In modern global competition, developing, codeveloping, or accessing cutting-edge knowledge are of critical importance, and alliances often represent one important mechanism to gain knowledge and promote organizational learning (Shenkar and Li 1999; Koza and Lewin 1998; Gulati 1999). Shenkar and Li (1999), for example, sought to answer whether firms in alliances seek knowledge in a complementary area or additional knowledge in the same area in which they already have a knowledge base, and Gulati (1999) addressed the role of network resources in determining alliance formation. Enjoying the benefits accruing to members of a network has become vital for survival in many industries, including airlines, autos, biotechnology, and multimedia, and so several studies have highlighted belonging to a network as an alliance motive (Millington and Bayliss 1995; Powell, Koput, and Smith-Doerr 1996).

PARTNER SELECTION/CHARACTERISTICS

A second identifiable stream of alliance research deals with the choice of an alliance partner that will enhance the likelihood of venture success. After all, alliances involve close interaction and interdependence between two parties making common cause when their interests run parallel to each other (Ohmae 1989). Lane and Beamish (1990) go so far as to say that "Identifying and selecting a partner is possibly the most important consideration in establishing a cooperative venture" (93), and yet, "As we talked with executives, we were amazed at how some partners were found. Some had been met 'fortuitously' at cocktail parties in Latin America or Trinidad, or in a hotel bar in Nigeria" (95).

What exactly constitutes "the right partner"? Several authors have suggested that partners should be complementary in the products, geographic presence, or functional skills that they bring to the venture (Harrigan 1985; Lynch 1989). Harrigan found, for example, that alliances are more likely to succeed when partners possess complementary missions, resource capabilities, managerial capabilities, and other attributes that create a strategic fit in which the bargaining power of the venture's sponsors is evenly matched. Put another way, partners' needs to be engaged in a particular alliance are stabilizing to the relationship, while a wide variety of asymmetries are destabilizing to the alliance. However, complementary contributions and matching needs, while necessary, are not sufficient. As

Beamish (1988) and other have emphasized, it is important to select a partner with whom trust already exists or can be established.

Although recognized as important, the notion of complementarity of partner contributions remained somewhat vague until the work of Geringer (1991). He separated task- and partner-related dimensions of partner selection criteria. Task-related criteria include factors associated with the operational skills and resources that an alliance requires for its competitive success (e.g., financial resources, technical know-how, access to distribution systems); partner-related criteria include factors associated with the efficiency and effectiveness of partners' cooperation (e.g., a partner's national or corporate culture and trust between top management teams). Observed variations in the choice of criteria used to select alliance partners, Geringer reasoned, may be attributable to differences in the strategic context of an alliance and its parent firms, that is, to the specific competitive circumstances confronting the proposed venture.

The theme of complementary contributions was recently picked up by Chung, Singh, and Lee (2000) and by Kashlak, Chandran, and Di Benedetto (1998). Partner selection studies have also been framed through perspectives of network position (Gulati 1995a, 1995b; Stuart 1998), knowledge transfer between partners (Simonin 1999a), cultural factors (Fedor and Werther 1995), and a firm's home-market relationships (Elg 2000).

CONTROL/CONFLICT ISSUES

PARENT CONTROL OVER ALLIANCES

A major dimension in the alliance literature involves issues of control. Desire for control sometimes poses intractable problems in alliances, precisely because alliances are jointly managed. As Killing (1982, 121) noted, "The problems in managing joint ventures stem from one cause: there is more than one parent." The resulting control problems are described well by Ohmae: "A real alliance compromises the fundamental independence of economic actors, and managers don't like that. After all, for them, management has come to mean total control. Alliances mean sharing control. The one precludes the other" (1989, 143).

Other things being equal, a partner desires more control the greater an alliance's strategic significance to the partner. More control may be gained through ownership (increasing equity share) or through bargaining power (making the alliance more dependent on the partner's proprietary resources that are costly or impossible to replace) (Brouthers and Bamossy 1997; Contractor and Kundu 1998; Das and Teng 1998; Gulati and Singh 1998; Hagedoorn and Narula 1996; Rao and Schmidt 1998; Young-Ybarra and Wiersema 1999).

CONFLICT IN ALLIANCES

Another near ubiquitous aspect of alliances is conflict (Rieger and Wong-Rieger 1990). Conflict may arise primarily through two sources: interfirm diversity and actual or potential opportunism of alliance partners (Arino and de la Torre 1998; Cullen, Johnson, and Sakano 1995; Inkpen and Dinur 1998; Khanna, Gulati, and Nohria 1998; Larsson et al. 1998; Lin and Germain 1998). Together, these sources may help explain a significant proportion of the high failure rates observed in alliances (Harrigan 1988). Each source will be discussed in turn.

Parkhe (1991) proposed that cross-border alliances bring together partners who may differ in two important ways, each potentially triggering conflict. Type I diversity includes the familiar interfirm differences (interdependencies) that alliances are specifically created to exploit. These differences form the underlying strategic motivations for entering into alliances. Thus, Type I diversity deals with the reciprocal strengths and complementary resources furnished by the alliance partners, differences that actually facilitate formulation, development, and collaborative effectiveness of alliances. Type II diversity refers to differences in partner characteristics that often negatively affect the longevity and effective functioning of alliances. (This thesis found empirical support in Parkhe 1993c and is also reflected in Shenkar and Zeira 1992). Type II diversity may stem from sharp differences in collaborating firms' cultural and political bases, as well as in firm-specific characteristics that may be tied to each firm's national heritage. A typology of the major dimensions of Type II interfirm diversity would include societal culture (metalevel of analysis), national context (macro), corporate culture (meso), strategic direction (meso), and management practices and organization (micro).

Over the life of the partnership, the dynamics of Types I and II are very different, since the two types are differently impacted by the processes of organizational learning and adaptation. While such processes may tend to reduce Type II diversity and fortify a relationship, they may also reduce Type I diversity and destabilize an alliance. For example, learning through an alliance may enable one partner to acquire the skills and technologies it lacked at the time of alliance formation (Hamel 1991). This partner may then enjoy a stronger bargaining hand, rewrite partnership terms more favorably to itself, or discard the other partner and terminate the alliance. Erosion of Type I diversity removes the raison d'être of the alliance and reduces longevity. Conversely, extreme asymmetries in partner capabilities may create imbalances in contributions to the alliance, which are also destabilizing.

Another conflict-inducing factor is the prospect of opportunistic behavior by an alliance partner. "Opportunism" is behavior by economic agents that involves "self-interest-seeking with guile" (Williamson 1975, 26). The prospect of such behavior can never be ignored in alliances, not because all economic agents behave opportunistically all of the time but because "some agents behave in this fashion and it is costly to sort out those who are opportunistic from those who are not" (Williamson and Ouchi 1981, 351), particularly in international alliances.

A rich body of literature has emerged from these fundamental considerations about voluntary interfirm cooperation. Scholars have recognized, for example, that (1) alliances involve mutual interdependence, such that one is vulnerable to another whose behavior is not under one's control (Zand 1972); (2) there is only partial overlap of goals of the cooperating parties (Ouchi 1980); and (3) each firm exercises only partial influence over the outcome of the alliance. The relationship environment is, therefore, often marked by uncertainty and vulnerability to opportunism.

Ex-ante and ex-post safeguards may be erected to defend against opportunism. Generically, such safeguards seek to alter an alliance's payoff structure in order to reduce gains from cheating, to increase gains from cooperation, or to increase costs of agreement violations. In essence, the purpose is to promote robust cooperation by restructuring the alliance and realigning partners' incentives. Important contributions in this area have come from game theory (Axelrod 1984), transaction cost economics (Williamson 1985), and contract law (Macneil 1978). Parkhe (1993b) merged game theoretic insights with the logic of transaction cost economics in a generalized model and found empirical support for the model's predictions regarding alliance structuring.

Yet larger questions remain. The costs of safeguards can be reduced if the perception of opportunism can be lowered, and perception of opportunism can be lowered if trust develops between alliance partners. In other words, trust can lubricate alliances and make alliances more efficient (inter)organizational modes. But what factors lead to the generation, growth, and destruction of trust? Can these factors be managed to accelerate what Zucker (1986) called "trust production"?

STABILITY/PERFORMANCE ASSESSMENT

The final major dimension emphasized in extant research deals with alliance outcomes. It quickly becomes apparent that performance measurement is a complex and controversial topic even at the individual firm level. The problems are compounded in alliances, where multiple parents attempt to influence alliance decisions, the true motivations of partners may be unknown to each other, and venture-specific data are seldom available.

Still, scholars have grappled with performance measurement issues, often by using "objective" measures. Objective measures include financial indicators (e.g., return on investment, return on equity, return on sales), market share, survival, and alliance duration (Geringer and Hebert 1989; see also Dussauge, Garrette, and Mitchell 2000; Kotabe and Swan 1995; Makino and Beamish 1998; Reuer 2000; Reuer and Koza 2000; Zaheer, McEvily, and Perrone 1998). These measures are open to many criticisms, however. The first is that any single measure is too narrow. As Venkatraman and Ramanujam (1986) argued, the breadth of the construct of performance cannot be captured unless financial, operational, and effectiveness measures are combined. Second, in the absence of knowledge of the concrete goals and actual (not declared) motivations of parent firms, it is difficult to compare alliance results against specific targets. Third, poor financial performance may be quite acceptable if an alliance is not a profit center but rather a source of learning that will synergistically contribute toward parent companies' overall competitiveness. Finally, alliance survival and duration may be associated not with alliance success but with high exit barriers.

Partly in response to these limitations, researchers began to use subtler criteria for assessing alliance outcomes, such as fulfillment of major strategic needs (an alliance can be said to be performing well when important strategic needs are being met very well) and indirect performance indicators (net spillover effects for parent firms, the alliance's profitability relative to its industry, and overall performance assessment by responsible parties) (Parkhe 1993b). Overall performance assessment is, of course, a subjective measure, hence subject to the familiar drawbacks of bias and recall associated with such measures. However, such a multidimensional operationalization of performance, resting on distinct, crucial aspects of the alliance phenomenon, may overcome some weaknesses of past performance measures.

Related to performance is the question of alliance stability. What does stability mean, and what factors contribute to alliance instability? Gomes-Casseres (1987) addressed these questions, taking into account alliance survival and duration but also going beyond. The significance of Gomes-Casseres's contribution lies in his insight to link alliance outcomes to the ongoing operations of parent firms. He identified three types of alliance instability: (1) an alliance may be liquidated completely; (2) an alliance may be sold to the local partner or to outsiders; and (3) one parent may buy out the other's interest in an alliance and create a wholly owned subsidiary. Thus viewed, instability does not always reflect poor performance, dissolution does not necessarily equal failure, and survival does not inevitably indicate success.

More recently, several researchers have undertaken systematic studies of the alliance stability/instability construct, including Chi (2000), Das and Teng (2000), Reuer and Leiblein (2000), Yan (1998), and Yan and Zeng (1999). For example, after a careful review and synthesis of the current alliance literature, Yan and Zeng proposed the following redefinition of instability: "Instability refers to the extent to which the [alliance] alters its strategic directions, renegotiates its contract/agreements, reconfigures its ownership and/or management structures, or changes the relationship with its parents or the relationship between the parents that may have a significant effect on the venture's performance" (1999, 405).

INTEGRATING ALLIANCE RESEARCH STREAMS

Four noteworthy streams in current alliance research have been discussed. Although such conceptualization is useful, it should be strongly emphasized that these streams represent inextricably interlinked processes, not surgically separable phenomena. For instance, the choice and availability of capable, trustworthy partners will favorably influence the selection of an alliance mode of organizational structure, reduce control/conflict problems, and improve stability/performance levels. Such pulling together of each of the four streams is evident, for example, in Serapio and Cascio 1996.

Indeed, as will be discussed shortly, there is a need to focus on such (invisible) management decision-making processes, not merely on the (visible) outcomes of those processes. As Wood and Gray (1991, 143) observed, most studies "leap from preconditions to outcomes, leaving us with a 'black box' to cover the area in between." As such, Parkhe (1993a) proposed that one way to accelerate alliance theory development would be to focus research on the concepts of trust, reciprocity, opportunism, and forbearance (fig. 8.1). In their essay "A Theory of Cooperation in International Business," Buckley and Casson (1988, 32) noted that the essence of voluntary interfirm cooperation lies in "coordination effected through mutual forbearance." Forbearance becomes possible only when there is reciprocal behavior (Axelrod 1984) and mutual trust (Thorelli 1986), which, in turn, only come about given an absence of opportunism (Williamson 1985).

Despite being at the "core" of alliances, these concepts are often substantially or totally ignored. Integrating past research and raising the level of alliance theory development will require greater attention to these core concepts in the future. Although some theoretical integration is now evident (e.g., Hitt et al. 2000; Tsang 2000), much work remains ahead in matching methods to the important research questions in alliances.

METHODOLOGICAL ORIENTATIONS

The current body of alliance research has been lauded for containing "many studies addressing diverse aspects of alliances in theoretically imaginative and methodologically sound ways" (Parkhe 1993a, 232). However, as in management research generally (Bettis 1991), alliance studies tend to overemphasize certain methodological approaches while neglecting others. As Bettis observed, "Current norms of the field seem strongly biased toward large sample multivariate statistical studies. This leads to a large database mentality, in which large-scale mail surveys and ready-made databases such as Compustat, CRSP, and PIMS are often favored. . . . Qualitative studies do appear in the journals but they are the exception" (1991, 316). Such a bias is reflected by a representative sample of alliance studies from the period 1995–2000, shown in table 8.1.

Inasmuch as the content and process of scientific inquiry are intertwined, this bias creates a mismatch: Large-scale mail surveys and ready-made databases are ill-equipped to capture the "soft" core concepts outlined in figure 8.1. Three conclusions follow. One, major gaps exist in the

TABLE 8.1. Select Alliance Studies: 1995–2001

Study	Research Problem	Primary Dimension in Figure 8.1	Major Data Sources	Data Analytic Technique
Ariño & de la Torre 1998	Model of collaboration process, application to a failed alliance	Control/conflict issues	Archival and interview data	Longitudinal case study
Brouthers & Bamossy 1997	Influence of key stakeholders on alliance negotiations	Control/conflict issues	Interviews	Case studies
Chi 2000	Model for the option to acquire or divest an alliance	Alliance stability/performance	N/A	N/A
Chung, Singh, & Lee 2000	Factors that drive alliance formation between firms	Partner selection/characteristics	Archival data	Logistic regression analysis
Contractor & Kundu 1998	Optimum choice of organizational mode	Control/conflict issues	Mail survey	Discriminant analysis, LOGIT
Cullen, Johnson & Sakano 1995	Antecedents of commitment in alliances	Control/conflict issues	Mail survey	OLS regression, structural equation modeling
Das & Teng 2000	Framework for alliance instabilities	Alliance stability/performance	N/A	N/A
Dussauge Garrette, & Mitchell 2000	The outcomes and durations of alliances among competitors	Alliance stability/performance	*Automotive News, Aviation Technology, Space Technology*	Maximum likelihood binomial logistic regression
Elg 2000	Role of home-market relationships in a company's choice of foreign partners	Partner selection/characteristics	N/A	N/A
Gulati 1995a	Choice of governance structures in alliances	Partner selection/characteristics	CATI database	Logit model
Gulati 1995b	How social structure affects alliance formation patterns	Partner selection/characteristics	Worldscope, CATI	Dynamic panel model

Gulati 1999	The role of network resources in determining alliance formation	Motives for alliance formation	Worldscope, COMPUSTAT, Nikkei; Disclosure	Dynamic panel model
Gulati & Singh 1998	Why firms choose different governance structures across their alliances	Control/conflict issues	CATI database	Multinomial logistic regression
Hagedoorn & Narula 1996	Company choices of organizational models	Control/conflict issues	CATI database	"Literature-based alliance counting"
Inkpen & Dinur 1998	Integrating alliance into a firm's knowledge creation system	Control/conflict issues	Field interviews	Longitudinal case study
Kashlak, Chandran, & DiBenedetto 1998	Test of reciprocity between U.S. and foreign companies in telecommunications	Partner selection/characteristics	FCC (Washington, DC)	Combination time series/cross-sectional
Khanna, Gulati, & Nohria 1998	How the tension between cooperation and competition affects the dynamics of learning alliances	Control/conflict issues	N/A	N/A
Kotabe & Swan 1995	The role of strategic alliances on product innovativeness	Alliance stability/performance	WSJ announcements	Content analysis, ANCOVA
Koza & Lewin 1998	Evolutionary framework of alliances	Motives for alliance formation	N/A	N/A
Larsson et al. 1998	Managing the interorganizational learning dilemma	Control/conflict issues	N/A	N/A
Madhok 1995	Rationale for cooperative approach toward alliances based on trust	Alliance stability/performance	N/A	N/A
Makino & Beamish 1998	Incidence, performance, and survival likelihood of alliances	Motives for alliance formation	Secondary data (Japanese sources)	Log-linear model, chi-square
Millington & Bayliss 1995	Incidence and motivation for alliances between U.K. and EU firms	Control/conflict issues	Extel U.K. Quoted Companies List	Archival, case study
Parkhe 1998a, 1998b	Understanding and building trust in international alliances	Control/conflict issues	N/A	N/A
Powell, Koput, & Smith-Doerr 1996	Tracking the locus of innovation: in individual firms or in networks of learning?	Motives for alliance formation	Bioscan	Panel regression model
Rao & Schmidt 1998	Influence tactics in international alliance negotiations	Control/conflict issues	Mail survey	Multiple regression, MANOVA

(continued)

TABLE 8.1.—Continued

Study	Research Problem	Primary Dimension in Figure 8.1	Major Data Sources	Data Analytic Technique
Reuer 2000	Effects of alliance formation and types of alliance termination	Alliance stability/performance	F&S Index, Lexis-Nexis	Event study
Reuer & Koza 2000	Relationship between asymmetric information and indigestibility perspectives of alliances	Alliance stability/performance	F&S Index, Lexis-Nexis	Event study methodology
Reuer & Leiblein 2000	Effect of investment in foreign subsidiaries and alliances on enhancing corporate flexibility and reducing risk	Alliance stability/performance	COMPUSTAT, CRSP, Directory of International Affiliations	OLS regression model
Shenkar & Li 1999	Do firms seek knowledge in a complementary area or in same area as currently?	Motives for alliance formation	Mail survey	Logistic regression model
Simonin 1999a	The role of "causally ambiguous" nature of knowledge in the knowledge transfer process	Control/conflict issues	Mail survey	Maximum likelihood LISREL VIII
Simonin 1999b	Role of knowledge ambiguity in the knowledge transfer process	Control/conflict issues	Mail survey	Maximum likelihood LISREL VIII
Stuart 1998	Predicting alliance formation from network-based mapping	Partner selection/characteristics	Dataquest	Random effects probit regression
Yan 1998	Tracing the destabilizing and stabilizing forces in alliances	Alliance stability/performance	N/A	N/A
Yan & Zeng 1999	Reconceptualization of the alliance instability construct	Alliance stability/performance	N/A	N/A
Young-Ybarra & Wiersema 1999	Determinants of strategic flexibility	Control/conflict issues	Not reported	Maximum likelihood LISREL VIII
Zaheer, McEvily, & Perrone 1998	Model of performance based on interpersonal and interorganizational trust	Alliance stability/performance	Mail survey	Maximum likelihood LISREL

literature regarding crucial, invisible alliance management processes. Two, addressing these gaps will require a significant reorientation in conceptual foci (from the rectangles to the inner circle of fig. 8.1). Three, this reorientation, in turn, will require the use of appropriate empirical research methods. These methods must be sufficiently powerful and rigorous in generating valid, reliable data that further our understanding of trust, reciprocity, opportunism, and forbearance.

One such method is case studies. In a departure from number-crunching studies, a case study would permit researchers to "get close to the action" of the various life-cycle stages of alliances (Reuer 2000), for example, through open-ended interviews with top management and persons directly involved in the alliance, attendance at select executive meetings, and even quantitative data from questionnaires (a survey embedded within a case study) (Yin 1984). In the interviews, key actors are asked about the facts of the alliance, in addition to their opinions and insights about the events (Eisenhardt 1989). (Mail surveys and secondary data typically sacrifice this richness and subtlety of understanding because there is little opportunity for clarification of questions or elaboration of answers.) Such interviews can be extremely fruitful, because interviewees can provide crucial insights, suggest sources of corroboratory evidence, and even initiate access to such sources.

However, interviews can be subject to problems of bias, poor recall, and poor or inaccurate articulation. Therefore, to test for convergence, the interview evidence must be triangulated with multiple data sources. These include archival records and documentation. Archival corroboration involves cross-reference to databases, news clippings, and other reports in the mass media. Documentation research involves the systematic collection and examination of relevant company records and documents, including, especially, the proposal, formal studies, and progress reports regarding the alliance.

The data thus obtained lend themselves to systematic and rigorous data analytic techniques, such as explanation building, pattern matching, and time-series analysis (Miles and Huberman 1984; Yin 1984). Parkhe (1993a, 249–51) showed that each technique is especially well suited for answering specific, probing research questions about "fuzzy" alliance management processes that have remained shielded from scientific inquiry.

Notwithstanding the unique potential of case studies for rigorous alliance theory advancement, no single methodological approach (including case studies) is self-sufficient and capable of producing a well-rounded theory that simultaneously maximizes the research quality criteria of construct validity, internal validity, external validity, and reliability. Since seemingly diverse approaches (such as inductive/deductive, theory generation/theory testing, and qualitative/quantitative) complement and reinforce each other, once the "soft" core concepts become better understood via case studies, the unique strengths of the other approaches should be exploited by undertaking studies that draw upon the emergent grounded theory from case studies but go further.

A good example of triangulation of data obtained using multiple data sources and multiple methodological approaches is found in Beamish 1988. His study of alliances in developing countries used case study research on a set of twelve "comparative core cases," personal interviews, and questionnaires. The questionnaire findings lent themselves to nonparametric statistical analysis, and this analysis was supplemented by interview data. A further strength of the research design of this study is that data were collected from the joint venture general manager, the MNE partner, and the local partner. Soliciting information from each major player in the alliance provides a more balanced picture of alliance operation and enhances confidence in the findings. Future researchers should attempt to emulate this feature of the Beamish study, although, admittedly, doing so would increase the resource commitment to the project.

Other innovative ways exist to research the complex phenomenon of alliances. For example, Larsson (1993) sought to combine the benefits of idiographic case studies and nomothetic surveys through the case survey methodology. This approach conducts quantitative analysis of patterns across case studies to produce generalizable, cross-sectional analysis and indepth, processual analysis. Given the previous discussion about the need for merging rich insights from case studies with the unique strengths of other approaches, the case survey methodology may occupy a particularly important place in future alliance research.

FUTURE RESEARCH OPPORTUNITIES

International alliances represent a fertile area for timely, exciting research questions on a topic of growing importance. Some of the problems and prospects were touched upon earlier. For example, although trust is alleged to be a central concept in alliances (Thorelli 1986), it remains poorly understood in terms of its conceptual domain, antecedents, and consequences. Methodologically, alliance-specific data are often unavailable, since companies tend to report consolidated company-wide data; in addition, it is desirable to view the entire life cycle of alliances as a series of interconnected stages rather than studying isolated elements.

These observations share a common thread. They are symptomatic of the need for a renewed focus on invisible management processes, a shift that must be accompanied by a reorientation in research designs. There are, however, encouraging signs. Of the thirty-eight representative alliance studies shown in table 8.1, approximately 13 percent focus on alliance motives, 18 percent on partner selection/characteristics, 40 percent on control/conflict issues, and 29 percent on alliance stability/performance issues. This breakdown marks a huge shift from past research, which concentrated primarily on counting and classifying alliance motives and partner characteristics, to more complex issues involving control, conflict, stability, and performance. Although table 8.1 certainly does not represent a comprehensive compilation of the entire universe of alliance studies published between 1995 and 2000, it seems safe to say that we have moved beyond early work to potentially more fruitful studies.

Building on and extending recent research, I propose three areas that are especially ripe for deeper empirical work and theoretical insights: "soft" aspects of collaboration, knowledge and organizational learning, and network embeddedness.

"SOFT" ASPECTS OF COLLABORATION

Formal contracts, though necessary, are not a substitute for informal understandings. Even though formal contracts can provide a basic framework, they cannot possibly anticipate all future contingencies, let alone adequately deal with them (Macneil 1978; Williamson 1985). Given the double uncertainty of unknown future events and a partner's responses to those events, trust emerges as a central organizing principle in alliances. Recognizing the critical lubricating role of trust (and associated variables), several studies have recently addressed the "soft" aspects of collaboration (fig. 8.1), including Peng and Shenkar 1997; Kashlak, Chandran, and Di Benedetto 1998; Parkhe 1998a, 1998b, 2000; Das and Teng 1998, 2000; Khanna, Gulati, and Nohria 1998; Yan and Zeng 1999; and Zaheer, McEvily, and Perrone 1998.

Yet, interesting and important questions remain, as depicted in the circle portion of figure 8.2. What is trust, how do we know when it exists,

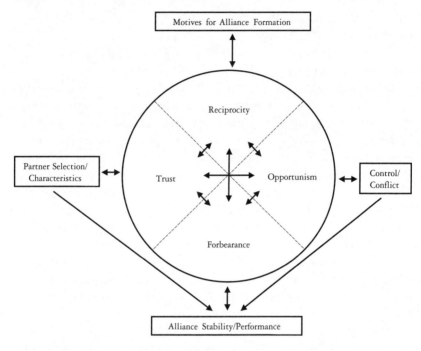

FIGURE 8.2. Extension of integrative framework: focus on "soft" aspects of collaboration

and how can it be measured? Does trust mean fundamentally the same thing across countries and across cultures, or are there important differences that international alliance managers and international management researchers must understand? How do the constructs of trust, reciprocity, opportunism, and forbearance relate to each other, and, based on this understanding, can trust be deliberately generated in an alliance?

KNOWLEDGE AND ORGANIZATIONAL LEARNING

Worldwide learning is one of the pillars of competitive success (Bartlett and Ghoshal 2000), and nowhere is this principle more forcefully applicable than in international alliances (Dussauge, Garrette, and Mitchell 2000; Simonin 1999a, 1999b; Shenkar and Li 1999; Inkpen and Beamish 1997; Inkpen and Dinur 1998; Larsson et al. 1998; Arino and de la Torre 1998; Powell, Koput, and Smith-Doerr 1996). Despite the recent surge of interest in this topic, however, much remains to be learned about the primary

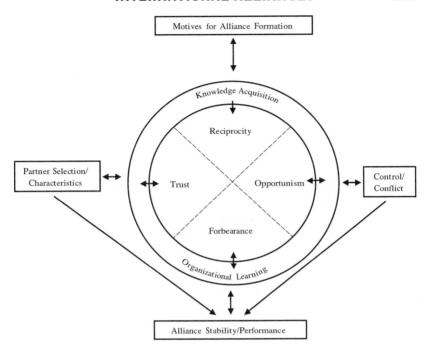

FIGURE 8.3. Extension of integrative framework: focus on knowledge and organizational learning

currency in this "information age," namely, knowledge. We need to better understand the conditions under which alliances provide a platform for firms to leverage each other's skills versus those under which alliances become vehicles for the theft of core technologies and the erosion of competitive strength. Are there in fact international asymmetries in the ability with which firms internalize a partner's skills (Hamel 1991)? What must managers do to effectively monitor information flows across the alliance membrane, protect their "family jewels," while at the same time participating in alliances and enhancing each partner's long-term competitiveness? Figure 8.3 represents a research agenda focused on these issues.

NETWORK EMBEDDEDNESS

It is becoming increasingly apparent that firms exist not in a social vacuum but in a social network of relationships, and this network drives and constrains the types of cooperative and competitive strategies a company may choose. In the industries of airlines, autos, biotechnology, and multimedia, it is networks, rather than individual companies, that are battling it out on a worldwide playing field.

Following this trend, the network paradigm is attracting considerable research attention (Stuart 1998; Gulati 1995a, 1995b, 1999; Gulati and Singh 1998). As shown in figure 8.4, important theoretical and empirical contributions are needed and possible in this area. Why is network formation more advanced in some industries than in others? Can we expect competition in all industries to migrate from individual firms to dyadic alliances to networks? What factors explain strategic blocks (relatively dense subnetworks of closely allied firms within a network)? What must each focal firm attempt to do, not only to position itself effectively within its own network but also to position the entire network effectively against competing networks?

These research questions are part of a larger mosaic of alliance theory development, which may best be appreciated by taking a metaperspective of the field. This perspective should integrate (1) diverse but related theoretical approaches that bear upon the alliance phenomenon; (2) the range of research designs that can (and should) be selectively employed in future research; and (3) the levels of analysis that must be systematically studied and integrated. Figure 8.5 provides such a metaperspective.

Some cells in figure 8.5 (e.g., surveys of individual managers using the strategic behavior approach) are overdeveloped, while other, potentially fruitful cells (e.g., multilevel case studies using the organizational learning perspective) are underdeveloped. The potential value of figure 8.5 lies in its full depiction of the intersection of theories, methods, and levels, from which the most intriguing, least explored combinations may be chosen for study. Clearly, certain methods are more compatible with particular theoretical approaches than others. As Kogut observed, "case studies of industries or a few ventures will be the most appealing methodology to provide initial insight into transaction cost and transfer of organizational know-how motivations" (1988, 329). Researchers must be careful not to become wedded to any particular theoretical or methodological approaches, for doing so binds judgment and creates a "trained incapacity" to appreciate factors outside of those approaches (Poole and Van de Ven 1989). Although each approach may provide a useful research lens, no approach alone is sufficient to encompass the complexity of international alliances.

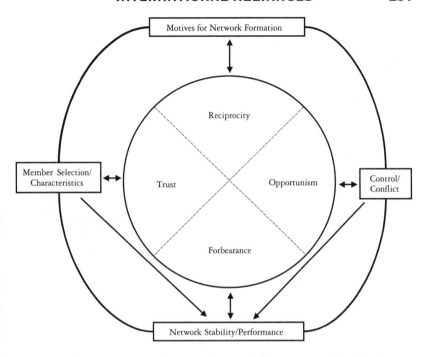

FIGURE 8.4. Extension of integrative framework: focus on network embeddedness

CONCLUSION

This chapter's brief review of the past, present, and future of alliance research suggests that this body of work has evolved tremendously since the early work of Friedman and Kalmanoff (1961). Although a great deal has been learned, much important work lies ahead.

International alliances are complex, mixed-motive (simultaneously competitive and cooperative), cross-border relationships. In global competition, they represent a way to *compete through cooperation.* Research on alliances has gravitated toward four major topics: motives for alliance formation, partner selection/characteristics, control/conflict, and alliance stability/performance. Although each topic is individually important, there has been little effort to reintegrate the insights into a higher-order theory of alliances.

The lack of such effort may be traced to the dominant methodological focus of current research (table 8.1), which leans strongly toward "hard,"

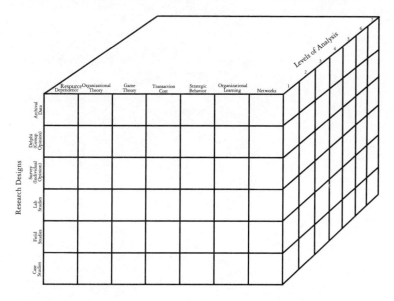

Levels of Analysis
1. Individual manager (alliance)
2. Individual managers (parent firms)
3. Organizational (alliance)
4. Organizational (parent firms)
5. Interorganizational (dyadic relationships between parents, between alliance and parents)
6. Network (alliance embedded in surrounding industry structure)
7. Multilevel (simultaneously individual, organizational, network levels)

FIGURE 8.5. A menu for alliance research: effective intersection of theories, methods, and levels

quantitative approaches. The need for the next phase of alliance research is to develop deeper understanding of invisible management processes, which involve crucial, "soft" variables (figure 8.1). Consequently, a methodological reorientation of future studies may be in order. Such reorientation would build upon the lessons from prior research and would permit theories of alliance processes to catch up with theories of alliance outcomes. As international alliances continue their powerful sweep across the global business landscape, alliance research will likely become even more timely and relevant to the study of international management.

REFERENCES

Andersen Consulting. 1999. Dispelling the myths of alliances. *Outlook* (October), special edition.

Arino, A., and Jose de la Torre. 1998. Learning from failure: Towards an evolutionary model of collaborative ventures. *Organization Science* 9:306–25.

Axelrod, R. 1984. *The evolution of cooperation.* New York: Basic Books.

Bartlett, C. A., and S. Ghoshal. 2000. *Transnational management.* Homewood, IL: Irwin.

Beamish, P. W. 1988. *Multinational joint ventures in developing countries.* London: Routledge.

Beamish, P. W., and John C. Banks. 1987. Equity joint ventures and the theory of multinational enterprises. *Journal of International Business Studies* (summer): 1–16.

Beamish, P. W., and J. P. Killing, eds. 1997. *Cooperative strategies.* San Francisco: New Lexington Press. (The three volumes in this collection include *Asian Pacific perspectives, North American perspectives,* and *European perspectives.*)

Bettis, R. A. 1991. Strategic management and the straightjacket: An editorial essay. *Organization Science* 2:315–19.

Brouthers, K. D., and G. J. Bamossy. 1997. The role of key stakeholders in international joint venture negotiations: Case studies from Eastern Europe. *Journal of International Business Studies* 28:285–308.

Buckley, P. J., and M. Casson. 1988. A theory of cooperation in international business. In F. J. Contractor and P. Lorange, eds., *Cooperative strategies in international business,* 31–53. Lexington, MA: Lexington Books.

Chi, T. 2000. Option to acquire or divest a joint venture. *Strategic Management Journal* 21:665–87.

Chung, S., H. Singh, and K. Lee. 2000. Complementarity, status similarity, and social capital as drivers of alliance formation. *Strategic Management Journal* 21:1–22.

Contractor, F. J., and S. K. Kundu. 1998. Modal choice in a world of alliances: Analyzing organizational forms in the international hotel sector. *Journal of International Business Studies* 29:325–58.

Contractor, F. J., and P. Lorange. 1988. Why should firms cooperate? In F. J. Contractor and P. Lorange, eds., *Cooperative strategies in international business.* Lexington, MA: Lexington Books.

Cullen, J. B., J. L. Johnson, and T. Sakano. 1995. Japanese and local partner commitment to international joint ventures: Psychological consequences of outcomes and investments in the international joint venture relationship. *Journal of International Business Studies* 26:91–115.

Das, T. K., and B-S. Teng. 1998. Between trust and control: Developing confidence in partner cooperation in alliances. *Academy of Management Review* 23:491–512.

———. 2000. Instabilities of strategic alliances: An internal tensions perspective. *Organization Science* 11:77–101.

Dussauge, P., and B. Garrette. 1995. Determinants of success in international strategic alliances: Evidence from the global aerospace industry. *Journal of International Business Studies* 26:505–30.

Dussauge, P., B. Garrette, and W. Mitchell. 2000. Learning from competing partners: Outcomes and durations of scale and link alliances in Europe, North America, and Asia. *Strategic Management Journal* 21:99–126.

Eisenhardt, K. M. 1989. Building theories from case study research. *Academy of Management Review* 14:532–50.

Elg, U. 2000. Firms' home-market relationships: Their role when selecting international alliance partners. *Journal of International Business Studies* 31:169–77.

Fedor, K. J., and W. B. Werther. 1995. Making sense of cultural factors in international alliances. *Organizational Dynamics* (spring):33–48.

Friedmann, W. G., and G. Kalmanoff, eds. 1961. *Joint international business ventures.* New York: Columbia University Press.

Geringer, J. M. 1991. Strategic determinants of partner selection criteria in international joint ventures. *Journal of International Business Studies* 22:41–62.

Geringer, J. M., and L. Hebert. 1989. Control and performance of international joint ventures. *Journal of International Business Studies* 20:235–54.

Gomes-Casseres, B. 1987. Joint venture instability: Is it a problem? *Columbia Journal of World Business* (spring):97–102.

Gulati, R. 1995a. Does familiarity breed trust? The implications of repeated ties for contractual choice in alliances. *Academy of Management Journal* 38:85–112.

———. 1995b. Social structure and alliance formation patterns: A longitudinal analysis. *Administrative Science Quarterly* 40:619–52.

———. 1998. Alliances and networks. *Strategic Management Journal* 19:293–317.

———. 1999. Network location and learning: The influence of network resources and firm capabilities on alliance formation. *Strategic Management Journal* 20:397–420.

Gulati, R., and H. Singh. 1998. The architecture of cooperation: Managing coordination costs and appropriation concerns in strategic alliances. *Administrative Science Quarterly* 43:781–814.

Hagedoorn, J., and R. Narula. 1996. Choosing organizational modes of strategic technology partnering: International and sectoral differences. *Journal of International Business Studies* 27:265–84.

Hagedoorn, J., and B. Sadowski. 1999. The transition from strategic technology alliances to mergers and acquisitions: An exploratory study. *Journal of Management Studies* 36 (1): 87–107.

Hamel, G. 1991. Competition for competence and interpartner learning within international strategic alliances. *Strategic Management Journal* 12:83–104.

Harrigan, K. R. 1985. *Strategies for joint ventures.* Lexington, MA: Lexington Books.

———. 1986. *Managing for joint venture success.* Lexington, MA: Lexington Books.

———. 1988. Strategic alliances and partner asymmetries. In F. Contractor and P. Lorange, eds., *Cooperative strategies in international business.* Lexington, MA: Lexington Books.

Hennart, Jean-François. 1988. A transaction costs theory of equity joint ventures. *Strategic Management Journal* 9:361–74.

———. 1991. The transaction costs theory of joint ventures: An empirical study of Japanese subsidiaries in the United States. *Management Science* 37:483–97.

Hergert, M., and D. Morris. 1988. Trends in international collaborative agreements. In F. Contractor and P. Lorange, eds., *Cooperative strategies in international business.* Lexington, MA: Lexington Books.

Hitt, M. A., M. T. Dacin, E. Levitas, J-L. Arregle, and A. Borza. 2000. Partner selection in emerging and developed market contexts: Resource-based and organizational learning perspectives. *Academy of Management Journal* 43:449–67.

Inkpen, A. C., and P. W. Beamish. 1997. Knowledge, bargaining power, and the instability of international joint ventures. *Academy of Management Review* 22:177–202.

Inkpen, A. C., and A. Dinur. 1998. Knowledge management processes and international joint ventures. *Organization Science* 9:454–68.

Kashlak, R. J., R. Chandran, and C. A. Di Benedetto. 1998. Reciprocity in international business: A study of telecommunications alliances and contracts. *Journal of International Business Studies* 29:281–304.

Khanna, T., R. Gulati, and N. Nohria. 1998. The dynamics of learning alliances: Competition, cooperation, and relative scope. *Strategic Management Journal* 19:193–210.

Killing, J. P. 1982. How to make a global joint venture work. *Harvard Business Review* May–June: 120–27.

Knecht, B. 1994. Crossborder deals jumped last year to record levels. *Wall Street Journal* January 25, C19.

Kogut, B. 1988. Joint ventures: Theoretical and empirical perspectives. *Strategic Management Journal* 9:319–32.

Kotabe, M., and K. S. Swan. 1995. The role of strategic alliances on high-technology new product development. *Strategic Management Journal* 16:621–36.

Koza, M. P., and A. Y. Lewin. 1998. The co-evolution of strategic alliances. *Organization Science* 9:255–64.

Lane, H. W., and P. W. Beamish. 1990. Cross-cultural cooperative behavior in joint ventures in LDCs. *Management International Review* 30:87–102.

Larsson, R. 1993. Case survey methodology: Quantitative analysis of patterns across case studies. *Academy of Management Journal* 36:1515–46.

Larsson, R., L. Bengtsson, K. Henriksson, and J. Sparks. 1998. The interorganizational learning dilemma: Collective knowledge development in strategic alliances. *Organization Science* 9:285–305.

Li, J., and O. Shenkar. 1997. The perspectives of local partners. In P. W. Beamish and J. P. Killing, eds., *Cooperative strategies: Asian Pacific perspectives,* 300–322. San Francisco: New Lexington Press.

Lin, X., and R. Germain. 1998. Sustaining satisfactory joint venture relationships: The role of conflict resolution strategy. *Journal of International Business Studies* 29:179–96.

Luo, Y. 1999. *Entry and cooperative strategies in international business expansion.* Westport, CT: Quorum Books.

Lynch, R. P. 1989. *The practical guide to joint ventures and corporate alliances.* New York: Wiley.

Macneil, I. R. 1978. Contracts: Adjustment of long-term economic relations under classical, neoclassical, and relational contract law. *Northwestern University Law Review* 72:854–902.

Madhok, A. 1995. Revisiting multinational firms' tolerance for joint ventures: A trust-based approach. *Journal of International Business Studies* 26:117–37.

Makino, S., and P. W. Beamish. 1998. Performance and survival of joint ventures with non-conventional ownership structures. *Journal of International Business Studies* 29:797–818.

Miles, M. B., and M. A. Huberman. 1984. *Qualitative data analysis.* Beverly Hills, CA: Sage.

Millington, A. I., and B. T. Bayliss. 1995. Transnational joint ventures between UK and EU manufacturing companies and the structure of competition. *Journal of International Business Studies* 26:239–54.

Ohmae, K. 1989. The global logic of strategic alliances. *Harvard Business Review* (March/April):143–54.

Oliver, C. 1990. Determinants of interorganizational relationships: Integration and future directions. *Academy of Management Review* 15:241–65.

Ouchi, W. G. 1980. Markets, bureaucracies, and clans. *Administrative Science Quarterly* 25:129–42.

Parkhe, A. 1991. Interfirm diversity, organizational learning, and longevity in global strategic alliances. *Journal of International Business Studies* 22:579–601.

———. 1993a. "Messy" research, methodological predispositions, and theory development in international joint ventures. *Academy of Management Review* 18:227–68.

———. 1993b. Strategic alliance structuring: A game theoretic and transaction cost examination of interfirm cooperation. *Academy of Management Journal* 36:794–829.

———. 1993c. Partner nationality and the structure-performance relationship in strategic alliances. *Organization Science* 4:301–24.

———. 1996. International joint ventures. In B. J. Punnett and O. Shenkar, eds., *Handbook for international management research,* 429–59. Cambridge, MA: Blackwell.

———. 1998a. Understanding trust in international alliances. *Journal of World Business* 33:219–40.

———. 1998b. Building trust in international alliances. *Journal of World Business* 33:417–37.

———. 2000. Hurdles in the hurtle toward an age of alliances. *Business Horizons.* September–October: 2–32.

Peng, P. W., and O. Shenkar. 1997. *The meltdown of trust: A process model of strategic alliance dissolution.* Paper presented at the annual meeting of the Academy of Management, Boston.

Poole, M. S., and A. H. Van de Ven. 1989. Using paradox to build management and organization theories. *Academy of Management Review* 14:562–78.

Powell, W. W., K. W. Koput, and L. Smith-Doerr. 1996. Interorganizational collaboration and the locus of innovation: Networks of learning in biotechnology. *Administrative Science Quarterly* 41:116–45.

Rao, A., and S. Schmidt. 1998. A behavioral perspective on negotiating international alliances. *Journal of International Business Studies* 29:665–94.

Reuer, J. J. 2000. Parent firm performance across international joint venture life-cycle stages. *Journal of International Business Studies* 31:1–20.

Reuer, J. J., and M. P. Koza. 2000. Asymmetric information and joint venture performance: Theory and evidence for domestic and international joint ventures. *Strategic Management Journal* 21:81–88.

Reuer, J. J., and M. J. Leiblein. 2000. Downside risk implications of multinationality and international joint ventures. *Academy of Management Journal* 43:203–14.

Rieger, F., and D. Wong-Rieger. 1990. Conflicts in international joint ventures as mismatches in strategic objectives and acculturation orientation. Paper presented at the annual meeting of the Strategic Management Society, Stockholm.

Root, F. R. 1987. *Entry strategies for international markets.* Lexington, MA: Lexington Books.

Serapio, M. G., and W. F. Cascio. 1996. End-games in international alliances. *Academy of Management Executive* 10 (1): 62–73.

Shenkar, O., and J. Li. 1999. Knowledge search in international cooperative ventures. *Organization Science* 10:134–43.

Shenkar, O., and Y. Zeira. 1992. Role conflict and role ambiguity of chief executive officers in international joint ventures. *Journal of International Business Studies* 23:55–75.

Simonin, B. L. 1999a. Ambiguity and the process of knowledge transfer in strategic alliances. *Strategic Management Journal* 20:595–623.

———. 1999b. Transfer of marketing knowhow in international strategic alliances: An empirical investigation of the role and antecedents of knowledge ambiguity. *Journal of International Business Studies* 30:463–90.

Stuart, T. E. 1998. Network positions and propensities to collaborate: An investigation of strategic alliance formation in a high-tech industry. *Administrative Science Quarterly* 43:668–98.

Stuckey, J. 1983. *Vertical integration and joint ventures in the aluminum industry.* Cambridge, MA: Harvard University Press.

Tallman, S. B., and O. Shenkar. 1994. A managerial decision model of international cooperative venture formation. *Journal of International Business Studies* 25:91–113.

Thorelli, H. B. 1986. Networks: Between markets and hierarchies. *Strategic Management Journal* 7:37–51.

Tsang, E. W. K. 2000. Transaction cost and resource-based explanations of joint ventures: A comparison and synthesis. *Organization Studies* 21:215–42.

Venkatraman, N., and V. Ramanujam. 1986. Measurement of business performance in strategy research: A comparison of approaches. *Academy of Management Review* 11:801–14.

Wille, J. R. 1988. Joint venturing strategies. In John D. Carter, Robert F. Cushman, and C. Scott Hartz, eds., *The handbook of joint venturing.* Homewood, IL: Dow Jones-Irwin.

Williamson, O. E. 1975. *Markets and hierarchies: Analysis and antitrust implications.* New York: Free Press.

———. 1985. *The economic institutions of capitalism.* New York: Free Press.

Williamson, O. E., and W. G. Ouchi. 1981. The markets and hierarchies program of research: Origins, implications, prospects. In A. Van de Ven and William F. Joyce, eds., *Perspectives on organization design and behavior.* New York: Wiley.

Wood, D. J., and B. Gray. 1991. Toward a comprehensive theory of collaboration. *Journal of Applied Behavioral Science* 27:139–62.

Yan, A. 1998. Structural stability and reconfiguration of international joint ventures. *Journal of International Business Studies* 29:773–96.

Yan, A., and M. Zeng. 1999. International joint venture instability: A critique of previous research, a reconceptualization, and directions for future research. *Journal of International Business Studies* 30:397–414.

Yin, R. K. 1984. *Case study research: Design and methods.* Beverly Hills, CA: Sage.

Young-Ybarra, C., and M. Wiersema. 1999. Strategic flexibility in information technology alliances: The influence of transaction cost economics and social exchange theory. *Organization Science* 10:439–59.

Zaheer, A., B. McEvily, and V. Perrone. 1998. Does trust matter? Exploring the effects of interorganizational and interpersonal trust on performance. *Organization Science* 9:141–59.

Zand, D. E. 1972. Trust and managerial problem solving. *Administrative Science Quarterly* 17:229–39.

Zucker, L. G. 1986. Production of trust. *Research in Organizational Behavior* 8:53–111.

CROSS-BORDER MERGERS
AND ACQUISITIONS

WHAT HAVE WE LEARNED?

Asli M. Arikan

Global cross-border merger-and-acquisition (M&A) activity grew by nearly 50 percent in 1999, and three-quarters of the cross-border deals took place in Western Europe (Wessel 2000). In some countries, cross-border M&A activity already exceeds domestic M&As. For instance, in 2000, cross-border M&As accounted for 54 percent of all Australian M&A activity (Lewis and Clyne 2001). Cross-border M&As in East Asia's crisis countries (Indonesia, Korea, Malaysia, and Thailand) rose sharply in value from U.S.$3 billion in 1996 to $22 billion in 1999, before falling slightly to $18 billion in 2000 (Ashoka and Negishi 2001). According to UNCTAD estimates for 1999, the total number of cross-border M&As was six thousand, with a total value of U.S.$720 billion (UNCTAD 2000, fig. I.4).

In this chapter cross-border M&A deals refer to deals involving firms from different nations. Cross-regional (interregional) M&A deals involve firms from different geographical regions, such as Europe and Asia. Intraregional M&A deals refer to transactions within the same geographical region. Finally, domestic M&A deals are those between firms registered in the same country. The bulk of the domestic M&A literature is concerned with U.S. domestic M&A deals as opposed to other countries' domestic M&As. Comparative M&A research concerns comparisons of domestic M&A activities in different countries but can extend to comparison of host, target, and dyad countries and hence to cross-border deals.

Figure 9.1 illustrates the various research designs available for comparative cross-border M&A research. It should also be noted that, with the exception of U.S. cross-border M&As, scant research is devoted to all the other possible comparative research designs.

The share of U.S. companies in worldwide M&A deals (both domestic and cross-border) decreased from 90 percent of worldwide M&A deal-transaction value in 1985 to 52 percent in 1999.[1] This decline corresponds to the increase in European and Asian deals (including both interregional and intraregional deals) in 1999, 42 percent and 6 percent, respectively. This statistic alone highlights the need to research non-U.S. domestic M&A (as well as intraregional cross-border) deals and provides opportunities for comparative research.

In all three regions (Europe, Asia, and the United States) the percentage (in terms of both the transaction value and the number of deals) of interregional deals (e.g., where at least one European and one Asian company is involved) is *higher* than intraregional deals (where both companies are from the same region). For example, the percentage of deals where at least one party is a European company is 46 percent of the worldwide M&A deals, whereas only 36 percent of the worldwide deals occur between European companies (intra-European deals).

The literature on U.S. domestic M&As is much more developed when compared to the non-U.S. domestic, cross-border (including cross-regional) M&A research. The main research clusters dealing with the phenomena of domestic M&As are shareholder wealth effects, strategic motivations and postevent performance results, industry consolidation and institutional environment, postevent integration phase, and differences and similarities in corporate cultures involved.

WHAT WE KNOW FROM DOMESTIC
U.S. M&A RESEARCH

Overall, empirical findings show that synergistic deals between strategically related companies result in higher postdeal returns for the acquiring firm due to economies of scale and scope, operating efficiencies (Bradley, Desai, and Kim 1988), and market power. Meanwhile, synergy realization is a function of the similarity and complementarity of the merging businesses, to the extent of interaction and coordination during the organizational integration process and the lack of employee resistance to the combined firm (Larsson and Finkelstein 1999). This finding highlights the

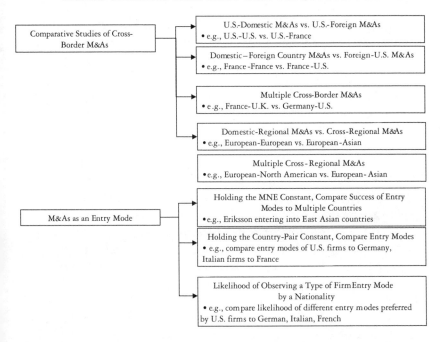

FIGURE 9.1. Empirical and case research typologies in cross-border mergers and acquisitions

importance of human resource management in the context of domestic M&As.

Shareholder wealth effects of M&As differ for targets and the acquirers: target shareholders earn on average a 20 to 30 percent premium while shareholders of acquiring firms on average break even at best (e.g., Jensen 1988; Jensen and Ruback 1983). There is also anecdotal evidence that the acquirers fail to realize expected synergies and thus rarely create economic wealth for their shareholders. One might speculate that the management of this complex corporate event is a main factor in determining the success of acquirers.

WEALTH EFFECTS OF CROSS-BORDER M&AS

A Bloomberg study of the thirty biggest cross-border deals completed in 1998 and 1999 showed an annualized return of less than 9 percent through March 2001 (Levy 2001). An analysis of eight cross-border deals announced since March 2000, with an average value of U.S.$470 million, has provided on average a modest return (McBeath and Bacha 2001). Thus, both cross-border and domestic (U.S.) M&As rarely create value for the acquirers' shareholders (Datta and Puia 1995).

Cultural distance, measured using the cultural distance index of Kogut and Singh (1988), is negatively related to the wealth effects for the acquirers' shareholders (Datta and Puia 1995). Managerial hubris (Roll 1986) has been one of the leading explanations of corporate diversification through M&A. The hubris hypothesis suggests that bidding managers make mistakes in evaluating target firms but undertake acquisitions presuming that their valuations are correct (Seth, Song, and Pettit 2000). The synergy hypothesis proposes that acquisitions take place when the combined value of the buyer and the target is higher than the sum of the stand-alone values of the two firms (Seth 1990; Bradley, Desai, and Kim 1988). Seth, Song, and Pettit (2000) tested managerial hubris against synergy as motives for foreign acquisitions of U.S. firms. Overall, the synergy hypothesis is the predominant explanation of acquisition motives. However, conditional on the existence of positive total postmerger value, the hubris hypothesis is supported in addition to the synergy explanation.

The wealth effects of cross-border acquisitions differ slightly from the case of domestic M&As. Dewenter (1995) compared the market reactions to takeover announcements of cross-border and domestic M&As in U.S. chemical and retail industries to test whether nationality of the acquirer makes a difference. The findings suggest that there is no statistically significant difference in the target shareholders' wealth gains in both cases. However, buyer nationality moderates the effect of transaction-related variables on the target premiums. Foreign buyers tend to pay higher premiums when they execute hostile takeovers when compared to the case of multiple rival bidders.

OVERVIEW OF CROSS-BORDER M&A EMPIRICAL STUDIES

When Daimler and Chrysler announced their grand transatlantic merger of equals in 1998, their purpose was to excel in every segment of cars and trucks on a global basis by uniting the most innovative and profitable American automaker with the prestigious manufacturer of Mercedes. . . . Both chairmen, Chrysler's Robert Eaton and Daimler's Juergen Schrempp, spouted effectively about future success—despite a 1998 joint study *conducted by their own two companies* that showed that 73 percent of the odds were stacked against the merger, they were able to sell it to their respective boards and shareholders—and to themselves.[2]

Research on cross-border acquisitions can be clustered into a number of streams: national cultural differences and its effects,[3] top management turnover and related conflicts, entry-mode choice, and knowledge transfer. In this section each of these main research streams will be highlighted by representative studies. Most of the studies focus on the postintegration stage. Very little emphasis, if any, is put on the preacquisition period. For instance, how do firms go about identifying suitable target local firms in a host country? Is there a gradual development of initial trading relationships into partnerships and further into internalization via acquisition? Do companies look for target firms in a region, and, if so, what are the comprehensive criteria for comparing these heterogeneous target firms from different countries?

INSTITUTIONAL ENVIRONMENT

Economics, taxes, and accounting and tax rules and regulations across countries have been shown to affect motivations behind cross-border acquisitions, as well as the performance of such ventures. In particular, the tax environment of the companies can affect every phase of cross-border acquisitions. In addition to the capital gains taxes, there might be transaction taxes, for example, stamp duty and other capital taxes, which can represent a significant additional cost to buying a foreign target (Driscoll et al. 2001). All of these issues might not be the central concern of management researchers, yet they represent additional sources of explanation (which need to be controlled for) for the very phenomena that we strive to understand and explain. Therefore, interdisciplinary research is particularly called for in this regard.

ROLE OF NATIONAL AND ORGANIZATIONAL CULTURES

Differences between the national cultures of firms engaging in M&As tend to be the most commonly used factor in differentiating performances between domestic and cross-border M&As. Managing organizational and national cultural differences as well as relative power issues are critical to the success of postacquisition integration (David and Singh 1993). Most of the limited number of studies that compare domestic versus cross-border M&As focus on the top management teams of the companies involved.

If we assume that top managers have valuable firm-specific information, a high turnover rate would be undesirable. On the other hand, from an organizational design perspective, the acquirer would want to replace the top management of the target firm to increase control. The relative standing theory (Frank 1985) asserts that individuals' perceptions of their status are based on how they compare their status to others in a proximate setting. Perceived cultural compatibility, loss of autonomy, and size are the constructs that measure relative standing. Moreover, relative standing theory (Frank 1985) predicts that the target firm's top executives are placed in a social setting in which they perceive their relative standing to have diminished compared to their previous status as well as to the top executives of the acquiring firm (Hambrick and Cannella 1993). Therefore, one would expect to see a high turnover rate of the target's top management team. But would cross-border M&As compound this negative relationship?

A study of 168 cross-border and 102 domestic acquisitions revealed that turnover rates of top executives of U.S. firms acquired by non-U.S. firms were significantly higher than the rates of domestic M&As. The nationality of the foreign acquirer was found to be an important predictor of turnover in certain acquisition categories (Krug and Hegarty 1997). In this study countries were clustered using Ronen and Shenkar's (1985) national culture categorization.

Postmerger integration phase is a vital component of a successful cross-border M&A activity. Theoretical research has argued that national cultural distance hinders cross-border acquisition performance by increasing the costs of integration. However, empirical findings regarding the effect of differences among national cultures in the context of cross-border M&As are mixed. For example, Morosini, Shane, and Singh (1998) provide findings that support *positive* association between national culture distance and cross-border acquisition performance of fifty-two cross-border acquisitions that took place between 1987 and 1992. Very et al.'s (1997) survey of top executives from recently acquired British and French companies reveals that the theory of relative standing explains poor postmerger performance. The findings suggest that cultural differences do not necessarily lead to postmerger lack of performance; however, loss of autonomy does. (Very et al. 1997).

Case studies also show mixed results. In a pilot study of six companies, national cultural differences between the target and the acquirer was one of the least significant variables affecting the success of postmerger integration (Kanter and Corn 1994). In contrast, Cartwright and Cooper (1993b) argue that neglecting cultural compatibility between the target and the acquirer leads to failure. Pablo (1994) found that, after controlling for industry and acquisition experience, other individual- or organizational-level factors such as task, cultural, and political characteristics of the acquisitions influence the successful postmerger integration.

Lubatkin et al. (1998) show that the administrative approaches used by firms with different nationalities (British and French) reflect their different heritages and that these differences were consistent with national differences and the theoretical perspectives of institutional development and cross-cultural studies. Over time, some firms develop an expertise in managing the integration process by coping with difficulties that result from firm-specific and nation-specific differences (Olie 1994; Calori, Lubatkin, and Very 1994). For example, a study of acquisitions in Hungary, the Czech Republic, Slovakia, and Poland shows that the appropriate management skills (knowledge of the partner's language and sensitivity toward cultural issues) are often underestimated compared to general business skills (Villinger 1996).

In recent years, cultural issues in M&As have been increasingly a research topic. In particular, integration processes and outcomes are affected by the human factors that most likely represent two different national contexts in the case of cross-border M&As. M&As result in high turnover of top management (e.g., Krug and Hegarty 1997), reduced job satisfaction and organizational commitment, and employee stress (e.g., Cartwright and Cooper 1995). Mainly, in an M&A event, human factors play a role in partner selection and cultural fit, management of postevent integration, and employee attitudes toward organizational change. In this context, successful integration means that the culture of the acquirers (dominant party) is imposed upon the target firm rather than introduced or adapted to the target's organizational culture (Cartwright 1998). It is important to note that most studies that dealt with the differences and similarities of corporate culture and the effect on M&A outcomes almost exclusively sampled *domestic* U.S. and U.K. corporate deals.

Yet, national *and* organizational cultural differences can play a significant role in the context of cross-border M&As. Morosini discusses the following example to illustrate the impact of organizational cultural differences in the context of the investment banking industry, which is considered to be a regulated and conventional global industry, thus easily compatible in terms of business practices around the globe. It has been observed that the aggressive, deal-oriented, and equity culture usually associated with Anglo-Saxon investment and merchant banks does not easily fuse with the more conservative culture of certain commercial banks, such as in Germany and Switzerland. "Thus, national cultural resistances and deep-rooted reactions can be greatly reinforced and further *anchored* as a result of differing corporate cultures that may exist at the base" of a cross-border M&A (Morosini 1999, 48; emphasis added).

Differences in national cultures of the firms involved in cross-border M&As also affect postevent business strategies. This is mainly because culture determines the types of sources of information to which members selectively attend and the way in which this information is evaluated and used in the organizational context (Schneider 1989). For example, Japanese firms make greater use of qualitative data than U.S. firms. Whether the relative weight placed on issues related to national culture will be greater than on issues related to corporate culture depends on the intensity of the influence of institutional context (national culture, governments, and ideologies) on business practices. In such cases, national and corporate cultures will be highly correlated, allowing the researcher to focus on one rather than both. In countries where the institutional context does not have an intensive effect on business practices, they are more likely to see a large differential between the national culture and the organizational culture of a specific firm. Therefore, it becomes imperative to account for both layers of culture in cross-border M&A studies.

HUMAN RESOURCE MANAGEMENT

A recent survey of top executives at 190 companies in Brazil, China, Hong Kong, the Philippines, Singapore, South Korea, and the United States revealed that three-quarters of executives were concerned with retaining key talent as one of the most critical factors of M&A integration success (Kay and Shelton 2000). As mentioned earlier, the departure of top executives has been extensively analyzed (e.g., Krug and Hegarty 1997), with most of the discussion related to national and corporate cultural differences and the effects on M&A integration and success.

However, there are more microlevel organizational behavior challenges due to the merging of two companies. This would be more of a concern in the context of cross-border M&As because the two sets of employees might represent two substantially different national cultures as well as corporate cultures. This is clearly one area where there is substantial room for innovative research to explore the micromechanisms of the cross-border M&A corporate event.

INTERNATIONALIZATION OF MNCS

If we look at the stock market reaction to multinational corporations (MNCs) announcing international acquisitions, evidence shows that there will be significant positive abnormal returns for shareholders of MNCs not operating in the target firm's country (Doukas and Travlos 1988). The positive abnormal returns will be higher when the U.S. firm expands into new industry and geographic markets—especially markets less developed than in the U.S. economy. Shareholders of MNCs gain the greatest benefits from foreign acquisitions when there is a simultaneous diversification across both industry and geography.

MNCs engage in cross-border M&As as an entry mode as an alternative to greenfield investments or international joint ventures (Kogut and Singh 1988). In this context, institutional environment, national cultures, and transaction costs economics have been utilized to predict success, as well as the occurrence of cross-border M&As (Brouthers and Brouthers 2000). In a related study, the findings suggest that Japanese firms entering the U.S. market prefer greenfield equity joint ventures over M&As when (1) the desired assets are linked to nondesired assets of the U.S. firm that is large and not divisionalized, (2) the Japanese firm has little prior exposure to the U.S. market and hence wants to avoid the post-M&A integration problems, (3) both the Japanese and the U.S. firm manufacture the same product, and (4) the industry that they are entering is growing neither very rapidly nor very slowly (Hennart and Reddy 1997). Japanese firms choose to enter into the United States via cross-border acquisition when (1) the Japanese firms tend to have weaker competitive advantages, (2) the industry is described as having a very high or slow growth rate, and (3) the scale of the investment is larger in comparison to the acquiring firm (Hennart and Park 1994).

Survival and location choices of entrants into new markets via cross-border acquisitions have also been research interests. McCloughan and Stone (1998) studied the survival of 252 foreign manufacturing plants in the northern region of the United Kingdom during the period 1970–93. The results suggest that greenfield entrants face a lower risk of failure than do acquisition entrants, particularly early in life. Moreover, the age of the indigenous plant at the point of the foreign takeover is positively related to the survival rates. In contrast, the home country of the parent firm and the location of the host country in the region did not have any significant explanatory power. A case study of the Gilette Company's acquisition of the Parker Pen Company illustrated that, to utilize global brands, MNCs need to strengthen local country units (Kanter and Dretler 1998). In this case study, multinational firms are argued to pursue cross-border acquisitions in a local country of operation to provide local integration across divisions to create within-country synergies.

Knowledge transfer is a key issue in interorganizational relationships. On the one hand, knowledge that is tacit, hard to codify, and context specific hinders successful transfer even within firms, let alone between firms. The problem of transfer would be more severe in the case of cross-border M&As. On the other hand, the value of the target to the acquirer might only reside in the target's firm-specific knowledge. In a multi-method study, Bresman, Birkinshaw, and Nobel (1999) investigated knowledge transfer in cross-border acquisitions using both questionnaire and case methodology. Findings based on the survey data suggest that the most important factors in successful transfer of technological know-how are the communication, visits, and meetings between the firms, as well as the time elapsed after the acquisition. In contrast, the transfer of patents depends on the size of the target, how recent the acquisition, and the articulability of the knowledge. In the initial postacquisition period, knowledge flows from the acquirer to the target, but over time it might evolve into a high-quality reciprocal knowledge transfer.

RESEARCH METHODS

Most of the studies on M&As use survey methodology to collect data, once the acquisitions are identified from the secondary data sources. Some studies, especially those examining countries other than the United States, supplement survey data with interviews. There is an emphasis on the use of descriptive statistics rather than formal models to test an hypothesis. However, in more recent studies one can see a more rigorous attempt to test various theories using formal models. In descriptive studies, it is not possible to determine causality; the research endeavor is largely limited to the establishment of relations between variables. However, in formal models, one has the opportunity to predict directional relations between the variables based on the theoretical approach employed. Such models also allow correction for sample selection biases using statistical techniques.

It is also imperative to develop a comparative perspective in assessing domestic M&As in order to have an appropriate benchmark for the cross-border M&A studies. Domestic M&As in the United States are presumed to be the control group in studies that deal with national cultural differences and top management turnover. However, an appropriate control group should be comparable to the acquirer company and represent the acquirer's domestic M&As rather than using a group of U.S. M&As. This approach immediately poses challenges in multicountry cross-border M&A research, yet it highlights the importance of constructing a suitable research design.

For example, if the sample has a cross-border M&A between France and England, and the purpose is to determine the differences between the two types, the appropriate base model is not the domestic U.S. M&A. Rather, one has to choose either domestic U.K. or domestic French M&As. However, it has to be stated that the data requirements are hard to meet in the international context, but that is precisely where the gaps lie in the literature. Overall, a very small number of developing or emerging countries have been studied in the context of cross-border M&As.

The time frame of the study and the time when the researcher is actually gathering primary data through case study or survey design are important in terms of both the reliability and the interpretation of the cross-border M&A empirical findings. The two main types of research are carried in either a retrospective or a longitudinal framework. Most of the empirical studies are concerned with the "after the fact" analysis. This is mainly because the firms involved in such corporate events tend to consider any data pertaining to the preacquisition and preintegration phases proprietary and refrain from disclosing relevant data to the researchers. It is even harder to have longitudinal studies of large samples. However, the challenges associated with longitudinal studies in cross-border M&A deals also present future research opportunities.

RESEARCH INSTRUMENTS

In domestic M&A research there is naturally more emphasis on the effects of differences in the corporate cultures of the merging companies on postevent integration processes and results. The survey instrument used to measure the factors of the organizational culture construct is developed in

Chatterjee et al. 1992. The purpose of the instrument is to unpack the perceptions of organizational cultural differences of top management teams of recently acquired firms. In table 9.1, the culture index used in each study is identified with the researchers who developed it. However, this construct is rarely used in the empirical studies that look at cross-border M&As. As mentioned earlier, however, comparative research of domestic M&As in different countries requires a consideration of the national cultural and institutional contexts in which those deals are embedded.

Hofstede's (1980, 1997) national culture index is the most commonly used instrument to measure national cultural differences in cross-border M&As. The cultural distance composite developed by Kogut and Singh (1988) is also used in a number of studies. The problems associated with this measure are discussed elsewhere in this handbook and hence are not elaborated here. In only one study that could be identified were both national and organizational culture instruments used simultaneously (Weber, Shenkar, and Raveh 1996). This is still an underdeveloped area within the cross-border M&A research stream.

DISCUSSION AND FUTURE RESEARCH DIRECTIONS

Given the anecdotal evidence of firms facing critical challenges when they acquire cross-border targets, the management literature leaves many unanswered questions. Although the domestic M&A literature has given substantial attention to corporate cultural differences and similarities between firms, hardly any research in cross-border M&As has looked into this issue. A main reason for this is that the data required for assessing corporate culture in a large sample study are very difficult to gather, especially in countries where reporting conventions are not as developed as in the United States or the United Kingdom. Also, there is the overgeneralization that the national culture is overimposing upon and engulfing the effects of corporate cultures in the context of cross-border M&As.

Future research venues are more likely to take into account both the corporate and the national cultural context of firms that engage in cross-border M&As. Moreover, although it is more difficult, there is an increasing trend of looking into cross-border M&As between less researched country dyads (e.g., emerging and developing countries). Single-industry cross-border M&As, especially, would be a fertile research area to untangle the effects of organizational cultures as well as national cultures, mainly

TABLE 9.1. Empirical Studies of Cross-Border M&As

Study	Research Question(s)	Type	Countries Involved	Main Data Source(s)	Sample Size	Period	Dependent Variable(s)	Method	Culture Index	Results
Anand & Delios 2002	Analyze the capability-seeking aspects of foreign direct investment by examining the relationship between upstream (technological) and downstream (marketing) capabilities and the choice between entry mode (acquisitions, greenfield)	Cross-border	Targets: U.S. Acquirers: Japan, U.K., Canada, Germany, France, the Netherlands, Switzerland	*Foreign Direct Investment in the United States*	Japan (4160 entries), U.K. (2778 entries), Canada (2316 entries), Germany (1540 entries), France (924 entries), the Netherlands (745 entries), Switzerland (556 entries)	1974–91	Proportion of entries by acquisition (acquisition = 1, greenfield = 0)	Grouped (4-digit SIC industry) probit model		Relative technological advantage (differences in R&D intensities) is a significant determinant of entry mode choice. The use of acquisition for foreign entry is attributed to the characteristics of capabilities sought in foreign investment.
Angwin 2000	Effects of national differences upon due diligence and the use of professional advisers	Cross-border	Germany, U.K., Sweden, France, Switzerland, Netherlands	Survey questionnaire, interviews	142	1985–95		Descriptive	Hofstede 1980	National differences play an important role in affecting acquirer's perceptions of the target, which in turn affect the management of deal negotiation and postacquisition phase.
Angwin & Savill 1997	Perceptions of European top executives	Cross-border	Germany, U.K., Sweden, France, Switzerland, Netherlands	Semi-structured survey, interviews	142	1985–95		Descriptive		Expansion in Europe is still a priority. Two main advantages of cross-border acquisitions is speed and

(continued)

TABLE 9.1.—*Continued*

Study	Research Question(s)	Type	Countries Involved	Main Data Source(s)	Sample Size	Period	Dependent Variable(s)	Method	Culture Index	Results
										control. Cross-border acquisitions are more risky than domestic.
Calori, Lubatkin, & Very 1994	Influence of national culture on the integration process of cross-border acquisitions	Cross-border	Targets: France, U.K. (surveyed) Acquirers: U.S., France, U.K.	*Acquisition Monthly* (1987–89), *Kompass France, Kompass Great Britain, Dun and Bradstreet Europe,* Survey questionnaire (1991, English, French)	75 firms	1987–89	Attitudinal and economic performance of the target firms	Discriminant analysis, multiple regressions	Hofstede 1980	National administrative heritage of firms that involve cross-border acquisitions should be helpful in anticipating cultural problems in the integration process.
Capron & Mitchell 1997	Motives and outcomes of horizontal cross-border acquisitions	Interregional cross-border and intraregional cross-border	Target– Acquirer: 1 European– European, 1 European– North American, 1 North American– North American, 1 North		4 firms, number of respondents not specified	1988–92		Case study, descriptive		Strong support for production efficiency and strategic reconfiguration explanation rather than market power as firm motivation.

Study	Topic	Type	Targets/Acquirers	Data source	Sample	Period	Method	Findings
			American–European (telecommunications equipment manuf. industry)					
Datta & Puia 1995	Impact of relatedness and cultural distance on wealthy effects of cross-border M&As	Cross-border	Targets: U.K., Canada, Australia, other non-U.S. countries Acquirers: U.S.	Wall Street Journal	112	1987–90	Cumulative abnormal returns in time periods of (−1, 0), (+5, −5), (−10, +10), (−15, +15), (−20, +20), (−30, +30)	Event study to get CAR, descriptive Kogut & Singh 1988	Cross-border acquisitions, on average, do not create value for the buyer's shareholders. Moreover, high cultural distance leads to lower wealth effects for the buyer shareholders.
Dewenter 1995	Intraindustry investment patterns of domestic and foreign acquirers	Cross-border	Targets: U.S. chemical firms Acquirers: not stated	Mergers & Acquisitions, Mergerstat Review, Japan Economic Institute	239 (domestic) 183 (foreign)	1978–89	Binary variable of relatedness	Logit regression	Foreign investors are more likely to make related acquisitions.
Flanagan, Milman, & D'Mello 1997	Differences in five Latin American countries and the U.S. in terms of M&A activity	Comparative domestic M&A	Targets: Argentina, Brazil, Chile, Mexico, Venezuela, U.S.	Securities Data Corporation, Worldwide M&A Database	Argentina (199), Brazil (220), Chile (124), Mexico (305), Venezuela (84), U.S. (38,481)	1985–94	Descriptive		Latin American region has more cross-border acquisitions when compared to the U.S.

(continued)

TABLE 9.1.— *Continued*

Study	Research Question(s)	Type	Countries Involved	Main Data Source(s)	Sample Size	Period	Dependent Variable(s)	Method	Culture Index	Results
Inkpen, Sundaram, & Rockwood 2000	Acquisitions by non-U.S. firms of U.S. targets in the Silicon-valley type industries	Cross-border	Targets: U.S. communications-, computer-related industries) Acquirers: non-U.S. (EU)	*Securities Data Corporation, Worldwide M&A Database,* interviews	6 deals for case study, 11,639 Silicon-valley type asset acquisitions for descriptive information	1990–99		Case study, descriptive		Failure to deal with integration properly can lead to demoralized staff and employee defections. Technology-based companies suffer more when they lose their key success factor when they have high turnover.
Kitching 1974		Comparative interregional vs. U.S. cross-border	Targets: European firms Acquirers: U.S. and European	Interview	407 1					U.S. acquirers have 50% chance of success. European acquirers have 54% chance of success.
Krug & Hegarty 1997	Top management turnover in domestic vs. cross-border acquisitions	Cross-border	Targets: U.S. Acquirers: U.S., Canada, Australia, U.K., Japan, and other non-U.S. countries	*Mergers & Acquisitions, Register, Million Dollar Directory*	68 cross-border, 102 domestic, 120 nonacquired U.S. firms	1986–88	Turnover rate over the 5-year post-event period	ANOVA, descriptive	Ronen & Shenkar 1985	Cross-border acquisitions are associated with higher top management turnover over time when compared to domestic M&As.
Krug & Nigh	Postacquisition top management depar-	Cross-border	Targets: U.S. Acquirers:	*Mergers & Acquisitions*	103	1986–89	Top management depar-	Linear regression	Kogut & Singh 1988	Greater cultural distance, higher levels of

					N	Period	Measure	Method	Theory	Findings
1998	tures in U.S. targets acquired by foreign firms		non-U.S.	(1998), *Standard & Poor's Register of Corporations, Directors, and Executives* (1996)			ture rates			international integration in target industry, poor preacquisition performance of the U.S. target lead to greater postacquisition top executive departures.
Morosini, Shane, & Singh 1998	Effects of national culture distance on cross-border acquisition performance	Cross-border	Targets of Italian acquirers: France, Germany, U.S., U.K., Switzerland, Austria, Spain Other targets: Italy Other acquirers: U.S., U.K., France, Belgium, Germany, Sweden, Switzerland, Finland, the Netherlands	KPMG Peat Marwick Consultants' M&A database, survey questionnaire (Italian, English), interviews	52	1987–92	Percentage rate of growth in sales ($U.S.) over 2-year postacquisition period	Ordinary least squares regression	Kogut & Singh 1988	There is positive association between national cultural distance and cross-border performance.

(continued)

TABLE 9.1.—*Continued*

Study	Research Question(s)	Type	Countries Involved	Main Data Source(s)	Sample Size	Period	Dependent Variable(s)	Method	Culture Index	Results
Olie 1994	Effects of firm-specific and nation-specific differences on the integration phase of cross-border mergers	Cross-border	Dutch-Germany mergers in 1969: fiber merger, aviation merger, and 1970 (1972) steel merger	Interviews	3	1969–	Historical account of each merger	Case study	Hofstede 1980	The aviation merger could not evolve more than a confederation of two companies, which had temporarily combined their financial interests. Similarly, the steel merger remained as an artificial construct. As the postmerger integration efforts intensify, the national cultural differences become more potent.
Segalla, Fischer, & Sandner 2000	Employee values concerning common corporate integration problems in cross-border M&As, JVs, & alliances	Cross-border	France, Germany, Italy, Spain, U.K. (banking industry)	Survey questionnaire, scenario	290	1994		Descriptive	Hofstede 1980	Process of integration is as important as the decision to merge.
Seth, Song, & Pettit 2000	Motives underlying the foreign acquisitions of U.S. firms and the extent of wealth creation and distribution between the buyer and the target	Cross-border	Targets: U.S. Acquirer: Foreign	*Mergers & Acquisitions Rosters on Foreign Investment in the U.S., Mergerstat Review*	100	1981–90	Total gain measured as CAR and summed for target and buyer	Regression		Synergy-seeking assumption is robust such that managers on average seek to create economic value. Value-destroying transaction is motivated by managerialism rather than hubris.

Uhlenbruck & De Castro 2000	Effects of strategic and organizational fit on postprivatization performance	Cross-border	Targets: Czech Republic, Germany, Hungary Acquirers: Australia, Austria, Belgium, Canada, Denmark, Finland, Luxembourg, Norway, Sweden, Switzerland, the Netherlands, U.K., U.S., western part of Germany	*World Bank, Investment Dealers Digest*, government agencies in charge of privatization, *Institutional Investor*, survey questionnaire (English and German), interviews	170	1989–93	ROA, ROS	Multivariate regression		Mixed
Vaara 2000	Sense-making approach to studying the (re)construction of cultural conceptions in the merger context	Cross-border	Finnish-Swedish M&As	Interviews (1992–97)	8	1984–97	Case study	Hofstede 1997		Identified three concurrent cultural sense-making processes: "search for rational understanding," "emotional identification," and "sociopolitical manipulation"

(continued)

TABLE 9.1.—Continued

Study	Research Question(s)	Type	Countries Involved	Main Data Source(s)	Sample Size	Period	Dependent Variable(s)	Method	Culture Index	Results
Very, Lubatkin, & Calori 1996	Influences of acculturative stress and/or attraction on the financial performance of recent domestic and cross-national mergers	Cross-border vs. domestic	Target: British, French Acquirers: British, U.S., French	*Acquisitions Monthly*, survey (English, French)	42 French (62 target firm managers) and 64 British (95 target firm managers) target firms	1987–89	Reported change in postmerger performance (earnings, sales, market share)	Linear regression	Hofstede 1980	Depending upon the dimension of acculturative stress, and the nationality of the acquirer and the target, cultural differences may elicit perceptions of attraction rather than stress.
Very et al. 1997	Relative standing (Frank 1985) of top managers and the performance of cross-border acquisitions	Cross-border vs. domestic	Target: British, French Acquirers: British, U.S., French	*Acquisitions Monthly*, survey (English, French)	42 French (62 target firm managers) and 64 British (95 target firm managers) target firms	1987–89	Reported change in postmerger performance (earnings, sales, market share)	Linear regression, ANOVA	Hofstede 1980	When the target's top management perceives their postevent relative standing to be lowered, they may feel a loss of autonomy, unappreciated, and inferior status, and these feelings more likely lead to culture clashes, dysfunctional behavior, and unanticipated decline in performance.
Very & Schweiger 2001	Comparative analysis of domestic vs. cross-border acquisitions	Cross-border vs. domestic	Acquirers: France, Germany, Italy, U.S.	In-depth interviews of one top manager per	26 firms (top managers)	In or after 1997		Descriptive	Kogut & Singh 1988	Two broad categories of problems are collecting reliable information about targets

| Weber, Shenkar, & Raveh 1996 | National and corporate cultures in domestic vs. cross-border mergers | Cross-border vs. domestic | Targets: U.S. firms Acquirers: non-U.S. and U.S. | Survey questionnaire | 52 | 1985–87, survey done in 1988 | Co-plot methodology | Hofstede 1980, Chatterjee et al. 1992 (corporate culture) | and integration. National and corporate cultures were problematic during the integration phase.

In IM&A's national culture differentials predict stress, negative attitudes toward the merger, and actual cooperation than corporate culture differentials do. Both national and corporate cultures determine merger process and outcomes. |

because one can gather common firm-performance measures that are not just self-reported perceptual accounts provided by firm employees. Overall, there is more research to be done to build the body of knowledge required to guide the managers in overcoming some of the obstacles in the area of cross-border M&As.

Domestic M&A literature could be a valuable guide for directing future research in cross-border M&As. For example, widely explored operational and microsynergistic motives and results of domestic M&As have not been explored in the context of cross-border M&As. In the domestic M&A literature, corporate culture has been the topic of significant exploration. In the context of cross-border M&As, national culture *and* organizational culture simultaneously play significant roles in most likely every phase of the M&A event. However, we have a very limited number of studies that look at these two levels of distinct culture constructs simultaneously (e.g., Weber, Shenkar, and Raveh 1996). The following list provides possible future research directions regarding cross-border M&As.

1. Management of expatriates and cross-border M&A activity
2. Industry-specific cross-border M&As versus domestic M&As
3. Human resource management and cross-border M&As (e.g., employee retention, employee satisfaction and compensation, staffing, and training)
4. Conflict management and the integration phase of cross-border M&As
5. Negotiation management in cross-border M&As
6. Leadership (e.g., cross-border "merger of equals")
7. Interplay between corporate cultures and national cultures in cross-border M&As
8. Longitudinal studies that encompass pre-event to postevent of cross-border M&A deals

NOTES

1. Figures were obtained from the database produced by Securities Data Company for the years 1985–99.

2. Peter Krass, in *Across the Board,* May/June 2001, Publication of the Conference Board. Emphasis is in the original.

3. For a detailed review of cross-border acquisitions and the role of national and organizational cultures, see Weber 1996.

REFERENCES

Anand, J., and A. Delios. 2002. Absolute and relative resources as determinants of international acquisitions. *Strategic Management Journal* 23 (2): 119–34.

Angwin, D. 2000. Mergers and acquisitions across European borders: National perspectives on preacquisition due diligence and the use of professional advisers. *Journal of World Business* 36 (1): 32–57.

Angwin, D., and B. Savill. 1997. Strategic perspectives on European cross-border acquisitions: A view from top European executives. *European Management Journal* 15 (4): 423–35.

Ashoka, M., and S. Negishi. 2001. Cross-border mergers and acquisitions in East Asia: Trends and implications. *Finance and Development* 38 (1).

Bradley, M., A. Desai, and E. H. Kim. 1988. Synergistic gains from corporate acquisitions and their division between the stockholders of target and acquiring firms. *Journal of Financial Economics* 21 (1): 3–40.

Bresman, H., J. Birkinshaw, and R. Nobel. 1999. Knowledge transfer in international acquisitions. *Journal of International Business Studies* 30 (3): 439–62.

Brouthers, K. D., and L. E. Brouthers. 2000. Acquisition of greenfield start-up? Institutional, cultural, and transaction cost influences. *Strategic Management Journal* 21 (1): 89–97.

Calori, R., M. Lubatkin, and P. Very. 1994. Control mechanisms in cross-border acquisitions—An international comparison. *Organization Studies* 15 (3): 361–79.

Cartwright, S. 1998. International mergers and acquisitions: The issues and challenges. In M. C. Gertsen, A. M. Soderberg, and J. E. Torp, eds., *Cultural dimensions of international mergers and acquisitions,* 5–15. Berlin and New York: Walter de Gruyter.

Cartwright, S., and C. L. Cooper. 1993a. Of mergers, marriage, and divorce: The issues of staff retention. *Journal of Managerial Psychology* 8 (6): 7–10.

———. 1993b. The psychological impact of merger and acquisition on the individual: A study of building society managers. *Human Relations* 46 (3): 327–47.

———. 1995. Organizational marriage: "Hard" versus "soft" issues. *Personnel Review* 24 (3): 32–42.

Chatterjee, S., M. H. Lubatkin, D. M. Schweiger, and Y. Weber. 1992. Cultural differences and shareholder value in related mergers: Linking equity and human capital. *Strategic Management Journal* 13 (5): 319–34.

Datta, D. K., and G. Puia. 1995. Cross-border acquisitions: An examination of the influence of relatedness and cultural fit on shareholder value creation in U.S. acquiring firms. *Management International Review* 35 (4): 337–59.

David, K., and H. Singh. 1993. Acquisition regimes: Managing cultural risk and relative deprivation in corporate acquisitions. *International Review of Strategic Management* 4:227–76.

Dewenter, K. L. 1995. Does the market react differently to domestic and foreign takeover announcements? Evidence from the U.S. chemical and retail industries. *Journal of Financial Economics* 37:421–41.

Doukas, J., and N. G. Travlos. 1988. The effect of corporate multinationalism on shareholders' wealth: Evidence from international acquisitions. *Journal of Finance* 43 (5): 1161–75.

Driscoll, S., T. Stuth, J. Rieger, and S. Kobayashi. 2001. Mergers and acquisitions. *International Tax Review* (July):15–25.

Flanagan, D. J., C. D. Milman, and J. P. D'Mello. 1997. A comparison of the characteristics of M&A activity in five Latin American countries and the United States: 1985–1994. *International Journal of Conflict Management* 7 (2): 5–20.

Frank, R. H. 1985. *Choosing the right pond: Human behavior and the quest for status.* Oxford: Oxford University Press.

Hambrick, D. C., and A. A. Cannella Jr. 1993. Relative standing: A framework for understanding departures. *Academy of Management Journal* 36 (4): 733–62.

Hennart, J.-F., and Y.-R. Park. 1994. Location, governance, and strategic determinants of Japanese manufacturing investment in the United States. *Strategic Management Journal* 15 (6): 419–36.

Hennart, J.-F., and S. Reddy. 1997. The choice between mergers and acquisitions: The strategy of Japanese investors in the United States. *Strategic Management Journal* 18(1):1–12.

Hofstede, G. 1980. *Culture's consequences.* Beverly Hills, CA: Sage.

———. 1997. *Cultures and organizations: Software of the mind.* New York: McGraw-Hill.

Inkpen, A. C., A. K. Sundaram, and K. Rockwood. 2000. Cross-border acquisitions of U.S. technology assets. *California Management Review* 42 (3): 50–71.

Jensen, M. C. 1988. Takeovers: Their causes and consequences. *Journal of Economic Perspectives* 2, no. 1 (winter).

Jensen, M. C., and W. H. Meckling. 1976. Theory of the firm: Management behavior, agency costs, and ownership structure. *Journal of Financial Economics* 3:305–60.

Jensen, M. C., and R. S. Ruback. 1983. The market for corporate control: The scientific evidence. *Journal of Financial Economics* 11, nos. 1–4 (April): 5–50.

Kanter, R. M., and R. I. Corn. 1994. Do cultural differences make a business difference? Contextual factors affecting cross-cultural relationship success. *Journal of Management Development* 13:5–23.

Kanter, R., and T. D. Dretler. 1998. "Global strategy" and its impact on local operations: Lessons from Gillette Singapore. *Academy of Management Executive* 12 (4): 60–68.

Kay, I. T., and M. Shelton. 2000. The people problem in mergers. *McKinsey Quarterly* 4:27–37.

Kogut, B., and H. Singh. 1988. The effect of national culture on the choice of entry mode. *Journal of International Business Studies* 19 (3): 411–32.

Krug, J. A., and W. H. Hegarty. 1997. Postacquisition turnover among U.S. top management teams: An analysis of the effects of foreign vs. domestic acquisitions of U.S. targets. *Strategic Management Journal* 18 (8): 667–75.

Krug, J. A., and G. Nigh. 1998. Top management departures in cross-border acquisitions: Governance issues in an international context. *Journal of International Management* 4:267–87.

Larsson, R., and S. Finkelstein. 1999. Integrating strategic, organizational, and human resource perspectives on mergers and acquisitions: A case survey of synergy realization. *Organization Science* 10 (1): 1–26.

Levy, A. 2001. Cross-border mergers: Promises unfulfilled. *Bloomberg Markets* 10, no. 4 (April).

Lewis, R., and S. Clyne. 2001. M&A yearbook: Australia. *Corporate Finance* (November):35–36.

Lubatkin, M., R. Calori, P. Very, and J. Veiga. 1998. Managing mergers across borders: A two-nation exploration of a nationally bound administrative heritage. *Organization Science* 9 (6): 670–84.

McBeath, I., and J. Bacha. 2001. Mergers and acquisitions: A consideration of the drivers and hurdles. *Journal of Commercial Biotechnology* 8 (2): 147–53.

McCloughan, P., and I. Stone. 1998. Life duration of foreign multinational subsidiaries: Evidence from UK northern manufacturing industry, 1970–93. *International Journal of Industrial Organization* 16 (6): 719–47.

Morosini, P. 1999. *Managing cultural differences.* Oxford: Elsevier Science.

Morosini, P., S. Shane, and H. Singh. 1998. National cultural distance and cross-border acquisition performance. *Journal of International Business Studies* 29 (1): 137–58.

Olie, R. 1994. Shades of culture and institutions in international mergers. *Organization Studies* 15 (3): 381–405.

Pablo, A. 1994. Determinants of acquisition integration level: A decision-making perspective. *Academy of Management Journal* 37 (4): 803–36.

Reddy, S. 1997. The choice between mergers/acquisitions and joint ventures: The case of Japanese investors in the United States. *Strategic Management Journal* 18 (1): 1–12.

Roll, R. 1986. The hubris hypothesis of corporate takeovers. *Journal of Business* 59:197–216.

Ronen, S., and O. Shenkar. 1985. Clustering countries on attitudinal dimensions: A review and synthesis. *Academy of Management Review* 10 (3): 435–54.

Schneider, Susan C. 1989. Strategy formulation: The impact of national culture. *Organization Studies* 10 (2): 149–68.

Segalla, M., L. Fischer, and K. Sandner. 2000. Making cross-cultural research relevant to European corporate integration: Old problem—new approach. *European Journal of Management* 18 (1): 38–51.

Seth, A. 1990. Value creation in acquisitions: A re-examination of performance issues. *Strategic Management Journal* 11 (1): 99–115.

Seth, A., K. P. Song, and R. Pettit. 2000. Synergy, managerialism or hubris? An empirical examination of motives for foreign acquisitions of U.S. firms. *Journal of International Business Studies* 31 (3): 387–406.

UNCTAD. 2000. World investment report 2000: Cross-border mergers and acquisitions and development. New York: UNCTAD.

Vaara, E. 2000. Constructions of cultural differences in post-merger change processes: A sensemaking perspective on Finnish-Swedish cases. *M@n@gement* 3 (3): 81–110.

Very, P., M. Lubatkin, and R. Calori. 1996. A cross-national assessment of acculturative stress in recent European mergers. *International Studies of Management and Organization* 26 (1): 59–86.

Very, P., M. Lubatkin, R. Calori, and J. Veiga. 1997. Relative standing and the performance of recently acquired European firms. *Strategic Management Journal* 18 (8): 593–614.

Very, P., and D. M. Schweiger. 2001. The acquisition process as a learning process: Evidence from a study of critical problems and solutions in domestic and cross-border deals. *Journal of World Business* 36 (1): 11–31.

Villinger, R. 1996. Post-acquisition managerial learning in central east Europe. *Organization Studies* 17 (2): 181–206.

Weber, Y. 1996. Cross-border mergers: The dominant mode of internalization. In B. J. Punnett and O. Shenkar, eds., *Handbook for international management research*, 403–28. Cambridge, MA: Blackwell.

Weber, Y., O. Shenkar, and A. Raveh. 1996. National and corporate cultural fit in mergers/acquisitions: An exploratory study. *Management Science* 42 (8): 1215–27.

Wessel, D. 2000. Cross-border mergers soared last year—Most deals were struck by Western Europeans; Britain overtook U.S. *Wall Street Journal*, July 19.

INTERNATIONAL AND CROSS-CULTURAL LEADERSHIP RESEARCH

Peter W. Dorfman

Moral superiority has been a major criterion for Chinese leadership since historic times, and this belief is still prevalent in every Chinese business circle. (Hui and Tan 1999)

Japanese and American management is 95 percent the same, and differs in all important respects. (T. Fujisawa, cofounder of Honda Motor Company)

Charismatic leadership may be acted in the highly assertive manner, as in the case of John F. Kennedy, Martin Luther King, Jr., or in a quiet, nonassertive manner, as in the case of Mahatma Gandhi, Nelson Mandela, and Mother Teresa. (House, Wright, and Aditya 1997)

To what extent is leadership influenced by one's culture? Judging by the preceding quotes, leadership processes are inexorably intertwined within one's culture. In the first edition of this handbook, I noted that, of the thousands of empirical leadership studies, relatively few were concerned with the impact of cultural influences on leadership (Dorfman 1996). Is this still true? Yes it is, but the situation has changed dramatically. Similar to the burgeoning interest in cross-cultural and international management (Adler 2002; Thomas 2002), there have been increased interest and

~
I wish to extend my appreciation to Jon Howell and Renee Brown for their helpful comments and suggestions for this chapter.

growth in research regarding cultural influences on leadership processes. This is clearly apparent as reflected in recent reviews of international leadership research and theory (e.g., House, Wright, and Aditya 1997), large-scale international leadership projects recently completed and under way (Smith and Peterson 1988; House et al. 1999; House et al. 2004), and leadership textbooks that include sections or chapters specifically concerned with cross-cultural leadership (e.g., Chemers 1997; Yukl 2002). Developing global leaders is the focus of a new book series devoted entirely to global leadership (Mobley, Gessner, and Arnold 1999; Mobley and McCall 2001; Mobley and Dorfman 2003). In addition, the premier leadership journal, *Leadership Quarterly,* publishes special issues on international and cross-cultural leadership research (see Peterson and Hunt 1997a, 1997b) and continues to feature articles with an international focus (e.g., Den Hartog et al. 1999).

This recent burgeoning of interest should not be surprising. "For all practical purposes, all business today is global" (Mitroff 1987). The economic integration of Europe into the European Union, regional and global trading entities (e.g., NAFTA, ASEAN), and the omnipresence of the World Trade Organization (WTO) are but a few examples of the increased interdependencies of nations. Practical knowledge in managing people of different national origins is particularly important because of the increasing number of multinational companies, strategic alliances of companies with vastly different organizational cultures, and international joint ventures. This collaboration and partnership among people of different national origins provides unique opportunities to understand the process by which culture influences leadership effectiveness. And we know that the success of any organization depends on effective leadership. However, despite this need to better understand how one's national culture and social institutions affect leadership (Cullen 2002), there is no generally accepted theory of cross-cultural leadership.

While recent literature reviewed in this chapter points to new theory development, much more is needed. This chapter updates my previous review of the literature in the first handbook, which addresses the following fundamental research questions. If the phenomenon of leadership is universal and found in all societies (Murdoch 1967; Bass 1990), to what extent is leadership culturally contingent? Which dimensions of cultural variation and theoretical frameworks are most useful to understand cultural contingencies? What are the mechanisms by which cultural variation affects individuals, groups, organizations, industries, and societies? What are the most useful and appropriate research designs to dissect the complex influence of national culture on organizational life?

At first glance, it might seem obvious that leadership processes should reflect the vast differences found among cultures. After all, ample evidence points to cultural differences in values, beliefs, traits, and decision styles that are consistent with different management practices (Arvey, Bhagat, and Salas 1991; Dowling, Welch, and Schuler 1999; Adler 2002). For instance, the individualistic performance appraisal, reward, and compensation human resource management practices characteristic of the United States are not the norm in more collectivistic Asian cultures (Latham and Napier 1989; Erez 1997). In Korean major corporations, called *chaebols,* the concept of meritorious pay for performance is often avoided because it is thought that seniority systems will more likely lead to group harmony (Steers, Shinn, and Ungson 1989). As another example, frank discussions with subordinates during work are much more likely in the individualistic United States than in the more collectivistic Japanese society (Smith 1989). In Japan, more subtle indirect tactics are used during work hours to avoid conflict, but candid and blunt discussions may take place when socializing (in bars) after work (Rao, Hashimoto, and Rao 1997).

Because of the complex interplay between effective management and leadership, it seems reasonable to expect that cultural differences should influence not only management processes but also leadership processes. A major premise of this chapter, as well as of my personal experience, is that the kind of leadership that will be attempted, and the effectiveness of leadership activities, is culturally contingent. As noted long ago by Haire, Ghiselli, and Porter (1966), it makes little sense to export participative and democratic leadership approaches to authoritarian cultures where managers are more likely to believe in the divine right of kings than Jeffersonian democracy. But what do we know about the impact of culture on leadership processes beyond a relatively simple point that leadership processes will reflect the culture in which they are embedded? Unfortunately, while a number of authors speculate about the impact of culture on leadership, the *empirical* cross-cultural leadership research literature is sparse, often nontheoretical, fraught with methodological problems, and fragmented across a wide variety of publication outlets. Far more questions exist than answers regarding the culturally contingent aspects of leadership.

This chapter will not attempt to review comprehensively the entire domain and content area of the international management and cross-cultural leadership literature. Excellent reviews can be found in the cross-cultural chapter of *Bass and Stogdill's Handbook of Leadership* (Bass 1990), Smith and Peterson's leadership text (1988), and literature reviews by House, Wright, and Aditya (1997), Peterson and Hunt (1997a, 1997b), and Dickson et al. (in press). Instead of a comprehensive review, this chapter is theory based and organized around contemporary leadership theories and themes. The relevant literature consists of leadership models and empirical leadership studies that focus on cross-cultural comparisons. Because most leadership theories have a distinctly Western origin, tests of these theories also have a distinctly Western character. However, the few models of leadership developed and tested outside a Western influence are also presented. Before reviewing the cross-cultural leadership literature, a summary of the history and present conceptualizations of leadership is presented. After a discussion of important conceptual and methodological issues, suggestions for future research and a model of cross-cultural leadership are given.

WHY IS THIS TOPIC IMPORTANT?

This question may be approached from both a practical and a theoretical perspective. From the practical viewpoint, the United States needs to compete internationally, and leadership is often credited with the success of international operations. Many U.S. multinational corporations (e.g., Ford Motor Company, Hewlett-Packard Corporation, Citicorp) consistently receive 40 percent or more of their revenues and profits from abroad (Shapiro 1991). The trend of the global economic village is clear, and the twenty-first century may very well become known as the century of the "global world" (McFarland, Senen, and Childress 1993). This "borderless world" (Ohmae 1990) has led to the rapid restructuring of organizations, as well as expansion in the number of managers working in foreign countries (i.e., expatriates). Despite current controversy about the desirability of globalization, Jack Welch, former CEO of General Electric, argues that, for organizations, globalization is a way of life and organizations must change by necessity to survive in this new environment (Welch 2001). The cultural diversity of employees found in multinational organizations presents quite a management challenge. The U.S. expatriate work force alone numbers in excess of one hundred thousand managers working in over 130 countries located in every continent in the world (Arvey, Bhagat, and Salas 1991; Howard 1992). Obviously, with the recent creation of the European

Union, a nontrivial question concerns the development of a "Euro-Manager," one who can work effectively within the wide variability of European cultures (Hazucha et al. 1999). A recent development for multinational organizations is to create a group of managers, called international cadre, who specialize in international assignments (Cullen 2002). What does the management literature provide us with in the way of practical knowledge and advice to assist leaders in adapting to cultural constraints? Unfortunately, not much in the way of well-grounded research. Thus, while a practical need exists for such information, little if any help is available at this time. The Global Leadership and Organizational Behavior Effectiveness (GLOBE) project, discussed later in this chapter, should eventually provide some much needed practical knowledge necessary for managers working in various cultures.

From a scientific and theoretical perspective, compelling reasons exist for considering the influence of culture on leadership processes. Because the general goal of science is to develop universally valid theories, laws, and principles, leadership researchers *should* strive to develop leadership theories that transcend cultures. Most likely, these theories will take the form of midrange theories such as those prevalent in the leadership literature (e.g., LMX theory from Graen and Uhl-Bien 1995). Conventional practice labels theories that transcend cultures as transcultural, culture free, etic or cultural universal. In contrast, research that reflects the diversity among cultures is often labeled cultural specific, culturally unique, or emic. We will return to these concepts later to clarify what has become a false dichotomy between these perspectives. The inherent limitations in transferring theories across cultures have been well noted in the literature (Poortinga and Malpass 1986; Chemers 1997)—what works in one culture may not *necessarily* work in another culture. However, through cross-cultural research we may determine which aspects of a leadership theory are culturally universal and which aspects are culturally unique. As Triandis (1993) suggests, leadership researchers will be able to "fine-tune" theories by investigating cultural variations as parameters of the theory. Cross-cultural research may also help uncover new theoretical relationships by forcing the researcher to consider a much broader range of noncultural variables (Chemers 1983). For instance, models promoting participatory leadership may be valid for relatively sophisticated employees in developed countries but less valid for employees in less developed countries where egalitarian values may not be highly valued. Additional situational factors to consider are religion, language, history, laws, political systems, and so forth. Cultural variations may, therefore, highlight relationships between theoretical constructs and specify important theoretical boundary conditions.

Because we are just beginning to understand how the role of culture influences leadership processes, numerous research questions remain as yet unanswered. Will characteristics of a society make it more or less susceptible to leadership influence? To what extent will prototypes of "ideal leaders" vary across cultures? Are the leadership functions identical across cultures, and, if so, will leadership styles and behaviors vary in accomplishing these functions? What principles and/or laws of leadership transcend cultures? We do not have comprehensive answers to these questions, but progress has been made in a number of areas.

LEADERSHIP DEFINED AND OVERVIEW OF LEADERSHIP PERSPECTIVES

The word "leadership" is a relatively new addition to the English language; it appeared approximately two hundred years ago in writings about political influence in the British Parliament. However, from Egyptian hieroglyphics, we know that symbols for "leader" have existed as early as five thousand years ago. Simply put, leaders have existed in all cultures throughout history. The verb "to lead" derives from the Latin *agere*, which means "to set in motion" (Jennings 1960). The Anglo-Saxon term *laedere* indicates that people are on a journey (Bolman and Deal 1995). In putting the two terms together, Adler (1999) suggests that a leader is "someone who sets ideas, people, organizations, and societies in motion; someone who takes the worlds of ideas, people, organizations, and societies on a journey. To lead such a journey requires vision, courage, and influence" (51).

One might be surprised to find that, while the subject of leadership has generated thousands of academic papers, articles, and books, there is no consensually agreed upon definition of leadership (Bass 1990). Most definitions of leadership include the core concept of *influence* and influence for the purpose of achieving something important. It is also a core element in Yukl's (2002) definition of leadership:

> Leadership is the process of influencing others to understand and
> agree about what needs to be done and how it can be done effectively,
> and the process of facilitating individual and collective efforts to
> accomplish the shared objectives. (7)

There are many more definitions of "leader" and "leadership" (Bass 1990), but for our purposes it is not necessary to review these or select one in preference to another. The point is that various definitions emphasize diverse aspects of leadership and may be equally valid. The practice and philosophy of leaders and leadership can be gleaned from writings as diverse in content, philosophy, and time as those found in Greek classics such as Homer's *Iliad,* the Old and New Testaments, essays about Confucius in China, and Machiavelli's rules and principles for obtaining and holding power in Italy.

Are leaders, and the associated conceptualization of leadership with its numerous nuances and abstractions, viewed differently across cultures? No definitive answer to this question presently exists, but evidence indicates that evaluative interpretations of leadership probably vary across cultures. Peterson and Hunt (1997a) suggest that the labels "leader" and "leadership" and many of the associated connotations are distinctly, if not uniquely, American. For instance, Americans put a premium on leadership. For most Americans, the term "leadership" evokes a positive connotation—it is a desirable characteristic. Organizational success and demise are often attributed solely (if not mistakenly) to the chief executive. Surprisingly, positive semantic evaluations of leadership are not universal. For example, Europeans seem less enthusiastic about leadership than do Americans. As Serge Moscovici writes, "When we Europeans say leader, we think, as if by conditioned reflex, of Hitler. . . . no one would forget the havoc the leadership principle wreaked in Germany's history and in ours. . . . In short, everything seems to indicate that leadership is an unintended and undesirable consequence of democracy, or a 'perverse effect' as we say in France" (Graumann and Moscovici 1986, 241–42). In Holland, consensus and egalitarian values are held in high esteem (Hofstede 1993), and anecdotal evidence suggests that the Dutch believe the concept of leadership is overvalued. Other nations also seem to downplay the importance of leadership. CEOs of large successful Japanese corporations, for example, credit subordinates for organizational accomplishments, while de-emphasizing their own role as contributors to organizational success (Bass and Yokochi 1991). It seems likely that the meaning and the importance of leadership vary across cultures.

Subtle and not so subtle cultural differences regarding the conceptualization of leadership await further research, but an anecdotal example of contrasting viewpoints can be observed with the international GLOBE leadership project. In August 1994, the first GLOBE research conference was held at the University of Calgary in Canada (House et al. 1994). Fifty-four researchers from thirty-eight countries gathered to develop a collective understanding of the project and to initiate its implementation. In this meeting considerable time was spent generating a working definition of "leadership" that reflected the diverse viewpoints held by GLOBE researchers. A consensus emerged, but only after hours of discussion with many contrasting viewpoints. The GLOBE project's universal definition of organizational leadership emerged as "the ability of an individual to influence, motivate, and enable others to contribute toward the effectiveness and success of the organizations of which they are members" (House et al. 1999, 184). Brett et al. (1997) observe that the initial interaction among GLOBE researchers demonstrated the effectiveness of an "n-way" approach to cross-cultural research. As such, the initial stages of an "n-way" model of conducting research begin with a research question and a multicultural team of scholars—this exactly describes the GLOBE research project.

HISTORICAL TRENDS AND STREAMS OF LEADERSHIP RESEARCH

The field of leadership is often portrayed as having passed through multiple distinct eras—from an earlier focus on "great man" and trait theories, to behavior and contingency theories, to more recent theories that stress charismatic, transformational, and visionary elements. In fact, the leadership field has recently undergone a transformation and rejuvenation with a general reorientation from looking at leadership "in" organizations to leadership "of" organizations (Boal and Hooijberg 2001). Each era of research activity can be characterized by a dominant research strategy and focus of interest (Chemers 1983). The implication of most historical reviews is that leadership research has progressed in a linear, predictable, and consistent fashion through these phases. However, one should understand that the field of leadership is often in a state of ferment and confusion (Yukl and Van Fleet 1992) with multiple foci occurring at the same time. If we can think of leadership research flowing as a stream, it flows in a meandering, intertwining, and consistently shifting manner. What follows is a brief, and therefore simplistic, introduction to the history of leadership research as viewed from a North American perspective.

"GREAT MAN" AND TRAIT THEORIES
(THE "RIGHT STUFF")

Not surprisingly, because the history of the world has been shaped by the leadership of great men and women, the study of leaders began as an effort to identify the personal characteristics and personality traits of leaders. Findings from early studies were disappointing, as researchers were not able to consistently identify personality traits or physical characteristics that were both necessary and sufficient for leadership success. More recent studies and reviews using sophisticated meta-analytic statistical techniques have revealed that some individual traits are consistently related to which individual will emerge as a leader (leadership emergence) but are somewhat less consistently related to leadership effectiveness. For example, successful leaders in Western nations often exhibit high energy and activity levels, self-confidence, persistence, tolerance of stress, decisiveness, emotional maturity, intellectual competencies, achievement orientation, and strong drives for responsibility (Kirkpatrick and Locke 1991). Recent research found in the assessment center literature (Howard and Bray 1988) strongly supports the notion that managerial success in the United States is dependent on a set of personal skills and attributes such as those just mentioned.

BEHAVIORAL APPROACH TO LEADERSHIP

Partly as a response to the disappointing results of the early trait approach to leadership, leadership researchers in the 1950s began to study what managers actually do on the job. The goal of the behavioral approach was to identify and measure relevant leadership actions and behavioral patterns that lead to high subordinate productivity and morale. Thus, the research focus changed from what leaders *are* to what leaders *do*. Researchers at Ohio State University (e.g., Fleishman 1953; Fleishman, Harris, and Burtt 1955) and at the University of Michigan (Likert 1961; Bowers and Seashore 1966; Likert 1967) found that subordinates perceived leader behaviors to fall into two independent categories. The first category concerns task-oriented behaviors, labeled "initiating structure." This category includes such structuring leader behaviors as assigning subordinates to tasks, coordinating activities, and criticizing poor work. The second category, labeled "consideration," concerns relationship-oriented behaviors such as showing concern for subordinates and acting friendly and supportive. However, the pure behavioral approach to leadership suffers from a failure to examine critical situational factors. Just as personal traits may be more or less important depending on the situation, leaders also need to tailor their leadership behaviors to the situation. To be effective, leaders must adapt their actions to suit the requirements of the task and the characteristics of the subordinates who perform the task (Yukl and Van Fleet 1992). This fact is incorporated in contingency theories. These specific theories are mentioned here because not only have they been empirically tested within a Western context, but they have also been examined from a cross-cultural perspective.

CONTINGENCY THEORIES OF LEADERSHIP

Contingency theories of leadership consider how situational factors alter the effectiveness of particular leader behaviors and styles of leadership. The assumption is that no leadership traits, behaviors, or styles automatically constitute effective leadership. The key is the fit between a leader's style and the situation the leader faces. For instance, the leadership styles of General George Patton (commanding the Third Army in World War II) and Mahatma Gandhi (resisting the British in India) were vastly different, but both were effective. According to contingency theories, leaders must correctly identify the critical characteristics of each situation, identify which leader behaviors are required, and then be flexible to exhibit these behaviors (Howell et al. 1990).

FIEDLER'S CONTINGENCY THEORY OF LEADERSHIP

Fiedler's contingency model of leadership (Fiedler 1967; Fiedler and Chemers 1984) may be the most widely researched model of leadership (Bass 1990). The basic premise is that the situation moderates the relationship between leader personality traits (currently referred to as the leader's basic motivational orientation) and effectiveness. The leadership situation is characterized by the quality of leader-member relations, the degree of task structure, and the leader's position power. The personality-motivational orientation of the leader, measured by the least preferred co-worker (LPC) score, indicates the extent to which the leader's primary motivation is oriented toward task or interpersonal success. According to the theory, task-motivated leaders perform best in situations in which they have very high or very low potential power to influence groups. Relationship-motivated leaders perform best in situations in which they have moderate control (Fiedler 1993).

Fiedler developed another contingency model (Fiedler 1986; Fiedler and Garcia 1987) called the "cognitive resources theory." The crux of the theory concerns how cognitive resources of the leader, for which experience and intelligence are critical, become related to group performance. The theory specifies that under conditions of low stress good decisions are made by leaders with high intellect. In contrast, under highly stressful conditions, a leader's experience will help him or her effectively deal with problems. Both outcomes only occur, however, if the leader is directive and the subordinates in the group actually require guidance to perform their tasks.

PATH-GOAL THEORY OF LEADERSHIP

The path-goal theory developed by Evans (1970) and House (1971) and recently updated by House (1996) provides another view of the link between leader behaviors, follower characteristics, and situational factors. Simply put, this theory is called "path-goal" because the leader's primary function is to motivate followers through increasing personal payoffs to subordinates for work goal achievement and making the paths to these payoffs easier to travel. Leaders are expected to clarify subordinate roles, increase resources and remove roadblocks, and increase opportunities for personal satisfaction. The path-goal theory (in the revised version by House and Mitchell [1974]) employs four specific leader behaviors: directive leadership, supportive leadership, achievement-oriented leadership, and participative leadership. The theory is very follower oriented, as characteristics of the followers, such as their competence and personality needs, influence the appropriate leader behavior. Finally, characteristics of the task and environment (e.g., task structure and complexity) are also considered. An example may clarify how the theory operates. For stressful, boring, or tedious tasks, supportive leadership will lead to increased subordinate effort and satisfaction. Thus, support will be welcomed if your task is to stuff envelopes for your favorite politician. The theory has been extended with the addition of several leadership behaviors, including "value-based behavior," that embody many of the elements of charismatic leadership. The original path-goal theory has spawned the leadership substitutes theory, the most systematic typology of moderators thus far proposed. Path-goal theory also serves as a very useful framework for cross-cultural research

(Dorfman et al. 1997), since "culture" may be the ultimate situational moderator (Triandis 1993).

LEADERSHIP SUBSTITUTES THEORY

Leadership substitutes theory can be considered a natural extension of path-goal theory by providing a framework for classifying the situational moderator variables found in path-goal theory. These situational variables may be attributes of the subordinates (e.g., experience and ability), task (e.g., intrinsically satisfying tasks), or organization (e.g., degree of formalization) that enhance, neutralize, or substitute for particular leader behaviors (Kerr and Jermier 1978; Howell, Dorfman, and Kerr 1986). For example, researchers have found that, in stressful organizational situations such as landing jet fighters on a nuclear aircraft carrier, directive leadership is relatively unimportant compared with the work experience and training of the crew. A common misunderstanding regarding substitutes theory is that substitutes eliminate the need for all types of leadership. In reality, some substitute variables such as worker professionalism may be true substitutes for certain leadership behaviors (e.g., directive leadership) but are enhancers for others (e.g., participative leadership) (Howell and Costley 2001).

PARTICIPATIVE LEADERSHIP AND THE NORMATIVE DECISION MODEL

Supervisors often struggle with the extent to which subordinates should become involved in organizational decisions. Vroom and Yetton (1973), and subsequently Vroom and Jago (1988), developed a model of participation (the normative decision model) that specifies the type of decision procedures most likely to be effective in alternative situations. The model was developed partly as a response to the rather simplistic acceptance and romance of participatory approaches. For Vroom and Yetton, the type of participatory approach should be evaluated in terms of the contribution to effective performance, not because it is the right or decent way to act. Use of the model does not result in a decision but prescribes the most appropriate decision *process* for the supervisor—autocratic, consultative, or complete delegation.

"NEW" LEADERSHIP: CHARISMATIC AND TRANSFORMATIONAL THEORIES

Charismatic and transformational theories help account for the enormous *emotional* impact that powerful leaders can have in creating organizational excitement and commitment. Charisma, a Greek word meaning "divinely inspired gift," embodies the leadership influence resulting from personal identification with extraordinary leaders. Such leaders are found in politics (Franklin D. Roosevelt, Mahatma Gandhi, John F. Kennedy), religion (Christ, Mohammed, Moses), and business (Bill Gates, Lee Iacocca). The major charismatic theories include those by House (1977), Conger and Kanungo (1987), and Shamir, House, and Arthur (1993). The major transformational theory of leadership was developed by Bass (1985, 1990, 1997), who was strongly influenced by the ideas of Burns (1978). In this same vein, Kouzes and Posner (1987) and Bennis and Nanus (1985) developed and articulated what are currently referred to as visionary theories. Visionary theories have a distinctly practical bent to them and can be quite useful for practicing managers.

Bass's (1985) transformational and transactional theory is representative of charismatic theories. According to Bass, followers may be motivated by leaders in two distinctly different but important ways. Transactional leadership motivates followers by providing task guidance, correcting performance flaws, and rewarding successful efforts—essentially using an exchange or transaction process with followers. Followers are motivated by self-interest and achieve an implicit bargain with the leader: "You work for me, do what I tell you, and I'll reward you when you perform well." In contrast, transformational leaders inspire followers to transcend their own interests for superordinate goals. They do this through a number of means—idealized influence or charisma, inspirational motivation, intellectual stimulation, and individualized consideration (Bass and Avolio 1993). Neo-charismatic theories developed by House and Shamir (1993) stress charismatic processes found in the transformational theories and, more specifically, the processes by which charismatic leadership influences followers.

THE MEANING OF CULTURE AND CROSS-CULTURAL IMPLICATIONS FOR MANAGEMENT AND LEADERSHIP

Debate has raged among academicians over defining the term "culture" (Swidler 1986), with the result that there may be as many different definitions and conceptualizations of "culture" as there are of "leadership." For Hofstede (1991, 1993), culture is the collective programming of the mind, or "software of the mind"—the mental programs that distinguish one group of people from another. Triandis (1980) offers a definition that encompasses objective and subjective elements—the latter of which includes the traditional focus on attitudes, norms, and values. Since many definitions of culture are valid (Triandis, Kurowski, and Gelfand 1994), leadership researchers need not become overly concerned with choosing *the* most appropriate definition of culture. But it is important to not use the term carelessly (Roberts 1970) and to remember that culture is a group-level construct that reflects the character of a group's unique social identity (Deutsch 1973; Brett et al. 1997). For leadership researchers the following caveat emptor is critical: Cross-*national* differences in organizational practices do not necessarily imply cross-*cultural* differences. That is, there is a whole host of situational variables in addition to culture (such as a country's legal and economic systems) that can lead to cross-national differences. The important point about culture is that it shapes the values, attitudes, and behaviors of a social group.

IMPACT OF CULTURE ON MANAGEMENT PROCESSES

Although scholars agree that the concepts of management and leadership are conceptually intertwined, they are not identical (Bass 1985). Managers may or may not be viewed as leaders, and leaders may or may not be good managers (Lord and Maher 1991). Managers with intercultural responsibilities clearly understand the difficulty of working across national and cultural borders, as is often required for joint ventures, strategic alliances, and mergers. In addition to obvious language problems that face managers in intercultural contexts, many management practices seem to be inexorably intertwined with cultural forces and seem strange, if not ridiculous, to members of contrasting cultures. For instance, the Japanese practice of overworking productive employees and letting the incompetent ones do little (e.g., placing a nonproductive employee near the window, thus being labeled as a "window person") may seem to be a wasteful and silly management practice to an American manager, whereas the American practice of "employee of the month" awards may seem equally strange to a manager in a more collectivist culture that emphasizes teamwork. Hofstede (1993) argues that there are no such things as universal management theories and that theories as well as practices stop at national borders.

Wonderful examples of cultural contingencies in management are provided by Laurent's (1983) series of questions asked to managers from various European cultures. Striking differences were found between managers of different nations regarding the desirability of specific management practices. For instance, when asked if it is often necessary to bypass the hierarchical line in order to have efficient work relationships, most Italian managers responded negatively. In contrast, most Swedish managers thought this behavior was perfectly reasonable. The reality of having two bosses, an aspect of the matrix type of organizational structure, was anathema for French and Italian managers, but was not nearly as much of a problem for U.S. managers. My personal experience in the Mexican *maquiladoras* (often called "twin plants") reflected an often overoptimistic *"no problema"* response to obviously difficult issues. The essential role of management may also be culturally contingent. In France, the manager's role is thought to be that of an expert, whereas in the United States the manager is viewed as a problem solver. A midlevel French supervisor may lose respect and power if she or he does not know the precise answer to a subordinate's question, whereas the same is not likely true for an American supervisor.

The study of influence tactics used by managers also shows some cross-cultural specifics (and seeming universals as well). In one study of Japanese managers, some of the influence tactics used mirrored those often found in the United States (Rao, Hashimoto, and Rao 1997). For instance, appeals to higher authority, assertiveness, and sanctions represented the same strategies in Japan and America. However, two tactics in particular— socializing after work and convincing subordinates that their personal development will be enhanced—were found to be strategies unique in character to Japanese managers. Furthermore, in a recent study contrasting American and Chinese managers, rational persuasion and exchange were rated as more effective by Americans, and coalition tactics, upward appeals, and gifts were more effective for Chinese (Fu and Yukl 2000). In the largest study of cross-cultural influence tactics to date, Kennedy, Fu, and Yukl (2003) found that consultation and collaboration were related to two cultural dimensions called individualism/collectivism and power distance. While these two influence tactics could predictably be linked to *low* power distance cultural values, I was surprised to learn that they were more prevalent for individualistic, not collectivistic, values. The likely explanation for the latter finding lies with the importance of in-groups versus out-groups in collectivistic societies. One may wish to collaborate, but only with trusted in-group members.

In summary, there is considerable literature linking cultural values to management techniques. Erez (1994) argues that this link is not just a coincidence.

Managerial techniques that fit in with individualistic values—individual job enrichment, individual goal setting, and individual incentives—emerge and become effective in individualistic cultures. In contrast, the management practices that correspond to collectivistic, group oriented values—quality circles, autonomous work groups, group goals, and participation in goal setting and decision making—emerge in more collectivist cultures such as Scandinavia, Japan, China, and Israel. (580)

CULTURAL INFLUENCE ON LEADERSHIP THROUGH MANAGERIAL ATTITUDES, VALUES, AND BELIEFS

It should come as no surprise that the cross-cultural management literature is replete with studies examining cross-national differences in managerial attitudes, values, and beliefs. Since excellent reviews of this literature are available (e.g., Ronen 1986; Bhagat et al. 1990; Arvey, Bhagat, and Salas 1991; Hofstede 1993, 2001), only the classic study by Haire, Ghiselli, and Porter (1966) is described to illustrate the importance of this research for cross-cultural leadership. The researchers' primary goal in the Haire, Ghiselli, and Porter (1966) study was to determine whether managerial attitudes are essentially the same across nations or whether they differ from country to country. Questionnaire responses were obtained from more than thirty-six hundred managers in fourteen nations. Eight leadership items covered issues relating to an average subordinate's capacity for leadership and initiative, a leader's attitude toward sharing information and participation, and attitudes toward authority and control. One striking finding regarding leadership was that, while managers from all countries espoused democratic management styles and favored participatory leadership, managers of most countries held a low opinion as to whether subordinates had the capacity for leadership and initiative. American managers, more than managers in other countries, believed that individuals have the necessary requisites for democratic leadership—the potential to exhibit initiative and share leadership responsibilities. Responses enabled the researchers to form clusters of nations with similar response patterns (e.g., Anglo compared to the Nordic European or Latin European cluster). One major finding is somewhat paradoxical—a strong pattern of cultural influence exists simultaneously with a considerable similarity of viewpoints for all managers. The simultaneous existence of similarity and diversity foreshadows forthcoming evidence related to leadership differences across cultures. Studies that increase the range of cultural values considered (e.g., Ralston et al. 1993; Trompenaars 1993) attest to continued interest in diverse cross-cultural beliefs and values. For leadership researchers to benefit from this line of research, more work is clearly needed to elucidate the mechanism by which managerial beliefs, values, and attitudes are linked to leadership processes. To this end, Chemers (1994) clearly identified how cultural differences in values are likely to impact three essential leadership functions—image management, relationship development, and resource utilization. As an example of how a culture's values might influence the kind of image expected of a leader, one only has to consider differences in the ideal leader described in American folk wisdom as independent and forceful, whereas the image of a leader in a more collectivist society such as Japan includes attributes of fairness and harmony.

IMPACT OF CULTURE ON LEADERSHIP PROCESSES

It has become almost axiomatic for researchers to argue that the kind of leadership attempted and the level of leadership success will depend on the congruence between the cultural values and leadership processes (e.g., Bass 1990). Obviously, authoritarian leadership behaviors are less likely to work in democratic cultures characterized by a long history of egalitarianism and low power stratification than they are in cultures with opposite beliefs and values. The prevailing view is that core beliefs and values consistent with these "cultural dimensions" guide managerial action. Without denigrating the importance of "values," an alternative mechanism is that culture limits the repertoire of acceptable strategies of action rather than being the end value toward which action is directed (Swidler 1986). That is, while people naturally know "how to act" in certain situations, they do not necessarily have to be able to espouse the "value" consistent with the action or cognitively realize that a particular behavior is directed toward a specific value. Although both the cultural dimensions/values and behavioral repertoire/routines explanations are valid causal mechanisms by which organizational behaviors become culturally contingent, the former are more established in the leadership literature.

In fact, Yukl (2002) argues that the quality of cross-cultural leadership research is dependent on the adequacy of the conceptual framework used to identify cultural dimensions. But which cultural dimensions are most important? How are these dimensions linked to leadership processes? These remain unresolved questions. Consider first the variety and range of cultural dimensions researched within the management and leadership literature. Agreement as to the adequacy, meaning, and measurement of Hofstede's initial four culture dimensions (power distance, individualism and collectivism, uncertainty avoidance, and masculinity and femininity) and currently a fifth dimension (long- versus short-term orientation) remains controversial. The GLOBE project mentioned previously builds on Hofstede's initial work and currently specifies nine cultural dimensions. In addition to the four original Hofstede dimensions, it adds cultural dimensions of performance orientation, future orientation, and humane orientation and further separates two of Hofstede's original four dimensions. On the basis of empirical data GLOBE researchers separated Hofstede's masculinity-femininity dimension into assertiveness and gender egalitarianism dimensions. Furthermore, they found that Hofstede's individualism-collectivism factor should be conceived as two aspects of collectivism—one reflecting the construct for in-groups such as families and organizations, the other reflecting societal values and practices. Trompenaars (1993) suggests other dimensions, most of which concern interpersonal relationships. For instance, his "achievement versus ascription" dimension concerns the importance placed on accomplishment and record (i.e., achievement) with the status attributed to you on the basis of birth, kinship, and who you know (i.e., ascription).

The question of which cultural dimensions are most important for leadership cannot be completely answered at this time. Triandis (1993), based on years of cross-cultural research, suggests that individualism-collectivism is one of the most important dimensions of cultural variation. He argues that leadership processes may differ in individualist and collectivist cultures in the following manner. For collectivist cultures, we might expect successful leaders to be supportive and paternalistic (i.e., maintaining the harmony of the workgroup, solving workers' personal problems, being generally helpful and considerate). For individualist cultures, support might be valued when needed, but achievement-oriented and participative leadership would be key leader behaviors. A strong case can also be made for the importance of the cultural dimension labeled "power distance" by Hofstede (1980) and the GLOBE project (House et al. 2004). It is relatively easy to envision why power stratification should be important for leadership processes. In cultures characterized by low power distance, subordinates expect superiors to consult them and use their suggestions, whereas in cultures characterized by high power distances, subordinates expect supervisors to act more directively and perhaps in an autocratic manner. Project GLOBE also found that the cultural dimension labeled performance orientation was particularly important in its relationship to many culturally endorsed leadership dimensions—for example, charismatic/valued-based leadership (Dorfman, Hanges, and Brodbeck 2004). Again, careful theorizing should help determine which cultural factors are most important in any given situation. For instance, we should find that in high uncertainty avoidance societies, leaders are likely to forcefully provide direction in tasks to be accomplished and the method to accomplish these tasks. Clearly, empirical research should help resolve the issue regarding which dimensions are most important for leadership. As a cross-cultural researcher who anticipates (relishes?) variance among cultures, I expect that the importance of cultural dimensions will vary systematically across cultures and specific leadership functions. We shall see.

IMPACT OF CULTURE ON DESCRIPTIONS
OF IDEAL LEADERS

The social information–processing literature (Rosch 1975; Croker, Fiske, and Taylor 1984) provides a nice conceptual framework to explain the mechanisms by which cultural values impact leadership. Models developed from this literature illustrate how cultures shape the basic ways people collect, store, organize, and process information about each other. For instance, Shaw (1990) suggests that much of the cross-national literature indicating differences in managerial beliefs, values, and styles can be interpreted as showing culturally influenced differences in leader prototypes. As typically conceived, prototypes contain a set of features or attributes that define the essential characteristics of a category, and for us one important category is that of "an effective business leader."

Are there universally endorsed prototypes of ideal leaders? Although it is unlikely that any single prototype of an effective leader conforms equally well across societies, there may be universally endorsed attributes as well as culturally specific attributes. A basic question then concerns the identification of the content of prototypes across cultures. However, it would also be useful to determine how the content of these cultural prototypes change for different leadership prototypes (e.g., business leader vs. political leader). Although these issues are no doubt complex, the cognitive/information processing approach to studying leadership (e.g., Lord, Foti, and Phillips 1982) is a useful paradigm to investigate questions of this sort regarding idealized leaders. The basic paradigm used by Lord and associates assumes that leadership involves a perceptual process—being perceived by others as a leader. A central question for Lord (e.g., Lord and Maher 1991) concerns how leadership is recognized based on followers' implicit ideas of what leaders are and how leadership is inferred based on positive or negative organizational outcomes.

What evidence exists to confirm the expected influence of cultural differences on implicit leadership theories? A study by O'Connell, Lord, and O'Connell (1990) found that culture plays a strong role in influencing the content of leader attributes and behaviors perceived as desirable and effective. Their study specifically examined the similarities and differences between Japanese and American conceptions of useful leadership attributes. For the Japanese, the traits of being fair, flexible, a good listener, outgoing, and responsible were highly rated for leadership effectiveness in many domains, such as business, media, and education. For Americans, traits of intelligence, honesty, understanding, verbal skills, and determination were strongly endorsed as facilitating leader effectiveness in numerous domains. A study by Gerstner and Day (1994) also provides additional evidence that ratings of leadership attributes and behaviors vary across cultures. University students from eight nations identified the fit between fifty-nine attributes (previously developed from Lord) and each student's image of a business leader. As expected, attributes that were seen as most characteristic of business leaders varied across cultures—no single trait was rated in the top five as being most prototypical across all eight nations. As another example of how leadership perceptions are influenced by culture, Chong and Thomas (1997) suggest that leadership prototypes of two ethnic groups in New Zealand influenced the *amounts* of leadership behaviors experienced. These three studies just described, while important, were limited in size, scope, and sample selection such that their theoretical significance and generalizability are limited beyond the specific cultures sampled.

Two studies recently published by GLOBE researchers (as part of the GLOBE project) further attest to the existence and importance of culturally influenced leadership theories (CLTs). Den Hartog et al. (1999) presented evidence that attributes of charismatic/transformational leadership are universally endorsed as contributing to outstanding leadership. This study also provides evidence that leadership prototypes vary by hierarchical levels within an organization; implicit leadership theories held for top managers and CEOs differ from those held for effective supervisors. Using a different subset of the GLOBE data for European cultures, Brodbeck et al. (2000), in a second study, presents convincing evidence that clusters of European cultures sharing similar cultural values also share similar leadership concepts. Specific leadership attributes and behaviors thought to be universally effective and those thought to be culturally contingent will be described later in this chapter.

Numerous questions related to leadership prototypes remain to tantalize cross-cultural researchers for years to come. For instance, if leadership prototypes differ among nations, are they equally compelling and influential? How do they develop? What psychological mechanisms link the prototypes to dominant cultural values? Are prototypes more functionally set for homogeneous societies such as Japan than for culturally diverse societies such as the United States? Are specific characteristics of each prototype, such as the default and constraint values associated with a prototype, similarly culturally contingent? Additional questions emerge relating to the expression and manifestation of the ideal prototype, as well as to the process by which outcomes are interpreted and credited (Chemers 1994).

CROSS-CULTURAL LEADERSHIP
RESEARCH STUDIES

Most studies conducted by leadership researchers in different parts of the world reflect an awareness and understanding of leadership research conducted in America and other Western countries (Smith and Peterson 1988). In addition, most of these studies are ethnocentric (research designed and tested in one culture and replicated in another culture) rather than truly comparative (designed to test similarities and differences across two or more cultures) (Adler 1984). There is nothing inherently wrong with testing the applicability of a particular theory developed in the West to other geographic regions or cultures. However, simple replications limit the kind of conclusions that can be inferred. One cannot conclude that similar findings in the second culture prove universality, nor do differences warrant the conclusion that "culture" is the causal factor (Roberts 1970). Numerous other explanations are possible, and it is critical for cross-cultural researchers to develop rigorous designs to reduce the potential for alternative explanations (Brett et al. 1997). In addition, it is important to remember that it is rare (and perhaps unheard of) to find *any* leadership theory developed in the West, and tested in the West, to be free from conflicted findings or unresolved issues. Therefore, when testing the transferability of theories across cultures, unsupported findings do not necessarily mean that culture is the "culprit." The following organizational schema mirrors as closely as possible the initial discussion of streams of leadership research. The fit is not exact, as I have chosen to deviate where necessary to include additional relevant literature.

BEHAVIORAL APPROACH TO LEADERSHIP

Findings from a number of cross-cultural studies have supported the importance of the task-oriented and relationship-oriented leadership dimensions (Ayman and Chemers 1983; Bond and Hwang 1986; Sinha 1980) that were originally conceptualized in the United States. Tscheulin (1973), for example, translated the original Ohio State University "Supervisory Behavior Description Questionnaire" scale into German and confirmed the existence of these two leadership factors in West Germany. After reviewing a number of studies, he concluded that "the similarity of results across almost 20 years with different cultures and different methods of analysis can be considered remarkable" (30). Fleishman and Simmons's (1970) research in Israel extended U.S. findings to Israeli foremen. They found that leadership patterns that combined high consideration with structure resulted in the highest supervisory ratings. Rim (1965), who studied Israeli head nurses and industrial supervisors, also found that the most influential people were those high in both consideration and structure. Similarly, Misumi's seminal research studies in Japan (Misumi 1985) also point to successful supervision requiring high levels of both kinds of leadership (his studies are described more fully in a separate section). Results of other studies in different cultures are not always so consistent. In a comparison of Turkish and American first-line supervisors, Kennis (1977) found that American supervisors were perceived to be more participative and considerate than Turkish supervisors but equal in structuring behaviors. However, whereas participation, consideration, and structure were related to satisfaction with supervision for Americans, only the consideration score was related to satisfaction with supervision for the Turkish sample. In contrast to the usual finding of consideration being important, Anderson (1983), in New Zealand, found that considerate leader behavior did not lead to higher subordinate performance. Studies using the task-oriented and relationship-oriented leadership styles have also been conducted with Chinese students, managers, and administrators (Meade 1970; Bond and Hwang 1986); Italian, Belgian, American, and U.K. managers (Thia-garajan and Deep 1970); New Zealand white and Polynesian managers (Anderson 1983); Philippine and Chinese managers (Bennett 1977); Japanese students, teachers, supervisors, and government administrators (Misumi and Shirakashi 1966; Misumi and Peterson 1985); Brazilian employees (Farris and Butterfield 1972); Iranian employees (Ayman and Chemers 1983); Indian employees (Kakar 1971; Sinha 1984); Canadian Anglophones and Francophones (Punnett 1991); Middle East managers (Scandura, Von Glinow, and Lowe 1999); and Israeli manual and clerical workers (Mannheim, Rim, and Grinberg 1967).

In general, cross-cultural studies support the importance of considerate leadership in increasing subordinates' satisfaction with supervision. The universality of leader supportiveness should not be surprising since supportive leaders show concern for followers and are considerate and available to listen to followers' problems (Dorfman et al. 1997). Contrary findings in this regard are infrequent, but they do occur. Bennett (1977) found that Filipino and Chinese bank managers were less relationship oriented than their Western counterparts and concluded that effectiveness of this leadership behavior may be dependent on cultural norms. A recent study of Middle East managers (Scandura, Von Glinow, and Lowe 1999) also found a very limited importance of supervisory consideration. In addition, evidence also exists that cultures differ in the perceived importance of managerial consideration/supportive behaviors (Bass et al. 1979) and often differ in the factor structure of the leadership scales measuring consideration (Mauer 1974; Anderson 1983; Ayman and Chemers 1983).

To summarize the impact of task orientation, results from studies conducted in both Western and non-Western cultures are very complex and defy simple explanation (Bass 1990). Korman's (1966) review of studies in the United States, for example, concludes that there is a lack of consistent results for task-oriented leadership. Not surprisingly, cross-cultural studies examining the impact of directive behaviors on employees also show conflicting, and not easily interpretable, results (Kakar 1971; Kennis 1977; Anderson 1983). Results by Dorfman et al. (1997) further confirm a cultural-specific interpretation for task-oriented leadership—it was important in some countries but not in others. A study by Scandura, Von Glinow, and Lowe (1999), discussed later in this chapter, found intriguing results where emphasis on task orientation, not consideration, was important for effective leadership in the Middle East.

Many of the studies just discussed have also been reviewed by Tannenbaum (1980), Bhagat et al. (1990), Bass (1990), and Smith and Peterson (1988). I found it particularly striking that somewhat differing conclusions were drawn by these reviewers regarding the two leadership functions of task-oriented and relationship-oriented behaviors. For instance, Bass (1990) notes that "considerable differences in the initiation of structure and consideration have been found among managers from different countries" (797). While noting that these leadership functions have not been consistently supported in individualistic countries (ironically where the theories were developed) Smith and Peterson (1988) conclude that "studies conducted in collectively oriented societies have given much more consistent support to theories of leaders style which specify two components of effectiveness" (98). In direct contrast, Bhagat et al. (1990) conclude "that the well known dimensions of 'consideration' and 'initiation of structure' are not as appropriate in non-Western cultures as they are in the USA" (89). Can these differing views be reconciled? This specific issue may be moot, as leadership theory has progressed far beyond the too simplistic two-dimension conception of leadership.

Several additional leader behaviors, such as leader reward and punishment behaviors, have also been studied in cross-cultural contexts. The behavior of leaders rewarding subordinates for good performance has been found to have positive impacts in very different cultures (e.g., Podsakoff et al. 1986; Dorfman et al. 1997). Leader rewards that are contingent on subordinates performing well (i.e., contingent rewards) consistently lead to high subordinate levels of commitment, job satisfaction, and satisfaction with supervision. Not surprisingly, regardless of the cultural context, subordinates everywhere welcome praise, recognition, and approval when they perform well. In contrast, the influence of contingent punishment leadership behaviors (Podsakoff et al. 1986) may be more culturally specific. The Dorfman et al. (1997) study confirmed the culture-specific interpretation of contingent punishment for countries in the Pacific-Asian Basin. This leader behavior had positive impacts only in the highly individualistic United States.

One methodological issue is particularly relevant to the literature just cited. As is the case with any questionnaire that is developed without consideration for the possible emic (i.e., insider familiar with the culture) nature of the construct in question, conclusions regarding the general absence of culturally contingent findings may be suspect. For instance, although a leader's rewarding behaviors may be important in all cultures, the American propensity for praising subordinates for good performance in front of others, thus glorifying one person's success, would be frowned upon in the Japanese culture. Obviously, cultural differences would be masked if a questionnaire were developed without this sensitivity. As another example, strict rules of *tatamae* (e.g., strict rules of social interaction to not express inner feelings so as to maintain harmony) prohibit Japanese from openly seeking rewards or professing expectations of rewards (Yokochi 1989). The degree to which expectations of rewards differ between samples, and the impact of a leader not providing these rewards, would remain masked in questionnaire research unless specific questions in the research instrument reflected these possible differences. In these cases, qualitative research might be better able to discover subtle differences between cultures.

CONTINGENCY THEORIES OF LEADERSHIP

FIEDLER'S CONTINGENCY THEORY OF LEADERSHIP

Some of the initial tests of Fiedler's contingency theory were carried out in Holland (Fiedler, Meuwese, and Oonk 1961) and Belgium (Fiedler 1966). And, according to Fiedler (1966), these initial tests were very supportive of his contingency model. It should also be noted that Fiedler's model has been used extensively in training multicultural groups. Furthermore, a study by Bennett (1977), using Filipino and Hong Kong Chinese bank managers, provides some evidence that culture plays a moderating role in the contingency model. Bennett found that high-performing Filipino managers were more task oriented, whereas high-performing Chinese managers were more relationship oriented. The author acknowledges that the study was not a thorough test of the contingency model because no attempt was made to assess the specific level of "leadership favorability" that is required for an adequate test of the model. However, the results led Bennett to make the observation that a person-oriented dimension of leadership (similar to consideration) may be dependent upon cultural norms for its effectiveness. In contrast, most other studies of considerate leadership conclude the opposite and find that it is the "initiating structure" leadership dimension that is culturally contingent. Tests of Fiedler's contingency model in Japan have been less than encouraging (Shirakashi 1968; Misumi and Peterson 1987). LPC scores seem to depend on the particular sample, and there are serious questions of the reliability and construct validity of the LPC measure in Japan. In addition, Misumi (1985) failed to find significant relationships between his four basic leader types and LPC scores.

More recently, Ayman and Chemers (1991) found mixed support for the LPC model in predicting subordinates' satisfaction within the "collectivist" country of Mexico. In this study Ayman and Chemers considered the impact of a personality trait labeled "self-monitoring" in addition to the usual defining factors of the theory. The complexity of their results defies a simple interpretation, but it does provide evidence for the importance of examining additional personality considerations when determining how a particular leadership theory operates across cultures. Triandis (1993) has developed a comprehensive set of propositions predicting how Fiedler's contingency model might hold up in collectivist cultures. Leaders in collectivist cultures will most often find themselves in situations of middle favorability—thus the relationship-oriented leader will be most effective in collectivist cultures. Another prediction states that most leaders in collectivist cultures will be nurturant, but these cultures will also have effective leaders who are *extremely* task oriented—the Idi Amin type. Finally, he concludes that there really is no need for contingency theories in collectivist cultures (consistent with Misumi's [1985] position).

PATH-GOAL THEORY OF LEADERSHIP

House's path-goal leadership theory was developed to predict subordinates' motivation, satisfaction, and performance as outcomes resulting from four types of leader behavior. The theory incorporates numerous moderator variables, and since culture is an important moderator, the theory has been useful in cross-cultural research. For instance, Dorfman and Howell (1988) investigated the moderating effect of culture in a somewhat unique manner. They hypothesized that, consistent with path-goal theory, culture may moderate the impact of leadership behaviors on important criteria. Dorfman and Howell did not directly contrast the moderating impact of culture by comparing the differing effects of leadership among several countries (i.e., "it works like this here, but not here perspective"). Instead, the researchers looked at the influence of culture by contrasting *individuals* who indicated a strong, as opposed to a weak, adherence to specific cultural values and beliefs (i.e., beliefs in individualism-collectivism, power distance, masculinity, and paternalism). This approach is consistent with the one used by Earley (1989, 1993) to employ an individual-level representation of a cultural-level construct. The researchers found that two leadership processes were moderated by cultural beliefs and two were not. In general, the results indicated that the leaders' contingent reward behaviors have consistent and nonmoderated positive impacts on subordinate satisfaction with supervision and organizational commitment in both cultures. In a similar manner, the researchers found that supportive leadership behaviors were not moderated by cultural beliefs. In contrast to contingent reward and support, the results for directive leadership indicated clear moderating effects of culture and partial moderating effects for contingent punishment. As expected, directive leadership had maximal effect on employee attitudes and performance for employees who personally held strong beliefs in cultural dimensions that were expected to promote directive leadership (e.g., belief in the appropriateness of high power distance between the supervisor and subordinate).

A cross-cultural field study by Dorfman et al. (1997) provides further evidence of the cross-cultural transferability of leadership behaviors. This study incorporated Yukl's multiple linkage model (1989) into the original path-goal theory to test the generalizability of six leader behaviors across five nations in North America and Asia. Yukl's model is a metatheory that includes a wider range of leadership behaviors, mediators, and moderators than the earlier path-goal theory. It also includes the "substitutes of leadership" typology of moderators that has been discussed previously. The findings showed complete universality for three leader behaviors (supportive behaviors, contingent reward, and charismatic) and cultural specificity for the remaining three leader behaviors (directive, participative, and contingent punishment behaviors). In comparing the impacts of leadership behaviors between Asian and Western culture clusters, the researchers were struck by the fact that the United States was unique in several respects from all other cultures studied. It was the *only* culture where leader directiveness had no effect on subordinate attitudes. It was the *only* culture where participative leadership had a significant positive effect on the job performance of subordinates. And it was the *only* culture where leaders' contingent punishment behavior strongly affected followers. The high individualism of the United States (Dorfman and Howell 1988; Hofstede 1991) combined with the highly participative U.S. management climate likely contribute toward the culturally unique results regarding leadership behaviors in the U.S. sample.

LEADERSHIP SUBSTITUTES THEORY

The transferability of leader substitutes across cultures is relatively untested. Misumi proposed that substitutes for leadership are probably less operative in Japan than in the United States (Misumi and Peterson 1985). For instance, large spatial distances between leaders and subordinates (which presumably neutralize certain leadership actions) are less prevalent in Japan, where supervisors are rarely isolated in separate offices like they tend to be in the United States. Also, the single-organizational career pattern may encourage employees in Japan to depend on their formal leaders for guidance, whereas U.S. employees would rely on professional socialization and occupational training (potential substitutes). Empirical research lends some support to Misumi's predictions. Dorfman et al. (1997) found that certain substitute/enhancer factors (e.g., worker professionalism and subordinate's years of work experience) were significant in all cultures studied except Japan. However, two substitutes and/or enhancers were found significant in *all* countries studied. Perceived leader expertise and subordinate years of schooling showed strong substitute/enhancer effects in all five cultures. Other studies testing the transferability of leader substitutes across cultures provide less support for the theory (e.g., Podsakoff et al. 1986; Fahr, Podsakoff, and Cheng 1987). Conclusions regarding the ultimate utility and usefulness of the substitutes theory in general are still premature. Nonetheless, because of the wide variety of organizational structures found across nations, it would be surprising to find that substitutes for leadership are unaffected by cultural differences.

PARTICIPATIVE LEADERSHIP AND
NORMATIVE DECISION THEORY

Participatory leadership can be conceptualized as existing along a dimension that ranges from autocratic decisions to complete delegation. The original Vroom and Yetton (1973) normative decision model and the revised model (Vroom and Jago 1988) delineate which decision procedures are most likely to be effective in alternative situations. As Yukl (1989) notes, this normative decision model is probably one of the best supported situational leadership theories, yet it, too, has theoretical aspects that are not strongly supported (Field 1982). Consistent with the general absence of literature investigating the generalizability of leadership theories across cultures, there is a paucity of research investigating the transferability of the normative decision theory. However, some preliminary cross-cultural results have confirmed that the model may be useful in understanding participatory leadership in other cultures.

Bottger, Hallein, and Yetton (1985) investigated the behavioral intent to engage in participatory leadership among 150 managers from Australia, Africa, Papua New Guinea, and the Pacific Islands. Using standard Vroom-Yetton methodology, whereby managers select an appropriate level of participation for problem solving among prespecified problem sets, they found that participation was highest for *all* managers in situations of low structure and low power compared to situations of high structure and high power. That is, when managers feel relatively powerless and problems are not structured, a participatory style is favored for managers from all nations. Nevertheless, managers from the developed nation of Australia were more participatory than managers from the other less developed nations in low power and low structure situations. The authors explain this finding as the result of differing levels of managerial education across countries rather than as the result of cultural influences. Their conclusion is thought-provoking, but cultural factors may have influenced the results, as no attempt was made to either measure or rule out alternative cultural hypotheses.

As with all tests of the Vroom-Yetton model of decision making that use a standard "problem set" methodology, it is crucial to verify that behavioral intentions can be used as a surrogate for actual leader behaviors in real situations. The validity of this technique has been supported using a sample of American managers (Jago and Vroom 1978). Obviously, if this standard problem set methodology is to be used in cross-cultural studies, similar validation evidence must also be obtained in other national samples. One such replication of the Jago and Vroom (1978) validation effort was conducted by Bohnisch et al. (1988) for Austrian managers. Similar to findings in America, the responses for the problem sets were significantly related to behavior in actual situations, although there is a less than perfect correspondence between the leaders' behavioral intentions and actual responses. Given the reasonable assurance of reliable methodology for Austrian managers, Jago and colleagues (recently reported by Reber, Jago, and Bohnisch 1993) investigated the differences between a matched sample of 161 American and 161 Austrian managers. Significant differences in decision-making proclivities included the finding that U.S. managers more frequently used the A-1 autocratic decision-making style than did the Austrian counterparts, whereas Austrian managers more frequently employed the G-II group decision-making style than did the U.S. counterparts. Consistent with these results, the "mean level of participation" score revealed that Austrian managers were significantly more participative than U.S. managers. Overall, the mean frequencies with which responses fell within the feasible set (across all cases in the problem set) were almost identical between the two samples (21.65 versus 20.82), but these differences were significant in favor of the Austrian managers outperforming the U.S. managers. Perhaps the most interesting finding concerns the results that, when conflict among subordinates is likely (problem attribute #7), U.S. managers become more autocratic while Austrian managers become more participative. In contrast, the two research populations were similar in their overall intention to use C-II decision making the most (leader makes the decision after sharing the information with the group). Both samples also proceeded to use A-II the least (individuals respond individually to the leader and the leader makes the decision). Rather than overinterpreting differences and similarities between the samples, it may be safest to conclude that the research methodology seems to be robust across these two cultures.

Contrasts among U.S. managers and additional European counterparts were also reported by Jago and colleagues (Jago et al. 1993). Participating managers completed a standard problem data set, as described previously (Vroom and Yetton 1973), by selecting a behavioral intention ranging from highly participative to highly autocratic. Overall results indicated that German, Austrian, and Swiss managers were the most participative, Polish and Czech managers were the most autocratic, and U.S. and French managers were between the extremes. Two other findings were particularly interesting. First, unlike managers of other nations, Polish managers were more likely to be participative on trivial matters, in contrast to important issues. Second, only the U.S. and Polish managers were likely to become autocratic when subordinate conflict was likely (a consistent finding in all previous research with U.S. managers). One further aspect of the study is particularly noteworthy. The researchers developed predictions of participation based on Hofstede's power distance scores, and results were generally supportive for the prediction that participation scores would be higher for lower power distance cultures. While one could quibble with this particular study's lack of confirmatory evidence regarding Hofstede's prior ranking of cultural differences among samples and the different time frames for collecting the data, the study should be commended for its logical conceptualization of culture as influencing participatory leadership.

Besides the stream of research initiated by Vroom and Yetton (1973), the studies by Heller and Wilpert (1981) and Heller et al. (1988) bear examining for their relevance to participatory leadership. These two studies were complex, time-consuming, large-scale cross-national research efforts that had the purpose of understanding how various macrofactors (e.g., country) and microfactors (e.g., specific task) influence leader decision-making and participatory processes in organizations. Heller and Wilpert obtained survey data (and feedback in the form of group discussions) from sixteen hundred managers sampled from 129 organizations across eight nations (Israel, Spain, the United Kingdom, Germany, Netherlands, the United States, France, and Sweden). Managerial decision making (DM) was conceived as varying along a continuum (decision without explanation, decision with explanation, prior consultation, joint decision, delegation), and a "decision centralization score" was computed for each manager indicating the manager's degree of centralized (authoritarian) versus participative decision making. Some of the findings that are relevant to participatory leadership include (1) small but consistent covariance between a subordinate's perceptions of supervisory participation and the subordinate's own job satisfaction, (2) significant differences among managers' self-descriptions of their decision-making styles across nations (e.g., Israeli managers described their DM as more centralized than did Swedish managers), (3) managers' DM style that was much more influenced by microlevel variables close to the decision maker (e.g., type of decision to be made) than by macrolevel variables such as country of the manager, and (4) an absence of country/culture clusters as might have been expected from prior theorizing (e.g., a Nordic vs. Latin European cluster).

The study by Heller et al. (1988) provides further evidence regarding DM processes across nations. This study, like the Heller and Wilpert study (1981), also employed multiple research methods using multinational samples (United Kingdom, Netherlands, and Yugoslavia). As previously found, DM varied greatly with the type of decision required, and the researchers were able to detect influences due to "organizational culture" that lead to more or less centralization. The evidence for country differences was not clear, and, as previously found by Heller and Wilpert (1981), no cultural patterns emerged as might be predicted by a cultural typology such as Hofstede's (1980).

The following additional areas concerning participation might be fruitful to explore using a cross-cultural "lens." First, it would be helpful to replicate some preliminary findings supporting the easily conceived proposition that leaders in cultures characterized by high power stratification and uncertainty avoidance should be less likely to engage in participatory practices than those found in low power stratification and non-risk-aversive cultures. Such effects were found by Kennis (1977) when comparing participatory leadership practices between U.S. and Turkish supervisors. Second, will research from non-Western culture clusters (Ronen and Shenkar 1985) universally support the well-documented finding in Western countries that supervisors are more apt to describe themselves as being more participative than are their subordinates (Yukl 1994)? At this point in time we simply have no evidence one way or another to support or refute the universality of this phenomenon found in Western societies. Yet, if participatory leadership is not a socially desirable aspect of leadership in non-Western nations, and therefore not part of a leadership prototype for effective leaders, we would not expect leaders to report higher levels of participation than would the subordinates. Third, are there cultural differences regarding whether supervisors have to solicit *and* implement recommendations from subordinates to be viewed as a participative supervisor, or is the solicitation of input sufficient? Assume that Mohr (1982) is correct in arguing that Americans express their sense of their participativeness in decision making by having an impact on the decision, not just the objective act of participation. Yet in Japan, it may be the mere act of presenting ideas to one's supervisors that characterizes participation. Perhaps it will be necessary to develop indigenous models of participation for specific culture clusters (Ronen and Shenkar 1985) to adequately understand participation across cultures. A single leadership model may not suffice. As Smith and Peterson (1988) note, "Participation in a Japanese work team, a Yugoslav Worker's council, an autonomous work group in the Volvo car plant, or a 'self-managed' U.S. software house are only in the broadest sense the same thing" (161).

CHARISMATIC AND TRANSFORMATIONAL LEADERSHIP ACROSS CULTURES

Charisma is a central concept in the new genre of leadership theories collectively referred to as charismatic theories (House and Shamir 1993). Charismatic leaders offer a compelling vision of what the organization may become and are able to transform the needs and aspirations of followers from self-interests to collective interests. Proponents of charismatic and transformational theories seem to come close to adopting a universalist position regarding cross-cultural transferability. Bass (1991, 1997) argues that it may be possible for a single transformational and transactional leadership theory to explain leadership and its consequences across differing cultures. According to Bass, leaders who engage in transformational behaviors will be more effective than those who do not, regardless of culture. House (1991; House, Wright, and Aditya 1997) has a similar belief in the robustness of charismatic leadership across cultures. There are, however, significant differences among these charismatic theories, and these differences may have implications for cross-cultural transferability. As noted by Chemers and Ayman (1993), the Bass transformational theory (see Bass 1990; Bass and Avolio 1990; Bass and Avolio 1993) focuses on the transformational characteristics of outstanding leaders across different cultures, whereas the charismatic leadership theory developed by House and Shamir (1993) addresses how differences in cultures will make followers more susceptible to a particular charismatic leader. Although these charismatic theories seem to adopt a universalist position, a closer look at the respective positions reveals a more complex understanding of possible cultural influences. For instance, Bass acknowledges that the transactional and transformational theory may have to be fine-tuned as it applies to different cultures, and the specific behaviors and decision styles may change to some extent. Consistent with this cultural contingency modification, Bass speculates that transformational leaders will be more participative in India and Japan than in Pakistan and Taiwan because worker participation is viewed more favorably in the former countries. House and Shamir (1993) also suggest that the strategies employed by the charismatic leader may be culturally contingent. For instance, Gandhi's exhortations for love and acceptance of others aroused the need for affiliation, whereas General George Patton evoked the negative image of the enemy, which aroused the power motive essential for combat. Nonetheless, according to charismatic theorists, the most effective leadership patterns (assuming the leader's goals and values are consistent with those of the organization) involve charismatic behaviors irrespective of the culture in which they are found. The GLOBE research project similarly found that many charismatic leader attributes are universally perceived to enhance effective leadership (this will be reviewed shortly).

In general, there is strong empirical evidence supporting the importance of charismatic leadership in the West. Despite substantive and legitimate criticism, including definition and measurement problems (Smith and Peterson 1988; Hunt 1991; Yukl 2002), charismatic theories fare quite well under empirical scrutiny. Numerous studies employing a variety of methods (including field studies, case histories, management games, interviews, and laboratory experiments) and samples (including middle- and lower-level managers, top-level corporate leaders, educational leaders, and national leaders) attest to the significant and robust impact of charismatic and transformational leadership (see House and Shamir 1993). Furthermore, Bass (1991) notes confirming cross-cultural evidence for the proposition that there is a hierarchy of leadership effectiveness among various leadership styles—transformational leaders are more effective than those practicing transactional leadership, who in turn are more effective than laissez-faire leaders (the latter are not effective). This hierarchy of relationships was found for field grade officers in Germany and Canada, New Zealand professionals and administrators, senior managers in Italy and Sweden, and middle-level managers in Japan, Belgium, Canada, Spain, Saudi Arabia, and India (Bass et al. 1987; Bass 1991; Bass and Yokochi 1991; Bass and Avolio 1993; Howell 1997). These studies generally support a near universal position regarding the potential impact of charismatic and transformational leadership across cultures. On a somewhat less supportive note, a recent methodologically sophisticated study by Shamir et al. (1998) examining the effects of charismatic leadership on individuals at multiple organizational levels within a single country found little support for Shamir, House, and Arthur's (1993) self-concept-based charismatic theory. Clearly, much remains to be learned about the process by which charismatic leadership affects followers. And certainly, when considered from a cross-cultural perspective, one should entertain a hypothesis that the *enactment* of charismatic leadership and transformational leadership will likely be culture specific. As one example, speeches by charismatic international business CEOs were analyzed and found to reflect their personal philosophy of international business (Den Hartog and Verburg 1997).

Empirical tests of the cross-cultural validity of charismatic theories have become extremely problematic. We also have to consider that the leadership constructs themselves are multifaceted and that definitions vary considerably among originators of the theories (cf. Bass 1985; House and Shamir 1993). Furthermore, even within a particular theory (e.g., Bass and Avolio 1989), the conceptualization and operational measurement of the construct has changed over time. Although this may be laudable in terms of the ultimate scientific goal of understanding leadership processes, it creates numerous problems for the cross-cultural researcher. For instance, how should researchers interpret recent findings by Echavarria and Davis (1994) in the Dominican Republic; Den Hartog, Van Muijen, and Koopman (1994) in the Netherlands; and Koh (1990) in Singapore? In each of these studies the factor structures are quite different from the original factor structure presented by Bass (1985). Should these researchers conclude that the fundamental concepts of transformational leadership are similar across cultures but that the enactment of the constructs differ, or should they conclude that this leadership construct is fundamentally different across cultures? Or do the differences simply reflect various degrees of sophistication of the research samples, since the respondents were given the unfamiliar task of rating supervisors in questionnaire format? The ambiguity of interpretation is unsettling.

Where does this extensive and burgeoning research literature leave us? For the time being we may speculate that transformational and charismatic leadership is important in all nations but that subtle differences are likely to exist from country to country. In addition, a significant question concerns the kind of *impact* expected for this leadership process. Some studies simply examine the relative influence of charismatic and/or transformational leadership in one country in contrast to another. For instance, Howell and Dorfman (1988) found different impacts of charismatic leadership on employees' satisfaction with work and supervision for Mexican and American employees. Although the impact was positive for both American and Mexican employees, charismatic leadership had a much stronger impact on American employees. More sophisticated research strategies pinpoint the specific types of transformational behaviors and/or the precise mechanisms by which these types of leader behaviors influence others. For instance, results of a recent study by Chen and Fahr (2001), using supervisor-subordinate dyads in Taiwan and the People's Republic of China (PRC), support the position that transformational leadership for both samples has more of a profound impact on employee job satisfaction and organizational commitment than does transactional leadership. More interestingly from a theoretical perspective is the fact that specific types of transformational behaviors have different effects in each country. The researchers note that "providing an appropriate model" and "demonstrating high expectations of performance" significantly influenced PRC employees' job attitudes and organizational citizenship, whereas "providing individualized support" and "fostering collaboration" had significant influence on Taiwan employees' job satisfaction and organizational citizenship. Again consistent with the universality position, Dorfman et al. (1997) found that charismatic leadership had consistently positive impacts on subordinate attitudes and perceptions among five countries in the Pacific Rim. However, within the three countries where job performance data was available, charismatic leadership directly influenced employee attitudes (satisfaction with work and supervision), not job performance. This finding illustrates a major controversy in the academic literature as to the extent that charismatic leadership affects performance in addition to attitudes and perceptions. This issue will be interesting to follow as additional cross-cultural studies are conducted. The unique perspectives provided by researchers of differing cultures, concomitant with better measurements of culture, should provide a most interesting window into the mechanisms by which charismatic leadership so profoundly influences followers.

INDIGENOUS NON-WESTERN LEADERSHIP THEORIES

LEADERSHIP IN JAPAN

Although a wealth of popular and academic literature exists describing Japanese management practices, the literature investigating Japanese leadership processes is relatively sparse. Notable exceptions include Misumi's seminal research studies (1985) and Graen and Wakabayashi's (1994) testing of leader-member exchange (LMX) theory in Japan. Misumi's research program in Japan has spanned more than forty years and, similar to U.S. leadership studies of the same time period, has investigated the impact of leadership styles on subordinate attitudes and performance. An interesting, and often unrecognized, point is that Misumi's conception of leadership was highly influenced by the work of Western social scientists. Admirably, his research program included both laboratory and field studies. Misumi's performance-maintenance (PM) theory of leadership (1985) identifies four types of leaders—classified by their focus on two basic leadership functions labeled "performance" and "maintenance." The performance function (P) reflects two aspects: a leader's planning, guiding, and developing work procedures, as well as pressure on subordinates to work hard and get the work done. The maintenance (M) function reflects the leader's promotion of group stability and social processes. These central leadership functions in the PM theory are similar to the task-oriented and support-oriented leadership functions previously addressed in Western theories of leadership. Misumi's results suggest that, for effective leadership in Japan, supervisors must emphasize performance-oriented (P) and maintenance-oriented (M) factors *together*. That is, the leader high in both functions (PM) is better than the leader low in both functions (pm) or than the leader high in one and low in the other (pM or Pm). Hui (1990) speculates that the PM leader is influential in Oriental cultures because the M gives subordinates the feeling that they are members of the supervisor's "in-group" and the P should lead to high productivity, which is beneficial to the entire group.

Recent tests of Misumi's PM theory conducted in nations other than Japan provide illuminating evidence regarding the issue of culture-free versus culture-specific leadership (Peterson, Smith, and Peng 1993; Peterson, Smith, and Tayeb 1993b; Peterson, Brannen, and Smith 1994). Misumi's PM leadership instrument was adapted for use in China, but researchers found it necessary to add an additional leadership factor, labeled "C" for character and morals, to adequately characterize Chinese leadership (Xu et al. 1985). Tests of the three-part leadership scale (CPM) consistently revealed three separate dimensions (Ling 1989; Ling and Fang 2003) that according to Wang (1994) now provide a reliable and valid assessment of leadership behavior in China. Research in the United States and Great Britain indicates similarities and differences between the American perceptions of task-oriented and relationship-oriented leader behaviors and Misumi's P and M leader behaviors. Misumi's maintenance (M) factor closely resembles the relationship-oriented factor found in U.S. leadership research; it has the same meaning and positive relationships to subordinate satisfaction and reduced stress in Japan as it does in the United States. However, certain items that reflect M in Japan (and Hong Kong) would be perceived as inappropriate to American managers and subordinates. For instance, discussing a subordinate's personal difficulties with other organizational members, but in the person's absence, is consistent with Japanese and Chinese managers high on the M factor (Smith et al. 1989). Misumi's performance (P) factor also includes some behaviors similar to the task-oriented factor found previously in the U.S. research, but there are intriguing differences between the Americans and the Japanese. The following P leadership behaviors may seem natural and acceptable to the Japanese but probably would be considered harsh or overly exacting for Americans: "Is your supervisor strict about the amount of work you do?" "Is your supervisor strict about observing regulations?" "Does your supervisor make you work to your maximum capacity?"

Misumi's work is unique and noteworthy for several reasons. First, although Misumi used questionnaire items to reflect leadership behaviors broadly applicable to many contexts, he also tailored items to the specific research setting. For instance, a broadly applicable M question might inquire if your supervisor supports you, whereas a distinct M question might ask if a teacher is friendly toward pupils in class. A second interesting aspect of Misumi's research concerns his observation that the meaning of a particular leader behavior may change in the context of other leader behaviors—a form of leadership interaction. That is, a P-type behavior exhibited by a supervisor high in M may be seen by subordinates as reflecting a "planning" function, whereas the same behavior may be seen as "pressuring for production" behavior for a leader low in M.

Graen's LMX theory was originally developed in the United States (Dansereau, Graen, and Haga 1975), but long-term programmatic research efforts with Japanese colleagues add greatly to our understanding of Japanese leadership processes (Wakabayashi and Graen 1984; Graen and Wakabayashi 1994). The LMX theory examines leadership as an exchange process between a leader and individual subordinates. Leaders establish vastly different exchange relationships between trusted subordinates (the in-group) and the remaining subordinates (the out-group). There is a relatively high level of mutual influence with the leader and in-group subordinates (high LMX). Leaders are likely to support and reward in-group subordinates, encourage them to participate in decisions, and directly help their careers. In exchange, subordinates are expected to work hard, be loyal to the leader, and be committed to their job. For out-group subordinates, the working relationships are characterized by unidirectional downward influence and contractual behavior exchange—subordinates comply with leader requests by performing only the required job duties.

As a result of this effort by Graen and Wakabayashi (e.g., Wakabayashi and Graen 1984; Graen and Wakabayashi 1994) substantial evidence exists that the quality of the supervisor-subordinate exchange relationship is as critical in Japan as it is in the United States. Part of this research program has focused on testing a strongly held belief in Japan (the Yoshoni [1968] model) that managerial career progress is a function of seniority, status of the college attended, and visibility of the job to the personnel department. Only later in midcareer will individual merit factor into promotion decisions. The result of a thirteen-year longitudinal study in a large Japanese corporation made it quite clear that, contrary to the Yoshino hypothesis, managerial progress was more strongly influenced by the working relationships between the manager and a superior early in a manager's career than the other hypothesized factors (Graen et al. 1990). While such a finding might not be surprising to an American, it is contrary to the common perceptions in Japan as to the nature of performance assessment and promotion. Thus, it seems that early career differentiation and promotion is the norm rather than deferred evaluation and promotion; it was the discretional role development activities of the supervisor rather than age and tenure that led to career progress. The programmatic series of research studies by Graen and colleagues are important not only for concrete findings, but also for demonstrating the importance of research to support or refute commonly held conceptions of leadership within a culture.

A recent revision of the LMX theory (Graen and Uhl-Bien 1991) more clearly specifies how the exchange relationship process develops. As proposed by the theory, the relationship-building process between leaders and followers occurs over three stages—from the initial "stranger" stage into the "acquaintance" stage and finally into the fully "mature" stage. Graen and Wakabayashi (1994) have extended this model to Japanese leadership and suggest that it has important relevance to leadership-making situations for Japanese transplants (Japanese companies located in the United States). They propose that cross-cultural learning by both the Japanese associates and American workers will reduce mutual fears and eventually result in an effective hybrid organizational culture. The goal of achieving a highly mature leadership relationship should reduce common misunderstandings that affect leadership effectiveness. For instance, although American workers may from the start expect participatory leadership practices from Japanese managers, this practice will likely occur only after the U.S. worker becomes a competent, experienced, and trusted employee, not a relative newcomer to the job. Graen's recent work has been extended to include models of team building for both international organizations as well as international research teams (Graen et al. 1997). In an intriguing article, Hui and Graen (1997) compare and contrast the Chinese concept of *guanxi* (a complex web of interpersonal relationships and reciprocal obligations) to the concept of relationship building in the LMX theory. They conclude that the development of "third" cultures such as a synthesis between the Chinese notion of *guanxi* and the American notion of LMX in international joint ventures will provide lasting benefits for both cultures.

LEADERSHIP IN INDIA

The confluence of Western organizational structures and management principles with Indian cultural influences is evident in the areas of leadership and power relationships (Sinha 1995). Indian culture is *vertical collectivist* (Triandis and Bhawuk 1997), characterized by familialism, patronage, personalized relationships, and obedience to authority (Sinha 1997). Yet, because of a strong desire to compete effectively in the global market, Indian organizations adopt Western management principles that they believe will lead to higher efficiency and productivity. As a result of this cultural confluence with modern management principles, Indian organizations have human resource functions such as performance appraisal and formal planning processes, but they do not operate as they do in the West (Virmani and Guptan 1991).

Similar to Misumi's research in Japan, early efforts to study leadership in India were influenced by conceptual links to Western social scientists. However, research results were often inconsistent and at odds with prevailing beliefs about the nature of effective leadership in Indian organizations. Research data often supported the interpretation that democratic, participative, and considerate leaders were most effective, whereas managers and workers often voiced a preference for paternalistic and nurturing leaders who are also authoritarian and assertive (Kakar 1971; Sinha 1994). Khandwalla's pioneering innovative (PI) theory (Khandwalla 1983) combines a participatory leadership style with a professional orientation that stresses innovation, sophisticated technologies, risk taking, and creativity. In contrast, leadership views of Singh and Paul (1985) contain more of an Indian ethos where the leader is expected to give unconditional care and affection to subordinates. To reconcile these somewhat inconsistent beliefs about effective leadership, Sinha (1980, 1984) developed a nurturant-task (NT) oriented model that incorporated a combination of leadership styles. The model suggests that an ideal leader in India is both nurturant and task oriented. According to the theory, NT leaders are warm and considerate, show affection, care for their subordinates, and are committed to their growth. However, their nurturance is contingent on the subordinate's task accomplishment—the leader becomes a benevolent source provided the subordinate respects and obeys the supervisor, works hard, and is highly productive. In Sinha's words, "the leader must keep *the task* as the basis for building *sneh-shradha* (affection-deference) relationships with subordinates" (1997, 65). The relationship is very much like that within the Japanese management-familial system in which the supervisor benevolently guides the subordinate, who in turn must reciprocate with complete obedience and absolute loyalty (Whitehill and Takezawa 1968).

Sinha (1980, 1984) presents research evidence that the effectiveness of NT is affected by a number of contingency variables such as the subordinate's desire for a dependency relationship and acceptance of a hierarchical relationship. In this sense, the model closely resembles predictions from other contingency theories such as the House path-goal theory. Sinha also hypothesizes that the most ideal leadership style shifts from the NT style to a more participative style as the subordinate develops and grows. Triandis (1994) makes an interesting observation that, even in cultures not typically appreciative of democratic relationships, participatory leadership can be effective given worker training to accept, expect, and appreciate such styles. We might expect that aspects of the NT model hold for other high power distance and collectivist cultures that value hierarchical and personalized relationships. It is likely not a coincidence that Sinha's NT leader resembles Misumi's PM leader in Japan, the benevolent-paternalistic leader in Iran (Ayman and Chemers 1983), the paternalistic *patron* in Mexico (Bass 1990), or the family-dominated leaders of Korean *chaebols* (Steers, Shinn, and Ungson 1989). Further information about managerial leadership in India is forthcoming in the GLOBE anthology (Chhokar, in progress).

LEADERSHIP IN MIDDLE EASTERN COUNTRIES

Modern Arab management practices have been influenced by Islamic religion, tribal and family traditions, the legacy of colonial bureaucracies, and contact with Western nations (Ali 1990). The pervasive influence of the Islamic religion is a key to understanding the Arab world and presumably leadership in the Arab world (Hagan 1995). In Arabic, the word for "leadership" is *al kiyada,* which refers to officers in the military or high-ranking members of the government. Historically, a leader is a great hero who leads warriors into battle; therefore, not unexpectedly, the concept of leadership is rooted in traditional military concepts of leadership (Scandura, Von Glinow, and Lowe 1999). In addition, tribal traditions influence all aspects of life, and as a consequence, managers are expected to act as fathers—viewing their role in a highly personalized manner characterized by providing and caring for employees and favoring individuals within the family and tribe over "outsiders." The legacy of a highly structured bureaucracy left by the ruling Ottoman Empire and European nations is superimposed on these Islamic family-tribal traditions. The combination of family and tribal norms, in addition to bureaucratic organizational structures, fosters authoritarian management practices that may be characterized as a "sheikocracy" leadership style (Al-Kubaisy 1985). This style is characterized by a patriarchal approach to managing that includes strong hierarchical authority, subordination of efficiency to human relations and personal connections, and sporadic conformity to rules and regulations contingent on the personality and power of those who make them.

The complex world of Arab management (viewed from an American perspective) promotes a duality of managerial thinking and practice that values modernity but maintains traditional values. To the culturally uninformed Western manager, the following management practices must seem strange indeed: establishing a huge number of rules and regulations while no attempt is made to implement them; designing selection and promotion systems according to the principle of merit but hiring and rewarding according to social ties and personal relations; and paying employees in the public sector who are not required to report for work if they come from powerful families (Khadra 1990). Partially due to the transitional stage of development in the region, the successful managerial leader must navigate between dual sets of values present in the culture (Abdalla and Al-Homoud 2001). Modernity and technological sophistication are often at odds with a more traditional and familial culture.

The prophetic-caliphal model of leadership developed by Khadra (1990) personifies many aspects of modern Arab culture just discussed. The model is based on an abstraction of the dynamics of Arab leadership and focuses on the antecedents and consequences of two distinctly different types of leaders. There is a strong predisposition for expecting a "great man" to emerge as a leader. The "great or prophetic leader" is perceived by followers as a person who has accomplished a miracle or other extraordinary action. This type of leader will engender follower feelings of love, strong attachment, unity of purpose, and voluntary submission to authority. In contrast, if the leader who emerges is simply an "ordinary" or "caliphal" man, conflict and strife will result and the leader must rule by coercion and fear. The prophetic-caliphal model requires further theoretical development, and many aspects of the model will be difficult to test in its present form. Nevertheless, Khadra (1990) presents evidence from a questionnaire survey that the model's principal constructs make sense to Arab managers. For example, approximately three out of four managers responded by agreeing or strongly agreeing to the following statements: "I consider the department in which I work as my private property and manage it the way I like," "I do not let anybody participate in the decisions I make," and "The prescribed procedures for work are mostly constraints that should not be adhered to." Given the overwhelming agreement with these questions in the survey, one can easily argue that results from more sophisticated studies of Arab leadership will undoubtedly confirm many culture-specific aspects of Arab leadership.

Leadership studies in the Middle East are almost nonexistent, but a few recent research studies shed some light on leadership in this area of the world. Scandura et al. (1999) found striking differences in effective leadership styles between a U.S. managerial sample and a sample of managers from the Middle East (Jordan and Saudi Arabia). Although they used the fairly old conception of leadership as being composed of two leadership styles, initiating structure and consideration, the results were dramatic. Whereas the people-oriented style (i.e., consideration) was related to job satisfaction and leader effectiveness for the U.S. sample, the task-oriented style (i.e., initiating structure) was not. Exactly opposite results were found for the Middle East sample. They conclude that strong and decisive leadership is expected from an Arab person, hence the effectiveness of setting high goals and standards of performance characteristic of "initiating structure," whereas a "considerate leader" might be perceived as being weak and indecisive.

A recent special issue of *Applied Psychology: An International Review* focuses on leadership and culture in the Middle East (Kabasakal and Dastmalchian 2001). Many of the research findings presented in these articles came from studies initiated as part of the GLOBE project (House et al. 1999). While the articles focus on Iran, Kuwait, Turkey, and Qatar, the cultural information applies to other Middle Eastern countries as well as other countries that have predominately Muslim populations. Some highlights of the studies include the following findings. An analysis of societal cultural norms indicate relatively low scores on future orientation and performance orientation that may be caused in part by the concept of "fate" in Islam. In contrast, the desirable leadership profile requires the leader to strongly endorse performance and future orientations (Kabasakal and Dastmalchian 2001). For Iran specifically and Middle Eastern countries generally, high power distance scores indicate the acceptance of unequal sharing of power in the society and high in-group collectivism scores indicate the importance of loyalty, pride, cohesiveness, and other in-group collectives. Scores on the "gender egalitarian" culture scale are low for the region and, interestingly, also are low when respondents indicated their desire for how things "should be" as contrasted with how things "are now" (Dastmalchian, Javidan, and Alam 2001). In addition, the Middle Eastern countries in general score quite highly on the "humane" culture dimension (Kabasakal and Dastmalchian 2001). Taken together, these cultural values explain the seemingly contradictory nature of contemporary managerial leadership practices in the region—desire for modernity while maintaining traditional cultural values. The GLOBE results support the following leadership profile: a culture-universal desire for charismatic/value-based and team-oriented leaders whose visionary and future-oriented leadership is directed at being more performance oriented. In addition, the culture-unique elements of a more traditional leadership profile in the Middle East countries include the endorsements of attributes such as familial, humble, faithful, self-protective, and considerate. Paternalistic and autocratic tendencies are found alongside of the desire for a highly considerate, supportive, and humble leader (Pasa, Kabasakal, and Bodur 2001). As a personal note, the terrible events of 9/11/2001 in the United States are a clarion call for the West to better understand the cultural and religious forces operating in the Middle East. For moderate leaders to succeed, they must neutralize the extremist factions while preserving traditional values characteristic of moderate Islam. The requirements for effective leadership in this region of the world are indeed daunting.

CONTEMPORARY LEADERSHIP RESEARCH: STUDIES IN PROGRESS AND NEW CONCEPTUAL MODELS

THE GLOBE PROJECT

House et al. (1994) and colleagues from more than sixty nations are engaged in a long-term programmatic series of cross-cultural leadership studies.[1] The scope of the project is immense, as managerial samples represent societies from all continents. Initial results of the first two phases of the study were published by House et al. (1999) and by Den Hartog et al. (1999). A complete discussion of the findings can be found in the book *Leadership, Culture, and Organizations: The GLOBE Study of 62 Societies* (House et al. 2004). The GLOBE project is currently in its third phase.

What is particularly noteworthy about this project is its use of a combination of quantitative and qualitative methods. Quantitative aspects include scales to measure societal culture, organizational culture, and leadership behaviors. An initial goal of the study was to develop and validate societal and organizational measures of culture. This was accomplished in the first phase of research. Nine psychometrically sound culture dimension scales were developed. They are (1) uncertainty avoidance, (2) power distance, (3) collectivism I: societal emphasis on collectivism, (4) collectivism II: in-group collectivistic practices, (5) gender egalitarianism, (6) assertiveness, (7) future orientation, (8) performance orientation, and (9) humane orientation. In addition, researchers are engaged in writing ethnographic studies of leaders in each nation/societal culture. Qualitative interpretations of culture have been developed through interviews, focus groups, and the use of unobtrusive measures. For the latter, an unobtrusive measure of power stratification might be the number of status-relevant titles in the organizations to be studied or the number of statues in a country glorifying military leaders.

If the measurement of societal and organizational culture was the first focus of the GLOBE project, the second focus was to determine the extent to which different cultures had similar beliefs regarding effective leader attributes and behaviors. The research question was framed as such: To what extent are specific leadership attributes and behaviors believed to be universally effective or ineffective, and, conversely, to what extent are specific attributes and behaviors culturally contingent? As examples of leadership attributes that might be culturally sensitive, it was hypothesized that leadership attributes such as hard work and achievement orientation will be universally applicable, whereas attributes such as leader spirituality, leader subtlety, and harmony will be more strongly endorsed by Asian cultures than Western cultures. House was particularly interested in the question of whether attributes related to charismatic leadership will be universally endorsed, as he predicted.

The GLOBE results indicate the following are leadership dimensions (and attributes comprising each dimension) universally believed to contribute to effective leadership: integrity (being trustworthy, just, and honest); visionary (having foresight and planning ahead); inspirational (being positive, dynamic, encouraging, motivating, building confidence), and team builder (being communicative, informed, and a coordinator and team integrator). Other dimensions include being decisive and diplomatic. The visionary and inspirational leadership dimensions are critical aspects of charismatic leadership and contain the most number of attributes universally perceived to lead to effective leadership. The portrait of a leader who is universally viewed as effective is clear: the person should exhibit integrity and charismatic qualities while being decisive, diplomatic, and administratively skilled when building effective teams. The GLOBE researchers' initial hypothesis was strongly supported with regard to the endorsement of charismatic/value-based attributes as contributing to effective leadership.

The following leadership dimensions and attributes were perceived as inhibiting effective leadership: self-protective (loner, asocial), malevolent (noncooperative and irritable), face saver, autocratic, and additional specific attributes including egocentric and ruthless. For me, the most interesting attributes are those that were neither universally perceived as positive or negative. They were mixed, in the sense that they were positively perceived to enhance effective leadership in some cultures and negatively perceived to inhibit effective leadership in other cultures. These attributes included ambitious, cautious, class-conscious, compassionate, domineering, elitist, enthusiastic, formal, independent, individualistic, logical, orderly, risk taker, self-effacing, sensitive, sincere, status-conscious, and worldly. With a list like this, it is no wonder that potential cultural clashes are likely among peoples from differing cultures.

So far, this section has described phases of the GLOBE project that on the one hand concern the measurement of culture and on the other hand concern leadership attributes perceived to be either effective or noneffective. Can linkages be found between culture and leadership? Fortunately, for GLOBE and the research community, the answer is an unequivocal "yes." Evidence using sophisticated statistical analysis (such as hierarchical linear modeling [HLM]) indicates that the GLOBE cultural dimensions relate to specific leadership attributes in ways that make sense. To summarize our findings, being charismatic (visionary, inspirational, self-sacrificial, integrity, decisive, and performance oriented) is considered more important for cultures with a high performance orientation. Being team oriented (collaborative, diplomatic, team integrator, and administratively competent) is more important for effective leadership in cultures that are more collectivistic than individualistic. Being participative (delegator, nonautocratic) is more important for leadership effectiveness in cultures low in power distance and uncertainty avoidance but high in performance orientation and gender egalitarianism.

GLOBE researchers use the term "societal culture" rather than "nation" or "national culture" because there may be two or more societal cultures in some nations (i.e., black and white cultures in South Africa). As part of the project, GLOBE researchers were able to group all sixty-two nations/societal cultures into ten country clusters. The Anglo societal culture, for instance, consists of the United States, Canada, England, Ireland, Australia, New Zealand, and South Africa (white sample). As seen in table 10.1, the societal clusters can be ranked as to the primary leadership characteristics believed to contribute to effective leadership. That is, as discussed previously, leadership prototypes based on implicit leadership can be developed for a national or societal culture as well as for individuals within the culture. The former are labeled by GLOBE researchers as "culturally endorsed leadership theories" (CLTs). Comparing two societal clusters can illustrate the relative importance of various CLT leadership attributes and skills. For instance, the cluster rankings for charismatic/valued-based attributes within the Anglo (English-speaking) cluster is the highest for all societal clusters. Participative and humane-oriented leadership are also viewed very positively and have high ranks. Self-protective leadership is considered an impediment to effective leadership for this cluster. This cluster ranks among the lowest clusters on this dimension. The Southern Asian cluster contains some important similarities and differences in comparison to the Anglo cluster. Charismatic/value-based was ranked high, which is similar to the Anglo cluster, and team-oriented lead-

TABLE 10.1. Summary of Societal Cluster Rankings on CLT Leadership Dimensions

	CLT Leadership Dimensions					
Societal Cluster	Charismatic/ Value-Based	Team- Oriented	Participative	Humane- Oriented	Autonomous	Self-Protective
Eastern Europe	M	M	L	M	H/H	H
Latin America	H	H	M	M	L	M/H
Latin Europe	M/H	M	M	L	L	M
Confucian Asia	M	M/H	L	M/H	M	H
Nordic Europe	H	M	H	L	M	L
Anglo	H	M	H	H	M	L
Sub-Saharan Africa	M	M	M	H	L	M
Southern Asia	H	M/H	L	H	M	H/H
Germanic Europe	H	M/L	H	M	H/H	L
Middle East	L	L	L	M	M	H/H

Notes: For letters separated by a slash, the first letter indicates rank with respect to the absolute score, the second letter with respect to relative score.

H = high rank; M = medium rank; L = low rank.

H or L (bold) indicates Highest or Lowest cluster score for a specific CLT dimension.

ership was ranked higher for the Southern Asia cluster than for the Anglo cluster. A dramatic difference occurs with the participative dimension. While participative leadership is viewed somewhat positively (raw score), it ranks among the lowest clusters in this dimension for the Southern Asia cluster. The humane-oriented leadership score, however, is the highest raw score and rank of all societal clusters. Self-protective leadership is viewed as slightly negative (raw score) but is less negative than for most other clusters. In sum, the ranking of societal clusters presented in table 10.1 highlights important differences among the clusters.

EVENT MANAGEMENT LEADERSHIP THEORY

Another large-scale programmatic leadership research project is a worldwide effort originated by Smith and Peterson (1994) and reported in a twenty-five-nation test of their event management leadership theory. The Smith and Peterson (1988) event management model addresses the way that events in organizational life are interpreted. It posits that people in explicit leadership roles compete with other sources to shape the meanings given to events. An organizational event is defined as any occurrence, novel, or routine impinging on any organization. For instance, managers often need to select new employees. In their twenty-five-country study, Smith and Peterson (1994) asked managers how much they relied upon eight sources of meaning (e.g., formal organization rules and national norms) for eight categories of events (e.g., selecting a new employee or handling poor subordinate performance). Results indicated that event management processes were related to cultural dimensions. For instance, managers in countries that Hofstede (1980) classified as high on individualism and low on power distance generally reported relying more heavily on their own experience and training and less heavily on formal rules and procedures than did managers in other countries. Managers in collectivist, high power distance countries (e.g., Iran, Korea, and the Philippines) showed an aversion to using subordinates as a source of guidance. In addition to such culture-specific variability, several cultural-universal results were obtained. For example, most managers reported interpreting events based on their own experience and training more than on any other source, while shunning reliance on superiors (Smith 2003).

The event management leadership process has been the focus of several studies in China (Smith, Peterson, and Wang 1996). Similar to previous studies, managers were asked to describe the extent to which they used five sources of influence for handling nine managerial events. Western managers (U.S. and British) relied more upon their own experience and training, but for Chinese managers, rules and procedures were more salient. Yet for both sets of managers, the perception was that events were evaluated more positively when the managers relied on their own experience and training. In another study (Smith, Wang, and Leung 1997), midlevel Chinese managers in Chinese joint ventures reported a much stronger reliance on widespread beliefs within their own country as a source of guidance than had been found in other nations in earlier studies. In a second study reported in this same article, events were more frequently problematic for Chinese managers when working with Western or Japanese partners than with ethnic Chinese. This result supports the hypothesis that the frequency of problem events increased with culture distance between Chinese leaders and their joint venture partners.

CULTURE, SELF-IDENTITY, AND WORK THEORY

Erez and Earley (1993) propose a new situational model of leadership and work motivation (Erez 1997) that focuses on the role of culture in influencing the leader-follower(s) relationship. Their model assumes that societal culture influences all aspects of leadership and work motivation, but the basic interpersonal and psychological mechanisms that embody these processes are similar across cultures. The crux of the model concerns both the leaders' and the followers' self-representation motives. According to the model, leaders and followers act to preserve and enhance their self-efficacy, self-enhancement, and self-consistency. While the model incorporates constructs commonly found in many leadership models (leader, follower, intervening variables), the cultural viewpoint emanates from considering how cultures impact three intervening variables: organizational and cultural structure, roles, and interpersonal relationships between leaders and followers. A consistent thread throughout the authors' discussion of the model would be that leaders in all cultures are likely to endorse and promote management practices that are culturally consistent. While other leadership models may lead to a similar conclusion, the Erez and Earley model specifies *how* and *why* leaders are likely to engage in activities and behaviors that are consistent with their culture through self-representational motives. For instance, a leader in the United States might endorse participatory practices because:

(1) It helps employees grow, (2) it is just and necessary, (3) it reaffirms the leader's membership in society, and (4) it promotes a positive self-image for the leaders by advocating values respected by

society. The first two examples are related to self-efficacy motives, the third example to a self-enhancement motive, and the fourth to a self-consistency motive. (Erez and Earley 1993, 182)

Consider how leadership processes might differ in individualist versus collectivistic cultures. According to Erez and Earley's model, leadership in collectivistic cultures would be successful to the extent it influences a group toward valued goals, as the leader must provide an opportunity for the followers to contribute to the group welfare. In contrast, in individualistic cultures, leaders should be effective to the extent that they form an emotional bond with the follower and provide valued outcomes and opportunities for personal growth and approval. The Erez and Earley leadership model signifies an exciting advancement in the field because it proposes specific mechanisms by which the macrolevel of cultural factors influence microlevel leader-follower behaviors in a culturally consistent manner.

A CULTURE-ENVELOPING MODEL OF LEADERSHIP

The cross-cultural model of leadership diagramed in figure 10.1 was developed as a result of the material I reviewed for this chapter. Culture is envisioned as an all-encompassing and enveloping influence on leadership theories and leadership processes. Like the Erez and Earley (1993) model, my model is based on social cognitive information processing and also is loosely organized around Yukl's (1989) integrated leadership model. Similar to Yukl's model, my model is presented as a general framework to guide research and thinking by identifying a few key variables rather than proposing a well-formulated theory with specific propositions. The three internal foci of the model represent (a) the leader's power, (b) personal characteristics of the leader, particularly the leader's image, and (c) interpersonal actions between the leader-followers and leader-groups. All are presumed to be heavily culturally contingent elements of leadership. First, culture is assumed to affect the *leader's power*—the actual and perceived capacity to influence others in the organization. For instance, a leader's potential capacity to influence others, almost by definition, should be potent in cultures characterized by strongly hierarchical power stratifications and by clearly defined masculine-feminine roles within society (e.g., Korea, Mexico). All leader-follower interactions operate dynamically through a filter of perceived and actual power. Second, because leadership effectiveness is inexorably intertwined with the process of being perceived

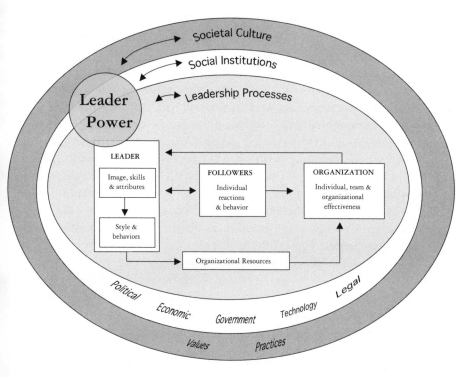

FIGURE 10.1. Culture-enveloping leadership model

as a leader (Lord and Maher 1991), personal characteristics of the leader, including the *image* a leader creates and maintains, are crucial (Chemers 1994). The prototype of an effective leader within a country reflects the ideal leader's image. In America it likely includes attributes such as independence, strong will, and inspirational; in Japan it likely reflects attributes such as interdependence, collaboration, and self-effacement. These prototypes in turn define the image-making behavior of the leader. Third, the model also suggests a culturally contingent manner in which the role of the leader is enacted through the *behavioral exchanges* between the leader and followers. For example, participatory leadership is neither expected nor likely to be effective in high power distance cultures. Although the model as proposed does not limit the number of cultural parameters, two key cultural dimensions are individualism-collectivism and power stratification.

(Other macrovariables besides culture [e.g., political, legal, and economic environment] influence leadership but are obviously not the focus of this model.)

It should be clear that, while the model focuses on power, personal leader characteristics, and interactions with followers, culture impacts these constructs through social cognitive processing of leaders and followers. It is through the schemas (scripts, prototypes) characterizing the mental landscape of leaders (Redding 1994) and followers that the meaning for many, if not all, leadership actions and behaviors can be completely understood. Other aspects of the model worth noting include the emphasis on individual *and* group processes and the reciprocal nature between the leaders and followers. Also, the model suggests that situational moderator variables, some of which can be described as "substitutes for leadership," are important to leaders in all cultures. Finally, the model suggests that culture will impact what is considered to be individual and group effectiveness. Individual success and resulting concomitant individual rewards from high individual performance will not be viewed favorably in collectivistic cultures, particularly if this success disturbs group harmony and cohesiveness (Chemers 1994).

CONCEPTUAL ISSUES AND MAJOR RESEARCH QUESTIONS

It should be evident from reading this chapter that the influence of culture on leadership processes has been conceptualized and researched in many ways. Yukl summarizes the kinds of questions asked in the cross-cultural leadership literature as What are the differences in the: (1) conceptualization of leadership behavior and leadership prototypes, (2) beliefs about effective leadership behavior, (3) actual patterns of leadership behaviors and styles, and (4) relationship of leadership behaviors to outcomes such as subordinate motivation, satisfaction, and performance? (Yukl 2002). More generally, as a prescriptive statement regarding how cross-cultural research should proceed, Brett et al. (1997) in their excellent chapter note that research designs should consist of "the original midrange model plus hypotheses about how culture will influence this model and assertions about equivalence" (99). Testing the generalizability of a given theory is one of the most compelling reasons for conducting international research (Brown and Sechrest 1980; Earley, Mosakowski, and Gibson 1995). The central question becomes, How does the normal operation of relationships within a theory change as we move across cultures? Using the Brett et al. (1997) terminology, cross-cultural hypotheses often take the following three forms: Type I proposes that culture has a main effect on the midrange model where cultural differences are thought to be antecedent constructs; Type II characterizes culture as a moderator of the strength or direction of the relationship between particular constructs in the model; Type III proposes that different constructs are needed to address the research question (i.e., emic constructs are required). Although the overlap between research models and questions proposed by Brett et al. and Yukl is not perfect, they are consistent with each other and provide a nice conceptualization of basic research questions with respect to cross-cultural leadership research.

THE ROLE OF CULTURE IN CROSS-CULTURAL LEADERSHIP THEORY

One often-employed research strategy for elucidating cultural contingencies of leadership consists of identifying specific dimensions of cultural variation and using these dimensions to understand how leadership changes from culture to culture. As Triandis (1993, 169) notes, through the study of cross-cultural leadership we may better understand how cultural variables function as parameters of leadership theories. "As we develop a better understanding of cross-cultural leadership, we will develop theorems of the form: If a culture is high in X, theory Y works as expected; if a culture is low in X, theory Y must be modified as follows." Recall that others (e.g., Earley 1989) similarly agree on the usefulness of exploring cultural differences from a culture dimension viewpoint. Using Fiedler's contingency theory as an example, Triandis (1993) offered many hypotheses elucidating how culture may impact this specific leadership theory. Recent leadership studies by Dorfman and Howell (1988), Den Hartog et al. (1999), Jago et al. (1993), and House et al. (2004) have taken this approach.

There are several important aspects of culture that should be considered as caveats for leadership researchers. First, cultures are not static; they are dynamic and continually evolving. Although the speed of evolution may not be great, the associated beliefs, values, and other elements of a culture at a single point in time may not necessarily be reflected in later time periods. Second, although cultures may be characterized correctly as being high or low on a specific dimension (e.g., power distance), this orientation will not likely be characteristic for *all* issues or situations (Triandis 1994).

For instance, Americans are considered to be extremely rugged individualists, yet they are inveterate joiners of groups and organizations. Third, individual differences exist in the adoption of cultural values such that not all individuals of a culture will have attributes of that culture. For instance, "even in highly individualistic cultures like the United States or Northwestern Europe, there are 'allocentrics' who have mostly collectivist attributes, and even in collectivist cultures, such as in the Far East there are 'idiocentrics' who have mostly individualistic attributes" (Triandis 1993, 191). Fourth, it is easy to gloss over significant differences that exist within a country (Punnett 1991) as well as to not attend to differences that exist among countries even though they may belong to a country cluster (Ronen and Shenkar 1985). To further complicate matters, we need to consider overlapping cultural entities, as many of us are identified with organizational cultures, and cultures endemic to our profession, in addition to a national culture. The combination of these caveats should lead us to take a cautious view regarding the cultural contingencies of leadership. Even for those who view culture as a significant influence on organizational behavior, some skepticism should be reserved as to the degree to which culture impacts organizational behavior—it is only one of many influences. Tightly constructed arguments for linking leadership processes to culture are necessary to advance the position that empirically derived cross-national differences in leadership processes reflect cross-cultural differences.

THE PERCEIVED IMPORTANCE OF LEADERSHIP DIFFERS AMONG CULTURES

It is hard to overstate the perceived importance of leadership to the American psyche. Even the few researchers who devalue the "real" impact of leadership (e.g., Pfeffer 1977; Meindl, Ehrlich, and Dukerich 1985) acknowledge that the belief in, or attribution of, leadership to organizational success is endemic to the U.S. culture. Social psychologists consider one particularly significant attribution error as the tendency to overly attribute the cause of an individual's performance to personal factors rather than situational factors (Ross 1977). Likewise, the American tendency to attribute organizational success to somebody rather than to something (i.e., situational factors) may reflect a similar information-processing error. After all, coaches are fired when athletic teams fail, and CEOs are replaced when stock prices plummet, even if external forces are the more obvious causal factors. Do citizens of other nations attribute the same importance of leadership to organizational success or failure? And, are attributions for the causes of leadership success similar across nations? Like most phenomena, cultural similarities and differences have been found for attributions made by respondents from different countries (Triandis 1994), and, therefore, we should not be too surprised to find differences in attributions for organizational success in people of different nations. Consider that Smith and Whitehead (1984) found cultural differences for attributions about organizational promotions and demotions; Americans used the internal factors of ability and effort, while Indians used the external factors of matrimony, corruption, and the influence of friends. Additional studies focusing on attributional differences using organizational respondents from many cultures may shed light on issues related to leadership emergence and leadership success across cultures.

Is the actual impact of leadership similar across nations, and is this impact affected by situational or contingency factors? Because leaders have been found in all societies throughout history, it is not hard to formulate an argument for leadership being universally important and having equal impact across cultures. Yet, the general lack of research addressing the issue of leadership impact precludes definitive answers. Peterson, Brannen, and Smith (1994) make cogent arguments speculating why organizational leadership effects should generally be weaker in the United States than in Japan. The thrust of their argument relates to the greater work centrality and acceptance of authority in Japan. This "enhances" the effect of leadership in Japan, whereas the higher level of individuality in the United States limits Americans' dependence on other people, including supervisors, so as to "neutralize" the impact of leadership in the United States (Howell, Dorfman, and Kerr 1986). However, an equally cogent argument can be made for expecting equal leadership impacts for Americans and Japanese. Part of this line of reasoning proceeds with noting that basic task and relationship facets of behaviors are found everywhere in work organizations, and it may only be the particular expressions of these functions that differ among societies. Future empirical research should provide answers to this argument considering all cultures. I think it is an important issue, and research should lead to the discovery of intriguing differences among cultures.

EXPLICIT AND IMPLICIT NATURE OF LEADERSHIP

Even if citizens of all countries attribute the same importance to leadership, are there differences in the degree to which leadership in work organizations is explicit or implicit? That is, to what degree are job expectations implicit, tacit, and clearly understood by subordinates? Or, is it necessary for leaders to frequently and explicitly convey job expectations? At this time we simply don't know, given an absence of literature regarding this issue. However, the Japanese culture again provides a good example of the implicit/explicit differences in espoused leadership requirements. As reported by Bass (1991), one historian suggested that there is no need for leaders of Japanese groups because everyone in the group knows how everybody else should behave in the group—group members create harmony by tacit understanding (Hayashi 1988). Furthermore, worker motivation is enhanced by the sense of group cohesiveness, where workers share in group norms of quality and productivity (Kashima and Callan 1994). Consistent with these norms, the Japanese image of a good midlevel manager is one who creates harmony in the group as opposed to being a technical expert in directing work behaviors (Sullivan, Suzuki, and Kondo 1986; Hayashi 1988). The mutual responsibility between the leader and subordinate emanating from the central concept of *amae* (dependence on another person's kindness and goodwill) and the importance of group harmony (*wa*) lend themselves to clearly understood implicit obligations. But, from Misumi's research (1985) we know that leadership remains an important process in Japanese organizations. And, it is also clear that Japanese supervisors are more likely to use "pressuring" leader behaviors than are American supervisors. However, at a minimum, one might expect that the Japanese concept of continually striving for improvements (*kaizen*) and of elevating teamwork to a fine art fundamentally influence how leaders manage group processes. Perplexing questions remain to be answered. For example, if Japanese group members continually work hard and strive for improvements, why is it necessary for Japanese leaders to engage in pressuring behaviors?

CULTURAL UNIVERSALS VERSUS CULTURAL SPECIFICS

To what extent is leadership culturally contingent? The extreme positions on this question are relatively easy to identify. A culture-free, or universalist, approach assumes that, because all leaders throughout the world have had to inspire, motivate, and provide guidance to people, core leadership processes should be similar across cultures. If so, it should be possible to identify universals of leadership—those attributes of leaders, leadership behaviors, and theories that remain invariant across cultures. The cultural universal position is consistent with an etic or comparative research approach; certain leadership constructs are universal in the sense that they are comparable, though probably not equally important, across cultures. For instance, Likert (1961, 1967) generally argued that his "Systems 3 and 4" styles of interpersonal relationships (consultative and democratic styles) would be the most effective leadership styles in terms of increased productivity and employee satisfaction, regardless of the country or the culture. Bass (1991) also maintains that the basic structure of leadership is universal and that behaviors that inspire and intellectually challenge followers should travel well across cultures. The GLOBE research project (House et al. 1999) found a number of leadership attributes that clearly are universally believed to enhance effective leadership. Many of these characteristics, presented previously in this chapter, reflect the importance of charismatic leadership attributes, including visionary and inspirational elements. An etic approach to leadership research allows us to empirically test whether there are universally effective leadership patterns.

Conversely, the culture-specific approach assumes that, because cultures are different, leadership processes should reflect these differences. The culture-specific perspective, which is consistent with an emic or insider approach to construct development (Berry 1980), reflects the idea that certain leadership constructs and behaviors are likely to be unique to a given culture. In-depth emic studies that are culture-specific provide descriptively rich information about how leadership constructs are enacted in those cultures. Emic studies should also reveal the subtle meaning of behaviors that would escape notice from those who are outside a culture. Consistent with the culture-specific position, Jackofsky, Slocum, and McQuaid (1988) found, with few exceptions, that the leadership styles of a sample of French, West German, Swedish, and Taiwanese CEOs were consistent with the corresponding society's cultural values. Some cross-cultural scholars are skeptical about the existence of leadership universals and seriously question whether the search for leadership universals is fruitful (e.g., Hofstede 1993). The GLOBE research project (House et al. 1999) also determined that there were leadership attributes that were seen as contributing to effective leadership in some societal cultures but not others.

Examples include leader attributes previously discussed, such as ambitious, compassionate, elitist, enthusiastic, independent, individualistic, logical, orderly, risk taker, self-effacing, sensitive, sincere, status-conscious, and worldly.

Support can be provided for both positions—cultural similarities *and* differences exist in managerial and leadership processes (Dorfman and Ronen 1991). In fact, neither of the extreme positions presents a viable or accurate picture of cross-cultural leadership. For instance, a few basic leadership functions, such as supportive leadership, are likely transcultural and exist in many cultures, even though the enactment or specific expression of those leadership functions varies according to cultural constraints. As Smith et al. (1989) demonstrated, specific behaviors that connote each leadership function are often culturally specific. And, the desirability or preference of subordinates for leaders to engage in specific leadership behaviors is likely to be culturally contingent. For instance, a low "pressuring" style of leadership was preferred for British and American employees, but the trend was in the opposite direction for Japanese employees (Smith et al. 1992). In addition, the impact of specific leadership functions on subordinate attitudes and criteria is likely to differ across cultures (Dorfman et al. 1997). However, additional research is greatly needed to identify clearly the situationally unique aspects from the general aspects of leadership effectiveness.

THE UNIVERSE OR DOMAIN OF LEADERSHIP BEHAVIORS AND STYLES

Has leadership research identified most, if not all, possible leadership behaviors critical for leadership success? Clearly, it would be presumptuous to assert that Western researchers have completely elucidated the entire range of leadership processes for all cultures, let alone for the less familiar African, Asian, and Middle Eastern cultures. For instance, one might consider the leadership styles of aboriginal tribal leaders (indigenous Australian, Eskimo, American Indian, African, etc.) and compare them to "modern" leaders. Would these tribal cultures provide a baseline for leadership styles and attributes? What has been added? What has dropped out or changed? (R. M. Brown, personal communication, September 16, 2001). Regarding Asia, researchers from Western cultures should not have been surprised to find that Chinese leadership necessitates the addition of leader behaviors specifically reflecting Confucian values of "personal moral character" (Xu 1987; Hui and Tan 1999). Misumi's (1985) seminal research studies in Japan have already provided a window into Japanese leadership. Yet we know very little about leadership processes in less well-studied continents such as Africa. As Blunt and Jones (1992) note, the absence of empirical investigation of leadership styles and practices among African cultures is associated with a corresponding dearth of indigenous (i.e., culturally specific models developed in Africa) models of leadership. It has been suggested that the combination of African culture with a colonial past yields a unique African management style whereby internal issues of resource allocation are more important than the achievement of organizational goals (Montgomery 1987).

How should we best search for universals and cultural specifics for leadership styles and behaviors? A similar problem was addressed by Schwartz (1992) while mapping out universals in the content and structure of "values" (e.g., power, tradition). It may be useful to ask and try to answer the following questions asked by Schwartz but now frame the questions within a leadership perspective:

1. "Have we identified a comprehensive set of leader behaviors and styles?" Although some leader behaviors seem to be universally important (e.g., task orientation), it would be presumptuous to suggest that all important leadership behaviors and processes have been elucidated.

2. "To what extent are universally recognized leadership behaviors conceptually and functionally equivalent?" As previously noted, many leader behaviors (processes, styles, functions) examined in Western societies seem to be both functionally and conceptually equivalent to those in widely diverse cultures.

3. "Are the antecedents and consequences to leadership behaviors similar across cultures?" We simply do not know the answer to this question. The GLOBE research project should provide some answers.

4. "To what extent are the specific expressions (or enactments, actions, or behaviors) of commonly identified styles of leadership culturally contingent?" The research by Peterson and Smith and colleagues (e.g., Smith and Tayeb 1988; Smith et al. 1989) begins to address this issue. But far more research is needed to replicate and extend their research regarding the generality/cultural specificity of specific leader actions and behaviors. Research

programs may benefit by using different analytical strategies, with multiple samples within a given culture, across a variety of cultures, and for various organizational settings, to determine precisely which behaviors (actions, etc.) are culturally specific and which transfer universally.

5. "Are configurations of leader behaviors, such as might be expected with transformational leadership, different among cultures?" Not only do we not know the answer to this question from a cross-cultural perspective, but we are also a long way from understanding the unique configuration of possible combinations of leader behaviors and styles within Western societies.

INTERCULTURAL INTERACTION

Adler (1984) emphasized the importance of conducting studies that are designed to answer the question, How should we best manage cross-cultural interaction within the same organization? Such synergistic studies should answer questions related to how and when supervisors should use indigenous and culturally specific patterns of management, patterns common to all cultures, or synergistic combinations of both. Such intercultural contacts within the same organization will become even more important as economic globalization progresses. Consider the complexity and potential chaos of managing Mexican *maquiladoras* (twin plant), manufacturing operations in Mexico owned by multinational firms. Managers from Asia, Europe, North America, and Latin America supervise a diverse work force composed of Mexican nationals, parent-country nationals, and third-country nationals. Obviously, language problems complicate the communication process between expatriate managers and subordinates, and behavioral cues may be misinterpreted. Graen and Wakabayashi (1994) describe a comparative study investigating the Japanese leadership-making process in manufacturing firms in Japan and compared this to the leadership-making process for Japanese-owned manufacturing transplants (new start-ups) in the United States. Using patterned interviews, case material, and documentation, the researchers examined the leadership process designed to ultimately implement a teamwork system that would be functionally equivalent to the home plant's. Graen and Wakabayashi discuss how an intercultural group can overcome its initial fears. For example, one American fear was that the American values of individualism would be subverted, whereas the Japanese fear was that American values would undermine traditional Japanese values of teamwork.

Two studies summarized by Peterson, Brannen, and Smith (1994) also address the problem of expatriate Japanese managers supervising American employees. As might be expected, successful operation of one acquired U.S. plant required overcoming "implicit management theories" held by both parties. Issues that had to be dealt with included the negative stereotypes Americans held of the Japanese and different understandings related to quality control, unionized labor structures, and an "extreme" American culture. A number of adjustments occurred in "typical" Japanese management behaviors, with some adaptations endorsing U.S. norms and values. A second study (Peterson, Brannen, and Smith 1994) described leadership processes in a Japanese-owned electronics manufacturing company in Georgia. Results of this study attest to the complex adjustment of actions and interpretations that occurs with intense intercultural interaction. Furthermore, a number of studies support the proposition that Japanese supervisors are viewed by non-Japanese subordinates as being strongly task oriented (e.g., Smith et al. 1992). Yet, Peterson, Brannen, and Smith (1994) speculate that not only may Japanese expatriate supervisors find that they have less influence over U.S. subordinates than they did over Japanese subordinates, but they may also have less influence than their American supervisor counterparts. This issue regarding the relative supervisory impact of expatriate managers versus host-country managers remains unresolved. On a more positive note, empirical results from the Peterson, Brannen, and Smith (1994) study indicated considerable consistency in predicting subordinates' attitudes, performance, attendance, and turnover *despite* supervisor nationality. Such intercultural interaction raises fascinating issues, yet with a few exceptions, the paucity of leadership studies so far prevents firm conclusions about effective leadership processes in these situations.

METHODOLOGICAL ISSUES

What follows is a discussion of several methodological problems and dilemmas that make international and cross-cultural research intrinsically difficult. However, no attempt will be made to address all of the vast number of potential methodological pitfalls that await cross-cultural researchers (cf. Adler 1984; Hui and Triandis 1985; van de Vijver and Leung 1997). The following discussion is selective and reflects a personal judgment as to those issues particularly important for leadership researchers. Various solutions to these problems are frequently the source of debate, but researchers seem to agree on one point—conducting comparative international and cross-cultural research is fundamentally much more difficult than most people realize (Arvey, Bhagat, and Salas 1991). Fortunately, expert guidance in conducting cross-cultural research is available in this handbook (and its previous edition). In addition, van de Vijver and Leung (1997) and Brett et al. (1997) provide additional information and direction for designing cross-cultural studies irrespective of the phenomenon of interest.

RIVAL HYPOTHESES CONFOUND

Many scholars (e.g., Roberts and Boyacigiller 1984; Triandis 1994; Brett et al. 1997) have addressed what might be labeled the "fundamental methodological issue." "When do findings of *cross-national* differences reflect true *cross-cultural* differences?" It is simply too easy for researchers to slip into the epistemological trap of inferring that culture is the root cause of cross-national differences. Besides culture, a myriad of other factors, including technological, political, economic, and organizational factors, influence organizational behavior (Child 1981). These other factors present competing hypotheses and rival explanations that need to be ruled out if cultural explanations are attributed as causes (Kelley, Whatley, and Worthley 1987). Unfortunately, culture may also influence many of these factors, thus presenting a Herculean task to disentangle the effects of culture from other influences.

STRATEGIES TO ADDRESS THE RIVAL
HYPOTHESIS CONFOUND

How should researchers avoid the trap of blindly inferring that cross-national differences are the result of cultural differences? While it may seem obvious, it is critical to pay careful attention to initially developing a rigorous research design that minimizes the potential for alternative explanations (Brett et al. 1997). As a prescriptive model for cross-cultural research, Brett et al. (1997) argue that it is advisable to use a combination of approaches, including inductive and deductive, qualitative and quantitative, and so forth. Starting with a multicultural team of scholars, the research question(s) and hypotheses should be jointly developed. While this goal of having no single culture dominate the research question or design is desirable, it is simply a fact that most leadership research and education have been centered in Western culture, with the United States dominating both. This fact may create problems in developing a true multicultural team, but it should not block the development of a culturally balanced study. For instance, although the GLOBE leadership project started under the auspices of Robert House, a leadership researcher clearly in the Western research camp, he incorporated ideas, hypotheses, specific questionnaire items, and interpretation of results from many members of the multicultural team. In fact, in the initial stages of the GLOBE project, the definition of "leadership" was developed in concert with many individuals across the globe.

Careful selection of cross-national samples is crucial to ruling out alternative explanations to cultural influence. As Arvey, Bhagat, and Salas (1991) note, "The sampling issue appears to loom large as a serious and critical element. How does a researcher ensure that all potential differences between samples in two countries/cultures are controlled in order to support a finding that differences on a particular dependent variable or the relationships between two variables are a function of nationality or culture?" (400). Sampling may take the form of systematic, random, or convenience sampling, with the latter least preferred (van de Vijver and Leung 1997). The third phase of the GLOBE leadership project is an example of using a systematic sampling process in leadership research. CEOs of entrepreneurial and nonentrepreneurial organizations along with their direct reports were sampled from numerous countries. Alternative explanations from rival hypotheses can be reduced by increasing the number of cultures studied, assuming that a compelling theoretical framework exists with commensurate measurement of cultures along relevant theoretical dimensions (van de Vijver and Leung 1997).

Peng, Peterson, and Shyi (1991) suggest that cross-cultural comparisons with perfectly matched samples are probably impossible but that potential confounds should be carefully considered and empirical checks should be conducted post hoc to estimate sample equivalence. At a minimum, the industry, job characteristics, and organizational level of the samples should match. Which additional variables should leadership researchers pay particular attention to, and should they use a covariance analysis later when analyzing data? Answers to these questions are best resolved on a case-by-case basis. For instance, consider a research investigation examining participatory leadership across cultures. In this situation it would be important to check and control for noncultural factors that have been found to influence participatory leadership such as age, education, hierarchical level, and managerial function (Jago et al. 1993). To illustrate how managerial functions may affect participation, Heller (1969) found that American managers in finance and accounting were more autocratic than those in purchasing and sales, who in turn were more autocratic than managers in personnel or those who were less specialized managers.

CROSS-CULTURAL CONSTRUCT AND MEASUREMENT EQUIVALENCE ISSUES

Do leadership constructs have the same commonality of meaning (construct or conceptual equivalence), similar purpose (functional equivalence), similar measurement properties (metric equivalence), and relationships among the constructs (structural equivalence) across cultures? As has been pointed out, even the translation of the term "leadership" is problematic in some cultures. My experience with the construct of participative leadership leads me to believe that it can have a very different meaning in America in contrast to Mexico. In addition to meeting the functional/conceptual equivalence criterion, direct comparisons among cultures using inferential statistics require metric equivalence—similar to the operationalization of constructs with items that mean the same thing across cultures. Yet we know that the precise behaviors that define leadership dimensions may be culturally contingent (Smith et al. 1989). For instance, although Smith et al. (1989) found some leadership behaviors clustered together similarly across cultures (e.g., fair treatment by a supervisor), others did not. In addition, actions by a leader may connote one leadership function in one culture but another in a different culture. As one particularly striking example, a supervisor discussing a subordinate's personal problems without the subordinate present was seen as being consistent with a maintenance leadership function in Japan, but not so for Americans.

Even for situations where questionnaire items signify the same leader functions, metric equivalence requires that numerical values on a scale must indicate precisely the same magnitude of the construct regardless of the population under consideration (Hui and Triandis 1985). Obviously, significant conceptual and measurement problems exist if differing factor structures are found to underlie responses from leadership questionnaires given to respondents from more than one culture. For instance, Koh (1990) found that in contrast to a four-factor solution predicted by Bass and Avolio's (1993) transformational leadership theory, a single transformational factor emerged in Singapore. Does this reflect a less discriminating conceptualization of transformational leadership, or does it reflect a need to use items developed specifically for that culture, or neither?

A current debate concerns the degree of metric equivalence necessary to conduct cross-cultural research. Hulin (1987), using item response theory, stakes out the strong position for metric equivalence. He suggests that using items in questionnaires that are culturally nonequivalent will render comparisons on such scales potentially meaningless—thus the quest for complete metric equivalence. Peterson, Smith, and colleagues position themselves differently (Smith et al. 1989; Peng, Peterson, and Shyi 1991). They argue that useful information will be suppressed if one goes over-board searching for perfect metric equivalence. Rather than insisting on a level of metric equivalence that most likely cannot be obtained, they suggest that imprecise equivalence should be accepted as inevitable and taken into account in the interpretation process. Debate on these two contrasting positions will no doubt continue for years to come.

STRATEGIES TO ADDRESS MEASUREMENT EQUIVALENCE ISSUES

Many methodological strategies are available to demonstrate or improve measurement equivalence in cross-cultural studies (Hui and Triandis 1985). Some of the commonly used methods are back translation (to assure a correct and conceptually similar translation) and factor analysis (to assess the internal structure coherence of the data). Newer approaches such as item response theory (IRT) and simultaneous factor analysis in several populations show promise but are not yet commonly found in the research literature. Furthermore, while van de Vijver and Leung (1997) present a convincing argument that researchers should use available statistical tools to detect item bias, the fact is that the overall picture of the state of the art regarding differential item functioning across cultures is gloomy (Bond 1993). What should researchers do to ensure measurement equivalence?

Since many of these strategies complement one another, an obvious suggestion would be for researchers to use multiple strategies to determine the existence of measurement equivalence. Although this multistrategy approach may seem daunting, Hui and Triandis (1985) argue that it is not as difficult as one might imagine.

One can improve an instrument by proper translation techniques and then establish conceptual/functional equivalence as well as instrument (constructs as operationalized) equivalence by the nomological network method and by examination of internal structure congruence. After that, the response pattern method and regression methods can be used to test item equivalence and scalar equivalence. (149)

Alternatively, if item bias is found, researchers may choose to remove biased items from their research instrument. Even such a reasonably sounding approach, however, presents a dilemma to cross-cultural researchers, as biased items may reflect important cross-cultural differences.

COMMON METHOD, SOURCE, AND RESPONSE BIASES

The use of survey research using questionnaires has been and likely will continue to be a frequently used research method for international research. Problems when using questionnaires in leadership research are well documented (e.g., Lord and Maher 1991); however, because attitudinal and perceptual measures represent unique responses of individuals, they lend themselves to this type of assessment. Furthermore, strong evidence exists for the validity of using questionnaires when items measure specific, concrete, and easily observable behaviors (Yukl and Van Fleet 1992). Yet, all research strategies, including survey research, should be concerned with biases that threaten the validity of cross-cultural comparisons. Using the taxonomy of biases proposed by van de Vijver and Leung (1997), these include construct biases (e.g., differential meaning and incomplete coverage of the construct), method biases (e.g., differential effects of social desirability or familiarity of response procedures), and item biases (e.g., poor item translation or wording that is inappropriate).

Response biases are extremely troublesome for cross-cultural survey research (Hui and Triandis 1989; Triandis 1994). Studies that focus on the magnitude, level, or frequency of use of variables across cultures are particularly problematic. Social desirability is but one response set to be addressed and will be discussed shortly. Another bias concerns the failure to use extreme ends of the scale. For Asian cultures, this is perhaps linked to the value of modesty and a desire to respond cautiously. In addition, Stening and Everett (1984) found differences within Asian cultures in their tendency to use the midpoint responses of the scale, with the Japanese most likely to do so and the Thai least likely. By contrast, the extreme response set bias is defined by excessive use of the scale endpoints (Hui and Triandis 1989). For Mediterranean cultures this may be due to a belief that extreme responses are sincere and reflect true feelings. However, it may also be caused by respondents not being familiar with graded responses such as those with Likert formats (van de Vijver and Leung 1997). For instance, Adler, Campbell, and Laurent (1989) found that responses from more than 50 percent of the respondents from the PRC choose entirely bimodal answers to five-point Likert scales! It was obviously impossible to use typical data analytic techniques in this situation. Another response set involves a tendency to respond either positively or negatively (labeled "acquiescence" in both cases) despite true feelings. In general, the lower the status and educational level of respondents, the stronger the acquiescence (Hofstede 1980). Furthermore, inconsistent test administration and differing motivation levels among respondents may exacerbate response bias problems in cross-cultural research.

Using my own research as an example (Dorfman and Howell 1988), we found that subordinates reported a higher level of supervisor participation for U.S. managers than for Mexican or Korean managers. This could reflect true differences or response biases of the type previously discussed. Not only are such level-oriented studies affected by biases, so are structure-oriented studies. The latter examine relationships among variables. For instance, Ganster, Hennessey, and Luthans (1983) note that biases may mask significant relationships between two variables (a suppressor effect), provide a false correlation (a spurious effect), or moderate the relationship between two variables (a moderator effect). Response biases will have the net effect of confounding the interpretation of research demonstrating, or not demonstrating, cross-national differences.

Common method bias is considered a significant measurement artifact and occurs when relations are explored among constructs measured in the same way (Spector 1987). It is particularly problematic when the data is obtained from only one source. Such common source bias is often a problem when self-report questionnaires are used exclusively (Glick, Jenkins, and Gupta 1986). Although controversy exists as to the real impact of common source and method biases (Wagner and Crampton 1993), it is clearly wise to use multiple methods and sources where possible. Triandis (1994) and many others warn against relying on a single method, particularly if it only employs self-report technologies (Campbell 1982).

Social desirability is defined as the tendency of individuals to present themselves in a favorable light. Podsakoff, Todor and Skov (1982) have noted the importance of controlling for social desirability in leadership studies using questionnaires. It is likely that social desirability varies across cultures (Hofstede 1980) and, therefore, may be a particularly problematic response bias in cross-cultural research (Randall, Huo, and Pawelk 1993). Obviously, if members of one culture tend to respond in a socially desirable manner more than members of another culture, particularly in terms of describing leadership styles and behaviors of their supervisors, apparent cultural differences may simply reflect differing response sets (Triandis 1972). The tendency to respond in a socially desirable manner may be particularly prevalent in cultures that are high in collectivism and power distance.

STRATEGIES TO ADDRESS COMMON METHOD, SOURCE, AND RESPONSE BIAS PROBLEMS

How should researchers control for these confounds? First, researchers should test for response biases using several available techniques (Spector 1987). For instance, researchers could examine the overall response distributions to determine the existence of the previously discussed response tendencies (i.e., use of the extreme responses in contrast to a neutral response). And confidence intervals may be calculated around the percentage uses of midpoint responses (Stening and Everett 1984). To control for the potential biasing effects of social desirability, researchers might measure social desirability and statistically partial out the impact of this potential bias. Other response sets such as avoiding endpoints of the scale can be dealt with in a number of ways. For instance, transforming raw scores to ranks may be appropriate in some studies (as is frequently done in determining work goal importance across cultures). Obviously, using ranks rather than raw scores loses "interval" information. Alternatively, raw scores can be converted to various types of standardized scores, thus retaining the relative distance of scores between data points. That is, variables may be standardized within each culture before proceeding with the analysis—unfortunately this eliminates true differences at the cross-cultural level. Alternatively, a "within unit-of-analysis standardization" procedure could be used where the unit of analysis may be the individual respondent. These responses can be aggregated to the cultural level (Leung and Bond 1989). GLOBE researchers, for most of their sixty-two-country sample, found a close correspondence between the standardized (i.e., bias free) measures and uncorrected (raw score) measures of specific culture dimensions. However, several countries had response biases that were more problematic than others.

Second, because many problems are inherent in analytical strategies using "mean level responses across cultures" (Peng, Peterson, and Shyi 1991), researchers should be extremely wary of analytical strategies for hypothesis testing that contrast mean level scores (e.g., the average level of job satisfaction or leader behavior for country A was X, which was significantly higher than for country B, which was Y). Direct comparisons across cultures using T-tests or MANOVA's assume scalar equivalence in addition to conceptual/functional equivalence—both of which are highly questionable assumptions. There is a growing recognition by reviewers that single method research strategies that use mean level responses as primary data are inappropriate for publication. The likelihood of inappropriate inferences because of subtle language differences combined with many response biases is simply too great. However, mean scores might be used as additional information and interpreted in congruence with findings obtained with other methods (Smith et al. 1992).

Third, the use of alternative methods to check for convergence is also an obvious recommendation for international leadership research. As noted by Yukl and Van Fleet (1992, 183), "The limitations of each type of methodology make it desirable to use multiple methods in research on leadership. . . . The purpose of the research should dictate the methodology and choice of samples, not the other way around." Qualitative and quantitative approaches are complementary and desirable. Qualitative methods are clearly appropriate in the initial stages of the research process, to make sure you are asking the right questions in subsequent quantitative analyses and to help interpret the results. Appropriately used qualitative methods such as patterned interviews, critical incidents, observation, audio tapes, archival records, and intensive case studies can provide a rich (emically focused) description of leadership processes (Bennis and Nanus 1985; Luthans, Welsh, and Rosenkrantz 1993; Welsh, Luthans, and Sommer 1993; Graen and Wakabayashi 1994). Carefully conducted interviews, for instance, can provide unique insights into a culture and managerial leadership processes within that culture. The following two studies, apparently conducted without knowledge of each other, show the strength of qualitative methods. By conducting in-depth interviews with Spanish managers, Aram and Walochik (1996) identified a distinct Spanish management style characterized by improvisation, informality, flexibility, and a relatively low level of reliance on organizational systems, procedures, and formal planning. Martinez (2000) found similar managerial styles using an ethnographic approach to interview Mexican entrepreneurs. In addition, she was able to reveal six roles of the Mexican *empresario* (e.g., establish trust in relationships) in addition to three broad themes (e.g., family model) underlying management styles. As one example of linking roles to themes, the importance of trust established within family bonds is extended to business and employee relationships (Martinez and Dorfman 1998). The relationships between roles and themes would have been very difficult to uncover using a pure quantitative research approach.

Nevertheless, response biases may affect nonquestionnaire research methods as well. Alternative methodologies have limitations, such as excessive subjectivity and poorly defined standards for evaluating research quality, and are subject to information processing distortions such as selective attention, memory limitations, interpretability problems, and attribution errors (Yukl and Van Fleet 1992). As discussed previously, the combination of quantitative and qualitative approaches used in the GLOBE leadership project presents a unique opportunity to observe the usefulness of complementary research approaches.

ETIC AND EMIC PERSPECTIVES: COMPLEMENTARY OR INCOMPATIBLE APPROACHES?

As noted by Brett et al. (1997) cross-cultural research is characterized by a number of dichotomies including the emic-etic perspective, local versus specific knowledge, and the search for similarities versus differences. Each perspective not only reflects a researcher's personal perspective regarding research in general but also tends to direct the research questions asked and methods used. Consider, for instance, the often proposed distinction between an etic and emic approach to cross-cultural research. As typically presented, the universal aspects of a culture are labeled etic and the unique aspects of a culture are labeled emic. Yet Pike's original development of both terms was much broader and qualitatively different from how they are currently used today in management studies. Properly interpreted, the etic is the universal set of a phenomenon composed of all emics. As brought to my attention by Sandra Martinez, the proper use of these terms in leadership research would be to define the universal (etic) aspects of leadership as being composed of *all* subsets (emics) of phenomena found in each culture (Martinez and Dorfman 1998). These subsets would include culture-specific as well as culture-common elements. Triandis (1980) and others have noted that it is also appropriate to distinguish emic and etic research approaches. Emic approaches are characterized by in-depth intracultural investigation, whereas the etic approach is characterized by a comparison of multiple systems viewed from an outside perspective with the constructs assumed to be universal (Berry 1980). Because the terms "etic" and "emic" carry so much excessive linguistic baggage, and controversy exists as to whether researchers are using the terms correctly, it may be best to use alternative terminology. The GLOBE research team has chosen to use the concept of "universal" and "culture specific" to replace "etic" and "emic," respectively.

Comparative cross-cultural leadership studies using a comparative research approach with universal (etic) constructs have often found similarities in the conceptualization and effectiveness of certain leadership functions (styles, behaviors, processes). As an example, the series of studies by Podsakoff (e.g., Podsakoff et al. 1986) have consistently found that leader reward and punishment behaviors are effective in both individualist and collectivist cultures. Perhaps, paradoxically, it is by the establishment of cross-cultural generalities through an interpretive insider approach that cultural differences can be understood. For instance, an examination of confirmatory factor analyses conducted within each culture may indicate how insiders reinterpret the original leadership construct. Numerous examples can be found in the leadership literature (Ayman and Chemers 1983; Smith et al. 1989; Koh 1990), pointing out changes in the internal structure of measures for different cultures. Dorfman et al. (1997) found that specific leadership behaviors (e.g., participatory leadership) were not equally effective across cultures. Thus, etic approaches to leadership research may lead to discovering both similarities and differences in leadership behaviors and their effectiveness among cultures. But numerous problems are inherent in etic designs that can trap the unwary researcher.

Because an etic design may overlook important concepts and ideas that are unique to a particular culture, emic or in-depth intracultural studies may not necessarily lead to a similar picture of a society as will etic or comparative studies (Smith and Tayeb 1988). Most important, an emic approach might decode the meanings of a supervisor's behavior that might be inaccessible to outsiders. For example, the leader's influence on a subordinate by rewarding quality work for Arab cultures may depend entirely on the status of the supervisor and the tribal-kinship relationships between the leader and the follower (Khadra 1990). As a second example, Ling

(1989) described the importance of defining leader behaviors that reflect "personal moral character" in addition to Western-derived leadership behaviors for Chinese managers. But, emic approaches, with their thorough understanding of individual cultures, preclude finding general principles and laws that are applicable to other cultures.

I think it is safe to conclude that emic and etic perspectives are complementary, not incompatible. As noted by Earley, Mosakowski, and Gibson (1995), some combination of emic and etic approaches is desirable for construct development. A pure etic approach may overlook the uniqueness of a given culture, whereas the pure emic approach limits the development of general principles. It should, therefore, come as no surprise that numerous writers suggest that we use multinational research teams, carefully investigate the phenomenon of interest within each society, and develop a true understanding of quantitative research findings through qualitative analysis (e.g., Boyacigiller and Adler 1991). In short, leadership researchers are advised to combine quantitative approaches with complementary qualitative evidence and give serious consideration to functional, conceptual, and metric equivalence issues. As described previously, the GLOBE programmatic leadership project developed by House et al. (1999) serves as an exemplar of using multiple approaches to study leadership across cultures. By using a combination of ethnographic studies and traditional questionnaire techniques, these researchers strive to advance both methodological and conceptual aspects of cross-cultural leadership research. Even so, the inherent tension between these basic approaches increases the inherent difficulty of conducting cross-cultural research. GLOBE researchers found this to be true from both a research design and an interpersonal perspective (Dorfman, Hanges, and Dickson 1998).

PSYCHOMETRIC ISSUES REGARDING THE OPERATIONALIZATION AND MEASUREMENT OF CULTURE

The difficulty of conceptualizing, operationalizing, and measuring culture is obviously formidable. Although a number of typologies have been proposed to assess cultural dimensions (Schwartz 1992; Trompenaars 1993), Hofstede's (1980; Hofstede 2001) conceptualization and measurement of cultural variations have been the most popular to date (Erez 1994). And his seminal research program has led to great advances in the field of cross-cultural management. Unfortunately, while Hofstede's five dimensions of culture are well conceptualized, the operationalization and measurement of the variables are problematic (Roberts and Boyacigiller 1984). Items in several of the scales are seemingly unrelated to the construct of interest, data are combined from differently formatted questions, and item scores are combined in an unusual fashion (Dorfman and Howell 1988). Hofstede's uncertainty avoidance scale, for example, comprises items that reflect these disparate constructs: level of perceived stress, length of time the individual believes she or he will work for the company, and beliefs regarding whether rules should be broken. Given these (and many other) statistical problems, one should develop a certain level of skepticism regarding the meaningfulness of "country scores," subsequent ranking of countries, and the placement of countries in simple high/low topologies for each of the cultural dimensions. Unwary leadership researchers may unwittingly stumble if culture is used as a parameter (moderator or a boundary condition for a theory) *and* tests of specific hypotheses rely on the precise rankings of countries using Hofstede's (1980) measures. The same is true for GLOBE country rankings. Researchers who intend to use Hofstede, GLOBE, or measures developed by other researchers should do so with caution, particularly if hypothesis development and analysis rely on the precise ranking of countries found in previous research.

SOLUTIONS TO OPERATIONALIZATION AND MEASUREMENT OF CULTURE

Several alternative conceptualizations and measures of cultural dimensions are available in addition to the Hofstede measure (Dorfman and Howell 1988; Earley 1989; Schwartz 1992; Trompenaars 1993; House et al. 1999). Assessing the construct validity of any instrument designed to measure cultural variations is a complex, difficult, lengthy, and dismaying task. Regardless of which cultural dimensions are used in the research, it would be prudent to verify empirically that a particular sample maps onto the cultural dimensions as hypothesized. That is, one should not simply assume, without additional verification, that because country X was more collective than country Y (using past rankings such as Hofstede, GLOBE, or others) that these rankings also hold with new samples. Researchers should use a variety of procedures to quantitatively and qualitatively triangulate the essence of the construct. For instance, it goes without saying that the researcher should thoroughly understand each culture under investigation, use previously developed measures of cultural variation where appropriate, verify empirically the predicted cultural variations for the sample under investigation, and use qualitative data to substantiate hypothesized variations. Essentially, I am advocating a construct validity approach to the measurement of cultural variations. Such efforts have been employed (cf., Earley 1989; House et al. 1999) and strengthen one's presumption of cultural variations.

CONCLUSIONS: WHERE DO WE GO FROM HERE?

Returning to the basic question regarding cultural contingencies for leadership theories, what can we conclude? Most empirical research supports the conclusion that, while several popular leadership theories developed in the West may be applicable to other cultures, cultural contingencies exist and will likely affect the strength of relationships between theoretical constructs, the conceptualization and measurement of constructs, and the specific expression of how leadership is enacted. At a minimum, cross-cultural researchers need to ask *when* and under what conditions, not *if,* culture is a contingency. Unfortunately, we are far from being able to delineate how cultural variations function as antecedents, moderators, or other kinds of variables within leadership theories. However, the literature base is growing and we are making progress!

Throughout this chapter I have identified specific research questions that, if answered, should lead to advancing the level of theoretical development in the field of international and cross-cultural research. What follows is my personal view as to the kinds of studies that are important to undertake. First, we are woefully ignorant about gender differences in leadership across cultures. There are some exceptions (Gibson 1995), but far more conceptualization and investigation of gender differences are needed. In so many societies, the relatively small number of female managers and CEOs compared to male managers creates a large barrier to research. However, as Adler (1999) notes, while there are relatively few female leaders of global companies and while women traditionally are underrepresented in managerial positions, a disproportionate number have founded and are leading entrepreneurial enterprises. Will some of the male/female cultural distinctions found in studies of female leaders in America generalize to other regions of the world? It is interesting to note that Adler (1999) suggests that the relational style of communicating that is associated with female managers in America is more typical of most non-American managers around the world than of the typical American male communication style.

As a second issue, we should also move beyond simplistic dichotomies implied in the terms "universal" versus "indigenous culture specific." We simply need to be more sophisticated when discussing these supposed dichotomies. As argued by Bond and Smith (1996), the etic-emic dilemma is no more inseparable than nature and nurture. Cross-cultural researchers often look for culturally specific aspects of phenomena under study perhaps because it seems more meaningful and fun. Researchers are adept in providing examples that reflect the unique or indigenous culture-specific aspects of leadership. Yet the leadership literature clearly indicates that there are universally meaningful leadership constructs and *similar* behaviors that manifest these constructs. For instance, the GLOBE leadership study found a number of leadership attributes (e.g., integrity) that are universally perceived to be highly relevant for effective leadership. In addition, a set of leadership practices such as providing support and rewarding good performance is clearly meaningful leadership practices in all societies. But what does "universal" really imply? Are we talking about universal in terms of meaning, function, measurement, or enactment? I think that we are approaching a research position that embraces both the search for universals and culture specifics—an approach labeled "hybrid research" by Earley and Singh (1995). This creative blending of approaches in comparative leadership studies can result in the same phenomenon having both universal and culturally specific explanations (Hui and Graen 1997).

A third issue concerns the almost inevitable merging and confluence of cultures and associated management practices. Will forces of globalization blur differences among nations, cultures, and organizations? It is often suggested that there is a substantial amount of cross-national convergence of management practices, values, and beliefs (Boyacigiller et al. 1996). This occurs as a result of interactions between organizations engaged in cross-border trading and widespread proliferation of management education programs that reflect Western assumptions, values, and practices. The growing influence of MNCs, IJVs, and relentless business competition will inevitably cause local and national firms to change management practices. The modern Indian organization is a case in point—it is a blend of nurturing and paternalistic leadership styles with Western management principles. The Arab leadership process is similarly a merging of Islamic religious beliefs, tribal traditions, legacies of colonial bureaucracies, and contact with Western nations. The Mexican entrepreneur, in a search for new management techniques to remain competitive, embraces U.S. management practices and principles such as total quality management but does so within a Mexican cultural tradition. In actuality, it is difficult to assess the extent of international convergence that may be taking place with regard to leadership practices because of the lack of historical baseline data (Martinez 2000). There is no evidence of a single model of management practices or of cultural values from which or toward which all nations are converging. It is most likely that there is some convergence toward U.S. practices, some toward Western European practices, and some toward Japanese practices. While some convergence is likely taking place with respect to management practices, there is also a great deal of stability with respect to the more fundamental aspects of both cultural practices and psychological commonalties within cultural entities.

Fourth, while empirical evidence is scarce, I suspect that cultures differ with respect to implicit versus explicit leadership requirements, the range and relative importance of leadership behaviors, and the variety of leadership influences such as commitment and satisfaction. We are at an initial stage in beginning to understand the entire range of worldwide leadership behaviors and styles, and it is thus likely that the field of cross-cultural leadership research will expand the domain of leadership behaviors and styles. For instance, leadership attributes and functions related to morality and the creation of harmonious interpersonal group relationships have emerged from indigenous studies in Asian countries. Thus, in a real sense, the emic discovery of morality as a critical leader attribute in Asian societies will expand the etic set of all leader behaviors and attributes. Will managerial leaders influence subordinates' commitment, job satisfaction, and job performance exactly the same across cultures, or will leaders have differing influence depending on the culture?

Fifth, the past controversy in the leadership literature concerning the relative merits of quantitative and positivist hypothesis testing versus qualitative and interpretive perspectives has been exaggerated. It should simply be a nonissue. The legitimacy of a variety of different methods for generating cross-cultural knowledge is obvious (Brett et al. 1997). Consider how the quantitative approach of determining the impact of universally meaningful leadership behaviors (e.g., participation) has been merged with the qualitative approach in determining how this leadership behavior is actually enacted in various cultures. One often proposed suggestion for increasing the quality of cross-cultural leadership research is to develop multinational research teams that involve true partnerships and to develop multiple research approaches consistent with these diverse orientations. This is easy to say but obviously difficult to achieve. It has been my experience that, because of the dominance of Western education at the doctoral level, with most of the published leadership literature originating in Western outlets and dominated by Americans, the membership of multinational teams inevitably includes Western-trained scholars. They often are reluctant to become true partners, as appropriate in truly decentered approaches to cross-cultural research where culturally diverse perspectives are considered in the initial conceptualization and research design.

Finally, there probably is no end to the variety of leadership topics that could be the focus of a cross-cultural leadership project. In the first edition of this handbook, I noted that a quick perusal through current leadership literature yielded the following list of currently popular leadership topics that could be effectively studied using a cross-cultural lens: influence tactics, leadership and corporate strategy, individual differences and leadership, global and executive leadership, and leadership of international mergers and joint ventures, among many others. To end on a very positive note for this edition of the handbook, I found meaningful cross-cultural research in all of these areas. Hopefully, the next edition of this handbook will contain more definitive findings with respect to these topics. We truly have a unique opportunity to further the theoretical understanding of leadership while providing practical help to leaders who are expected to function effectively in increasingly multinational contexts.

NOTE

1. In the interest of full disclosure, I have been intimately involved in the GLOBE project, first as a co-country investigator for Mexico and then in the coordinating role as a co-principal investigator for additional phases of GLOBE.

REFERENCES

Abdalla, I. A., and M. A. Al-Homoud. 2001. Exploring the implicit leadership theory in the Arabian Gulf States. *Applied Psychology: An International Review* 50 (4): 506–31.

Adler, N. J. 1984. Understanding the ways of understanding: Cross-cultural management methodology reviewed. In R. Farmer, ed., *Advances in international comparative management* 1:31–67.

————. 1999. Global leadership: Women leaders. In W. Mobley, M. J. Gessner, and V. Arnold, eds., *Advances in global leadership,* 1:49–73. Stamford, CT: JAI Press.

————. 2002. *International dimensions of organizational behavior.* 4th ed. Cincinnati, OH: South-Western College Publishing.

Adler, N. J., N. Campbell, and A. Laurent. 1989. In search of appropriate methodology: From outside the People's Republic of China looking in. *Journal of International Business Studies* 20 (1): 61–74.

Ali, A. J. 1990. Management theory in a transitional society: The Arab's experience. *International Studies of Management and Organization* 20 (7): 7–35.

Al-Kubaisy, A. 1985. A model in the administrative development of Arab Gulf countries. *Arab Gulf* 17 (2): 29–48.

Anderson, L. R. 1983. Management of the mixed-cultural work group. *Organizational Behavior and Human Performance* 31:303–30.

Aram, J. D., and K. Walochik. 1996. Improvisation and the Spanish manager. *International Studies of Management and Organization* 26 (4): 73–89.

Arvey, R. D., R. S. Bhagat, and E. Salas. 1991. Cross-cultural and cross-national issues in personnel and human resource management: Where do we go from here? In G. R. Ferris and K. M. Rowland, eds., *Research and personnel and human resources management,* 9:367–407. Greenwich, CT: JAI Press.

Ayman, R., and M. M. Chemers. 1983. Relationship of supervisory behavior ratings to work group effectiveness and subordinate satisfaction among Iranian managers. *Journal of Applied Psychology* 68 (2): 338–41.

————. 1991. The effect of leadership match on subordinate satisfaction in Mexican organizations: Some moderating influences of self-monitoring. *Applied Psychology: An International Review* 40 (3): 299–314.

Bass, B. M. 1985. *Leadership and performance beyond expectations.* New York: Free Press.

————. 1990. *Bass and Stogdill's handbook of leadership: Theory, research, and managerial applications.* 3d ed. New York: Free Press.

————. 1991. Is there universality in the Full Range model of leadership? Paper presented at the annual meeting of the National Academy of Management, Miami.

————. 1997. Does the transactional-transformational leadership paradigm transcend organizational and national boundaries? *American Psychologist* 52 (2): 130–39.

Bass, B. M., and B. J. Avolio. 1989. Potential biases in leadership measures: How prototypes, leniency, and general satisfaction relate to ratings and rankings of transformational and transactional leadership constructs. *Educational and Psychological Measurement* 49:509–27.

————. 1990. *Transformational leadership development: Manual for the Multifactor Leadership Questionnaire.* Palo Alto, CA: Consulting Psychologist Press.

————. 1993. Transformational leadership: A response to critiques. In M. M. Chemers and R. Ayman, eds., *Leadership theory and research,* 49–80. San Diego: Academic Press.

Bass, B. M., P. C. Burger, R. Doktor, and G. V. Barrett. 1979. *Assessment of managers: An international comparison.* New York: Free Press.

Bass, B. M., D. A. Waldman, B. J. Avolio, and M. Bebb. 1987. Transformational leadership and the falling dominoes effect. *Group and Organizational Studies* 12:73–87.

Bass, B. M., and J. Yokochi. 1991. Charisma among senior executives and the special case of Japanese CEO's. *Consulting Psychology Bulletin* (winter/spring):31–38.

Bennett, M. 1977. Testing management theories cross-culturally. *Journal of Applied Psychology* 62 (5): 578–81.

Bennis, W. G., and B. Nanus. 1985. *Leaders: The strategies of taking charge.* New York: Harper and Row.

Berry, J. W. 1980. Social and cultural change. In H. C. Triandis and R. W. Brislin, eds., *Handbook of cross-cultural psychology.* Boston: Allyn and Bacon.

Bhagat, R. S., B. L. Kedia, S. E. Crawford, and M. Kaplan. 1990. Cross-cultural and cross-national research in organizational psychology: Emergent trends and directions for research in the 1990's. In C. L. Cooper and I. Robertson, eds., *International review of industrial and organizational psychology.* New York: John Wiley.

Blunt, P., and M. J. Jones. 1992. *Managing organizations in Africa.* Berlin: Walter de Gruyter.

Boal, K. B., and R. Hooijberg. 2001. Strategic leadership research: Moving on. *Leadership Quarterly* 11 (4): 515–49.

Bohnisch, W., J. W. Ragan, G. Reber, and A. Jago. 1988. Predicting Austrian leader behavior from a measure of behavioral intent: A cross-cultural replication. In *Management under differing labour market and employment systems,* 313–22. Berlin: Walter de Gruyter.

Bolman, L., and T. Deal. 1995. *Leading with soul.* San Francisco: Jossey-Bass.

Bond, L. 1993. Comments on O'Neill and McPeek's paper. In P. W. Holland and H. Wainer, eds., *Differential item functioning,* 277–79. Hillsdale, NJ: Lawrence Erlbaum.

Bond, M., and K. K. Hwang. 1986. The social psychology of the Chinese people. In M. H. Bond, ed., *The psychology of the Chinese people.* Hong Kong: Oxford University Press.

Bond, M. H., and P. B. Smith. 1996. Cross-cultural social and organizational psychology. *Annual Review of Psychology* 47:205–36.

Bottger, P. C., I. H. Hallein, and P. W. Yetton. 1985. A cross-national study of leadership: Participation as a function of problem structure and leader power. *Journal of Management Studies* 22:358–68.

Bowers, D. C., and S. E. Seashore. 1966. Predicting organizational effectiveness with a four factor theory of leadership. *Administrative Science Quarterly* 11:238–63.

Boyacigiller, N., and N. Adler. 1991. The parochial dinosaur: Organizational science in a global context. *Academy of Management Review* 16:262–90.

Boyacigiller, N. A., M. J. Kleinberg, M. E. Phillips, and S. A. Sackmann. 1996. Conceptualizing culture. In B. J. Punnett and O. Shenkar, eds., *Handbook for international management research,* 157–208. Cambridge, MA: Blackwell.

Brett, J. M., et al. 1997. New approaches to the study of culture in industrial/organizational psychology. In P. C. Earley and M. Erez, eds., *New perspectives on international industrial/organizational psychology,* 75–129. San Francisco, CA: New Lexington Press.

Brodbeck, F. C., et al. 2000. Cultural variation of leadership prototypes across twenty-two European countries. *Journal of Occupational and Organizational Psychology* 73:1–29.

Brown, E. D., and L. Sechrest. 1980. Experiments in cross-cultural research. In H. C.

Triandis and J. W. Berry, eds., *Handbook of cross-cultural psychology,* vol. 2. Boston: Allyn and Bacon.

Burns, J. M. 1978. *Leadership.* New York: Harper and Row.

Campbell, J. P. 1982. Editorial: Some remarks from the outgoing editor. *Journal of Applied Psychology* 67:691–700.

Chemers, M. M. 1983. Leadership theory and research: A systems-process integration. In P. B. Paulus, ed., *Basic group processes.* New York: Springer-Verlag.

———. 1994. A theoretical framework for examining the effects of cultural differences on leadership. Paper presented at the Twenty-third International Congress of Applied Psychology, Madrid, Spain.

———. 1997. *An integrative theory of leadership.* London: Lawrence Erlbaum.

Chemers, M. M., and R. Ayman. 1993. Directions for leadership research. In M. M. Chemers and R. Ayman, eds., *Leadership theory and research,* 321–32. San Diego: Academic Press.

Chen, X. P., and J. L. Fahr. 2001. Transformational and transactional leader behaviors in Chinese organizations: Differential effects in the People's Republic of China and Taiwan. In W. H. Mobley and M. W. McCall, eds., *Advances in global leadership,* vol. 2. Oxford: Elsevier Science.

Child, J. 1981. Culture, contingency, and capitalism in the cross-national study of organizations. In L. L. Cummings and B. M. Staw, eds., *Research in organizational behavior,* 3:303–56. Greenwich, CT: JAI Press.

Chhokar, J. S. In progress. Leadership and culture in India: The GLOBE Research Project. In J. Chhokar, F. Brodbeck, and R. J. House, eds., *Managerial cultures of the world: GLOBE in-depth studies of the cultures of 25 countries,* vol. 2. Thousand Oaks, CA: Sage.

Chong, L. M. A., and D. C. Thomas. 1997. Leadership perceptions in cross-cultural context: Pakeha and Pacific islanders in New Zealand. *Leadership Quarterly* 8 (3): 275–93.

Conger, J. A., and R. Kanungo. 1987. Toward a behavioral theory of charismatic leadership in organizational settings. *Academy of Management Review* 12:637–47.

Croker, J., S. T. Fiske, and S. E. Taylor. 1984. Schematic bases of belief change. In J. R. Eisen, ed., *Attitudinal judgment,* 197–226. New York: Springer-Verlag.

Cullen, J. B. 2002. *Multinational management: A strategic approach.* 2d ed. Cincinnati, OH: South-Western College Publishing.

Dansereau, F., G. B. Graen, and W. Haga. 1975. A vertical dyad linkage approach to leadership in formal organizations. *Organizational Behavior and Human Performance* 13:46–78.

Dastmalchian, A., M. Javidan, and K. Alam. 2001. Effective leadership and culture in Iran: An empirical study. *Applied Psychology: An International Review* 50 (4): 532–51.

Den Hartog, et al. 1999. Culture specific and cross culturally generalizable implicit leadership theories: Are attributes of charismatic/transformational leadership universally endorsed? *Leadership Quarterly* 10:219–56.

Den Hartog, D. N., J. J. Van Muijen, and P. L. Koopman. 1994. Transactional versus transformational leadership: An analysis of the MLQ in the Netherlands. Paper presented at the Twenty-third International Congress of Applied Psychology, Madrid, Spain.

Den Hartog, D., and R. M. Verburg. 1997. Charisma and rhetoric: Communicative techniques of international business leaders. *Leadership Quarterly* 8 (4): 355–91.

Deutsch, M. 1973. *The resolution of conflict: Constructive and destructive processes.* New Haven, CT: Yale University Press.

Dickson, M., D. Den Hartog, J. K. Mitchelson. In press. Research on leadership in a cross-cultural context. Making progress, and raising new questions. *Leadership Quarterly.*

Dorfman, P. W. 1996. International and cross-cultural leadership research. In B. J. Punnett and O. Shenkar, eds., *Handbook for international management research,* 267–349. Oxford, U.K.: Blackwell.

Dorfman, P., P. J. Hanges, and F. C. Brodbeck. 2004. Leadership and cultural variation: The identification of culturally endorsed leadership profiles. In R. J. House et al., eds., *Leadership, culture, and organizations: The GLOBE study of 62 societies.* Thousand Oaks, CA: Sage.

Dorfman, P. W., P. J. Hanges, and M. W. Dickson. 1998. Challenges in cross-cultural research: The GLOBE project—A mini-United Nations or the champion Chicago Bulls? Paper presented at the International Conference of Applied Psychology, San Francisco.

Dorfman, P. W., and J. P. Howell. 1988. Dimensions of national culture and effective leadership patterns. *Advances in international comparative management* 3:127–50.

———. 1997. Managerial leadership in the United States and Mexico: Distant neighbors or close cousins? In C. S. Granrose and S. Oskamp, eds., *Cross cultural work groups.* Thousand Oaks, CA: Sage.

Dorfman, P. W., J. P. Howell, S. Hibino, J. K. Lee, U. Tate, and A. Bautista. 1997. Leadership in Western and Asian countries: Commonalities and differences in effective leadership processes across cultures. *Leadership Quarterly* 8 (3): 233–74.

Dorfman, P. W., and S. Ronen. 1991. The universality of leadership theories: Challenges and paradoxes. Paper presented at the annual meeting of the National Academy of Management, Miami, FL.

Dowling, P. J., D. E. Welch, and R. S. Schuler. 1999. *International human resource management: Managing people in a multinational context.* 3d ed. Cincinnati, OH: South-Western College Publishing.

Earley, P. C. 1989. Social loafing and collectivism: A comparison of the United States and the People's Republic of China. *Administrative Science Quarterly* 34:565–81.

———. 1993. East meets West meets Mideast: Further explorations of collectivistic and individualistic work groups. *Academy of Management Journal* 36 (2): 319–48.

Earley, P. C., E. Mosakowski, and C. Gibson. 1996. A framework for understanding experimental research in an international and intercultural context. In B. J. Punnett and O. Shenkar, eds., *Handbook for international management research.* Cambridge, MA: Blackwell.

Earley, P. C., and H. Singh. 1995. International and intercultural management research: What next? *Academy of Management Journal* 38:1–14.

Echavarria, N. U., and D. D. Davis. 1994. A test of Bass's Model of Transformational and Transactional Leadership in the Dominican Republic. Paper presented at the Twenty-third International Congress of Applied Psychology, Madrid, Spain.

Erez, M. 1994. Toward a model of cross-cultural industrial and organizational psychology. In H. C. Triandis, M. D. Dunnette, and L. M. Hough, eds., *Handbook of industrial and organizational psychology*, 2d ed., vol. 4. Palo Alto, CA: Consulting Psychologists Press.

———. 1997. A culture-based model of work motivation. In P. C. Earley and M. Erez, eds., *New perspectives on international industrial/organizational psychology*, 193–242. San Francisco: New Lexington Press.

Erez, M., and P. C. Earley. 1993. *Culture, self-identity, and work*. New York: Oxford University Press.

Evans, M. G. 1970. The effects of supervisory behavior on the path-goal relationship. *Organizational Behavior and Human Performance* 5:277–98.

Fahr, J. L., P. M. Podsakoff, and B. S. Cheng. 1987. Culture-free leadership effectiveness versus moderators of leadership behavior: An extension and test of Kerr and Jermier's substitute for leadership model in Taiwan. *Journal of International Business Studies* 18:43–60.

Farris, G. F., and D. A. Butterfield. 1972. Control theory in Brazilian organizations. *Administrative Science Quarterly* 17 (4): 574–85.

Fiedler, F. E. 1966. The effect of leadership and cultural heterogeneity on group performance: A test of the contingency model. *Journal of Experimental Social Psychology* 2:237–64.

———. 1967. *A theory of leadership effectiveness*. New York: McGraw-Hill.

———. 1986. The contribution of cognitive resources to leadership performance. *Journal of Applied Social Psychology* 16:532–48.

———. 1993. The leadership situation and the black box in contingency theories. In M. M. Chemers and R. Ayman, eds., *Leadership theory and research*. San Diego: Academic Press.

Fiedler, F. E., and M. M. Chemers. 1984. *Improving leadership effectiveness: The leader match concept*. New York: John Wiley.

Fiedler, F. E., and J. E. Garcia. 1987. *New approaches to leadership: Cognitive resources and organizational performance*. New York: John Wiley.

Fiedler, F. E., W. Meuwese, and S. Oonk. 1961. An exploratory study of group creativity in laboratory tasks. *Acta Psychologica* 18:100–119.

Field, R. H. 1982. A test of Vroom-Yetton normative model of leadership. *Journal of Applied Psychology* 67:523–32.

Fleishman, E. A. 1953. The description of supervisory behavior. *Personnel Psychology* 37:1–6.

Fleishman, E. A., E. F. Harris, and H. E. Burtt. 1955. *Leadership and supervision in industry*. Columbus, OH: Bureau of Educational Research, Ohio State University.

Fleishman, E. A., and J. Simmons. 1970. Relationship between leadership patterns and effectiveness ratings among Israeli foremen. *Personnel Psychology* 23:169–72.

Fu, P. P., and G. A. Yukl. 2000. Perceived effectiveness of influence tactics in the United States and China. *Leadership Quarterly* 11:251–66.

Ganster, D. C., H. W. Hennessey, and F. Luthans. 1983. Social desirability response effects: Three alternative methods. *Academy of Management Journal* 26:321–31.

Gerstner, C. R., and D. V. Day. 1994. Cross-cultural comparison of leadership prototypes. *Leadership Quarterly* 5 (2): 121–34.

Gibson, C. 1995. An investigation of gender differences in leadership across four countries. *Journal of International Business Studies* 26 (2): 255–79.

Glick, W., G. Jenkins, and N. Gupta. 1986. Method versus substance: How strong are underlying relationships between job characteristics and attitudinal outcomes? *Academy of Management Journal* 29:441–64.

Graen, G. B., et al. 1997. Cross-cultural research alliances in organizational research: Cross-cultural partnership-making in action. In P. C. Earley and M. Erez, eds., *New perspectives on international industrial/organizational psychology,* 160–90. San Francisco: New Lexington Press.

Graen, G. B., and M. Uhl-Bien. 1991. The transformation of professionals into self-managing and partially self-designing contributions: Toward a theory of leadership-making. *Journal of Management Systems* 3 (3): 33–48.

———. 1995. Relationship-based approach to leadership: Development of leader-member exchange (LMX) theory of leadership over 25 years: Applying a multi-level multi-domain perspective. *Leadership Quarterly* 6: 219–47.

Graen, G. B., and M. Wakabayashi. 1994. Cross-cultural leadership making: Bridging American and Japanese diversity for team advantage. In H. C. Triandis, M. D. Dunnette, and L. M. Hough, *Handbook of industrial and organizational psychology,* 2d ed., 4:415–46. Palo Alto, CA: Consulting Psychologists Press.

Graen, G. B., et al. 1990. International generalizability of American hypotheses about Japanese management progress: A strong inference investigation. *Leadership Quarterly* 1:1–23.

Graumann, C. F., and S. Moscovici. 1986. *Changing conceptions of leadership.* New York: Springer-Verlag.

Hagan, C. M. 1995. Comparative management: Africa, the Middle East, and India. Working Paper. Florida Atlantic University, Boca Raton.

Haire, M., E. E. Ghiselli, and L. Porter. 1966. *Managerial thinking: An international study.* New York: Wiley.

Hayashi, S. 1988. *Culture and management in Japan.* Tokyo: University of Tokyo Press.

Hazucha, J. F., et al. 1999. *In search of the Euro-manager: Management competencies in France, Germany, Italy, and the United States,* vol. 1. Stamford, CT: JAI Press.

Heller, F. A. 1969. *Managerial decision making.* London: Human Resources Center, Tavistock Institute of Human Relations.

Heller, F. A., P. Drenth, P. L. Koopman, and V. Rus. 1988. *Decisions in organizations.* Great Britain: Sage.

Heller, F. A., and B. Wilpert. 1981. *Competence and power in managerial decision-making: A study of senior-levels of organization in eight countries.* London: Wiley.

Hofstede, G. 1980. *Culture's consequences: International differences in work-related values.* London: Sage.

———. 1991. *Cultures and organizations: The software of the mind.* New York: McGraw-Hill.

————. 1993. Cultural constraints in management theories. *Academy of Management Executive* 7 (1): 81–94.

————. 2001. *Culture's consequences: Comparing values, behaviors, institutions, and organizations across nations.* Thousand Oaks, CA: Sage.

House, R. J. 1971. A path-goal theory of leader effectiveness. *Administrative Science Quarterly* 16:321–38.

————. 1977. A 1976 theory of charismatic leaders. In J. G. Hunt and L. L. Larson, eds., *Leadership: The cutting edge.* Carbondale: Southern Illinois University Press.

————. 1991. The universality of charismatic leadership. Paper presented at the annual meeting of the National Academy of Management, Miami.

————. 1996. Path-goal theory of leadership: Lessons, legacy, and a reformulated theory. *Leadership Quarterly* 7 (3): 323–52.

House, R. J., P. J. Hanges, M. Agar, and S. A. Ruiz-Quintanilla. 1994. Conference on global leadership and organizational behavior (GLOBE), Calgary, Canada.

House, R. J., P. J. Hanges, M. Javidan, P. W. Dorfman, V. Gupta, and GLOBE Associates. 2004. *Leadership, culture, and organizations: The GLOBE study of 62 societies.* Thousand Oaks, CA: Sage.

House, R. J., P. J. Hanges, S. A. Ruiz-Quintanilla, P. W. Dorfman, M. Javidan, M. Dickson, V. Gupta, and 170 co-authors. 1999. Cultural influences on leadership and organizations: Project GLOBE. In W. F. Mobley, M. J. Gessner, and V. Arnold, eds., *Advances in global leadership,* 1:171–233. Stamford, CT: JAI Press.

House, R. J., and T. R. Mitchell. 1974. Path-goal theory of leadership. *Contemporary Business* 3:81–98.

House, R. J., and B. Shamir. 1993. Toward the integration of transformational, charismatic, and visionary theories. In M. M. Chemers and R. Ayman, eds., *Leadership theory and research: Perspectives and directions,* 81–107. San Diego: Academic Press.

House, R. J., N. S. Wright, and R. N. Aditya. 1997. Cross-cultural research on organizational leadership: A critical analysis and a proposed theory. In P. C. Earley and M. Erez, eds., *New perspectives in international industrial/organizational psychology,* 535–625. San Francisco: New Lexington Press.

Howard, A., and D. W. Bray. 1988. *Managerial lives in transition: Advancing age and changing times.* New York: Guilford Press.

Howard, C. G. 1992. Profile of the twenty-first-century expatriate manager. *HR Magazine* 37 (6): 43–102.

Howell, J. P. 1997. Substitutes for leadership: Their meaning and measurement—an historical assessment. *Leadership Quarterly* 8 (2): 113–16.

Howell, J. P., D. Bowen, P. W. Dorfman, S. Kerr, and P. M. Podsakoff. 1990. Substitutes for leadership: Effective alternatives to ineffective leadership. *Organizational Dynamics* (summer): 21–38.

Howell, J. P., and D. L. Costley. 2001. *Understanding behaviors for effective leadership.* Upper Saddle River, NJ: Prentice-Hall.

Howell, J. P., and P. W. Dorfman. 1988. *A comparative study of leadership and its substitutes in a mixed cultural work setting.* Paper presented at the Western Academy of Management, Big Sky, MT.

Howell, J. P., P. W. Dorfman, and S. Kerr. 1986. Moderator variables in leadership research. *Academy of Management Review* 11:88–102.

Hui, C. H. 1990. Work attitudes, leadership styles, and managerial behaviors in different cultures. In R. W. Brislin, ed., *Applied cross-cultural psychology. Cross-cultural Research and Methodology series,* vol. 14. Newbury Park, CA: Sage.

Hui, C., and G. Graen. 1997. Guanxi and professional leadership in contemporary Sino-American joint ventures in mainland China. *Leadership Quarterly* 8 (4): 451–65.

Hui, C. H., and G. C. Tan. 1999. The moral component of effective leadership: The Chinese case. In W. Mobley, M. J. Gessner, and V. Arnold, eds., *Advances in global leadership,* 1:249–66. Stamford, CT: JAI Press.

Hui, C. H., and H. C. Triandis. 1985. Measurement in cross-cultural psychology: A review and comparison of strategies. *Journal of Cross-Cultural Psychology* 16 (2): 131–52.

———. 1989. Effects of culture and response format on extreme response styles. *Journal of Cross-Cultural Psychology* 20:296–309.

Hulin, C. L. 1987. A psychometric theory of evaluation of item and scale translations: Fidelity across languages. *Journal of Cross-Cultural Psychology* 18 (2): 115–42.

Hunt, J. G. 1991. *Leadership: A new synthesis.* Newbury Park, CA: Sage.

Jackofsky, E. F., J. W. Slocum Jr., and S. J. McQuaid. 1988. Cultural values and the CEO: Alluring companions? *The Academy of Management Executive* 2 (1): 39–49.

Jago, A., and V. H. Vroom. 1978. Predicting leader behavior from a measure of behavioral intent. *Academy of Management Journal* 21:715–21.

Jago, A. G., G. Reber, W. Bohnisch, J. Maczynski, J. Zavrel, and J. Dudorkin. 1993. Culture's consequences? A seven nation study of participation. Proceedings of the twenty-fourth annual meeting of the Decision Sciences Institute, Washington, DC.

Jennings, E. 1960. *The anatomy of leadership.* New York: Harper and Row.

Kabasakal, H., and A. Dastmalchian. 2001. Introduction to the special issue on leadership and culture in the Middle East. *Applied Psychology: An International Review* 50 (4): 479–88.

Kakar, S. 1971. Authority patterns and subordinate behavior in Indian organizations. *Administrative Science Quarterly* 16:298–307.

Kashima, Y., and V. J. Callan. 1994. The Japanese work group. In H. C. Triandis, M. D. Dunnette, and L. M. Hough, eds., *Handbook of industrial and organizational psychology,* 2d ed., vol. 4. Palo Alto, CA: Consulting Psychologists Press.

Kelley, L., A. Whatley, and R. Worthley. 1987. Assessing the effects of culture on managerial attitudes: A three-culture test. *Journal of International Business Studies* 18 (summer):17–31.

Kennedy, J. C., P. P. Fu, and G. A. Yukl. 2003. Influence tactics across twelve cultures. In W. Mobley and P. Dorfman, eds., *Advances in global leadership,* vol. 3. Oxford: JAI Press.

Kennis, I. 1977. A cross-cultural study of personality and leadership. *Group and Organizational Studies* 2 (1): 49–60.

Kerr, S., and J. M. Jermier. 1978. Substitutes for leadership: Their meaning and measurement. *Organizational Behavior and Human Decision Processes* 22:375–403.

Khadra, B. 1990. The prophetic-caliphal model of leadership: An empirical study. *International Studies of Management and Organization* 20 (3): 37–51.

Khandwalla, P. N. 1983. PI management. *Vikalpa* 8:220–38.

Kirkpatrick, S. A., and E. A. Locke. 1991. Leadership: Do traits matter? *The Academy of Management Executive* 5 (2): 48–60.

Koh, W. L. 1990. An empirical validation of the theory of transformational leadership in secondary schools in Singapore. Ph.D. diss., University of Oregon.

Korman, A. K. 1966. Consideration, initiating structure, and organizational criteria. *Personnel Psychology* 18:349–60.

Kouzes, J. M., and B. Z. Posner. 1987. *The leadership challenge: How to get extraordinary things done in organizations.* San Francisco: Jossey-Bass.

Latham, G. P., and N. K. Napier. 1989. Chinese human resource management practices in Hong Kong and Singapore: An exploratory study. In G. Ferris and K. Rowland, eds., *Research in personnel and human resource management.* Greenwich, CT: JAI Press.

Laurent, A. 1983. The cultural diversity of Western conceptions of management. *International Studies of Management and Organization* 13 (2): 75–96.

Leung, K., and M. H. Bond. 1989. On the empirical identification of dimensions for cross-cultural comparisons. *Journal of Cross-Cultural Psychology* 20:133–51.

Likert, R. 1961. *New patterns of management.* New York: McGraw-Hill.

———. 1967. *The human organization.* New York: McGraw-Hill.

Ling, W. Q. 1989. Pattern of leadership behavior assessment in China. *Psychologia* 32:129–34.

Ling, W. Q., and L. Fang. 2003. The Chinese leadership theory. In W. H. Mobley, M. J. Gessner, and V. Arnold, eds., *Advances in global leadership,* vol. 3. Stamford, CT: JAI Press.

Lord, R. G., R. J. Foti, and J. S. Phillips. 1982. A theory of leadership categorization. In J. G. Hunt, U. Sekaran, and C. A. Schriesheim, eds., *Leadership: Beyond establishment views,* 104–21. Carbondale: Southern Illinois University Press.

Lord, R. G., and K. J. Maher. 1991. *Leadership and information processing: Linking perceptions and performance,* vol. 1. Cambridge, MA: Unwin Hyman.

Luthans, F., D. H. B. Welsh, and S. A. Rosenkrantz. 1993. What do Russian managers really do? An observational study with comparisons to U.S. managers. *Journal of International Business Studies* 24 (4): 741–62.

Mannheim, B. F., Y. Rim, and G. Grinberg. 1967. Instrumental status of supervisors as related to workers' perceptions and expectations. *Human Relations* 20:387–97.

Martinez, S. M. 2000. An ethnographic study of the Mexican entrepreneur: A configuration of themes and roles impacting managerial leadership in an emerging economy. Ph.D. diss., Department of Management, New Mexico State University.

Martinez, S. M., and P. W. Dorfman. 1998. The Mexican entrepreneur: An ethnographic study of the Mexican Empresario. *International Studies of Management and Organization* 28 (2): 97–123.

Mauer, K. F. 1974. The utility of the leadership opinion questionnaire in the South Africa mining industry. *Journal of Behavioral Science* 74:67–72.

McFarland, L. J., S. Senen, and J. R. Childress. 1993. *Twenty-first century leadership.* New York: Leadership Press.

Meade, R. D. 1970. Leadership studies of Chinese and Chinese-Americans. *Journal of Cross-Cultural Psychology* 1 (4): 325–32.

Meindl, J. R., S. B. Ehrlich, and J. M. Dukerich. 1985. The romance of leadership. *Administrative Science Quarterly* 30:78–102.

Misumi, J. 1985. *The behavioral science of leadership: An interdisciplinary Japanese research program.* Ann Arbor: University of Michigan Press.

Misumi, J., and M. F. Peterson. 1985. The performance-maintenance (PM) theory of leadership: Review of a Japanese research program. *Administrative Science Quarterly* 30:196–223.

Misumi, J., and S. Shirakashi. 1966. An experimental study of the effects of supervisory behavior on productivity and morale in a hierarchical organization. *Human Relations* 19 (3): 297–307.

Mitroff, I. I. 1987. *Business not as usual.* San Francisco: Jossey-Bass.

Mobley, W., and P. W. Dorfman, eds. 2003. *Advances in global leadership,* vol. 3. Oxford: JAI Press.

Mobley, W., M. J. Gessner, and V. Arnold, eds. 1999. *Advances in global leadership,* vol. 1. Stamford, CT: JAI Press.

Mobley, W. H., and M. W. McCall, eds. 2001. *Advances in global leadership,* vol. 2. Oxford: Elsevier Science.

Mohr, L. B. 1982. *Explaining organizational behavior.* San Francisco: Jossey-Bass.

Montgomery, J. D. 1987. Probing managerial behaviour: Image and reality in Southern Africa. *World Development* 15 (7): 911–29.

Murdoch, G. 1967. *Ethnographic atlas.* Pittsburgh: University of Pittsburgh Press.

O'Connell, M. S., R. G. Lord, and M. K. O'Connell. 1990. Differences in Japanese and American leadership prototypes: Implications for cross-cultural training. Paper presented at the Academy of Management, San Francisco, CA.

Ohame, K. 1990. *The borderless world.* New York: Harper Business.

Pasa, S. F., H. Kabasakal, and M. Bodur. 2001. Society, organisations, and leadership in Turkey. *Applied Psychology: An International Review* 50 (4): 559–89.

Peng, T. K., M. F. Peterson, and Y. Shyi. 1991. Quantitative methods in cross-national management research: Trends and equivalence issues. *Journal of Organizational Behavior* 12:87–107.

Peterson, M. F., M. Y. Brannen, and P. B. Smith. 1994. Japanese and U.S. leadership: Issues in current research. In S. B. Prassad, ed., *Advances in International Comparative Management* 9:57–82.

Peterson, M. F., and J. G. Hunt. 1997a. International perspectives on international leadership. *Leadership Quarterly* 8 (3): 203–31.

———. 1997b. Overview: International and cross-cultural leadership research (part II). *Leadership Quarterly* 8 (4): 339–42.

Peterson, M. F., P. B. Smith, and T. K. Peng. 1993. Japanese and American supervisors of a U.S. workforce: An international analysis of behavior meanings and leadership style correlates. Unpublished manuscript.

Peterson, M. F., P. B. Smith, and M. H. Tayeb. 1993. Development and use of English versions of Japanese PM leadership measures in electronics plants. *Journal of Organizational Behavior* 14:251–67.

Pfeffer, J. 1977. The ambiguity of leadership. *Academy of Management Review* 2:104–12.

Podsakoff, P. M., P. W. Dorfman, J. P. Howell, and W. D. Todor. 1986. Leader reward and punishment behaviors: A preliminary test of a culture-free style of leadership effectiveness. In R. Famer, ed., *Advances in International Comparative Management* 2:95–138.

Podsakoff, P. M., W. D. Todor, and R. Skov. 1982. Effects of leader contingent and non-contingent reward and punishment behavior in subordinate performance and satisfaction. *Academy of Management Journal* 25:810–21.

Poortinga, Y. H., and R. S. Malpass. 1986. Making inferences from cross-cultural data. In W. J. Lonner and J. W. Berry, eds., *Field methods in cross-cultural research*, 12–46. Beverly Hills, CA: Sage.

Punnett, B. J. 1991. Language, cultural values, and preferred leadership styles: A comparison of Anglophones and Francophones in Ottawa. *Canadian Journal of Behavioral Science* 23 (2): 241–44.

Ralston, D. A., D. J. Gustafson, F. M. Cheung, and R. H. Terpstra. 1993. Differences in managerial values: A study of U.S., Hong Kong, and PRC managers. *Journal of International Business Studies* 24 (2): 249–75.

Randall, D. M., P. Y. Huo, and P. Pawelk. 1993. Social desirability bias in cross-cultural ethics research. *International Journal of Organizational Analysis* 1:185–202.

Rao, A., K. Hashimoto, and A. Rao. 1997. Universal and culturally specific aspects of managerial influence: A study of Japanese managers. *Leadership Quarterly* 8 (3): 295–312.

Reber, G., A. Jago, and W. Bohnisch. 1993. Interkulturelle unterschlede im fuhrungsuer-halten. *Globalisierung der Wirtschaft, Einwirkungen auf die Betriebswirtschaftslehre*, 217–40. Stuttgart: Verlag Paul Haupt.

Redding, S. G. 1994. Comparative management theory: Jungle, zoo, or fossil bed? *Organization Studies* 15 (3): 323–59.

Roberts, K. H. 1970. On looking at an elephant: An evaluation of cross-cultural research related to organizations. *Psychological Bulletin* 74:327–50.

Roberts, K. H., and N. Boyacigiller. 1984. Cross-national organizational research: The grasp of the blind man. In B. M. Staw and E. E. Cummings, eds., *Research in organizational behavior*, 6:423–75. Greenwich, CT: JAI Press.

Ronen, S. 1986. *Comparative and multinational management.* New York: John Wiley and Sons.

Ronen, S., and O. Shenkar. 1985. Clustering countries on attitudinal dimensions: A review and synthesis. *Academy of Management Review* 10:435–54.

Rosch, E. 1975. Universals and cultural specifics in human categorization. In R. Brislin, S. Bochner, and W. Lonner, eds., *Cross-cultural perspectives in learning*, 177–206. New York: Sage.

Ross, L. 1977. The intuitive psychologist and his shortcomings: Distortions in the attributional process. *Advances in Experimental Social Psychology* 32:174–221.

Scandura, T. A., M. A. Von Glinow, and K. B. Lowe. 1999. When East meets West: Leadership "best practices" in the United States and the Middle East. In W. Mobley, M. J. Gessner, and V. Arnold, eds., *Advances in global leadership*, 1:235–48. Stamford, CT: JAI Press.

Schwartz, S. H. 1992. Universals in the content and structure of values: Theoretical advances and empirical tests in twenty countries. In M. P. Zanna, ed., *Advances in experimental social psychology,* vol. 25. New York: Academic Press.

Shamir, B., R. J. House, and M. B. Arthur. 1993. The motivational effects of charismatic leadership: A self-concept theory. *Organization Science* 4:1–17.

Shamir, B., E. Zakay, E. Breinin, and M. Popper. 1998. Correlates of charismatic leader behavior in military units: Subordinates' attitudes, unit characteristics, and superiors' appraisals of leader performance. *Academy of Management Journal* 41 (4): 387–409.

Shapiro, A. C. 1991. *Foundations of multinational financial management.* Boston: Allyn and Bacon.

Shaw, J. B. 1990. A cognitive categorization model for the study of intercultural management. *Academy of Management Review* 15 (4): 626–45.

Shirakashi, S. 1968. An experimental study of leadership effectiveness in a small group: A test of the contingency model. *Japanese Journal of Educational and Social Psychology* 8 (2): 249–67.

Singh, N. K., and O. Paul. 1985. *The corporate soul: Dynamics of effective management.* New Delhi: Vikas.

Sinha, J. B. P. 1980. *The nurturant task leader.* New Delhi: Concept.

———. 1984. A model of effective leadership styles in India. *International Studies of Management and Organization* 14 (3): 86–98.

———. 1994. Cultural imbeddedness and the developmental role of industrial organizations in India. In H. C. Triandis, M. D. Dunnette, and L. M. Hough, eds., *Handbook of industrial and organizational psychology,* 2d ed., 4:727–64. Palo Alto, CA: Consulting Psychologists Press.

———. 1997. A cultural perspective on organizational behavior in India. In P. C. Earley and M. Erez, eds., *New perspectives on international industrial/organizational psychology,* 53–74. San Francisco: New Lexington Press.

Smith, P. B. 2003. Leaders' sources of guidance and the challenge of working across cultures. In W. Mobley and P. Dorfman, eds., *Advances in global leadership,* vol. 3. Oxford: JAI Press.

Smith, P. B., J. Misumi, M. H. Tayeb, M. F. Peterson, and M. H. Bond. 1989. On the generality of leadership style across cultures. *Journal of Occupational Psychology* 30:526–37.

Smith, P. B., and M. F. Peterson. 1988. *Leadership, organizations, and culture: An event management model.* London: Sage.

Smith, P. B., M. F. Peterson, J. Misumi, and M. H. Bond. 1992. A cross-cultural test of Japanese PM leadership theory. *Applied Psychology: An International Review* 42 (1): 5–19.

Smith, P. B., M. F. Peterson, and Z. M. Wang. 1996. The manager as mediator of alternative meanings: A pilot study from China, the U.S.A. and U.K. *Journal of International Business Studies* 27 (1): 115–38.

Smith, P. B., and M. K. Peterson. 1994. Leadership as event-management: A cross-cultural survey based upon middle managers from twenty-five nations. Paper presented at the Cross-Cultural Studies of Event Management session at the International Congress of Applied Psychology, Madrid, Spain.

Smith, P. B., and M. H. Tayeb. 1988. Organizational structure and processes. In M. H. Bond, ed., *The cross-cultural challenge to social psychology.* Cross-cultural Research and Methodology series, 2:153–64. Newbury Park, CA: Sage.

Smith, P. B., Z. M. Wang, and K. Leung. 1997. Leadership, decision-making, and cultural context: Event management within Chinese joint ventures. *Leadership Quarterly* 8 (4): 413–31.

Smith, P. B., and G. T. Whitehead. 1984. Attributions for promotion and demotion in the U.S. and India. *Journal of Social Psychology* 124:27–34.

Spector, R. E. 1987. Method variance as an artifact in self-report affect and perceptions at work: Myth or significant problem? *Journal of Applied Psychology* 72:438–43.

Steers, R. M., Y. K. Shinn, and G. R. Ungson. 1989. *The Chaebol: Korea's new industrial might.* New York: Harper.

Stening, B. W., and J. E. Everett. 1984. Response styles in a cross-cultural managerial study. *Journal of Social Psychology* 122:151–56.

Sullivan, J., T. Suzuki, and Y. Kondo. 1986. Managerial perceptions of performance. *Journal of Cross-Cultural Psychology* 17 (4): 379–98.

Swidler, A. 1986. Culture in action: Symbols and strategies. *American Sociological Review* 51:273–86.

Tannenbaum, A. S. 1980. Organizational psychology. In H. C. Triandis and R. W. Brislin, eds., *Handbook of cross-cultural psychology,* 281–334. Boston: Allyn and Bacon.

Thiagarajan, K. M., and S. D. Deep. 1970. A study of supervisor-subordinate influence and satisfaction in four cultures. *Journal of Social Psychology* 82:173–80.

Thomas, D. C. 2002. *Essentials of international management: A cross-cultural perspective.* Thousand Oaks, CA: Sage.

Triandis, H. C. 1972. *The analysis of subjective culture.* New York: Wiley.

————. 1980. Introduction. In H. C. Triandis and W. W. Lambert, eds., *Handbook of cross-cultural psychology,* 1–14. Boston: Allyn and Bacon.

————. 1993. *The contingency model in cross-cultural perspective.* San Diego: Academic Press.

————. 1994. *Culture and social behavior.* New York: McGraw-Hill.

Triandis, H. C., and D. P. S. Bhawuk. 1997. Culture theory and the meaning of relatedness. In P. C. Earley and M. Erez, eds., *New perspectives on international industrial/organizational psychology,* 13–52. San Francisco: New Lexington Press.

Triandis, H. C., L. L. Kurowski, and M. J. Gelfand. 1994. Workplace diversity. In H. C. Triandis, M. D. Dunnette, and L. M. Hough, eds., *Handbook of industrial and organizational psychology,* 2d ed., vol. 4. Palo Alto, CA: Consulting Psychologists Press.

Trompenaars, F. 1993. *Riding the waves of culture: Understanding cultural diversity in business.* London: Breatley.

Tscheulin, D. 1973. Leader behaviors in German industry. *Journal of Applied Psychology* 57:28–31.

van de Vijver, F., and K. Leung. 1997. *Methods and data analysis for cross-cultural research.* Thousand Oaks, CA: Sage.

Virmani, B. R., and S. U. Guptan. 1991. *Indian management.* New Delhi: Vision.

Vroom, V. H., and A. Jago. 1988. *The new leadership: Managing participation in organizations.* Englewood Cliffs, NJ: Prentice-Hall.

Vroom, V. H., and P. W. Yetton. 1973. *Leadership and decision-making.* Pittsburgh: University of Pittsburgh Press.

Wagner, J. A., and S. M. Crampton. 1993. Percept-percept inflation in micro organizational research: An investigation of prevalence and effect. Paper presented at the annual meeting of the Academy of Management, Madison, WI.

Wakabayashi, M., and G. B. Graen. 1984. The Japanese career progress study: A seven-year follow-up. *Journal of Applied Psychology* 69:603–14.

Wang, Z. M. 1994. Culture, economic reform, and the role of industrial and organizational psychology in China. In H. C. Triandis, M. D. Dunnette, and L. M. Hough, eds., *Handbook of industrial and organizational psychology,* 2d ed., 4:689–725. Palo Alto, CA: Consulting Psychologists Press.

Welch, J. 2001. *Jack: Straight from the gut.* New York: Warner Brothers.

Welsh, D. H. B., F. Luthans, and S. M. Sommer. 1993. Managing Russian factory workers: The impact of U.S.-based behavioral and participative techniques. *Academy of Management Journal* 36 (1): 58–79.

Whitehill, A. M., and S. Takezawa. 1968. *The other worker.* Honolulu, HI: East-West Center Press.

Xu, L. C. 1987. A cross-cultural study on the leadership behavior of Chinese and Japanese executives. *Asia Pacific Journal of Management* 4 (3): 203–9.

Xu, L. C., L. Chen, and A. Y. Xue. 1985. The role of psychology in enterprise management [in Chinese]. *Acta Psychologica Sinica* 17 (4): 339–45.

Yokochi, N. 1989. Leadership styles of Japanese business executives and managers: Transformational and transactional. Ph.D. diss., United States International University, San Diego, CA.

Yoshoni, M. 1968. *Japan's managerial system.* Cambridge, MA: MIT Press.

Yukl, G. A. 1989. *Leadership in organizations.* 2d ed. Englewood Cliffs, NJ: Prentice-Hall.

———. 1994. *Leadership in organizations.* 3d ed. Englewood Cliffs, NJ: Prentice-Hall.

———. 2002. *Leadership in organizations.* 5th ed. Upper Saddle River, NJ: Prentice-Hall.

Yukl, G. A., and D. Van Fleet. 1992. Theory and research on leadership in organizations. In M. D. Dunnette and L. M. Hough, eds., *Handbook of industrial and organizational psychology,* 2d ed., 3:147–97. Palo Alto, CA: Consulting Psychologists Press.

INTERNATIONAL HUMAN
RESOURCE MANAGEMENT

Randall S. Schuler, Pawan S. Budhwar, and Gary W. Florkowski

International human resource management (IHRM) is about the world-wide management of human resources (Adler and Ghadar 1990; Tung 1984; Punnett and Ricks 1992; Brewster 1993, 1996; Brewster and Hegewisch 1994; Cascio and Bailey 1995; Harzing and Van Ruysseveldt 1995; Hendry 1996; Dowling 1998; Poole 1999; Harris and Brewster 1999a). The purpose of IHRM is to enable the firm, the multinational enterprise (MNE), to be successful globally. This entails being (a) competitive throughout the world, (b) efficient, (c) locally responsive, (d) flexible and adaptable within the shortest of time periods, and (e) capable of transferring learning across its globally dispersed units. These requirements are significant, and the magnitude of the reality is indisputable: for example, a substantial majority of industries in North America and Europe are under full-scale attack by foreign competitors (Bartlett and Ghoshal 1991, 1998). On the other hand, most of the emerging markets are now bombarded by foreign direct investments (FDIs) by the MNEs of developed nations (UNCTAD 1999).

IHRM for many firms is likely to be critical to their success, and effective IHRM can make the difference between survival and extinction for many MNEs. Yet, for reasons of cost, time, and difficulty, IHRM research has been limited and largely focused on a few issues. Calls are now being made to advance our understanding of this important area in several ways, including (1) developing models and frameworks to reflect the complex set of environmental factors that impinge upon the global management of human resources (Adler and Ghadar 1990; Shenkar 1995; Harris and

Brewster 1999a; Mendenhall and Oddou 2000; Sparrow and Hiltrop 1997; Budhwar and Sparrow 2002); (2) researching international human resource activities in a way that recognizes their systematic interaction (Punnett and Ricks 1992; Begin 1997; Clark et al. 1999); and (3) utilizing more theoretical perspectives to predict and explain relationships (Arvey, Bhagat, and Salas 1991; Black and Mendenhall 1990; Schuler, Dowling, and De Cieri. 1993; Teagarden et al. 1995; Taylor, Beechler, and Napier 1996; Budhwar and Debrah 2000).

In this chapter, we review what is being done in the IHRM field. A strategic framework is utilized to organize our review and evaluation of the existing literature and research. While MNEs are our primary focus, issues associated with traditional comparative human resource management research are examined as well. Implications and suggestions for future research agendas are offered throughout (Schuler, Budhwar, and Florkowski 2002).

A MODEL OF IHRM

Our model of IHRM is based on the framework offered by Schuler, Dowling, and De Cieri (1993); it draws on Sundaram and Black's (1992) definition of an MNE as:

> any enterprise that carries out transactions in or between two sovereign entities, operating under a system of decision making that permits influence over resources and capabilities, where the transactions are subject to influence by factors exogenous to the home country environment of the enterprise. (733)

This definition serves to highlight the differences between managing global firms and domestic firms and thus establishes the basis for conceptualizing IHRM as substantially more encompassing than domestic human resource management (Bartlett and Ghoshal 1991, 1992, 1998; Adler and Bartholomew 1992; Casson 1982; Hennart 1982; Kogut 1989; Toyne 1989; Teece 1983; Williamson 1985; Buckley and Casson 1976; Black, Gregersen, and Mendenhall 1992; Sparrow 1995; Brewster et al. 1996; De Cieri and Dowling 1997; Roberts, Kossek, and Ozeki 1998; Clark et al. 1999; Dowling, Welch, and Schuler 1999). A consequence of this for most MNEs is a human resource department that develops and administers the following policies and practices but across a wide variety of nations, each with its own social, cultural, legal, economic, political, and historical characteristics (Morgan 1986): human resource planning; staffing; performance evaluation; training and development; compensation and benefits; and labor relations/safety and health.

The rise of the MNE is being accelerated because the costs associated with the development and marketing of new products are too great to be amortized over only one market, even a large one such as the United States or Europe (Bartlett and Ghoshal 1991, 1998; Caves 1996; Buckley and Casson 1998; Harzing 1999a). However, some products and services demand accommodation to location customs, tastes, habits, and regulations. For many multinationals, the likelihood of competing in several diverse environments has never been greater. While these scenarios suggest paths that MNEs have indeed taken to be competitive, they are superseded by the need to manage globally, as if the world were one vast market, and simultaneously to manage locally, as if the world were a vast number of separate and loosely connected markets (Bartlett and Ghoshal 1991; Caligiuri and Stroh 1995; Merchant 2000).

Bartlett and Ghoshal's (1991, 1998) basic premise is that MNEs are represented by units spread throughout the world that need to be coordinated or integrated in some form and to some degree (Harzing 2000). The differentiation and integration of units (Lawrence and Lorsch 1967) need to be done with attention to being globally competitive, efficient, responsive, and flexible to local needs and conditions, as well as being able to transfer learning across units (Buckley and Casson 1998; Rangan 1998). In essence, MNEs are firms that need to be global and local (multidomestic) at the same time. MNEs, however, need to achieve different levels of globalness and localness. And there are varying ways to attain similar levels of globalness and localness (Bartlett 1992; Adler and Ghadar 1990; Caligiuri and Stroh 1995; Dowling 1998; Wells 1998).

Simultaneous concerns for being global, transferring learning, and being multidomestic (thereby facilitating local sensitivity) generate important issues relevant to IHRM. For example, can MNEs link their globally dispersed units through human resource policies and practices? How do MNEs facilitate a multidomestic response that is simultaneously consistent with the need for global coordination and the transfer of learning and innovation across units through human resource policies and practices?

The growing importance of MNEs and use of complex global strategic business decisions have generated a similar phenomenon in the area of

IHRM, namely, the linkage of IHRM with the strategic needs of the business (Galbraith and Kazanjian 1986; Bartlett and Ghoshal 1991, 1998; Tayeb 1995; Wright and Snell 1998). Thus, a more strategic perspective of IHRM has developed (Schuler, Dowling, and De Cieri 1993; Bartlett and Ghoshal 1992; Adler and Bartholomew 1992; Black, Gregersen, and Mendenhall 1992, Black et al. 1999; Taylor, Beechler, and Napier 1996; Festing 1997; Brewster, Larsen, and Mayrhofer 1997; Schuler and Jackson 1999).

Further reasons for the development of a more strategic perspective of IHRM include the recognition that (a) human resource management at any level is important to strategy implementation (Hamel and Prahalad 1986; Hambrick and Snow 1989; Wright and Snell 1998); (b) major strategic components of MNEs have a significant influence on international management issues, functions, policies, and practices (Edstrom and Galbraith 1977; Roberts, Kossek, and Ozeki 1998); (c) many of these characteristics of IHRM can influence the attainment of the concerns and goals of MNEs (Kobrin 1992); and (d) a wide variety of factors make the relationship between MNEs and IHRM complex, thereby making the study of IHRM challenging as well as important (Bartlett and Ghoshal 1991, 1998, 2000; Oddou and Derr 1999; Dowling, Welch, and Schuler 1999; Evans 1992).

By including a more strategic perspective, today's model of IHRM incorporates the broader, contextual reality described by Adler and Ghadar (1990). While Schuler, Dowling, and De Cieri (1993) describe this phenomenon as the development of a field called "strategic international human resource management," we treat it as the evolution of IHRM to encompass a strategic perspective and use their framework as a contemporary description of IHRM. In both cases, the traditional comparative aspect of IHRM and this more recent strategic perspective of IHRM are joined. This facilitates the implementation of the research agenda in IHRM called for by Adler and her colleagues. The model for IHRM that is used here to inventory and appraise what we know today, as well as to suggest a research agenda for tomorrow, appears in figure 11.1. This model is now accepted and further validated by many researchers in the field (e.g., Taylor, Beechler, and Napier 1996; De Cieri and Dowling 1997; Festing 1997; Poole 1999; Budhwar and Sparrow 2002).

As shown in figure 11.1 there are three major components of IHRM: issues, functions, and policies and practices. We confine our discussion to these items, referring interested readers to Schuler, Dowling, and De Cieri

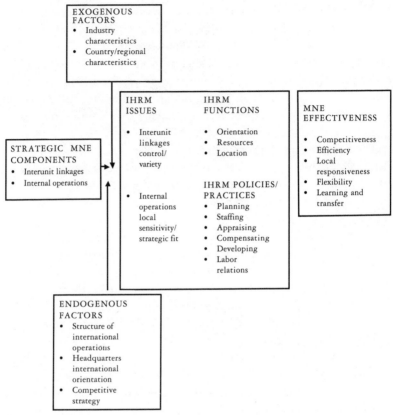

Source: Adapted from Schuler, Dowling, and De Cieri 1993

FIGURE 11.1. Integrative framework of international human resource management in MNEs

1993 and 1999 for a thorough description of the entire model. All aspects of the model, however, are woven into the research agenda that is articulated.

IHRM ISSUES

IHRM issues are best conceptualized in terms of interunit and intraunit needs and challenges. Although the MNE is separated across several nations, it remains a single enterprise and therefore must consider how to balance competing pressures for differentiation and integration (Lawrence and Lorsch 1967; Galbraith 1987). Multinationals must decide how to be sensitive to unique demands of the indigenous environment without inhibiting their ability to coordinate the internal operations of local units in pursuit of global strategies. Because these issues of differentiation and integration are often facilitated by human resource management activities, they represent a critical component in IHRM. An example of this dual focus is found in most American-based MNEs, which tend to assign primary responsibility to their subsidiaries for local compensation and benefits, training, and labor relations, with regional units assuming secondary (i.e., coordinating) responsibility (Reynolds 1992; Merchant 2000).

IHRM FUNCTIONS

IHRM functions represent three areas: an MNE's human resource orientation, the resources (time, energy, money) allocated to its human resource organization, and the location of those resources and HR decision making. Considerable resources can be devoted to human resource management on a transnational scale. The center can staff a rather extensive HR department dedicated exclusively to IHRM tasks, such as deciding how to select and repatriate international assignees (Caligiuri 2000; Caligiuri and Lazarova 2000; Osland 2000), as well as how to compensate these employees (Peterson, Napier, and Shin 1996). It can also hire a staff of individuals to focus on managerial training and development, largely to develop a global management cadre (Black and Gregersen 2000). Accordingly, the resources devoted to and the location of IHRM operations can be expected to vary considerably across MNEs (Alder and Ghadar 1990; Bird, Taylor, Beechler 1998; Merchant 2000). Dowling (1988) documented several types of IHRM structures within MNEs, including a totally centralized HR function; centralized HR policy development with regional input in implementation; corporate, group, and divisional HR units with unique responsibilities; and centralized HR decision making for parent-country nationals (PCNs) and third-country nationals (TCNs). Of course, IHRM resource consumption should diminish as the number of PCNs and TCNs decreases and as overseas units are awarded greater decision-making autonomy (i.e., decentralization).

IHRM POLICIES AND PRACTICES

IHRM policies and practices, which constitute the last component of the model, involve the development of general guidelines on how individuals will be managed and specific HR initiatives. IHRM policies and practices relevant to the needs of MNEs include those related to planning, staffing, appraising, compensating, training, and developing, as well as to labor relations (Dowling, Schuler, and Welch 1994; Dowling, Welch, and Schuler 1999). To illustrate, an MNE might have an HR policy that indicates that performance will be rewarded. Given that this is a rather general statement, each MNE unit could be free to develop specific practices that are simultaneously consistent with local conditions and the general policy. Under this policy, one local unit might develop an individual incentive plan for the general manager tied to the sales of the local operation while another unit might institute a group incentive plan for the entire top management team tied to host-country sales (Fulkerson and Schuler 1992).

As suggested by Evans (1986), Bartlett and Ghoshal (1991), Adler and Ghadar (1990), and Teagarden et al. (1995), understanding and doing research in IHRM must encompass a rather complex reality. The model in figure 11.1 has tried to capture this fact. It will now be used to organize and critique what has been published in the IHRM domain. Our discussion is divided into three broad categories: IHRM and MNE effectiveness; the impact of MNEs on host industrial relations (IR) systems[1]; and national HRM systems and competitive advantage.

IHRM AND MNE EFFECTIVENESS

Because IHRM issues are the main drivers of IHRM functions, policies, and practices, the ensuing discussion is structured around these issues, beginning with interunit linkages.

INTERUNIT LINKAGES

Within our framework of IHRM shown in figure 11.1, the interunit linkages have been a traditional focal point for discussion of IHRM (Pucik and Katz 1986; Pucik 1988; Phatak 1992, 1995; Bartlett and Ghoshal 1991, 1998). These discussions typically have focused on recognizing the variety of several worldwide units while controlling and coordinating that variety (Doz and Prahalad 1986; Edstrom and Galbraith 1977). Indeed, the key objective in interunit linkages appears to be balancing the needs of variety (diversity), coordination, and control for purposes of global competitiveness, flexibility, and organizational learning (Bartlett and Ghoshal 1991, 1998, 2000; Barkema et al. 1997). The nature of this balance is expected to vary depending on the characteristics of the particular MNE, such as its stage of globalization (Alder and Ghadar 1990; Milliman, Von Glinow, and Nathan 1991; Caligiuri and Stroh 1995; Pan and Li 2000).

IHRM POLICIES AND PRACTICES

IHRM policies and practices may strengthen interunit linkages in numerous ways, including (a) comprehensive human resource planning, ensuring that the MNE has the appropriate people in place around the world at the right time; (b) staffing policies that capitalize on the worldwide expertise of expatriates, TCNs, and host-country nationals (HCNs); (c) performance appraisals that are anchored in the competitive strategies of MNE headquarters and host units; (d) compensation policies that are strategically and culturally relevant; and (e) training and development initiatives that prepare individuals to operate effectively in their overseas locations and to cooperate with other MNE units. How organizations develop, effectively implement, and institutionalize such policies should be at the heart of our research agenda for IHRM. Some research has been initiated in this regard. For example, Roberts, Kossek, and Ozeki (1998), on the basis of interviews with IHRM managers, have identified three practical challenges to managing the global workforce: deployment, knowledge and innovation dissemination, and talent identification and development. They have also identified four strategies to meet these challenges. These are aspirational careers, awareness-building assignments, strategic teams, and virtual solutions. Finally, they propose a diagnostic framework for each of the challenges and for when to use each of the strategies. Yet, previous studies have been skewed heavily toward the effects that staffing or development practices have on individuals—primarily expatriated employees (Tung and Punnett 1993; Brewster and Scullion 1997; Harris and Brewster 1999a). One could argue that this focus is consistent with the efforts of many MNEs (especially those based in North America) to manage interunit operations through PCNs. Even within Europe such an ethnocentric approach is adopted by most organizations to organize their IHRM (Mayrhofer and Brewster 1996). As more firms think and act globally, however, there is a compelling need to devise and sustain effective transnational human resource management systems (Adler and Bartholomew 1993; Edwards, Ferner, and Sisson 1996).

Given these caveats, linkage-related IHRM research is subsequently reviewed. Although HCNs and TCNs may enhance such linkages in vital ways, previous investigations have concentrated on the reactions these groups have to host-level HRM policies and practices. As a result, we will examine that segment of the literature in the section titled "Internal Operations in IHRM."

HUMAN RESOURCE PLANNING

Human resource planning should be an indispensable means of engineering effective interunit linkage, most notably by synchronizing the staffing, appraisal, and compensation subsystems of IHRM. Such planning must be comprehensive in scope—cognizant of, and responsive to, the MNE's industry characteristics, product stage, organizational phase of international development, global structure, and competitive strategies (Bartlett and Ghoshal 1991, 1998). These considerations are reflected in the following critical human resource planning issues facing MNEs:

- Identifying top management potential at the earliest possible career stage
- Identifying critical success factors for the future international manager
- Providing developmental opportunities
- Tracking and maintaining commitments to individuals in international career paths
- Tying strategic business planning to human resource planning, and vice versa
- Dealing with the organizational dynamics of multiple (decentralized) business units while attempting to achieve global and regional (e.g., Europe) focused strategies
- Providing meaningful assignments at the right time to ensure adequate international and domestic human resources

Similarly, Wong (2000) has identified ten major planning and processing activities that international HR executives need to address: (1) assignment and cost planning, (2) candidate selection, (3) assignment terms and condition documentation, (4) relocation processing and vendor management, (5) cultural and language orientation/training, (6) compensation administration and payroll processing, (7) tax administration, (8) career planning and development, (9) handling of spouse and dependent matters, and (10) immigration processing.

How best to do any of these activities remains a challenge for some MNEs; how best to do them in an integrative manner through HR planning initiatives is a major challenge for most MNEs (Phatak 1992; Evans 1986, 1992; Bartlett and Ghoshal 1991). More specific questions about each of these items will be addressed.

INTERNATIONAL HUMAN RESOURCE STAFFING: THE MIX OF PCNS, TCNS, AND HCNS

Staffing is a major IHRM practice that MNEs have used to help coordinate and control their far-flung global operations (Pucik and Katz 1986; Zeira and Banai 1981; Hendry 1992; Dowling and Schuler 1990; Mayrhofer and Brewster 1997; Caligiuri and Stroh 1995; Dowling, Welch, and Schuler 1999; Pucik and Saba 1998). Traditionally, MNEs sent PCNs abroad to ensure that the policies and procedures of the home office were being carried out to the letter in foreign operations (Punnett and Ricks 1992; Hailey 1992; Brewster and Scullion 1997). As costs became prohibitive and career issues made these assignments less attractive, MNEs turned increasingly to TCNs and HCNs to satisfy international staffing needs (Heenan and Perlmutter 1979; Black, Gregersen, and Mendenhall 1992; Black et al. 1999). Kobrin (1988) argued that U.S.-based multinationals may have gone too far in this regard, seriously eroding their capacity to formulate and implement globally competitive strategies.

MNEs nevertheless continue to expatriate PCNs as technical troubleshooters, structure reproducers, and general management operatives. Precise data are lacking on the extent to which there is cross-cultural or industry variation in the utilization of short- versus long-term tours of duty and single postings versus career rotations. Tung (1982) found that Japanese MNEs expatriated more frequently when filling senior and middle management positions in advanced industrialized economies than did European or U.S. firms. The staffing approach for lower managerial positions was polycentric (i.e., staffed from the host labor market) in the advanced industrialized countries regardless of MNE home country; however, Japanese multinationals displayed levels considerably below those for their Western-based counterparts. European and Japanese firms behaved very similarly in newly industrializing economies, often reporting that 40 to 50 percent of host managerial positions were occupied by PCNs. In general, U.S. companies are least likely to staff management vacancies in these locations with PCNs; nevertheless, U.S. companies do use PCNs. The same survey (Tung 1982) identified several changing reasons for using expatriates, including:

Protecting company interests	→ Broadening global perspectives
Providing functional perspectives	→ Broadening global knowledge
	→ Providing developmental assignments
Building local talent via PCN training	→ Orchestrating better career planning
Managing mature businesses	→ Managing new and joint ventures

More recently, Peterson, Napier, and Shin (1996) examined the similarities and differences among the expatriate management programs across British, German, Japanese, and U.S. MNCs. They report similarities in the policies related to selection primarily on technical and interpersonal skills; primary reliance on managers choosing the expatriate rather than self-nomination; training programs consisting of country and cultural awareness, as well as language training, if applicable; common expatriate compensation packages; common performance appraisal methods throughout the MNE; and labor relations policy based on the union situation in the host country. Differences across the four countries included greater use of TCNs by U.S.- and British-owned MNCs; very modest use of inpatriates by Japanese MNCs; and wide use of separate employment contracts while on expatriate status by German and British MNCs (Peterson, Napier, and Shin 1996, 556).

MNEs remain concerned about the best way to identify and select expatriates for foreign assignments (Black, Gregersen, and Mendenhall 1992; Black et al. 1999; Harzing 1995; Torbiorn 1997; Haines and Saba 1999). Davison and Punnett (1995) argue that international managers and researchers need to avoid an "ostrich-like" attitude of "gender and race blindness" when dealing with international assignments. The existing research suggests that the foreign assignment selection process should be done systematically, based upon the critical dimensions of the foreign assignment. The list that follows displays eleven such dimensions identified in an unpublished report by the Personnel Decisions Research Institute (1987). The trend here appears to be in the direction of developing a selection process based on the identification of critical job dimensions and the development of predictors that can be used to increase the probability of success (Hough 1989; Dowling, Schuler, and Welch 1994; Dowling, Welch, and Schuler 1999). Ultimately, researchers must isolate the relative impact that individual characteristics (e.g., knowledge, skills, abilities) have on successful completion of international assignments as opposed to organizational factors (e.g., appraisal and compensation policies, support systems) (Arvey, Bhagat, and Salas 1991).

CRITICAL DIMENSIONS FOR FOREIGN ASSIGNMENT SELECTION

A. Accept Foreign Assignments
- Discussions with spouse/family/significant others
- Awareness of own and family needs/goals
- Considerations of personal/family responsibilities/obligations
- Planning for care of dependents
- Considering impact of job on professional development and career progression
- Learning about cultural differences before going abroad

B. Spouse and Family Support
- Providing support to family
- Receiving support from family
- Willingness to make sacrifices for family members
- Attentiveness to needs of family members

C. Knowledge of Foreign Language
- Ability to understand and communicate orally in the foreign language
- Ability to read and write in the foreign language

D. Adjustment to Living Abroad
- Sensitivity to and acceptance of cultural differences
- Acceptance of different mores (values, behavior, attitudes)
- Developing/maintaining relationships
- Involvement in host community
- Coping with different/difficult living circumstances
- Locating resources (housing, food, etc.) in foreign countries

E. ADJUSTMENT TO FOREIGN BUSINESS PRACTICES
- Knowledge of foreign business practices
- Sensitivity to appropriate business protocol/practices
- Engaging in appropriate business practices
- Interacting with business contacts, clients, and staff in a socially acceptable manner

F. ESTABLISHING/MAINTAINING BUSINESS CONTACTS
- Identifying business contacts
- Establishing rapport with contacts, clients, and co-workers
- Being open and honest in dealing with others
- Developing a network of business contacts
- Using contacts to achieve objectives

G. TECHNICAL COMPETENCE
- Possessing thorough technical knowledge
- Keeping up-to-date and fully informed about technical developments and work-related matters
- Using technical knowledge in solving difficult problems and in making high-quality decisions

H. WORKING WITH OTHERS
- Maintaining smooth and effective working relationships with management and co-workers
- Working as an effective team member
- Coordinating with other units or foreign companies/governments to achieve company goals
- Assisting supervisors, peers, and subordinates

I. COMMUNICATING/PERSUADING
- Providing thorough, clear, and timely information to others, both orally and written
- Presenting own positions clearly and decisively
- Being persuasive in promoting one's own ideas

J. INITIATIVE/EFFORT
- Taking on additional duties or responsibilities willingly
- Following up on requests to others when necessary

- Persisting and overcoming difficult obstacles
- Working long hours to meet deadlines

K. Company Support

- Providing information on matters such as housing, community services/support systems, insurance, and banks
- Providing adequate information on new job
- Providing timely living arrangements/allowances
- Providing adequate information/assistance for reentry into U.S. job market
- Providing timely responses to business-related matters
- Fulfilling company commitments

The "Spouse and Family Support" dimension in the preceding list typically rests on assumptions that the spouse is female and will not be working abroad in a career-related position (Punnett, Crocker, and Stevens 1992). However, dual-income and dual-career couples are becoming an increasingly important segment of professional managers in the United States (Harvey and Wiese 1998). It is now expected that dual-career couples will increasingly be involved in international assignments, many of which will entail the expatriation of women managers (Adler 1994; Tung 1988; Handler and Lane 1997; Harvey and Buckley 1998). There remains a paucity of research on the initiatives that U.S.- and non-U.S.-based MNEs are undertaking to capitalize on these developments (e.g., spousal employment search services, waivers of immigration restrictions on working spouses), a deficiency that should be remedied in subsequent IHRM investigations.

Along with this research on expatriation is the work on repatriation. The quality of the repatriation process is viewed as critical to the overall career success of expatriates. It has also been linked to the adjustment process and turnover of expatriates following their return home (Brewster 1988; Adler 1991; Black, Gregersen, and Mendenhall 1992; Black et al. 1999; Brewster and Scullion 1997; Harris and Brewster 1999a; Stroh 1995). Much progress has been made in capturing the complexity of the repatriation process. For example, Black, Gregersen, and Mendenhall (1992) and Black et al. (1999) have presented a rich framework incorporating many variables associated with the anticipatory and in-country repatriation adjustment process. Based on their framework, they presented eighteen propositions waiting to be tested. Alternatively, Welch et al. (1992) described the process of repatriation as having four phases: preparation, physical relocation, transition, and readjustment. While some would argue that this conceptualization really goes far beyond the process of "coming home," others would claim that it represents all the variables that potentially impact the longevity and performance of the individual once repatriated. Stroh (1995) examined the main turnover predictors among repatriates in fifty-one U.S.-based MNCs. Her study revealed the following indicators as the main predictors of repatriate turnover: corporate values related to the importance of overseas assignment to the organization; whether the organization has a career development plan for repatriates; and the perceived impact of corporate turbulence on being able to place repatriates adequately upon their return. Hammer, Hart, and Rogan (1998) examined the adjustment of U.S. corporate managers and spouses to their professional and social environments upon their return to the United States. They investigated the relationship of background variables (e.g., age, prior national experience), host-country variables, and reentry variables of expectations to reentry satisfaction and reentry difficulties for forty-four returning managers and thirty-three spouses from two MNCs. They found support for the relationship between reentry expectations and overall reentry satisfaction for managers and reentry expectations, reentry satisfaction, and reentry difficulties for spouses. Such ongoing research—along with earlier discussed frameworks in the field such as Welch et al. 1992; Black, Gregersen, and Mendenhall 1992; and Black et al. 1999—reflects the trends in IHRM to be more systematic, inclusive, and contextual. In doing so, they offer fertile ground for future research.

Further research opportunities abound in the area of staffing with TCNs and HCNs. While the use of more TCNs and HCNs may solve staffing needs, it raises concerns about the ability to satisfy the needs of coordination and control (Ouchi and MacGuire 1975; Hailey 1992; Tayeb 1995; Torbiorn 1997; Harzing 1999a; Dowling, Welch, and Schuler 1999). As Pucik and Katz (1986) argued, firms can redress such needs by establishing rules and procedures for HCNs or TCNs to carry out or by socializing the HCNs or TCNs to think and behave like expatriates. Of course, these pure archetypes might not be found as MNEs seek the most appropriate solution to fit the circumstances. For example, under conditions of rapid change, high uncertainty, and the need for social information to be gathered and utilized, MNEs would more likely socialize individuals (Van Maanen and Schein 1979). Under conditions of stability, certainty, and the need for technical information to be utilized, firms would more likely establish rules and procedures for individuals to carry out (Banai 1992). Since MNEs rarely find just one set of conditions or another, combinations of the two approaches are commonplace.

Concerns remain about the biasing effects that the culture and norms of parent firms can have on socialization processes (Pucik and Katz 1986). These ethnocentric forces can compromise the MNE's ability to identify and benefit from cultural synergies in their operating units. One means of combating management ethnocentrism would be to engage more TCNs in preference to PCNs, individuals who would be expected to have been previously socialized (Cappelli and McElrath 1992). But we still cannot define the best way to socialize a culturally diverse set of individuals. It appears, however, that, as MNEs become more global, their socialization process needs to be less ethnocentric—cultural differences are too important to ignore or deny (Adler and Ghadar 1990; Adler 1997). In fact, facilitating and diffusing cultural synergies may be critical to economic success as industries become more transnational in nature (Adler and Bartholomew 1992; Adler 1997; Porter and Tansky 1999). Recently, Caligiuri (2000) examined the relationship between host national contact and cross-national adjustment of expatriates. Her findings suggest that greater contact with host nationals positively relates to cross-cultural adjustment when an expatriate possesses the personality trait of openness. The personality characteristic of sociability was also related to cross-cultural adjustment.

On the way to developing a global workforce and a cadre of global managers, MNEs need to open their recruitment process and enhance the attractiveness of global assignments (Adler and Bartholomew 1992; Adler 1994; Izraeli and Adler 1994; Harvey et al. 1999; Haines and Saba 1999). Remaining to be researched, however, is the relationship between an open recruiting process and MNE effectiveness. Indeed, yet to be investigated is the extent to which there are gaps between what MNEs "now do" in recruiting and what they "should do." One possible way to investigate this question is to use the "Retention Audit" illustrated in table 11.1.

Staffing research has targeted expatriates, TCNs, and HCNs, but this approach is less true of works examining appraisals, compensation, and training. This shortcoming is being redressed gradually as MNEs seek to globalize their operations.

APPRAISING PERFORMANCE

While the expatriate is on assignment, the individual performance must be appraised (Dowling, Schuler, and Welch 1994; Brewster and Scullion 1997; Dowling, Welch, and Schuler 1999). Peterson, Napier, and Shin (1996), in their comparative IHRM study of British, German, Japanese and U.S. multinationals, found that expatriates had performance appraisals while serving in the foreign assignment. Their appraisal mechanisms varied from quantitative (e.g., graphic scale) to qualitative (e.g., MBO [management by objective] or narrative). As discussed previously, many types of assignments exist entailing numerous job performance dimensions. For the expatriate assignment, in contrast to the domestic assignment, MNEs need to evaluate dimensions of performance not specifically job related, such as cross-cultural interpersonal qualities; sensitivity to foreign norms, laws, and customs; adaptability to uncertain and unpredictable conditions; and the host location's integration with other MNE units. The significance of these factors will vary by the type of expatriate. Thus far, the research on

TABLE 11.1.   Retention Audit

Please describe the retention practices of your division/business on two dimensions: circle the number describing now" and square the number describing "should be."

In our Retaining Decisions	Not at All	Low Extent	Somewhat	A Great Deal	Complete
1. Global career paths are critical in one's career.	1	2	3	4	5
2. Cross-business and cross-division career paths are critical.	1	2	3	4	5
3. Global career development is in the hands of a corporate unit.	1	2	3	4	5
4. Promotion and compensation practices and policies reward the managers who develop globally.	1	2	3	4	5
5. Managers have a "career home" in a business/division rather than a geographical area.	1	2	3	4	5
6. Performance reviews, rewards, and incentives meet world-class standards.	1	2	3	4	5
7. Continual challenges to the way we do things are made.	1	2	3	4	5

© Randall S. Schuler, Rutgers University

expatriate performance appraisal has not fully addressed the relative impact of these uniquely international dimensions of performance, regardless of the type of expatriate assignment (Dowling, Schuler, and Welch 1994; Peterson et al. 1996). Thus, the research opportunities in this area are relatively unlimited.

While the performance appraisals of expatriates who are assigned to special technical projects and short-term stays tend to be operational and task focused, evaluations of the expatriate manager tend to be more strategic, more related to the operation of the entire unit and how it relates to the other locations (Phatak 1992; Evans 1986; Selmer and de Leon 1997). Appraising the performance of this manager, therefore, becomes an important issue at the interunit linkage level of IHRM (Fulkerson and Schuler 1992; Dowling, Welch, and Schuler 1999). Units within a large MNE may pursue different strategic missions, face different legal conditions, and encounter far different competitive situations. Consequently, MNEs must account for these environmental conditions when constructing appraisal formats and individual objectives for unit managers (Pucik 1988; Lindholm, Tahvanainen, and Ingmar 1999). While it appears that this approach to PCN appraisal is not unknown within large multinationals (Fulkerson and Schuler 1992), there is little empirical evidence to suggest how widespread the practice is or under what conditions (e.g., degree of trust) it is more effective. It does appear, however, that performance appraisal of expatriate managers can be a critical means whereby MNEs link their units together (e.g., by appraising cooperative behaviors and incorporating the various environmental dimensions into each manager's appraisal format differently). It can also facilitate the development of a common appraisal format that recognizes and makes situational differences legitimate, so that the relative contributions of managers around the world can be tracked, evaluated, and compared. This strategically and culturally standardized information should guide managerial career development, future promotion decisions, and compensation adjustments. As the next two sections detail, though, there is little evidence that strong linkages actually exist.

COMPENSATING THE EXPATRIATE

It has been argued that expatriate compensation can be as significant as appraisal in fostering interunit linkages and the attainment of international strategic objectives (Dowling, Schuler, and Welch 1994; Reynolds 1992; Dowling, Welch, and Schuler 1999). "In theory, [PCNs] should have no more or less at risk economically than their domestic counterparts" (Reynolds 1992, 75). The reality is that expatriates tend to have greater income security because performance evaluations usually are a rather modest determinant of their total compensation package. While PCNs may have fewer opportunities to invest in tax shelters and other economic amenities than their functional equivalents at home, they can cost MNEs up to five times as much (Dowling, Schuler, and Welch 1994, 149). A side effect of this cost differential is the substantial disparity between the salary of PCNs and that of HCNs or TCNs. This disparity has the potential to create status distinctions in an MNE's global workforce, thereby inhibiting interunit linkages. The extent to which this actually occurs, however, is not documented publicly. It appears, however, that expatriate compensation as practiced by U.S. MNEs tends to reflect the assumption of the home country (e.g., money is the most important motivator) and thus has been very culture bound (Schuler and Rogovsky 1998; Bradley, Hendry, and Perkins 1999).

Similar patterns are evident in the provision of benefits. U.S. and Japanese multinationals normally limit TCNs to the fringe benefits available to indigenous employees at the same time as PCNs receive home-country entitlements (Towers-Perrin 1987). European MNEs are more egalitarian as a rule, extending home-country benefits to TCNs and PCNs.

Given how little we know about "standard" international compensation and benefits administration, research opportunities abound (Sparrow 1999). Some of the key issues to be investigated include the following: How can MNEs develop pay structures that are cost-effective, fair, and adaptable to different employee groups? How can MNEs develop more culturally sensitive compensation schemes that recognize country differences, yet are equally motivating and still equitable? How can international-assignee compensation be better linked to the strategy and industry characteristics of a given MNE?

These broader-based research issues buttress several more specific ones identified by a recent survey of international HR professionals associated with the Institute of International Human Resources. Among the topics identified are the following:

1. Managing expatriate expectations
2. Adding "appropriate" value to expatriate compensation packages

3. "Localization" of expatriate compensation
4. Cost containment
5. Global pension schemes
6. Integration of HR planning with expatriate compensation
7. Management development as a crucial factor in expatriate compensation planning
8. Regionalization
9. Revisiting the "balance sheet" concept
10. Centralizing and decentralizing the assignment policy

Addressing these several general and specific issues in expatriate compensation is likely to provide a full research agenda for those interested in IHRM reward structures.

TRAINING AND DEVELOPING

The training and development aspect of IHRM presents another means of linking the dispersed units of an MNE. Traditionally, research has focused on the predeparture training extended to PCNs and their families. Lack of preparation generally has been associated with a higher expatriate failure rate; U.S. multinationals tend to engage in less training than do their European and Japanese counterparts (Tung 1982; Ronen 1986; Noble 1997). Moreover, U.S. MNEs ordinarily place less emphasis on language, interpersonal skills, and culture sensitivity in their training programs than do MNEs based elsewhere (Brewster 1988; McEnery and DesHarnals 1990; Tung 1982; Dowling, Welch, and Schuler 1999; Harris and Brewster 1999b). Consequently, it is not surprising that U.S. MNEs experience higher expatriate failure rates than do other multinationals. At times such claims are contradictory; for example, Peterson, Napier, and Shin (1996, 550) report lower failure rates than those reported by Tung (1982). However, as suggested previously, the findings of Peterson, Napier, and Shin (1996) also confirm higher expatriate failure rates in U.S. multinationals in comparison to Western European and Japanese MNCs. As much of this research is based on self-reported data, more rigorous designs are needed to better control potential cultural biases (e.g., home-country differences in the willingness to disclose organizational shortcomings or seek early repatriation).

Increasingly, scholars and professionals are casting the training and developing of international assignees into a much larger frame, one consistent with a broader, more theoretical, and systematic description of IHRM, per figure 11.1. For example, the family is now recognized as a very significant factor in expatriate success (Dowling, Schuler, and Welch 1994; Dowling, Welch, and Schuler 1999; Adler 1997; Handler and Lane 1997; Harris and Brewster 1999b), particularly when dual-career issues are involved (Punnett, Crocker, and Stevens 1992; Reynolds and Bennett 1991; Hammer, Hart, and Rogan 1998; Harvey and Buckley 1998; Harvey and Wiese 1998). Better paradigms (i.e., social learning theory) have begun to emerge concerning the impact and likely success of cross-cultural training (Black and Mendenhall 1990; Porter and Tansky 1999; Downes and Thomas 1999). International HR planning is seen more often as a key orchestrator of expatriate career development, incorporating expatriate assignment decisions and the repatriation process (Black, Gregersen, and Mendenhall 1992; Black et al. 1999; Tregaskis 1998).

Perhaps most indicative of this shift in perspective is the contention that training and development is no more important for PCNs than it is for individuals from other parts of the world (Adler and Bartholomew 1992). In fact, global firms can enhance their interunit linkages by creating a pool of global managers with citizenship from anywhere in the world (Fulkerson and Schuler 1992; Bartlett and Ghoshal 2000). Management development activities could be housed in corporate or global headquarters with local, regional, and other HR units assisting in program design and delivery (Evans 1992; Scullion 1992; Vanderbroeck 1992; Tichy 1992; Bartlett and Ghoshal 1991, 1992, 1998; Dowling, Welch, and Schuler 1999). The efficacy of this or other structural approaches remains an empirical question. A look at these issues might relate answers to the questionnaire in table 11.2 to measures of MNE effectiveness.

SUPERORDINATE VALUES FOR IHRM PRACTICE DEVELOPMENT

Part of the challenge in developing HR practice to facilitate interunit linkages is to allow simultaneously for some flexibility. Flexibility supports change and enables adaptation to local conditions. Flexibility is attained in part by ensuring that practices are not carved in stone (mentally or physically) and that practices are formulated within a larger context, most notably an overriding human resource philosophy and core human resource policies (Schuler 1992; Buckley and Casson 1998; Rangan 1998). Statements of human resource philosophy proscribe limits on the actual treatment of individuals regardless of location through its top-down impact on

HR policy-making (Schuler 1992). Core IHRM policies, in turn, operationalize this philosophy and arguably constrain the set of IHRM practices in use (i.e., types of compensation, staffing procedures, appraisal methods, and training and development modes). There are many choices in the array of possible IHRM practices (Schuler and Jackson 1987; Sparrow and Hiltrop 1994); because these practices will influence the behaviors of individuals, they need to be closely aligned with other IHRM activities (Begin 1992; Wright and Snell 1998).

Developing core IHRM policies that facilitate interunit linkages may be easier said than done, especially if units have dramatically different local environments or are pursuing different competitive strategies with different technologies. This confounding may make the task more challenging,

ABLE 11.2. Selection Audit

ease describe the selection practices of your division/business on two dimensions: circle the number describing "is w" and square the number describing "should be."

our Selection Decisions	Not at All	Low Extent	Somewhat	A Great Deal	Completely
. Business needs and the availability of candidates worldwide are considered.	1	2	3	4	5
. There is extensive understanding of local conditions.	1	2	3	4	5
. World-class standards are used.	1	2	3	4	5
. Job applicants are told that global assignments are part of their career.	1	2	3	4	5
. Ability to work with and learn from colleagues of many nations is considered.	1	2	3	4	5
. Selection methods are attractive and appropriate to local conditions.	1	2	3	4	5
. Incentives to join the firm appeal to a broad range of cultures.	1	2	3	4	5
. Benchmarking of the best practices is done regularly.	1	2	3	4	5
. All levels of employees are considered for international assignments.	1	2	3	4	5
. Global assignments are seen as essential in building a truly globally competitive company.	1	2	3	4	5

© Randall S. Schuler, Rutgers University

but it does not make it impossible. Perhaps, however, it does require more resources to systematically devise HR practices that are anchored in common human resource policies. Longitudinal investigations of the growth and allocation patterns of IHRM budgets within MNEs may shed some light on this matter.

The discussion now turns to findings associated with the internal operations of MNE units.

INTERNAL OPERATIONS IN IHRM

Internal operations require the same degree of research attention as interunit linkages, since both have an influence on MNE effectiveness (Porter 1990; Punnett and Ricks 1992; Taylor, Beechler, and Napier 1996). Local units must recognize and abide by indigenous employment law, tradition, and custom, unless variances or exemptions have been granted by the host government; thus, overseas units need to be given some autonomy to adapt HR practices to local conditions (Rugman and Verbeke 1998). Yet, because they need to be coordinated with the rest of the MNE (e.g., to facilitate the transfer of local managers) some commonality must exist regarding human resource policies. The local unit needs to develop HR practices that advance its own competitive strategy as well (Schuler and Jackson 1987; Morrison and Roth 1992; De Cieri and Dowling 1997; Festing 1997). Exactly how this fit might be obtained is only suggested in the following discussion, but the implication here is that the local unit needs to transcend mere conformity with indigenous culture.

IHRM POLICIES AND PRACTICES

There are at least three ways of enhancing internal operations through IHRM policies and practices. The first entails matching and adapting HR practices to closely accommodate the unit's competitive strategy, local culture, and governing legal system. The second necessitates creating a modus operandi whereby HRM practices can be modified swiftly to respond to changing host conditions. The third calls for a set of IHRM policies at the MNE level that can encompass and legitimize the HRM practices of the local units.

MATCHING AND ADAPTING HR PRACTICES

One means of ensuring that HR practices are consistent with labor-market requirements would be to staff the HR function with HCNs. In fact, this is one of the positions that MNEs seem most prone to fill with indigenous persons (Copp 1977; Dowling and Schuler 1990; Jedel and Kujawa 1977; Dowling, Welch, and Schuler 1999; Torbiorn 1997). To complement this fit, the location manager, in turn, needs to inform the HR manager of the unit's business needs, in particular its competitive strategy.

The process of systematically aligning human resource practices, policies, and philosophies with each other and the unit's strategic needs is similar for domestic corporations and MNEs. A major difference, however, lies in the need to balance the competitive strategy and cultural imperatives (Phatak 1992, 1995; Punnett and Ricks 1992; Adler 1991, 1997). The cultural imperative is an encompassing term that can include aspects of the local culture, economy, legal system, religious beliefs, and education. Its importance to IHRM resides in the definition of acceptable, legitimate, and feasible work practices and behaviors (Adler 1991, 1997; Schneider 1986; Laurent 1986; Adler and Bartholomew 1992)—acceptable in terms of questions such as "Can we pay workers different rates, and thereby differentiate them, according to performance?"; legitimate in terms of questions such as "Are there any legal statutes prohibiting us from not paying workers overtime for work done on Saturday and Sunday?"; and feasible in terms of questions such as "While this society espouses hierarchical, authoritarian, and paternalistic values, can we empower the workforce to make workplace decisions in order to facilitate our quality strategy?"

All of these components should influence decisions about where to locate units and which HR practices to use therein. The extent to which MNEs deliberate on these matters prior to host entry has not been examined in previous studies.

Local units also must be ready to ensure that HR practices, once developed, can be adapted to fit the evolving needs and goals of MNEs. For example, host management might institute much more comprehensive succession planning and development schemes than are warranted in the host environment to accommodate the larger multinational's potential staffing and transfer needs. In all likelihood, this will be done for a limited pool of individuals (i.e., persons targeted as global managers). Future investigations need to identify and critique the incentive mechanisms that MNE headquarters utilize to secure ongoing cooperation in this regard, especially when host units are pursuing distinct business strategies. Another key issue is the relative impact that organizational and personal factors have on the lag period within MNEs for responsive adaptations in HR practice.

CREATING A MODUS OPERANDI

It is equally important for human resource policies and practices to reflect changes in the local environment. To facilitate this, host management must establish procedures for, and recognize the legitimacy of, altering HR practices to fit new conditions (Brewster and Tyson 1991; Latta 1999; Walsh 1996). This will help ensure the needed flexibility that is a concern and goal for MNEs today. Exactly what these mechanisms are, and what role culture plays in them, awaits future study.

DEVELOPING GLOBAL HR POLICIES

The center has a fundamental responsibility and strategic interest in developing broad HR policies that are appropriate enough for local units to adapt to their local environment and competitive strategy needs. This discussion complements the earlier discussion under the section "Interunit Linkages." There it was argued that policies have to be created to facilitate interunit linkage and transfer of learning, while still recognizing the needs of the local units. That discussion suggested that host units must not only systematically analyze their own environmental needs but also must ensure that those factors are folded into the process whereby global HR policies are created (Bartlett and Ghoshal 2000; Schuler 2000). As local units become more geographically and culturally dispersed, it becomes more difficult for headquarters to identify and track factors bearing on competitiveness. For example, internal labor-market data that are useful to the larger MNE but unnecessary for local compliance may not need to be maintained by host units unless headquarters exercises some control over local HR information systems (Florkowski and Nath 1993; Niederman 1999).

Schuler, Dowling, and De Cieri (1993) proposed that MNEs will devote more resources to the development and implementation of such overarching policies as environmental heterogeneity. Subsequent investigations must verify the extent to which this is true.

HRM AND INTERNATIONAL JOINT VENTURES

Shenkar and Zeira (1987) and Shenkar and Li (1999) indicated that research on the HRM aspects of international joint ventures (IJVs) has been sporadic and limited. Additional IJV studies have emerged since then, most of which further conceptualize the HRM challenges of these strategic initiatives. For example, Zeira and Shenkar (1990) devised a research framework for IJV personnel policies that ties a typology of venture employees with characteristics of the parent firms. Others have discussed how sociocultural factors affect the transferability of HRM practices from foreign parents to their overseas ventures (Teagarden and Von Glinow 1990; Von Glinow and Teagarden 1988; Tayeb 1995; Edwards, Ferner, and Sisson 1996; Recht and Wilderom 1998; Ferner and Varul 2000; Chan 1999).

Less attention has been focused on the practices associated with partner selection, IJV start-up, or venture control. Geringer (1991) used proxies for managerial and technical talent as possible predictors of partner selection—the only HRM-related variables that have been tested so far. Yet, a comprehensive case study indicates that screening potential partners on the basis of managerial and HRM compatibility increases the likelihood of successful venture operations (Schuler et al. 1991; Schuler, Dowling, and De Cieri 1992, 2000; Schuler and Van Sluijs 1992; Van Sluijs and Schuler 1994). One survey found that less than 5 percent of the total time associated with venture creation was spent resolving HRM-linked issues (Coopers and Lybrand 1986). This foreshadows an abdication of venture control, since HRM-based mechanisms may be a more significant determinant of IJV control-system effectiveness than are ownership position and related formal controls (Frayne and Geringer 1990; Cyr 1997; Harzing 1999b).

Each of these topics invites a stream of research, demonstrating that the need for more rigorous empirical studies of HRM in IJVs intensified rather than abated in the 1990s. Schuler (2000) has done an extended review on HR issues and activities in IJVs. He discusses in-depth most of the previously raised issues. What follows is a summary of HR-related issues in IJVs.

KEY HR ISSUES IN IJVs

In today's globalized world, partnerships, alliances, and IJVs among two or more firms are becoming increasingly common (Sparks 1999). The existing IHRM literature highlights issues such as the importance of IJVs (Cyr 1995), reasons for the formation of JVs (Barkema et al. 1997), success and failures of JVs (Harbison 1996), conflict in IJVs (Fey and Beamish 2000), culture and control IJVs (Cyr 1997), and learning in and from IJVs (Barkema et al. 1997; Lei, Slocum, and Pitts 1997; Child and Faulkner 1998). All these issues have implications for the management of HRs in IJVs.

Considering the fact that international alliances and joint ventures are particularly difficult to manage (Killing 1983) and HR issues and activities are directly associated with the success of IJVs (Child and Faulkner 1998; Cyr 1995), we highlight the key HR issues in IJVs that form an important research agenda.

Of most reasons for the formation of IJVs, the one that appears to be gaining substantial momentum involves learning and knowledge, sharing, and transfer (Grant and Spender 1996; Child and Faulkner 1998; Shenkar and Li 1999). In this regard, the role and importance of HRM issues and activities in IJVs become of prime importance.

IMPORTANCE OF HRM IN IJVs

The importance of HRM in organizations is now widely acknowledged (Jackson and Schuler 2000; Poole 1999). In the context of the IJV, HRM has the potential to be even more important: its impact is on several organizations, not just one, and is in several societal contexts, not just one (Dowling, Welch, and Schuler 1999).

More specifically, within the IJV context there is a multitude of organizational issues that are at the same time human resource issues (Child and Faulkner 1998; Pucik 1988). Broadly presented, they can be categorized by organizational level and individual/group level.

ORGANIZATIONAL LEVEL

At this level the organizational/HR issues involve the following:

- *Parent-to-parent relationships,* such as seeking and selecting; building trust and cooperation; and learning about each other and from each other
- *Parent-to-IJV relationships,* such as identifying the reasons to establish the IJV, the appropriate structural relationship, for example, degree of control versus autonomy, methods of integration, the assignment of managers and nonmanagers for and to the IJV, and the management and transfer of learning and knowledge
- *IJV-environmental context relationship,* such as the identification of the relevant stakeholders and their objectives and acquiring knowledge of the relevant laws, political system, social system, culture, customs, language, tradition, and labor market

- *Parent characteristics,* including such issues as the values, vision, culture, practices, structure, and strategy that will enable the parent to learn from the IJV itself and the other parent—in other words, organizational capability (Cyr 1995; Lei, Slocum, and Pitts 1997; Makhija and Ganesh 1997)

Developing and utilizing an organizational-level capability appear to be more important for competitive partners that engage in IJVs (Pucik 1988).

INDIVIDUAL/GROUP LEVEL
Several organizational/HR issues at the individual/group level in IJVs involve the following:

- *Learning, sharing, and transferring of knowledge* to enable the other employees and team to learn and grow
- *Competencies* (knowledge, skills, abilities, personality, and habits) to perform the organizational roles
- *Behaviors, actions, and attitudes* that are consistent with needs of the business, customers, and colleagues
- *Motivation and commitment* to be productive, stay with the firm, and attract others to the firm
- *Lack of business success in the IJV* due to human resource issues such as lack of competent and motivated staff, staff not matched with the requirements of the competitive strategy or staff not socialized and committed to the IJV itself, or staff not able to manage dual loyalties

Virtually all of the issues in the previous lists are significant in the IJV process and involve and depend upon HRM. These issues have significant HR implications for HR activities in IJVs (Schuler 2000; Jackson and Schuler 2000).

HR ACTIVITIES
The HR activities included here relate to, are associated with, and impact the organizational level and the individual/group level of the human resource issues indicated previously. These include policies and practices associated with the following issues:

- Environmental analysis
- Organizational structure, design, strategy, values, mission, and culture
- Human resource planning
- Job design and job analysis
- Recruitment, selection, and orientation
- Training, socialization, and assimilation
- Performance and career management
- Renumeration (compensation)
- Employee welfare
- Communications (Pucik 1988; Cyr 1995)

These policies and practices are regarded by practitioners and academics alike as the core of HRM today, especially with the growing emphasis on strategic HRM (Schuler and Jackson 1999; Jackson and Schuler 2000). The relationships of HR policies and practices with the IJV process are developed through an analysis of the HR implications associated with the organizational/HR issues identified earlier. These issues and implications are further categorized as they unfold in the IJV process in stages with the HR implications for specific HR activities. Researchers in the field (see Pucik 1988; Makhija and Ganesh 1997; Lei, Slocum, and Pitts 1997) suggest four stages of the IJV process: (1) formation (the partnership stage), (2) development (the IJV itself), (3) implementation (the IJV itself), and (4) advancement (the IJV and beyond).

These four stages include the activities even before the IJV itself is formed and conclude with the relationship among the three entities, two partners, and one IJV. While the literature generally treats one partner as being in the same country as the IJV, this need not be the case in this model. A three-country IJV, however, makes the entire process more complex and the HRM more extensive and important. The organizational/HR issues in each stage of the IJV process are numerous and so are their implications for HRM. There is then a multitude of organizational and HRM issues at each stage that are filled with HR implications. Some of these implications are presented in table 11.3.

These implications form the basis for describing the HR activities in the IJV process and should form the agenda for future research. Apart from these issues, research should continue to focus on the issues related to general HRM function (such as recruitment and selection, training and development, performance appraisal) and IHRM (for example, expatriation, repatriation, compensation, dual careers).

AUDITING IHRM INITIATIVES

To ensure that all the HR-related challenges are met, MNEs need to systematically evaluate their functional capacity and responsiveness in IHRM.

TABLE 11.3.   HR Implications in the Four Stages of the IJV Process

IJV Stage Organizational/HR Issues	HR Implications
Stage 1—Formation	The more important learning is, the greater the role for HRM
Identifying reasons	Knowledge needs to be managed
Planning for utilization	Systematic selection is essential
Selecting dedicated manager	Cast a wide net in partner search
Finding potential partners	Be thorough for compatibility
Selecting likely partners	Ensure extensive communications
Resolving critical issues	More skilled negotiators are more effective
Negotiating the arrangement	Integrative strategies for learning
Stage 2—Development	Concerns of multiple sets of stakeholders need to be considered for long-term viability and acceptance.
Locating the IJV	The structure will impact the learning and
Establishing the right structure	knowledge management process. These
Getting the right senior managers	are impacted by the quality of IJV managers
	Recruiting selecting and managing senior staff can make or break the IJV
Stage 3—Implementation	These will provide meaning and direction to the IJV and employees
Establishing the vision, mission, values strategy, and structure	These will impact what is learned and shared
Developing HR politics and practices	Need to design policies and practices with local-global considerations
Staffing and managing the employees	The people will make the place
Stage 4—Advancement and Beyond	Partners need to have the capacity to learn from each other
Learning from the partner	HR systems need to be established to support
Transferring the new knowledge to the parents	knowledge flow to the parent and learning by the parent
Transferring the new knowledge to other locations	Sharing through the parent is critical

Source: Schuler 2000

While there has been a growing body of literature devoted to HRM auditing (e.g., Biles and Schuler 1986; Dyer 1991; Gomez-Mejia 1985; Jennings, McCarthy, and Undy 1990; Ulrich 1989, 1999; Walker and Bechet 1991), this matter receives surprisingly little attention in practice—the closest approaches are payroll audits or formal reviews of employment law compliance in domestic operations. Ethnocentrism tends to afflict these auditing paradigms as well, given their inherent reliance on a single cultural, regulatory, and structural context for human resource policies (Mayrhofer and Brewster 1996). With few exceptions, they also fail to assess how well HRM profiles *fit* the business's environment, structure, and strategy or what changes need to occur to foster better alignment.

Florkowski and Schuler (1994) proposed auditing strategic IHRM activities from multiconstituent, strategic fit, and efficiency-effectiveness perspectives. This synergistic approach examines the potential for conflict among the audit's stakeholders; the need to differentiate its contents based on competitive strategy, organizational life-cycle stage, and national culture; and the ways that effectiveness can be operationalized in multinational settings. Several propositions were developed that require close empirical scrutiny. There are also other ways of conducting IHRM audits. For example, Ulrich (1999) suggests that HR audits can be conducted by assessing (1) HR practices (i.e., assessing the array of services offered by an HR department), (2) HR professionals (for example, doing a 360° feedback on the extent to which an HR professional demonstrates competence), and (3) HR functions or departments (such as by computing functional competence, investigating overall indicators of HR functions, or measuring the competence against established benchmark standards).

So far, discussion has concentrated exclusively on the internal policies and practices of MNEs as they relate to HRM. Two other aspects of IHRM research that warrant attention are the effects of MNEs on the industrial relations systems of host countries and the comparisons of national HRM systems. The former offers insight into the propensity of multinational firms to act as change agents in their operating environments, while the latter begins to clarify the impact that societal HRM policies may have on the international competitiveness of firms operating in particular host settings.

IMPACT OF MNEs ON HOST IR SYSTEMS

So far, we have discussed indigenous labor-market practices as though they were exogenous from the perspective of MNEs. Yet, transnational decision-making structures, superior financial resources, and more extensive information systems arguably equip multinationals to substantially influence, if not dictate, industrial relations patterns in host countries. Weinberg (1977) alleged that MNEs utilize these advantages to secure regressive changes in collective bargaining and labor legislation, gravitating toward the lowest level of social responsibility tolerated in a given host country. Selective examples of U.S.-owned operations in Europe were presented to buttress this view. The Organization for Economic Cooperation and Development (OECD) has voiced similar concerns, culminating in nonbinding guidelines for the HRM activities of multinationals operating in member countries. Respect for and compliance with local employment standards are stressed throughout the guidelines (see Campbell and Rowan 1983; Lee 1997; Bamber and Lansbury 1998). Some nations (i.e., Pakistan, Thailand, and Kenya) have gone so far as to incorporate "cultural preservation" criteria in their national development policies to limit the sociocultural impact of foreign-owned firms (Schregle 1985, 58). National and local governments of HCNs dictate to a great extent the employment regulations and related guidelines (Katz and Elsea 1997; Saundry and Turnbull 1999; Peng 2000).

Such dynamics raise critical issues for international HRM researchers. Paramount among them is whether the characterization of MNEs as cultural tsunamis stems from overpublicized, isolated incidents or from patterned practice. With one exception (Jain 1990), prior studies have not systematically cataloged the HRM profiles of foreign-owned businesses and compared them with the structural configuration evident in matched domestic companies.[2] Marginson et al. (1995) found that the majority of the firms in their study monitored labor performance across units in different countries. The point made by Rowan (1977) is still valid and needs serious consideration:

> [I]t would make much more sense to compare British Petroleum with Exxon, Nestle with General Foods, Imperial Chemicals Industries with DuPont, or Lever Brothers (Unilever) with Procter & Gamble. The comparison would then be with similar companies operating in similar markets under similar conditions. (83–84)

Instead, there has been a tendency to assess multinationals' sphere of influence on workplace or institutional relationships by aggregating case studies across industries without adequate controls or by soliciting generic perceptions of foreign-owned firms via questionnaires.

The first type of design appears in Blanpain 1977. Mixing a diverse set of case reports, he argues that MNEs have not significantly altered major components of the IR systems in the United Kingdom or Belgium. On the other hand, due to the growth of the European Union, there is a trend emerging toward the internationalization of industrial relations (Streeck 1998). However, such a development has its own problems (Blyton and Turnbull 1996). Although larger organizations tended to export "innovative" policies at the outset, each system rejected those deemed to be culturally unacceptable within a relatively short period of time. Jedel and Kujawa (1977) utilized the second approach to compare foreign- and U.S.-owned businesses in the United States. On balance, neither group of managerial respondents expected MNEs to diffuse HRM innovations into the U.S. labor market. Those affiliated with British enterprises held the strongest belief in this regard. Furthermore, most of the foreign parent organizations had staffed the senior industrial relations position in a polycentric manner, increasing the likelihood of adaptation to local conditions. This is now a more general trend. Presently, MNEs generally delegate the management of labor relations to their foreign subsidiaries. However, a policy of decentralization does not keep corporate headquarters from exercising some coordination over labor relations strategy. Generally, corporate headquarters will become involved in or oversee labor agreements made by foreign subsidiaries because these agreements may affect the international plans of the firm and/or create precedents for negotiations in other countries (Dowling, Welch, and Schuler 1999, 234–35).

Besides being somewhat dated, neither investigation examines the overseas behavior of Japanese firms. Ishida (1986) asked Japanese expatriates to evaluate the extent to which numerous "Japanese" HRM policies could be, and have been, transferred abroad. Seniority-based wage and promotions systems were judged to be nontransferable in the United States, West Germany, and Southeast Asia, while the outlook for information sharing, participation, and workforce flexibility initiatives was more optimistic in all three places. Respondents in Southeast Asia also perceived that their units were further along in becoming "Japanized" than did expatriates in the West. Similar findings are reported by Shadur, Rodwell, and Bamber (1995) in their comparative study of Japanese and non-Japanese companies in three Australian industries.

While instructive, the preceding studies did not document how HRM transfer patterns actually vary across Japanese subsidiaries. Jain (1990) reported that conformist pressures were evident in Canadian units, where the parents' decision-making, group work, and industrial relations practices underwent substantial modification. In contrast, policies related to internal promotions, employment security, and benefits remained largely intact. Southeast Asian subsidiaries were not immune to isomorphic pressures either, with Singaporean units emulating parent-country practices more closely than were operations in Malaysia or India. Oliver and Wilkinson (1989) likewise found that Japanese businesses in the United Kingdom departed from only one major feature of that country's industrial relations model—an absence of multiunion bargaining relationships.

The United States has shown particular interest in the industrial relations and equal employment opportunity (EEO) posture of Japanese subsidiaries. Acknowledging several well-known incidents where unfair labor practice charges had been levied against Japanese-owned firms, Marett (1984) indicated that site locations did not necessarily coincide with regions having low unionization levels. Staffing patterns at Japanese-owned facilities have raised the specter of discrimination, though. For example, their auto plants are consistently situated in areas that have lower black-to-white population ratios than is the norm for U.S. auto plants (Cole and Deskin 1988). A subset of U.S.- and Japanese-owned greenfield sites further revealed that the latter had hired significantly fewer minorities than labor market demographics would predict.[3] Even if this evidence is taken at face value, it is unlikely that U.S. companies will be encouraged to disregard EEO mandates any more than they already are prone to do. Nearly 60 percent of the Japanese firms doing business in the United States faced possible EEO litigation by the late 1980s (Labor Letter 1989), suggesting once again that the host system actively works to neutralize objectionable MNE policies (Dowling, Welch, and Schuler 1999).

With much of the Western world mesmerized by Japanese-style management over the last few decades, it is not surprising to find a paucity of research on the effects that foreign-owned firms are having on that country's labor market practices. This may prove to be a fruitful area of study over the next decade as Japan undergoes economic restructuring to rebound from the recent global economic downturn. Aggressive long-term downsizing and the refusal to honor job contracts extended to college graduates are two departures from traditional Japanese HRM practices appearing with greater frequency (Miller 1993). Sano (1993) reports that large Japanese firms are placing increased emphasis on short-term individual performance in reward decisions, drawing more heavily from external labor markets, and shifting to flatter organizational structures. So far, these actions have been depicted as domestic initiatives rather than as spillover effects from operations that are foreign controlled. The impetus for sustained change in the HRM system may shift, though, as Japanese markets and investment opportunities become more accessible to the international community.

It is worth noting that virtually all of the investigations previously discussed focused on highly industrialized host countries. The extent to which MNEs drive the HRM policies in developing countries, places where the former's economic leverage should be at its zenith, is also of interest (Wells 1998). Regrettably, the literature offers little insight on this point (Napier and Vu 1998). Schregle (1985) discusses the lingering influence that colonizing nations often have on the postindependence labor laws of former colonies. To illustrate, French-speaking African countries drew heavily from France's Labour Code for Overseas Territories when enacting their own national labor codes. Sardi and Williamson (1989) detail the industrial relations strategy of a vertically integrated multinational operating in Nigeria; however, no comparisons were made with indigenous competitors in the same lines of business, nor was an evaluation made of the implications those strategies had for the larger labor market. Bangert and Poor (1993) studied 165 IJVs in Hungary and concluded that foreign parents were having a major impact on the HRM policies evolving in that country's transitional economy. Mankidy (1995) and Ratnam (1995) have shown a strong influence of the "British regime" (even after over fifty years of independence) on present Indian labor laws. While valuable, the qualitative insights of the studies mentioned would have been bolstered substantially by more rigorous quantitative analyses. For example, regressions could have been run in which HRM policy sophistication indices (see Delaney, Lewin, and Ichniowski 1989) were treated as dependent variables and various financial, organizational, and operational variables as predictors.

Much still needs to be learned about the dynamics of the adaptation process of MNEs within and across host countries. Several studies indicate that the IR decision making is decentralized as a rule (e.g., Reynolds 1992; Roberts and May 1974; Dowling, Welch, and Schuler 1999; Breitenfellner 1997). Yet, Hamill (1984) cautioned that there might not be uniform application of a single policy within MNEs. He uncovered varying levels of home office involvement across units based on such factors as differences in intersubsidiary product integration, unit life-cycle stage, local performance, and the scale of parent investment. Other unanswered questions include, Is there a learning curve phenomenon across MNEs, in which previous host-country experiences progressively reduce the magnitude and time of adjustment when expansion into new host nations occurs? If not, then what are the structural and cultural impediments to effective learning and its transfer? One could argue that firms with transnational HR systems (Adler and Bartholomew 1993; Bartlett and Ghoshal 1998) have a competitive advantage in recognizing and responding to these challenges (Amit and Belcourt 1999). How is the learning rate affected by host mix and home-country base? An appropriate analogy may be the impact that cultural toughness has on expatriate acculturation (Mendenhall and Oddou 1985; Mendenhall and Stahl 2000). MNEs functioning primarily in very "foreign" cultural environments should have a harder time avoiding indigenous backlashes and instituting swift, corrective measures than should those confined to more familiar cultural terrains. This problem will be exacerbated when high levels of regulatory heterogeneity, complexity, and relevancy coincide with low levels of regulatory stability and predictability (Florkowski and Nath 1993; Rugman and Verbeke 1998; Lee 1997).

NATIONAL HRM SYSTEMS AND COMPETITIVE ADVANTAGE

The existing literature is replete with cross-country comparisons of selected HRM practices (e.g., Poole 1986; Von Glinow and Chung 1989; Brewster and Hegewisch 1994; Brewster et al. 1996; Budhwar and Sparrow 1998; Sparrow and Budhwar 1997; Sparrow, Schuler, and Jackson 1994). However, this genre of work typically documents procedural or ideological differences in HRM without empirically linking such variation to behavioral or economic outcomes for organizations or societies. In an increasingly global economy, researchers need to address how country-level HRM systems impact international trade and the competitiveness of national economies (e.g., Brown and Garman 1990; Kochan, Dyer, and Batt 1992). Recently, Debrah, McGovern, and Budhwar (2000) highlighted the benefits of appropriate human resource development policies for the participating governments of a "South-east Asian growth triangle" operated by Singapore, Malaysia, and Indonesia. Accompanying methodological and substantive issues are discussed next.

COMPARATIVE FRAMEWORK

Devising an analytic scheme that effectively captures and evaluates the diversity of HRM structures, processes, policies, and policy effects across nations remains a challenge for researchers. Yeung and Wong (1990) devised a 2 x 2 classification matrix reflecting societal variations in human resource orientation and administration. The first dimension indicates whether performance or individual welfare is emphasized in the workplace, while the second refers to a reliance on internal or external labor markets. China, Japan, the United States, and the Scandinavian cluster were used to illustrate the resultant four cells. Although this framework highlights some fundamental HRM differences, its overall utility is very limited. For example, macrolevel linkages among governments, employers, and organized labor are not addressed. The same holds true for the legal systems regulating employment relationships. Most significantly, the model provides no insight into the stability of HRM patterns over time or the likely direction of future changes.

Convergence theory (Kerr et al. 1973) offers a more dynamic, albeit deterministic, view of societal HRM systems. It postulates that global market and technological forces induce economically advanced societies to erect very similar, increasingly tripartite, superstructures for industrial relations in the long run. Large macrolevel differences in these arrangements essentially indicate that nations occupy different points on the maturity curve for industrialization. However, available evidence does not support a homogenization of institutions and practices within or among developed economies (e.g., Dore 1973; Maurice, Sellier, and Silvestre 1986; Poole 1986; Sparrow and Budhwar 1997; McGaughey and De Cieri 1999). McGaughey and De Cieri (1999), however, argue that organizations are becoming more similar in terms of macrolevel variables (convergence) but are maintaining their culturally based dissimilarities in terms of microlevel variables (divergence).

Begin (1992, 1997) discusses national HRM systems in terms of lifecycle transitions, stressing their ongoing synchronization with a country's dominant industrial structure. He uses information from six countries as case studies. These countries are Japan, the United States, the United Kingdom, Germany, Sweden, and Singapore. Unlike the preceding model, changes do not necessarily reflect movement toward a final set of institutional configurations, nor are they irreversible. According to Begin, HRM systems containing limited, informal rules should emerge when a nation's firms are operating predominantly in simple but dynamic environments. As that technologically simple environment becomes more stable, there is an expectation that organizations that function as machine bureaucracies will proliferate and eventually alter the general character of HRM systems in that society. This aggregate "shift" in organizational form and its accompanying formalization of virtually all HRM activities allegedly mark the arrival of a mature market economy.

Movement to the next evolutionary stage of more temporary and adaptable organizations will not be triggered unless a preponderance of firms enter and compete in more complex, dynamic environments.[4] Here, businesses secure and maintain international competitive advantage through continual innovation, which is fueled by relaxed work/job allocation systems as well as development- and retention-oriented systems for staffing, governance, and rewards (Begin 1997). Likely candidates for this transition are newly industrialized economies where substantial increases in the standard of living jeopardize initial factor-cost advantages associated with labor. To illustrate, Singapore is aggressively pursuing this end through government policies designed to create a technically sophisticated educational system, to expand indigenous research facilities, and to foster more technological partnerships with MNEs (Debrah, McGovern, and Budhwar 2000).

A societal decline in innovative activity eventually leads to some form of retrenchment in HRM systems. When major industries cease to innovate because they have entered a wealth phase, organizational rigidities set in and productivity improvements lessen. Professional bureaucracies eventually supplant ad hoc structures so long as indigenous firms utilize the technology advances pioneered elsewhere. Increased emphasis is placed on formal security, governance, and reward systems at the expense of those pertaining to the structuring of work, staffing, and development. Nations failing to keep abreast of the state of the art in technology risk backsliding further into the machine bureaucracy phase with its restrictive HRM systems. Indigenous employees also find themselves confronted with a declining standard of living because productivity gains do not generate enough revenue to advance the general social welfare.

Numerous research issues are embedded in Begin's (1997) broad framework. To begin with, how do national reward structures affect a country's competitiveness within and across these life-cycle stages? The level, form, and stability of these components over time are paramount concerns. The ability to compete within and across life-cycle stages may also be a function of organized labor's control over labor costs and industrial conflict levels. Each of these items is addressed more fully next.

REWARD POLICIES

COMPENSATION

The U.S. Bureau of Labor Statistics has compiled standardized information on international compensation policies in the manufacturing sector. Unpublished reports are available on hourly compensation costs, which include payments made directly to employees and employer benefit contributions, adjusted for exchange rates.[5] Table 11.4 contains recent time-series data for Canada, the United States, Mexico, Japan, South Korea, Taiwan, France, Germany, Italy, and the United Kingdom. Begin (1997) classified Mexico, South Korea, Taiwan, Canada, and the United Kingdom as countries where the dominant HRM systems are machine bureaucracies.[6] A low-wage strategy seems to endow the first three nations with a distinct labor factor advantage relative to the other two in this stage, not to mention those occupying more industrially advanced states. Continuing with Begin's paradigm, adhocracies or professional bureaucracies are dominant among the remaining countries in table 11.4. Cost competition within this group intensified in the 1980s and early 1990s, which is best

TABLE 11.4. Hourly Compensation Costs for Production Workers: Index: U.S. 100

Country	1983	1984	1985	1986	1987	1988	1989	1990	1991	1992
United States	100	100	100	100	100	100	100	100	100	100
Canada	87	85	84	87	89	97	104	107	110	105
Mexico	10	9	12	8	7	9	10	11	13	15
Japan	58	58	49	90	80	91	87	85	93	100
Korea	15	14	10	17	12	17	23	26	28	30
Taiwan	12	14	12	19	17	20	25	26	28	32
France	73	73	58	79	91	93	88	102	98	104
Germany	80	79	74	107	126	131	124	147	145	160
Italy	71	71	59	95	96	101	101	117	117	120
United Kingdom	66	68	48	68	67	76	74	88	88	91

Source: U.S. Bureau of Labor Statistics, unpublished data

illustrated in the disappearing Japanese-American wage differential. French manufacturers also came ever closer to parity with their American rivals. By 1992, Italy and Germany were encumbered with labor costs that were substantially higher than those found elsewhere.

A major shortcoming in this kind of analysis is the failure to integrate productivity and quality measures. These items constitute the return on investment from compensation expenditures. In the United States, for example, many firms that initially relocated in Mexico because of lower wages are repatriating their operations because of low productivity and ancillary costs (Mayer 1993). While standardized productivity data are available for many countries (e.g., Staff 1991), pertinent quality indices generally are not. Such information must become more accessible before meaningful comparisons can be made. Also, there is a need to understand the assumptions that underlie much reward behavior and the implications of perceived changes in trust, motivation, and commitment. It is also important to understand what pay means to people in different cultures (Sparrow 2000, 203).

BENEFITS

Appropriately configured benefit plans may be instrumental in securing an employee mix that promotes competitive advantage for individual firms (Bowen and Wadley 1989; Lazear 1990; Hempel 1999; Boxall 1995). To what extent can this be extrapolated to national economies? Aggregated policies may have distinctive signatures regarding the proportion of total rewards comprising benefits, the benefit options typically offered, and the extent to which these items are privately or publicly financed.

For example, a recent study found that South Korean and Japanese employers consistently disbursed less of their rewards in the form of benefits than did other nations over the period under study. The United States fell in the middle of the pack, at odds with the common perception of American firms having outlier status. It is interesting to note that the United Kingdom gravitated closer to the Japanese than to the American mix as the 1980s unfolded. German and French companies, in contrast, repeatedly allocated higher proportions of compensation to benefits (Towers-Perrin 1999).

Can national productivity or quality differentials be attributed in part to such variations? We are not aware of any research that has examined this issue directly. Several U.S. studies indicate that employees tend to underestimate substantially the benefit costs borne by the employer *(Employee Benefit Plan Review* 1984; Lewellen and Lanser 1973; Wilson, Northcraft, and Neale 1985). If this can be generalized across cultures, then feelings of pay inequity and its dysfunctional organizational consequences should become more widespread in national labor markets as employers channel larger fractions of their labor costs into benefits. Differences in the way benefits are paid for may be more telling of a country's competitiveness (White, Druker, and Chiu 1998). To illustrate, national health care and/or pension systems potentially free up employer resources to invest in new benefit categories or pay-for-performance schemes. This social reallocation of costs may have a more significant impact on international trade than the relative level of benefits per se (Belous 1984, 23). Recently, Sparrow examined the dynamics of international reward management in a number of countries. Discussing the importance of culture value orientations, distributive justice, and pay differentials, he concludes that MNEs attempting to harmonize reward systems will face predictable patterns of resistance across different nations. Highlighting the importance of local institutional context, Sparrow (2000, 210) suggests that there should be considerable local autonomy of practice allowed within MNEs and distinctive pay and benefit practices will remain within domestic organizations.

TRADE UNIONS

Research shows that U.S. unions generally exert more influence over wages than do their counterparts in other industrialized nations (Blanchflower and Freeman 1992; Katz and Darbishire 2000). A U.S. government study criticized the way that labor leaders wield this power, concluding that import penetration levels stem largely from high union wages in the United States (U.S. Federal Trade Commission 1987). Other evidence indicates that import activity creates substantial downward pressures on U.S. union-nonunion wage differentials and union-sector employment (Macpherson and Stewart 1990; Abowd and Lemieux 1991).

This research suggests that the economic policies of U.S. unions are one reason why U.S. firms have difficulty competing with foreign producers. Yet, unionization rates are not systematically higher in high net-importing industries than they are in low net-importing ones (Karier 1991a, 1991b). Furthermore, LeGrande (1988) found that changes in the value of the U.S. dollar against foreign currencies had a much more significant effect on the relative labor costs of domestic and foreign manufacturers during the 1980s than did collectively bargained wage levels. If so, then securing wage concessions does not go to the heart of the competitiveness problem—unstable exchange rates—which cannot be redressed at the bargaining table. More empirical work is needed to reconcile such divergent findings. It may be particularly fruitful to examine the relationship between union density and import penetration in industries outside the United States.

The propensity for industrial conflict should significantly impede a society's ability to devise and administer competitive HRM systems regardless of the market niche that has been targeted. Ofori-Dankwa (1993) conjectured that conflict levels are dictated by a country's dominant union paradigm and environmental munificence (i.e., resource- or institutional-based buffering). During periods of positive munificence, nations characterized by unions that operate with a high-political, low-economic paradigm (e.g., France) should display less conflict than those saddled with unions embracing a low-political, high-economic orientation (e.g., the United States). The converse is predicted in times of negative munificence, as politically active labor organizations seek to embarrass the opposing ("antilabor") party in power. High-political, high-economic paradigms (e.g., Great Britain, Sweden) should engender responses that are more sensitive to specific combinations of positive/negative resource and institutional buffering (Puchala 1999).

While these hypothesized relationships are intriguing, there are formidable impediments to testing them at this time. Industrial conflict measures are not standardized transnationally, raising serious construct validity concerns in intercountry comparisons. Identical workplace disputes can be treated differently based on the prevailing decision rules governments use for statistical record keeping. There also are several aspects of strikes to consider, including frequency, breadth, duration, and impact (Stern 1978). How does one integrate these factors to provide a comprehensive evaluation of societal performance? Poole (1986) developed strike activity profiles for eighteen countries utilizing the first three dimensions. While this scheme does facilitate assessments within each of the five patterns that were presented, it is less clear how one makes interprofile judgments without referring to some quantification of impact. For example, is it more desirable to see duration, breadth, or frequency as the dominant structural feature of strikes? One must decide this on the basis of cultural preferences unless information about impact is integrated.

There is even less work regarding union political activities and institutional buffering (Weiss 1998). Neither construct has been sufficiently operationalized for cross-cultural studies. The conventional wisdom is that European unions are much more engrossed in politics than are their U.S. cohorts, but it is hard to separate well-publicized, militant rhetoric from actual involvement or effectiveness (e.g., per capita dues allocated to political activity, the relative structure of those activities, impact on regulatory processes, and outcome). Such indicators may be relevant in sorting out unions' concentration on strategic, as opposed to functional or workplace, issues among nations (Kochan, McKersie, and Cappelli 1984; Teague 2000; Marginson and Sisson 1998; Ramsay 1997).

CONCLUSION

Over the last decade or so, IHRM research has covered a lot of ground; however, the published research to date raises many more questions that should be the focus of future research. This review of the literature was couched in a strategic context based on the expectation that IHRM increasingly will become a source of competitive advantage in global as well as multidomestic markets. Accordingly, there is a strong need to improve our understanding of the approaches that MNEs utilize to satisfy the competing needs for integration and differentiation in their operations. Adler and Bartholomew (1992) found that a growing proportion of published organizational behavior/IHRM research is focusing on international interactions (i.e., interactions among organizational members from two or more countries). Improving the ability of MNEs to manage cultural interactions enhances the prospects of satisfying both needs.

Specific IHRM policies and practices have commanded varying levels of research attention, clustering primarily in staffing and training. We have pointed out where future studies can make incremental advances in these functional areas, as well as in those areas that have been largely overlooked in the past. Even stronger is the need to *empirically* link IHRM policies with behavioral and financial outcomes and a firm's performance in individual business units and the overall firm.

This goes beyond descriptive case studies and surveys conveying frequency distributions, modes of analysis that still represent a large proportion of reported research in this field. More rigorous designs must be devised that better operationalize IHRM variables, formally test a priori hypotheses about their impact on efficiency and effectiveness, and incorporate adequate controls (see also Boyacigiller and Adler 1991, 279–80; Buller and McEvoy 1993; Guest 1997). Such refinements will greatly improve our ability to document the value-added that flows from IHRM initiatives—a prerequisite to meaningful comparisons of transnational HR systems and less sophisticated alternatives. Qualitative research remains an essential tool in studying the process by which IHRM policies evolve, diffuse, and are institutionalized in multinationals.

Finally, researchers should not lose sight of the interface between HRM systems that MNEs utilize and the national HRM systems that comprise their operating environment. Prior studies indicate that multinationals have a limited capacity to alter the entrenched features of indigenous employment relationships. It remains unclear how multinationals react to impending HRM life-cycle transitions in a given country. Are MNEs prone to adapt to such changes faster than their domestic competitors? What role do MNEs play in the rate of change and stabilization of new HRM systems? Do host countries selectively pressure multinationals with "deviant" HRM systems to conform to prevailing practices based on their home country? For example, advanced industrialized nations may enforce their employment laws more vigorously against MNEs from other developed nations with objectionable trade barriers than against those based elsewhere. Ultimately, international human resource management research must unite these micro- and macrolevel perspectives.

As demonstrated by this review, interested scholars have myriad opportunities to help international business organizations develop and sustain human resource–based competitive advantages. Researchers and firms that chart these waters effectively will secure enviable market positions in the decades ahead.

NOTES

1. Some controversy exists regarding the extent to which MNEs operate as change agents within the industrial relations systems of host countries. Available evidence on this point is reviewed later in the chapter.

2. Hamill (1983, 1984) analyzed numerous labor relations practices of U.S.- and British-owned MNEs in three British industries and found some differences. As noted earlier, Tung (1982) found that the deployment patterns for host top management differed by MNE home-country and assignment region. Training content also varied with home office location. Other investigations have compared the compensation/benefits packages of MNEs and domestic firms in industrialized host countries, reporting that multinationals

generally meet or exceed what domestic firms provide (International Labour Office 1976). It is our contention that the complete set of HRM policies must be inventoried and evaluated to ascertain their cultural ramifications, as well as their ability to elicit the role behaviors essential to a particular competitive strategy (Schuler and Jackson 1987).

3. However, the authors noted that U.S. firms in other industries have not behaved markedly different when launching greenfield operations.

4. Begin (1997) also contends that ad hoc HRM systems may serve as an alternative starting point, although it is difficult to envision how this would occur.

5. The former component encompasses take-home pay, payments for nonwork time (i.e., holidays, vacations), and the cost of in-kind benefits; the latter covers payments for legally required insurance programs and collectively bargained/private benefits.

6. The first three countries are solidifying their recent entry into this life-cycle stage, the fourth never really evolved beyond it, while the fifth receded back into it during the post–World War II era.

REFERENCES

Abowd, J. M., and T. Lemieux. 1991. The effects of international competition on collective bargaining outcomes: A comparison of the United States and Canada. In J. M. Abowd and R. B. Freeman, eds., *Immigration, trade, and the labor market.* Chicago: University of Chicago Press.

Adler, N. J. 1991. *International dimensions of organizational behavior.* Boston: PWS-Kent.

———. 1994. Competitive frontiers: Women managing across borders. In N. J. Adler and D. N. Izraeli, eds., *Competitive frontiers: Women managers in a global economy.* Cambridge, MA: Blackwell.

———. 1997. *International dimensions of organizational behavior.* 3d ed. Cincinnati: South-Western College Publishing.

Adler, N. J., and S. Bartholomew. 1992. Academic and professional communities of discourse: Generating knowledge on transnational human resource management. *Journal of International Business Studies* 23:551–69.

———. 1993. Managing globally competent people. *Academy of Management Executive* 6 (3): 52–65.

Adler, N. J., and N. Boyacigiller. 1993. Going beyond traditional HRM scholarship. In D. M. Saunders, ed., *New Approaches to Employee Management,* vol. 3. Greenwich, CT: JAI Press.

Adler, N. J., and E. Ghadar. 1990. Strategic human resource management: A global perspective. In R. Pieper, ed., *Human Resource Management in International Comparison.* Berlin: de Gruyter.

Amit, R., and M. Belcourt. 1999. Human resources management processes: A value-creating source of competitive advantage. *European Management Journal* 17 (2): 174–81.

Arvey, R. D., R. S. Bhagat, and E. Salas. 1991. Cross-cultural and cross-national issues in personnel and human resources management: Where do we go from here? In K. M. Rowland, ed., *Research in Personnel and Human Resources Management,* vol. 9. Greenwich, CT: JAI Press.

Bamber, G. J., and R. D. Lansbury, eds. 1998. *International and comparative employment relations: A study of industrialized market economies.* London: Sage.

Banai, M. 1992. The ethnocentric staffing policy in multinational corporations: A self-fulfilling prophecy. *International Journal of Human Resource Management* 3:451–72.

Bangert, D., and J. Poor. 1993. Foreign involvement in the Hungarian economy: Its impact on human resource management. *International Journal of Human Resource Management* 4:817–40.

Barkema, H. G., O. Shenkar, F. Vermeulen, and J. H. J. Bell. 1997. Working abroad, working with others: How firms learn to operate international joint ventures. *Academy of Management Journal* 40 (2): 426–42.

Bartlett, C. 1992. Christopher Bartlett on transnationals: An interview. *European Management Journal* (September):271–76.

Bartlett, C. A., and S. Ghoshal. 1991. *Managing across borders: The transnational solution.* London: London Business School.

———. 1992. What is a global manager? *Harvard Business Review* (September–October):124–32.

———. 1998. *Managing across borders: The transnational solution.* 2d ed. London: Random House.

———. 2000. Going global: Lessons for late movers. *Harvard Business Review* (March–April):132–42.

Begin, J. P. 1992. Comparative human resource management (HRM): A systems perspective. *International Journal of Human Resource Management* 3:379–408.

———. 1997. *Dynamic human resource systems: Cross-national comparisons.* Berlin and New York: Walter de Gruyter.

Belous, R. S. 1984. An international comparison of fringe benefits: Theory, evidence, and policy implications. Report 84-815E. Washington, DC: Congressional Research Service.

Biles, G. E., and R. S. Schuler. 1986. *Audit handbook of human resource practices: Auditing the effectiveness of the human resource functions.* Alexandria, VA: American Society for Personnel Administration.

Bird, A., S. Taylor, and S. Beechler. 1998. A typology of international human resource management in Japanese multinational corporations: Organizational implications. *Human Resource Management* 37 (2): 159–72.

Black, J. S., and H. B. Gregersen. 2000. High impact training: Forging leaders for the global frontier. *Human Resource Management* 39 (2–3): 173–84.

Black, J. S., H. B. Gregersen, and M. Mendenhall. 1992. *Global assignments.* San Francisco: Jossey-Bass.

Black, J. S., H. B. Gregersen, M. Mendenhall, and L. K. Stroh. 1999. *Globalizing people through international assignments.* Reading, MA: Addison-Wesley.

Black, J. S., and M. Mendenhall. 1990. Cross-cultural training effectiveness: A review and a theoretical framework for future research. *Academy of Management Review* 15 (1): 113–36.

Blanchflower, D. G., and R. B. Freeman. 1992. Unionism in the United States and other advanced OECD countries. *Industrial Relations* 31:56–79.

Blanpain, R. 1977. Multinationals' impact on host country industrial relations. In R. F.

Banks and J. Stieber, eds., *Multinationals, unions, and labor relations in industrialized countries.* Ithaca, NY: Cornell University.

Blyton, P., and P. Turnbull. 1996. Confusing convergence: Industrial relations in the European airline industry. *European Journal of Industrial Relations* 2 (1): 7–20.

Bowen, D. E., and C. A. Wadley. 1989. Designing a strategic benefits plan. *Compensation and Benefits Review* 215:44–56.

Boxall, P. F. 1995. Building the theory of comparative HRM. *Human Resource Management Journal* 5:5–17.

Boyacigiller, N. A., and N. J. Adler. 1991. The parochial dinosaur: Organizational science in a global context. *Academy of Management Review* 16:262–90.

Bradley, P., C. Hendry, and S. Perkins. 1999. Global or multi-local? The significance of international values in reward strategy. In C. Brewster and H. Harris, eds., *International HR,* 120–42. London and New York: Routledge.

Breitenfellner, A. 1997. Global unionism: A potential player. *International Labour Review* 136 (4): 531–55.

Brewster, C. 1988. *The management of expatriates.* Human Resource Research Centre Monograph Series, no. 2. Bedford, UK: Cranfield School of Management.

———. 1993. Developing a "European" model of human resource management. *International Journal of Human Resource Management* 4:765–84.

———. 1995. Towards a European model of human resource management. *Journal of International Business Studies* 26:1–22.

Brewster, C., and A. Hegewisch, eds. 1994. *Policy and practice in European human resource management.* London: Routledge.

Brewster, C., H. H. Larsen, and W. Mayrhofer. 1997. Integration and assignment: A paradox in human resource management. *Journal of International Management* 13:1–23.

Brewster, C., and H. Scullion. 1997. A review and agenda for expatriate HRM. *Human Resource Management Journal* 7 (3): 32–41.

Brewster, C., O. Tregaskis, A. Hegewisch, and L. Mayne. 1996. Comparative research in human resource management: A review and an example. *International Journal of Human Resource Management* 7:586–604.

Brewster, C., and S. Tyson. 1991. *International comparisons in human resource management.* London: Pitman.

Brown, D. K., and D. M. Garman. 1990. Human resource management and international trade. *Industrial Relations* 29:189–213.

Buckley, P. J., and M. C. Casson. 1976. *The future of the multinational enterprise.* London: Macmillan.

———. 1998. Models of the multinational enterprise. *Journal of International Business Studies* 29 (1): 21–44.

Budhwar, P., and Y. A. Debrah. 2000. Rethinking comparative and cross national human resource management research. *International Journal of Human Resource Management* 12 (3): 497–515.

Budhwar, P., and P. R. Sparrow. 1998. National factors determining Indian and British HRM practices: An empirical study. *Management International Review* 38 (2): 105–21. Special issue.

———. 2002. An integrative framework for determining cross national human resource management practices. *Human Resource Management Review* 12 (3): 377–403.

Buller, R. E., and G. M. McEvoy. 1993. International management research: Challenges and exemplars. Unpublished manuscript.

Caligiuri, P. M. 2000. Selecting expatriates for personality characteristics: A moderating effect of personality on the relationship between host national contact and cross-cultural adjustment. *Management International Review* 40 (1): 61–80.

Caligiuri, P. M., and M. Lazarova. 2000. Strategic repatriation policies to enhance global leadership development. In M. Mendenhall, T. Kuehlmann, and G. Stahl, eds., *Developing global business leaders: Policies, processes, and innovation.* New York: Quorum Books.

Caligiuri, P. M., and L. K. Stroh. 1995. Multinational corporation management strategies and international human resources practices: Bringing IHRM to the bottom line. *International Journal of Human Resource Management* 6 (2): 495–507.

Campbell, D. C., and R. L. Rowan. 1983. *Multinational enterprises and the OECD industrial relations guidelines.* Philadelphia: Industrial Research Unit, University of Pennsylvania.

Cappelli, P., and R. McElrath. 1992. The transfer of employment practices through multinationals. Working paper, Wharton School, University of Pennsylvania.

Cascio, W., and E. Bailey. 1995. International human resource management: The state of research and practice. In O. Shenkar, ed., *Global perspectives of human resource management,* 15–36. Englewood Cliffs, NJ: Prentice Hall.

Casson, M. C. 1982. Transaction costs and the theory of the multinational enterprise. In A. Rugman, ed., *New theories of the multinational enterprise.* New York: St. Martin's Press.

Caves, R. E. 1996. *Multinational enterprise and economic analysis.* 2d ed. Cambridge: Cambridge University Press.

Chan, A. W. 1999. Managing HRs across the border: Two cases of Hong Kong-based joint ventures in China. *International Journal of Management* 16 (4): 586–93.

Child, J., and D. Faulkner. 1998. *Strategies of cooperation,* Oxford: Oxford University Press.

Clark, T., H. Gospel, and J. Montgomery. 1999. Running on the spot? A review of twenty years of research on the management of human resources in comparative and international perspective. *International Journal of Human Resource Management* 10 (3): 520–44.

Cole, R. E., and D. R. Deskin. 1988. Racial factors in site location and employment patterns of Japanese auto firms in America. *California Management Review* 31:9–21.

Coopers and Lybrand/Yankelovich, D. Skelly, and White, Inc. 1986. *Collaborative ventures: A pragmatic approach to business expansion in the eighties.* New York: Coopers and Lybrand.

Copp, R. 1977. Locus of industrial relations decision making in multinationals. In R. F. Banks and J. Stieber, eds., *Multinationals, unions, and labor relations in industrialized countries.* Ithaca, NY: Cornell University.

Cyr, D. J. 1995. *The human resource challenge of international joint ventures.* Westport, CT: Quorum.

———. 1997. Culture and control: The tale of East-West joint ventures. *Management International Review* 1:127–44. Special issue.

Davison, E. D., and B. J. Punnett. 1995. International assignments: Is there a role for gender and race in decisions? *International Journal of Human Resource Management* 6 (2): 411–41.

Debrah, Y. A., I. McGovern, and P. Budhwar. 2000. Complementarity or competition: The development of human resources in a growth triangle. *International Journal of Human Resource Management* 11 (2): 314–35.

De Cieri, H., and P. J. Dowling. 1997. Strategic human resource management: An Asia-Pacific perspective. *Management International Review* 1:21–42. Special issue.

Delaney, J. T., D. Lewin, and C. Ichniowski. 1989. Human resource policies and practices in American firms. BLMR Report 137. Washington, DC: U.S. Government Printing Office.

Dore, R. 1973. *British factory, Japanese factory: The origins of national diversity in industrial relations.* Berkeley, CA: University of California Press.

Dowling, P. J. 1988. International HRM. In L. Dyer, ed., *Human resource management: Evolving roles and responsibilities.* Washington, DC: Bureau of National Affairs.

———. 1998. Completing the puzzle: Issues in the development of the field of international human resource management. Keynote address to the sixth International Human Resource Management Conference, Paderborn, June 1998.

Dowling, P. J., and R. S. Schuler. 1990. *International dimensions of human resource management.* Boston: PWS-Kent.

Dowling, P. J., R. S. Schuler, and D. E. Welch. 1994. *International dimensions of human resource management.* 2d ed. Belmont, CA: Wadsworth.

Dowling, P. J., D. E. Welch, and R. S. Schuler. 1999. *International dimensions of human resource management.* 3d ed. Cincinnati: South-Western College Publishing.

Downes, M., and A. S. Thomas. 1999. Managing overseas assignments to build organizational knowledge. *Human Resource Planning* 22 (4): 33–48.

Doz, Y. L., and C. K. Prahalad. 1986. Controlled variety: A challenge for human resource management in the MNC. *Human Resource Management* 25:55–71.

Dyer, L. 1991. Evolving role of the human resource organization. Working paper, Center for Advanced Human Resource Studies, ILR School, Cornell University.

Edstrom, A., and J. Galbraith. 1977. Transfer of managers as a coordination and control strategy in multinational organizations. *Administrative Science Quarterly* 22:248–63.

Edwards, P., A. Ferner, and K. Sisson. 1996. The conditions for international human resource management: Two case studies. *International Journal of Human Resource Management* 7 (1): 20–40.

Employee Benefit Plan Review. 1984. (October):46–47.

Evans, P. 1986. The context of strategic human resource management policy in complex firms. *Management Forum* 6:105–7.

———. 1992. Management development as glue technology. *Human Resource Planning* 15:85–106.

Ferner, A., and M. Varul. 2000. "Vanguard" subsidiaries and the diffusion of new practices: A case study of German multinationals. *British Journal of Industrial Relations* 38 (1): 115–40.

Festing, M. 1997. International human resource management strategies in multinational corporations: Theoretical assumptions and empirical evidence from German firms. *Management International Review* 1:43–63. Special issue.

Fey, C. F., and P. W. Beamish. 2000. Joint venture conflict: The case of Russian international joint ventures. *International Business Review* 9:139–62.

Florkowski, G. W., and R. Nath. 1993. MNC responses to the legal environment of international human resource management. *International Journal of Human Resource Management* 4:305–24.

Florkowski, G. W., and R. S. Schuler. 1994. Auditing human resource management in the global environment. *International Journal of Human Resource Management* (December): 827–52.

Frayne, C. A., and J. M. Geringer. 1990. The strategic use of human resource management practices as control mechanisms in international joint ventures. In K. M. Rowland, ed., *Research in personnel and human resource management,* vol. 2. Greenwich, CT: JAI Press.

Fulkerson, J. R., and R. S. Schuler. 1992. Managing worldwide diversity at Pepsi-Cola International. In Susan Jackson, ed., *Diversity in the workplace.* New York: Guilford.

Galbraith, J. R. 1987. Organization design. In J. W. Lorch, ed., *Handbook of organization behavior.* Englewood Cliffs, NJ: Prentice-Hall.

Galbraith, J. R., and R. Kazanjian. 1986. *Strategy implementation: The role of structure in process.* St. Paul: West Publishing.

Geringer, J. M. 1991. Strategic determinants of partner selection criteria in international joint ventures. *Journal of International Business Studies* 22:41–62.

Gomez-Mejia, L. R. 1985. Dimensions and correlates of the personnel audit as an organizational assessment tool. *Personnel Psychology* 38:293–308.

Grant, R. M., and J. C. Spender. 1996. Knowledge and the firm: An overview. *Strategic Management Journal* 12:83–103.

Guest, D. E. 1997. Human resource management and performance: A review and research agenda. *International Journal of Human Resource Management* 8 (3): 263–76.

Hailey, J. 1992. Localization and expatriation: The continuing role of expatriates in developing countries. Paper presented at the 1992 European Institute for Advanced Studies in Management workshop, Cranfield, England.

Haines, V. Y., III, and T. Saba. 1999. Understanding reactions to international mobility policies and practices. *Human Resource Planning* 22 (3): 40–52.

Hambrick, D. C., and C. C. Snow. 1989. Strategic reward systems. In C. C. Snow, ed., *Strategy, organization design, and human resource management.* Greenwich, CT: JAI Press.

Hamel, G., and C. K. Prahalad. 1986. Do you really have a global strategy? *Harvard Business Review* (July–August):139–48.

Hamill, J. 1983. The labor relations practices of foreign-owned and indigenous firms. *Employee Relations* 51:14–16.

———. 1984. Labor relations decision making within multinational corporations. *Industrial Relations Journal* 15 (2): 30–34.

Hammer, M. R., W. Hart, and R. Rogan. 1998. Can you go home again? An analysis of the repatriation of corporate managers and spouses. *Management International Review* 38 (1): 67–86.

Handler, C. A., and I. M. Lane. 1997. Career planning and expatriate couples. *Human Resource Management Journal* 7 (3): 67–79.

Harbison, J. R. 1996. *Strategic alliances: Gaining a competitive advantage.* New York: The Conference Board.

Harris, H., and C. Brewster. 1999a. International human resource management: The European contribution. In C. Brewster and H. Harris, eds., *International HR,* 1–18. London and New York: Routledge.

———. 1999b. An integrative framework for pre-departure preparation. In C. Brewster and H. Harris, eds., *International HR,* 223–40. London and New York: Routledge.

Harvey, M. G., and M. R. Buckley. 1998. The process for developing an international program for dual-career couples. *Human Resource Management Review* 8 (1): 99–123.

Harvey, M., M. F. Price, C. Speier, and M. M. Novicevic. 1999. The role of inpatriates in a globalization strategy and challenges associated with the inpatriation process. *Human Resource Planning* 22 (1): 38–50.

Harvey, M. G., and D. Wiese. 1998. The dual-career couple: Female expatriates and male trailing spouses. *Thunderbird International Business Review* 40 (4): 359–88.

Harzing, A. W. 2000. An empirical analysis and extension of the Bartlett and Ghoshal typology of multinational companies. *Journal of International Business Studies* 31 (1): 101–20.

Harzing, A. W. 1995. The persistent myth of high expatriate failure rates. *International Journal of Human Resource Management* 6 (2): 457–74.

———. 1999a. *Managing the multinationals: An international study of control mechanisms.* Cheltenham: Edward Elgar.

———. 1999b. MNE staffing policies for the managing director position in foreign subsidiaries: The results of an innovative research method. In C. Brewster and H. Harris, eds., *International HR,* 67–88. London and New York: Routledge.

Harzing, A. W., and J. Van Ruysseveldt, eds. 1995. *International human resource management.* London: Sage.

Heenan, D. A., and H. V. Perlmutter. 1979. *Multinational organization development.* Reading, MA: Addison-Wesley.

Hempel, P. S. 1999. Designing multinational benefits programs: The role of national culture. *Journal of World Business* 33 (3): 277–94.

Hendry, C. 1992. Human resource management in the international firm. Paper presented to the VET Forum Conference "Multinational Companies and Human Resources: A Moveable Feast?" University of Warwick, June 22–24.

———. 1996. Continuities in human resource processes in internationalization and domestic business management. *Journal of Management Studies* 33:475–94.

Hermart, J. E. 1982. *A theory of the multinational enterprise.* Ann Arbor: University of Michigan Press.

Hough, J. 1989. Critical dimensions for foreign assignment selection. Minneapolis, MN: Personnel Decisions Research Institute. Internal document.

International Labour Office. 1976. *Multinationals in Western Europe: The industrial relations experience.* Geneva: ILD.

Ishida, H. 1986. Transferability of Japanese human resource management abroad. *Human Resource Management* 25:103–20.

Izraeli, D. N., and N. J. Adler. 1994. Competitive frontiers: Women managers in a global economy. In N. J. Adler and D. N. Izraeli, eds., *Competitive frontiers: Women managers in a global economy.* Cambridge, MA: Blackwell.

Jackson, S. E., and R. S. Schuler. 2000. *Managing human resources: A partnership perspective.* 7th ed. Cincinnati, OH: South-Western Publishing.

Jain, H. C. 1990. Human resource management in selected Japanese firms, their foreign subsidiaries, and locally owned counterparts. *International Labour Review* 129:73–89.

Jedel, M. J., and D. Kujawa. 1977. Industrial relations profiles of foreign-owned manufacturers in the United States. In R. F. Banks and J. Stieber, eds., *Multinationals, unions, and labor relations in industrialized countries.* Ithaca, NY: Cornell University.

Jennings, C., W. E. J. McCarthy, and R. Undy. 1990. *Employee relations audits.* London: Routledge.

Karier, T. 1991a. Unions and the U.S. comparative advantage. *Industrial Relations* 30:1–19.

———. 1991b. Unions: Cause or victim of U.S. trade deficit? *Challenge* 34:34–41.

Katz, H. C., and O. Darbishire. 2000. *Converging divergences: Worldwide changes in employment systems.* Ithaca: ILR Press.

Katz, J. P., and S. W. Elsea. 1997. A framework for assessing international labor relations: What every HR manager needs to know. *Human Resource Planning* 20 (4): 16–25.

Kerr, C., J. Dunlop, E. Harbison, and C. Myers. 1973. *Industrialism and industrial man: The problems of labour and management in economic growth.* Rev. ed. Harmondsworth: Penguin.

Killing, J. P. 1983. *Strategies for joint venture success.* New York: Praeger.

Kobrin, S. J. 1988. Expatriate reduction and strategic control in American multinational corporations. *Human Resource Management* 27:63–75.

———. 1992. Multinational strategy and international human resource management policy. Unpublished paper, Wharton School, University of Pennsylvania.

Kochan, I. A., L. Dyer, and R. Batt. 1992. International human resource studies: A framework for future research. *Research frontiers in industrial relations and human resources.* Madison, WI: Industrial Relations Research Association.

Kochan, I. A., R. McKersie, and P. Cappelli. 1984. Strategic choice and industrial relations theory. *Industrial Relations* 23:16–39.

Kogut, B. 1989. A note on global strategies. *Strategic Management Journal* 10:383–89.

Labor Letter. 1989. *Wall Street Journal,* August 28, A1.

Latta, G. W. 1999. The impact of European integration on human resource management. *Benefits and Compensation International* 28 (6): 20–24.

Laurent, A. 1986. The cross-cultural puzzle of international human resource management. *Human Resource Management* 25:91–102.

Lawrence, P. R., and J. W. Lorsch. 1967. *Organization and environment.* Cambridge, MA: Harvard University Press.

Lazear, E. P. 1990. Pensions and deferred benefits as strategic compensation. *Industrial Relations* 29:263–80.

Lee, E. 1997. Globalization and labour standards: A review of issues. *International Labour Review* 136 (2): 173–89.

Lei, D., J. W. Slocum Jr., and R. A. Pitts. 1997. Building cooperative advantage: Managing strategic alliances to promote organizational learning. *Journal of World Business* 32 (3): 202–23.

LeGrande, L. 1988. Wage rates and exchange rates. Washington, DC: Congressional Research Service. Staff report.

Lewellen, W. G., and H. P. Lanser. 1973. Executive pay preferences. *Harvard Business Review* 51 (5): 115–22.

Lindholm, N., M. Tahvanainen, and B. Ingmar. 1999. Performance appraisal of host country employees: Western MNEs in China. In C. Brewster and H. Harris, eds., *International HR*, 143–59. London and New York: Routledge.

Locke, R., and K. Thelen. 1995. Apples and oranges revisited: Contextualized comparisons and the study of comparative labor politics. *Politics and Society* 23:337–67.

Macpherson, D. A., and J. B. Stewart. 1990. The effect of international competition on union and nonunion wages. *Industrial and Labor Relations Review* 43:434–46.

Makhija, M. V., and U. Ganesh. 1997. The relationship between control and partner learning in learning related joint ventures. *Organizational Science* 8 (2): 508–24.

Mankidy, J. 1995. Changing perspectives of workers participation in India with particular reference to banking industry. *British Journal of Industrial Relations* 33 (3): 443–58.

Marett, P. C. 1984. Japanese-owned firms in the United States: Do they resist unionism? *Labor Law Journal* 35:240–50.

Marginson, P. 1992. European integration and transnational management-union relations in the enterprise. *British Journal of Industrial Relations* 30:529–45.

Marginson, P., P. Armstrong, P. K. Edwards, and J. Purcell. 1995. Extending beyond borders: Multinational companies and international management of labour. *International Journal of Human Resource Management* 6 (3): 702–19.

Marginson, P., and K. Sisson. 1998. European collective bargaining: A virtual prospect? *Journal of Common Market Studies* 36 (4): 505–28.

Maurice, M., E. Sellier, and J. Silvestre. 1986. *The social foundations of industrial power: A comparison of France and Germany.* Cambridge, MA: MIT Press.

Mayer, N. 1993. Costs, low productivity in Mexico forcing U.S. firms home. *Pittsburgh Post-Gazette*, July 10, B10.

Mayrhofer, W., and C. Brewster. 1996. In praise of ethnocentricity: Expatriate policies in European multinationals. *International Executive* 38 (6): 749–78.

McEnery, J., and G. DesHarnals. 1990. Culture shock. *Training and Development Journal* (April):43–47.

McGaughey, S. L., and H. De Cieri. 1999. Reassessment of convergence and divergence dynamics: Implications for international HRM. *International Journal of Human Resource Management* 10:235–50.

Mendenhall, M., and G. Oddou. 1985. The dimensions of expatriate acculturation. *Academy of Management Review* 10:39–47.

———, eds. 2000. *Readings and cases in international human resource management.* 3d ed. Cincinnati, OH: South-Western College Publishing.

Mendenhall, M., and G. K. Stahl. 2000. Expatriate training and development: Where do we go from here? *Human Resource Management* 39 (2–3): 251–65.

Merchant, H. 2000. Configurations of international joint ventures. *Management International Review* 40 (2): 107–40.

Miller, K. L. 1993. Stress and uncertainty: The price of restructuring. *Business Week,* March 29, 74.

Milliman, J., M. A. Von Glinow, and M. Nathan. 1991. Organizational lifecycles and strategic international human resource management in multinational companies: Implications and congruence theory. *Academy of Management Review* 18:269–92.

Morgan, P. V. 1986. International human resource management: Fact or fiction? *Personnel Administrator* 31 (9): 44–46.

Morrison, A. J., and K. Roth. 1992. A taxonomy of business-level strategies in global industries. *Strategic Management Journal* 13:399–418.

Napier, N. K., and V. T. Vu. 1998. International human resource management in developing and transitional economy countries: A breed apart? *Human Resource Management Review* 8 (1): 39–77.

Neef, A., and C. Kask. 1991. Manufacturing productivity and labor costs in fourteen economies. *Monthly Labor Review* 114 (12): 24–37.

Niederman, F. 1999. Global information systems and human resource management: A research agenda. *Journal of Global Information Management* 7 (2): 33–39.

Noble, C. 1997. International comparisons of training policies. *Human Resource Management Journal* 7 (1): 5–18.

Oddou, G., and C. B. Derr. 1999. *Managing internationally.* Orlando: Dryden Press.

Ofori-Dankwa, J. 1993. Murray and Resef revisited: Toward a typology/theory of paradigms of national trade union movements. *Academy of Management Review* 18:269–92.

Oliver, N., and B. Wilkinson. 1989. Japanese manufacturing techniques and personnel and industrial relations practice in Britain: Evidence and implications. *British Journal of Industrial Relations* 27:75–91.

Osland, J. S. 2000. The journey inward: Expatriate hero tales and paradoxes. *Human Resource Management* 39 (2–3): 227–38.

Ouchi, W., and M. MacGuire. 1975. Organizational control: Two functions. *Administrative Science Quarterly* 20:559–69.

Pan, Y., and X. Li. 2000. Joint venture formation of very large multinational firms. *Journal of International Business Studies* 31(1):179–89.

Peng, M. W. 2000. Controlling the foreign agent: How governments deal with multinationals in a transition economy. *Management International Review* 40 (2): 141–65.

Personnel Decisions Research Institute. 1987. *Critical dimensions for foreign assignment selection.* Minneapolis, MN: Personnel Decisions Research Institute.

Peterson, R. B., N. Napier, and W. S. Shin. 1996. Expatriate management—The differential role of national multinational corporation ownership. *International Executive* 38 (4): 543–62.

Peterson, R. B., J. Sergant., N. Napier, and W. S. Shin. 1996. Corporate expatriate HRM policies, internationalization, and performance in the world's largest MNCs. *Management International Review* 36 (3): 215–30.

Phatak, A. V. 1992. *International dimensions of management.* 3d ed. Boston: PWS-Kent.

————. 1995. *International dimensions of management.* 4th ed. Cincinnati: South-Western College Publishing.

Poole, M. 1986. *Industrial relations: Origins and patterns of national diversity.* London: Routledge and Kegan Paul.

————, ed. 1999. *Human resource management: Critical perspectives on business and management.* Vols. 1, 2, and 3. London: Routledge.

Porter, G., and J. W. Tansky. 1999. Expatriate success may depend on a "Learning orientation": Considerations for selection and training. *Human Resource Management* 38 (1): 47–60.

Porter, M. E. 1990. *Competitive advantage of nations.* New York: Free Press.

Puchala, D. J. 1999. Institutionalism, intergovernmentalism, and European integration: A review article. *Journal of Common Market Studies* 37 (2): 317–31.

Pucik, V. 1988. Strategic alliances, organizational learning, and competitive advantage: The HRM agenda. *Human Resource Management* 27 (1): 77–93.

Pucik, V., and J. H. Katz. 1986. Information control and human resource management in multinational firms. *Human Resource Management* 25 (1):121–32.

Pucik, V., and T. Saba. 1998. Selecting and developing the global versus the expatriate manager: A review of the state-of-the-art. *Human Resource Planning* 21 (4): 40–54.

Punnett, B. J., O. Crocker, and M. A. Stevens. 1992. The challenge for women expatriates and spouses: Some empirical evidence. *International Journal of Human Resource Management* 3:585–92.

Punnett, B. J., and D. A. Ricks. 1992. *International business.* Boston: PWS-Kent.

Ramsay, H. 1997. Solidarity at last? International trade unionism approaching the millennium. *Economic and Industrial Democracy* 18 (4): 503–37.

Rangan, S. 1998. Do multinationals operate flexibly? Theory and evidence. *Journal of International Business Studies* 29 (2): 217–37.

Ratnam, V. C. S. 1995. Economic liberalisation and the transformation of industrial relations policies in India. In A. Verma, T. A. Kochan, and R. D. Lansbury, eds., *Employment relations in the growing Asian economies,* 248–314. London: Routledge.

Recht, R., and C. Wilderom. 1998. Kaizen and culture: On the transferability of Japanese suggestion systems. *International Business Review* 7:7–22.

Reynolds, C. 1992. Are you ready to make IHR a global function? *HR News: International HR* (February):C1–C3.

Reynolds, C., and R. Bennett. 1991. The career couple challenge. *Personnel Journal* 70 (3): 46–48.

Roberts, B. C., and J. May. 1974. The response of multinational enterprises to international trade union pressures. *British Journal of Industrial Relations* 12:403–17.

Roberts, K., E. E. Kossek, and C. Ozeki. 1998. Managing the global workforce: Challenges and strategies. *Academy of Management Executive* 12 (4): 93–106.

Ronen, S. 1986. *Comparative and multinational management.* New York: Wiley and Sons.

Rowan, R. L. 1977. Comment. In R. F. Banks and J. Stieber, eds., *Multinationals, unions, and labor relations in industrialized countries.* Ithaca, NY: Cornell University.

Rugman, A. M., and A. Verbeke. 1998. Multinational enterprises and public policy. *Journal of International Business Studies* 29 (1): 115–36.

Sano, Y. 1993. Changes and continued stability in Japanese HRM systems: Choice in the share economy. *International Journal of Human Resource Management* 4:11–27.

Sardi, S., and C. Williamson. 1989. Management and industrial relations strategies of multinational corporations in developing countries. *Journal of Business Research* 18:179–93.

Saundry, R., and P. Turnbull. 1999. Contractual (in)security, labour regulation, and competitive performance in the port industry: A contextualized comparison of Britain and Spain. *British Journal of Industrial Relations* 37 (2): 273–96.

Schneider, S. 1986. National vs. corporate culture: Implications for human resource management. *Human Resource Management* 27 (2): 133–48.

Schregle, J. 1985. Labour law and industrial relations in the Third World. In R. Blanpain, ed., *Comparative Labour Law and Industrial Relations.* 2d ed. New York: Kluwer Law and Taxation Publishers.

Schuler, R. S. 1992. Strategic human resource management: Linking the people with the strategic needs of the business. *Organizational Dynamics* (summer):18–31.

———. 2000. Human resource issues and activities in international joint ventures. *International Journal of Human Resource Management* 12:1–52.

Schuler, R. S., P. S. Budhwar, and G. W. Florkowski. 2002. International human resource management: Review and critique. *International Journal of Management Reviews* 4:41–70.

Schuler, R. S., P. J. Dowling, and H. De Cieri. 1992. The formation of an international joint venture: Marley Automotive Components. *European Management Journal* 10:304–9.

———. 1993. An integrative framework of strategic international human resource management. *International Journal of Human Resource Management* 4:717–64.

———. 1999. An integrative framework of strategic international human resource management. In R. S. Schuler and S. E. Jackson, eds., *Strategic human resource management: A reader,* 319–55. London: Blackwell.

———. 2000. The formation of an international joint venture: Marley Automotive Components. In M. Mendenhall and G. Oddou, eds., *Readings and cases in international human resource management,* 394–405. 3d ed. Cincinnati: South-Western College Publishing.

Schuler, R. S., and S. E. Jackson. 1987. Linking competitive strategy and human resource management practices. *Academy of Management Executive* 3:207–19.

———, eds. 1999. *Strategic human resource management: A reader.* London: Blackwell.

Schuler, R. S., S. E. Jackson, P. J. Dowling, and H. De Cieri. 1991. Formation of an international joint venture: Davidson Instrument Panel. *Human Resource Planning* 141:51–59.

Schuler, R. S., and N. Rogovsky. 1998. Understanding compensation practice variations across firms: The impact of national culture. *Journal of International Business Studies* 29:159–77.

Schuler, R. S., and E. Van Sluijs. 1992. Davidson-Marley BV: Establishing and operating an international joint venture. *European Management Journal* 10:428–37.

Scullion, H. 1992. Strategic recruitment and development of the international managers: Some European considerations. *Human Resource Management Journal* 3:57–69.

Selmer, J., and C. de Leon. 1997. Succession procedures for expatriate chief executives. *Human Resource Management Journal* 7 (3): 80–88.

Shadur, M. A., J. J. Rodwell, and G. J. Bamber. 1995. The adoption of international best practices in a Western culture: East meets West. *International Journal of Human Resource Management* 6 (3): 735–57.

Shenkar, O., ed. 1995. *Global perspectives of human resource management.* Englewood Cliffs, NJ: Prentice Hall.

Shenkar, O., and J. Li. 1999. Knowledge search in international cooperative ventures. *Organizational Science* 10 (2): 34–44.

Shenkar, O., and Y. Zeira. 1987. Human resource management in joint ventures: Directions for research. *Academy of Management Review* 12:546–57.

Sparks, D. 1999. Partners. *Business Week,* October 5, 106.

Sparrow, P. R. 1995. Towards a dynamic and comparative model of European human resource management: An extended review. *International Journal of Human Resource Management* 6:481–505.

———. 1999. International rewards systems: To converge or not to converge? In C. Brewster and H. Harris, eds., *International HR,* 102–19. London and New York: Routledge.

———. 2000. International reward management. In G. White and J. Druker, eds., *Reward management,* 196–214. London: Routledge.

Sparrow, P. R., and P. Budhwar. 1997. Competition and change: Mapping the Indian HRM recipe against world wide patterns. *Journal of World Business* 32:224–42.

Sparrow, P. R., and J. M. Hiltrop. 1994. *European human resource management in transition.* London: Prentice Hall.

———. 1997. Redefining the field of European human resource management: A battle between national mindsets and forces of business transition. *Human Resource Management* 36:201–19.

Sparrow, P. R., R. S. Schuler, and S. E. Jackson. 1994. Convergence or divergence: Human resource practices and policies for competitive advantage world-wide. *International Journal of Human Resource Management* 5:267–99.

Stern, R. N. 1978. Methodological issues in quantitative strike analysis. *Industrial Relations* 17:32–42.

Streeck, W. 1998. The internationalization of industrial relations in Europe: Prospects and problems. *Politics and Society* 26 (4): 429–59.

Stroh, L. K. 1995. Predicting turnover among expatriates: Can organizations affect retention rates? *International Journal of Human Resource Management* 6 (2): 443–56.

Sundaram, A. K., and J. S. Black. 1992. The environment and internal organization of multinational enterprises. *Academy of Management Review* 17:729–57.

Tayeb, M. 1995. The competitive advantage of nations: The role of HRM and its sociocultural context. *International Journal of Human Resource Management* 6:588–605.

Taylor, S., S. Beechler, and N. Napier. 1996. Toward an integrative model of strategic international human resource management. *Academy of Management Review* 21 (4): 959–85.

Teagarden, M. B., and M. A. Von Glinow. 1990. Contextual determinants of HRM effectiveness in cooperative alliances: Mexican evidence. *Management International Review* 30:23–36. Special issue.

Teagarden, M. B., M.A. Von Glinow, D. E. Bowen, C. A. Frayne, S. Nason, Y. P. Huo, J. Milliman, M. E. Arias, M. C. Butler, J. M. Geringer, N. H. Kim, H. Scullion, K. B. Lowe, and E. A. Drost. 1995. Toward a theory of comparative management research: An idiographic case study of the best international human resources management project. *Academy of Management Journal* 38 (5): 1261–87.

Teague, P. 2000. Macro-economic constraints, social learning, and pay bargaining in Europe. *British Journal of Industrial Relations* 38 (3): 429–52.

Teece, D. 1983. A transaction cost theory of the multinational enterprise. In M. Casson, ed., *The growth of international business.* London: Allen and Unwin.

Tichy, N. 1992. Global development. In V. Pucik, N. M. Tichy, and C. K. Barnett, eds., *Globalizing management.* New York: Wiley and Sons.

Torbiorn, I. 1997. Staffing for international operations. *Human Resource Management Journal* 7 (3): 42–52.

Towers-Perrin. 1987. *Worldwide total remuneration.* New York: TowersPerrin.

———. 1999. *Worldwide total renumeration.* New York: TowersPerrin.

Toyne, B. 1989. International exchange: A foundation for theory building in international business. *Journal of International Business Studies* 20:1–18.

Tregaskis, O. 1998. HRD in foreign MNEs. *International Studies of Management and Organization* 28 (1): 136–63.

Tung, R. L. 1982. Selection and training procedures of U.S., European, and Japanese multinationals. *California Management Review* 25:57–71.

———. 1984. Strategic management of human resources in the multinational enterprise. *Human Resource Management* 23 (2): 129–43.

———. 1988. *The new expatriates: Managing human resources abroad.* Cambridge, MA: Ballinger.

Tung, R., and B. J. Punnett. 1993. Research in international human resource management. In D. Wong-Rieber and F. Rieger, eds., *International management research: Looking to the future.* New York: Walter de Gruyter.

Ulrich, D. 1989. Assessing human resource effectiveness: Stakeholder, utility, and relationship approaches. *Human Resource Planning* 12:301–16.

———. 1999. Measuring human resources: An overview of practice and a prescription for results. In R. S. Schuler and S. E. Jackson, eds., *Strategic human resource management: A reader,* 462–82. London: Blackwell.

UNCTAD. 1999. World investment report 1999. <http://www.unctad.org>

U.S. Federal Trade Commission. 1987. International competitiveness and the trade deficit. Washington, DC. Staff report.

Vanderbroeck, P. 1992. Long-term human resource development in multinational organizations. *Sloan Management Review* (fall):95–99.

Van Maanen, E., and E. Schein. 1979. Toward a theory of organizational socialization. In L. L. Cummings, ed., *Research in organizational behavior,* vol. 1. Greenwich, CT: JAI Press.

Van Sluijs, E., and R. S. Schuler. 1994. As the IJV grows: Lessons and progress at Davidson-Marley BV. *European Management Journal.*

Von Glinow, M. A., and B. J. Chung. 1989. Comparative human resource management practices in the United States, Japan, Korea, and the People's Republic of China. In K. M. Rowland and G. R. Ferris, eds., *Research in personnel and human resource management,* suppl. 1. Greenwich, CT: JAI Press.

Von Glinow, M. A., and M. B. Teagarden. 1988. The transfer of human resource technology in Sino-U.S. cooperative ventures: Problems and solutions. *Human Resource Management* 27:201–29.

Walker, J. W., and T. P. Bechet. 1991. Defining effectiveness and efficiency measures in the context of human resource strategy. Paper presented at the fourth Biennial Research Symposium, Human Resource Planning Society, Newport, RI.

Walsh, J. 1996. Multinational management strategy and human resource decision making in the single European market. *Journal of Management Studies* 33 (5): 633–48.

Weinberg, N. 1977. Multinationals and unions as innovators and change agents. In R. F. Banks and J. Siebers, eds., *Multinationals, unions, and labor relations in industrialized countries.* Ithaca, NY: Cornell University.

Weiss, L. 1998. *The myth of powerless state.* London: Polity.

Welch, D., T. Adams, B. Betchley, and M. Howard. 1992. The view from the other side: The handling of repatriation and other expatriation activities by the Royal Air Force. *Proceedings of the AIB Southeast Asia Conference.* Published by the conference.

Wells, L. T., Jr. 1998. Multinationals and the developing countries. *Journal of International Business Studies* 29 (1): 101–14.

White, G., J. Druker, and R. Chiu. 1998. Paying their way: A comparison of managerial reward systems in the London and Hong Kong banking industries. *Asia Pacific Journal of Human Resources* 36 (1): 54–71.

Williamson, O. E. 1985. *The economic institutions of capitalism.* New York: Free Press.

Wilson, M., G. B. Northcraft, and M. A. Neale. 1985. The perceived value of fringe benefits. *Personnel Psychology* 38:309–20.

Wong, N. 2000. Mark your calender! Important tasks for international HR workforce. *Costa Mesa* 79 (4): 72–74.

Wright, P. M., and S. A. Snell. 1998. Toward a unifying framework for exploring fit and flexibility in strategic human resource management. *Academy of Management Review* 23 (4): 756–72.

Yeung, A. K. O., and G. Y. Wong. 1990. A comparative analysis of the practices and performance of human resource management systems in Japan and the PRC. In K. M. Rowland, ed., *Research in personnel and human resources management,* suppl. 2. Greenwich, CT: JAI Press.

Zeira,, Y., and M. Banai. 1981. Attitudes of host-country organizations towards MNCs' staffing policies: A cross-country and cross-industry analysis. *Management International Review* 2:38–47.

Zeira, Y., and O. Shenkar. 1990. Interactive and specific parent characteristics: Implications for management and human resources in international joint ventures. *Management International Review* 30:7–22. Special issue.

INTERNATIONAL BUSINESS NEGOTIATIONS RESEARCH

REVISITING "BRICKS, MORTAR, AND PROSPECTS"

Stephen E. Weiss

In international business, negotiation is ubiquitous. This is not surprising if it is defined as "the deliberate interaction of two or more social units (at least one of them a business entity), originating from different nations, that are attempting to define or redefine the terms of their interdependence in a business matter" (Weiss 1993, 270, adapting Walton and McKersie 1965, 3). Researchers have studied negotiation—and will likely continue to study it—in cross-border activities as wide-ranging as sales (e.g., Kale and Barnes 1992; Mintu-Wimsatt and Gassenheimer 2000), licensing (e.g., Parker 1996; Root and Contractor 1981), joint ventures (e.g., Weiss 1987a; Yan and Gray 1994), mergers and acquisitions (e.g., de Beaufort and Lempereur 1996; Sebenius 1998), labor relations (e.g., Bellace and Latta 1983; Northrup and Rowan 1976), MNE–host government relations (e.g., Fagre and Wells 1982; Ramamurti 2001), and cultural aspects of these and other endeavors (e.g., Cai, Wilson, and Drake 2000; Graham et al. 1988).

It has not always been construed so broadly, however. One of the few explicit, alternative definitions of international business negotiation reflects the emphasis in the 1960s and 1970s, in the field of international business, on the foreign operations of MNEs (Root 1993, 11–12). This view was limited to "negotiations between potential or actual foreign investors and host governments regarding . . . a foreign direct investment" (Stoever 1981, 1).

415

The beginnings of U.S.-based management research on international negotiation go back at least to 1970, the publication date of *International Business Negotiations: A Study in India* (Kapoor).[1] In its preface, Fayerweather wrote of the "deplorably barren" state of research literature on negotiations between MNEs and nation states.[2] The postwar literature on international political negotiations at that point already included three seminal works: Schelling's (1960) *The Strategy of Conflict,* Ikle's (1976 [1964]) *How Nations Negotiate,* and Sawyer and Guetzkow's (1965) internationally oriented social-psychological analysis.[3]

During the 1970s, as research by political scientists and social psychologists gained momentum (e.g., chronologically, Rubin and Brown 1975; Zartman 1976; Druckman 1977; Pruitt 1981), management strategy researchers produced a number of books and articles on MNE–host government negotiations (e.g., Fayerweather and Kapoor 1976; Smith and Wells 1976). By 1980, this work, dubbed the "bargaining school" of MNE–host government relations, constituted a stream of research that would be extended by many subsequent studies (e.g., Doz and Prahalad 1980; Gomes-Casseres 1990; Vachani 1995).

During the same period, other management researchers began studying "cross-cultural" business negotiation. These efforts can also be traced back to 1970, when *Harvard Business Review* published an insightful comparison of Japanese and American negotiations by Van Zandt. This body of work was not as well defined as the bargaining school and would long be criticized for its hodgepodge development and quality.[4] At the end of the decade, Graham (1984b, 51) commented, "we know little [beyond the 'descriptive and anecdotal'] about business negotiations in different cultures."

The early 1980s initiated a major transformation of the field of negotiation. The general audience book *Getting to Yes* (Fisher and Ury 1981) attracted tremendous attention; others (e.g., Raiffa 1982) followed. That uptake stimulated wide-ranging research on negotiation, though most of it was U.S.-based and considered generic.

A number of scholars did begin to focus on cultural differences in bargaining behavior in the early 1980s. Fisher's (1980) *International Negotiation* encouraged these efforts. Management researchers compared American and Chinese, and American and Japanese, behavior via surveys (e.g., Tung 1982, 1984) and experimental role plays (e.g., Harnett and Cummings 1980; Graham 1983).[5] Some of this work was elaborated upon in books that became part of a rapidly growing "negotiating with ___" literature in both academic and popular circles (e.g., Graham and Sano 1989; Foster 1992; Pye 1992).[6]

By 1992, a reviewer for the *Negotiation Journal* who had lamented the historical neglect of international dimensions of negotiation in general audience books exclaimed, "the 1990s are beginning to look like the decade that will change all that. The decade has at least begun with a flourish" (Groth 1992, 242). He was referring to international negotiation generally (e.g., Kremenyuk 1991), but his comment also applied to international business negotiations. An excellent general audience book on the subject, *Making Global Deals* (Salacuse 1991), had just appeared.

Research on cross-cultural negotiation certainly gained momentum in the 1990s. One could even suggest that it has reached a second stage of development conceptually and methodologically. Early work has been thoroughly reviewed (Cai and Drake 1998; Gelfand and Dyer 2000), researchers are asking more compelling, sophisticated questions about moderating as well as direct effects, and their efforts are clustered in research groups that can be systemically followed (e.g., Brett and associates; Triandis and associates).

Since the completion of the first version of this survey (Weiss 1996), research on international business negotiations as a whole has intensified.[7] Several recent milestones have marked its progress. The first edited book of research on the subject, *International Business Negotiations* (Ghauri and Usunier), appeared in 1996. In 1998, the *Journal of International Business Studies* dedicated an issue to the subject, as did, in 1999, the three-year old journal *International Negotiation*. In 1998, the CIBER center at Duke University's Fuqua School began what has become an annual public workshop for faculty on teaching international business negotiation. It is, as this chapter is intended to show, a fascinating field of research with a significant history and a promising future.

With the preceding history as background, this chapter concentrates on the conceptual foundations, methods, and substantive knowledge for—and from—research on international business negotiations. It targets the "bricks," "mortar," and skills of the field. The first section describes established paradigms, frameworks, and stage models. The next section discusses research methods and ongoing challenges such as the development of "twin-sided data." A subsequent section samples the substantive lessons in existing work and delineates areas of emphasis and neglect. The prospects for future research then outlined include intercultural interaction, intergroup relationships, "no-agreement outcomes" (a.k.a. "failures"), testing prescriptions, and extra-U.S. research on negotiation processes and outcomes.

CONCEPTUAL FOUNDATIONS

Fundamentally, negotiation consists of two or more parties, mixed motives (common and conflicting interests), "mutual movement" (Zartman 1976, 8), and a goal—not a certainty—of reaching agreement. These elements present numerous foci for research. The most common—and basic—have been, Why do certain outcomes occur, and what is the process (how do negotiators "move")?

Let us first consider research on international business negotiation most broadly, from perspectives provided by paradigms, and then take up particular analytic frameworks and other conceptualizations. Paradigms represent coherent and usually large bodies of work. Individual frameworks generally offer more focused views that may or may not fit within an existing paradigm. Thus they both provide ways to organize thinking and situate finer-grain studies (see Lewicki, Weiss, and Lewin 1992).

One of the first lenses developed for negotiation researchers is the still widely cited "preliminary social-psychological model of [international] negotiation" formulated by Sawyer and Guetzkow (1965). Their model consists of five elements that stretch across three time periods: (1) antecedent parties' *goals,* which influence the concurrent (2) negotiation *process,* which, in turn, determines the consequent (3) negotiation *outcome;* in addition, antecedent (4) *background factors* influence goals and process, whereas concurrent (5) *conditions* influence the negotiation process. This model is a touchstone by which to compare and assess the added value of the following research paradigms, analytic frameworks, and stage models.

PARADIGMS

There are two major paradigms in international business negotiations research, each with its own take on negotiation and body of studies that complement and cross-reference each other. They might be called the "macrostrategic" (bargaining school) and the "comparative, microbehavioral" (cross-cultural) paradigms. Both focus on negotiation outcomes and their determinants more than on the dynamics of mutual movement. In a sense, both paradigms take a strategic view of negotiation. But they clearly differ with respect to the actors and facets of negotiation that they investigate.

MACROSTRATEGIC ("BARGAINING SCHOOL")

This research paradigm centers on the concept of bargaining power and its sources and effects. The bargaining school of MNE–host government relations, which epitomizes this paradigm, holds that the parties negotiate this relationship. Their relative bargaining power, in particular, determines the terms. MNE power is conceived in terms of resources such as capital, technology, access to foreign markets, and product differentiation, while the negotiation outcome—or "bargaining success"—is proxied by the MNE's percentage of ownership of its foreign operation (see fig. 12.1.)

This relationship changes over time, according to the theory of the "obsolescing bargain" (Vernon 1968, 1980). In initial negotiations over market entry, an MNE often obtains favorable terms from a host government. However, as soon as the MNE makes a fixed investment, its power begins to diminish. Over time, the government gains relatively more bargaining power, renegotiates the initial bargain, and improves its terms (Stoever 1979, 7).

The researchers often identified with this stream of research have been associated with Harvard and its Multinational Enterprise Databank[8] (e.g., Vernon 1968; Fagre and Wells 1982; Encarnation and Wells 1985; Gomes-Casseres 1990). Early on, another group worked out of New York University (Kapoor 1970; Fayerweather and Kapoor 1976; Stoever 1981; Sakuma 1987). Over the years, a number of other researchers have aligned their work with the bargaining school (e.g., Young and Hood 1977; Bennett and Sharpe 1979; de la Torre 1981; Grieco 1982; Lecraw 1984; Grosse and Aramburu 1990; Blodgett 1991; Ramamurti 2001). Several researchers have focused specifically on the obsolescing bargain (Stoever 1979; Jenkins 1986; Kobrin 1987; Vachani 1995).

These researchers' studies have often investigated U.S.- or European-owned MNEs' negotiations with less developed country governments over direct investments in extractive industries (e.g., Smith and Wells 1976). Some studies have also been done on manufacturing (e.g., Kobrin 1987) and diverse sectors (e.g., Vachani 1995). In the language of Sawyer and Guetzkow (1965), the goal has been to correlate antecedent background factors (i.e., party attributes such as R&D spending) with consequent outcomes (e.g., ownership of foreign subsidiaries). The organizations involved

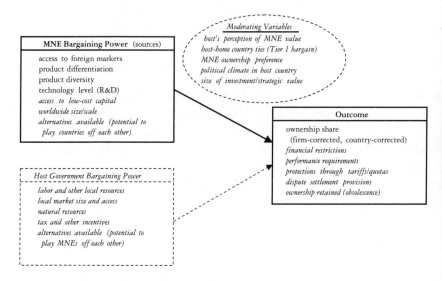

Source: Based on Fagre and Wells 1982; Vachani 1995; Ramamurti 2001
Note: Dashed lines and italics indicate modifications of original view.

FIGURE 12.1. The bargaining school of MNE–host government relations: original and evolving views

have been treated as monolithic parties, and the analysis has been based on "large *n*" samples.

With respect to results, this research has found significant, positive (yet small) correlations between ownership and an MNE's level of technology and access to foreign markets (e.g., Fagre and Wells 1982). This basic relationship has been probed by examining governments' internal dynamics (e.g., Philip 1976; Encarnation and Wells 1985), introducing variables for government power (e.g., Lecraw 1984), and incorporating MNEs' actual ownership preferences rather than assuming preferences of 100 percent (e.g., Gomes-Casseres 1990). The most recent refinements include specification of moderating variables such as host-country political climate (Vachani 1995) and addition of another "tier" of bargaining, namely, that between an MNE's home government and the host government (Ramamurti 2001, 23). (For more on this topic, see the section titled "Existing Substantive Knowledge.")

Many of these topics are also of interest to researchers studying international joint ventures. They use bargaining power to explain partnership agreements. In the process, they have grappled with the difficulty of meaningfully defining bargaining power (e.g., "a bargainer's ability to favorably change the 'bargaining set'" [Lax and Sebenius 1986, in Yan and Gray 1994, 1480; see also Dupont 1996, 43ff]) and operationalizing it in nontautological ways.[9] These researchers have contributed ideas on different components of power (Yan and Gray 1994), the role of stakeholders in negotiations (Brouthers and Bamossy 1997), and causes of joint venture instability or changes in the bargain over time (Inkpen and Beamish 1997).

COMPARATIVE, MICROBEHAVIORAL

This paradigm centers on face-to-face interaction between individual negotiators, which adherents view as *the* point of contact in negotiation (Graham 1987, 164–65). One could say that the mutual movement that characterizes negotiation can only occur through interaction. Here, the focus is on what individuals do (e.g., make offers, disclosures, threats) and on how culture, specifically, influences this behavior.

In terms of Sawyer and Guetzkow's (1965) model, microbehavioral researchers study the negotiation process, resulting outcomes, and background factors (primarily culture). Goals and conditions were not considered until very recently (Cai and Drake 1998; Gelfand and Dyer 2000) (see figure 12.2). A growing majority of these studies have been based on negotiation experiments, as compared to the actual negotiations analyzed by the bargaining school. Geographically, they have concentrated on comparing Americans with Japanese (e.g., Graham 1981; Brett and Okumura 1998) and with Chinese (e.g., Tung 1982; Tinsley and Pillutla 1998).

There are three major groups of researchers, or bodies of work, within the comparative, microbehavioral paradigm: Graham and his associates; survey-based work; and "cultural values" researchers. Most productive from the mid-1980s to the mid-1990s, Graham and his associates recruited subjects from various cultures to participate in experiments involving a dyadic, intracultural sales negotiation over three commodities (the "Kelley [1966] game") (chronologically, Graham 1983, 1985; Adler, Graham, and Schwartz Gerkhe 1987; Campbell et al. 1988; Graham et al. 1988; Adler, Brahm, and Graham 1992; Graham, Evenko, and Rajan 1992; Graham 1993). These researchers investigated the effects of "bar-

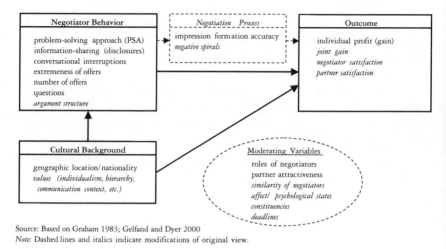

Source: Based on Graham 1983; Gelfand and Dyer 2000
Note: Dashed lines and italics indicate modifications of original view.

FIGURE 12.2. The comparative, microbehavioral paradigm: original and evolving views

gainer characteristics" such as culture and self-esteem, and "situational constraints" such as the role of the negotiator as buyer or seller, on "process-related factors" (e.g., information-providing strategies) and on negotiation outcomes (e.g., individual profit levels). The scope of these comparative data is extraordinary: By late 1993, they represented one thousand subjects from seventeen countries.

The second body of work rests on surveys of individuals' actual intercultural negotiation experiences and is exemplified by a cohesive series of studies of American-Chinese negotiations (Brunner and Taoka 1977; DePauw 1981; Tung 1982; Lee and Lo 1988; Eiteman 1990; and Americans plus others with the Chinese, Stewart and Keown 1989). They targeted similar topics, relied on self-report questionnaires administered to the American side, and in at least one instance directly replicated a previous study (Brunner and Taoka 1977, by Lee and Lo 1988). The questions here concern negotiator behavior and process, comparing Chinese to Americans, but this work differs from Graham's comparative research in addressing counterparts' behavior in *inter*cultural negotiations.[10] This research also stretches beyond the microbehavioral realm by inquiring about the influence of variables such as trade relations and product characteristics on negotiating success.

The cultural values researchers, a group that emerged in the 1990s, include two major subgroups: one based at the University of Illinois (Triandis, Carnevale, and their associates), the other at Northwestern University (Brett and her associates). Both groups have taken experimental approaches to examine relationships between values such as individualism/collectivism, hierarchy/egalitarianism (or "power distance"), and high/low context communication, on the one hand, and negotiation behavior and outcomes, on the other (for the values, see Hall 1976; Hofstede 1984; Schwartz 1994). They share a concern for greater methodological rigor in this paradigm, which they have demonstrated by, among other things, conceptualizing these relationships in some detail and testing their subjects' cultural values rather than assuming them on the basis of nationality or citizenship (Brett et al. 1998).

With respect to results, Graham's group has uncovered cultural differences in the effect of the negotiator's role on the profit obtained. Japanese buyers have performed significantly better than sellers, for example, whereas no role effect has occurred with Americans. The group's findings on negotiator use of a "problem-solving approach" (PSA) and a number of other variables have been mixed (see table 12.2 later in the chapter). Survey research has shown that American negotiators in the mid-1970s emphasized some knowledge of Chinese culture as a primary factor in negotiating successfully but ten years later placed more emphasis on the uniqueness of a company's product. Lastly, values researchers have discovered some significant differences in the tactics negotiators employ, while the outcomes achieved have tended to be similar across cultures (Brett 2001, xx). In a comprehensive review of cross-cultural research, however, Gelfand and Dyer (2000, 68) concluded that "there is [still] an abundance of conflicting and unexpected patterns in the literature, making it difficult to make any generalizations."

Other criticisms of this research have pointed at simplistic conceptualizations, the reliance upon the measures for values that are available (Weiss 1999; Wilson et al. 1995, 222), and the paucity of intercultural as opposed to intracultural data (Cai and Drake 1998). One could add that the interactional component—the process—in international negotiations has still not received much attention. Are there action, reaction, and reaction-to-reaction sequences in the behaviors of a negotiator from culture A and a negotiator from culture B that can be described and explained?

Varied research related to this paradigm continues on a number of fronts, however. On the comparative side, it includes goal setting and framing (e.g., Neale, Northcraft, and Huber 1987; Cai, Wilson, and Drake 2000), conflict-handling styles (Jehn and Weldon 1991; Leung and Tjosvold 1998), and complex rather than singular definitions of value dimensions (Cho and Cho 2001). For intercultural negotiation, there is work on framing (e.g., Kimmel 1993; Lituchy 1992), affect (George, Jones, and Gonzalez 1998; Kumar 1997), information processing and integrative potential (Brett and Okumura 1998), and appropriate negotiation strategies (Francis 1991; Weiss 1994b). (Methodological aspects of this research are discussed further under the section "Research Methods," and additional results may be found in the section "Existing Substantive Knowledge.")

In sum, the macrostrategic and microbehavioral paradigms represent substantial bodies of research on international business negotiations, but they developed independently and have, by and large, explored distinct areas. It is interesting to note that Tinsley, Curhan, and Kwak (1999) have observed that juxtaposing the two perspectives seems to pose a dilemma: The macroperspective, as seen in the comparative advantage theory of international trade, underscores the benefits of differences between parties, whereas the microview, seen in cognitive theories, highlights the drawbacks. Only a few such works have attempted to bridge these perspectives (e.g., Rao and Schmidt 1998; Weiss 1993); they remain largely isolated from each other.

ANALYTIC FRAMEWORKS

Models and frameworks of analysis designed expressly for international business negotiation present another set of views of the phenomenon. This section sketches six of them: one associated with the macrostrategic paradigm (Fayerweather and Kapoor 1976), three with the comparative, microbehavioral paradigm, (Weiss with Stripp 1998 [1985]; Graham 1987; Brett 2000), and two that combine the preceding perspectives (Tung 1988; Weiss 1993). The first framework concentrates on negotiation conditions; the remaining five encompass process and outcomes. (The titles of the next six sections reflect the researchers' own labels.)

THE CONTEXT OF NEGOTIATION

Laid out in diagrams without much explanation, this early framework for international business negotiations by Fayerweather and Kapoor (1976,

29–32) consists of five major factors: the negotiation situation, functional areas (e.g., finance), the "four C's" (common interests, conflicting interests, compromise, and criteria for undertaking negotiation and achieving agreement), the environment (political, economic, cultural, and social systems), and "perspective" (broad factors such as previous negotiation experiences that influence the negotiation at hand). An additional factor is a negotiator's "integrative expression" of many skills, including the functional skills mentioned previously, the ability to understand group dynamics, and awareness of one's own capabilities. Every party to a negotiation finds itself in such a context, so that understanding the negotiation requires consideration of multiple contexts, that is, consideration of *each* party's "context" or "negotiation situation" (Fayerweather and Kapoor 1976, 33, figs. 3–5).

As Tung (1988, 206) has noted, this framework largely ignores behavioral variables and has not facilitated the development of testable hypotheses (cf. Lecraw and Morrison 1991; Phatak and Habib 1996). Furthermore, it does not show how the five factors interact or how to deal with multiple contexts (e.g., the "environment" is specific to and at least partly different for each party in international negotiation).

NEGOTIATOR'S FRAMEWORK FOR
CULTURAL COMPARISONS

Targeting the process of negotiation, and presuming that groups or teams were involved, Weiss with Stripp (1998 [1985]) propounded twelve aspects that could vary across cultures. This framework shaped many discussions of cross-cultural negotiation (e.g., Moran and Stripp 1991; Salacuse 1991, 58–70; Foster 1992, 41, 264ff). It did not, however, explicate relationships among the variables.

These relationships—which derived from Sawyer and Guetzkow's (1965) ideas (goals → process → outcome)—are more apparent in a reformulation of the framework (Weiss 1994b, 53). It lays out four sets of variables: (1) the general model of the negotiation process, (2) the role of the individual, (3) aspects of interaction, and (4) outcome. "General model" comprises the basic concept of the negotiation process and the most significant type of issue, and "role" includes selection of negotiators, individuals' aspirations, and decision making in groups. "Interaction" consists of two subgroups of variables labeled "dispositions" (orientation toward time, risk-taking propensity, bases of trust) and "process" (concern with protocol, communication complexity, and nature of persuasion). Lastly, "outcome" represents the form of a satisfactory agreement. Only some of the variables have been investigated empirically (e.g., aspiration [individualism] and communication context).

MODEL OF INTERORGANIZATIONAL NEGOTIATIONS

While not labeled "international" or "cross-cultural," Graham's (1987) "model of interorganizational negotiations" has framed his research on cultural differences. It sets forth four *classes* of constructs (in parentheses): (1) *situational constraints* (e.g., power relationship) and (2) *bargainer characteristics* (e.g., culture, interpersonal orientation), which are antecedent factors that influence (3) concurrent, *process-related factors* (e.g., initial demands, impression-formation accuracy) that, finally, determine (4) consequent *negotiation outcomes* (e.g., negotiator profits, client satisfaction, interpersonal attraction). Explicitly based on Sawyer and Guetzkow's (1965) model, Graham's (1987, 173) model highlights the mediating role of concurrent factors and treats as secondary the direct relationship between antecedent and consequent constructs.

In contrast to Fayerweather and Kapoor (1976), this model emphasizes bargainers' characteristics and behavior. But it construes situational constraints more narrowly.

MODEL OF INTERCULTURAL NEGOTIATION

Brett (2000) has proposed that in a cross-cultural, bilateral negotiation, culture affects each negotiator's preferences and strategy. The two negotiators' preferences determine integrative potential, while their strategies determine patterns of interaction. Integrative potential and interaction patterns jointly determine the type of negotiation outcome.

Specifically, Brett relates the cultural component to three values. Individualism/collectivism influences an individual's preferences, hierarchy/egalitarianism affects strategy, and high versus low context communication influences information gathering. Alternatively put, these values respectively correspond to the motivation for searching for information, the value assigned to information sharing, and ways of information searching.

CONCEPTUAL FRAMEWORK OF INTERNATIONAL BUSINESS NEGOTIATIONS

Almost twenty years after the publication of Kapoor's (1970) book, Tung (1988) observed that research on the subject had been "sporadic" and conducted in the absence of a "conceptual framework." In response, she designed a framework in which (1) environmental context affects the (2) negotiation context and (3) negotiator characteristics, which then both influence (4) "strategy selection and process/ progress." This last, composite element determines (5) the negotiation outcome, which feeds back on negotiation context and negotiator characteristics.

This model both resembles Graham's (1987) model and differs from it. They share the inclusion of negotiator (bargainer) characteristics and the conditions → process → outcome line of reasoning in Sawyer and Guetzkow's (1965) model. But Tung's conceptual framework distinctively encompasses broad, albeit not operationally specified, environmental variables.

THE RBC PERSPECTIVE

Lastly, Weiss (1993) conceived a parsimonious model for interorganizational negotiations centering on three key facets: the parties' relationship, their behaviors, and related conditions. The relationship—the connection between the parties—serves as the focal point because it epitomizes the interdependent and interactive nature of negotiation. Behaviors and conditions shape the relationship according to a core $_B \nearrow \overset{R}{\leftarrow} \nwarrow _C$ logic.

Relationships and behaviors may be analyzed on organizational, group/team, and individual levels. There are four types of conditions. The first is circumstances: the physical and social features of the site in which all negotiators find themselves. Each party is then individually affected by its capabilities (skills, resources, and traits that enable it to influence a counterpart and open it to be influenced); cultures (e.g., ethnic, organizational, national); and environments (noncultural factors beyond the organization). The last two conditions may overlap for parties, although perceptions and responses to them may well differ. Finally, beyond the core $_B \nearrow \overset{R}{\leftarrow} \nwarrow _C$ dynamic, RBC factors affect each other in other ways, especially over time (e.g., $R_t \rightarrow B_{t+1}$).

Like Graham's and Tung's conceptualizations, the RBC Perspective incorporates behaviors *and* conditions and, like Fayerweather and Kapoor's model, offers a broad view of conditions. In contrast, this model posits relationships between factors, treats the "negotiation outcome" as an element of the negotiators' relationship, and acknowledges different levels of analysis.[11] Given its scope, it serves, in a subsequent section, as a basis for classifying existing knowledge about international business negotiations.

STAGE MODELS

A third and last major area for broad conceptualizations has been the movement of negotiation across time. This relates to the process component of some frameworks mentioned previously and to relationships in the RBC Perspective. Since the early days of the field, various researchers and practitioners have described negotiation as a sequence of phases or stages, each characterized by certain types of negotiator behavior.

Most writers admit that these models cannot be rigidly applied (Dupont 1990, 52–57; Salacuse 1991, 25). Others argue that linear, phase structures contain a strong Western bias (Trompenaars and Hampden-Turner 1998, 123ff). Many models are at least grounded in actual negotiation experience (e.g., Graham 1981), but few have been rigorously validated (Holmes 1992).

Several stage models have been developed for international business negotiations. It is instructive to compare them to what is probably the most detailed process model available in negotiation research (Gulliver 1979). Designed for cross-cultural if not explicitly business use, it actually comprises two models: one is developmental, the other cyclical. The nine stages of the developmental model appear at the top of figure 12.3.[12] Of the six business models in the figure, three are included simply for comparison (e.g., Cavusgil and Ghauri 1990; Griffin and Daggart 1990; March 1985). The remaining three are the most widely recognized in the field.

FOUR STAGES (GRAHAM)

Based on his early research on negotiations in Japan and in the United States, Graham (1981, 6) proposed that all business negotiations traverse four stages. Nontask sounding includes all activities related to "getting to know one another" but not information related to the business of the meeting. Task-related exchange of information about parties' needs and preferences follows. The next stage, persuasion, consists of parties' attempts to modify each other's expectations. Then the parties complete an agreement, often by putting together a series of concessions or smaller agreements. According to Graham (1981), the content, duration, and importance of these stages differ across cultures. For example, Japanese engage in sounding much longer than do Americans and emphasize exchange of information, whereas Americans focus on persuasion (cf. Brett and Okumura 1998). (See research propositions related to this model in Siminitras and Thomas 1998.)

Researcher	Stages									Total No.
	1	2	3	4	5	6	7	8	9	
General Cross-Cultural										
Gulliver[1]	search for arena	agenda setting and issue definition	establishing maximal limits	narrowing differences	preliminaries to final bargaining	final bargaining	ritual affirmation	execution of agreement	aftermath	9
Business										
Cavusgil and Ghauri	offer/informal meetings	strategy formulation/face-to-face negotiation					implementation			5
Graham	nontask sounding bargaining	task-related info exchange		persuasion		concessions & agreement				4
Griffin and Daggart	preparation	bargaining					ceremony	implementation		4
March[2]	prenegotiation	opening moves				agreement or frustration	post-negotiation			4 to 7+
McCall and Warrington[3]	prenegotiation	distributive bargaining		integrative bargaining		decision-making and action	post-negotiation			5
Salacuse[4]	prenegotiation		conceptualization			working out details				3

Notes: Although different researchers' stages have been aligned as closely as possible, their correspondence is not exact due to differences in stage definitions and durations.

1. This "developmental" process model is one of two components—concurrent processes—in Gulliver's overall model of negotiation. The second process, which is cyclical, is information exchange.
2. Frustration leads either to last resort tactics and eventually agreement or to postponement (after a time, parties may—or may not—review and revitalize the negotiations and recommence with prenegotiation).
3. Based on Douglas 1962 and Morely and Stephenson 1977.
4. Based on Zartman and Berman 1982. See also Ikle (1976 [1964]).

Source: Gulliver 1979; Cavusgil and Ghauri 1990, 64–66, 68–78; Graham 1981; Griffin and Daggart 1990; March 1985; McCall and Warrington 1984, 22–34; Salacuse 1991, 25–27.

FIGURE 12.3. Stage models of international business negotiation

FIVE (THREE PLUS TWO) STAGES
(MCCALL AND WARRINGTON)

For cross-cultural marketing, British researchers McCall and Warrington (1984, 22–34) enlarged a model developed by their compatriots Morely and Stephenson (1977), who, in turn, had borrowed from the American labor-management research of Douglas (1962). Their first stage, prenegotiation, involves the buyer's and seller's individual assessments of the environmental factors likely to influence their objectives, their negotiations within their own organizations, and efforts to obtain negotiating authority. Moving from that stage to the next may call for the seller to make a presentation to the buyer ("Facilitating Stage A"). Three other facilitating stages (B–D) follow each ensuing main stage but need not be described here. During distributive bargaining (Stage I), the parties strongly indicate the outcomes they desire and test and identify each other's limits. As they signal areas of possible movement, without necessarily committing themselves, they reach a more personal level and integrative bargaining (Stage II). This stage entails attentiveness to parties' styles, eliciting information about the issues, and maintaining flexibility of movement by linking issues. Decision making and action (Stage III) indicates the point at which parties must decide on what to accept. The fifth stage, postnegotiation, refers to finalizing an agreement, usually by drawing up a legal contract.

DEAL-MAKING PHASES (SALACUSE)

Lastly, adapting ideas from political scientists Zartman and Berman (1982) and Ikle ([1964] 1976), Salacuse (1991, 25–27) has described three "fundamental" phases for international business negotiations. During prenegotiation, which involves both independent and face-to-face activity, parties determine whether or not they will negotiate and, if so, how. In other words, this phase includes diagnosis, information gathering, a decision to negotiate, and setting an agenda. During the second phase—conceptualization—parties attempt to agree on a formula or concept for their transaction and perhaps write a letter of intent. They work toward these goals by pursuing a definition of interests, proposals and counterproposals, and creative options. Third, in working out the details, which depends heavily on technical expertise, parties explore the implications of their formula, undertake technical analysis, consider implementation, and document their agreement as clearly and unambiguously as possible.

All three of these models recognize activities preliminary to active negotiation. McCall and Warrington (1984, 79) viewed their five-stage model as compatible with Graham's (1981). Yet, their sequences for distributive and integrative bargaining appear to be reversed. (These terms—"distributive" and "integrative"—refer respectively to the competitive division of a fixed pie, which emphasizes individual gains, and to a focus on increasing total joint gain by bridging interests or expanding the pie [for details see Walton and McKersie 1965; Lax and Sebenius 1986; Putnam 1990].) Perhaps the most distinctive difference among the three models lies in their depictions of the heart of the interaction as an exchange of concessions versus development of a common formula.

RESEARCH METHODS

Moving from conceptual foundations to methods of investigation introduces the real—and probably biggest—challenges for the international business negotiations researcher. Like other researchers, the international business negotiations researcher faces basic methodological choices in research design, data collection, and data analysis. They are complicated by the international and cultural dimensions of the subject, but the nature of negotiation—multifaceted, interactive, dynamic—also complicates matters.

CASE STUDIES, SURVEYS, AND EXPERIMENTS

The negotiation literature contains examples of most social science research designs. In a systematic review covering the period 1976–93, Weiss (1994a) found that the methods most frequently employed, in order of frequency, were the case study (e.g., Weiss 1987a; Young and Hood 1977), questionnaire survey (e.g., Brunner and Taoka 1977; Kobrin 1987), and various experimental designs (e.g., Francis 1991; Graham 1983). All three methods continue to be used (e.g., Yan and Gray 1994; Rao and Schmidt 1998; Tinsley 1998). One can also find a number of statistical studies based on large, existing databases such as those of the World Bank, Harvard's Multinational Enterprise Databank, and the Profit Impact of Marketing Strategies (PIMS) (e.g., Gomes-Casseres 1990, 8).

The case study of a real, nonexperimental negotiation puts researchers and their audiences "close to the action" (Parkhe 1993, 248ff), minimizes the external validity issue inherent in experiments (Eliashberg, Lilien, and Kim 1995), and generally facilitates "thick description" (Geertz 1973).

Data sources for international business negotiations research have included primary sources such as structured and other postnegotiation interviews with participants (e.g., Brouthers and Bamossy 1997; Encarnation and Wells 1985, 53), company archives (e.g., DePauw 1981, 110–79), and government documents (e.g., Young and Hood 1977). To supplement these data, researchers have also used secondary sources such as periodicals and other published literature.

Most of the case studies to date have not followed explicit or common criteria (see Yin 1984). Very few studies articulate the conceptions of negotiation by which they have been constructed (cf. Allison 1971), and there are few examples of multiple case studies built on a common structure that facilitates comparisons and knowledge cumulation (Brouthers and Bamossy 1997; Weiss 1987a, 1990, 1993; Yan and Gray 1994). Moreover, the depth of analysis is often constrained, due perhaps to the difficulty, for researchers, of obtaining critical information (for more on this, see the section "General Concerns"). There are also few examples of direct observation of negotiations in situ (e.g., Brannen 1995; Wright 1990), *systematic* participant observation (see Fetterman 1989; cf. Araskog 1989; Wasserstein 2000), and tape or video recordings of naturally occurring international business negotiation (e.g., Firth 1991).

Survey research also focuses on real negotiations but additionally makes quantitative analysis possible. The questionnaires used thus far have ranged in kind from the wide-angle and "exploratory" (e.g., Tung's [1982] inquiries about U.S. firms' historical relationships with China, conduct of negotiations, perceptions of Chinese decision-making styles, success factors, and negotiation preparations) to the tight, cohesive instrument previously validated in the United States (e.g., Jehn and Weldon's [1991] application of Thomas-Kilman conflict-handling modes with Chinese respondents). Questionnaires have also been used to confirm or correct publicly gathered information (e.g., Kobrin 1987, 625, on parents' ownership of subsidiaries).

As to format and administration, international business negotiations questionnaires have run from thirty-eight items (e.g., Brunner and Taoka 1977) to seventy-two items—nineteen pages (e.g., Tung 1982). Most entail Likert-style response options, although some researchers (e.g., Eiteman 1990) have deliberately eschewed the "check-a-box" format in favor of open-ended questions. Distribution of the questionnaires (see Dillman 1978, 1991) has included mail only (e.g., Tung 1982), advance facsimile or telephone notification combined with one or two subsequent mailings (Rao and Schmidt 1998), mail and follow-up visits with nonrespondents during which the nonrespondents complete the questionnaires (e.g., Stewart and Keown 1989), and interview only with the researcher recording responses (e.g., Lecraw 1984, 32). Response rates for mailed questionnaires have reportedly ranged from 12 percent (out of an original mailing of 1,156 in Tung [1982, 26]) to 59–64 percent (e.g., Brunner and Taoka 1977; Kobrin 1987). Resulting data have been analyzed qualitatively (e.g., Eiteman 1990) and quantitatively via ANOVA (e.g., Jehn and Weldon 1991), factor analysis (e.g., Tung 1982), and TOBIT multiple regression (Kobrin 1987, 629).

Such surveys present researchers with at least three types of challenges: cross-cultural validity, respondent bias, and the vicissitudes of international undertakings. In studying Chinese and American conflict-handling styles, for example, Jehn and Weldon (1991) applied U.S.-based constructs and scales to survey items but found that they really needed to investigate the responses directly via factor analysis. As a consequence, they reached different factor conclusions (for more on cross-cultural validity, see later discussion). Second, questionnaires administered *after* a negotiation are vulnerable to respondents' fundamental attribution errors, post hoc rationalizations, and other psychological and perceptual biases. Also, respondents may differ across cultures in their attitudes toward providing factual versus desired and written versus verbal information and in their willingness to divulge any information at all to researchers.[13] Third, researchers in international business negotiations, like other international researchers described in this book, encounter translation and back translation issues (Triandis 1972, 45–46) and mundane problems such as delays and high costs.

The last of the three major research methods, experiments, offers a researcher the greatest opportunity for direct observation and rigorous analysis of the dynamic, interactive aspects of negotiation. The international business negotiations experiments conducted thus far have usually been either paper-and-pencil scenario designs or face-to-face interactions between subjects, coupled with pre- and/or postnegotiation questionnaires. The face-to-face experiments tend to involve brief, well-contained tasks carried out in intracultural settings (cf. the large-scale sixteen-person negotiation simulation in Winham and Bovis 1979).

For example, Harnett and Cummings (1980, 136ff) chose a bilateral monopoly game (a sales negotiation over price and quantity for a single product) to investigate executives' bargaining behavior in eight countries. The negotiators could only communicate via written offers and counter-offers. Graham, whose work was described earlier, has relied on Kelley's (1966) thirty-minute, one-on-one person negotiation involving the sale of televisions, typewriters, and air conditioners. Neale, Northcraft, and Huber's (1987) study of Chinese and American negotiation behavior is based on a twenty-five-minute competitive market involving several retailers and manufacturers who negotiate the delivery, discount, and financing terms for one product and complete as many deals as they can. In this study, the researchers made minor modifications in instructions (e.g., changing the product from refrigerators for Americans to bicycles for the Chinese) and used English instructions for their Chinese subjects, whereas Harnett and Cummings (1980) and Graham translated game instructions and materials into their subjects' native languages (see also Brett et al. 1998.)

Intercultural experiments are far less common, although their number is rising. Examples include the Kelley game described previously (Adler and Graham 1989), a task involving the disposition of parcels of farmland (Lituchy 1992), an industrial product sale negotiated by American-Korean dyads (Kimmel 1993), and a one-on-one American-Japanese negotiation over syndication rights to a television show (Brett and Okumura 1998). Notable paper-and-pencil experiments on intercultural negotiations include Francis 1991 and Tse, Francis, and Walls 1994.

For both intracultural and intercultural settings, data have been based on pre- and postnegotiation questionnaires completed by participants (e.g., see appendix of Adler and Graham 1989) and built-in measures of the negotiated final outcomes (e.g., profit). An important contribution from comparative research in the late 1990s has been the inclusion of prenegotiation, cultural values questionnaires for confirmatory tests (e.g., Tinsley and Pillutla 1998). The values of the subjects in various country groups have not, as in prior research, simply been assumed or ignored. These various data have been analyzed by ANOVA (e.g., Kimmel 1993) and regression (e.g., Graham 1983), among other techniques. Videotaping proceedings, while enticing, has been associated so far with only "exploratory" qualitative analysis (e.g., Graham 1985, 1992; cf. Cai, Wilson, and Drake 2000), and other possible data sources such as audio tape and transcripts have been largely untapped (cf. Adair and Brett 2001).

There are some drawbacks and challenges in this research, just as in others. The most obvious may be the validity of generalizing behavioral conclusions to real negotiations, particularly given the types of subjects and tasks in experiments to date (see Eliashberg, Lilien, and Kim 1995). Student behavior may seem unrepresentative of manager behavior prima facie (Graham 1984b, 56, based on Fouraker and Siegel 1963). At the same time, researchers who have employed managers in executive training programs ("convenience samples" in Graham, Evenko, and Rajan 1992) have assumed, not demonstrated, their representativeness. Managers who participate in negotiation workshops conducted by foreign experts may be unusual subgroups in their countries and moreover, may behave in ways particular to the workshop setting. This generalizability debate begs for empirical data.

Furthermore, as negotiation researchers discovered in the 1970s (see Pruitt 1981), an experiment requiring subjects to negotiate one issue tends to elicit or reveal only aspects of distributive—competitive—bargaining behavior as opposed to other aspects of behavior or choices between different types of negotiation. An experimenter must search out such biases. The problem of correspondence between experiment and phenomenon in situ seems especially problematic in attempts to relate short, experimental negotiations between two individuals to protracted, multi-issue international negotiations between two or more organizations (cf. Weick 1965, as quoted in Harnett and Cummings 1980, 8).

GENERAL CONCERNS

Important methodological concerns, for both established researchers and those new to the field, cut across all of the aforementioned research methods. One is the anthropologist's classic distinction between etic and emic perspectives (Pike 1966). Three others stem specifically from the nature of negotiation: having access to real negotiations, developing "twin-sided data" and "two-direction comparisons," and limiting the distortion caused by reductionist or naive approaches.[14]

By and large, international business negotiations researchers have neglected the relevance and consequences of etic and emic perspectives in their work. Briefly, an emic approach examines behavior from within a cultural system, so that the analyst "discovers" its structure and relates analytic criteria to internal characteristics. An etic approach studies behavior from a position outside the system, where the analyst creates or imposes a structure and treats his or her criteria as absolute or universal (Berry 1980, 11–12, as quoted in Gudykunst and Ting-Toomey 1988, 226; see also Hall 1985). A pseudo-etic perspective (Triandis 1972, 39) refers to emic (often American) concepts and instruments simply translated and applied elsewhere. Etic- and emic-based issues are starting to be raised in international business negotiations research literature, primarily by methodologically oriented scholars who entered the field in the 1990s (e.g., Lytle et al. 1995; Jehn and Weldon 1992).

Consider, for example, American meanings of such common concepts as collaborating and integrative negotiating behavior. A French negotiation scholar has concluded after decades of observation that the French simply do not comprehend "principled negotiation" (Fisher and Ury 1981). This concept, which refers to an emphasis on interests, inventing options, and objective criteria, "does not translate" (personal communication).

Collaborating, one of five conflict-handling styles identified by Kilmann and Thomas (1977), is distinguished in the United States by high concern for self and high concern for others. When Jehn and Weldon (1992) surveyed Chinese managers, however, the managers' responses showed no recognition of a concern-for-others dimension. Coding responses according to the five categories employed in the United States resulted in one significant difference between Chinese and American frequencies, namely, with compromising. Yet when the two researchers set aside these categories to factor analyze responses directly, other characterizations of styles and significant differences emerged (e.g., immediate, direct attention to task-related conflicts versus stalling, extending the time frame).

Experimental designs and interpretations of results may also be affected by unwittingly imported emic biases. For instance, in the Bolter Turbine sales negotiation simulation (Graham 1984a), role directions for the sales representative state that this sale will affect his or her annual bonus. Japanese managers and executives who have played that role in my classes have repeatedly pointed out that in their companies an annual bonus would "never" be tied to one sale (personal communication). Similarly, one may raise questions about the meaningfulness of counting ostensibly similar words (e.g., "no's") across cultures and the cross-cultural equivalence of categories developed in the United States (e.g., Angelmar and Stern 1978). These content analytic schemes rely on explicit, verbal communication. To what extent can such a system detect the implicit signals typical in a high context culture? The very willingness to demonstrate one's behavior in a contrived setting so a researcher can examine it is culturally shaped and variable (Triandis 1972, 36–37). In the end, this etic-emic concern is not a matter of choosing one perspective over the other but one of recognizing the drawbacks of relying on only one of them.

The increasing use of cultural values constructs and measures in experiments and surveys also warrants a cautionary note. Their principal appeal in many studies seems to be their quantification, as reflected in the limited discussion of the values themselves, simple conceptualizations of their role in negotiation, and inattention to other cultural variables and other techniques by which to address culture (Weiss 1999, 70–72, 77). Individualism and collectivism, typically viewed as polar opposites, may actually be more appropriately treated as separate dimensions (e.g., Cho and Cho 2001). This work also often presumes a one-to-one correspondence between culture and behavior, but multiple values most likely determine a behavior, just as multiple behaviors may result from one value (see Cai, Wilson, and Drake 2000; Gelfand and Dyer 2000).[15]

Among negotiation-specific concerns, direct access to real negotiation sessions is an especially high hurdle for a researcher. While these are the very actions and interactions that intrigue researchers, negotiators understandably fear the negative effects on performance, process, and outcomes that researchers may cause merely by their presence. In some cases, researchers may be able to leverage their expertise. It is said that, in his consulting contract with the Papua New Guinean government in the 1970s, Harvard professor Lou Wells negotiated a clause granting him future access to data and permission to publish analyses of the negotiations for which he provided advice (see Allan, Hammond, and Wells 1974).[16] These opportunities are rare, though, and unless the researcher is a go-between for the parties or is affiliated with one (see Douglas 1962), even these opportunities may perpetuate the problem of one-sidedness discussed shortly.

Alternatives to direct access or participation, such as other meaningful contact with the participants or access to documents, can also elicit concern from negotiators. Sometimes, however, especially upon the completion of a negotiation, a researcher can persuade the participants to open up. The researcher should consider how to address concerns such as the intended use of the information, what may and may not be disclosed publicly, and the prepublication review of manuscripts. Once a negotiator grants an interview, a researcher should diligently try to maintain trust and gain respect; almost any interviewee can open or close doors to other interviewees.

Given the reluctance of negotiators to provide primary information about their sessions, it is not surprising that those researchers who do gain it often obtain permission from only one side or end up with a disproportionate amount of information about one side. The resulting picture of a phenomenon that is by its very essence interactive cannot help but be one-sided. That happens even in some experiments (e.g., Francis 1991) and surveys (e.g., Rao and Schmidt 1998, 673 n. 1). Twin-sided data are clearly preferable, whether they are needed to analyze negotiators' communications or explain the attainment of an agreement (see Brouthers and Bamossy 1997; Faure 2000).

Virtually every study reviewed for this chapter focuses on negotiations that resulted in agreement, yet not all negotiations reach agreement. What we know about international business negotiations thus carries a serious, "single-direction" bias (Roberts 1970). Negotiators may be more reluctant to discuss their negotiation failures than successes, but some researchers set them aside even when they have gained access (e.g., Eiteman 1990, 60). Whatever the circumstances, until researchers decipher causes of no-agreement outcomes (for early inroads, see Downie 1991; Underdal 1983), conclusions about the determinants of negotiation outcomes should be treated as partial or tentative.

Last is the concern about distortion. Real international business negotiations, especially between organizations, appear multifaceted, intrinsically complicated, and dynamic. To the extent that frameworks of *analysis* lead to pictures made up of fragmented and frozen elements, the frameworks need to be used with caution (e.g., Weiss 1993, table 2).

In the same vein, researchers tend somewhat unrealistically to treat negotiation always as a formal process that unfolds at a green baize-covered conference table. But much negotiation occurs informally, in hallways and between subgroups, and tacitly. That is where the real progress and breakthroughs may occur; what happens back at a conference table may simply have been "precooked" (Kaufman 1989, 7). That is, negotiators at the table may simply announce an already made deal or play out a prearranged script to reach a prearranged destination. Thus researchers should not naively concentrate on the negotiating table in their attempts to describe process and explain outcomes.

In sum, the range of these methodological concerns underscores the difficulty—and importance—of carefully designed, conscientiously pursued research in this field (see Triandis 1972, 55–57). No single method appears ideal. Several negotiation researchers advocate the use of multiple methods of data collection and analysis to examine negotiations (e.g., Druckman 1986; George, Jones, and Gonzalez 1998).

EXISTING SUBSTANTIVE KNOWLEDGE: A SAMPLE

What have we learned about international business negotiations through the lenses and methods previously discussed? What empirical results have been obtained? If we set aside the boundaries of the macrostrategic and microbehavioral paradigms, what can we say we know about international business negotiations as a whole?

Over the last thirty years, management research and popular literature have offered numerous observations and lessons. A search in ABI Inform for publications related to international negotiation during half of that period (1986–98) produced 5,138 citations. Clearly, there is a vast amount of information available, though it varies markedly in quality and reliability.

To answer these questions with a degree of confidence, this section focuses on articles in the *Journal of International Business Studies* (*JIBS*), the premier journal in the United States for international business. *JIBS* is peer reviewed, which promises a measure of intersubjectivity, and is not restricted to a single research paradigm. Titles of all articles published between 1976 and mid-2001 were searched for the words "negotiation" or "bargaining." The nineteen resulting articles represent a subset of knowledge feasible to cover here in some detail.

Table 12.1 classifies these articles within the inclusive RBC Perspective described earlier in this chapter. The cell in which an author's name is printed in boldface signifies the article's primary emphasis or focus; regular typeface citations in other cells locate the article's secondary themes. For example, de la Torre's (1981) article concentrates on the essence of the relationship between companies and governments (interorganizational—prenegotiation) but also discusses important types of preparation (behavior—prenegotiation) and negotiation behavior (behavior—negotiation) for each side. These classifications cannot capture all of the topics addressed in the articles, but the table does convey their main substantive emphases. For that matter, the overall pattern of boldface articles and regular typeface

TABLE 12.1. *Journal of International Business Studies,* Articles on International Business Negotiation, 1976–2001 (By predominant analytical orientation, *n* = 19)

	Prenegotiation	Negotiation	Postnegotiatic
RELATIONSHIPS BETWEEN PRIMARY PARTIES			
Interorganizational	de la Torre 1981 (2)	Contractor 1985 (1)	
		Lecraw 1984	
		Tung 1982	
		Vachani 1995	
		Weiss 1990 (2)	
Intergroup			
Interpersonal		George, Jones, & Gonzalez 1998	
		Graham 1983	
		Graham, Evenko, & Rajan 1992	
		Tse, Francis, & Walls 1994	
Cross-level		Francis 1991 (1)	
BEHAVIORS OF PRIMARY PARTIES			
Organizations	Contractor 1985	de la Torre 1981	
	de la Torre 1981	Ramamurti 2001	
	Tung 1982	Tung 1982 (3)	
		Vachani 1995	
		Weiss 1990	
internal			
Groups (Teams)			
internal		Money 1998	
Individuals		Francis 1991	
		George, Jones, & Gonzalez 1998 (3)	
		Graham 1983 (3)	
		Graham 1985 (1)	
		Graham, Evenko, & Rajan 1992 (2)	
		Money 1998 (2)	
		Rao & Schmidt 1998 (2)	
		Tinsley & Pillutla 1998	
		Tse, Francis, & Walls 1994	
CONDITIONS			
Circumstances	Brouthers & Bamossy 1997	Brouthers & Bamossy 1997 (2)	
		George, Jones, & Gonzalez 1998	
Capabilities		Brouthers & Bamossy 1997	
		Brunner & Taoka 1977	
		Fagre & Wells 1982	
		Graham 1983	
		Lecraw 1984 (1)	
		Ramamurti 2001	
		Rao & Schmidt 1998	
		Vachani 1995 (2)	
Cultures		Brunner & Taoka 1977 (2)	
		George, Jones, & Gonzalez 1998	

Graham 1983, 1985
Graham, Evenko, & Rajan 1992
Money 1998
Rao & Schmidt 1998
Tinsley & Pillutla 1998 (2)
Tung 1982
Tse, Francis, & Walls 1994 (2)

Environments
Brunner & Taoka 1977
Ramamurti 2001 (2)
Weiss 1990

Source: Adapted from Weiss 1993, 276.
Note: Boldface citation locates an article's primary focus of study. The number in parentheses indicates the number of other RBC top-addressed as secondary emphases in an article. Secondary emphases are identified by regular typeface.

articles and empty cells constitutes a fair representation of the coverage and gaps in the entire research literature on international business negotiations.

RELATIONSHIPS

In the RBC Perspective, "relationships" refers to the connection between the primary parties and includes aspects such as their common and conflicting interests, the balance of power, the character of their interaction, and negotiation outcomes.

INTERORGANIZATIONAL

Half of the nineteen articles address negotiations between organizations. Three articles (Contractor 1985; de la Torre 1981; Weiss 1990) emphasize the relationship between them. Another three articles (Fagre and Wells 1982; Lecraw 1984; Vachani 1995) concentrate more on one party and its capabilities, so they appear later under the section "Capabilities." And the remaining three articles (Brouthers and Bamossy 1997; Ramamurti 2001; Tung 1982) have to do with some other facet of the framework. Let us probe these articles primarily in the order of their boldface appearance in table 12.1.

De la Torre's (1981, 9, 25) article focuses on the relationship between foreign private investors and developing host countries and "what happens when the twain meet." He argues that neither side tends to consider adequately the other's general objectives, options, and contexts. For instance, governments should understand the importance of market attractiveness and investment climate in firms' investment decisions, and firms should appreciate governments' overall development strategies and their difficulties in developing internal consensus. After reviewing the literature, de la Torre concludes that for better foreign investor–host government relationships, governments should make national development priorities explicit, centralize investment decisions, and set investment regulations that may be flexibly applied. The two sides' negotiations would also be improved by access to more relevant, accurate information (e.g., country economic data, terms of previous agreements between the government and other investors) and by more sophisticated analysis (e.g., social cost-benefit analyses under varying conditions).

Different compensation schemes in joint venture agreements are the subject of Contractor's (1985) article. Although direct investment, licensing, and trade have traditionally been framed as mutually exclusive options, Contractor explores how firms benefit from mixes of equity ownership, royalty payments, and transfer pricing. Each joint venture partner's share of earnings depends on the nature of the mix, the selling price of the joint venture product, and the quantity produced. According to Contractor's formal models, the optimal behavior for a foreign firm seeking solely to maximize profit (issues of risk aside) is to maximize equity share. On the other hand, the optimal mix for a local firm depends on the circumstances. If a host government considers final product prices, tax revenues, and the venture's foreign exchange needs, its best stance, based on these models, is to allow equity investment as the only form of foreign investment and not to cap the foreign partner's share (cf. de la Torre 1981, 19).

Weiss (1990) analyzes IBM Corporation's 1983–86 negotiations with the government of Mexico to establish a wholly owned microcomputer assembly operation. Based on the RBC Perspective, this case study considers the parties involved, their relationships, behaviors, and influencing conditions. There were a number of subparties (e.g., on the IBM side, IBM World Trade Americas/Far East, its Latin American division, and IBM de Mexico, S.A.), advisors (e.g., IBM's Mexican outside counsel), and other interested actors (e.g., the U.S. Embassy in Mexico). Both IBM and the Mexican government had multiple interests in this negotiation, which was influenced by environmental conditions such as the historical U.S.-Mexico relationship and rapid changes in the global computer industry. The talks lasted twenty-three months. During that period, government officials bargained with each other intensively, the National Commission on Foreign Investment rejected two investment applications from IBM, and IBM shifted from active advocacy to a "quiet" strategy. Both parties treated the negotiations as an educational process: IBM updated government officials on computer technology, and the government deepened IBM's knowledge of local conditions.

INTERGROUP

None of the *JIBS* articles provides substantial coverage of intergroup or interteam relationships in any time period of negotiation. (This is a long-standing gap that is addressed later in the section "Future Research.")

INTERPERSONAL

As table 12.1 shows, four studies touch on relationships between individual negotiators. George, Jones, and Gonzalez (1998) discuss "negative spirals": the increasingly negative, affective reactions that lead to less cooperative interactions in cross-cultural negotiations. In two comparative studies, Graham (1983) and his associates (Graham et al. 1992) found that Americans, Japanese, and Soviets who used a cooperative, problem-solving approach experienced similar approaches by their counterparts. Tse, Francis, and Walls's (1994) research reveals the preferred means of the Chinese and Canadians of dealing with person-related conflict. (For the principal summaries of these studies, see the sections "Individuals" [under "Behavior"] and "Cultures" [under "Conditions"]).

CROSS-LEVEL

Among the nineteen articles, only Francis's (1991) is based on relationships that are asymmetric (involving different levels of social grouping), although it does not analyze them as such. Her experimental study targeted individuals' reactions to adaptation behavior exhibited by a foreign group. Americans assessed effectiveness, "likableness," and other attributes of Japanese sales teams who behaved in American ways to no degree, a moderate degree, or a substantial degree. Japanese who displayed *moderate* adaptation received the most likable and comfortable ratings. Those who adapted substantially were rated as more likely to engender suspicion and less likely to land a contract. Thus, while similarity/attraction promotes the adoption of a counterpart's behavior, it appears that at some level of adaptation, especially in intergroup relations, counterparts become concerned about preserving the distinctiveness of their group. A replication study with Korean teams did not entirely support the effectiveness of moderate adaptation but did confirm the negative reactions associated with substantial adaptation.

BEHAVIORS

The second major facet of the RBC Perspective—behaviors of the primary parties—refers straightforwardly to behaviors directed toward or affecting the counterpart as a party to the negotiation. Such behavior takes place in various arenas, not just at the negotiating table. Verbal styles, bargaining tactics, and even perceptions—with somewhat of a stretch—pertain to this facet.

ORGANIZATIONS

Chinese negotiating style and U.S. firms' success factors in the 1970s represent the main findings in Tung's (1982) report of a survey of U.S. firms. Respondents pointed out Chinese counterparts' indirectness, concern for long-term associations, and extended time for decision making. Over 60 percent of the respondents rated the U.S. firm's "attitude" (i.e., preparation, patience, sincerity) as the most important factor in concluding negotiations successfully. (A more objective analysis of the survey data by Tung [1982, 35] shows that three factors significantly correlated with a firm's successfulness: its years of experience trading with the Chinese, the number of previous negotiations with the Chinese, and knowledge gained by reading books on Chinese industrial practices.) Fewer respondents agreed on causes of failure. About one-third emphasized cultural differences (e.g., communication breakdowns), while another one-third downplayed them. For both success and failure, product characteristics represented the second most responsible factor (cf., more recently, Stewart and Keown 1989). Preparations (behavior—prenegotiation) such as hiring experts to train negotiators and simulated negotiations also correlated with success, albeit at different levels of significance.

GROUPS (TEAMS)

At the group level, whether it be the behavior of groups in negotiation or of individuals within groups (internal), we see again that *JIBS* articles have ignored this topic. Money's (1998) recent model of multilateral negotiation includes a variable labeled "clique formation," which he proposes to be positively correlated with negotiators' low individualism, high uncertainty avoidance, and low masculinity.

INDIVIDUALS

In contrast to group behavior, individual negotiators' behavior has received a great deal of attention in *JIBS,* as well as in the field generally. Graham's studies (1983, 1985, 1992) are a prime example. They investigated American, Brazilian, Japanese, and Soviet behavior in intracultural negotiation experiments. Use of a problem-solving approach and other behaviors were measured through self-reports by negotiators and through counterparts' perceptions in postnegotiation questionnaires. In addition, Graham (1985, 1992) videotaped negotiations. Results for the four countries are summarized in table 12.2, along with results from some other countries.

With respect to Japanese negotiating style, Graham (1985) found that they made more extreme initial offers in their negotiations than did Americans in theirs (Americans made "fair" offers), said "no" less often, remained silent longer, and used aggressive tactics only later in negotiation and in the buyer, not seller, role. (Similarities between the Japanese and Americans included their common frequency in asking questions.) In the Japanese negotiations, counterparts also tended to reciprocate when the negotiator used a problem-solving approach. But negotiation behavior does not explain much variance in individuals' profit levels; more variance is explained by an individual's preestablished role as buyer or seller (Graham 1983, 55; cf. Brett and Okumura 1998).

Brazilians, in comparison to Americans, made more extreme first offers (even more extreme than the Japanese), fewer promises and commitments, and more commands, and they interacted longer (Graham 1985, 84, 88). Furthermore, they interrupted each other more often ("fighting for the floor"), made greater eye contact and more physical contact, and uttered an extraordinary number of "no"s. To explain high profit levels here, Graham (1983, 56) cites the effective use of powerful and deceptive strategies (see "BRZ" in table 12.2).

Soviet negotiators interrupted each other more often than did Americans yet made fewer direct references to the other negotiator (use of "you"). Graham (1992, 409) states, though, that the overall picture of Soviet behavior is "not so clear." Soviets exhibited more problem-solving behavior than did Americans, and a strong, significant relationship emerged between negotiators' and counterparts' uses of a problem-solving approach.

TABLE 12.2. Comparative Results from Graham et al.'s Intracultural (Kelley) Negotiation Experiments (n = 40 to 80, with exception of USA [n = 134])

	North America			W. Europe			E. Europe		Asia							Latin America	
	USA	CDN^A	CDN^F	FRN	GRM	UK	CZC	SOV	CHN^N	CHN^S	HK	JPN	KOR	PHL	TWN	BRZ	MEX
OUTCOMES (means)																	
Buyer's profit	46.8[a]	47.9	42.3	49.0	42.8	50.0	42.6	45.4	45.6	45.7	49.2	51.6	46.8	44.5	44.3	47.3	48.6
Seller's profit	43.5	42.5	44.1	42.2	39.0	44.3	41.8	40.5	46.7	40.0	44.7	44.3	38.6	39.5	40.1	45.5	37.7
Joint profit	90.3	90.4	86.4	91.2	81.8	94.3	84.4	85.9	92.3	85.7	93.9	95.9	85.4	84.0	84.4	92.8	86.3
$Profit_{Buyer} > Profit_{Seller}$	n.s.	*	n.s.	n.s.	n.s.	*	n.s.	n.s.	n.s.	n.s.	*	*	*	n.s.	n.s.	n.s.	*
PROCESS ~ OUTCOME[1]																	
$PSA_N \rightarrow Profit_N$	n.s.	*	n.s.	n.s.	*	*	n.s.	*	n.s.			n.s.	n.s.		*	n.s.	*
$PSA_C \rightarrow Profit_N$	*	*	*	n.s.	n.s.	n.s.		n.s.	n.s.	*		n.s.	n.s.		n.s.	n.s.	n.s.
$ATT_N \rightarrow SAT_C$	*[b]	*	n.s.	*	*	n.s.		*	*			*[c]	*		*		*
$PSA_N \rightarrow SAT_C$	*	*	*	n.s.	*	n.s.		*	*(–)	n.s.	*	n.s.	n.s.	n.s.	n.s.		n.s.
PROCESS ~ PROCESS[1]																	
$PSA_N \rightarrow PSA_C$	*	*	n.s.	n.s.	n.s.	n.s.	*	*	*	*		*	*		n.s.		*

Sources: For all profit means and their significance, including CHINA-North, South, Graham 1993

For all significance results of correlations: BRZ: Graham 1983; CDN (Anglo, French), MEX: Adler, Graham, & Schwarz Gehrke 1987; CHN^N: Graham, Mintu, & Rodgers 1994; FRN, GRM, UK: Campbell et al. 1988; JPN, KOR, TWN, USA: Graham et al. 1988; SOV: Graham, Evenko, & Rajan 1992

Notes: [1]Based on partial correlation coefficients.

ATT: Attractiveness

PSA: Problem-solving approach (cooperative, integrative, and information-exchange-oriented behavior)

SAT: Satisfaction

N: Negotiator   C: Counterpart

*significance at p ≤ .05

n.s. not significant at .05 or better

blank indicates no results published

[a]Some of these mean profit statistics differ from those reported in other articles (e.g., Graham 1983)

[b]Positively signed in Graham et al 1988; negatively signed in Graham 1984

[c]Significant for one measure of ATT, not for the other

For Soviet negotiators, however, using a problem-solving approach had a much stronger *negative* effect on individual profits and mattered less in satisfying counterparts.

The three remaining articles in the individuals' behavior category reach beyond the traditional topics and methods of comparative, microbehavioral research. George, Jones, and Gonzalez (1998) draw attention to the nature and effects of emotion in cross-cultural negotiation (see also Adler, Ronen, and Silverstein 1998; Kumar 1999). Citing existing research, they show how negotiator affect primes one's substantive information processing in such a way that one will select information congruent with those feelings. Negative affect causes and sustains negative spirals. More generally, the authors suggest that affect in negotiation is determined by three factors: individual differences (e.g., affective disposition), cross-cultural differences (e.g., rules for expressing emotion), and context (e.g., negotiators' relationship).

Money (1998) departs from tradition by being the only author of the nineteen to focus not on bilateral negotiations but on multilateral ones such as those undertaken to form SEMATECH and Airbus. He still targets individuals' behavior—in particular, their level of problem solving—and the negotiated outcome. In his model, behavior and outcome are shaped by clique formation and emergent roles, which are themselves influenced by national culture, other organizational factors (e.g., size, experience), and individual characteristics (e.g., personality). The behavior of negotiators in cliques—coalitions—may be the most interesting element of this preliminary model.

Finally, Rao and Schmidt's (1998) empirical study provides some answers to questions about how American executives try to influence counterparts in international joint venture negotiations. The authors draw on organizational- and individual-level theories—specifically, transactions cost, power dependence, and game theory—to identify six independent variables: conflict frames, trust, power, cultural distance, time horizon, and interpersonal orientation. Their dependent variable was the type of influence tactic: soft (e.g., emphasize friendliness), hard (e.g., make a threat), and rational (i.e., use logic and data). Executives involved in eighty-one joint venture negotiations in twenty-five different countries, between 1989 and 1991, completed questionnaires. According to self-reports, these U.S. negotiators most frequently used rational tactics, then hard ones, and, finally, soft tactics. The time horizon of the collaboration positively influenced the use of rational tactics. The tactical usage best explained by Rao and Schmidt is soft tactics: 29 percent of their variance is correlated with variables in the study, most notably, partner's alternatives, cultural distance, and trust in partner. (The first two variables are positively signed, whereas trust in partner is negative.[17])

CONDITIONS

The third of the three RBC facets of negotiation—conditions—refers to "factors that stimulate, restrict or otherwise modify the primary parties' behavior and relationships in . . . negotiation" (Weiss 1993, 286ff). Four types of conditions were defined in the section "Analytic Frameworks." The first—circumstances—envelopes both, or all, primary parties; the remaining three may be visualized as concentric rings around each party separately.

CIRCUMSTANCES

As table 12.1 shows, only one *JIBS* article emphasizes the effects of circumstances on negotiation process and outcomes. Brouthers and Bamossy (1997) empirically investigated the role of key stakeholders—in this case, local governments controlling the ownership of state-owned enterprises (SOEs)—in joint venture negotiations. They sampled eight negotiations between West European firms and SOEs in Central/Eastern Europe from 1990 to 1994, admirably interviewing negotiators from both sides for each negotiation. Among a multifaceted set of results, the authors found that stakeholders exerted significant influence on seven of the eight negotiations and wielded the most influence in those involving strategic industries such as telecommunications. In two cases, the stakeholders weakened the SOE's position. The stakeholders most often made their moves before and after, not during, negotiation. In prenegotiation periods, these included forcing the SOE to negotiate, signaling objectives for the SOE, using their resources tactically, and altering industry structure. Other tactics observed, but less frequently, were replacing key managers, limiting SOE equity in the joint venture, hiring Western investment bankers to advise the SOE, and limiting market share for the joint venture. (On stakeholders, see also Phatak and Habib 1996.)

Other works in table 12.1 give some attention to circumstances. For example, George, Jones, and Gonzalez (1998) posit the relevance to negotiators' interactions of previous joint experiences, the language chosen for negotiation, and time pressures. In passing, Tung (1982, 31) describes the number of members of Chinese negotiating teams and the provision of interpreters, and Weiss (1990, 579, 582) mentions the communication channels used (letter and telephone) in the IBM-Mexico negotiations.

CAPABILITIES

Parties' capabilities (e.g., skills, resources, traits, roles) are considered in a number of articles, for this category is closely aligned with the bargaining school paradigm. All three articles in boldface in table 12.1 concentrate on MNE bargaining power and resources in the MNE–host government relationship. However, the second and third articles also offer some insight into the government side of the relationship.

Fagre and Wells's (1982) study demonstrates that U.S. firms' percentage of ownership of their Latin American subsidiaries through the mid-1970s was significantly correlated with the parent firms' level of technology, access to foreign markets, product differentiation, and product diversity. With the inclusion of one more factor (size of subsidiary), these variables account for 12 to 14 percent of the variance in ownership of subsidiaries across Latin America and up to 25 percent for Mexico, depending on the use of actual or corrected ownership percentages.

Lecraw (1984) confirmed the significance of these MNE capabilities with data on various MNEs' subsidiaries in Southeast Asia. In addition, he analyzed MNE-subsidiary linkages and government capabilities, namely, host-country attractiveness and potential MNE investors. These three factors *negatively* affected the equity levels that parents obtained in subsidiaries. Depending on the outcome measure used, 47 to 63 percent of the variance in these MNE-government negotiation outcomes is attributable to these MNE and government capabilities.

Nearly a dozen years later, Vachani (1995) argued that no one had yet empirically investigated the temporal dimension—the actual obsolescence—of the obsolescing bargain. He studied the level of ownership retained by U.S.-, U.K.-, and other European-owned companies in India over a fifteen-year period. His data on sixty-one companies show a consistent decline in ownership over this period, with U.K. companies ending up in 1987 with just under 30 percent and U.S. and other European companies retaining roughly 15 percent of the ownership shares they held in 1973. Vachani significantly explains 41 percent of the variance in retained ownership with the size of investment and technology level (both positively signed); also significant are time, U.S. parent, receipt of benefits from host government, and marketing expertise (all negatively signed).

Surprisingly, a larger sunk investment did not make an MNE more vulnerable and export performance was not significant and not positively, but negatively, signed. Vachani attributes the latter to the "low tech" nature of the exports involved.

Graham's studies also touch on this RBC category because they incorporate negotiators' roles. In one experiment (Graham 1983, 54, table 3), Japanese buyers earned significantly greater individual profits than sellers. American and Brazilian buyers also fared better, but not significantly.[18]

CULTURES

Cultural differences have certainly been covered in *JIBS* articles. In addition to the articles listed in the "Cultures" cell in table 12.1, the boldface articles in "Behaviors—Individuals" also discuss culture directly, if not predominantly. These two categories most closely represent the comparative, microbehavioral paradigm. The studies by Weiss (1990), Francis (1991), and Tung (1982) also offer observations about cultural aspects of international business negotiations. But here, let us turn to the findings in the three boldface titles not yet discussed, all of which concern Chinese and North American negotiators.

In one of the earliest surveys of American businessmen in the People's Republic of China, Brunner and Taoka (1977) probed views on a wide range of topics. What did they learn with respect to culture? Respondents strongly agreed that the Chinese were "extremely tough negotiators" (72), took longer than Europeans to respond to proposals, required more interaction than Americans expected before they extended trust, and preferred group decisions over individual ones. Other relevant findings have to do with other negotiating practices, the negotiating atmosphere, and specifications in contracts. One more lesson the two authors offer, without actually stating, is that individuals' experiences and opinions can vary substantially: Out of thirty-eight survey questions, twenty-four elicited answers with moderate to high variation among respondents.

In 1998, Tinsley and Pillutla experimentally tested how and why Americans and Hong Kong Chinese differ in their views of appropriate negotiation strategies (i.e., norms). They expected such differences to stem from differences in cultural values such as self-enhancement (individualism), self-transcendence (collectivism), and conservatism/openness to change. The conceivable negotiation strategies were self-interested, altruistic, joint problem solving, competitive, and equality (compromise). In questionnaires completed after participating in intracultural negotiations, American students favored self-interest and problem-solving norms, whereas Hong Kong Chinese preferred equality norms. Americans favored high joint gain outcomes, while Hong Kong Chinese rated equal outcomes as most satisfactory.

These results run counter to a standing view that high collectivism is associated with cooperation and joint problem solving. The Hong Kong Chinese did test significantly higher in collectivism than did the Americans. The authors explain, however, that collectivism may be an insufficient condition for joint problem solving because problem solving requires innovation, that is, openness to change. When collectivism or cooperation is linked to conservatism, as occurred in this study, it leads to an equality norm.

Tse, Francis, and Walls (1994) also investigated preferred strategies, but for conflicts handled by Chinese and Canadian executives. Their experiment called for the executives to respond to joint project scenarios that varied with respect to the partner involved (same culture or foreign) and the conflict (task based or person based). Options included five positive conflict resolution strategies (be friendly, compromise, seek more information, consult superior, delay decision) and two negative strategies (threaten to withdraw, discontinue negotiation). Responses were most strongly affected by the country of the respondent. Chinese executives generally recommended negative strategies more often than Canadians did. For positive strategies, Chinese preferred "consult superior" more than Canadians did but "delay decision" less than Canadians. Several interesting results also appeared in country-conflict interaction effects. Chinese recommended discontinuing negotiation much more strongly when conflict was person based than task based. Canadians recommended "be friendly" more highly when conflict was person based than task based, yet Chinese preferred just the opposite. Neither the Chinese nor the Canadians significantly changed their strategies when dealing with intercultural versus intracultural conflict (nationality of partner).

ENVIRONMENTS

Finally, these nineteen *JIBS* articles display little interest in the noncultural environment of negotiating parties. Brunner and Taoka (1977) mention the effects of factors such as the U.S.-China trade relationship and foreign competition in China on American negotiators' efforts. Weiss's

(1990) IBM-Mexico case study refers to conditions such as the global computer market, the Mexican economy, and diplomatic ties between the United States and Mexico. But only the most recent article in the series really deals with this topic.

Ramamurti (2001) argues that the traditional model of the bargaining school has become outdated, made irrelevant by developments over the last thirty years. Host government policies on foreign direct investment changed from regulation in the 1970s to promotion in the 1980s and 1990s. Ramamurti states that such investment and trade policies are the result not simply of national policy-making but of negotiations between an MNE's home government and the host government, both bilaterally and through multilateral institutions. These "Tier 1 bargains" set macrorules for foreign direct investment that condition microlevel, "Tier 2" negotiations between the MNE and host government.[19] Ramamurti proposes that empirical studies, which are needed to validate his model, will find that in the 1990s a weak MNE from a strong country had more bargaining power than a strong MNE from a weak country (whereas the opposite would hold in the traditional model).

OTHER RELEVANT RESEARCH

While the *JIBS* articles in table 12.1 accurately portray the substantive emphases in the literature on international business negotiations, additional work is worth noting. Some of it relates to empty cells in the table. Other work addresses topics covered in the table but has investigated them from a different perspective or with different results. This work is typically not situated within the field of negotiation. Examples include research on international joint ventures, conflict management, and multicultural teams.

Among the empty cells in table 12.1, the internal behavior of organizations in negotiations has attracted some attention. Encarnation and Wells (1985) have examined how governments organize for their foreign investment negotiations with corporations. In a study of two joint venture negotiations, Weiss (1997, 268, 275–76) learned that intraorganizational conflict and *keiretsu* pressure were major causes of one negotiation outcome.

The postnegotiation period, while again relatively neglected, is precisely the focus of a series of studies by Stoever (1979, 1981) on "renegotiations" between host governments and foreign companies. He outlined factors that trigger renegotiation (e.g., change in government, unusual visibility of a company's project, unpopular actions by the company's home government) and various characteristics of the interaction that follows (e.g., its threatening quality for the foreign company). His case studies include copper mining in Zambia and ITT's operations in Chile in the early 1970s.[20]

As to other fields or bodies of work, interorganizational relationships (e.g., Oliver 1990), and international joint ventures in particular, offer the negotiation researcher much to consider. Existing knowledge about joint ventures includes the motivations for joint ventures (e.g., Contractor and Lorange 1988; Kogut 1988), selection of partners (e.g., Geringer 1991), resource contributions and bargaining power in negotiations (e.g., Blodgett 1991; Harrigan 1985; Yan and Gray 1994), conflict resolution (e.g., Lin and Germain 1998), and structuring different types of relationships (e.g., Beamish 1985; Killing 1983; Walsh, Wang, and Xin 1999).

Conflict resolution/management research has also produced germane empirical findings. For instance, Sullivan et al. (1981) discovered that Japanese managers preferred to resolve joint venture disputes and build trust through conferral rather than arbitration, *except* when an American was in charge of operations. In that case, Japanese preferred to have binding arbitration written into joint venture contracts (cf. Dyer and Song 1997). More recently, Morris et al. (1998) found that Chinese managers preferred to avoid explicit negotiation in workplace conflict, whereas American managers took a competitive approach. These choices are respectively explained by the underlying values of social conservatism and self-enhancement. This body of comparative research has concentrated on Asia (e.g., Leung and Tjosvold 1998; Ting-Toomey et al. 1991) but is expanding to include European and other countries (e.g., Tinsley 1998; van Oudenhoven, Mechelse, and de Dreu 1998).

Finally, the activities of multicultural teams, a relatively new area of research, have been the subject of rich, ethnographic, and distinctly intercultural studies. They delve into how managers create—or negotiate— new, hybrid cultures and the levels of heterogeneity optimal for performance (e.g., Earley and Mosakowski 2000; Salk and Brannen 2000). Salk (1996–97) cautions that, in practice, managers cite "cultural differences" for various purposes, including preservation of their social identities. Their use of the term is not as straightforward or objective as it appears in research: Characterizations of team members from other countries may differ significantly from their actual behavior.

FUTURE RESEARCH

There is still much about international business negotiations to try to understand. The amount of unexplained variance in analyses to date readily attests to that. In table 12.1, there are completely empty and other neglected cells. Even the cells with boldface entries have not been exhaustively explored; only some of the facets that they represent have been examined in the works listed. Beyond the general topics that each cell represents lie numerous applications and contexts. Imagine the list of possibilities created by multiplying the number of types of business activities by country pairs or combinations across the globe and then multiplying that by different industry or company pairings.

From such a vast universe, one could easily suggest a number of topics for future research. The challenge is to identify areas of work that will significantly advance the field. That goal motivates this final section, which singles out a few topics and recommends two reorientations for researchers.

PROSPECTIVE TOPICS

The foregoing sections of this chapter suggest four major aspects of international business negotiations for further research: interaction between the parties; intergroup (interteam) relationships; influencing conditions; and no-agreement outcomes. Each is a fundamental topic and intrinsic to the core goals of describing process and explaining outcomes. All four topics can accommodate both macrostrategic and microbehavioral perspectives. At the same time, these paradigms may be enriched—perhaps bridged or integrated—by covering these topics.

INTERACTION BETWEEN THE PARTIES

So far, neither the macrostrategic nor microbehavioral paradigm has revealed much about the essential mutual movement—the continuous, back-and-forth dynamic—between international negotiators. Microbehavioral literature provides data on individuals' global, postnegotiation impressions of counterpart behavior and the frequencies of individuals' actions, but not descriptions of interaction sequences. (See also intercultural negotiations in the upcoming section "Three Additional Topics.") Macrostrategic research has omitted behavior altogether. Thus the process—the pulsing heart of negotiation—remains either a "black box" (Gelfand and Dyer 2000, 78) or a jumble of loose pieces.

In what ways, for instance, do counterparts respond to negotiators' various requests for information, and how do effective negotiators respond to those responses? How is a party's greater bargaining power manifest in its actions and in counterpart reactions during negotiation? Does perception of power vary during negotiation, with factors such as issues? How do the myriad exchanges and action chains in a negotiation combine to define the negotiation process, and how do these "mini-exchanges"—or which of them—determine the final outcome?

Some of these questions may be answered by paying more attention to the temporal dimension of negotiation (see e.g., Adair and Brett 2001). The stage models discussed earlier (recall figure 12.3) represent a step in this direction, although they have yet to be rigorously validated and historically such conceptualizations have been limited by the methods available to test them (namely, static categorization schemes). According to Holmes (1992, 100), small group decision research has developed techniques well suited to process analysis of negotiations—techniques such as flexible phase mapping, gamma analysis, and optimal matching (see also Druckman 1986). Future international research may also benefit from considering patterns of interaction that are not strictly linear or sequential and from reassessing principally American definitions of what constitutes negotiation and the boundaries of the "negotiation period" and pre- and postnegotiation.

INTERGROUP (INTERTEAM) RELATIONSHIPS

As table 12.1 shows, studies in the United States have neglected group activity. This is not unique to international business negotiations research. Commenting on American management theories generally, Hofstede (1993, 92) has observed: "A stress on interactions among individuals obviously fits a culture identified as the most individualistic in the world, but it will not be so well understood by the four-fifths of the world population for whom the group prevails over the individual." Moreover, international negotiations often involve teams of negotiators.

There are basic questions to tackle in this area. What are the key internal and horizontal dynamics of negotiations between teams? How do different distributions of bargaining power among team members affect these dynamics? Which factors influence negotiation outcomes? How do negotiations between culturally heterogeneous teams differ from those between homogeneous teams?

International business negotiation researchers may draw on the sizeable body of general, "within-group" literature on workgroups and teams (e.g., Donnellon 1996; Gersick 1988; Jehn, Northcraft, and Neale 1999), along with the smaller literature on intergroup relations (e.g., Brett and Rognes 1986; Kramer 1991) and on negotiating groups (e.g., Carlisle and Leary 1981). The research on multicultural teams discussed earlier in this chapter should also offer some insights.

INFLUENCING CONDITIONS

After an exhaustive review of negotiation research in marketing, Eliashberg, Lilien, and Kam (1995, G56–57) concluded: "strategy MUST depend on the specific situation" (authors' emphasis). Other reviewers have equally stressed the importance of contexts (e.g., Cai, Wilson, and Drake 2000; Simintiras and Thomas 1998). Yet macrostrategic researchers have concentrated almost exclusively on capabilities (and resource-based power, in particular), while microbehavioral researchers have targeted only national cultures.

There are many other potentially significant conditions to investigate. To what extent do circumstances such as prior relationships predetermine negotiator behavior and negotiation outcomes? How much explanatory value can context-based notions of power (Yan and Gray 1994) and environmental conditions such as the host-home government relationship (Ramamurti 2001) add to macrostrategic explanations? How do cross-level and asymmetric negotiations—between, say, an individual (small business owner) and a group (MNE team) or between unequally sized teams—differ from same-level or symmetric negotiations? Do high stakes affect international negotiator behavior, given the many other factors in play? How do organizational and professional cultures influence the impact of national culture? Such questions involve not only main effects between condition and behavior, and condition and outcome, but relationships among conditions and moderating effects of conditions on relationships between other variables.

NO-AGREEMENT OUTCOMES

Although this term, rather than "failures," has become part of negotiation researchers' lexicon (e.g., Sebenius 1983), it has received little empirical attention (for reasons, see Kesner and Shapiro 1991). Existing literature still has the single-direction bias toward agreement outcomes discussed in the section on research methods (for an exception, see Weiss 1997). Not knowing much about these outcomes is a particularly salient gap in our knowledge about international business negotiations.

THREE ADDITIONAL TOPICS
While the previous topics pertain to both existing research paradigms, one might also note narrower but important additional topics. Let us consider just three of them: intercultural negotiations, multiparty negotiations, and testing prescriptions.

INTERCULTURAL NEGOTIATIONS
As seen in earlier sections, microbehavioral research has been characterized by comparisons of intracultural negotiations. By definition, however, international business negotiation is intercultural negotiation, and researchers cannot take for granted that intraculturally based descriptions, explanations, or predictions apply to intercultural negotiations. In the limited research directly on this issue, most studies have shown that negotiators behave differently in the two situations (e.g., Brett and Okumura 1998; cf. Tse, Francis, and Walls 1994). Even relatively young individuals considered part of cosmopolitan elites retain differences distinguishable by national background (Morris et al. 1998). Clearly, intercultural negotiations per se deserve more direct examination.[21]

MULTIPARTY NEGOTIATIONS
Fayerweather and Kapoor (1976, 31) pointed out long ago that MNE–host government negotiations over direct investments are "rarely bilateral . . . but multilateral." The overwhelming majority of existing management research, at both the macrolevel and the microlevel, still concerns bilateral negotiations. The use of multimember strategic alliances (e.g., Airbus, the Star Alliance) and their expanding scope since the 1980s (e.g., "relationship enterprises," in "The Global Firm: R.I.P." 1993), and other multiparty business relationships, underscore the contemporary relevance of this topic. Money's (1998) *JIBS* article represents a foray into this area. Political science literature should also hold some useful leads (e.g., Zartman 1994).

TESTING PRESCRIPTIONS
Like other management researchers and perhaps even more because of the practical nature of the subject, international business negotiation

researchers aspire to assist negotiators and improve practice.[22] Recommendations and management implications are set forth in almost every book and article on the subject, whether general audience or research oriented. But very few prescriptions for strategy or action have themselves been empirically tested. Within the microbehavioral paradigm, the long-standing assumption and common recommendation to adopt the counterpart's approach was found, once tested, to be counterproductive (Francis 1991). Other strategies have been conceptualized (Weiss 1994b) but not yet tested. For macrostrategic research involving large-scale negotiations between organizations, de la Torre's (1981, 25) observation from years ago still applies today: "We need to learn a great deal more about these ['increasingly complex'] negotiating processes in order to reach any normative conclusions and translate them into training programs." These programs, too, should be subject to study and evaluation.

PURSUING METHODOLOGICAL RIGOR BUT WITH CIRCUMSPECTION

The 1996 version of this review recommended greater attention to methodological rigor—both qualitative and quantitative—and to cross-cultural validity. The concerns that prompted that call still appear in the research methods section of this chapter, but there has been major progress in the late 1990s. More experimental studies are measuring subjects' cultural values instead of assuming them and examining intracultural—within-sample—as well as intercultural variation (e.g., Tinsley and Pillutla 1998), and survey researchers are standardizing responses to control for response bias before making cross-cultural comparisons (e.g., Morris et al. 1998). These kinds of steps should continue.

At the same time, researchers might well make room for more circumspection in their work. Many studies of cultural aspects of negotiation have relied upon—and perhaps been instigated by—one quantitative technique: Hofstede's value questionnaire (or, increasingly, Schwartz's). What aspects does this approach sidestep? Existing research consists of many individual studies, each written to show how it "breaks new ground." Too little space is devoted to placing them in the larger context of the field or phenomenon as a whole and to drawing connections with other studies, including those outside one's operating paradigm.

At this point in its development, the field stands to benefit considerably from studies designed to confirm previous findings and then to test their robustness or generalizability across subjects (or respondents), negotiating conditions, and methods. Surveys and experiments could be replicated with similar samples. Those previously run with convenience samples could be rerun with other, preferably random samples. Data from scenario-based experiments, postnegotiation role-play questionnaires, and surveys could be compared with data from direct observation of behavior in situ and examined with multiple analytic techniques (see George, Jones, and Gonzalez 1998; Vachani 1995).

This orientation should encourage researchers to devote more effort to grappling with apparent contradictions and conflicts in their findings. In Tinsley and Pillutla's (1998) experiments, for example, Hong Kong Chinese negotiators behaved less integratively than did Americans, while the opposite occurred in Graham's role plays (see table 12.2). In other experiments (Graham 1993), his Japanese negotiators achieved higher joint gains than did Americans and differed significantly in their results by role; neither was the case in Brett and Okumura's (1998, 502, 504) experiments (see also Harnett and Cummings 1980, 144). All in all, more multimethod, multisample research, spearheaded by interesting and probing questions, would enable researchers to assimilate findings, increase confidence levels, and better consolidate knowledge.

LEARNING FROM AND WITH RESEARCHERS IN OTHER COUNTRIES

As a first rule for good cross-cultural research, Triandis (1972, 55) has recommended contacting "competent social scientists in the cultures in which you plan to work." There are a number of examples of collaboration in research on international business negotiations, especially among comparative, microbehavioral researchers and especially since the mid-1990s. Triandis et al.'s (2001) work on culture and deception, for instance, is the fruit of a sixteen-person research team.[23]

Assembling an international research team is not only a way of expanding one's geographical scope and of gaining access to data; more important, it is a countermeasure for playing to one's own biases and a means of developing cross-cultural validity in research. For this, researchers from other countries must be involved in conceptualizations and in research design. The studies reviewed in this chapter have practically all been based on U.S. research paradigms and methods, and a perusal of their reference lists suggests that American researchers have largely neglected other countries' negotiation literatures. The studies contain little discussion about emic perspectives, yet Cohen (1997), among others, has convincingly argued that "bargaining," "negotiation," and "compromise" (and, most likely, "proposal" and "agreement" as well) can each carry very different meanings across cultures. Such differences could affect the very target of one's research.

There are significant, historical and growing negotiation literatures in countries besides the United States. In France, for example, one can find dozens of books, not to mention articles, on negotiation (e.g., de Callières 1963 [1716]; Chalvin 1984; Dupont 1990; Rojot 1991). In China, according to a recent review, there are fourteen textbooks just on international business negotiation (Zhao 2000). While many of these books include coverage of U.S. research, they also lay out different views of negotiation and critiques of some U.S.-based views (see, e.g., Faure et al. 2000, 184–87). By considering these bodies of work, researchers in the United States can learn more about international negotiation and about how others think about it.

CONCLUSION

To many people, international business negotiations research appears to be a field of management research only a few years old, yet its origins, as we have seen, go back at least thirty years. In the United States, the field has an identifiable, if fragmented, history. The macrostrategic and comparative, microbehavioral paradigms are well established. Various frameworks and models are in place, major methodological challenges have been identified, and several substantive areas have been investigated. These are all "bricks" with which and on which to build.

The field holds much promise. While there is still a lot to understand about international negotiation processes and outcomes, increasing numbers of scholars worldwide are being drawn to it. In this broad field, new and well-established researchers can find interesting topics to explore. These topics comprise not only a fascinating subject for research but an essential dimension of international management.

NOTES

1. The labeling of research as "U.S.-based" throughout this article has a triple purpose. First and foremost, it explicitly identifies the research as only from the United States as opposed to globally comprehensive. I do not wish to imply that research on interna-

tional business negotiations takes place only in the United States or that only U.S. research is worth attention; actually, as I will argue later in this chapter, I believe Americans should pay much more attention to other countries' researchers and literatures. Second, U.S. research has been relatively self-contained, and concentrating solely on it enables one to see how that research body developed to what it is today. Third, it is a more manageable amount of literature to cover in the space of a book chapter.

2. Even eleven years later, de la Torre (1981,10) still characterized the literature on host country–foreign investor negotiations as "scant."

3. Other major research on negotiation prior to 1970 developed in the fields of labor relations (e.g., Douglas 1962; Walton and McKersie 1965) and conflict analysis and conflict resolution (e.g., Rapoport 1960; Boulding 1962; and Burton 1969). Note also that the *Journal of Conflict Resolution* was founded in 1956.

4. As in other fields, the label "cross-cultural" has been applied to studies offering pancultural ("generic") negotiation models, to those comparing negotiations within one culture to negotiations in another, and to studies of negotiations between parties from different cultures. One might differentiate these studies with the labels "universal," "comparative," and "multicultural" (Weiss 1987b, 3). (See also Janosik's [1987] distinctions among four cultural perspectives: learned behavior, shared values, culture as dialectic, and culture in context.) The confusion has been exacerbated by researchers' failure to distinguish between the source of their data and the focus of their analyses. Some researchers draw data from international negotiations yet focus entirely on one party's behavior from a comparative perspective (e.g., in political science [Blaker 1977]). Other researchers develop data on intracultural negotiations yet treat their findings as valid for intercultural negotiations. They assume parties will behave similarly in intercultural negotiations.

While international business negotiations research, strictly speaking, would involve only intercultural or multicultural negotiations, resolving this debate and recategorizing works lie beyond the scope of this chapter. Furthermore, useful lessons may be found in and sparked by comparative studies, so they are included here. This chapter will, however, distinguish between the intracultural and the intercultural.

5. Management research on cultural differences, like that on MNE-government negotiations, paralleled research in other fields. They include cultural anthropology, sociology, psychology (e.g., Porat 1970), social psychology (e.g., Druckman et al. 1976), sociolinguistics (e.g., Gumperz 1975), and communications (e.g., Ting-Toomey 1985).

6. Since this chapter is devoted to research, it does not cover the popular or trade literature. It is huge, supplied by diverse sources, and of widely varying quality and reliability. The better works do, however, offer and trigger insights for the management researcher.

7. A search in *ABI Inform* for all articles on international negotiation published from January 1999 to May 2001 produced 947 references. In the same vein, an undated search of the U.S. Library of Congress for "international business negotiation" generated over 10,000 references. (This is only a relative, not precise, count, however, because a quick scan revealed the inclusion of references to noninternational business negotiations as well as to nonbusiness international negotiations.)

8. The Multinational Enterprise Databank covers 187 U.S. Fortune 500 firms with at least six foreign investments over the period 1965–75 (Gomes-Casseres 1990, 7).

9. The bargaining school, particularly for MNE-government relations, should also take up another concern: It still assumes a basically competitive frame on negotiation in a field that, as a whole, has shifted emphasis to integrative potential, value creation, and mutual gain or, in some corners, to the mix of value creation and value claiming. While bargaining school researchers may not wish to totally abandon their perspective, they could nevertheless incorporate these ideas and enrich their conceptualizations of power and the situations and processes in which it is exercised.

10. For a recent survey study of Filipinos and Americans, see Mintu-Wimsatt and Gassenheimer 2000.

11. For an empirical test of the model, see Shemwell 1996.

12. The cyclical model entails information exchange and learning. Gulliver (1979) saw the two models as necessarily intertwined. He likened progress in negotiation—and the relationship between the models—to the movement of a car: wheels constantly rotate about their axles while the car as a whole moves forward (82).

13. For example, an American expert on Japanese industry and business told me that, for one project on research and development practices, he could not use any of the responses to his survey because each respondent had answered according to his organization's party line (personal communication). The researcher threw out the survey and started over. See also Latin American attitudes toward information handling and disclosure in Woodworth and Nelson 1980.

14. Such concerns have raised doubts about the very value of cross-cultural negotiation research up to the mid-1990s. Lytle (1993) has stated: "These studies generally fail to provide convincing evidence that culture is the variable producing the differences between groups." Gelfand and Dyer (2000, 68) and Wilson et al. (1995, 214, 222) have concurred. Lytle cites three underlying problems: (1) the absence of a priori, theoretically based hypotheses predicting why cultures should differ in their negotiation processes; (2) the failure to provide a model detailing how culture will affect negotiations; and (3) generalization of findings to contexts not directly explored, that is, assuming that intracultural negotiation processes apply in intercultural contexts. Elsewhere, Lytle et al. (1995) additionally point to weak construct validity and not specifying whether culture is a direct effect or moderator.

15. Anne Lytle cogently reinforced this point at the annual meeting of the International Association for Conflict Management, June 2001, in Paris, France.

16. Some scholars (e.g., Kogut [1994]) have argued that a researcher should absolutely separate consulting from research and simply not use or develop data from the former for the latter. In general, I share that "pure research" view, for methodological and ethical reasons, but I also believe the field of international business negotiations would gain much from greater access to real negotiations, which may require some compromise (albeit negotiated with the client and explicitly noted in research reports).

17. The trust result runs counter to Rao and Schmidt's hypothesis. As a possible explanation, they suggest that, once trust is established, negotiators may think counterparts can withstand "frank talk"; soft tactics, which may have been used to create the trust, are no longer necessary.

18. In contrast, Harnett and Cummings (1980, 144) have reported that in their

experiments American buyers' profits were significantly greater than sellers' and that Japanese buyers' profits were *smaller* than sellers', but not significantly. See also Brett and Okumura (1998), whose Japanese respondents to a prenegotiation questionnaire viewed the role of the negotiator as more important than did American respondents, although there was "reasonable variance" among the Japanese.

19. This two-tier idea resembles the concepts of "two-level bargaining" and "nested negotiations" in research on international political negotiations (see Mayer 1988; Putnam 1988), both of which have a sizeable following in that literature.

20. Research on Chinese negotiations with foreign-owned MNEs may stimulate a reexamination of the division of "negotiation time" into these three periods, because the Chinese reportedly continue negotiating after a contract is signed (e.g., Chen 1993). They do not delineate as definitively as Americans do between "precontract" and "postnegotiation." See the "Future Research" section of this chapter.

21. A particular topic within this area that could be studied much more intensively is negotiators' ethics. The topic has received only some attention in general negotiation literature (e.g., Reitz, Wall, and Love 1998; Shell 1999, 201ff) and even less in international business negotiations (Usunier and Ghauri 1996).

22. As Triandis (2001, 18) has also written, "everything on this topic [cross-cultural management] is applied."

23. Another major presence in international negotiation research, general in scope rather than specific to business, is the PIN Group originally based at the Institute for Applied Systems Analysis in Vienna. They have sponsored some ten books, including Kremenyuk 1991.

REFERENCES

Adair, W., and J. Brett. 2001. The effects of culture and time on behavioral patterns in deal-making negotiations. Paper presented at the annual meeting of the International Association for Conflict Management, June, Paris.

Adler, N. J., R. Brahm, and J. L. Graham. 1992. Strategy implementation: A comparison of face-to-face negotiations in the People's Republic of China and the United States. *Strategic Management Journal* 13:449–66.

Adler, N. J., and J. L. Graham. 1989. Cross-cultural interaction: The international comparison fallacy? *Journal of International Business Studies* (fall):515–37.

Adler, N. J., J. L. Graham, and T. Schwarz Gehrke. 1987. Business negotiations in Canada, Mexico, and the United States. *Journal of Business Research* 15:411–29.

Adler, R. S., B. Rosen, and E. M. Silverstein. 1998. Emotions in negotiation: How to manage fear and anger. *Negotiation Journal* 14 (2): 161–79.

Allan, G. B., J. S. Hammond, and L. T. Wells Jr. 1974. *Bougainville Copper Ltd. (B) HBS Case no. 9-174-104.* Boston: HBS Case Services.

Allison, G. T. 1971. *The essence of decision.* Boston: Little, Brown.

Angelmar, R., and L. W. Stern. 1978. Development of a content analytic system for analysis of bargaining communication in marketing. *Journal of Marketing Research* 15 (February):93–102.

Araskog, R. V. 1989. *The ITT wars.* New York: Henry Hold.

Beamish, P. W. 1985. The characteristics of joint ventures in developed and developing countries. *Columbia Journal of World Business* 20 (3): 13–19.

Bellace, J. R., and G. W. Latta. 1983. Making the corporation transparent: Prelude to multinational bargaining. *Columbia Journal of World Business* 18 (2): 14–19.

Bennett, D. C., and K. E. Sharpe. 1979. Agenda-setting and bargaining power: The Mexican state versus transnational automobile corporations. *World Politics* (October): 57–89.

Berry, J. 1980. Introduction to methodology. In H. Triandis and J. Berry, eds., *Handbook of cross-cultural psychology,* vol. 2. Boston: Allyn and Bacon.

Blaker, M. 1977. *Japanese international negotiating style.* New York: Columbia University Press.

Blodgett, L. L. 1991. Partner contributions as predictors of equity share in international joint ventures. *Journal of International Business Studies* 22 (1): 63–78.

Boulding, K. 1962. *Conflict and defense.* New York: Harper and Row.

Brannen, M. Y. 1995. Does culture matter? Negotiating a complementary culture to support technological innovation. In J. K. Liker, J. E. Ettlie, and J. C. Campbell, eds., *Engineered in Japan–Japanese technology-management practices,* 321–45. New York: Oxford University Press.

Brett, J. M. 2000. Culture and negotiation. *International Journal of Psychology* 35 (2): 97–104.

———. 2001. *Negotiating globally.* San Francisco: Jossey-Bass.

Brett, J. M., and T. Okumura. 1998. Inter- and intracultural negotiation: U.S. and Japanese negotiators. *Academy of Management Journal* 41 (5): 495–510.

Brett, J. M., and J. K. Rognes. 1986. Intergroup relations in organizations: A negotiations perspective. In P. Goodman and associates, eds., *Designing effective work groups,* 202–36. San Francisco: Jossey-Bass.

Brett, J. M., et al. 1998. Culture and joint gains in negotiation. *Negotiation Journal* 14 (1): 61–86.

Brouthers, K. D., and G. J. Bamossy. 1997. The role of key stakeholders in international joint venture negotiations: Case studies from Eastern Europe. *Journal of International Business Studies* 28:285–308.

Brunner, J. A., and G. Taoka. 1977. Marketing and negotiating in the People's Republic of China: Perceptions of American businessmen who attended the 1975 Canton Fair. *Journal of International Business Studies* 8 (2): 69–82.

Burton, J. W. 1969. *Conflict and communication.* New York: Free Press.

Cai, D. A., and L. E. Drake. 1998. The business of business negotiation: Intercultural perspectives. *Communication Yearbook* 21:153–89.

Cai, D. A., S. R. Wilson, and L. E. Drake. 2000. Culture in the context of intercultural negotiation: Individualism-collectivism and paths to integrative agreements. *Human Communication Research* 26 (4): 591–617.

Campbell, N. C. G., et al. 1988. Marketing negotiations in France, Germany, the United Kingdom, and the United States. *Journal of Marketing* 52:49–62.

Carlisle, J., and M. Leary. 1981. Negotiating groups. In R. Payne and C. Cooper, eds., *Groups at work,* 165–88. Chichester, UK: John Wiley and Sons.

Cavusgil, S. T,. and P. N. Ghauri. 1990. *Doing business in developing countries.* London: Routledge.

Chalvin, D. 1984. *L'entreprise négociatrice.* Paris: Dunod.

Chen, M. 1993. Understanding Chinese and Japanese negotiating styles. *International Executive* 35 (2): 147–59.

Cho, Y.-H., and Y.-H. Cho. 2001. Dual orientations of individualism-collectivism and conflict resolution modes in a collectivist country. Paper presented at the annual meeting of the International Association for Conflict Management, June, Paris.

Cohen, R. 1997. *Negotiating across cultures: Communication obstacles in international diplomacy.* Rev. ed. Washington, DC: U.S. Institute of Peace Press.

Contractor, F. 1985. A generalized theorem for joint-venture and licensing negotiations. *Journal of International Business Studies* 16 (2): 23–50.

Contractor, F., and P. Lorange, eds. 1988. *Cooperative strategies in international business.* Lexington, MA: Lexington Books.

de Beaufort, V., and A. Lempereur. 1996. Preparing mergers and acquisitions in the European Union: The asset of cooperative negotiation. In P. Ghauri and J.-C. Usunier, eds., *International business negotiations,* 273–301. Oxford: Pergamon.

de Callières, F. 1963 [1716]. *On the manner of negotiating with princes.* Trans. A. F. Whyte. Notre Dame: Notre Dame University Press.

de la Torre, J. 1981. Foreign investment and economic development: Conflict and negotiation. *Journal of International Business Studies* 12 (2): 9–32.

DePauw, J. W. 1981. *U.S.-Chinese trade negotiations.* New York: Praeger.

Dillman, D. A. 1978. *Mail and telephone surveys: The total design method.* New York: Wiley.

———. 1991. Design and administration of mail surveys. *Annual Review of Sociology* 17:225–49.

Donnellon, A. 1996. *Team talk: The power of language in team dynamics.* Boston: Harvard Business School Press.

Douglas, A. 1962. *Industrial peacemaking.* New York: Columbia University Press.

Downie, B. M. 1991. When negotiations fail: Causes of breakdown and tactics for breaking the stalemate. *Negotiation Journal* 7 (2): 175–86.

Doz, Y. L., and C. K. Prahalad. 1980. How MNCs cope with host government intervention. *Harvard Business Review* (March–April):149–57.

Druckman, D. 1986. Stages, turning points, and crises. *Journal of Conflict Resolution* 30:327–60.

———, ed. 1977. *Negotiations: Social-psychological perspectives.* Beverly Hills: Sage.

Druckman, D., et al. 1976. Cultural differences in bargaining behavior: India, Argentina, and the United States. *Journal of Conflict Resolution* 20 (3): 413–52.

Dupont, C. 1990. *La négociation: Conduite, théorie, applications.* 3d ed. Paris: Dalloz.

———. 1996. A model of the negotiation process with different strategies in international business negotiations. In P. Ghauri and J.-C. Usunier, eds., *International business negotiations,* 39–67. Oxford: Pergamon.

Dyer, B., and X. Song. 1997. The impact of strategy on conflict: A cross-national comparative study of U.S. and Japanese firms. *Journal of International Business Studies* 28 (3): 467–93.

Earley, P. C., and E. Mosakowski. 2000. Creating hybrid team cultures: An empirical test of transnational team functioning. *Academy of Management Journal* 43 (1): 26–49.

Eiteman, D. K. 1990. American executives' perceptions of negotiating joint ventures with the People's Republic of China: Lessons learned. *Columbia Journal of World Business* 25 (4): 59–67.

Eliashberg, J., G. Lilien, and N. Kim. 1995. Searching for generalizations in business marketing negotiations. *Marketing Science* 14 (3): G47–G60.

Encarnation, D., and L. T. Wells Jr. 1985. Sovereignty en garde: Negotiating with foreign investors. *International Organization* 39 (1): 47–78.

Fagre, N., and L. T. Wells Jr. 1982. Bargaining power of multinationals and host governments. *Journal of International Business Studies* 13 (2): 9–23.

Fang, T. 1998. *Chinese business negotiating style.* Thousand Oaks, CA: Sage.

Faure, G. O. 2000. Negotiation on joint ventures in China. In V. Kremenyuk and G. Sjostedt, eds., *International economic negotiation: Models versus reality,* 65–97. Cheltenham, UK: Edward Elgar.

Faure, G. O., et al. 2000. *La negociation: Situations-problematique-applications.* Paris: Dunod.

Fayerweather, J., and A. Kapoor. 1976. *Strategy and negotiation for the international corporation.* Cambridge, MA: Ballinger.

Fetterman, D. M. 1989. *Ethnography: Step by step.* Applied Social Research Methods Series, vol. 17. Newbury Park, CA: Sage.

Firth, A. 1991. Discourse at work: Negotiating by telex, fax, and phone. Ph.D. diss., University of Aalborg.

Fisher, G. 1980. *International negotiation: A cross-cultural perspective.* Yarmouth, ME: Intercultural Press.

Fisher, R., and W. Ury. 1981. *Getting to yes.* Boston: Houghton-Mifflin.

Foster, D. A. 1992. *Bargaining across borders.* New York: McGraw-Hill.

Fouraker, L. E., and S. Siegel. 1963. *Bargaining behavior.* New York: McGraw-Hill.

Francis, J. N. P. 1991. When in Rome? The effects of cultural adaptation on intercultural business negotiations. *Journal of International Business Studies* 22:403–28.

Geertz, C. 1973. *The interpretation of cultures: Selected essays.* New York: Basic Books.

Gelfand, M. J., and N. Dyer. 2000. A cultural perspective on negotiation: Progress, pitfalls, and prospects. *Applied Psychology: An International Review* 49 (1): 62–99.

George, J. M., G. R. Jones, and J. A. Gonzalez. 1998. The role of affect in cross-cultural negotiations. *Journal of International Business Studies* 29 (4): 749–72.

Geringer, J. M. 1991. Strategic determinants of partner selection criteria in international joint ventures. *Journal of International Business Studies* 22:41–62.

Gersick, C. J. G. 1988. Time and transition in work teams: Toward a new model of group development. *Academy of Management Journal* 31:9–41.

Ghauri, P., and J.-C. Usunier, eds. 1996. *International business negotiations.* Oxford: Pergamon.

The global firm: R.I.P. 1993. *The Economist,* February 6, 69.

Gomes-Casseres, B. 1990. Firm ownership preferences and host government restrictions: An integrated approach. *Journal of International Business Studies* 21 (1): 1–23.

Graham, J. L. 1981. A hidden cause of America's trade deficit with Japan. *Columbia Journal of World Business* (fall):5–15.

————. 1983. Brazilian, Japanese, and American business negotiations. *Journal of International Business Studies* (spring/summer):47–61.

————. 1984a. Bolter Turbine, Inc. negotiation simulation. *Journal of Marketing Education* 4 (spring):28–36.

————. 1984b. A comparison of Japanese and American business negotiations. *International Journal of Research in Marketing* 1:51–68.

————. 1985. The influence of culture on the process of business negotiations: An exploratory study. *Journal of International Business Studies* 16 (1): 81–96.

————. 1987. A theory of interorganizational negotiations. In J. N. Sheth, ed., *Research in Marketing,* 9:163–83. Greenwich, CT: JAI Press.

————. 1993. The Japanese negotiation style: Characteristics of a distinct approach. *Negotiation Journal* (April):123–40.

Graham, J. L., L. I. Evenko, and M. N. Rajan. 1992. An empirical comparison of Soviet and American business negotiations. *Journal of International Business Studies* 23 (3): 387–418.

Graham, J. L., D. K. Kim, C. Lin, and M. Robinson. 1988. Buyer-seller negotiations around the Pacific Rim: Differences in fundamental exchange processes. *Journal of Consumer Research* 15:48–54.

Graham, J. L., A. T. Mintu, and W. Rodgers. 1994. Explorations of negotiation behavior in ten foreign cultures using a model developed in the United States. *Management Science* 40 (1): 72–95.

Graham, J. L., and Y. Sano. 1989. *Smart bargaining: Doing business with the Japanese.* Rev. ed. New York: Ballinger.

Grieco, J. M. 1982. Between dependency and autonomy: India's experience with the international computer industry. *International Organization* 36 (3): 609–32.

Griffin, T. J., and W. R. Daggart. 1990. *The global negotiator.* New York: Harper-Business.

Grosse, R., and D. Aramburu. 1990. A bargaining view of government/MNE relations. *International Trade Journal* 6 (2): 209–38.

Groth, B. 1992. Book review—Negotiating in the global village: Four lamps to illuminate the table. *Negotiation Journal* 8 (3): 241–57.

Gudykunst, W. B., and S. Ting-Toomey. 1988. *Culture and interpersonal communication.* Newbury Park, CA: Sage.

Gulliver, P. H. 1979. *Disputes and negotiations.* New York: Academic Press.

Gumperz, J. J. 1975. Cross-cultural communication and public negotiations. Proposal and progress reports for research sponsored by U.S. Dept. of Health, Education, and Welfare. Mimeo (unpublished).

Hall, E. P. 1985. The etic-emic distinction. In B. Dervin and M. Voigt, eds., *Progress in communication science,* 7. Norwood, NJ: Ablex.

————. 1976. *Beyond culture.* Garden City, NY: Anchor Books.

Harnett, D. L., and L. L. Cummings. 1980. *Bargaining behavior: An international study.* Houston: Dame.

Harrigan, K. R. 1985. *Strategies for joint ventures.* Lexington, MA: Lexington Books.

Hofstede, G. 1984. *Culture's consequences.* Abridged version. Cross-Cultural Research and Methodology Series, vol. 5. Beverly Hills, CA: Sage.

————. 1993. Cultural constraints in management theories. *Executive* 7 (1): 81–94.

Holmes, M. E. 1992. Phase structures in negotiation. In L. L. Putnam and M. E. Roloff, eds., *Communication and negotiation,* Annual Reviews of Communication Research, 20:83–104. Newbury Park, CA: Sage.

Ikle, F. C. 1976 [1964]. *How nations negotiate.* Greenwich, CT: Kraus Reprint.

Inkpen, A. C., and P. W. Beamish. 1997. Knowledge, bargaining power, and the instability of international joint ventures. *Academy of Management Review* 22 (1): 177–202.

Janosik, R. J. 1987. Rethinking the culture-negotiation link. *Negotiation Journal* 3:385–95.

Jehn, K. A., G. B. Northcraft, and M. A. Neale. 1999. Why differences make a difference: A field study of diversity, conflict, and performance in workgroups. *Administrative Science Quarterly* 44 (4): 741–63.

Jehn, K., and E. Weldon. 1991. Conflict-handling styles: A comparative study of managers and professionals in the People's Republic of China and the United States. Paper presented at the annual meeting of the Academy of Management, Miami, FL, August 10–12.

————. 1992. A comparative study of managerial attitudes toward conflict in the United States and the People's Republic of China: Issues of theory and measurement. Paper presented at the annual meeting of the Academy of Management, Las Vegas, NV, August 9–12.

Jenkins, B. 1986. Reexamining the obsolescing bargain. *International Organization* 40 (1): 139–65.

Kale, S. H., and J. W. Barnes. 1992. Understanding the domain of cross-national buyer-seller interaction. *Journal of International Business Studies* 23:101–32.

Kapoor, A. 1970. *International business negotiations: A study in India.* New York: New York University Press.

Kaufman, J. 1989. Toward an integral analysis of international negotiations. In F. Mautner-Markhof, ed., *Processes of international negotiations,* 7–13. Boulder: CO: Westview.

Kelley, H. H. 1966. A classroom study of the dilemmas in interpersonal negotiations. In K. Archibald, ed., *Strategic interaction and conflict.* Berkeley, CA: University of California, Berkeley, Institute of International Studies.

Kesner, I. F., and D. L. Shapiro. 1991. Did a "failed" negotiation really fail? Reflections on the Arthur Andersen-Price Waterhouse merger talks. *Negotiation Journal* 7 (4): 369–78.

Killing, J. P. 1983. *Strategies for joint venture success.* New York: Praeger.

Kilmann, R., and K. Thomas. 1977. Developing a forced-choice measure of conflict-handling behavior: The MODE instrument. *Education and Psychological Measurement* 37:309–25.

Kimmel, S. 1993. When strong expectations are dangerous: The effect of cultural expectations, information gathering, and perspective taking ability on intercultural negotiation. Ph.D. diss., University of Michigan School of Business.

Kobrin, S. J. 1987. Testing the bargaining hypothesis in the manufacturing sector in developing countries. *International Organization* 41:609–38.

Kogut, B. 1988. Joint ventures: Theoretical and empirical perspectives. *Strategic Management Journal* 9:319–32.

———. 1994. Introductory remarks: International organizational studies: Fad or future? Michigan International Organizational Studies Conference, University of Michigan Business School, February.

Kramer, R. M. 1991. Intergroup relations and organizational dilemmas: The role of categorization processes. In B. Staw and L. L. Cummings, eds., *Research in organizational behavior,* 13:191–228. Greenwich, CT: JAI Press.

Kremenyuk, V. A., ed. 1991. *International negotiation: Analysis, approaches, issues.* San Francisco: Jossey-Bass.

Kumar, R. 1997. The role of affect in negotiations: An integrative overview. *Journal of Applied Behavioral Science* 33:84–100.

———. 1999. Communicative conflict in intercultural negotiations: The case of American and Japanese business negotiations. *International Negotiation* 4 (1): 63–78.

Lax, D. A., and J. K. Sebenius. 1986. *Manager as negotiator.* New York: Free Press.

Lecraw, D. J. 1984. Bargaining power, ownership, and profitability of subsidiaries of transnational corporations in developing countries. *Journal of International Business Studies* 15 (1): 27–43.

Lecraw, D. J., and A. J. Morrison. 1991. Transnational corporation-host country relations: A framework for analysis. *Essays in international business,* no. 9. Columbia: University of South Carolina Center for International Business Education and Research.

Lee, K. H., and T. W. C. Lo. 1988. American business people's perceptions of marketing and negotiating in the People's Republic of China. *International Marketing Review* (summer):41–51.

Leung, K., and D. Tjosvold. 1998. *Conflict management in the Asia Pacific.* Singapore: Wiley.

Lewicki, R. J., S. E. Weiss, and D. Lewin. 1992. Models of conflict, negotiation, and third party processes: A review and synthesis. *Journal of Organizational Behavior* 13:209–52.

Lin, X., and R. Germain. 1998. Sustaining satisfactory joint venture relationships: The role of conflict resolution strategy. *Journal of International Business Studies* 29 (1): 179–96.

Lituchy, T. R. 1992. International and intranational negotiations in the United States and Japan: The impact of cultural collectivism on cognition behaviors and outcomes. Ph.D. diss., University of Arizona College of Business and Public Administration.

Lytle, A. L. 1993. The influence of culture in negotiation: A comparison of intracultural and intercultural interaction. Paper presented at the annual meeting of the Academy of Management, Atlanta, GA, August 8–11.

Lytle, A. L., J. M. Brett, Z. I. Barness, C. H. Tinsley, and M. Janssens. 1995. A paradigm for quantitative cross-cultural research in organizational behavior. In B. M. Staw and L. L. Cummings, eds., *Research in organizational behavior,* 17:167–214. Greenwich, CT: JAI Press.

March, R. 1985. East meets West at the negotiating table. *Winds* (April):55–57.

Mayer, F. W. 1988. Bargains within bargains: Domestic politics and international negotiation. Ph.D. diss., Harvard University Kennedy School of Government.

McCall, J. B., and M. B. Warrington. 1984. *Marketing by agreement: A cross-cultural approach to business negotiation*. Chichester, UK: John Wiley and Sons.

Mintu-Wimsatt, A., and J. B. Gassenheimer. 2000. The moderating effects of cultural context in buyer-seller negotiation. *Journal of Personal Selling and Sales Management* 20 (1): 1–9.

Money, R. B. 1998. International multilateral negotiations and social networks. *Journal of International Business Studies* 29 (4): 695–710.

Moran, R. T., and W. G. Stripp. 1991. *Dynamics of successful international business negotiations*. Houston: Gulf.

Morely, I., and G. Stephenson. 1977. *The social psychology of bargaining*. London: Allen and Unwin.

Morris, M. W., et al. 1998. Conflict management style: Accounting for cross-national differences. *Journal of International Business Studies* 29 (4): 729–48.

Neale, M. A., G. B. Northcraft, and V. L. Huber. 1987. Framing, goal-setting, and the Chinese: Integrative negotiation among Chinese students. Paper presented at the annual meeting of the Academy of Management, New Orleans, LA, August 9–12.

Northrup, H. R., and R. L. Rowan. 1976. Multinational bargaining approaches in the Western European flat glass industry. *Industrial and Labor Relations Review* 30 (1): 32–46.

Oliver, C. 1990. Determinants of interorganizational relationships. *Academy of Management Review* 15:241–65.

Parker, V. 1996. Negotiating licensing agreements. In P. Ghauri and J.-C. Usunier, eds., *International business negotiations*, 203–30. Oxford: Pergamon.

Parkhe, A. 1993. "Messy" research, methodological predispositions, and theory development in international joint ventures. *Academy of Management Review* 18 (2): 227–68.

Phatak, A. V., and M. M. Habib. 1996. The dynamics of international business negotiations. *Business Horizons* 39 (3): 30–38.

Philip, G. 1976. The limitations of bargaining theory: A case study of the International Petroleum Company in Peru. *World Development* 4 (3): 213–39.

Pike, K. 1966. Etic and emic standpoints for the description of behavior. In A. G. Smith, ed., *Communication and culture*, 152–63. New York: Holt, Rinehart, and Winston.

Porat, A. M. 1970. Cross-cultural differences in resolving union-management conflicts through negotiations. *Journal of Applied Psychology* 54:441–51.

Pruitt, D. G. 1981. *Negotiation behavior*. New York: Academic.

Putnam, L. L. 1990. Reframing integrative and distributive bargaining: A process perspective. In B. H. Sheppard, M. H. Bazerman, and R. J. Lewicki, eds., *Research on negotiation in organizations*, 2:3–30. Greenwich, CT: JAI Press.

Putnam, R. D. 1988. Diplomacy and domestic politics: The logic of two-level games. *International Organization* 42:427–60.

Pye, L. W. 1992. *Chinese negotiating style: Commercial approaches and cultural principles*. Rev. ed. New York: Quorum.

Raiffa, H. 1982. *The art and science of negotiation*. Cambridge, MA: Belknap.

Ramamurti, R. 2001. The obsolescing "bargaining model"? MNC-host developing country relations revisited. *Journal of International Business Studies* 32 (1): 23–39.

Rao, A., and S. M. Schmidt. 1998. A behavioral perspective on negotiating international alliances. *Journal of International Business Studies* 29 (4): 665–94.

Rapoport, A. 1960. *Fights, games, and debates.* Ann Arbor: University of Michigan Press.

Reitz, H. J., J. A. Wall Jr., and M. S. Love. 1998. Ethics in negotiation: Oil and water or good lubrication? *Business Horizons* 41 (3): 5–15.

Roberts, K. 1970. On looking at an elephant: An evaluation of cross-cultural research related to organizations. *Psychological Bulletin* 5:327–50.

Rojot, J. 1991. *Negotiation: From theory to practice.* London: Macmillan.

Root, F. R. 1993. A retrospective look at international business as a field of study. *AIB Newsletter* (summer):11–14.

Root, F. R., and F. J. Contractor. 1981. Negotiating compensation in international licensing agreements. *Sloan Management Review* 22 (2): 23–32.

Rubin, J. Z., and B. Brown. 1975. *The social psychology of bargaining and negotiation.* New York: Academic.

Sakuma, M. 1987. *Negotiation strategy.* Tokyo: Jitsumu Kyoiku Shuppan. In Japanese.

Salacuse, J. W. 1991. *Making global deals.* Boston: Houghton Mifflin.

Salk, J. E. 1996–97. Partners and other strangers. *International Studies of Management and Organization* 26 (4): 48–72.

Salk, J. E., and M. Y. Brannen. 2000. National culture, networks, and individual influence in a multinational management team. *Academy of Management Journal* 43 (2): 191–202.

Sawyer, J., and H. Guetzkow. 1965. Bargaining and negotiation in international relations. In H. Kelman, ed., *International behavior: A social-psychological analysis,* 465–520. New York: Holt, Rinehart, Winston.

Schelling, T. C. 1960. *The strategy of conflict.* New York: Oxford University Press.

Schwartz, S. 1994. Beyond individualism/collectivism: New cultural dimensions of values. In U. Kim, H. C. Triandis, and H. Hakhoe, eds., *Individualism and collectivism: Theory, method, and applications,* 85–119. Thousand Oaks, CA: Sage.

Sebenius, J. K. 1983. Negotiation arithmetic: Adding and subtracting issues and parties. *International Organization* 37 (2): 282–316.

———. 1998. Negotiating cross-border acquisitions. *Sloan Management Review* 39 (2): 27–41.

Shell, G. R. 1999. *Bargaining for advantage.* New York: Penguin.

Shemwell, S. M. 1996. Cross-cultural negotiations between Japanese and American businessmen: A systems analysis. Ph.D. diss., Nova Southeastern University, Houston, TX.

Simintiras, A. C., and A. H. Thomas. 1998. Cross-cultural sales negotiations: A literature review and research propositions. *International Marketing Review* 15 (1): 10–28.

Smith, D. N., and L. T. Wells. 1976. *Negotiating third world mineral agreements: Promises as prologue.* Cambridge, MA: Ballinger.

Stewart, S., and C. F. Keown. 1989. Talking with the dragon: Negotiating in the People's Republic of China. *Columbia Journal of World Business* 24 (3): 68–72.

Stoever, W. A. 1979. Renegotiations: The cutting edge of relations between MNCs and LDCs. *Columbia Journal of World Business* 14 (1): 5–14.

————. 1981. *Renegotiations in international business transactions.* Lexington, MA: Lexington.

Sullivan, J., et al. 1981. The relationship between conflict resolution approaches and trust—a cross-cultural study. *Academy of Management Journal* 24 (2): 803–15.

Ting-Toomey, S. 1985. Toward a theory of conflict and culture. In W. B. Gudykunst, L. P. Stewart, and S. Ting-Toomey, eds., *Communication, culture, and organizational processes.* International and Intercultural Communication Annual, 9:71–86. Beverly Hills: Sage.

Ting-Toomey, S., et al. 1991. Culture, face maintenance, and styles of handling interpersonal conflict: A study in five cultures. *International Journal of Conflict Management* 2 (4): 275–95.

Tinsley, C. H. 1998. Models of conflict resolution in Japanese, German, and American cultures. *Journal of Applied Psychology* 83:316–23.

Tinsley, C. H., J. Curhan, and R. Kwak. 1999. Adopting a dual lens approach for overcoming the dilemma of differences in international business negotiations. *International Negotiation* 4 (1): 5–22.

Tinsley, C. H., and M. M. Pillutla. 1998. Negotiating in the United States and Hong Kong. *Journal of International Business Studies* 29 (4): 711–28.

Triandis, H. C. 1972. *The analysis of subjective culture.* New York: Wiley.

Triandis, H. C., P. Carnevale, M. Gelfand, C. Robert, S. A. Wasti, T. Probst, E. Kashima, T. Dragonas, D. Chan, X. P. Chen, U. Kim, C. de Dreu, E. van de Vliert, S. Iwao, K. Ohbuchi, and P. Schmitz. 2001. Culture and deception in business negotiations: A multilevel analysis. *International Journal of Cross-Cultural Management* 1 (1): 73–90.

Trompenaars, F., and C. Hampden-Turner. 1998. *Riding the waves of culture: Understanding cultural diversity in global business.* New York: McGraw-Hill.

Tse, D. K., J. Francis, and J. Walls. 1994. Cultural differences in conducting intra- and inter-cultural negotiations: A Sino-Canadian comparison. *Journal of International Business Studies* 25 (3): 537–55.

Tung, R. L. 1982. U.S.-China trade negotiations: Practices, procedures, and outcomes. *Journal of International Business Studies* 13 (2): 25–38.

————. 1984. How to negotiate with the Japanese. *California Management Review* 26 (4): 62–77.

————. 1988. Toward a conceptual paradigm of international business negotiations. In R. D. Farmer, ed., *Advances in international comparative management,* 3:203–219. Greenwich, CT: JAI Press.

Underdal, A. 1983. Causes of negotiation "failure." *European Journal of Political Research* 11 (2): 183–96.

Usunier, J. C., and A. Ghauri. 1996. Some general guidelines for negotiating international business. In P. N. Ghauri and J. C. Usunier, eds., *International business negotiations,* 383–407. Oxford: Pergamon.

Vachani, S. 1995. Enhancing the obsolescing bargain theory: A longitudinal study of foreign ownership of U.S. and European multinationals. *Journal of International Business Studies* 26 (1): 159–80.

van Oudenhoven, J. P., L. Mechelse, and C. K. de Dreu. 1998. Managerial conflict management in five European countries: The importance of power distance, uncertainty avoidance, and masculinity. *Applied Psychology: An International Review* 47 (3): 439–55.

Van Zandt, H. F. 1970. How to negotiate in Japan. *Harvard Business Review* (November–December):45–56.

Vernon, R. 1968. Conflict and resolution between foreign director investors and less developed countries. *Public Policy* 17:333–51.

———. 1980. The obsolescing bargain: A key factor in political risk. In M. B. Winchester, ed., *The international essays for business decision-makers*, 5:281–86. Houston: Center for International Business.

Walsh, J. P., E. Wang, and K. R. Xin. 1999. Same bed, different dreams: Working relationships in Sino-American joint ventures. *Journal of World Business* 34 (1): 69–93.

Walton, R. E., and R. B. McKersie. 1965. *A behavioral theory of labor negotiations.* New York: McGraw-Hill.

Wasserstein, B. 2000. *Big deal: 2000 and beyond.* Rev. ed. New York: Warner Books.

Weick, K. E. 1965. Laboratory experimentation with organizations. In J. G. March, ed., *Handbook of organizations*, 194–260. Chicago: Rand McNally.

Weiss, S. E. 1987a. Creating the GM-Toyota joint venture: A case in complex negotiation. *Columbia Journal of World Business* 22 (2): 23–37.

———. 1987b. Negotiation and culture: Some thoughts on models, ghosts, and options. *Dispute Resolution Forum* (National Institute for Dispute Resolution) (September):3–6.

———. 1990. The long path to the IBM-Mexico agreement: An analysis of the micro-computer investment negotiations, 1983–1986. *Journal of International Business Studies* 21:565–96.

———. 1993. Analysis of complex negotiations in international business: The RBC perspective. *Organization Science* 4 (2): 269–300.

———. 1994a. Empirical knowledge of international negotiation: A cross-disciplinary base for future theory and research. Working paper, York University Faculty of Administrative Studies, Toronto.

———. 1994b. Negotiating with "Romans," part I. *Sloan Management Review* 35 (2): 51–61.

———. 1996. International negotiations: Bricks, mortar, and prospects. In B. J. Punnett and O. Shenkar, eds., *Handbook for international management research*, 209–65. Cambridge, MA: Blackwell.

———. 1997. Explaining negotiation outcomes: Toward a grounded model for negotiations between organizations. In R. J. Lewicki, R. J. Bies, and B. H. Sheppard, eds., *Research on negotiation in organizations*, 6:247–333. Greenwich, CT: JAI Press.

———. 1999. Opening a dialogue on negotiation and culture: A "believer" considers skeptics' views. In D. M. Kolb, ed., *Negotiation eclectics: Essays in memory of Jeffrey Z. Rubin*, 67–84. Cambridge, MA: PON Books.

Weiss, S. E., with W. G. Stripp. 1998 [1985]. Negotiating with foreign businesspersons: An introduction for Americans with propositions on six cultures. In S. Niemeier, C. P. Campbell, and R. Dirven, eds., *The cultural context in business communication*, 51–118. Amsterdam: John Benjamins.

Wilson, S. R., et al. 1995. Cultural and communication processes in international business negotiations. In A. M. Nicotera, ed., *Conflict and organizations: Communicative processes,* 201–37. Albany, NY: SUNY Press.

Winham, G. R., and H. E. Bovis. 1979. Distribution of benefits in negotiation. *Journal of Conflict Resolution* 23 (3): 408–24.

Woodworth, W., and R. Nelson. 1980. Information in Latin American organizations. *Management International Review* 20 (2): 61–69.

Wright, L. L. 1990. Cross-cultural project negotiations in the consulting engineering industry: A study of Canadian-Indonesian negotiations. Ph.D. diss., University of Western Ontario School of Business Administration.

Yan, A., and B. Gray. 1994. Bargaining power, management control, and performance in United States-China joint ventures: A comparative case study. *Academy of Management Journal* 37 (6): 1478–1517.

Yin, R. K. 1984. *Case study research.* Applied Social Research Methods, vol. 5. Beverly Hills, CA: Sage.

Young, S., and N. Hood. 1977. Multinational and host governments: Lessons from the case of Chrysler UK. *Columbia Journal of World Business* 12 (2): 97–106.

Zartman, I. W., ed. 1976. *The 50% solution.* Garden City, NJ: Anchor.

———. 1994. *International multilateral negotiation.* San Francisco: Jossey-Bass.

Zartman, I. W., and M. R. Berman. 1982. *The practical negotiator.* New Haven, CT: Yale University Press.

Zhao, J. J. 2000. The Chinese approach to international business negotiation. *Journal of Business Communication* 37 (3): 209–237.

Part 5

CONCLUSION

INTERNATIONAL MANAGEMENT RESEARCH AT THE DAWN OF THE TWENTY-FIRST CENTURY

Betty Jane Punnett and Oded Shenkar

At the dawn of the twenty-first century, the world of business is increasingly global: Global is sometimes thought of as meaning less diversity and increased similarity around the world, but that is illusory. What is real about globalism is the enhanced interaction and heightened interdependence among the business world's component parts, in spite of major continuing differences among people and environments. Cross-border communication, travel, trade, and investment continue to rise, but national, regional, and subnational differences not only persist, they often become more salient because of increased interaction among people of different cultural and institutional backgrounds. This increased interaction and interdependence mean that international managers must familiarize themselves with the expectations and desires of colleagues, superiors, and subordinates from multiple and varied locations, while concomitantly supporting coordination and control of dispersed activities that are crucial for success in a globally competitive marketplace. More than ever, managers need to understand the intersection of these forces of globalization and localization, as well as their ramifications for the managerial role, contradictory as these may be. In this concluding chapter, we examine those ramifications and consider the role of international management research in this environment.

The era in which we live might well be considered a period of "false globalization," where the McDonald's of the world articulate artificial similarities across a planet that remains very much divided in terms of culture, society, and economy. In this environment, international managers play a prominent role, from negotiating alliances, through dealing with government officials, to motivating a diverse workforce. International management research, in turn, plays a critical role in supporting the international manager and the international firm facing an increasingly complex and rapidly changing world. By exploring the dynamics of cross-cultural negotiations, explaining how to conduct international surveys, and predicting what leadership styles will be appropriate in a given context (to name a few of the topics covered in this handbook), international management research assists managers and firms as they internationalize. The *Handbook for International Management Research* was prepared in this spirit. Its vision is that academic rigor and practical relevance are closely linked. We think that an advance in academic rigor implies that international managers can use knowledge and tools with greater confidence. While much research remains to be done, international management, and consequently international management research, is more important than ever, not only to business but also to the cultural, social, and political spheres within which business is embedded.

In this brief concluding chapter to this handbook, we touch on a number of issues that illustrate the relevance of international management research to today's world. We begin with a discussion of globalization—what it is, what it is not, and what it means for managers in both domestic and international organizations. Using this discussion as a platform, we consider globalization and its impact on the convergence and divergence of societies around the world. We consider major trends and developments at the dawn of the twenty-first century, such as the gap between rich and poor nations, the rise of small firms and strategic alliances, and the emergence of conflict and terrorism on a global scale. We look at the role of the world manager in this environment and explore how international management research, in an ethical and responsible fashion, can help create awareness, enhance understanding, and provide tools with which to enhance performance of international managers.

GLOBALIZATION: WHAT IT IS, WHAT IT IS NOT

The term "globalization" is often used quite loosely, with no systematic attempt to describe what it actually means. The vagueness is part neglect—the term is simply taken for granted—and part intention—a reflection of political and social realities. Vagueness enables various and diverse constituencies to interpret "globalization" in a way that suits their purpose and thus to take a stand in support of, or in opposition to, globalization. Each of the two camps tends to overreach, seeing globalization either as a panacea or as the root cause of all that is wrong in the world. We do not intend to resolve the globalization debate here but rather to describe the reality of globalization from a business and management perspective and to highlight the relevance of international management research to the issues raised by globalization.

In the broadest terms, globalization refers to the growth of international contacts, trade and investment, and the integration of world economies. Globalization is based on a number of relatively simple (yet often hyped) premises:

1. Technological developments have increased the ease and speed of international communication and travel to an unprecedented level.
2. Increased communication, new technologies, and travel have made the world "smaller."
3. A smaller world means that people are more aware of events outside their home country.
4. Increased awareness results in deeper understanding of the business opportunities, and threats, that lie beyond national boundaries.
5. A better understanding of opportunities and threats is a catalyst for international trade and foreign investment.
6. Increased trade and investment results in economies around the world becoming interdependent and more closely integrated.
7. Economic integration has been accompanied by the emergence of international organizations such as the World Trade Organization (WTO) and regional agreements such as the North American Free Trade Agreement that challenge some fundamental assumptions about the role of the state, the corporation, and the manager.

The reality encapsulated in these simple premises results in what has been termed "globalization." It is also important to understand what globalization is not. Globalization does not imply that people around the world are, or are becoming, more alike. Interaction may breed more understanding and tolerance for differences, but it can also breed suspicion and stereotyping, especially in a context that separates groups, for instance, into supervisors and subordinates, haves and have nots, locals and foreigners, and so on. Before we consider the role of the manager in the global environment, let us briefly summarize the positions for and against globalization with which managers have to contend.

GLOBALIZATION AND ANTIGLOBALIZATION

The mere mention of the word "globalization" generates passionate responses—both positive and negative—from different groups. During the 1980s and the 1990s, there were significant efforts to promote free trade and investment based on a belief that this trend would be good for all, developed and developing countries alike. Institutions, such as the World Bank and regional development banks, saw globalization as an essential part of the economic, political, and social agenda. The WTO was established at the beginning of 1995 to carry forward the work of the General Agreement on Tariffs and Trade, which had negotiated freer trade among its members during a series of negotiating rounds, starting in the 1950s. By and large, foreign investment regimes were liberalized, a trend that continued well into the 1990s. Governments increasingly competed for foreign investment, with multiple nations and states often bidding for the same project.

During the early 1990s, there were reasons to feel that globalization was working. The economic success of Singapore, the rapid economic growth in the Asian Tigers (as the rapidly growing Asian economies of Taiwan, South Korea, Singapore, and Hong Kong were called), and the industrialization of countries with largely agricultural economies, such as Brazil and Mexico, suggested that the results of globalization were indeed good for all nations, large or small, rich or poor. The United States, the biggest investor as well as the biggest investment target, was a symbol of the success of globalization. The United States experienced one of its most sustained periods of growth during that time, which was, to many, proof that globalization was working, that a new economic era, immune to economic shocks and recession, had dawned. Others saw a different picture—domestic producers going out of business, towns devastated by the loss of a major employer who moved abroad in search of cheaper labor, a nation at a risk of losing its industrial core and increasingly vulnerable to the whims of foreigners.

The belief in a brave and prosperous new world shaped by globalization was never universally shared. The Seattle meetings of the WTO (referred to as "the battle in Seattle" or the "Seattle debacle") turned into a fiasco, with a very loose coalition of antiglobalization groups—from animal rights groups to environmental groups to industrial unions embarking on a struggle that often turned violent. The antiglobalization forces have not coalesced into a coherent whole, because they represent extremely diverse and often contradictory views. Radical groups, with their own political agenda, sought to hijack the movement, undermining the legitimacy of genuine concerns. Yet, the vehemence of their protests made it clear that globalization was not a panacea for the world's problems.

Economic crises have also raised the spectrum of globalization as a potentially negative force. Globalization has often become a scapegoat for social and corporate ills, but it also became evident that an interdependent world meant sharing the pain as well as the prosperity. Terms such as "contagion" came into common use following the Asian financial crisis that quickly spread from Thailand to Korea and Indonesia, among others, and eventually rocked Latin American markets. A related term, "the domino effect," once utilized to describe the spread of communism, was borrowed to describe the risk of downward interdependencies in a global environment. The pendulum began to swing away from praise for globalization to a belief that it was actually the cause of the economic woes of the early twenty-first century. If globalization was overpraised before, it was now overblamed for problems that were often entirely of nations' own making, such as lack of transparent institutions, corruption, and the like.

More recently, we have observed the commencement of a more balanced view, an understanding that globalization is neither a panacea nor a demon, that it can produce both positive and negative outcomes, that it benefits some while hurting others, across and within nations. It is also becoming evident that globalization has winners and losers in the corporate world and that there are important determinants of who will succeed, and how, in the global business world. Understanding how to manage in a global environment is one of those determinants. International managers play a critical role in the efficacy of their firms, and international management research can guide them in fulfilling this critical role.

A crucial question that arises within the globalization debate and that is critical to the development of managerial response to globalization is the degree to which countries and cultures are becoming more similar or more dissimilar with time. The following section examines the forces that lead to similarity—convergence—and those that lead to dissimilarity—divergence.

CONVERGENCE AND DIVERGENCE

In the 1980s, Levitt often talked of a force that was driving the world toward a convergence of values. More travel and sophisticated communications mean that people have become much more aware of what is happening in other parts of the world. Much of the media is now global, such that the people of Afghanistan can find out what is happening in the United States. Movies made in India are shown around the world, as are American movies. Blue jeans and T-shirts have become the preferred dress for young people almost everywhere; a Middle Eastern businessman is as likely to wear a Western suit as a traditional Middle Eastern robe; an African professor in Canada will wear traditional dress one day and gray flannels with a blue blazer the next. Chinese restaurants abound in New York and London, and Kentucky Fried Chicken and McDonald's are found from Beijing to Tokyo to Moscow.

The growth in firms operating cross-nationally contributes, to an extent, to the convergence of attitudes, values, and behavior. Managers, when operating in different countries, import aspects of their home culture, some of which will be appealing to those with whom they work and adopted by them. Many multinationals standardize policies, procedures, and human resource practices throughout the nations in which they operate and attempt to develop a unifying corporate culture. Shared worldwide concerns, such as global warming, also suggest a potential converging of values, as does regional economic integration, exemplified by the European Union.

In contrast to the convergence argument, many believe that cross-national differences continue and are equally important, if not more so, today. For example, managers in the English-speaking Caribbean were asked what advice they would give to a foreign manager coming to the region; overwhelmingly, they responded that things were done differently there and that the foreign manager would need to spend the time to learn how things were done in the region (Punnett, 2002). The terrorist attacks of September 11, 2001, brought home these differences for many people in the United States. The many disputes around the world today—from

Afghanistan to Zimbabwe—based on an "us" versus "them" mentality—illustrate that cross-national and cross-cultural differences have by no means disappeared. The same is true of intracountry diversity: If you take the London subway or walk down the street in Toronto, you cannot help but notice the many languages that are spoken, the different forms of dress that are worn, the different greetings that are used, and the different foods that are prepared by different groups. Italian communities in Toronto are still very Italian, Chinese communities in New York still very Chinese, and West Indian communities in London very West Indian. If people retain many of their national and cultural characteristics when they immigrate and live in a mixed society, they will surely retain them at home.

The evidence of cross-national and cross-cultural divergence, or distinctiveness, is as compelling, if not more so, as the evidence of convergence. Ease of communication and travel often generates divergence. Extensive exposure to foreigners and foreign media may increase awareness of the home values, which may be seen as particularly "good" in contrast to foreign values. A sense of domination by foreigners can result in a determination to maintain one's own value system. Canadians, for example, feel that they are very influenced by the United States and react by being more Canadian; some people in the United States are concerned about Japanese influence and react by perceiving Japanese ways as negative. The collapse of the Soviet Union suggests that strong cultural value differences can be maintained by groups within a union, in spite of efforts to eliminate them. Similarly, French Canadians wish to be recognized as a distinct society within Canada and Native American groups argue for self-government based on cultural uniqueness.

It can also be argued that the activities of multinational and global companies contribute to divergence. Some companies provide products or services specifically developed for particular countries or regions, and some adapt their decisions to fit the needs of different locations, perpetuating differences. The Internet may potentially be a force for both convergence and divergence because it provides an opportunity for people around the world to communicate easily with each other. This increased communication means that people can easily learn about each other, which is likely to contribute to converging values. At the same time, it can be argued that the Internet allows small numbers of people who share a particular view to communicate with each other and develop divergent value systems. The real impact remains to be identified.

A balanced view will show concurrent convergence and divergence forces that often cut across each other. One can conclude that convergence will occur in some aspects of culture and divergence in others—in some ways, people are becoming more similar, but in many ways they retain their distinctiveness. International managers should be aware of the forces leading to both convergence and divergence and consider their likely impact. International management researchers add value by explaining and predicting where convergence and divergence are likely, how they impact organizational variables, and how managers can respond to them.

THE MANAGERIAL ROLE IN A GLOBAL ENVIRONMENT

A manager does not need to be working for a multinational to feel the impact of globalization and to become a player in international business— a small business in the United States may not think much of globalization until it finds itself faced with foreign competition on its own home turf. Global integration means that the action taken (or not taken) by firms on faraway shores may be increasingly relevant to any business, whether it thinks of itself as "domestic," "regional," "international," or "global." Operating in a global environment, managers need to be aware of both the pros and cons of globalization. They need to know about its benefits, for example, the sourcing opportunities available in foreign markets, as well as its adversarial impact, for example, the loss of jobs in the communities in which they live.

What is the role of the international manager in a global environment? It is clear that the role extends well beyond the business sphere. For example, international negotiations involve multiple constituencies, such as unions and governments; international human resource management necessitates getting into family issues, such as spouse adjustment and children's education; and managing a joint venture or an acquisition necessitates sensitivity to people issues that often involve communities as well as nongovernmental organizations.

These extreme requirements create a new managerial role that is much broader than the one many managers have been used to. This expansion of horizons, which will eventually impact the way managers operate domestically as well, is dependent on the availability and dissemination of relevant knowledge. The new managerial role requires more than dissemination, however. Since the international environment is not only complex but also fast changing, managers must also be able to *create* knowledge, either because the knowledge they seek is unavailable or because it needs to be firm specific to develop a competitive strategy. The skills and tools of international management research are thus an integral part of the managerial role.

GLOBALIZATION AND
MANAGERIAL CHALLENGES

In this section we consider a number of selected issues that international managers need to understand in the context of globalization today. The issues are all associated with globalization, and they are part of a broader vision for the managerial role that we see as a key legacy of the internationalization of business. We look at the gap between rich and poor countries, a role for smaller firms, and conflict and terrorism. We conclude by discussing the positive role that alliances can play at the beginning of the twenty-first century.

THE GAP BETWEEN RICH AND POOR COUNTRIES

The developing world has often been a focus of both pro- and antiglobalization forces—the first group arguing that globalization is the route to economic prosperity for developing countries, the second seeing it as the force that has widened the gap between rich and poor nations.

The disparity between the developed and the developing countries—the rich and poor nations of the world—can be clearly seen from the following statistics (United Nations 2001):

- The richest 20 percent of the world has 86 percent of the world's Gross Domestic Product (GDP), the middle 60 percent has 13 percent, and the poorest 20 percent has only 1 percent.
- Gross National Product (GNP) per capita in the developed world is $22,785, and in the developing world it is $5,725.
- The disparity between rich and poor countries is growing. Comparisons of the top 20 percent with the bottom 20 percent over the past almost two centuries show a dramatic increase—in 1820 the ratio was 3:1, in 1870, 7:1; in 1913, 11:1; in 1960, 30:1; in 1990, 60:1; and in 1997, 74:1.

There is no question that the rich have been growing richer and that the poor are not catching up. But is globalization to blame? Antiglobalization groups point to this disparity as evidence that globalization has not helped the poorer 80 percent of the world. In contrast, proglobalization groups argue that incomes in the poorer countries have been increasing and that these countries do not trade as much as the richer ones and therefore cannot expect to have benefited as much. This argument says that more, not less, trade and investment is needed and that, in an age of globalization, openness to the world is the one single guarantee for progress. And yet openness depends on knowledge, on awareness of world markets and their requirements, on learning how to negotiate a cross-border deal and how to make it happen once the contract has been signed.

Managers need to understand both viewpoints, because both have relevance and value and are likely to be taken by key constituencies with whom they will interact. Effective international managers will take a balanced (though not dispassionate) approach to the issue and in so doing can be greatly assisted by international management research. The academic research provides valuable objectivity, which is not unduly influenced by region, industry, product, or location. Better yet, academic researchers will often control for those factors, providing valuable insights into the firm that is changing its domain or location—a highly probable event in a global, competitive business environment.

The results of research focusing on developing country issues can be especially helpful to developed country managers who may be unfamiliar with this part of the world. Unfortunately, there is relatively little research on management in many parts of the developing world. The vast majority of international management research has focused on the United States and its major trading partners to the neglect of other locations (Thomas, Shenkar, and Clarke 1994). As we noted in the introduction to this handbook, this is one of the important gaps in international management research that needs to be remedied.

THE RISE OF SMALL FIRMS

An expected response to globalization has been a growth in large, global firms. There are a number of what might be called mega-firms that dominate certain industries and sectors. This enlargement of firms has been supported by a high intensity of cross-border mergers and alliances. Perhaps a less expected response is the growth in small firms with international, and sometimes global, operations. The opening of trade and investment opportunities has made it possible for smaller companies to seek out small, niche markets in a variety of locations. Very often, these niches are not of interest to the large companies and provide an ideal opportunity for small companies. The Internet has encouraged this development, as managers of small companies can do a substantial amount of investigation of foreign locations without leaving their offices, homes, or home offices.

The growing visibility of mega-multinational firms has shadowed the smaller firms that have more than maintained their own in the global business environment. It is little known, for instance, that smaller and medium firms have been *increasing* their share of U.S. exports for over a decade now. Yet, for a number of reasons, these firms are rarely the subjects of management research. First, management research has been increasingly dominated by large data sets of public companies that are easily manipulated, thus excluding small, private outfits. Second, the easier entry for survey research and interviews in the larger companies makes it unlikely that researchers will seek smaller firms. This is especially true in the international environment, where both researchers and executives have less familiarity. A case in point is the vast U.S. literature on Japanese management, which by and large omitted the smaller companies while focusing on the Toyota-size conglomerates that employ less than one-third of the Japanese workforce.

In the same way that some locations have been forgotten in international management research, the smaller firm has been all but neglected precisely at a time when entrepreneurship and related topics, so closely tied to the smaller firm, have been flourishing. Changing that will require creating awareness and developing the research strategies, designs, and tools that are necessary to conduct research in such firms. Some of the research strategies detailed in this handbook—for example, the one on qualitative research—are especially relevant for researching the smaller firm in international markets.

CONFLICT AND TERRORISM

Conflict and terrorism seem to be the norm at the dawn of the twenty-first century. The terrorist attacks in the United States on September 11, 2001, brought international terrorism to the forefront of the world psyche. Many countries had previously experienced terrorism, and conflicts in many parts of the world had had dire consequences, but the suicide attacks on the

Twin Towers of the World Trade Center in New York were dramatic images for most people. The Twin Towers were a symbol of globalization, and their collapse illustrated the vulnerability of globalization to local interests and violent, fractious elements. The attacks also underscored for Americans the reality that not everyone subscribes to the American Way and that some vehemently resent it. While most people hope that conflict and terrorism will abate, managers must be realistic and be prepared for them to continue. This means learning to live with uncertainty while broadening the knowledge base from which to draw when the need arises.

The business environment at the dawn of the twenty-first century is complex, and understanding it is difficult for any individual manager. International management research can play a pivotal role in providing information for developing this understanding. Part of the contribution of this research is to place management and business issues within the cultural, social, and political context within which business takes place. This is especially difficult to do outside of one's own society and workplace, but it is precisely here that comparative research can help us not only in expanding our global horizons but also in gaining better understanding of our own environment.

THE GROWTH OF ALLIANCES

Traditional multinational enterprises have often been criticized for extracting benefits from their host-country investments without giving much in return. More than 95 percent of the world's largest multinationals are based in the United States, the European Union, and Japan, and naturally these firms' profits will accrue disproportionately to their home country. Thus, the burden of producing a more evenhanded globalization falls on alliances, an arrangement that is more egalitarian in nature and is built more on the premise of cooperative relations and trust than on control.

The last two decades saw a dramatic increase in the number of strategic alliances of various kinds, from licensing and airline code sharing to joint ventures (including mergers and acquisitions). Despite the growth and the cumulative experience in managing this type of organization, the rate of alliance failure, especially for cross-border alliances, remains very high. The combination of these two factors created a keen interest in alliance understanding, both in academia and among business practitioners.

Alliances represent an unprecedented challenge to management research, a challenge that is likely to grow in the coming decades. To a great extent, theories, models, and methodologies presume a unitary organization with a clear ownership structure, transparent governance, and a single chain of command. While current scholarship acknowledges alliances as "hybrids" and recognizes the blurring of organizational boundaries that come with it, it is far from being able to address the complexity and ambiguity of managing in a twilight zone of vague borders and responsibilities. Many questions remain open, for example, Do alliances necessitate special motivational and leadership schemes? What skills are necessary for a manager to be successful in running an alliance? How should we conduct ethical and objective research when research needs to be supported by multiple entities that differ in what they consider acceptable and ethical?

Current events, including shifting political coalitions and joint military operations, remind us of the interface between the political and the organizational in more than one way. First, firm alliances are embedded in a political context: There is a strong correlation between political and military alliances, on the one hand, and the potential for organizational alliances, on the other hand. Countries that are hostile to each other are less likely to have, or even permit, the formation of alliances among their firms. Second, there are important lessons to be learned by management scholars from the alliances established centuries and even millennia ago by states and governments. This is one place from which to draw inspiration as we seek tools and frames of reference with which to address the alliance challenge. Since current events show that globalization is not synonymous with uniformity in thought or in practices, the history of international relations is a useful way to start.

INTERNATIONAL MANAGEMENT IN A GLOBAL CONTEXT

Managing in this world of conflicting opinions, extremes of wealth and poverty, strategic alliances, and so on, means that effective managers need to be especially aware of multiple factors in their environments. Sensitivity to cross-national differences is only one aspect of managing in a global environment. Learning how to manage across those differences is another. Managers need to learn the reality of globalization but also the myths, as the latter may surface in their dealings with various key constituencies. In the following pages, we provide some contours for the emerging role of the international manager.

THE WORLD MANAGER

The advance of globalization increasingly raises the profile of a so-called global manager who is at ease everywhere and can be effective in any environment. The successful placement of a Brazilian expatriate by French carmaker Renault to its Nissan affiliate in Japan has become a symbol of the global manager, emulated by DaimlerChrysler in the United States and Japan and by many others. At the same time, there are clear signs that managers remain entrenched in their domestic environment. Boards such as DaimlerChrysler's are by and large dominated by the acquiring firm and its home country nationals, and so is senior management. Multinationals such as ABB often require potential recruits to speak the home country language (in the case of ABB, German).

These inconsistent signals suggest that the concept of a global manager is far from being determined, nor is it clear that we will have global managers ten or twenty years from now. Instead of a global manager we will likely seek a "world manager," someone who understands other environments and can serve as a bridge and a boundary spanner between host and foreign environments. This manager will face an amalgam of pressures stemming from globalization and localization forces. Furthermore, he or she will face a pendulum oscillating between globalization and localization and will have to learn to live with the complexities and apparent contradictions related to such shifts. The world manager will also have to learn to manage continuously shifting alliances—something that, as noted earlier, is going to be an increasing requirement of his or her role.

The coming years will put an enormous pressure on these global or world managers. Their need to be attuned to local signals, on a global scale, is quite different from what convergence and divergence proponents had in mind in the discussions of the 1980s and 1990s. Management researchers should consider the leadership and human resource implications of these changes and develop ideas on how to create an operational environment that allows managers to survive and prosper in this environment.

THINKING GLOBALLY AND ACTING LOCALLY

The discussion of the current business environment suggests that the maxim "think globally and act locally" remains a truism. Globalization appears to be a continuing reality for managers, and thus they need to "think globally." A global philosophy is necessary for managers to succeed in this environment—the world is a potential place to do business. At the same time, the fragmentation engendered by conflicts and terrorism and the forces that encourage distinctiveness among countries and cultures demand that managers be especially sensitive to national and cultural differences.

It is easy to talk about the need to combine thinking globally with acting locally. It is not easy for a manager to accomplish this duality in reality. Thinking globally implies certain standardization in approaches. Acting locally implies adapting approaches to local conditions. In a 1983 doctoral seminar, Fayerweather (with more than thirty years of experience and research) talked of the inevitable conflict in multinational companies between forces for integration and those for fragmentation and the need to choose between the two. Much of the literature talks in these terms—for example, firms are either global or multidomestic, rationalized or dispersed, centralized or decentralized, and so forth. The advice to think globally and act locally indicates that a manager can incorporate both dimensions—integration and fragmentation—into decisions. This allows the firm to have, in a sense, the best of both worlds.

For an international manager to follow through on this advice, a thorough knowledge and appreciation of the global possibilities and similarities among countries, as well as a clear understanding of differences, are essential. The effective international manager today considers the global possibilities and is prepared for local eventualities. This is a difficult combination, and researchers can contribute substantially to managers' effectiveness by providing input on both the global possibilities and the local realities.

MANAGING MULTIPLE STAKEHOLDERS

The nature of the business environment described previously means that international managers will interact with an increasingly large number of stakeholders. Managers cannot think of themselves as simply responsible for activity X in country Y. Managers are representatives of the parent company and, as a derivative, representative of the parent country. Their decisions and actions will reflect well or poorly on both the parent company and the parent country. Managers are also representatives of the subsidiary where they are located. The success, or lack thereof, will depend on managers' decisions and actions.

Managers may see themselves as primarily responsible to shareholders, but they interact with employees, customers, creditors, colleagues, government representatives, and a host of others who are stakeholders, because they are impacted by the company and, thus, the manager's decisions and actions. In today's world, additional global stakeholder groups have come to the fore—various special interest groups that believe they are affected by the company's activities (for example, environmental groups) or those that believe they should take responsibility for others who are affected (for example, advocates against child labor). Managers ignore these groups at their peril, because they are often backed by large numbers of like-minded persons around the world and can exert concerted pressure on companies.

Managing the interests of multiple stakeholders is complex, because stakeholder groups are likely to have differing objectives and divergent views of what is acceptable in business activities. This is made more complex in an international environment where cross-national variations in politics, culture, technology, and so on, exacerbate the variations among stakeholder groups. To be effective in such an environment, international managers rely on information that is timely, reliable, and valid to help them balance the competing demands of stakeholders.

THE ROLE OF INTERNATIONAL MANAGEMENT RESEARCH IN A GLOBAL CONTEXT

The foregoing discussion of the world of business today and the role of the international manager in this environment portrays a complexity that is a challenge for managers. How do managers manage effectively in this environment? They rely, of course, on a variety of information sources, both within the company and from outside, to help make sense of the environment. They recognize the value of experts who can elucidate cross-national exigencies. This is where international management research can play a critical role in effective international management.

A CRITICAL NEED FOR INFORMATION AND KNOWLEDGE

In the business environment described here, the international manager has a substantial need for reliable and valid information and knowledge. For example, an American manager working in the Middle East has to manage in the midst of intense feelings (both positive and negative) about Americans, has to deal with conflict and terrorism, and finds cultural similarities and dramatic differences. Such a manager has to do a credible job technically and has to deal effectively with the wider environment. The manager can deal with the technical aspects of the job, even though those details too might vary from location to location. Dealing with the wider environment is more difficult and requires a different kind of information and knowledge, one that is often more tacit and yet rooted in empirical reality.

Academic research provides a sound basis for managers in these circumstances. Research demonstrates the suppositions and propositions that are supported and those that are not. Managers can turn to academic results with confidence in the reliability and validity of the findings. Published academic journal articles have passed the test of peer reviews and can be accepted as providing results and recommendations that are well thought out. To this extent international management research is relevant to the practice of international management.

RESEARCH AS A SOUND BASIS FOR MANAGEMENT DECISIONS AND ACTION

Managers making decisions and taking action in a global environment need a wealth of information if their decisions and actions are to be appropriate and not cause cross-national friction and conflict. It is impossible for any manager, even with an extensive staff, to gather the information pertinent to every decision and action. International managers must rely on input from outside sources; not least among them is international management research. Academic research is undertaken to describe what happens in the business world and to test hypothesized relationships among variables of interest to managers. The chapters in this handbook demonstrate the multiple aspects of the international management world that have been investigated, as well as the many that remain to be investigated. This research is a valuable source of information for practicing managers.

Unfortunately, oftentimes academics and managers speak a rather different language. Scholars may pose research questions in academic terms—for example, "to test the convergence of managerial value systems in free-trade regions"—and the immediate relevance of the results may not be obvious to the practicing manager. The manager is more likely to ask, "Will Canadian, Mexican, and U.S. managers become more alike because of NAFTA?" Research-based information can provide the answer, but the manager may not realize this. International management researchers need to make a special effort to ensure that their results are disseminated in a form that is easily accessed by managers. This is often a tall task in an academic environment that rewards knowledge creation rather than dissemination.

OBJECTIVES OF AND LIMITS TO INTERNATIONAL MANAGEMENT RESEARCH

Academic research can provide valuable information, knowledge, and insights for practicing managers. There are, however, choices inherent in the research that may make it more theoretical than practical. Most academics have been trained to seek "the truth." They recognize that this is unattainable, but it is nevertheless the aim of their research. Academics are, thus, not satisfied with probable likelihood; they want to demonstrate statistical significance. This scholarly approach is often criticized for limiting the relevance of international management research, but it need not be so. Academics and management practitioners need to work together to ensure that research addresses questions of importance to managers and that results, from sound research, are available to managers in a manager-friendly format.

Academics are schooled to be conservative; therefore, they generally do not see their role as "paving the way" for managers. More often, academics observe what is happening and investigate why it happens. Good academic research is based on demonstrating internal/external reliability and validity and is necessarily slow. The academic researcher, correctly from a scholarly perspective, may take many months to design a research project—including exhaustive literature reviews, development and pretesting of instruments, identification of appropriate samples, and so on. The practicing manager, in contrast, is faced with decisions that have to be made immediately and actions that must take place in the near term. This often leads to a conflict between scholars and practitioners. Simply put, the manager wants answers now, while the academic wants answers that are scientifically sound. The manager is often happy to settle for approximately right answers, while the academic is not.

Academic research is also geared toward total objectivity. This should be a real benefit to managers. Research conducted internally by a company, or by consultants working for a company, usually has stakeholders who influence the form of the research, as well as the outcomes. Scholars in the field of international management are careful to separate their research from any particular stakeholder interests. This means that scholarly, academic research can provide managers with an objective view of a situation of interest. This issue of objectivity recently came to the fore with discussions of possible conflict of interest by financial analysts, and the predominantly positive (though not perfect) record of academia on this account should be reassuring.

Many academic organizations now publish both scholarly and practitioner journals (for example, the *Academy of Management Executive* is intended especially for practitioners); others publish topical newsletters or similar publications (for example, the Academy of International Business's *Insights*). Many academics also provide consulting services to businesses, and this keeps the academics aware of practitioners' concerns, while also ensuring that managers are aware of the results of research. The gap between researchers and practitioners remains a concern, however. The *Handbook for International Management Research* should provide a partial bridge across this gap. It is our hope that practitioners will not be put off because the title of this book contains the word "research." Rather, practitioners should see this handbook as providing a unique source of research results. Much of the practitioner role, from gathering information to analyzing it and making systematic decisions, parallels the research process. A mutual appreciation of the contributions of academics and practitioners will be much more constructive than the often adversarial nature articulated in the "ivory tower" image. Scholars must seek to incorporate current issues into their thinking, and executives must be proactive in identifying those issues and in providing feedback of the practicality of models and tools designed outside the field.

SUMMARY AND CONCLUSIONS

This concluding chapter of the *Handbook for International Management Research* has sought to describe the international management environment at the dawn of the twenty-first century and to identify the important and relevant role that research plays in improving international managers' effectiveness. We have described today's environment as essentially one of contrasts and ambiguities, which makes the manager's role especially delicate and complex. The international manager's role is not simply a business role—he or she is a cross-cultural diplomat, whose decisions and actions can have wide personal and social ramifications. To be effective, both from a business perspective and in this wider role, the international manager relies on information. Scholars can play a vital part by providing information that is reasoned and objective.

We believe that this handbook can contribute to the international management field—both from a scholarly and a practical perspective. Our primary audience for this book is academic. The book chapters should provide guidance to researchers and help ensure that research is relevant and valid—both academically and practically. Although we have not designed the handbook for an audience of practicing managers, we believe that managers will find much of value in its chapters, as each identifies the body of knowledge that currently exists, as well as questions to be investigated. If, as we suggest, managers take at least the partial research role of identifying relevant research questions, both they and their academic counterparts will greatly benefit.

REFERENCES

Fayerweather, J. 1983. Doctoral seminar, New York University.
Punnett, B. J. 2002. Culture and management in the English-speaking Caribbean. Speech given to St. Vincent and the Grenadines Chamber of Commerce, February.
Thomas, A. 1996. A call for research in forgotten locations. In B. J. Punnett and O. Shenkar, eds., *Handbook for international management research*. Cambridge, MA: Blackwell.
Thomas, A. S., O. Shenkar, and L. Clarke. 1994. The globalization of our mental maps: Evaluating the geographic scope of *JIBS* coverage. *Journal of International Business Studies* 25 (4): 675–86.
United Nations. 2001. *World development report*. Oxford: Oxford University Press.

Part 6

APPENDIX

RETRIEVING INFORMATION FOR INTERNATIONAL MANAGEMENT RESEARCH

ELECTRONIC AND PRINT SOURCES

Ilgaz Arikan and Meri Meredith

The Internet has had a significant impact on international management research. First, accessing data sources and library holdings has become more convenient and less expensive. Second, interaction among researchers has been facilitated by the exchange of knowledge across various telecommunication media. In this appendix, we provide a quick reference guideline for those doing academic research in international management using the Internet as well as traditional library resources.

By using the Internet, researchers have quick but unfiltered access to a wealth of information at their fingertips. All postings on the Internet either on databases or on Web-based pages are electronic files. Any person with access to the Internet site has the power to add, delete, or edit these files and may not be subject to a peer-review process. Before the wide use of Internet search engines, only published studies were easy to locate because they were indexed. These studies are usually peer reviewed, and this screening process ensures methodologically and theoretically valid pieces to be available to other scientists.

COMMONLY USED SEARCHABLE DATABASES AND INDEXES

For convenience to the reader, the scope of these databases is given as follows:[1]

I: individual-level data and author search
F: firm-level data
N: industry-level data
C: country-level data

Some of the following databases and on-line sources may not be directly related to international management topics, and their contribution may provide a somewhat indirect link. This is due to the nature of quantitative reporting capability of many of the database providers. For example, some of the databases and sites emphasize more specific international business functions, such as marketing, trade statistics, accounting, and financial management. However, these can be correlated with many of the international management research interests. The data from these sources may need to be correlated depending on specific research questions international management scholars will ask. Several examples are provided here.

Political Risk Yearbook contains financial, political, and economic risk information on 106 countries. On several variables each country's risk factors are tracked for ten years, and brief summaries are provided to explain changes on social conditions and international relationships. While most of the information provided is based on accounting measures of macroeconomic variables, it might provide insight into individual decision making such as investment decisions, formation of joint ventures, and alliances. Coupled with a corruption index, this database can provide insight into various questions on differences between ethical perceptions of leaders, cross-cultural leadership issues, and so forth.

On the other hand, some resources may have a more direct impact on international management research. *Human Resources Series Policies and Practices* covers international human resources topics such as hiring, termination, productivity management, labor relations, compensation, and benefits. *Economist Intelligence Unit's Country Commerce,* which contains information on sixty countries' local companies—including labor relations, contractual agreements, corporate and personnel taxation, and merger and acquisition practices—can also provide significant insights into HRM practices in international contexts.

PRINT RESOURCES

Although the main scope of this appendix is on-line sources for international management research, there are several print sources that need to be mentioned.

CONSUMER INTERNATIONAL (N, C)
Euromonitor International, 122 S. Michigan Ave., Suite 1200, Chicago, IL 60603 312–922–1115

This source brings together in one volume all available market information on consumer trends in all the major non-European countries, the scope being all the major retail items purchased for household use. Covers approximately 120 consumer products with forecasts up to 2000. *Consumer Asia 2001, Consumer China 2001, Consumer Eastern Europe 2001/2002, Consumer Europe 2001/2002, Consumer Latin America 2001,* and *Consumer USA* are companion volumes. *Consumer Spending Forecasts for the World's Largest Economies, 1995–2005* covers twenty-six countries in eight major categories such as clothing, housing, food, and drink. *World Consumer Income and Expenditure Patterns 2001.*

COUNTRIES OF THE WORLD AND THEIR LEADERS (C)
The Gale Group, 27500 Drake Rd., Farmington Hills, MI 48331–3535 800–877–4253

This is a compilation of U.S. government department reports on contemporary political and economic conditions, government personnel and policies, political parties, religions, history, education, press, radio, television, climate, visa and world health information, and customs and duty tips. Also contains background notes. There are sections on international treaty organizations, U.S. embassies, and how and where to seek the State Department's assistance when doing business abroad.

DIRECTORY OF CORPORATE AFFILIATIONS (F, N)
Lexis/Nexis Group, 121 Chanlon Rd., New Providence, NJ 07974 908–464–6800

This source provides acquisition and merger information for major U.S. corporations and their divisions, including companies on the NYSE, AMEX, OTC and private companies. Volume 1 contains the Master Index, which is an alphabetical cross-reference index for more than 121,000 divisions, subsidiaries, affiliates and the parent companies. It also contains Brand Name and Geographical Indexes.

Volume 2 contains the Master Index of SIC codes and Personnel Index. Volume 3 contains public companies. Volume 4 contains private companies. Volume 5 contains international companies. There is a Merger, Acquisitions, and Name Change Index from 1976 to the present.

DIRECTORY OF AMERICAN FIRMS OPERATING IN FOREIGN COUNTRIES (F, N, C)

Uniworld Business Publications, Inc., 257 Central Park West, Suite 10A, New York, NY 10024-4110 212–496–2448

This three-volume directory lists American companies that own or have considerable capital investment in foreign businesses. Nonprofit organizations and institutions are not included. Volume 1 is an alphabetical listing of U.S. companies with addresses, products, officers, and list of countries of operation. In volumes 2 and 3, U.S. companies are listed within specific countries. The *Directory of Foreign Firms Operating in the United States* lists information on foreign businesses that own or have large investments in U.S. firms.

DIRECTORY OF UNITED STATES IMPORTERS (F)

The Gale Group, 27500 Drake Rd., Farmington Hills, MI 48331–3535 800–877–4253

Journal of Commerce, 445 Marshal St., Phillipsburg, NJ 08865

The coverage of importers is for the United States, Canada, and Puerto Rico. An alphabetical index is included for companies and products. Companies are also listed by state. Includes customs information for importing, trade commissions, consulates, embassies, foreign trade zones, and so forth. A companion volume is the *Directory of United States Exporters*.

DUN & BRADSTREET/GALE GROUP INDUSTRY HANDBOOK (N)

The Gale Group, 27500 Drake Rd., Farmington Hills, MI 48331–3535 800–877–4253

These two dependable and quality publishers have teamed up to offer an in-depth look at specific industries not published to date. The industries covered are chemicals and pharmaceuticals (vol. 1); broadcasting and telecommunications, and computers and software (vol. 2); construction and agriculture (vol. 3); entertainment and hospitality (vol. 4); and insurance and health and medical services (vol. 5). This handbook is a compilation of information on an industry with an overview, including its history, important participants, current trends, and future directions. Chapter 2 presents the number of establishments, employment, compensation, revenues, ratios, and performance indicators. Chapter 3 shows industry norms and ratios. Chapter 4 is a directory of major companies in the industry. Chapter 5 shows companies in rank order, first by sales and then by employment. Chapter 6 presents a summary of recent mergers and acquisitions within the industry. Chapter 7 lists both domestic and international associations directly involved in the industry or supporting the industry's activities with a URL or email address. Chapters 8, 9, and 10 list major consultants, trade information resources, and trade show activity including frequency of events, audience, and principal exhibits. There is a Master Index, a geographical index, and a SIC code index. The appendix presents a SIC to NAICS and a NAICS to SIC code lookup. Finally, statistics presented in chapter 2 show value of shipments and projected value of shipments.

ENCYCLOPEDIA OF BUSINESS INFORMATION SOURCES (F, N)
The Gale Group, 27500 Drake Rd., Farmington Hills, MI 48331–3535 800–877–4253

This fifteenth edition is a bibliographic guide to over 33,000 citations covering more than 1,100 business, financial, and industrial topics. Also included are descriptions of Web sites and Internet addresses and an alphabetical listing of all sources cited with contact information. There is extensive cross-referencing since some of the headings are a bit antiquated; for example, cellular telephone is found under the heading "Mobile Telephony Industry." There are eighteen types of sources from indexes and abstracts, encyclopedias, financial ratios, statistics, on-line and Internet databases to research centers and trade and professional societies.

EXPORTERS' ENCYCLOPEDIA (N)

Dun & Bradstreet, Inc., Parsippany, NJ 07054 800–526–0651

This encyclopedia contains procedures that are fundamental for success, from inception to execution. There are six sections to the volume: 1. Export Order, 2. Export Markets, 3. Export Know-how, 4. Communications Data, 5. Information Sources/Services, and 6. Transportation Data that has information on foreign trade zones and world trade centers. There is a supplemental volume, *Importers Manual USA.* This is a single-source reference encyclopedia for importing to the United States. There are sections on international law, international banking, packaging, shipping, insurance, and U.S. customs entry. There are general, country, and commodity indexes.

GLOBAL MARKET SHARE PLANNER (F, C)

Euromonitor International, 122 S. Michigan Ave., Suite 1200, Chicago, IL 60603 312–922–1115

This six-volume series concentrates on the key international consumer markets in thirty countries and key Foreign Major Consumer Groups sectors. The top 200 multinationals are analyzed in detail by experienced company research teams using locally based and London-based experts. Volume 1, *Global Market Share Rankings,* identifies the leading 1,800 regional and major subsidiaries that dominate the fast-moving consumer markets. Volume 2, *Major Performing Rankings,* ranks each of the 2,500 companies by commercial and financial criteria including market share and profit margin ranked nationally, regionally, and internationally. Volume 3, *World's Major Multinationals,* contains in-depth profiles of the top 200 companies operating worldwide in these markets. Volumes 4–6, *Major Market Share Companies,* covers leading companies in the Americas, Europe, South Africa, and Asia Pacific with contact details as well as ownership structure, a financial profile, main products and brands, and market share performance. Products covered are alcoholic drinks, bakery products, canned foods, cat and dog food, confectionary, dairy, desserts, disposable paper, frozen foods, hot drinks, household and cleaning, snacks, cosmetics and toiletries, OTC healthcare, and soft drinks. This series is updated quarterly.

THE HANDBOOK OF HUMAN RESOURCE MANAGEMENT (I, F, C)
Brian Towers, ed., Oxford: Blackwell Publishers, 1996
http://www.blackpublishing.co.uk

This second edition traces the transition from personnel management to human resource management. The handbook has been updated to provide wide-ranging overviews of developments worldwide from the United Kingdom, Continental Europe, United States, and Australia, including Japanese HRM practices in the United Kingdom and the United States.

HOOVER'S HANDBOOK OF AMERICAN BUSINESS (F)
Hoover's, Inc., 1033 La Posada Dr., Austin, TX 78752
512–374–4500
http://www.hoovers.com

This handbook contains a two-page synopsis of the top 500 companies in America with listings of who, what, where, and when, as well as a listing of the companies' key competitors. Companies are profiled with approximately fifty lists in which the companies are ranked, for example, by sales, employees, and so forth.

HOW TO FIND INFORMATION ABOUT COMPANIES (F)
Washington Researchers, Ltd., 416 Hungerford Dr., Suite 315, Rockville, MD 20850 301–251–9550

This is a three-volume set with many published resources, databases, CD-ROMs, and government documents. It discusses corporate cultures, plants and facilities, products and services, R&D, management and labor, finances, strategic plans, divisions, subsidiaries, private companies, foreign firms, and service companies.

Companions to this set are *How to Find Information about Divisions, Subsidiaries, and Products; How to Find Information about Foreign and Global Companies; How to Find Information about Private Companies;* and *How to Find Information about Service Companies.*

HUMAN RESOURCES SERIES POLICIES
AND PRACTICES (I)

West Group, P.O. Box 64833, St. Paul, MN 55164–0833
800–328–4880, X66470

This three-volume set is updated on a monthly basis. It covers HR management, record keeping and HRIS, International HR, hiring, termination, fair employment practices, quality/productivity management, performance appraisal, training and communication, discipline, grievances and absenteeism, labor relations, compensation and benefits, work and family, leaves of absence, and occupational safety, health, and security. There is an extensive index and a monthly newsletter.

INTERNATIONAL BUSINESS INFORMATION: HOW TO FIND
IT, HOW TO USE IT (I, F)

Ruth A. Pagell and Michael Halperin, eds., Chicago: Glenlake Publishing, 1999. 1261 West Glenlake, Chicago, IL 60660

This book is designed to be a valuable guide for anyone performing international business research. The sources included are highly selective. The indexes, abstracts, and full text databases described should be adequate to identify material that treats theoretical and conceptual issues. Dow Jones Interactive Publishing, Knight Ridder Information Services, and Financial Times Information have created the *World Reporter Database,* which is available through DIALOG, DataStar, Dow Jones, and FT Profile. Coverage of NAFTA has increased, and there are descriptions of Web sites interwoven throughout the chapters. It should be noted that sometimes the answers to apparently simple and plausible questions are nowhere to be found.

**INTERNATIONAL ENCYCLOPEDIA OF BUSINESS AND
MANAGEMENT (C)**
Routledge, 29 West 35th St., New York, NY 10001 212–
216–7800

This is an international work of business reference on management.
There are 500 entries covering such subjects as accounting, business
history and economics, finance, human resource management,
industrial/labor relations, international business, management education, comparative management, MIS, manufacturing management, marketing, operations management, operations research,
organizational behavior, and strategy. Coverage includes all aspects
of management and is international in both subject matter and
authorship. Cross-cultural aspects such as accounting in Asia or
banking in Japan are examples of geographical perspectives.

**INTERNATIONAL MARKETING DATA
AND STATISTICS (N, C)**
Euromonitor International, 122 S. Michigan Ave., Suite 1200,
Chicago, IL 60603 312–922–1115

This source contains statistics on demographic trends and forecasts,
economic indicators, banking and finance, external trade, labor
forces, industrial, energy, defense, environmental consumer, retail,
advertising, housing, agriculture, and regional comparisons. All
regions of the world are covered except Europe. *European Marketing
Data and Statistics* contains the European Statistics.

INTERNATIONAL MARKETING FORECASTS (N, C)
Euromonitor International, 122 S. Michigan Ave., Suite 1200,
Chicago, IL 60603 312–922–1115

Euromonitor has consolidated its in-house database and added to it
expert economists' opinions and computer forecasting models to
produce opinions of the way markets will develop in the next
twelve years. Using 1999 as the base year and taking into account

twenty years of historic data as well as a large range of socioeconomic predictions, data is provided on 320 different markets in fifty-two counties. The GDP real growth table is the starting point for many forecasts in association with population growth. Areas covered are demographics by age and gender, economic, labor force, income and earnings, expenditures, retailing, household durables, media, and communications. Meats, fish, baby food, disposable paper products, electronic appliances, consumer electronics, and leisure goods are some of the products covered. *European Marketing Forecasts 2001* covers the European side.

Mergent's Manuals (F)

Mergent, 60 Madison Ave., New York, NY 10010 800–342–5647, X7601

The manuals contain information on publicly owned companies. Included is financial information (income statements, balance sheets, financial and operating ratios) based on reports from the corporations and the SEC; description of business with a list of subsidiaries; and a capital structure section (details on capital stock and long-term debt). Special features of the manuals (blue pages) include geographical and business classification indexes, various special indexes, and charts. Depth of coverage varies. Each manual is updated with supplements.

Nelson's Directory of Investment Research (F)

Nelson Information, P.O. Box 591, Port Chester, NY 10573 http://www.nelnet.com

This directory identifies Wall Street research analysts. Volume 1 covers the United States and volume 2 covers international companies. There are seven parts to volume 1; the largest section covers 4,500 U.S. companies with a short profile and indicates which analysts cover that company. Often covered are the top officers and their duration in the company. Volume 2 covers 4,500 companies headquartered outside the United States.

THE OFFICIAL EXPORT GUIDE (C)
Primedia Directories, 10 Lake Dr., Hightstown, NJ 08520
800–221–5488

This is possibly the most comprehensive guide to the process of
exporting from the United States to all the countries of the world.
It is organized into nine sections. There is a glossary of international
trade terms. There are articles by industry experts offering practical
information and tips on the many aspects of international trade.
There is a basic "How to Export" section. There are country profiles
that cover 215 countries and territories. Included in this section are
data on best export opportunities, existing trade and entry trade,
warehousing, and free trade zones. The shipping services section
covers freight forwarders who provide freight rates and modular
transportation. It also provides lists of the U.S. headquarters of
international air cargo, small package carriers, ocean cargo carriers
and agents, rail services, translation and legal services, and export
trading companies. In the information sources section there are literally thousands of listings for specific country and industry officers,
international and private organizations, embassies, and consulates.
Schedule B contains mandatory numbers required to report export
shipments. Finally, there is a section on mandatory and hazardous
materials regulations, as well as samples of export documents. The
companion volume on importing is the *U.S. Customs House Guide.*

PASSPORT TO THE WORLD (C)
World Trade Press, 1505 Fifth Ave., San Rafael, CA 94901
800–833–8586

This is a series of twenty-four country-specific pocket-size guides to
help people learn about the business culture and etiquette of the
people of a country. Each one is crammed with hard-to-find information on cultural stereotypes, regional differences, value comparisons, women in business, strategies for success, communications
styles, making connections, reading the people, entertaining, conducting business meetings, and so forth.

PORTABLE ENCYCLOPEDIA FOR DOING BUSINESS (C)
World Trade Press, 1505 Fifth Ave., San Rafael, CA 94901
800–833–8586

This encyclopedia contains information on the economy, current
issues, opportunities, foreign investment and trade, trade agreements, foreign trade zones, import and export policy, procedures
industry reviews, trade fairs, business culture and travel, laws and
taxation, and important addresses. Companions are *A Short Course in
International Contracts, A Short Course in International Marketing, A
Short Course in International Negotiating,* and *A Short Course in International Payments.*

PRINCIPAL INTERNATIONAL BUSINESSES 2000/01 (F)
Dun & Bradstreet, Inc., Parsippany, NJ 07054 800–526–0651

This source contains information on 55,000 leading businesses in
133 countries listed alphabetically by country. Address, cable or
telex number, sales, employees, SIC, and chief executive are listed.
Alphabetic and product classification indexes are at the back of the
volume.

RETAIL TRADE INTERNATIONAL 2000 (N, C)
Euromonitor International, 122 S. Michigan Ave., Suite 1200,
Chicago, IL 60603 312–922–1115

This seven-volume report, in its eleventh edition, provides an in-
depth review and analysis of retail trade worldwide. The aim of the
report is to present a comprehensive survey of world retail trends
and developments and to provide not only the statistical data but
also an analysis and evaluation of the data on a national level.
Included in the country analysis are key findings, macroeconomic
factors, retail sales, retail infrastructure, key retailing issues, retail
business, food distribution, nonfood distribution, major retailers,
and an outlook. The timescale for historical trends is 1993–98 with
forecast trends projected to 2003. Fifty-two countries are covered.
An analyst with specific retail and/or country expertise, often based
in the country or region itself, has written each country section.

Retail sales as a proportion of GDP or consumer expenditures as a proportion of retail sales are examples of the statistical data.

WORLD RETAIL DIRECTORY AND SOURCEBOOK 1999/2000

This is a comprehensive guide to more than 2,600 retailers in over ninety countries. Section one has rankings of the world's major retailers, section two presents global trends in retailing with an overview of the industry, section three gives profiles of the 2,600 retailers, and section four features key information sources organized by major trade and business associations, major trade and business journals, and major research publishers. Great emphasis has been placed on classifying companies by their type of operations or retail format in order to facilitate easy comparison between countries.

WHO OWNS WHOM: CONTINENTAL EUROPE (F)

Dun & Bradstreet, Inc., Parsippany, NJ 07054 800–526–0651

This is a directory of parent, associate, and subsidiary companies. Volume 1 is a listing of parent companies by country with a separate list of foreign parent companies at the end. Volume 2 cross-references subsidiary and associate companies to their parent company. There are separate indexes at the back of the volumes for numeric titles, umlaut entries, and so forth.

WORLD BUSINESS DIRECTORY (F)

The Gale Group, 27500 Drake Rd., Farmington Hills, MI 48331–3535 800–877–4253

Published by the World Trade Centers Association, this four-volume set lists more than 100,000 top trading companies. Contains hard to find data on companies from Eastern Europe, People's Republic of China, and the former Soviet Union.

WORLD DEVELOPMENT REPORT (C)

Oxford University Press, 20 Madison Ave., New York, NY 10016

This annual report discusses infrastructures and environmental topics. It includes the World Development Indicators that offer selected social and economic statistics for more than 200 countries and territories. Some of the tables are GNP per capita, average annual rate of inflation, OECD imports of manufactured goods, income distribution, and PPP estimates of GNP. Its strength is in its twenty-one tables. They are Size of the Economy; Quality of Life; Population and Labor Force; Poverty; Distribution of Income and Consumption; Education; Health; Land Use and Agricultural Productivity; Water Use, Deforestation, and Protected Areas; Energy Use and Emissions; Growth of the Economy; Structure of Output; Structure of Demand; Central Government Finances; Balance of Payments Current Account and International Reserves; Private Sector Finance; Role of Government in the Economy; Power and Transportation; Communications, Information, and Science, and Technology; Global Trade; and Aid and Financial Flows; there is also table 1a, Key Indicators for Other Economies.

WORLD ECONOMIC FACTBOOK (C)
Euromonitor International, 122 S. Michigan Ave., Suite 1200, Chicago, IL 60603 312–922–1115

Represents a unique compilation of hard to get political and economic information on 207 countries laid out in a concise and standard format for easy comparison. Thus each country can be ranked from 1 to 207 to show its relative position in GDP, inflation, population, and so forth. Such items as political risk, main industries, consumption, trading partners, imports, exports, and tourism revenues and expenditures are included. It is a two-page snapshot of a country's environment.

WORLD INVESTMENT DIRECTORY (C)
United Nations, New York, NY 10017

This six-volume set contains foreign direct investment in one hundred countries, as well as a listing of companies and the countries in which they have a strong presence. There are tables for a summary of international investment position, for foreign direct investment flows by industry and geography, for largest foreign affiliates in host economy and largest transnational corporations abroad, and, finally, for the legal framework for transnational corporations. It is hoped that this work will be continually updated since foreign direct investment has become a significant sector of the global economy.

WORLD MARKET SHARE REPORTER (C)

The Gale Group, 27500 Drake Rd., Farmington Hills, MI 48331–3535 800–877–4253

This unique resource can be used for competitive analysis, diversification planning, marketing research, and other forms of economic and policy analysis. There are over sixteen hundred entries from more than 270 geographic locations and covers 433 SIC codes. There are four categories of shares: corporate, industry, brand, and product; commodity; service; and facility. It should be noted that the *World Market Share Reporter* does not cover North America, Canada, or Mexico. The *Market Share Reporter* covers these regions.

WORLDWIDE BRANCH LOCATIONS OF MULTINATIONAL COMPANIES (F)

The Gale Group, 27500 Drake Rd., Farmington Hills, MI 48331–3535 800–877–4253

This resource identifies and, in most cases, provides descriptive data on approximately twenty-six thousand overseas subsidiaries, branches, manufacturing plants, and offices of five hundred of the world's principal multinationals. Two hundred of the companies are American. The rest are headquartered in Japan, Canada, the United Kingdom, France, Germany, and Sweden. The book is arranged in two sections—by branches and by company headquarters. Three indexes provide access by geography, SIC code, and an alphabetical listing of both branches and parents.

INFORMATION RETRIEVAL

The traditional context of information retrieval is based on subject headings, descriptors, and type of documents. These are cataloged in a systematic order and easily accessed using a selection criterion. Internet search engines use similar criteria, but instead of using meaningful and evaluative selection criteria, they utilize algorithms to select words from the body of text, headers, or abstracts, and their output depends on the downloadability of documents into search engine servers. Some programs equate relevance, based on the repetition of terms in the body of a document. This increases efficiency in locating appropriate resources.

DOCUMENTATION OF ELECTRONIC SOURCES

All academic publications provide a list of references or works consulted to give due credit to the owner(s) of that particular work. To ensure consistency in publications as far as references are concerned, each journal, or outlet, has its own rules about the "proper way to document." While these proper ways to document other journal articles, books, papers, chapters in edited books, and dissertations are clearly noted in each volume of journals, many management journals have not provided guidelines for electronic sources.[2] Documenting electronic sources varies in form across disciplines. In the United States, there are two main documentation styles: MLA (Modern Language Association) and APA (American Psychological Association). Most commonly, the MLA style is used in the humanities and the APA in the natural and social sciences. There are also various less widely used discipline-specific styles. The following address provides useful links to various style guides.

http://owl.english.purdue.edu/handouts/research/r_docelectric.html

One possible way of documenting a source is to list the items in the order of author, date of publication, name of article, publisher information, Web site access date, and the URL address. For example,

Taylor, T. (20 March 2000). The elements of citation. Basic CGOS style. Columbia University Press. Retrieved January 4, 2001, from the World Wide Web:
http://www.columbia.edu/cu/cup/cgos/idx_basic.html

COMMONLY USED SEARCH ENGINES

Most commonly used search programs retrieve citations using descriptive words that might appear in the title, abstract, keywords, body of the text, or the citations. While it is possible to refine the search to authors, abstracts, titles, or geographies, usually an Internet-based search yields more unsorted results.

To search databases that are not on the Web, different programs are used. For example, ABI/INFORM Global provides in-depth coverage of business conditions, trends, corporate strategies and tactics, management techniques, competitive and product information, and a wide variety of other topics. This database provides informative indexing and substantive abstracts to articles from more than thirteen hundred leading business and management publications, including over 350 English-language titles from outside the United States. Updated weekly, the database covers business-related periodicals since 1971. Many of the titles in ABI/Inform link to the full-text articles as well. Database Producer is Proquest. While most of the Internet-based search engines provide free service to researchers, a search engine like ABI/INFORM will have limited accessibility. For example, a researcher at the Ohio State University can access ABI/INFORM through the university library system, since this database is licensed for use only by students, staff, and faculty of OhioLINK member institutions.

OWNERSHIP AND COPYRIGHT ISSUES ON THE WEB

Given the short history of electronic documents and their accessibility, the copyright laws have not been effectively developed. Copyright Law of the United States of America contained in Title 17 of the U.S. Code governs the intellectual property laws.[3] The U.S. Copyright Office at the Library of Congress has made a revision of the law and included the exceptions of the 1998 Digital Millennium Copyright Act (Public Law 105-304 in April 1999) and the 1998 Sonny Bono Term Extension Act (Public Law 105-298).

One other important feature of intellectual property on the Internet is its duration in circulation. While traditional print-form media such as journal articles, books, and dissertations exist almost indefinitely after their publication, Internet resources are posted rather than published, and they can be pulled off the servers at the discretion of the person in charge of posting these files. It is, therefore, almost impossible to assert that a document will have a permanent link (URL address).

AN EXAMPLE OF ON-LINE RESEARCH

Let us assume we are interested in doing a study on corruption and cultural differences. Most probably, we would need to administer a survey of Hofstede's cultural dimensions and measure corruption, economic and political development, risk indices, and so forth. With the use of the Internet, this study is made easy. For example, Hofstede's cultural dimensions survey is available for download on the Internet at the Institute for Research on Intercultural Cooperation (IRIC) Web site. One can download this questionnaire, choose among the many translations, and send out. For the corruption indices, the International Country Risk Guide can be used. Along with political and economic development indices such as Freedom in the World by the Freedom House, the Global Development Network Growth Database by the World Bank might be utilized for this study. Literature review can be supported by the on-line library search using ABI/Inform and ABC POLI SCI. These two databases for journals and other full-text materials are commonly available through many if not all university libraries. The surveys can be mailed or administered by one of many commercial surveyor companies such as NCS Pearson, Survey Trends, or Rao Soft. The following is a list of the Internet sources discussed here:

Hofstede's Cultural Dimensions Survey	http://cwis.kub.nl/~fsw_2/iric/index2.htm
Corruption and Country Risk Indices	http://www.prsgroup.com/icrg/icrg.html
Political Freedom Indices	http://www.freedomhouse.org/research/
Global Development Indices	http://www.worldbank.org/research/growth /GDNdata.htm
NCS Pearson	http://www.ncspearson.com/ncscorp /survey/index.htm
Survey Trends	http://www.surveytrends.com
Rao Soft	http://www.raosoft.com
ABI/Inform and ABC POLI SCI	Library links

Most probably, upon completion of the manuscript, the researcher would want to get some feedback from his or her peers and would circulate this study by emailing it as an attachment, saving money and time. He or she could also post the manuscript on a Web site as a working paper, allowing other researchers to access it and further the knowledge.

ALTERNATIVE LIBRARIES

Traditionally, institutional libraries subscribe to on-line journals and databases from various publishers and make these resources available to their patrons. Usually the wealth of the libraries' resources is dependent on how much financial support is provided, and the librarians decide on subscriptions based on usage of these journals and databases. Recently, many publishers have started compiling journals and databases and making them available for electronic distribution besides providing the services to traditional institutional libraries. Some of their features are free for all, while for some other services a fee is charged for accessing, downloading, and/or printing. In some cases, these sources do exist in university libraries as a link for on-line resources, and in some others cases, they may not be provided. Some of these individual subscription services of academic library collections are as follows.[4]

EBRARY.COM
http://www.ebrary.com

Ebrary.com is an on-line subscription service that offers, via the Internet, worldwide access to a comprehensive on-line library of authoritative copyrighted content. This is a partnering with the world's most influential publishers of professional, academic, and scholarly content. The team running this site has extensive experience in technology, library science, and electronic distribution. You name your price. There is an "ask-an-expert" feature. A one-month subscription is $9.95.

E-GLOBALLIBRARY.COM
http://www.e-globallibrary .com

E-global library mirrors the library support services typically provided by academic libraries. It contains vast compendiums of information in the forms of bibliographic databases that include articles, directory databases that contain listings and contact information, data-focused databases that contain statistics and data sets, and business-oriented databases that provide company profiles and related information. The basic services include online tutorials, research guides, and a core collection of Internet resources and career development resources. The premium services include access to electronic research databases, on-call reference assistance, and document delivery. For those institutions able to offer their on-line students access to their library's on-campus databases, e-global library will simply "pass through" students via the appropriate URL at no charge. E-global library was developed in 1987 by a team of twenty-five professional, subject-expert librarians who have evaluated thousands of Internet resources. They do daily verification of all links, develop seventy-four new guides each year, and review existing research guides quarterly.

QUESTIA.COM
http://www.questia.com

This is an on-line subscription-based service that offers free searching and unlimited access to tens of thousands of scholarly books and journals that support an undergraduate curriculum in the liberal arts. The price is $19.95 for a monthly subscription or $14.95 for a forty-eight-hour subscription. One can also create citations in the proper format. There is 24/7 support. However, there is no downloading, and printing can only be done one page at a time. One can bookmark, annotate, and highlight materials.

XANEDU.COM
http://www.Xanedu.com

XanEdu is a business-orientated on-line subscription service offered through an agreement with Bell and Howell, who is recognized for its collection, organization, and distribution of high-quality, value-added information to faculty, researchers, and students. There is an MBA research engine geared to MBA topics. Also available at this site is the Encyclopedia Britannica and the "Best of the Web" sites. The service is free to faculty, who can customize their course packets and integrate these resources that are content copyright cleared. These CoursePacks, Case Packs, or LitPacks Online are priced for students. One can search and view the full text for free. One pays only to print, to copy and paste, or to download the sections or articles.

RESOURCES ON THE INTERNET

ABI/INFORM (I, F, N, C)
http://www.proquest.com

This resource indexes and abstracts over one thousand business periodicals. Full text is available on four hundred titles. Adjacency searching is the default in this database. It can be searched by company name, keyword, subject, periodical title, or exact phrase. Very recent articles may not have full-text availability. It is available from home, lab, or office.

ACADEMIC UNIVERSE (LEXIS/NEXIS) (F, N, C)
http://www.lexisnexis.com

Academic Universe provides access to a wide range of news, business, legal, and reference information. News is segmented into top, general, company, government, political, and legal. There is company financial information such as 10Ks, proxies, annual reports to shareholders, EDGAR filings, country and state profiles, biographical information, general medical and health topics, medical abstracts, accounting, auditing, and tax.

ASSOCIATIONS UNLIMITED (F, N, C)
http://www.galegroup.com

This database contains information for approximately 460,000 international and U.S. national, regional, state, and local nonprofit membership organizations in all fields, including IRS data on U.S. 501© nonprofit organizations. Included among these organizations are SHRM Global Forum (Society for Human Resource Management) (http://www.shrmglobal.org); IHRIM (International Association for Human Resources Information Management) (http://www.ihrim.org) and International Association of Management (email: aomgt@infi.net). This last one publishes the *Journal of Information Technology Management*, which contains case studies and professional academic and practitioner-related articles.

BLOOMBERG FINANCIAL SERVICES (I, F, N, C)
http://www.Bloomberg.com

Bloomberg Financial Markets is a global, multimedia distributor of information services combining news, data, and analysis for global financial markets and businesses. It provides real-time pricing, data, history, analytics, and electronic communications 24 hours a day, 365 days a year. The news service has three hundred reporters and editors in fifty-two bureaus worldwide who provide around-the-clock coverage of the world's governments, corporations, industries, and financial markets. In conjunction with the service there is a magazine, forum, TV and radio news, and an energy newsletter. The forum is a powerful, innovative way to obtain executive interviews, CEO analyst roundtables, and expert interviews. I/B/E/S is the earnings estimate service, which covers over sixteen thousand companies in forty-two countries and is updated daily. The EDGAR filings are available within fifteen minutes of being filed electronically.

BRIDGE INFORMATION SYSTEM (N, C)
http://www.bridge.com

This financial analyst system tracks markets from equities and futures exchanges as well as nonexchange economic and market data sources. Bridge offers the most complete, timely, and accurate data available from both primary and emerging markets. It provides real-time stock quotes, graphics, technical and fundamental displays, market displays, charts, option system, and the latest news.

BUSINESS REFERENCE SUITE (F, N)
http://www.galegroup.com

This is a package containing three databases: Business and Industry, Business and Management Practices, and Tablebase. Business and Industry draws its content from over one thousand of the world's most authoritative business publications, including premier trade and business journals, leading industry newsletters, plus a broad collection of regional, national, and international newspapers covering events in over 190 countries. Sixty-seven percent of the articles are available in full-text format. The beauty of this database is the intelligent indexing and the searchable fields of concept terms, marketing terms, industry names, and document type. The Business and Management Practices database covers practical, how-to information about how companies are being managed from three hundred core publications and management articles from three hundred additional sources. Sixty-three percent of the database is in full-text format. Business and Industry covers none of these core publications. The third database, Tablebase, is exclusively tabular data on companies, industries, and products from privately published statistical annuals, trade associations, government agencies, nonprofit research groups, industry reports by investment research groups, and business and industry. There are over twenty thousand tables added per year. Rankings, market share, forecasts, demographics, and other statistics are found in this resource.

CEOEXPRESS COMPANY (I, F)
http://www.ceoexpress.com

This database was developed to organize the best resources on the Web for busy executives. CEOExpress takes all the information and, by employing expert human editors and "mind ergonomics," pares it down to the 20 percent that is most critical and useful. That information is delivered to the user's desktop in a clear, easy-to-use format. This is one-stop shopping for the busy executive with hundreds of links to valid sites. Some of the many categories are international business, international news, government agencies, statistics, Internet research, law, SEC, company research, industry snapshots, and reference. The company launched six new sites in 2000 and 2001: WiredCEO, JournalistExpress, MDExpress, LawyerExpress, CEOExpressSelect, and CLOExpress, a "best logistics resources on the Internet" for chief logistics officers.

THE CONFERENCE BOARD (I, F, N, C)
http://www.conference-board.org

The Conference Board is a widely recognized organization known for its research on employee relations and surveys. It has over eighty years of survey expertise in management and operations research.

More than thirty-three hundred companies in sixty-seven nations comprise its global network. The reports generated by this organization are regarded as top-quality research.

CORPTECH DIRECTORY OF TECHNOLOGY COMPANIES (I, F)

http://www.corptech.com

This database contains information on approximately fifty thousand public and private manufacturers and developers of high-tech products. The basic data is free. However, for a fee a customized report can be created. Part of the database is corporate and executives histories, executives title and responsibility, acquisition candidates, and operating units.

COUNTRY COMMERCE (N, C)

Economist Intelligence Unit
http://www.eiu.com

This is an EIU reference service covering sixty countries. It outlines business requirements for operating successfully in the world's major markets. It contains information on how to set up local companies and joint ventures, trading and licensing conditions, rules on foreign investment, contractual arrangements (especially for security and enforcement), labor laws and practices, local attitudes, procedures for mergers and acquisitions, restrictions on imports and exports, regulations on capital movements, corporate and personnel taxation, and competition and price control policies.

COUNTRY FINANCE (N, C)

Economist Intelligence Unit
http://www.eiu.com

Formerly Financing Foreign Operations, the Economist Intelligence Unit is a service covering financing conditions and techniques such as short-term financing; overdrafts and loans; trade bill discounting, commercial paper, factoring, and banks (domestic, foreign, and developmental); national monetary policy; investment incentives; tax incentives; trade financing; and insurance such as export credit programming for forty-seven countries. Each country is updated twice a year with twelve countries in rapid transition being updated quarterly. The EIU services are very expensive and not widely held in public libraries. They are available electronically for a fee at the EIU Web site.

COUNTRY PROFILE (N, C)
Economist Intelligence Unit
Web site: http://www.eiu.com

This is a quarterly EIU service that updates the political and economic status of 180 countries. It summarizes the past quarter of political and economic events, details the country's political and economic structure, and gives EIU expert outlook for the next two to eighteen months. The review section gives an analysis of key political developments; changes in the government's attitude toward business enterprises; trends in production and demand; and developments in monetary and fiscal conditions, wages and prices, merchandise trade, capital flows, exchange rates, and foreign debt. There are weekly and biweekly newsletters that update each country's status.

DATASTREAM (F, N)
http://www.datastream.com

Known for its historical analytical depth and breath, this database contains equity prices, volumes, market capitalization, earnings, and dividend data for around 50,000 equities covering 64 developed and emerging markets with over 25 years of history for key developed markets; global equity indices covering 38 markets, 16 regions, 127 sectors spanning over 25 years of history; extensive worldwide unit trust pricing and dividend coverage for 11 countries, including over 10,000 U.K. trusts; over 200,000 international macroeconomic time-series available with indicators for around 175 countries sourced from central banks; foreign exchange rates for over 63 currencies; over 2,000 interest rates, over 200,000 bonds from 32 markets, 19,000 warrants from over 50 markets, commodities covering 1,500 spot prices and major indices, and so forth.

Economist Intelligence Unit (EIU) (N, C)
http://www.eiu.com

EIU provides In Country Profiles, on 165 countries updated on an annual basis. The profiles cover the political and economic aspects of the country, as well as important historical data and future trends.

Emerald Intelligence and Fulltext (I, F, N, C)
http://www.emeraldinsight.com

Emerald Fulltext is a database containing full-text articles from over one hundred peer-reviewed and scholarly journals that have an international management focus of research into practice. Such prominent journals as *Management Decision, International Journal of Operations & Production Management, Cross Cultural Management,* and *Supply Chain Management* are included. The database can be accessed through CatchWord, EBSCO Online, and OCLC FirstSearch or through library consortia. Over 90 percent are refereed journals. The database is updated weekly in advance of the printed journal. MCB University Press, which produces Emerald, is a niche publisher of high-quality academic research and applied titles. The company was started by a group of senior business school academics who were dissatisfied with the publishing outlets available internationally for authors.

Factiva (I, F, N, C)
http://www.factiva.com   800–369–7466

Dow Jones Interactive contains a wealth of information, but beware of hidden pricing. In the Business Newsstand one has access to full-text same-day headlines for the *Wall Street Journal, New York Times, Washington Post,* and *Los Angeles Times.* The Publications Library provides indexing on six thousand publications, many of which are available in full text. One can search a single journal title or several titles simultaneously. The Web Center searches two thousand Web sites, which the editors have chosen on the basis of content, speed, navigation, and design. The Center indexes sites up to four times daily. The Custom Clips database allows one to create an SDI (Selective Dissemination of Information) and a personal or group folder, which can be sent to email addresses. There is a Company & Industry database, which provides D&B reports, market research reports, and EIU reports. There is a charge for each viewed record. The Historical Market Data Center provides twenty-five years' worth of pricing on stocks, bonds, mutual funds, and market indexes. Capital Changes Reporter is also available in this database.

FIRST CALL (F, N)
http://www.firstcall.com

First Call provides analysts reports, notes that are real-time delivery of morning meeting comments, intra-day research broadcasts, and special equity notes from two hundred top brokerage and investment firms worldwide. It also offers growth rates and consensus estimates. It contains earnings estimates from over six hundred global brokerage firms covering more than eighteen thousand companies worldwide.

HARVARD BUSINESS SCHOOL PUBLISHING (I, F, N)
http://www.hbsp.harvard.edu

The mission of Harvard Business School Publishing is to improve the practice of management and its impact on a changing world. It is known for its case studies on international management and human resource research. Because of its close association with the Harvard Business School it has access to the latest thinking in management by its faculty and many other prominent business thinkers worldwide. It is important to note that searching this Web site is not self-evident, and one needs some guidance. The first step is to click on the "advanced search" button, then in the "product category" click "case studies" and in the keyword box put a subject such as "human resources," not "human resource management" or "people management."

INTERNATIONAL MONETARY FUND (N, C)
http://www.imf.org

The International Monetary Fund (IMF) is an intergovernmental institution that seeks to stabilize exchange rates between currencies and to maintain their convertibility. There are 155 member nations. It publishes a large volume of statistics on balance of payments, trade directions, and the flow of monies. *International Financial Statistics (IFS)* and *Government Finance Statistics Yearbook* are published by the IMF. *IFS* is the principle statistical publication of the IMF, and it contains data on a country's exchange rate, international liquidity, money and banking, interest rates, production, consumer and production prices, trade, and international banking. It also includes both the GDP and the GNP. The *International Financial Statistics Yearbook* contains a thirty-year annual time-series of the same data.

INVESTEXT PLUS (F, N, C)

http://www.thomsonfinancial.com

This database is a large collection of investment research reports on companies, industries, and investment in North America, Europe, Asia/Pacific, Latin America, Africa, and the Middle East. The reports are generated by 13 of the top U.S. firms, 11 of the top European firms, and 18 of the top Wall Street Journal 1998 allstars, as well as 500 investment banks and 190 trade associations. These reports are full text in their original published formats, complete with charts, photographs, and graphics. The documents are organized into three categories: company, industry, and geographic and topical subjects. Here one can monitor industry trends, track company financials, or research merger and acquisition activity. They are downloadable. It is wise to read several reports from different sources in order to do a thorough analysis. Ten thousand of the four hundred thousand reports contain peer group comparisons, credit ratings, and key ratios.

JOURNAL OF COMMERCE (N, C)

http://www.joc.com

The *Journal of Commerce (JOC)* has been the leader in reporting international and transportation news since 1827. Shipping schedules are found in this resource. It is a member of the Economist Group, known for their accuracy and quality research. *JOC* also publishes usable business news and many stories gathered from around the world that do not appear anywhere else. There are reports on financing, global trade, imports, exports, transportation, foreign investments and markets, logistics, industry trends, and so forth. It publishes over two hundred special supplements throughout the year, providing in-depth coverage on topics ranging from geographic regions and insurance to port authorities, commodities, and other aspects of international trade. There are certain statistical tables available only in the printed version and other tables available only in the Web version. Subscribers to the print version have free access to the Internet version. One nice feature of the on-line version is the Regulations Watch.

LATIN AMERICAN NETWORK INFORMATION CENTER (C)
http://lanic.utexas.edu /

The Latin American Network Information Center (LANIC) is affiliated with the Institute of Latin American Studies (ILAS) at the University of Texas at Austin (UT Austin). LANIC is a key component of the International Information Systems also based at UT Austin. It contains forty-one searchable subject areas that focus on Central America, South America, and Caribbean countries. Its primary objective is to facilitate access to Internet-based information on, from, or about Latin America. The site has a Frequently Asked Questions (FAQ) section; questions can be emailed to info@lanic.utexas.edu.

MERGENT ONLINE (FORMERLY MOODY'S) (I, F, N)
http://www.mergentonline.com   800–342–5647

This service provides access to more than ten thousand U.S. companies, including real-time access to SEC (EDGAR) filings dating back to 1993, as well as real-time news headlines and complete text. The financial statements are as reported, providing balance sheet and income statement details. All of the information, including text descriptions, are updated daily. Additional coverage includes company history, business, property, subsidiaries, officers, directors, exchange and ticker symbol, address, telephone number, annual stock price ranges, transfer agent, stock splits, dividend payment history, number of employees, and so forth.

Michigan State University—CIBER (I, F, N, C)
http://ciber.bus.msu.edu/busres.htm

This site is known for its excellent links to other resources and is highly recommended. A subset of this site is the International Trade Leads. It contains the *Journal of International Marketing,* international and domestic news, periodicals, journals, research papers, regional- or country-specific information, statistical data, government resources, international trade shows, business events, and much more. When you click on "Referring Sites" you will find government agencies, organizations, universities, courses, publications and guides, commercial companies dealing in international trade, personal pages, indexes, and search engines. The International Trade Leads lists seventy-two links to such sites as Partnerbase (a dedicated resource for companies seeking international trade partners) and the IEBB (Import-Export Bulletin Board), which hosts an interactive professional discussion chat forum where one can interact in real time with experts in the letter of credit, freight forwarding, customer broker, and logistics areas. The *Journal of Commerce* sponsors the IEBB. The Electronic Trading Opportunity System (ETO) includes a news week service, and the Internet site lists trade opportunities categorized under products. The Trading Floor is a very interactive and complete Internet site with a list of required documentation for every country. There is a subscription fee. Finally, the Department of Commerce's *Export Marketing Magazine* has an Internet site that showcases U.S. importers and exporters.

National Trade Data Bank (NTDB) (I, F, N, C)
http://www.stat-usa.gov

The NTDB contains export promotional and international trade information collected by fifteen U.S. government agencies. There are Commerce Business Daily leads, Defense Logistics Agency leads, Trade Opportunity leads, Agricultural trade leads, and United Nations trade leads. There are more than two hundred thousand documents in this database. It has the latest census data on U.S. imports and exports by commodity and country. Here one can get to the International Marketing Insight Reports, Industry Sector Analysis Reports, Best Market Reports, and Country Commercial Guides. The complete Commercial Service International Contacts (CSIS) contains names and addresses of over eighty thousand individuals and firms abroad who are interested in importing U.S. products. The State Department country reports on economic policy and trade practices, the publications Export Yellow Pages, National Trade Estimates Report on Foreign Trade Barriers, the Export Promotion Calendar, and much more are included in this database. It is available at any one of the eleven hundred U.S. federal depository libraries.

THE OFFICIAL EXPORT GUIDE (C)

http://primediainfo.com

This is possibly the most comprehensive guide to the process of exporting from the United States to all the countries of the world. It is organized into nine sections. There is a glossary of international trade terms. There are articles by industry experts offering practical information and tips on the many aspects of international trade. There is a basic "How to Export" section. There are country profiles that cover 215 countries and territories. Included in this section are data on best export opportunities, existing trade and entry trade, warehousing, and free trade zones. The shipping services section covers freight forwarders who provide freight rates and modular transportation. It also provides lists of the U.S. headquarters of international air cargo, small package carriers, ocean cargo carriers and agents, rail services, translation and legal services, and export trading companies. In the information sources section there are literally thousands of listings for specific country and industry officers, international and private organizations, embassies, and consulates. Schedule B contains mandatory numbers required to report export shipments. Finally, there is a section on mandatory and hazardous materials regulations, as well as samples of export documents.

POLITICAL RISK YEARBOOK (C)

http://www.prsgroup.com/

This eight-volume resource contains political, financial, and economic risk information on 106 countries. Each study contains an expert assessment of the power structure, eighteen-month and five-year forecasts, information on social conditions and international relationships, a ten-year history fact sheet, a two-page summary with key economic forecasts, regional economic comparisons, and a recent chronology. There are graphical comparisons of the country's economic performance over time and in relation to other countries. This work focuses on international business needs—finding developing markets, currency movements, and making judgments about capital investment or corporate security. The five-year political and economic forecasts present most likely, second most likely, and third most likely five-year regime scenarios. There are forecasts of turmoil, investment restrictions, trade restrictions, and domestic and international economic problems, making these volumes highly important in assessing long-range trade prospects.

REUTER'S BUSINESS INSIGHT (N, C)
http://www.reuters.com

This database contains global analyst research reports in the areas of consumer goods, energy, finance, healthcare, commerce, and technology with in-depth forecasts. There are over one thousand journalists and photographers working in over one hundred bureaus worldwide. Reuters is known for its primary research, breaking news, interviews with key industry players, and industry forecasts. The reports are global or regional in scope, with the latest news and market commentaries as well as fast follow-up analyses.

THOMSON (F, N)
http://www.thomson.com

Thomson covers approximately 90 percent of the world stock market value and includes records for more than seventeen thousand active companies representing over fifty countries. Records cover fundamental financial data, all filings with the SEC, auditors report and opinion, accounting practices, product and geographic segment data when given, ratios, and foreign business statistics. Also included are records on some U.S. private companies, U.K. private companies, and Canadian companies. This is the Worldscope database, which contains records on approximately five thousand U.S. companies, and the rest are from around the world.

THUNDERBIRD, THE AMERICAN GRADUATE SCHOOL OF INTERNATIONAL MANAGEMENT (I, F, N, C)
http://www.t-bird.edu/default.asp

The strength of this Web site is a tripartite system focusing on global business, international affairs, and modern languages. It appears to be one of the most comprehensive Internet sites for international business links. There are links to the Institute for International Business Ethics (IBE), International Campus Consortium, and the North American Free Trade Agreement (NAFTA) Center, among others. This site has a strong emphasis on multilingual and multicultural programs and international research. It also offers Commercial Services and a Business Information Service that will (for a fee) provide expert research on a company or a country. Thunderbird is very heavily networked, which can be useful in getting to the correct source quickly. Especially useful are a case series link and a link to the International Business Information Center/Library (IBIC) site, which in turn offers links to electronic resources and a global gateway linked to three very important Internet sites: Gary Price's Lists of Lists, the free version of the U.S. Securities and Trade Commission's EDGAR database, and the direct link to World Stats. The *Thunderbird International Business Review* and the *Journal of Language for International Business* are also available at this site.

TRADE POLICY REVIEW (N, C)
http://www.wto.org

There are sixty reports on sixty countries included on this Internet site. The objectives of the Trade Policy Review mechanism are to contribute to improved adherence by all World Trade Organization members to rules, discipline, and commitments made under the Multilateral Trade Agreements. There are sections on sectoral issues and future multilateral trading systems and policies. More important, there are sections on systemic trade policy issues. Examples of answers to important questions that can be found on this site include the following: average industrial tariffs are now below 5 percent and should be under 3 percent in the year 2000; significant peaks remain in textiles, clothing, automobiles, and certain consumer electronics; in agriculture, very high rates remain for such important products as cereals, meat, dairy, poultry, sugar, and tobacco; and metric-only labeling that can cause difficulty for U.S. exporters is required by international ISO standards.

TRADE SHOW CENTRAL (F, N)

http://www.tscentral.com/

The Internet site Trade Show Central emerged early in 1996 in response to changing industry needs. Its goal is to provide the trade show and professional events industry a single point of access to information, products, and services. In 1998 it changed its name to reflect an expanded focus not only on trade shows but also on seminars, conferences, and conventions and meetings for all types of organizations. In addition to obtaining free comprehensive event data, detailed venue information, and an event industry supplier's database, visitors benefit from value-added products and on-line travel centers. Trade Show Central specializes in delivering a wide range of management products and services for event organizers, sponsors, and exhibitors, including Web advertising and promotion, on-line event registration, floor plan management, event representation, direct marketing, Web cast production, premium incentives, and Web site development. This is also a job openings database to which visitors are encouraged to email their resume.

NOTES

1. This classification is aimed to provide a rough estimate of the search materials and is not exhaustive. It is possible that a database may contain all of these criteria.

2. For example, *Journal of International Business Studies* does not provide a guideline for on-line resource citation at their submission guideline site (http://www.jibs.net/Submi _papers.asp). *Academy of Management Review and Academy of Management Journal* requires that "A reference to an electronic document should include the author's name, if known; the full title of the document; the full title of the work it is part of, if there is one; the ftp, http, or other address; and the date the document was accessed" (http://www.aom.pace.edu/amj/style_guide.html).

3. For further information on the U.S. copyright laws please log on at http://lcweb .loc.gov/copyright/title17/.

4. The subscription fees, terms of subscription, and coverage of databases are subject to change at the discretion of the publisher. The parameters provided here are as of December 2001.

QUICK REFERENCE GUIDE

INTERNET SEARCH ENGINES

Alta Vista	http://www.altavista.com
Direct Hit	http://www.directhit.com
Google	http://www.google.com
HotBot	http://hotbot.lycos.com
iWon	http://home.iwon.com
Lycos	http://www.lycos.com
Northern Light	http://www.northernlight.com
WebCrawler	http://www.webcrawler.com

ON-LINE JOURNALS, CENTERS, AND ORGANIZATIONS

Applied Psychology: An International Review	http://www.blackwellpublishers.co.uk
International Journal of Human Resource Management	http://www.rosina.catchword.com
International Journal of Intercultural Relations	http://www.elsevier.com/locate/ijintrel
International Review of Industrial and Organizational Psychology	http://www.wiley.com/Corporate /Website/Objects/Products /0,9049,90620,00.html
Journal of Applied Psychology	http://www.apa.org/journals/apl.htm
Journal of Commerce (international and transportation news since 1827)	http://www.joc.com
Journal of Cross-Cultural Psychology	http://www.fit.edu/CampusLife/clubs -org/iaccp/JCCP/Jccp.html
Management International Review	http://www.uni-hohenheim.de/~mir

Trade Policy Review	http://www.wto.org
Academy of International Business	http://www.aibworld.net
International Monetary Fund	http://www.imf.org
Latin American Network Information Center	http://lanic.utexas.edu
Michigan State University CIBER	http://www.ciber.bus.msu.edu /busres.htm
The Official Export Guide	http://www.primediainfo.com
Thunderbird	http://www.t-burd.edu/default.asp

DATABASES

Business Reference Suite	http://www.galegroup.com
CEOExpress	http://www.ceoexpress.com
Datastream	http://www.datastream.com
Economist Intelligence Unit	http://eiu.com
Emerald Intelligence & Full Text	http://www.emeraldinsight.com
Factiva	http://www.factiva.com
National Trade Data Bank	http://www.stat-usa.gov
Political Risk Yearbook	http://www.prsgroup.com
Thomson	http://www.thomson.com

ALTERNATIVE LIBRARIES

Ebrary (academic online library for business research)	http://www.ebrary.com
E-globallibrary (on-line bibliographic databases, statistics, and company information)	http://www.e-globallibrary.com
Questia (academic library for liberal arts research)	http://www.questia.com
XanEdu (business-oriented classroom teaching and course support)	http://Xanedu.com

CONTRIBUTORS

ASLI M. ARIKAN is an instructor in strategy and policy at Boston University's School of Management. Her research interests are corporate strategy, management of investments, technology and innovation, theory of the firm, and corporate finance. She has an MBA from the University of North Carolina and a BS in Industrial Engineering from the Istanbul Technical University, Turkey.

ILGAZ ARIKAN is an instructor in strategy and policy at Boston University's School of Management. His research interests are competitive strategy and game theory, international business strategy, and auctions and rent generation through various market mechanisms. He has an MBA from the University of North Carolina and a BS in Economics and a BA in International Business from the Marmara University, Istanbul, Turkey. He was the founder and the CEO of an international trading and consulting company from 1992 to 1994.

PAWAN S. BUDHWAR is a senior lecturer in the HRM Section at Cardiff Business School, Cardiff University, United Kingdom. He received his doctorate from Manchester Business School, United Kingdom. His current research interests include IHRM, HRM, quality of life and firms' performance, transformational leadership, and management in developing countries.

RABI S. BHAGAT is a professor of organizational behavior and international management at the University of Memphis. He received his Ph.D. from the University of Illinois at Urbana-Champaign. His teaching and research interests include organizational behavior, organizational theory, and in particular cross-cultural and cross-national studies. He has published articles in leading academic journals and research volumes. He was elected a fellow of the American Psychological Association, the Society for

Industrial and Organizational Psychologists, and the International Academy for Intercultural Research. His current research interests include cultural variations in human stress and cognition in organizations, knowledge management processes in global corporations, and developing the global mind-set.

NAKIYE A. BOYACIGILLER is a professor of international management at San Jose State University. Her research interests include cross-national organization behavior and strategic international human resource management. She has published many articles in academic journals and books and serves on six editorial boards, including the *Journal of International Business Studies, Organization Science,* and the recently launched *International Journal of Cross-Cultural Management.* Boyacigiller's current research, funded by the National Science Foundation, is a study of organization culture and human resource management practices in multinational corporations and their influence on corporate performance (with S. Beechler, S. Taylor, and O. Levy). She is also editing a book titled *Teaching and Experiencing Cross-Cultural Management: Lessons from Master Teachers* (with R. Goodman and M. Phillips).

PETER W. DORFMAN is a full professor and the department head of the Department of Management at New Mexico State University. His research interests span both the human resources management and the organizational behavior fields. His articles on leadership, cross-cultural management, and employee discrimination have appeared in the *Journal of Applied Psychology, Academy of Management Journal, Academy of Management Review, Journal of Management, Advances in International Comparative Management,* and *Advances in Global Leadership,* among others. He is currently investigating the impact of cultural influences on managerial behavior and leadership styles. In addition, he is an expert witness and consultant in employee discrimination and sexual harassment cases.

GARY W. FLORKOWSKI is an associate professor of business administration at the Katz Graduate School of Business at the University of Pittsburgh. He received his Ph.D. from Syracuse University in personnel and industrial relations. He has published articles and book chapters in the fields of IHRM, incentive compensation, and HRM regulatory compliance. His current research interests include the infusion of information technology in HR and industrial relations processes, IHRM, and global e-business regulation.

ITZHAK HARPAZ is the director of the Center for the Study of Organizations and Human Resource and is on the faculty of the Graduate School of Business at the University of Haifa, Israel. He received his Ph.D. from the University of Minnesota in human resource management and industrial relations. His main areas of expertise include organizational behavior, human resource management, industrial relations, and cross-cultural comparative management. He has published several books and many articles in professional and scientific journals on these topics.

BEN L. KEDIA holds the Robert Wang Chair of Excellence in International Business and is director of the Wang Center for International Business Education and Research (CIBER) and director of the International MBA Program at the University of Memphis. He received his Ph.D. from Case Western Reserve University. He has published articles in leading academic journals and textbooks. His current research interests include international strategy, knowledge transfer, and privatization in transition economies.

JILL KLEINBERG is an associate professor of organizational behavior and international management at the University of Kansas. A Japan specialist, her research adopts an anthropological ethnographic perspective on cross-cultural management and emergent organizational cultures. Her current research, funded by the Japanese Ministry of Education and the University of Kansas Center for International Business Education and Research, focuses on Japanese firms operating in the U.S.-Mexico border region; one issue of concern is the negotiation of cultural identity in the cross-national, cross-cultural work setting.

KWOK LEUNG is a professor of management at City University of Hong Kong. He received his Ph.D. in psychology at the University of Illinois. His main research interests include justice, conflict, research methodology, and culture, topics on which he has published widely. He is the editor of the *Asian Journal of Social Psychology* and an associate editor of the *Asia Pacific Journal of Management*. He coauthored *Methods and Data Analysis for Cross-Cultural Research* (Sage, 1997) and co-edited *Progress in Asian Social*

Psychology (Wiley, 1997) and *Conflict Management in Asia Pacific Rim* (Wiley, 1998). He is now co-editing *Handbook of Asian Management* (Kluwer, forthcoming).

MERI MEREDITH is the reference librarian in the Business Library at the Ohio State University. She obtained her BA in French from George Washington University and her MLS from Indiana University, Bloomington. She has over twenty years of experience in business reference work, first in the corporate world, then as an entrepreneur, and the last ten years at OSU. She has published several articles on international business in refereed journals. She is presently working on a book about dealing with an international clientele. She is active in the Special Libraries Association and is in *Who's Who in the World.*

KAREN SOUTH MOUSTAFA is a Ph.D. candidate in management at the University of Memphis. Prior to joining the doctoral program, she obtained her MA from the University of Auckland, New Zealand. She has had extensive experience as a manager in the healthcare industry, both in the United States and in New Zealand. She has recently coauthored a chapter in *Cross-Cultural Foundations: Traditions for Managing in a Global World* and has presented papers at several national and regional meetings of the Academy of Management. Her research interests include cultural variations in temporal orientation and cross-cultural organizational theory.

ARVIND PARKHE is a professor of strategy and international business and Cochran Senior Research Fellow in the Fox School of Business and Management, Temple University. His research focuses on the formation, structuring, and effective management of strategic alliances, international joint ventures, and global networks.

LILIANA M. PEREZ is a Ph.D. candidate in management at the University of Memphis. She has recently published an article in *Competitiveness Review* and has presented several papers at the national meetings of the Academy of Management and the Academy of International Business. Her current research interests include international alliances, knowledge creation and transfer, and information technology.

MARGARET E. PHILLIPS is an associate professor of international business at the George L. Graziadio School of Business and Management at

Pepperdine University. Her research, teaching, and consulting interests include cultural influences on behavior in and of organizations, management development in multicultural contexts, qualitative research methods, and the management of the arts. Phillips often works with teams, such as the one she worked with for this handbook. She coauthored "The Complex Culture of International Project Teams" with R. Goodman and S. Sackmann in *Modern Organizations and Emerging Conundrums* (Lexington Books, 1999) and is currently co-editing *Teaching and Experiencing Cross-Cultural Management: Lessons from Master Teachers.*

BETTY JANE PUNNETT is a chaired professor of international business and management at the University of the West Indies, Cave Hill Campus. She holds a Ph.D. in international business from New York University. Punnett has published extensively in the field, focusing most recently on the Caribbean. She recently completed a text on international business in the Caribbean and Latin America and is completing a text on international perspectives on organizational behavior and human resource management. She edits *Insights* for the Academy of International Business.

SONJA A. SACKMANN is professor in the Department of Economics, Management, and Organization Sciences at the University Bw Munich, Germany, and Partner, MZ St. Gallen, Switzerland. Her research interests include issues of culture in suborganizational, organizational, and multinational settings, including diversity, identity and cooperation, leadership, and issues of organizational change and development. She is the author of *Cultural Knowledge in Organizations: Exploring the Collective Mind, Unternehmenskultur (Corporate Culture),* and essays in numerous academic journals, both in English and German.

RANDALL S. SCHULER is professor of human resource strategy and Director of the Center for Global Strategic Human Resource Management in the Department of Human Resource Management at Rutgers University in New Brunswick, New Jersey. His interests are global human resource management, cross-border alliances, strategic human resource management, the human resource management function in organizations, and the interface of business strategy and human resource tasks. He has authored or edited over forty books, contributed dozens of chapters to books, and published over one hundred articles in professional journals and academic proceedings.

ODED SHENKAR is the Ford Motor Company Chair in Global Business Management and a professor of management and human resources at the Fisher College of Business at the Ohio State University. He received his Ph.D. from Columbia University. The author or editor of five books and numerous articles on comparative and international management, Shenkar is on the editorial board of seven major journals in the United States, Europe, and Asia. He is especially involved in research on China and on international strategic alliances.

STEVEN K. SU is a professor in the Department of Organizational Behavior at INSEAD in Singapore and Fontainebleau, France. He received his Ph.D. in business from Stanford University. His research focuses primarily on issues of conflict and negotiation. Recent studies conducted by Su and his colleagues examine the cross-cultural dynamics of the employment relationship and conflict and negotiation.

STEPHEN E. WEISS is a tenured associate professor at the Schulich School of Business, York University, Toronto. He teaches negotiation, international business, and strategy and has received Schulich's top award for MBA teaching. He has written extensively on international negotiation for publications such as the *Journal of International Business Studies, Organization Science,* and *Sloan Management Review.* He also provides negotiation training and consultation for a broad range of clients. He spent part of 2002 in France as a visiting professor at HEC School of Management.

LORNA L. WRIGHT is the director of the International MBA Program and an associate professor at the Schulich School of Business, York University, Toronto. Previously she was at Queen's School of Business, Queen's University. She holds an M.I.M. from the American Graduate School of International Management and a Ph.D. from the University of Western Ontario. Her research focuses on international negotiations, strategic alliances, and Canadian SME success internationally. She has extensive research and work experience in Canada, Japan, and Southeast Asia; speaks Thai and Indonesian fluently; and has knowledge of Japanese. Wright is on the editorial board of the *Journal of Asian Business* and has served in a variety of advisory positions dealing with Canada-Asia relations.

INDEX